Blackstone's Statutes on

Contract, Tort & Restitution

Blackstone's Statutes on

Contract, Tort & Restitution

2011–2012

22nd edition

edited by

F. D. Rose

PhD, LLD, DCL, of Gray's Inn, Barrister-at-Law
Professor of Commercial Law, University of Bristol

OXFORD
UNIVERSITY PRESS

OXFORD
UNIVERSITY PRESS

Great Clarendon Street, Oxford OX2 6DP

Oxford University Press is a department of the University of Oxford.
It furthers the University's objective of excellence in research, scholarship,
and education by publishing worldwide in

Oxford New York

Auckland Cape Town Dar es Salaam Hong Kong Karachi
Kuala Lumpur Madrid Melbourne Mexico City Nairobi
New Delhi Shanghai Taipei Toronto

With offices in

Argentina Austria Brazil Chile Czech Republic France Greece
Guatemala Hungary Italy Japan Poland Portugal Singapore
South Korea Switzerland Thailand Turkey Ukraine Vietnam

Oxford is a registered trade mark of Oxford University Press
in the UK and in certain other countries

Published in the United States
by Oxford University Press Inc., New York

First published by Blackstone Press

First edition 1987	Ninth edition 1998	Seventeenth edition 2006
Second edition 1989	Tenth edition 1999	Eighteenth edition 2007
Third edition 1991	Eleventh edition 2000	Nineteenth edition 2008
Fourth edition 1993	Twelfth edition 2001	Twentieth edition 2009
Fifth edition 1994	Thirteenth edition 2002	Twenty-first edition 2010
Sixth edition 1995	Fourteenth edition 2003	Twenty-second edition 2011
Seventh edition 1996	Fifteenth edition 2004	
Eighth edition 1997	Sixteenth edition 2005	

British Library Cataloguing in Publication Data

Data available

Typeset by Newgen Imaging Systems (P) Ltd., Chennai, India
Printed in Great Britain
on acid-free paper by
MPG Books Group

ISBN 978-0-19-969247-7

10 9 8 7 6 5 4 3 2 1

For Christabel

Contents

Editor's preface   *xv*
New to this edition   *xvii*

Part I   Statutes   1

Statute of Frauds 1677   1
Fires Prevention (Metropolis) Act 1774   1
Statute of Frauds Amendment Act 1828   1
Parliamentary Papers Act 1840   2
Libel Act 1843   3
Libel Act 1845   3
Mercantile Law Amendment Act 1856   3
Offences Against the Person Act 1861   4
Apportionment Act 1870   4
Law of Libel Amendment Act 1888   5
Factors Act 1889   6
Slander of Women Act 1891   6
Marine Insurance Act 1906   7
Law of Property Act 1925   9
Law Reform (Miscellaneous Provisions) Act 1934   10
Law Reform (Married Women and Tortfeasors) Act 1935   11
Law Reform (Frustrated Contracts) Act 1943   12
Law Reform (Contributory Negligence) Act 1945   13
Crown Proceedings Act 1947   14
Law Reform (Personal Injuries) Act 1948   15
National Parks and Access to the Countryside Act 1949   15
Reserve and Auxiliary Forces (Protection
    of Civil Interests) Act 1951   16
Defamation Act 1952   16
Occupiers' Liability Act 1957   17
Law Reform (Husband and Wife) Act 1962   19
Criminal Law Act 1967   19
Misrepresentation Act 1967   20
Civil Evidence Act 1968   21
Theatres Act 1968   22
Trade Descriptions Act 1968   22
Employers' Liability (Compulsory Insurance) Act 1969   22
Employer's Liability (Defective Equipment) Act 1969   22
Administration of Justice Act 1970   23
Taxes Management Act 1970   24
Animals Act 1971   28
Carriage of Goods by Sea Act 1971   32
Unsolicited Goods and Services Act 1971   38
Defective Premises Act 1972   41
Supply of Goods (Implied Terms) Act 1973   44
Consumer Credit Act 1974   48
Health and Safety at Work Act 1974   56
Rehabilitation of Offenders Act 1974   58

Reservoirs Act 1975   59
Congenital Disabilities (Civil Liability) Act 1976   59
Dangerous Wild Animals Act 1976   61
Fatal Accidents Act 1976   62
Protection from Eviction Act 1977   64
Torts (Interference with Goods) Act 1977   65
Unfair Contract Terms Act 1977   71
Civil Liability (Contribution) Act 1978   77
State Immunity Act 1978   79
Customs and Excise Management Act 1979   79
Pneumoconiosis etc. (Workers' Compensation) Act 1979   80
Sale of Goods Act 1979   81
Vaccine Damage Payments Act 1979   99
Highways Act 1980   101
Limitation Act 1980   102
[Senior Courts Act 1981]   119
Administration of Justice Act 1982   121
Civil Aviation Act 1982   121
Forfeiture Act 1982   122
Supply of Goods and Services Act 1982   123
Building Act 1984   133
Occupiers' Liability Act 1984   133
Police and Criminal Evidence Act 1984   134
Housing Act 1985   137
Landlord and Tenant Act 1985   137
Insolvency Act 1986   137
Latent Damage Act 1986   138
Consumer Protection Act 1987   139
Minors' Contracts Act 1987   147
Copyright, Designs and Patents Act 1988   148
Housing Act 1988   149
Road Traffic Act 1988   150
Road Traffic (Consequential Provisions) Act 1988   157
Employment Act 1989   158
Law of Property (Miscellaneous Provisions) Act 1989   158
Broadcasting Act 1990   160
Courts and Legal Services Act 1990   161
Environmental Protection Act 1990   161
Food Safety Act 1990   168
Water Industry Act 1991   168
Water Resources Act 1991   169
Access to Neighbouring Land Act 1992   172
Carriage of Goods by Sea Act 1992   177
Social Security Contributions and Benefits Act 1992   180
Trade Union and Labour Relations (Consolidation) Act 1992   181
Railways Act 1993   191
Criminal Justice and Public Order Act 1994   192
Value Added Tax Act 1994   195
Criminal Injuries Compensation Act 1995   197
Landlord and Tenant (Covenants) Act 1995   201
Merchant Shipping Act 1995   203
Arbitration Act 1996   204
Damages Act 1996   205

Defamation Act 1996   209
Police Act 1996   218
Local Government (Contracts) Act 1997   219
Protection from Harassment Act 1997   219
Social Security (Recovery of Benefits) Act 1997   221
Data Protection Act 1998   233
Human Rights Act 1998   234
Late Payment of Commercial Debts (Interest) Act 1998   244
National Minimum Wage Act 1998   249
Contracts (Rights of Third Parties) Act 1999   250
Countryside and Rights of Way Act 2000   254
Finance Act 2000   256
Financial Services and Markets Act 2000   256
Freedom of Information Act 2000   263
Postal Services Act 2000   263
Powers of Criminal Courts (Sentencing) Act 2000   264
Enterprise Act 2002   267
Proceeds of Crime Act 2002   267
Anti-social Behaviour Act 2003   268
Criminal Justice Act 2003   273
Health and Social Care (Community Health and
    Standards) Act 2003   274
Civil Partnership Act 2004   277
Gambling Act 2005   278
Mental Capacity Act 2005   279
Companies Act 2006   288
Compensation Act 2006   294
Government of Wales Act 2006   296
National Health Service Act 2006   296
NHS Redress Act 2006   297
Corporate Manslaughter and Corporate Homicide Act 2007   301
Income Tax Act 2007   304
Legal Services Act 2007   304
Tribunals, Courts and Enforcement Act 2007   305
Dormant Bank and Building Society Accounts Act 2008   306
Banking Act 2009   307
Equality Act 2010   307
Third Parties (Rights against Insurers) Act 2010   311
Damages (Scotland) Act 2011   314

Part II   Proposed Statutes   **320**

(Draft) Negligence (Psychiatric Illness) Bill   320
(Draft) Unfair Contract Terms Bill   322
Defamation Bill   339
Consumer Insurance (Disclosure and Representations) Bill   348

Part III   Statutory Instruments   **352**

Package Travel, Package Holidays and Package
    Tours Regulations 1992   352
Employers' Liability (Compulsory Insurance) Regulations 1998   358
Provision and Use of Work Equipment Regulations 1998   359

Unfair Terms in Consumer Contracts Regulations 1999   364
Consumer Protection (Distance Selling) Regulations 2000   370
Electronic Commerce (EC Directive) Regulations 2002   381
Electronic Signatures Regulations 2002   382
Late Payment of Commercial Debts Regulations 2002   385
Financial Services (Distance Marketing) Regulations 2004   385
Damages (Variation of Periodical Payments) Order 2005   386
General Product Safety Regulations 2005   389
Regulatory Reform (Unsolicited Goods and Services Act 1971)
    (Directory Entries and Demands for Payment) Order 2005   406
Transfer of Undertakings (Protection of Employment)
    Regulations 2006   407
Business Protection from Misleading Marketing Regulations 2008   408
Consumer Protection from Unfair Trading Regulations 2008   409

Part IV EU Materials   **414**

Treaty Establishing the European Economic Community
    (Treaty of Rome, 1957)   414
Regulation (EC) No 864/2007 (Non-contractual obligations) (Rome II)   415
Regulation (EC) No 593/2008 (Law applicable to contractual
    obligations) (Rome I)   415

Part V International Materials   **416**

United Nations Convention on the Use of Electronic
    Communications in International Contracts   416

Part VI Codes   **418**

Draft Common Frame of Reference   418

Index   *477*

Alphabetical contents

A Access to Neighbouring Land Act
      1992 . . . 172
   Administration of Justice Act 1970 . . . 23
   Administration of Justice Act 1982 . . . 121
   Animals Act 1971 . . . 28
   Anti-social Behaviour Act 2003 . . . 268
   Apportionment Act 1870 . . . 4
   Arbitration Act 1996 . . . 204
B Banking Act 2009 . . . 307
   Broadcasting Act 1990 . . . 160
   Building Act 1984 . . . 133
   Business Protection from Misleading Marketing
      Regulations 2008 . . . 408
C Carriage of Goods by Sea Act 1971 . . . 32
   Carriage of Goods by Sea Act 1992 . . . 177
   Civil Aviation Act 1982 . . . 121
   Civil Evidence Act 1968 . . . 21
   Civil Liability (Contribution) Act 1978 . . . 77
   Civil Partnership Act 2004 . . . 277
   Companies Act 2006 . . . 288
   Compensation Act 2006 . . . 294
   Congenital Disabilities (Civil Liability)
      Act 1976 . . . 59
   Consumer Credit Act 1974 . . . 48
   Consumer Insurance (Disclosure and
      Representations) Bill . . . 348
   Consumer Protection Act 1987 . . . 139
   Consumer Protection (Distance Selling)
      Regulations 2000 . . . 370
   Consumer Protection from Unfair Trading
      Regulations 2008 . . . 409
   Contracts (Rights of Third Parties) Act
      1999 . . . 250
   Copyright, Designs and Patents Act
      1988 . . . 148
   Corporate Manslaughter and Corporate
      Homicide Act 2007 . . . 301
   Countryside and Rights of Way
      Act 2000 . . . 254
   Courts and Legal Services Act 1990 . . . 161
   Criminal Injuries Compensation Act
      1995 . . . 197
   Criminal Justice Act 2003 . . . 273
   Criminal Justice and Public Order Act
      1994 . . . 192
   Criminal Law Act 1967 . . . 19
   Crown Proceedings Act 1947 . . . 14

   Customs and Excise Management Act
      1979 . . . 79
D Damages Act 1996 . . . 205
   Damages (Scotland) Act 2011 . . . 314
   Damages (Variation of Periodical Payments)
      Order 2005 . . . 386
   Dangerous Wild Animals Act 1976 . . . 61
   Data Protection Act 1998 . . . 233
   Defamation Act 1952 . . . 16
   Defamation Act 1996 . . . 209
   Defamation Bill . . . 339
   Defective Premises Act 1972 . . . 41
   Dormant Bank and Building Society Accounts
      Act 2008 . . . 306
   Draft Common Frame of Reference . . . 418
E Electronic Commerce (EC Directive)
      Regulations 2002 . . . 381
   Electronic Signatures Regulations
      2002 . . . 382
   Employers' Liability (Compulsory Insurance)
      Act 1969 . . . 22
   Employers' Liability (Compulsory Insurance)
      Regulations 1998 . . . 358
   Employer's Liability (Defective Equipment) Act
      1969 . . . 22
   Employment Act 1989 . . . 158
   Enterprise Act 2002 . . . 267
   Environmental Protection Act 1990 . . . 161
   Equality Act 2010 . . . 307
F Factors Act 1889 . . . 6
   Fatal Accidents Act 1976 . . . 62
   Finance Act 2000 . . . 256
   Financial Services and Markets Act
      2000 . . . 256
   Financial Services (Distance Marketing)
      Regulations 2004 . . . 385
   Fires Prevention (Metropolis) Act 1774 . . . 1
   Food Safety Act 1990 . . . 168
   Forfeiture Act 1982 . . . 122
   Freedom of Information Act 2000 . . . 263
G Gambling Act 2005 . . . 278
   General Product Safety Regulations
      2005 . . . 389
   Government of Wales Act 2006 . . . 296
H Health and Safety at Work Act 1974 . . . 56
   Health and Social Care (Community Health
      and Standards) Act 2003 . . . 274

Highways Act 1980 . . . 101
Housing Act 1985 . . . 137
Housing Act 1988 . . . 149
Human Rights Act 1998 . . . 234
I   Income Tax Act 2007 . . . 304
Insolvency Act 1986 . . . 137
L   Landlord and Tenant Act 1985 . . . 137
Landlord and Tenant (Covenants) Act
     1995 . . . 201
Late Payment of Commercial Debts (Interest)
     Act 1998 . . . 244
Late Payment of Commercial Debts
     Regulations 2002 . . . 385
Latent Damage Act 1986 . . . 138
Law of Libel Amendment Act 1888 . . . 5
Law of Property Act 1925 . . . 9
Law of Property (Miscellaneous Provisions)
     Act 1989 . . . 158
Law Reform (Contributory Negligence)
     Act 1945 . . . 13
Law Reform (Frustrated Contracts)
     Act 1943 . . . 12
Law Reform (Husband and Wife)
     Act 1962 . . . 19
Law Reform (Married Women and Tortfeasors)
     Act 1935 . . . 11
Law Reform (Miscellaneous Provisions) Act
     1934 . . . 10
Law Reform (Personal Injuries) Act
     1948 . . . 15
Legal Services Act 2007 . . . 304
Libel Act 1843 . . . 3
Libel Act 1845 . . . 3
Limitation Act 1980 . . . 102
Local Government (Contracts) Act
     1997 . . . 219
M   Marine Insurance Act 1906 . . . 7
Mental Capacity Act 2005 . . . 279
Mercantile Law Amendment Act 1856 . . . 3
Merchant Shipping Act 1995 . . . 203
Minors' Contracts Act 1987 . . . 147
Misrepresentation Act 1967 . . . 20
N   National Health Service Act 2006 . . . 296
National Minimum Wage Act 1998 . . . 249
National Parks and Access to the Countryside
     Act 1949 . . . 15
Negligence (Psychiatric Illness) Bill
     (Draft) . . . 320
NHS Redress Act 2006 . . . 297
O   Occupiers' Liability Act 1957 . . . 17
Occupiers' Liability Act 1984 . . . 133
Offences Against the Person Act 1861 . . . 4
P   Package Travel, Package Holidays and Package
     Tours Regulations 1992 . . . 352

Parliamentary Papers Act 1840 . . . 2
Pneumoconiosis etc. (Workers' Compensation)
     Act 1979 . . . 80
Police Act 1996 . . . 218
Police and Criminal Evidence Act 1984 . . . 134
Postal Services Act 2000 . . . 263
Powers of Criminal Courts (Sentencing) Act
     2000 . . . 264
Proceeds of Crime Act 2002 . . . 267
Protection from Eviction Act 1977 . . . 64
Protection from Harassment Act 1997 . . . 219
Provision and Use of Work Equipment
     Regulations 1998 . . . 359
R   Railways Act 1993 . . . 191
Regulation (EC) No 593/2008 (Law
     applicable to contractual obligations)
     (Rome I) . . . 415
Regulation (EC) No 864/2007 (Non-
     contractual obligations) (Rome II) . . . 415
Regulatory Reform (Unsolicited Goods and
     Services Act 1971) (Directory Entries and
     Demands for Payment) Order 2005 . . . 406
Rehabilitation of Offenders Act 1974 . . . 58
Reserve and Auxiliary Forces (Protection of
     Civil Interests) Act 1951 . . . 16
Reservoirs Act 1975 . . . 59
Road Traffic Act 1988 . . . 150
Road Traffic (Consequential Provisions)
     Act 1988 . . . 157
S   Sale of Goods Act 1979 . . . 81
Senior Courts Act 1981 . . . 119
Slander of Women Act 1891 . . . 6
Social Security Contributions and Benefits
     Act 1992 . . . 180
Social Security (Recovery of Benefits)
     Act 1997 . . . 221
State Immunity Act 1978 . . . 79
Statute of Frauds 1677 . . . 1
Statute of Frauds Amendment Act 1828 . . . 1
Supply of Goods and Services Act
     1982 . . . 123
Supply of Goods (Implied Terms)
     Act 1973 . . . 44
T   Taxes Management Act 1970 . . . 24
Theatres Act 1968 . . . 22
Third Parties (Rights against Insurers)
     Act 2010 . . . 311
Torts (Interference with Goods) Act
     1977 . . . 65
Trade Descriptions Act 1968 . . . 22
Trade Union and Labour Relations
     (Consolidation) Act 1992 . . . 181
Transfer of Undertakings (Protection of
     Employment) Regulations 2006 . . . 407

Treaty Establishing the European Economic
   Community (Treaty of Rome, 1957) . . . 414
Tribunals, Courts and Enforcement
   Act 2007 . . . 305
U Unfair Contract Terms Act 1977 . . . 71
Unfair Contract Terms Bill (Draft) . . . 322
Unfair Terms in Consumer Contracts
   Regulations 1999 . . . 364

United Nations Convention on the Use
   of Electronic Communications in
   International Contracts (2005) . . . 416
Unsolicited Goods and Services Act 1971 . . . 38
V Vaccine Damage Payments Act 1979 . . . 99
Value Added Tax Act 1994 . . . 195
W Water Industry Act 1991 . . . 168
Water Resources Act 1991 . . . 169

Editor's preface

As in previous editions, this book sets out to present the principal legislative contributions to the law of contract, tort and unjust enrichment, together with a selection of specific provisions of a more specialist legislative nature which affects the general law on civil liability and reveals something of its wider context.

It has always been intended that this book should include the core materials to be consulted by students of Contract, Restitution and Torts, a selection of other materials in the area of civil liability, and a few related regulatory and public law provisions. Case law and statute do not exist in isolation, any more than the three main subjects of this book do. They are all part of a dynamic legal architecture, combining elements of old and new, beautiful and ugly, awkward and useful. A citizen may prefer an area of outstanding natural beauty to an industrial estate or a plainly functional new hospital, but the modern landscape cannot be accurately recorded without noting all of its constituents or their different contributions.

When I began this series of statute books, over twenty years ago, this book was less than a third of the size it is now. One must have mixed views about the accretion of legislative material on what is still regarded as an essentially case law subject; but it is inescapable that the area of civil liability is under constant modification by the legislature and that the modern lawyer must be up to date, not only with new developments, but with the persistent revision of familiar legislation. A proper understanding of the law and how it is developing therefore means that an awareness of proposed and impending reforms, and of codes which influence the way in which the law operates in practice, are essential.

As a consequence of a growing number of interests with their own increasingly detailed rules, the law on civil liability inevitably overlaps with many other areas of law and it has been noticeable, on the initial compilation and annual revision of this collection of materials, how far this traditionally case law subject has been affected by a growing amount of specialist legislation. Detailed attention to such enactments is unlikely to be practicable or appropriate in most courses on civil liability and is more likely to occur in other, more public law orientated, courses. But it is a notable feature of the modern law of civil liability that the basic case law principles do not reveal the extent to which, in particular, potentially tortious conduct is legitimated and regulated by legislation. Moreover, modern statutes are increasingly likely to provide for the consequences of transgressions and contract failure; and there is a developing tendency to make criminal wrongdoing the subject of civil procedures. A brief selection of such materials is appropriate in a book such as this.

However, it has always been the distinctive policy behind this book to undertake a fresh and thorough revision of materials each year, in order to provide an up-to-date collection which both saves readers work and time in identifying the current status of the leading materials and also offers a research tool for demonstrating the varied way in which the common law of obligations has been modified by formal materials.

Legislative intervention in what has traditionally been regarded as an essentially case law area has been relentless over the last four decades. One feature of the Coalition Government is that it has, for the moment at least, eased, if not to some extent gone into reverse. Thus, it has been announced that the previous Government's draft Civil Law Reform Bill has been shelved, meaning that, if no alternative way forward is found, much work by the Law Commission in this area has proved fruitless. Nonetheless, albeit at a leisurely pace, a new Defamation Bill is wending its way through Parliament and the Law Commission's draft Consumer Insurance (Disclosure and Representations) Bill has been transformed into a Government Bill and therefore likely soon to become law. Moreover, there has been the normal amendment and correction of existing legislation; and the opportunity has been taken to reduce the overall extent of this collection.

As usual, in most cases the material in this book is reproduced in its complete, most recent form, all amendments being incorporated within square brackets; occasional omissions are indicated by three dots. Supplementary notes and details of amending provisions, easily available elsewhere, are generally omitted for reasons of space.

I continue to be grateful to my wife, Lynda, for her contribution to revision of these materials.

As always, I gladly acknowledge the holders' rights in copyright materials. And I continue to be grateful for suggestions as to possible revisions of this collection of materials, whether for additions or deletions.

Francis Rose
16 May 2011

New to this edition

The twenty-second edition of *Blackstone's Statutes on Contract, Tort & Restitution* has been fully revised and updated to include all relevant legislation and materials through to May 2011.

- Damages (Scotland) Act 2011
- Consumer Insurance (Disclosure and Representations) Bill 2011
- Defamation Bill 2010

Part I

Statutes

Statute of Frauds 1677

(29 Chas. II, c. 3)

4   No action against executors, etc. upon a special promise, or upon any agreement, or contract for sale of lands, etc. unless agreement, etc. be in writing and signed

[...] noe action shall be brought [...] whereby to charge the defendant upon any special promise to answere for the debt default or miscarriages of another person [...] unlesse the agreement upon which such action shall be brought or some memorandum or note thereof shall be in writeing and signed by the partie to be charged therewith or some other person thereunto by him lawfully authorised.

Fires Prevention (Metropolis) Act 1774

(14 Geo. III, c. 78)

86   No action to lie against a person where the fire accidentally begins

And [...] no action, suit or process whatever shall be had, maintained or prosecuted against any person in whose house, chamber, stable, barn or other building, or on whose estate any fire shall [...] accidentally begin, nor shall any recompence be made by such person for any damage suffered thereby, any law, usage or custom to the contrary notwithstanding; [...] provided that no contract or agreement made between landlord and tenant shall be hereby defeated or made void.

Statute of Frauds Amendment Act 1828

(9 Geo. IV, c. 14)

6   Action not maintainable on representations of character, etc., unless they be in writing signed by the party chargeable

...No action shall be brought whereby to charge any person upon or by reason of any representation or assurance made or given concerning or relating to the character, conduct, credit, ability, trade, or dealings of any other person, to the intent or purpose that such other person may obtain credit, money, or goods upon, unless such representation or assurance be made in writing, signed by the party to be charged therewith.

Parliamentary Papers Act 1840

(3 & 4 Vict., c. 9)

1   Proceedings, criminal or civil, against persons for publication of papers printed by order of Parliament, to be stayed upon delivery of a certificate and affidavit to the effect that such publication is by order of either House of Parliament

It shall and may be lawful for any person or persons who now is or are, or hereafter shall be, a defendant or defendants in any civil or criminal proceeding commenced or prosecuted in any manner soever, for or on account or in respect of the publication of any such report, paper, votes, or proceedings by such person or persons, or by his, her, or their servant or servants, by or under the authority of either House of Parliament, to bring before the court in which such proceeding shall have been or shall be so commenced or prosecuted, or before any judge of the same (if one of the superior courts at Westminster), first giving twenty-four hours notice of his intention so to do to the prosecutor or plaintiff in such proceeding, a certificate under the hand of [the Speaker of the House of Lords], or of the clerk of the Parliaments, or of the speaker of the House of Commons, or of the clerk of the same house, stating that the report, paper, votes, or proceedings, as the case may be, in respect whereof such civil or criminal proceeding shall have been commenced or prosecuted, was published by such person or persons, or by his, her, or their servant or servants, by order or under the authority of the House of Lords or of the House of Commons, as the case may be, together with an affidavit verifying such certificate; and such court or judge shall thereupon immediately stay such civil or criminal proceeding; and the same, and every writ or process issued therein, shall be and shall be deemed and taken to be finally put an end to, determined, and superseded by virtue of this Act.

2   Proceedings to be stayed when commenced in respect of a copy of an authenticated report, etc

In case of any civil or criminal proceeding hereafter to be commenced or prosecuted for or on account or in respect of the publication of any copy of such report, paper, votes, or proceedings, it shall be lawful for the defendant or defendants at any stage of the proceedings to lay before the court or judge such report, paper, votes, or proceedings, and such copy, with an affidavit verifying such report, paper, votes, or proceedings, and the correctness of such copy, and the court or judge shall immediately stay such civil or criminal proceedings; and the same, and every writ or process issued therein, shall be and shall be deemed and taken to be finally put an end to, determined, and superseded by virtue of this Act.

3   In proceedings for printing any extract or abstract of a paper, it may be shewn that such extract was bona fide made

It shall be lawful in any civil or criminal proceeding to be commenced or prosecuted for printing any extract from or abstract of such report, paper, votes, or proceedings, to give in evidence [...] such report, paper, votes, or proceedings, and to show that such extract or abstract was published bona fide and without malice; and if such shall be the opinion of the jury, a verdict of not guilty shall be entered for the defendant or defendants.

4   Act not to affect the privileges of Parliament

Provided always, that nothing herein contained shall be deemed or taken, or held or construed, directly or indirectly, by implication or otherwise, to affect the privileges of Parliament in any manner whatsoever.

Libel Act 1843

(6 & 7 Vict., c. 96)

1 Offer of an apology admissible in evidence of mitigation of damages in action for defamation

[...] In any action for defamation it shall be lawful for the defendant (after notice in writing of his intention so to do, duly given to the plaintiff at the time of filing or delivering the plea in such action,) to give in evidence, in mitigation of damages, that he made or offered an apology to the plaintiff for such defamation before the commencement of the action, or as soon afterwards as he had an opportunity of doing so, in case the action shall have been commenced before there was an opportunity of making or offering such apology.

2 In an action against a newspaper for libel, the defendant may plead that it was inserted without malice and without neglect and may pay money into court as amends

[...] In an action for libel contained in any public newspaper or other periodical publication it shall be competent to the defendant to plead that such libel was inserted in such newspaper or other periodical publication without actual malice, and without gross negligence, and that before the commencement of the action, or at the earliest opportunity afterwards, he inserted in such newspaper or other periodical publication a full apology for the said libel, or, if the newspaper or periodical publication in which the said libel appeared should be ordinarily published at intervals exceeding one week, had offered to publish the said apology in any newspaper or periodical publication to be selected by the plaintiff in such action; [...] and to such plea to such action it shall be competent to the plaintiff to reply generally, denying the whole of such plea.

Libel Act 1845

(8 & 9 Vict., c. 75)

2 Defendant not to file such plea without paying money into court by way of amends

[...] It shall not be competent to any defendant in such action, whether in England or Ireland, to file any such plea, without at the same time making a payment of money into court by way of amends [...], but every such plea so filed without payment of money into court shall be deemed a nullity, and may be treated as such by the plaintiff in the action.

Mercantile Law Amendment Act 1856

(19 & 20 Vict., c. 97)

3 Consideration for guarantee need not appear in writing

No special promise to be made by any person [...] to answer for the debt, default, or miscarriage or another person, being in writing, and signed by the party to be charged therewith, or some other person by him thereunto lawfully authorised, shall be deemed invalid to support an action, suit, or other proceeding to charge the person by whom such promise shall have been made, by reason only that the consideration for such promise does not appear in writing, or by necessary inference from a written document.

5   A surety who discharges the liability to be entitled to assignment of all securities held by the creditor

Every person who, being surety for the debt or duty of another, or being liable with another for any debt or duty, shall pay such debt or perform such duty, shall be entitled to have assigned to him, or to a trustee for him, every judgment, specialty, or other security which shall be held by the creditor in respect of such debt or duty, whether such judgment, specialty, or other security shall or shall not be deemed at law to have been satisfied by the payment of the debt or performance of the duty, and such person shall be entitled to stand in the place of the creditor, and to use all the remedies, and, if need be, and upon a proper indemnity, to use the name of the creditor, in any action or other proceeding, at law or in equity, in order to obtain from the principal debtor, or any co-surety, co-contractor, or co-debtor, as the case may be, indemnification for the advances made and loss sustained by the person who shall have so paid such debt or performed such duty, and such payment or performance so made by such surety shall not be pleadable in bar of any such action or other proceeding by him: Provided always, that no co-surety, co-contractor, or co-debtor shall be entitled to recover from any other co-surety, co-contractor, or co-debtor, by the means aforesaid, more than the just proportion to which, as between those parties themselves, such last-mentioned person shall be justly liable.

Offences Against the Person Act 1861

(24 & 25 Vict., c. 100)

44   If the magistrates dismiss the complaint, they shall make out a certificate to that effect

If the Justices, upon the Hearing of any [...] Case of Assault or Battery upon the Merits, where the Complaint was preferred by or on the Behalf of the Party aggrieved, [...] shall deem the Offence not to be proved, or shall find the Assault or Battery to have been justified, or so trifling as not to merit any Punishment, and shall accordingly dismiss the Complaint, they shall forthwith make out a Certificate [...] stating the Fact of such Dismissal, and shall deliver such Certificate to the Party against whom the Complaint was preferred.

45   Certificate or conviction shall be a bar to any other proceedings

If any Person, against whom any such Complaint as [is mentioned in section 44 of this Act] shall have been preferred by or on the Behalf of the Party aggrieved, shall have obtained such Certificate, or, having been convicted, shall have paid the whole Amount adjudged to be paid, or shall have suffered the Imprisonment or Imprisonment with Hard Labour awarded, in every such Case he shall be released from all further or other Proceedings, Civil or Criminal, for the same Cause.

Apportionment Act 1870

(33 & 34 Vict., c. 35)

2   Rents, &c. to accrue from day to day and be apportionable in respect of time

[...] From and after the passing of this Act all rents, annuities, dividends, and other periodical payments in the nature of income (whether reserved or made payable under an instrument in writing or otherwise) shall, like interest on money lent, be considered as accruing from day to day, and shall be apportionable in respect of time accordingly.

3   Apportioned part of rent, &c. to be payable when the next entire portion shall have become due

The apportioned part of any such rent, annuity, dividend, or other payment shall be payable or recoverable in the case of a continuing rent, annuity, or other such payment when the entire portion of which such apportioned part shall form part shall become due and payable, and not before, and in the case of a rent, annuity, or other such payment determined by re-entry, death, or otherwise when the next entire portion of the same would have been payable if the same had not so determined, and not before.

5   Interpretation of terms

In the construction of this Act—

The word 'rents' includes rent service, rentcharge, and rent seck, and also tithes and all periodical payments or renderings in lieu of or in the nature of rent or tithe.

The word 'annuities' includes salaries and pensions.

The word 'dividends' includes (besides dividends strictly so called) all payments made by the name of dividend, bonus, or otherwise out of the revenue of trading or other public companies, divisible between all or any of the members of such respective companies, whether such payments shall be usually made or declared at any fixed times or otherwise; and all such divisible revenue shall, for the purposes of this Act, be deemed to have accrued by equal daily increment during and within the period for or in respect of which the payment of the same revenue shall be declared or expressed to be made, but the said word 'dividend' does not include payments in the nature of a return or reimbursement of capital.

6   Act not to apply to policies of assurance

Nothing in this Act contained shall render apportionable any annual sums made payable in policies of assurance of any description.

7   Nor where stipulation made to the contrary

The provisions of this Act shall not extend to any case in which it is or shall be expressly stipulated that no apportionment shall take place.

Law of Libel Amendment Act 1888

(51 & 52 Vict., c. 64)

5   Consolidation of actions

It shall be competent for a judge or the court, upon an application by or on behalf of two or more defendants in actions in respect to the same, or substantially the same, libel brought by one and the same person, to make an order for the consolidation of such actions, so that they shall be tried together; and after such order has been made, and before the trial of the said actions, the defendants in any new actions instituted in respect to the same, or substantially the same, libel shall also be entitled to be joined in a common action upon a joint application being made by such new defendants and the defendants in the actions already consolidated.

In a consolidated action under this section the jury shall assess the whole amount of the damages (if any) in one sum, but a separate verdict shall be taken for or against each defendant in the same way as if the actions consolidated had been tried separately; and if the jury shall have found a verdict against the defendant or defendants in more than one of the actions so consolidated, they shall proceed to apportion the amount of damages which they shall have so found between and against the said last-mentioned defendants; and the judge at the trial, if he awards to the plaintiff the costs of the action, shall thereupon make such order as he shall deem just for the apportionment of such costs between and against such defendants.

Factors Act 1889

(52 & 53 Vict., c. 45)

1 Definitions

For the purposes of this Act—

(1) The expression 'mercantile agent' shall mean a mercantile agent having in the customary course of his business as such agent authority either to sell goods or to consign goods for the purpose of sale, or to buy goods, or to raise money on the security of goods:

(2) A person shall be deemed to be in possession of goods or of the documents of title to goods, where the goods or documents are in the actual custody or are held by any other person subject to his control or for him or on his behalf:

(3) The expression 'goods' shall include wares and merchandise:

(4) The expression 'document of title' shall include any bill of lading, dock warrant, warehouse-keeper's certificate, and warrant or order for the delivery of goods, and any other document used in the ordinary course of business as proof of the possession or control of goods, or authorising or purporting to authorise, either by endorsement or by delivery, the possessor of the document to transfer or receive goods thereby represented:

(5) The expression 'pledge' shall include any contract pledging, or giving a lien or security on, goods, whether in consideration of an original advance or of any further or continuing advance or of any pecuniary liability:

(6) The expression 'person' shall include any body of persons corporate or unincorporate.

2 Powers of mercantile agent with respect to disposition of goods

(1) Where a mercantile agent is, with the consent of the owner, in possession of goods or of the documents of title to goods, any sale, pledge, or other disposition of the goods, made by him when acting in the ordinary course of business of a mercantile agent, shall, subject to the provisions of this Act, be as valid as if he were expressly authorised by the owner of the goods to make the same; provided that the person taking under the disposition acts in good faith, and has not at the time of the disposition notice that the person making the disposition has not authority to make the same.

(2) Where a mercantile agent has, with the consent of the owner, been in possession of goods or of the documents of title to goods, any sale, pledge, or other disposition, which would have been valid if the consent had continued, shall be valid notwithstanding the determination of the consent; provided that the person taking under the disposition has not at the time thereof notice that the consent has been determined.

(3) Where a mercantile agent has obtained possession of any documents of title to goods by reason of his being or having been, with the consent of the owner, in possession of the goods represented thereby, or of any other documents of title to the goods, his possession of the first-mentioned documents shall, for the purposes of this Act, be deemed to be with the consent of the owner.

(4) For the purposes of this Act the consent of the owner shall be presumed in the absence of evidence to the contrary.

Slander of Women Act 1891

(54 & 55 Vict., c. 51)

1 Amendment of law

Words spoken and published [...] which impute unchastity or adultery to any woman or girl shall not require special damage to render them actionable.

Provided always, that in any action for words spoken and made actionable by this Act, a plaintiff shall not recover more costs than damages, unless the judge shall certify that there was reasonable ground for bringing the action.

Marine Insurance Act 1906

(6 Edw. VII, c. 41)

17   Insurance is uberrimae fidei

A contract of marine insurance is a contract based upon the utmost good faith, and, if the utmost good faith be not observed by either party, the contract may be avoided by the other party.

18   Disclosure by assured

(1) Subject to the provisions of this section, the assured must disclose to the insurer, before the contract is concluded, every material circumstance which is known to the assured, and the assured is deemed to know every circumstance which, in the ordinary course of business, ought to be known by him. If the assured fails to make such disclosure, the insurer may avoid the contract.

(2) Every circumstance is material which would influence the judgment of a prudent insurer in fixing the premium, or determining whether he will take the risk.

(3) In the absence of inquiry the following circumstances need not be disclosed, namely:

(a) any circumstance which diminishes the risk;

(b) any circumstance which is known or presumed to be known to the insurer. The insurer is presumed to know matters of common notoriety or knowledge, and matters which an insurer in the ordinary course of his business, as such, ought to know;

(c) any circumstance as to which information is waived by the insurer;

(d) any circumstance which it is superfluous to disclose by reason of any express or implied warranty.

(4) Whether any particular circumstance, which is not disclosed, be material or not is, in each case, a question of fact.

(5) The term 'circumstance' includes any communication made to, or information received by, the assured.

20   Representations pending negotiation of contract

(1) Every material representation made by the assured or his agent to the insurer during the negotiations for the contract, and before the contract is concluded, must be true. If it be untrue the insurer may avoid the contract.

(2) A representation is material which would influence the judgment of a prudent insurer in fixing the premium, or determining whether he will take the risk.

(3) A representation may be either a representation as to a matter of fact, or as to a matter of expectation or belief.

(4) A representation as to a matter of fact is true, if it be substantially correct, that is to say, if the difference between what is represented and what is actually correct would not be considered material by a prudent insurer.

(5) A representation as to a matter of expectation or belief is true if it be made in good faith.

(6) A representation may be withdrawn or corrected before the contract is concluded.

(7) Whether a particular representation be material or not is, in each case, a question of fact.

22   Contract must be embodied in policy

Subject to the provisions of any statute, a contract of marine insurance is inadmissible in evidence unless it is embodied in a marine policy in accordance with this Act. The policy may be executed and issued either at the time when the contract is concluded, or afterwards.

33   Nature of warranty

(1) A warranty, in the following sections relating to warranties, means a promissory warranty, that is to say, a warranty by which the assured undertakes that some particular thing shall or shall not be done, or that some condition shall be fulfilled, or whereby he affirms or negatives the existence of a particular state of facts.

(2) A warranty may be express or implied.

(3) A warranty, as above defined, is a condition which must be exactly complied with, whether it be material to the risk or not. If it be not so complied with, then, subject to any express provision in the policy, the insurer is discharged from liability as from the date of the breach of warranty, but without prejudice to any liability incurred by him before that date.

34   When breach of warranty excused

(1) Non-compliance with a warranty is excused when, by reason of a change of circumstances, the warranty ceases to be applicable to the circumstances of the contract, or when compliance with the warranty is rendered unlawful by any subsequent law.

(2) Where a warranty is broken, the assured cannot avail himself of the defence that the breach has been remedied, and the warranty complied with, before loss.

(3) A breach of warranty may be waived by the insurer.

35   Express warranties

(1) An express warranty may be in any form of words from which the intention to warrant is to be inferred.

(2) An express warranty must be included in, or written upon, the policy, or must be contained in some document incorporated by reference into the policy.

(3) An express warranty does not exclude an implied warranty, unless it be inconsistent therewith.

49   Excuses for deviation or delay

(1) Deviation or delay in prosecuting the voyage contemplated by the policy is excused—

    (a) where authorised by any special term in the policy; or

    (b) where caused by circumstances beyond the control of the master and his employer; or

    (c) where reasonably necessary in order to comply with an express or implied warranty; or

    (d) where reasonably necessary for the safety of the ship or subject-matter insured; or

    (e) for the purpose of saving human life, or aiding a ship in distress where human life may be in danger; or

    (f) where reasonably necessary for the purpose of obtaining medical or surgical aid for any person on board the ship; or

    (g) where caused by the barratrous conduct of the master or crew, if barratry be one of the perils insured against.

(2) When the cause excusing the deviation or delay ceases to operate, the ship must resume her course, and prosecute her voyage, with reasonable dispatch.

82   Enforcement of return

Where the premium or a proportionate part thereof is, by this Act, declared to be returnable,—

    (a) If already paid, it may be recovered by the assured from the insurer; and

    (b) If unpaid, it may be retained by the assured or his agent.

83   Return by agreement

Where the policy contains a stipulation for the return of the premium, or a proportionate part thereof, on the happening of a certain event, and that event happens, the premium, or, as the case may be, the proportionate part thereof, is thereupon returnable to the assured.

84   Return for failure of consideration

(1) Where the consideration for the payment of the premium totally fails, and there has been no fraud or illegality on the part of the assured or his agents, the premium is thereupon returnable to the assured.

(2) Where the consideration for the payment of the premium is apportionable and there is a total failure of any apportionable part of the consideration, a proportionate part of the premium is, under the like conditions, thereupon returnable to the assured.

(3) In particular—

(a) Where the policy is void, or is avoided by the insurer as from the commencement of the risk, the premium is returnable, provided that there has been no fraud or illegality on the part of the assured; but if the risk is not apportionable, and has once attached, the premium is not returnable;

(b) Where the subject-matter insured, or part thereof, has never been imperilled, the premium, or, as the case may be, a proportionate part thereof, is returnable: Provided that where the subject-matter has been insured 'lost or not lost' and has arrived in safety at the time when the contract is concluded, the premium is not returnable unless, at such time, the insurer knew of the safe arrival;

(c) Where the assured has no insurable interest throughout the currency of the risk, the premium is returnable, provided that this rule does not apply to a policy effected by way of gaming or wagering;

(d) Where the assured has a defeasible interest which is terminated during the currency of the risk, the premium is not returnable;

(e) Where the assured has over-insured under an unvalued policy, a proportionate part of the premium is returnable;

(f) Subject to the foregoing provisions, where the assured has over-insured by double insurance, a proportionate part of the several premiums is returnable: Provided that, if the policies are effected at different times, and any earlier policy has at any time borne the entire risk, or if a claim has been paid on the policy in respect of the full sum insured thereby, no premium is returnable in respect of that policy, and when the double insurance is effected knowingly by the assured no premium is returnable.

87 Implied obligations varied by agreement or usage

(1) Where any right, duty, or liability would arise under a contract of marine insurance by implication of law, it may be negatived or varied by express agreement, or by usage, if the usage be such as to bind both parties to the contract.

Law of Property Act 1925

(15 & 16 Geo. V, c. 20)

41 Stipulations not of the essence of a contract

Stipulations in a contract, as to time or otherwise, which according to rules of equity are not deemed to be or to have become of the essence of the contract, are also construed and have effect at law in accordance with the same rules.

49 Applications to the court by vendor and purchaser

(2) Where the court refuses to grant specific performance of a contract, or in any action for the return of a deposit, the court may, if it thinks fit, order the repayment of any deposit.

(3) This section applies to a contract for the sale or exchange of any interest in land.

56 Persons taking who are not parties and as to indentures

(1) A person may take an immediate or other interest in land or other property, or the benefit of any condition, right of entry, covenant or agreement over or respecting land or other property, although he may not be named as a party to the conveyance or other instrument.

136   Legal assignments of things in action

(1) Any absolute assignment by writing under the hand of the assignor (not purporting to be by way of charge only) of any debt or other legal thing in action, of which express notice in writing has been given to the debtor, trustee or other person from whom the assignor would have been entitled to claim such debt or thing in action, is effectual in law (subject to equities having priority over the right of the assignee) to pass and transfer from the date of such notice—

(a) the legal right to such debt or thing in action;

(b) all legal and other remedies for the same; and

(c) the power to give a good discharge for the same without the concurrence of the assignor:

Provided that, if the debtor, trustee or other person liable in respect of such debt or thing in action has notice—

(a) that the assignment is disputed by the assignor or any person claiming under him; or

(b) of any other opposing or conflicting claims to such debt or thing in action; he may, if he thinks fit, either call upon the persons making claim thereto to interplead concerning the same, or pay the debt or other thing in action into court under the provisions of the Trustee Act 1925.

(2) This section does not affect the provisions of the Policies of Assurance Act 1867.

146   Restrictions on and relief against forfeiture of leases and underleases

(1) A right of re-entry or forfeiture under any proviso or stipulation in a lease for a breach of any covenant or condition in the lease shall not be enforceable, by action or otherwise, unless and until the lessor serves on the lessee a notice—

(a) specifying the particular breach complained of; and

(b) if the breach is capable of remedy, requiring the lessee to remedy the breach;

(c) in any case, requiring the lessee to make compensation in money for the breach;

and the lessee fails, within a reasonable time thereafter, to remedy the breach, if it is capable of remedy, and to make reasonable compensation in money, to the satisfaction of the lessor, for the breach.

(2) Where a lessor is proceeding, by action or otherwise, to enforce such a right of re-entry or forfeiture, the lessee may, in the lessor s action, if any, or in any action brought by himself, apply to the court for relief; and the court may grant or refuse relief, as the court, having regard to the proceedings and conduct of the parties under the foregoing provisions of this section, and to all the other circumstances, thinks fit; and in case of relief may grant it on such terms, if any, as to costs, expenses, damages, compensation, penalty, or otherwise, including the granting of an injunction to restrain any like breach in the future, as the court, in the circumstances of each case, thinks fit.

(11) This section does not, save as otherwise mentioned, affect the law relating to re-entry or forfeiture or relief in case of non-payment of rent.

(12) This section has effect notwithstanding any stipulation to the contrary.

205   General definitions

(1) In this Act unless the context otherwise requires, the following expressions have the meanings hereby assigned to them respectively, that is to say: . . .

(xvii) 'Notice' includes constructive notice;

(xx) 'Property' includes any thing in action, and any interest in real or personal property;

. . .

Law Reform (Miscellaneous Provisions) Act 1934

(24 & 25 Geo. V, c. 41)

1   Effect of death on certain causes of action

(1) Subject to the provisions of this section, on the death of any person after the commencement of this Act all causes of action subsisting against or vested in him shall survive against, or, as the case

may be, for the benefit of, his estate. Provided that this subsection shall not apply to causes of action for defamation [...].

[(1A) The right of a person to claim under section 1A of the Fatal Accidents Act 1976 (bereavement) shall not survive for the benefit of his estate on his death.]

(2) Where a cause of action survives as aforesaid for the benefit of the estate of a deceased person, the damages recoverable for the benefit of the estate of that person:—

    [(a) shall not include—

        (i)   any exemplary damages;

        (ii) any damages for loss of income in respect of any period after that person's death;]

    (b) [...]

    (c) where the death of that person has been caused by the act or omission which gives rise to the cause of action, shall be calculated without reference to any loss or gain to his estate consequent on his death, except that a sum in respect of funeral expenses may be included.

(4) Where damage has been suffered by reason of any act or omission in respect of which a cause of action would have subsisted against any person if that person had not died before or at the same time as the damage was suffered, there shall be deemed, for the purposes of this Act, to have been subsisting against him before his death such cause of action in respect of that act or omission as would have subsisted if he had died after the damage was suffered.

(5) The rights conferred by this Act for the benefit of the estates of deceased persons shall be in addition to and not in derogation of any rights conferred on the dependants of deceased persons by [the Fatal Accidents Act 1976...] and so much of this Act as relates to causes of action against the estates of deceased persons shall apply in relation to causes of action under the said Act as it applies in relation to other causes of action not expressly excepted from the operation of subsection (1) of this section.

(6) In the event of the insolvency of an estate against which proceedings are maintainable by virtue of this section, any liability in respect of the cause of action in respect of which the proceedings are maintainable shall be deemed to be a debt provable in the administration of the estate, notwithstanding that it is a demand in the nature of unliquidated damages arising otherwise than by a contract, promise or breach of trust.

Law Reform (Married Women and Tortfeasors) Act 1935

(25 & 26 Geo. V, c. 30)

3   Abolition of husband's liability for wife's torts and ante-nuptial contracts, debts and obligations

Subject to the provisions of this Part of this Act, the husband of a married woman shall not, by reason only of his being her husband, be liable—

    (a) in respect of any tort committed by her whether before or after the marriage, or in respect of any contract entered into, or debt or obligation incurred, by her before the marriage; or

    (b) to be sued, or made a party to any legal proceeding brought, in respect of any such tort, contract, debt, or obligation.

4   Savings

    (2) For the avoidance of doubt it is hereby declared that nothing in this Part of this Act—

        (a) renders the husband of a married woman liable in respect of any contract entered into, or debt or obligation incurred, by her after the marriage in respect of which he would not have been liable if this Act had not been passed;

    (b) exempts the husband of a married woman from liability in respect of any contract entered into, or debt or obligation (not being a debt or obligation arising out of a commission of a tort) incurred, by her after the marriage in respect of which he would have been liable if this Act had not been passed;

    (c) prevents a husband and wife from acquiring, holding, and disposing of, any property jointly or as tenants in common, or from rendering themselves, or being rendered, jointly liable in respect of any tort, contract, debt or obligation, and of suing and being sued either in tort or in contract or otherwise, in like manner as if they were not married;

    (d) prevents the exercise of any joint power given to a husband and wife.

Law Reform (Frustrated Contracts) Act 1943

(6 & 7 Geo. VI, c. 40)

1 Adjustment of rights and liabilities of parties to frustrated contracts

(1) Where a contract governed by English law has become impossible of performance or been otherwise frustrated, and the parties thereto have for that reason been discharged from the further performance of the contract, the following provisions of this section shall, subject to the provisions of section two of this Act, have effect in relation thereto.

(2) All sums paid or payable to any party in pursuance of the contract before the time when the parties were so discharged (in this Act referred to as 'the time of discharge') shall, in the case of sums so paid, be recoverable from him as money received by him for the use of the party by whom the sums were paid, and, in the case of sums so payable, cease to be so payable:

Provided that, if the party to whom the sums were so paid or payable incurred expenses before the time of discharge in, or for the purpose of, the performance of the contract, the court may, if it considers it just to do so having regard to all the circumstances of the case, allow him to retain or, as the case may be, recover the whole or any part of the sums so paid or payable, not being an amount in excess of the expenses so incurred.

(3) Where any party to the contract has, by reason of anything done by any other party thereto in, or for the purpose of, the performance of the contract, obtained a valuable benefit (other than a payment of money to which the last foregoing subsection applies) before the time of discharge there shall be recoverable from him by the said other party such sum (if any), not exceeding the value of the said benefit to the party obtaining it, as the court considers just, having regard to all the circumstances of the case and, in particular,—

    (a) the amount of any expenses incurred before the time of discharge by the benefited party in, or for the purpose of, the performance of the contract, including any sums paid or payable by him to any other party in pursuance of the contract and retained or recoverable by that party under the last foregoing subsection, and

    (b) the effect, in relation to the said benefit, of the circumstances giving rise to the frustration of the contract.

(4) In estimating, for the purposes of the foregoing provisions of this section, the amount of any expenses incurred by any party to the contract, the court may, without prejudice to the generality of the said provisions, include such sum as appears to be reasonable in respect of overhead expenses and in respect of any work or services performed personally by the said party.

(5) In considering whether any sum ought to be recovered or retained under the foregoing provisions of this section by any party to the contract, the court shall not take into account any sums which have, by reason of the circumstances giving rise to the frustration of the contract, become payable to that party under any contract of insurance unless there was an obligation to insure imposed by an express term of the frustrated contract or by or under any enactment.

(6) Where any person has assumed obligations under the contract in consideration of the conferring of a benefit by any other party to the contract upon any other person, whether a party to the

contract or not, the court may, if in all the circumstances of the case it considers it just to do so, treat for the purposes of subsection (3) of this section any benefit so conferred as a benefit obtained by the person who has assumed the obligations as aforesaid.

2 Provision as to application of this Act

(1) This Act shall apply to contracts, whether made before or after the commencement of this Act, as respects which the time of discharge is on or after the first day of July, nineteen hundred and forty-three, but not to contracts as respects which the time of discharge is before the said date.

(2) This Act shall apply to contracts to which the Crown is a party in like manner as to contracts between subjects.

(3) Where any contract to which this Act applies contains any provision which, upon the true construction of the contract, is intended to have effect in the event of circumstances arising which operate, or would but for the said provision operate, to frustrate the contract, or is intended to have effect whether such circumstances arise or not, the court shall give effect to the said provision and shall only give effect to the foregoing section of this Act to such extent, if any, as appears to the court to be consistent with the said provision.

(4) Where it appears to the court that a part of any contract to which this Act applies can properly be severed from the remainder of the contract, being a part wholly performed before the time of discharge, or so performed except for the payment in respect of that part of the contract of sums which are or can be ascertained under the contract, the court shall treat that part of the contract as if it were a separate contract and had not been frustrated and shall treat the foregoing section of this Act as only applicable to the remainder of that contract.

(5) This Act shall not apply—

    (a) to any charterparty, except a time charterparty or a charterparty by way of demise, or to any contract (other than a charterparty) for the carriage of goods by sea; or

    (b) to any contract of insurance, save as is provided by subsection (5) of the foregoing section; or

    (c) to any contract to which [section 7 of the Sale of Goods Act 1979] (which avoids contracts for the sale of specific goods which perish before the risk has passed to the buyer) applies, or to any other contract for the sale, or for the sale and delivery, of specific goods, where the contract is frustrated by reason of the fact that the goods have perished.

3 Short title and interpretation

(2) In this Act the expression 'court' means, in relation to any matter, the court or arbitrator by or before whom the matter falls to be determined.

Law Reform (Contributory Negligence) Act 1945

(8 & 9 Geo. VI, c. 28)

1 Apportionment of liability in case of contributory negligence

(1) Where any person suffers damage as the result partly of his own fault and partly of the fault of any other person or persons, a claim in respect of that damage shall not be defeated by reason of the fault of the person suffering the damage, but the damages recoverable in respect thereof shall be reduced to such extent as the court thinks just and equitable having regard to the claimant's share in the responsibility of the damage:

Provided that—

    (a) this subsection shall not operate to defeat any defence arising under a contract;

    (b) where any contract or enactment providing for the limitation of liability is applicable to the claim, the amount of damages recoverable by the claimant by virtue of this subsection shall not exceed the maximum limit so applicable.

(2) Where damages are recoverable by any person by virtue of the foregoing subsection subject to such reduction as is therein mentioned, the court shall find and record the total damages which would have been recoverable if the claimant had not been at fault.

(5) Where, in any case to which subsection (1) of this section applies, one of the persons at fault avoids liability to any other such person or his personal representative by pleading the Limitation Act, 1939, or any other enactment limiting the time within which proceedings may be taken, he shall not be entitled to recover any damages [...] from that other person or representative by virtue of the said subsection.

(6) Where any case to which subsection (1) of this section applies is tried with a jury, the jury shall determine the total damages which would have been recoverable if the claimant had not been at fault and the extent to which those damages are to be reduced.

4   Interpretation

The following expressions have the meanings hereby respectively assigned to them, that is to say—

'court' means, in relation to any claim, the court or arbitrator by or before whom the claim falls to be determined;

'damage' includes loss of life and personal injury; [...]

'fault' means negligence, breach of statutory duty or other act or omission which gives rise to liability in tort or would, apart from this Act, give rise to the defence of contributory negligence.

Crown Proceedings Act 1947

(10 & 11 Geo. VI, c. 44)

2   Liability of the Crown in tort

(1) Subject to the provisions of this Act, the Crown shall be subject to all those liabilities in tort to which, if it were a private person of full age and capacity, it would be subject—

(a) in respect of torts committed by its servants or agents;

(b) in respect of any breach of those duties which a person owes to his servants or agents at common law by reason of being their employer; and

(c) in respect of any breach of the duties attaching at common law to the ownership, occupation, possession or control of property:

provided that no proceedings shall lie against the Crown by virtue of paragraph (a) of this subsection in respect of any act or omission of a servant or agent of the Crown unless the act or omission would apart from the provisions of this Act have given rise to a cause of action in tort against that servant or agent or his estate.

(2) Where the Crown is bound by a statutory duty which is binding also upon persons other than the Crown and its officers, then, subject to the provisions of this Act, the Crown shall, in respect of a failure to comply with that duty, be subject to all those liabilities in tort (if any) to which it would be so subject if it were a private person of full age and capacity.

(3) Where any functions are conferred or imposed upon an officer of the Crown as such either by any rule of the common law or by statute, and that officer commits a tort while performing or purporting to perform those functions, the liabilities of the Crown in respect of the tort shall be such as they would have been if those functions had been conferred or imposed solely by virtue of instructions lawfully given by the Crown.

(4) Any enactment which negatives or limits the amount of the liability of any Government department [, part of the Scottish Administration,] or officer of the Crown in respect of any tort committed by that department [, part] or officer shall, in the case of proceedings against the Crown under this section in respect of a tort committed by that department [, part] or officer, apply in relation to the Crown as it would have applied in relation to that department [, part] or officer if the proceedings against the Crown had been proceedings against that department or officer.

(5) No proceedings shall lie against the Crown by virtue of this section in respect of anything done or omitted to be done by any person while discharging or purporting to discharge any responsibilities

of a judicial nature vested in him, or any responsibilities which he has in connection with the execution of judicial process.

(6) No proceedings shall lie against the Crown by virtue of this section in respect of any act, neglect or default of any officer of the Crown, unless that officer has been directly or indirectly appointed by the Crown and was at the material time paid in respect of his duties as an officer of the Crown wholly out of the Consolidated Fund of the United Kingdom, moneys provided by Parliament, [the Scottish Consolidated Fund,] or any other Fund certified by the Treasury for the purposes of this subsection or was at the material time holding an office in respect of which the Treasury certify that the holder thereof would normally be so paid.

Law Reform (Personal Injuries) Act 1948

(11 & 12 Geo. VI, c. 41)

1   Common employment

(1) It shall not be a defence to an employer who is sued in respect of personal injuries caused by the negligence of a person employed by him, that that person was at the time the injuries were caused in common employment with the person injured.

(3) Any provision contained in a contract of service or apprenticeship, or in an agreement collateral thereto, (including a contract or agreement entered into before the commencement of this Act) shall be void in so far as it would have the effect of excluding or limiting any liability of the employer in respect of personal injuries caused to the person employed or apprenticed by the negligence of persons in common employment with him.

2   Measure of damages

(4) In an action for damages for personal injuries (including any such action arising out of a contract), there shall be disregarded, in determining the reasonableness of any expenses, the possibility of avoiding those expenses or part of them by taking advantage of facilities available under [the National Health Service Act 2006 or the National Health Service (Wales) Act 2006] or the [National Health Service (Scotland) Act 1978] or of any corresponding facilities in Northern Ireland.

3   Definition of 'personal injury'

In this Act the expression 'personal injury' includes any disease and any impairment of a person's physical or mental condition, and the expression 'injured' shall be construed accordingly.

National Parks and Access to the Countryside Act 1949

(12, 13 & 14 Geo. VI, c. 97)

60   Rights of public where access agreement or order in force

(1) Subject to the following provisions of this Part of this Act, where an access agreement or order is in force as respects any land a person who enters upon land comprised in the agreement or order for the purpose of open-air recreation without breaking or damaging any wall, fence, hedge or gate, or who is on such land for that purpose after having so entered thereon, shall not be treated as a trespasser on that land or incur any other liability by reason only of so entering or being on the land: Provided that this subsection shall not apply to land which for the time being is excepted land as hereinafter defined.

(2) Nothing in the provisions of the last foregoing subsection shall entitle a person to enter or be on any land, or to do anything thereon, in contravention of any prohibition contained in or having effect under any enactment.

Reserve and Auxiliary Forces (Protection of Civil Interests) Act 1951

(14 & 15 Geo. VI, c. 65)

13   Effect of failure to observe restrictions under Part I

(2) In any action for damages for conversion or other proceedings which lie by virtue of any such omission, failure or contravention, the court may take account of the conduct of the defendant with a view, if the court thinks fit, to awarding exemplary damages in respect of the wrong sustained by the plaintiff.

Defamation Act 1952

(15 & 16 Geo. VI & 1 Eliz. II, c. 66)

2   Slander affecting official, professional or business reputation

In an action for slander in respect of words calculated to disparage the plaintiff in an office, profession, calling, trade or business held or carried on by him at the time of the publication, it shall not be necessary to allege or prove special damage, whether or not the words are spoken of the plaintiff in the way of his office, profession, calling, trade or business.

3   Slander of title, etc.

(1) In an action for slander of title, slander of goods or other malicious falsehood, it shall not be necessary to allege or prove special damage—

    (a) if the words upon which the action is founded are calculated to cause pecuniary damage to the plaintiff and are published in writing or other permanent form; or

    (b) if the said words are calculated to cause pecuniary damage to the plaintiff in respect of any office, profession, calling, trade or business held or carried on by him at the time of the publication.

(2) Section one of this Act shall apply for the purposes of this section as it applies for the purposes of the law of libel and slander.

5   Justification

In an action for libel or slander in respect of words containing two or more distinct charges against the plaintiff, a defence of justification shall not fail by reason only that the truth of every charge is not proved if the words not proved to be true do not materially injure the plaintiff's reputation having regard to the truth of the remaining charges.

6   Fair comment

In an action for libel or slander in respect of words consisting partly of allegations of fact and partly of expression of opinion, a defence of fair comment shall not fail by reason only that the truth of every allegation or fact is not proved if the expression of opinion is fair comment having regard to such of the facts alleged or referred to in the words complained of as are proved.

9   Extension of certain defences to broadcasting

(1) Section three of the Parliamentary Papers Act, 1840 (which confers protection in respect of proceedings for printing extracts from or abstracts of parliamentary papers) shall have effect as if the reference to printing included a reference to broadcasting by means of wireless telegraphy.

10   Limitation on privilege at elections

A defamatory statement published by or on behalf of a candidate in any election to local government authority [to the Scottish Parliament] or to Parliament shall not be deemed to be published on a privileged occasion on the ground that it is material to a question in issue in the election, whether or not the person by whom it is published is qualified to vote at the election.

11   Agreements for indemnity

An agreement for indemnifying any person against civil liability for libel in respect of the publication of any matter shall not be unlawful unless at the time of the publication that person knows that the matter is defamatory, and does not reasonably believe that there is a good defence to any action brought upon it.

12   Evidence of other damages recovered by plaintiff

In any action for libel or slander the defendant may give evidence in mitigation of damages that the plaintiff has recovered damages, or has brought actions for damages, for libel or slander in respect of the publication of words to the same effect as the words on which the action is founded, or has received or agreed to receive compensation in respect of any such publication.

13   Consolidation of actions for slander etc.

Section five of the Law of Libel Amendment Act 1888 (which provides for the consolidation, on the application of the defendants, of two or more actions for libel by the same plaintiff) shall apply to actions for slander of title, slander of goods or other malicious falsehood as it applies to actions for libel; and references in that section to the same, or substantially the same, libel shall be construed accordingly.

16   Interpretation

(1) Any reference in this Act to words shall be construed as including a reference to pictures, visual images, gestures and other methods of signifying meaning.

Occupiers' Liability Act 1957

(5 & 6 Eliz. II, c. 31)

1   Preliminary

(1) The rules enacted by the two next following sections shall have effect, in place of the rules of the common law, to regulate the duty which an occupier of premises owes to his visitors in respect of dangers due to the state of the premises or to things done or omitted to be done on them.

(2) The rules so enacted shall regulate the nature of the duty imposed by law in consequence of a person's occupation or control of premises and of any invitation or permission he gives (or is to be treated as giving) to another to enter or use the premises, but they shall not alter the rules of the common law as to the persons on whom a duty is so imposed or to whom it is owed; and accordingly for the purpose of the rules so enacted the persons who are to be treated as an occupier and as his visitors are the same (subject to subsection (4) of this section) as the persons who would at common law be treated as an occupier and as his invitees or licensees.

(3) The rules so enacted in relation to an occupier of premises and his visitors shall also apply, in like manner and to the like extent as the principles applicable at common law to an occupier of premises and his invitees or licensees would apply, to regulate—

    (a) the obligations of a person occupying or having control over any fixed or moveable structure, including any vessel, vehicle or aircraft; and

    (b) the obligations of a person occupying or having control over any premises or structure in respect of damage to property, including the property of persons who are not themselves his visitors.

[(4) A person entering any premises in exercise of rights conferred by virtue of—

    (a) section 2(1) of the Countryside and Rights of Way Act 2000, or

    (b) an access agreement or order under the National Parks and Access to the Countryside Act 1949,

is not, for the purposes of this Act, a visitor of the occupier of those premises.]

2   Extent of occupier's ordinary duty

(1) An occupier of premises owes the same duty, the 'common duty of care', to all his visitors, except in so far as he is free to and does extend, restrict, modify or exclude his duty to any visitor or visitors by agreement or otherwise.

(2) The common duty of care is a duty to take such care as in all the circumstances of the case is reasonable to see that the visitor will be reasonably safe in using the premises for the purposes for which he is invited or permitted by the occupier to be there.

(3) The circumstances relevant for the present purposes include the degree of care, and of want of care, which would ordinarily be looked for in such a visitor, so that (for example) in proper cases—

(a) an occupier must be prepared for children to be less careful than adults; and

(b) an occupier may expect that a person, in the exercise of his calling, will appreciate and guard against any special risks ordinarily incident to it, so far as the occupier leaves him free to do so.

(4) In determining whether the occupier of premises has discharged the common duty of care to a visitor, regard is to be had to all the circumstances, so that (for example)—

(a) where damage is caused to a visitor by a danger of which he had been warned by the occupier, the warning is not to be treated without more as absolving the occupier from liability, unless in all the circumstances it was enough to enable the visitor to be reasonably safe; and

(b) where damage is caused to a visitor by a danger due to the faulty execution of any work of construction, maintenance or repair by an independent contractor employed by the occupier, the occupier is not to be treated without more as answerable for the danger if in all the circumstances he had acted reasonably in entrusting the work to an independent contractor and had taken such steps (if any) as he reasonably ought in order to satisfy himself that the contractor was competent and that the work had been properly done.

(5) The common duty of care does not impose on an occupier any obligation to a visitor in respect of risks willingly accepted as his by the visitor (the question whether a risk was so accepted to be decided on the same principles as in other cases in which one person owes a duty of care to another).

(6) For the purposes of this section, persons who enter premises for any purpose in the exercise of a right conferred by law are to be treated as permitted by the occupier to be there for that purpose, whether they in fact have his permission or not.

3   Effect of contract on occupier's liability to third party

(1) Where an occupier of premises is bound by contract to permit persons who are strangers to the contract to enter or use the premises, the duty of care which he owes to them as his visitors cannot be restricted or excluded by that contract, but (subject to any provision of the contract to the contrary) shall include the duty to perform his obligations under the contract, whether undertaken for their protection or not, in so far as those obligations go beyond the obligations otherwise involved in that duty.

(2) A contract shall not by virtue of this section have the effect, unless it expressly so provides, of making an occupier who has taken all reasonable care answerable to strangers to the contract for dangers due to the faulty execution of any work of construction, maintenance or repair or other like operation by persons other than himself, his servants and persons acting under his direction and control.

(3) In this section, 'stranger to the contract' means a person not for the time being entitled to the benefit of the contract as a party to it or as the successor by assignment or otherwise of a party to it, and accordingly includes a party to the contract who has ceased to be so entitled.

(4) Where by the terms or conditions governing any tenancy (including a statutory tenancy which does not in law amount to a tenancy) either the landlord or the tenant is bound, though not by contract, to permit persons to enter or use premises of which he is the occupier, this section shall apply as if the tenancy were a contract between the landlord and the tenant.

(5) This section, in so far as it prevents the common duty of care from being restricted or excluded, applies to contracts entered into and tenancies created before the commencement of this

Act, as well as to those entered into or created after its commencement; but, in so far as it enlarges the duty owed by an occupier beyond the common duty of care, it shall have effect only in relation to obligations which are undertaken after the commencement or which are renewed by agreement (whether express or implied) after that commencement.

5   Implied term in contracts

(1)   Where persons enter or use, or bring or send goods to, any premises in exercise of a right conferred by contract with a person occupying or having control of the premises, the duty he owes them in respect of dangers due to the state of the premises or to things done or omitted to be done by them, in so far as the duty depends on a term to be implied in the contract by reason of its conferring that right, shall be the common duty of care.

(2)   The foregoing subsection shall apply to fixed and moveable structures as it applies to premises.

(3)   This section does not affect the obligations imposed on a person by or by virtue of any contract for the hire of, or for the carriage for reward of persons or goods in, any vehicle, vessel, aircraft or other means of transport, or by virtue of any contract of bailment.

(4)   This section does not apply to contracts entered into before the commencement of this Act.

6   Application to the Crown

This Act shall bind the Crown, but as regards the Crown liability in tort shall not bind the Crown further than the Crown is made liable in tort by the Crown Proceedings Act, 1947, and that Act and in particular section two of it shall apply in relation to duties under sections two to four of this Act as statutory duties.

Law Reform (Husband and Wife) Act 1962

(10 & 11 Eliz. II, c. 48)

1   Actions in tort between husband and wife

(1)   Subject to the provisions of this section, each of the parties to a marriage shall have the like right of action in tort against the other as if they were not married.

(2)   Where an action in tort is brought by one of the parties to a marriage against the other during the subsistence of the marriage, the court may stay the action if it appears—

    (a)   that no substantial benefit would accrue to either party from the continuation of the proceedings; or

    (b)   that the question or questions in issue could more conveniently be disposed of on an application made under section seventeen of the Married Women's Property Act 1882 (determination of questions between husband and wife as to the title to or possession of property);

and without prejudice to paragraph (b) of this subsection the court may, in such an action, either exercise any power which could be exercised on an application under that said section seventeen, or give such directions as it thinks fit for the disposal under that section of any question arising in the proceedings.

Criminal Law Act 1967

(1967, c. 58)

3   Use of force in making arrest, etc.

(1)   A person may use such force as is reasonable in the circumstances in the prevention of crime, or in effecting or assisting in the lawful arrest of offenders or suspected offenders or of persons unlawfully at large.

14   Civil rights in respect of maintenance and champerty

(1) No person shall, under the law of England and Wales, be liable in tort for any conduct on account of its being maintenance or champerty as known to the common law, except in the case of a cause of action accruing before this section has effect.

(2) The abolition of criminal and civil liability under the law of England and Wales for maintenance and champerty shall not affect any rule of that law as to the cases in which a contract is to be treated as contrary to public policy or otherwise illegal.

Misrepresentation Act 1967

(1967, c. 7)

1   Removal of certain bars to rescission for innocent misrepresentation

Where a person has entered into a contract after a misrepresentation has been made to him, and—

    (a) the misrepresentation has become a term of the contract; or

    (b) the contract has been performed;

or both, then, if otherwise he would be entitled to rescind the contract without alleging fraud, he shall be so entitled, subject to the provisions of this Act, notwithstanding the matters mentioned in paragraphs (a) and (b) of this section.

2   Damages for misrepresentation

(1) Where a person has entered into a contract after a misrepresentation has been made to him by another party thereto and as a result thereof he has suffered loss, then, if the person making the misrepresentation would be liable to damages in respect thereof had the misrepresentation been made fraudulently, that person shall be so liable notwithstanding that the misrepresentation was not made fraudulently, unless he proves that he had reasonable ground to believe and did believe up to the time the contract was made that the facts represented were true.

(2) Where a person has entered into a contract after a misrepresentation has been made to him otherwise than fraudulently, and he would be entitled, by reason of the misrepresentation, to rescind the contract, then, if it is claimed, in any proceedings arising out of the contract, that the contract ought to be or has been rescinded, the court or arbitrator may declare the contract subsisting and award damages in lieu of rescission, if of opinion that it would be equitable to do so, having regard to the nature of the misrepresentation and the loss that would be caused by it if the contract were upheld, as well as to the loss that rescission would cause to the other party.

(3) Damages may be awarded against a person under subsection (2) of this section whether or not he is liable to damages under subsection (1) thereof, but where he is so liable any award under the said subsection (2) shall be taken into account in assessing his liability under the said subsection (1).

3   Avoidance of provision excluding liability for misrepresentation

[If a contract contains a term which would exclude or restrict—

    (a) any liability to which a party to a contract may be subject by reason of any misrepresentation made by him before the contract was made; or

    (b) any remedy available to another party to the contract by reason of such a misrepresentation,

that term shall be of no effect except in so far as it satisfies the requirement of reasonableness as stated in section 11(1) of the Unfair Contract Terms Act 1977; and it is for those claiming that the term satisfies that requirement to show that it does.]

Civil Evidence Act 1968

(1968, c. 64)

11　Convictions as evidence in civil proceedings

(1) In any civil proceedings the fact that a person has been convicted of an offence by or before any court in the United Kingdom or by a court-martial there or elsewhere shall (subject to subsection (3) below) be admissible in evidence for the purpose of proving where to do so is relevant to any issue in those proceedings, that he committed that offence, whether he was so convicted upon a plea of guilty or otherwise and whether or not he is a party to the civil proceedings; but no conviction other than a subsisting one shall be admissible in evidence by virtue of this section.

(2) In any civil proceedings in which by virtue of this section a person is proved to have been convicted of an offence by or before any court in the United Kingdom or by a court-martial there or elsewhere—

(a) he shall be taken to have committed that offence unless the contrary is proved; and

(b) without prejudice to the reception of any other admissible evidence for the purpose of identifying the facts on which the conviction was based, the contents of any documents which is admissible as evidence of the conviction, and the contents of the information, complaint, indictment or charge-sheet on which the person in question was convicted, shall be admissible in evidence for that purpose.

(3) Nothing in this section shall prejudice the operation of section 13 of this Act or any other enactment whereby a conviction or a finding of fact in any criminal proceedings is for the purposes of any other proceedings made conclusive evidence of any fact.

(4) Where in any civil proceedings the contents of any document are admissible in evidence by virtue of subsection (2) above, a copy of that document, or of the material part thereof, purporting to be certified or otherwise authenticated by or on behalf of the court or authority having custody of that document shall be admissible in evidence and shall be taken to be a true copy of that document or part unless the contrary is shown.

13　Conclusiveness of convictions for purposes of defamation actions

(1) In an action for libel or slander in which the question whether [the plaintiff] did or did not commit a criminal offence is relevant to an issue arising in the action, proof that at the time when that issue falls to be determined, [he] stands convicted of that offence shall be conclusive evidence that he committed that offence; and his conviction thereof shall be admissible in evidence accordingly.

(2) In any such action as aforesaid in which by virtue of this section [the plaintiff] is proved to have been convicted of an offence, the contents of any document which is admissible as evidence of the conviction, and the contents of the information, complaint, indictment or charge-sheet on which [he] was convicted, shall, without prejudice to the reception of any other admissible evidence for the purpose of identifying the facts on which the conviction was based, be admissible in evidence for the purpose of identifying those facts.

[(2A) In the case of an action for libel or slander in which there is more than one plaintiff—

(a) the references in subsections (1) and (2) above to the plaintiff shall be construed as references to any of the plaintiffs, and

(b) proof that any of the plaintiffs stands convicted of an offence shall be conclusive evidence that he committed that offence so far as that fact is relevant to any issue arising in relation to his cause of action or that of any other plaintiff.]

(3) For the purposes of this section a person shall be taken to stand convicted of an offence if but only if there subsists against him a conviction of that offence by or before a court in the United Kingdom or by a court-martial there or elsewhere.

Theatres Act 1968

(1968, c. 54)

4   Amendment of law of defamation
    (1) For the purposes of the law of libel and slander [. . .] the publication of words in the course of a performance of a play shall, subject to section 7 of this Act, be treated as publication in permanent form.
    (2) The foregoing subsection shall apply for the purposes of section 3 (slander of title, etc.) of the Defamation Act 1952 as it applies for the purposes of the law of libel and slander.
    (3) In this section 'words' includes pictures, visual images, gestures and other methods of signifying meaning.

Trade Descriptions Act 1968

(1968, c. 29)

35   Saving for civil rights
A contract for the supply of any goods shall not be void or unenforceable by reason only of a contravention of any provision of this Act.

Employers' Liability (Compulsory Insurance) Act 1969

(1969, c. 57)

1   Insurance against liability for employees
    (1) Except as otherwise provided by this Act, every employer carrying on any business in Great Britain shall insure, and maintain insurance, under one or more approved policies with an authorised insurer or insurers against liability for bodily injury or disease sustained by his employees, and arising out of and in the course of their employment in Great Britain in that business, but except in so far as regulations otherwise provide not including injury or disease suffered or contracted outside Great Britain.
    (2) Regulations may provide that the amount for which an employer is required by this Act to insure and maintain insurance shall, either generally or in such cases or classes of case as may be prescribed by the regulations, be limited in such manner as may be so prescribed.

2   Employees to be covered
    (1) For the purposes of this Act the term 'employee' means an individual who has entered into or works under a contract of service or apprenticeship with an employer whether by way of manual labour, clerical work or otherwise, whether such contract is expressed or implied, oral or in writing.
    (2) This Act shall not require an employer to insure—
        (a) in respect of an employee of whom the employer is the husband, wife, [civil partner,] father, mother, grandfather, grandmother, step-father, step-mother, son, daughter, grandson, granddaughter, stepson, stepdaughter, brother, sister, half-brother, half-sister; or
        (b) except as otherwise provided by regulations, in respect of employees not ordinarily resident in Great Britain.

Employer's Liability (Defective Equipment) Act 1969

(1969, c. 37)

1   Extension of employer's liability for defective equipment
    (1) Where after the commencement of this Act—
        (a) an employee suffers personal injury in the course of his employment in consequence of a defect in equipment provided by his employer for the purposes of the employer's business; and

(b) the defect is attributable wholly or partly to the fault of a third party (whether identified or not),

the injury shall be deemed to be also attributable to negligence on the part of the employer (whether or not he is liable in respect of the injury apart from this subsection), but without prejudice to the law relating to contributory negligence and to any remedy by way of contribution or in contract or otherwise which is available to the employer in respect of the injury.

(2) In so far as any agreement purports to exclude or limit any liability of an employer arising under subsection (1) of this section, the agreement shall be void.

(3) In this section—

'business' includes the activities carried on by any public body;

'employee' means a person who is employed by another person under a contract of service or apprenticeship and is so employed for the purposes of a business carried on by that other person, and 'employer' shall be construed accordingly;

'equipment' includes any plant and machinery, vehicle, aircraft and clothing;

'fault' means negligence, breach of statutory duty or other act or omission which gives rise to liability in tort in England and Wales or which is wrongful and gives rise to liability in damages in Scotland; and

'personal injury' includes loss of life, any impairment of a person's physical or mental condition and any disease.

(4) This section binds the Crown, and persons in the service of the Crown shall accordingly be treated for the purposes of this section as employees of the Crown if they would not be so treated apart from this subsection.

Administration of Justice Act 1970

(1970, c. 31)

40 Punishment for unlawful harassment of debtors

(1) A person commits an offence if, with the object of coercing another person to pay money claimed from the other as a debt due under a contract, he—

(a) harasses the other with demands for payment which, in respect of their frequency or the manner or occasion of making any such demand, or of any threat or publicity by which any demand is accompanied, are calculated to subject him or members of his family or household to alarm, distress or humiliation;

(b) falsely represents, in relation to the money claimed, that criminal proceedings lie for failure to pay it;

(c) falsely represents himself to be authorised in some official capacity to claim or enforce payment; or

(d) utters a document falsely represented by him to have some official character or purporting to have some official character which he knows it has not.

(2) A person may be guilty of an offence by virtue of subsection (1)(a) above if he concerts with others in the taking of such action as is described in that paragraph, notwithstanding that his own course of conduct does not by itself amount to harassment.

(3) Subsection (1)(a) above does not apply to anything done by a person which is reasonable (and otherwise permissible in law) for the purpose—

(a) of securing the discharge of an obligation due, or believed by him to be due, to himself or to persons for whom he acts, or protecting himself or them from future loss; or

(b) of the enforcement of any liability by legal process.

[(3A) Subsection (1) above does not apply to anything done by a person to another in circumstances where what is done is a commercial practice within the meaning of the Consumer Protection from Unfair Trading Regulations 2008 and the other is a consumer in relation to that practice.]

Taxes Management Act 1970

(1970, c. 9)

[**30   Recovery of overpayment of tax, etc.**

(1) Where an amount of [income tax or capital gains tax] has been repaid to any person which ought not to have been repaid to him, that amount of tax may be assessed and recovered as if it were unpaid tax.

(1A) Subsection (1) above shall not apply where the amount of tax which has been repaid is assessable under section 29 of this Act.

(1B) Subsections (2) to (8) of section 29 of this Act shall apply in relation to an assessment under subsection (1) above as they apply in relation to an assessment under subsection (1) of that section; and subsection (4) of that section as so applied shall have effect as if the reference to the loss of tax were a reference to the repayment of the amount of tax which ought not to have been repaid.

(2) In any case where—

    (a) a repayment of tax has been increased in accordance with section 824 [...] of the principal Act or section 283 of the 1992 Act (supplements added to repayments of tax, etc.); and

    (b) the whole or any part of that repayment has been paid to any person but ought not to have been paid to him; and

    (c) that repayment ought not to have been increased either at all or to any extent;

then the amount of the repayment assessed under subsection (1) above may include an amount equal to the amount by which the repayment ought not to have been increased.

(3) In any case where—

    (a) a payment, other than a repayment of tax to which subsection (2) above applies, is increased in accordance with section 824 or 825 of the principal Act or section 283 of the 1992 Act; and

    (b) that payment ought not to have been increased either at all or to any extent;

then an amount equal to the amount by which the payment ought not to have been increased may be assessed and recovered as if it were unpaid income tax [...].

(5) An assessment under this section shall not be out of time under section 34 of this Act if it is made before the end of whichever of the following ends the later, namely—

    (a) the [year of assessment] following that in which the amount assessed was repaid or paid as the case may be, or

    (b) where a return delivered by the person concerned [...] is enquired into by an officer of the Board, the period ending with the day on which, by virtue of section 28A(5) of this Act, the officer's enquiries are treated as completed.

(6) Subsection (5) above is without prejudice to section 36 of this Act.

(7) In this section any reference to an amount repaid or paid includes a reference to an amount allowed by way of set-off.]

[**33   Recovery of overpaid tax etc**

Schedule 1AB contains provision for and in connection with claims for the recovery of overpaid income tax and capital gains tax.]

[**Section 33**   **SCHEDULE 1AB**

RECOVERY OF OVERPAID TAX ETC

1   Claim for relief for overpaid tax etc

    (1) This paragraph applies where—

(a) a person has paid an amount by way of income tax or capital gains tax but the person believes that the tax was not due, or

(b) a person has been assessed as liable to pay an amount by way of income tax or capital gains tax, or there has been a determination or direction to that effect, but the person believes that the tax is not due.

(2) The person may make a claim to the Commissioners for repayment or discharge of the amount.

(6) The Commissioners are not liable to give relief in respect of a case described in sub-paragraph (1)(a) or (b) except as provided—

(a) by this Schedule and Schedule 1A (following a claim under this paragraph), or

(b) by or under another provision of the Income Tax Acts or an enactment relating to the taxation of capital gains.

(7) For the purposes of this Schedule an amount paid by one person on behalf of another is treated as paid by the other person.

2 Cases in which Commissioners not liable to give effect to claim

(1) The Commissioners are not liable to give effect to a claim under this Schedule if or to the extent that the claim falls within a case described in this paragraph (see also paragraph 4(5)).

(2) Case A is where the amount paid, or liable to be paid, is excessive by reason of—

(a) a mistake in a claim, election or notice,

(b) a mistake consisting of making or giving, or failing to make or give, a claim, election or notice,

(c) a mistake in allocating expenditure to a pool for the purposes of the Capital Allowances Act or a mistake consisting of making, or failing to make, such an allocation, or

(d) a mistake in bringing a disposal value into account for the purposes of that Act or a mistake consisting of bringing, or failing to bring, such a value into account.

(3) Case B is where the claimant is or will be able to seek relief by taking other steps under the Income Tax Acts or an enactment relating to the taxation of capital gains.

(4) Case C is where the claimant—

(a) could have sought relief by taking such steps within a period that has now expired, and

(b) knew, or ought reasonably to have known, before the end of that period that such relief was available.

(5) Case D is where the claim is made on grounds that—

(a) have been put to a court or tribunal in the course of an appeal by the claimant relating to the amount paid or liable to be paid, or

(b) have been put to Her Majesty's Revenue and Customs in the course of an appeal by the claimant relating to that amount that is treated as having been determined by a tribunal (by virtue of section 54 (settling of appeals by agreement)).

(6) Case E is where the claimant knew, or ought reasonably to have known, of the grounds for the claim before the latest of the following—

(a) the date on which an appeal by the claimant relating to the amount paid, or liable to be paid, in the course of which the ground could have been put forward (a "relevant appeal") was determined by a court or tribunal (or is treated as having been so determined),

(b) the date on which the claimant withdrew a relevant appeal to a court or tribunal, and

(c) the end of the period in which the claimant was entitled to make a relevant appeal to a court or tribunal.

(7) Case F is where the amount in question was paid or is liable to be paid—

(a) in consequence of proceedings enforcing the payment of that amount brought against the claimant by Her Majesty's Revenue and Customs, or

(b) in accordance with an agreement between the claimant and Her Majesty's Revenue and Customs settling such proceedings.

(8) Case G is where—

    (a) the amount paid, or liable to be paid, is excessive by reason of a mistake in calculating the claimant's liability to income tax or capital gains tax (other than a mistake in a PAYE assessment or PAYE calculation), and

    (b) liability was calculated in accordance with the practice generally prevailing at the time.

(9) Case H is where—

    (a) the amount paid, or liable to be paid, is excessive by reason of a mistake in a PAYE assessment or PAYE calculation, and

    (b) the assessment or calculation was made in accordance with the practice generally prevailing at the end of the period of 12 months following the tax year for which the assessment or calculation was made.

(10) For the purposes of Cases G and H—

    (a) "PAYE assessment" means an assessment on the claimant made in accordance with section 709 of ITEPA 2003 (assessment in connection with PAYE deductions), and

    (b) "PAYE calculation" means a calculation of the amount of a deduction or repayment made or to be made under PAYE regulations in respect of tax estimated to be payable by the claimant.

3 Making a claim

(1) A claim under this Schedule may not be made more than 4 years after the end of the relevant tax year.

(2) In relation to a claim made in reliance on paragraph 1(1)(a), the relevant tax year is—

    (a) where the amount paid, or liable to be paid, is excessive by reason of a mistake in a return or returns under section 8, 8A or 12AA of this Act, the tax year to which the return (or, if more than one, the first return) relates, and

    (b) otherwise, the tax year in respect of which the payment was made.

(3) In relation to a claim made in reliance on paragraph 1(1)(b), the relevant tax year is the tax year to which the assessment, determination or direction relates.

(4) A claim under this Schedule may not be made by being included in a return under section 8, 8A or 12AA of this Act.

4 The claimant: one person accountable for amounts payable by another etc

(1) Sub-paragraph (2) applies where, under a relevant enactment, a person ("P") is accountable to the Commissioners for—

    (a) an amount representing income tax or capital gains tax that is or is estimated to be payable by another person ("T"), or

    (b) any other amount that, under a relevant enactment, has been or is to be set off against a liability of T.

(2) A claim under this Schedule in respect of the amount may be made only by T.

(3) Sub-paragraph (4) applies where—

    (a) a person ("P") has paid an amount described in sub-paragraph (1)(a) or (b) in the belief that P was accountable to the Commissioners for the amount under a relevant enactment, but

    (b) P was not so accountable.

(4) A claim under this Schedule in respect of the amount may be made only by P.

(5) The Commissioners are not liable to give effect to a claim under sub-paragraph (4) if or to the extent that the amount has been repaid to T or set against amounts payable to the Commissioners by T.

(6) "Relevant enactment" means—

    (a) PAYE regulations,

    (b) Chapter 3 of Part 3 of the Finance Act 2004 or regulations under that Chapter (construction industry scheme), or

    (c) any other provision of or made under the Taxes Acts.

5   The claimant: partnerships

(1) This paragraph applies where—

(a) a trade, profession or business is carried on by two or more persons in partnership,

(b) an amount is paid, or liable to be paid, by one or more of those persons in accordance with a self-assessment, and

(c) the amount is excessive by reason of a mistake in a partnership return.

(2) A claim under this Schedule in respect of the amount—

(a) may be made by the relevant partner nominated to make the claim by all of the relevant partners, and

(b) may not be made by any other person.

(3) In relation to such a claim, references in this Schedule to the claimant are to any of the relevant partners.

(4) "Relevant partner" means—

(a) a person who was a partner in the partnership at any time during the period in respect of which the partnership return was made, or

(b) the personal representative of such a person.

6   Assessment of claimant in connection with claim

(1) This paragraph applies where—

(a) a claim is made under this Schedule,

(b) the grounds for giving effect to the claim also provide grounds for a discovery assessment or determination on the claimant in respect of any chargeable period, and

(c) such an assessment or determination could be made but for a relevant restriction.

(2) "Discovery assessment or determination" means—

(a) an assessment under section 29(1), or

(b) a discovery assessment or discovery determination under Schedule 18 to the Finance Act 1998 (company tax return etc).

(3) The following are relevant restrictions—

(a) the conditions in section 29(3) to (5),

(b) the restrictions in paragraphs 42 to 45 of Schedule 18 to the Finance Act 1998, and

(c) the expiry of a time limit for making a discovery assessment or determination.

(4) Where this paragraph applies—

(a) the relevant restrictions are to be disregarded, and

(b) the discovery assessment or determination is not out of time if it is made before the final determination of the claim.

7   Amendment of partnership return etc in connection with claim

(1) This paragraph applies where—

(a) a claim is made under this Schedule,

(b) the claimant is one of two or more persons carrying on a trade, profession or business in partnership,

(c) the grounds for giving effect to the claim also provide grounds for amending, under section 30B(1) (discovery of loss of tax from partnership), a return made by the partnership or any of the partners in respect of any period, and

(d) such an amendment could be made but for a relevant restriction.

(2) The following are relevant restrictions—

(a) the conditions in section 30B(4) to (6), and

(b) the expiry of a time limit for making an assessment under that section.

(3) Where this paragraph applies—

(a) the relevant conditions are to be disregarded, and

(b) the amendment is not out of time if it is made before the final determination of the claim.

8 Contract settlements

(1) In paragraph 1(1)(a) the reference to an amount paid by way of income tax or capital gains tax includes an amount paid under a contract settlement in connection with income tax or capital gains tax believed to be due from any person.

(2) Sub-paragraphs (3) to (6) apply if the person who paid the amount under the contract settlement ("the payer") and the person from whom the tax was due ("the taxpayer") are not the same person.

(3) In relation to a claim under this Schedule in respect of that amount—

(a) the references to the claimant in paragraph 2(5) to (7) (Cases D, E and F) have effect as if they included the taxpayer,

(b) the references to the claimant in paragraph 2(8) and (10) (Cases G and H) have effect as if they were references to the taxpayer,

(c) the references to the claimant in paragraphs 6(1)(b) and 7(1)(b) have effect as if they were references to the taxpayer, and

(d) references to tax in Schedule 1A (as it applies to a claim under this Schedule) include such an amount.

(4) Sub-paragraph (5) applies where the grounds for giving effect to a claim by the payer in respect of the amount also provide grounds for a discovery assessment or determination on the taxpayer in respect of any chargeable period.

(5) The Commissioners may set any amount repayable to the payer by virtue of the claim against any amount payable by the taxpayer by virtue of the assessment or determination.

(6) The obligations of the Commissioners and the taxpayer are discharged to the extent of any set-off under sub-paragraph (5).

(7) In this paragraph—

"contract settlement" means an agreement made in connection with any person's liability to make a payment to the Commissioners under or by virtue of an enactment;

"discovery assessment or determination" has the same meaning as in paragraph 6.

9 Interpretation

(1) In this Schedule "the Commissioners" means the Commissioners for Her Majesty's Revenue and Customs.

(2) For the purposes of this Schedule a claim is not finally determined until it, or the amount to which it relates, can no longer be varied (whether on appeal or otherwise).

Animals Act 1971

(1971, c. 22)

1 New provisions as to strict liability for damage done by animals

(1) The provisions of sections 2 to 5 of this Act replace—

(a) the rules of the common law imposing a strict liability in tort for damage done by an animal on the ground that the animal is regarded as ferae naturae or that its vicious or mischievous propensities are known or presumed to be known;

(b) subsections (1) and (2) of section 1 of the Dogs Act 1906 as amended by the Dogs (Amendment) Act 1928 (injury to cattle or poultry); and

(c) the rules of the common law imposing a liability for cattle trespass.

(2) Expressions used in those sections shall be interpreted in accordance with the provisions of section 6 (as well as those of section 11) of this Act.

2 Liability for damage done by dangerous animals

(1) Where any damage is caused by an animal which belongs to a dangerous species, any person who is a keeper of the animal is liable for the damage, except as otherwise provided by this Act.

(2) Where damage is caused by an animal which does not belong to a dangerous species, a keeper of the animal is liable for the damage, except as otherwise provided by this Act, if—

 (a) the damage is of a kind which the animal, unless restrained, was likely to cause or which, if caused by the animal, was likely to be severe; and

 (b) the likelihood of the damage or of its being severe was due to characteristics of the animal which are not normally found in animals of the same species or are not normally so found except at particular times or in particular circumstances; and

 (c) those characteristics were known to that keeper or were at any time known to a person who at that time had charge of the animal as that keeper s servant or, where that keeper is the head of a household, were known to another keeper of the animal who is a member of that household and under the age of sixteen.

3　Liability for injury done by dogs to livestock

Where a dog causes damage by killing or injuring livestock, any person who is a keeper of the dog is liable for the damage, except as otherwise provided by this Act.

4　Liability for damage and expenses due to trespassing livestock

(1) Where livestock belonging to any person strays on to land in the ownership or occupation of another and—

 (a) damage is done by the livestock to the land or to any property on it which is in the owner-ship or possession of the other person; or

 (b) any expenses are reasonably incurred by that other person in keeping the livestock while it cannot be restored to the person to whom it belongs or while it is detained in pursuance of section 7 of this Act, or in ascertaining to whom it belongs;

the person to whom the livestock belongs is liable for the damage or expenses, except as otherwise provided by this Act.

(2) For the purposes of this section any livestock belongs to the person in whose possession it is.

5　Exceptions from liability under sections 2 to 4

(1) A person is not liable under sections 2 to 4 of this Act for any damage which is due wholly to the fault of the person suffering it.

(2) A person is not liable under section 2 of this Act for any damage suffered by a person who has voluntarily accepted the risk thereof.

(3) A person is not liable under section 2 of this Act for any damage caused by an animal kept on any premises or structure to a person trespassing there, if it is proved either—

 (a) that the animal was not kept there for the protection of persons or property; or

 (b) (if the animal was kept there for the protection of persons or property) that keeping it there for that purpose was not unreasonable.

(4) A person is not liable under section 3 of this Act if the livestock was killed or injured on land on to which it had strayed and either the dog belonged to the occupier or its presence on the land was authorised by the occupier.

(5) A person is not liable under section 4 of this Act where the livestock strayed from a highway and its presence there was a lawful use of the highway.

(6) In determining whether any liability for damage under section 4 of this Act is excluded by subsection (1) of this section the damage shall not be treated as due to the fault of the person suffering it by reason only that he could have prevented it by fencing; but a person is not liable under that sec-tion where it is proved that the straying of the livestock on to the land would not have occurred but for a breach by any other person, being a person having an interest in the land, of a duty to fence.

6　Interpretation of certain expressions used in sections 2 to 5

(1) The following provisions apply to the interpretation of sections 2 to 5 of this Act.

(2) A dangerous species is a species—

 (a) which is not commonly domesticated in the British Islands; and

(b) whose fully grown animals normally have such characteristics that they are likely, unless restrained, to cause severe damage or that any damage they may cause is likely to be severe.

(3) Subject to subsection (4) of this section, a person is a keeper of an animal if—

(a) he owns the animal or has it in his possession; or

(b) he is the head of a household of which a member under the age of sixteen owns the animal or has it in his possession;

and if at any time an animal ceases to be owned by or to be in the possession of a person, any person who immediately before that time was a keeper thereof by virtue of the preceding provisions of this subsection continues to be a keeper of the animal until another person becomes a keeper thereof by virtue of those provisions.

(4) Where an animal is taken into and kept in possession for the purpose of preventing it from causing damage or of restoring it to its owner, a person is not a keeper of it by virtue only of that possession.

(5) Where a person employed as a servant by a keeper of an animal incurs a risk incidental to his employment he shall not be treated as accepting it voluntarily.

7   Detention and sale of trespassing livestock

(1) The right to seize and detain any animal by way of distress damage feasant is hereby abolished.

(2) Where any livestock strays on to any land and is not then under the control of any person the occupier of the land may detain it, subject to subsection (3) of this section, unless ordered to return it by a court.

(3) Where any livestock is detained in pursuance of this section the right to detain it ceases—

(a) at the end of a period of forty-eight hours, unless within that period notice of the detention has been given to the officer in charge of a police station and also, if the person detaining the livestock knows to whom it belongs, to that person; or

(b) when such amount is tendered to the person detaining the livestock as is sufficient to satisfy any claim he may have under section 4 of this Act in respect of the livestock; or,

(c) if he has no such claim, when the livestock is claimed by a person entitled to its possession.

(4) Where livestock has been detained in pursuance of this section for a period of not less than fourteen days the person detaining it may sell it at a market or by public auction, unless proceedings are then pending for the return of the livestock or for any claim under section 4 of this Act in respect of it.

(5) Where any livestock is sold in the exercise of the right conferred by this section and the proceeds of the sale, less the costs thereof and any costs incurred in connection with it, exceed the amount of any claim under section 4 of this Act which the vendor had in respect of the livestock, the excess shall be recoverable from him by the person who would be entitled to the possession of the livestock but for the sale.

(6) A person detaining any livestock in pursuance of this section is liable for any damage caused to it by a failure to treat it with reasonable care and supply it with adequate food and water while it is so detained.

(7) References in this section to a claim under section 4 of this Act in respect of any livestock do not include any claim under that section for damage done by or expenses incurred in respect of the livestock before the straying in connection with which it is detained under this section.

8   Duty to take care to prevent damage from animals straying on to the highway

(1) So much of the rules of the common law relating to liability for negligence as excludes or restricts the duty which a person might owe to others to take such care as is reasonable to see that damage is not caused by animals straying on to a highway is hereby abolished.

(2) Where damage is caused by animals straying from unfenced land to a highway a person who placed them on the land shall not be regarded as having committed a breach of the duty to take care by reason only of placing them there if—

    (a) the land is common land, or is land situated in an area where fencing is not customary, or is a town or village green; and

    (b) he had a right to place the animals on that land.

9 Killing of or injury to dogs worrying livestock

(1) In any civil proceedings against a person (in this section referred to as the defendant) for killing or causing injury to a dog it shall be a defence to prove—

    (a) that the defendant acted for the protection of any livestock and was a person entitled to act for the protection of that livestock; and

    (b) that within forty-eight hours of the killing or injury notice thereof was given by the defendant to the officer in charge of a police station.

(2) For the purposes of this section a person is entitled to act for the protection of any livestock if, and only if—

    (a) the livestock or the land on which it is belongs to him or to any person under whose express or implied authority he is acting; and

    (b) the circumstances are not such that liability for killing or causing injury to the livestock would be excluded by section 5(4) of this Act.

(3) Subject to subsection (4) of this section, a person killing or causing injury to a dog shall be deemed for the purposes of this section to act for the protection of any livestock if, and only if, either—

    (a) the dog is worrying or is about to worry the livestock and there are no other reasonable means of ending or preventing the worrying; or

    (b) the dog has been worrying livestock, has not left the vicinity and is not under the control of any person and there are no practicable means of ascertaining to whom it belongs.

(4) For the purposes of this section the condition stated in either of the paragraphs of the preceding subsection shall be deemed to have been satisfied if the defendant believed that it was satisfied and had reasonable ground for that belief.

(5) For the purposes of this section—

    (a) an animal belongs to any person if he owns it or has it in his possession; and

    (b) land belongs to any person if he is the occupier thereof.

10 Application of certain enactments to liability under sections 2 to 4

For the purposes of [the Fatal Accidents Act 1976,] the Law Reform (Contributory Negligence) Act 1945 and [the Limitation Act 1980] any damage for which a person is liable under sections 2 to 4 of this Act shall be treated as due to his fault.

11 General interpretation

In this Act—

  'common land', and 'town or village green' have the same meanings as in the Commons Regulation Act 1965;

  'damage' includes the death of, or injury to, any person (including any disease and any impairment of physical or mental condition);

  'fault' has the same meaning as in the Law Reform (Contributory Negligence) Act 1945;

  'fencing' includes the construction of any obstacle designed to prevent animals from straying;

  'livestock' means cattle, horses, asses, mules, hinnies, sheep, pigs, goats and poultry, and also deer not in the wild state and, in section 3 and 9 also, while in captivity, pheasants, partridges and grouse;

  'poultry' means the domestic varieties of the following, that is to say, fowls, turkeys, geese, ducks, guinea-fowls, pigeons, peacocks and quails; and 'species' includes sub-species and variety.

12   Application to Crown

(1) This Act binds the Crown, but nothing in this section shall authorise proceedings to be brought against Her Majesty in her private capacity.

(2) Section 38(3) of the Crown Proceedings Act 1947 (interpretation of references to Her Majesty in her private capacity) shall apply as if this section were contained in that Act.

Carriage of Goods by Sea Act 1971

(1971, c. 19)

1   Application of Hague Rules as amended

(1) In this Act, 'the Rules' means the International Convention for the unification of certain rules of law relating to bills of lading signed at Brussels on 25 August 1924, as amended by the Protocol signed at Brussels on 23 February 1968 [and by the Protocol signed at Brussels on 21 December 1979.]

(2) The provisions of the Rules, as set out in the Schedule to this Act, shall have the force of law.

(3) Without prejudice to subsection (2) above, the said provisions shall have effect (and have the force of law) in relation to and in connection with the carriage of goods by sea in ships where the port of shipment is a port in the United Kingdom, whether or not the carriage is between ports in two different States within the meaning of Article X of the Rules.

(4) Subject to subsection (6) below, nothing in this section shall be taken as applying anything in the Rules to any contract for the carriage of goods by sea, unless the contract expressly or by implication provides for the issue of a bill of lading or any similar document of title.

(5) [...]

(6) Without prejudice to Article X(c) of the Rules, the Rules shall have the force of law in relation to—

> (a) any bill of lading if the contract contained in or evidenced by it expressly provides that the Rules shall govern the contract, and
>
> (b) any receipt which is a non-negotiable document marked as such if the contract contained in or evidenced by it is a contract for the carriage of goods by sea which expressly provides that the Rules are to govern the contract as if the receipt were a bill of lading,

but subject, where paragraph (b) applies, to any necessary modifications and in particular with the omission in Article III of the Rules of the second sentence of paragraph 4 and of paragraph 7.

(7) If and so far as the contract contained in or evidenced by a bill of lading or receipt within paragraph (a) or (b) of subsection (6) above applies to deck cargo or live animals, the Rules as given the force of law by that subsection shall have effect as if Article I(c) did not exclude deck cargo and live animals.

In this subsection 'deck cargo' means cargo which by the contract of carriage is stated as being carried on deck and is so carried.

[1A   Conversion of special drawing rights into sterling

(1) For the purposes of Article IV of the Rules the value on a particular day of one special drawing right shall be treated as equal to such a sum in sterling as the International Monetary Fund have fixed as being the equivalent of one special drawing right—

> (a) for that day; or
>
> (a) if no sum has been so fixed for that day, for the last day before that day for which a sum has been so fixed.

(2) A certificate given by or on behalf of the Treasury stating—

> (a) that a particular sum in sterling has been fixed as aforesaid for a particular day; or
>
> (b) that no sum has been so fixed for a particular day and that a particular sum in sterling has been so fixed for a day which is the last day for which a sum has been so fixed before the particular day,

shall be conclusive evidence of those matters for the purposes of subsection (1) above; and a document purporting to be such a certificate shall in any proceedings be received in evidence and, unless the contrary is proved, be deemed to be such a certificate.

(3) The Treasury may charge a reasonable fee for any certificate given in pursuance of subsection (2) above, and any fee received by the Treasury by virtue of this subsection shall be paid into the Consolidated Fund.]

2   Contracting States, etc.

(1) If Her Majesty by Order in council certifies to the following effect, that is to say, that for the purposes of the Rules—

    (a) a State specified in the Order is a contracting State, or is a contracting State in respect of any place or territory so specified; or

    (b) any place or territory specified in the Order forms part of a State so specified (whether a contracting State or not),

the Order shall, except so far as it has been superseded by a subsequent Order, be conclusive evidence of the matters so certified.

(2) An Order in Council under this section may be varied or revoked by a subsequent Order in Council.

3   Absolute warranty of seaworthiness not to be implied in contracts to which Rules apply

There shall not be implied in any contract for the carriage of goods by sea to which the Rules apply by virtue of this Act any absolute undertaking by the carrier of the goods to provide a seaworthy ship.

SCHEDULE
THE HAGUE RULES AS AMENDED
BY THE BRUSSELS PROTOCOL 1968

Article I

In these Rules the following words are employed, with the meanings set out below—

    (a) 'Carrier' includes the owner or the charter who enters into a contract of carriage with a shipper.

    (b) 'Contract of carriage' applies only to contracts of carriage covered by a bill of lading or any similar document of title, in so far as such document relates to the carriage of goods by sea, including any bill of lading or any similar document as aforesaid issued under or pursuant to a charter party from the moment at which such bill of lading or similar document of title regulates the relations between a carrier and a holder of the same.

    (c) 'Goods' includes goods, wares, merchandise, and articles of every kind whatsoever except live animals and cargo which by the contract of carriage is stated as being carried on deck and is so carried.

    (d) 'Ship' means any vessel used for the carriage of goods by sea.

    (e) 'Carriage of goods' covers the period from the time when the goods are loaded on to the time they are discharged from the ship.

Article II

Subject to the provisions of Article VI, under every contract of carriage of goods by sea the carrier, in relation to the loading, handling, stowage, carriage, custody, care and discharge of such goods, shall be subject to the responsibilities and liabilities, and entitled to the rights and immunities hereinafter set forth.

Article III

(1) The carrier shall be bound before and at the beginning of the voyage to exercise due diligence to—

(a) Make the ship seaworthy.

(b) Properly man, equip and supply the ship.

(c) Make the holds, refrigerating and cool chambers, and all other parts of the ship in which goods are carried, fit and safe for their reception, carriage and preservation.

(2) Subject to the provisions of Article IV, the carrier shall properly and carefully load, handle, stow, carry, keep, care for, and discharge the goods carried.

(3) After receiving the goods into his charge the carrier or the master or agent of the carrier shall, on demand of the shipper, issue to the shipper a bill of lading showing among other things—

(a) The leading marks necessary for identification of the goods as the same are furnished in writing by the shipper before the loading of such goods starts, provided such marks are stamped or otherwise shown clearly upon the goods if uncovered, or on the cases or coverings in which such goods are contained, in such a manner as should ordinarily remain legible until the end of the voyage.

(b) Either the number of packages or pieces, or the quantity, or weight, as the case may be, as furnished in writing by the shipper.

(c) The apparent order and condition of the goods. Provided that no carrier, master or agent of the carrier shall be bound to state or show in the bill of lading any marks, number, quantity, or weight which he has reasonable ground for suspecting not accurately to represent the goods actually received, or which he has had no reasonable means of checking.

(4) Such a bill of lading shall be prima facie evidence of the receipt by the carrier of the goods as therein described in accordance with paragraph 3(a), (b) and (c). However, proof to the contrary shall not be admissible when the bill of lading has been transferred to a third party acting in good faith.

(5) The shipper shall be deemed to have guaranteed to the carrier the accuracy at the time of shipment of the marks, number, quantity and weight, as furnished by him, and the shipper shall indemnify the carrier against all loss, damages and expenses arising or resulting from inaccuracies in such particulars. The right of the carrier to such indemnity shall in no way limit his responsibility and liability under the contract of carriage to any person other than the shipper.

(6) Unless notice of loss or damage and the general nature of such loss or damage be given in writing to the carrier or his agent at the port of discharge before or at the time of the removal of the goods into the custody of the person entitled to delivery thereof under the contract of carriage, or, if the loss or damage be not apparent, within three days, such removal shall be prima facie evidence of the delivery by the carrier of the goods as described in the bill of lading.

The notice in writing need not be given if the state of the goods has, at the time of their receipt, been the subject of joint survey or inspection.

Subject to paragraph 6bis the carrier and the ship shall in any event be discharged from all liability whatsoever in respect of the goods, unless suit is brought within one year of their delivery or of the date when they should have been delivered. This period may, however, be extended if the parties so agree after the cause of action has arisen.

In the case of any actual or apprehended loss or damage the carrier and the receiver shall give all reasonable facilities to each other for inspecting and tallying the goods.

(6bis) An action for indemnity against a third person may be brought even after the expiration of the year provided for in the preceding paragraph if brought within the time allowed by the law of the Court seized of the case. However, the time allowed shall be not less than three months, commencing from the day when the person bringing such action for indemnity has settled the claim or has been served with process in the action against himself.

(7) After the goods are loaded the bill of lading to be issued by the carrier, master, or agent of the carrier, to the shipper shall, if the shipper so demands, be a 'shipped' bill of lading, provided that if the shipper shall have previously taken up any document of title to such goods, he shall surrender the

same as against the issue of the 'shipped' bill of lading, but at the option of the carrier such document of title may be noted at the port of shipment by the carrier, master, or agent with the name or names of the ship or ships upon which the goods have been shipped and the date or dates of shipment, and when so noted if it shows the particulars mentioned in paragraph 3 of Article III, shall for the purpose of this article be deemed to constitute a 'shipped' bill of lading.

(8) Any clause, covenant, or agreement in a contract of carriage relieving the carrier or the ship from liability for loss or damage to, or in connection with, goods arising from negligence, fault, or failure in the duties and obligations provided in this article or lessening such liability otherwise than as provided in these Rules, shall be null and void and of no effect. A benefit of insurance in favour of the carrier or similar clause shall be deemed to be a clause relieving the carrier from liability.

Article IV

(1) Neither the carrier nor the ship shall be liable for loss or damage arising or resulting from unseaworthiness unless caused by want of due diligence on the part of the carrier to make the ship seaworthy, and to secure that the ship is properly manned, equipped and supplied, and to make the holds, refrigerating and cool chambers and all other parts of the ship in which goods are carried fit and safe for their reception, carriage and preservation in accordance with the provisions of paragraph 1 of Article III. Whenever loss or damage has resulted from unseaworthiness the burden of proving the exercise of due diligence shall be on the carrier or other person claiming exemption under this article.

(2) Neither the carrier nor the ship shall be responsible for loss or damage arising or resulting from—

- (a) Act, neglect, or default of the master, mariner, pilot, or the servants of the carrier in the navigation or in the management of the ship.
- (b) Fire, unless caused by the actual fault or privity of the carrier.
- (c) Perils, dangers and accidents of the sea or other navigable waters.
- (d) Act of God.
- (e) Act of war.
- (f) Act of public enemies.
- (g) Arrest or restraint of princes, rulers or people, or seizure under legal process.
- (h) Quarantine restrictions.
- (i) Act or omission of the shipper or owner of the goods, his agent or representative.
- (j) Strikes or lockouts or stoppage or restraint of labour from whatever cause, whether partial or general.
- (k) Riots and civil commotions.
- (l) Saving or attempting to save life or property at sea.
- (m) Wastage in bulk or weight or any other loss or damage arising from inherent defect, quality or vice of the goods.
- (n) Insufficiency of packing.
- (o) Insufficiency or inadequacy of marks.
- (p) Latent defects not discoverable by due diligence.
- (q) Any other cause arising without the actual fault or privity of the carrier, or without the fault or neglect of the agents or servants of the carrier, but the burden of proof shall be on the person claiming the benefit of this exception to show that neither the actual fault or privity of the carrier nor the fault or neglect of the agents or servants of the carrier contributed to the loss or damage.

(3) The shipper shall not be responsible for the loss or damage sustained by the carrier or the ship arising or resulting from any cause without the act, fault or neglect of the shipper, his agents or his servants.

(4) Any deviation in saving or attempting to save life or property at sea or any reasonable deviation shall not be deemed to be an infringement or breach of these Rules or of the contract of carriage, and the carrier shall not be liable for any loss or damage resulting therefrom.

(5) (a) Unless the nature and value of such goods have been declared by the shipper before shipment and inserted in the bill of lading, neither the carrier nor the ship shall in any event be or become liable for any loss or damage to or in connection with the goods in an amount exceeding [666.67 units of account] per package or unit or [2 units of account per kilogramme] of gross weight of the goods lost or damaged, whichever is the higher.

(b) The total amount recoverable shall be calculated by reference to the value of such goods at the place and time at which the goods are discharged from the ship in accordance with the contract or should have been so discharged.

The value of the goods shall be fixed according to the commodity exchange price, or, if there be no such price, according to the current market price, or, if there be no commodity exchange price or current market price, by reference to the normal value of goods of the same kind and quality.

(c) Where a container, pallet or similar article of transport is used to consolidate goods, the number of packages or units enumerated in the bill of lading as packed in such article of transport shall be deemed the number of packages or units for the purpose of this paragraph as far as these packages or units are concerned. Except as aforesaid such article of transport shall be considered the package or unit.

[(d) The unit of account mentioned in this Article is the special drawing right as defined by the International Monetary Fund. The amounts mentioned in subparagraph (a) of this paragraph shall be converted into national currency on the basis of the value of that currency on a date to be determined by the law of the court seized of the case.]

(e) Neither the carrier nor the ship shall be entitled to the benefit of the limitation of liability provided for in this paragraph if it is proved that the damage resulted from an act or omission of the carrier done with intent to cause damage, or recklessly and with knowledge that damage would probably result.

(f) The declaration mentioned in sub-paragraph (a) of this paragraph, if embodied in the bill of lading, shall be prima facie evidence, but shall not be binding or conclusive on the carrier.

(g) By agreement between the carrier, master or agent of the carrier and the shipper other maximum amounts than those mentioned in sub-paragraph (a) of this paragraph may be fixed, provided that no maximum amount so fixed shall be less than the appropriate maximum mentioned in that sub-paragraph.

(h) Neither the carrier nor the ship shall be responsible in any event (nor loss or damage to, or in connection with, goods if the nature or value thereof has been knowingly misstated by the shipper in the bill of lading.

(6) Goods of an inflammable, explosive or dangerous nature to the shipment whereof the carrier, master or agent of the carrier has not consented with knowledge of their nature and character, may at any time before discharge be landed at any place, or destroyed or rendered innocuous by the carrier without compensation and the shipper of such goods shall be liable for all damages and expenses directly or indirectly arising out of or resulting from such shipment. If any such goods shipped with such knowledge and consent shall become a danger to the ship or cargo, they may in like manner be landed at any place, or destroyed or rendered innocuous by the carrier without liability on the part of the carrier except to general average, if any.

Article IV bis

(1) The defences and limits of liability provided for in these Rules shall apply in any action against the carrier in respect of loss or damage to goods covered by a contract of carriage whether the action be founded in contract or in tort.

(2) If such an action is brought against a servant or agent of the carrier (such servant or agent not being an independent contractor), such servant or agent shall be entitled to avail himself of the defences and limits of liability which the carrier is entitled to invoke under these Rules.

(3) The aggregate of the amounts recoverable from the carrier, and such servants and agents, shall in no case exceed the limit provided for in these Rules.

(4) Nevertheless, a servant or agent of the carrier shall not be entitled to avail himself of the provisions of this article, if it is proved that the damage resulted from an act or omission of the servant or agent done with intent to cause damage or recklessly and with knowledge that damage would probably result.

Article V

A carrier shall be at liberty to surrender in whole or in part all or any of his rights and immunities or to increase any of his responsibilities and obligations under these Rules, provided such surrender or increase shall be embodied in the bill of lading issued to the shipper. The provisions of the Rules shall not be applicable to charter parties, but if bills of lading are issued in the case of a ship under a charter party they shall comply with the terms of these Rules. Nothing in these Rules shall be held to prevent the insertion in a bill of lading of any lawful provisions regarding general average.

Article VI

Notwithstanding the provisions of the preceding articles, a carrier, master or agent of the carrier and a shipper shall in regard to any particular goods be at liberty to enter into any agreement in any terms as to the responsibility and liability of the carrier for such goods, and as to the rights and immunities of the carrier in respect of such goods, or his obligation as to seaworthiness, so far as this stipulation is not contrary to public policy, or the care or diligence of his servants or agents in regard to the loading, handling, stowage, carriage, custody, care and discharge of the goods carried by sea, provided that in this case no bill of lading has been or shall be issued and that the terms agreed shall be embodied in a receipt which shall be a non-negotiable document and shall be marked as such.

Any agreement so entered into shall have full legal effect. Provided that this article shall not apply to ordinary commercial shipments made in the ordinary course of trade, but only to other shipments where the character or condition of the property to be carried or the circumstances, terms and conditions under which the carriage is to be performed are such as reasonably to justify a special agreement.

Article VII

Nothing herein contained shall prevent a carrier or a shipper from entering into any agreement, stipulation, condition, reservation or exemption as to the responsibility and liability of the carrier or the ship for the loss or damage to, or in connection with, the custody and care and handling of goods prior to the loading on, and subsequent to the discharge from, the ship on which the goods are carried by sea.

Article VIII

The provisions of these Rules shall not affect the rights and obligations of the carrier under any statute for the time being in force relating to the limitation of the liability of owners of sea-going vessels.

Article IX

These rules shall not affect the provisions of any international Convention or national law governing liability for nuclear damage.

Article X

The provisions of these Rules shall apply to every bill of lading relating to the carriage of goods between ports in two different States if:

      (a) the bill of lading is issued in a contracting State,

or

      (b) the carriage is from a port in a contracting State,

or

      (c) the contract contained in or evidenced by the bill of lading provides that these Rules or legislation of any State giving effect to them are to govern the contract, whatever may be the nationality of the ship, the carrier, the shipper, the consignee, or any other interested person.

Unsolicited Goods and Services Act 1971

(1971, c. 30)

2 Demands and threats regarding payment

(1) A person who, not having reasonable cause to believe there is a right to payment, in the course of any trade or business makes a demand for payment, or asserts a present or prospective right to payment, for what he knows are unsolicited goods sent (after the commencement of this Act) to another person with a view to his acquiring them [for the purposes of his trade or business], shall be guilty of an offence and on summary conviction shall be liable to a fine not exceeding [level 4 on the standard scale].

(2) A person who, not having reasonable cause to believe there is a right to payment in the course of any trade or business and with a view to obtaining any payment for what he knows are unsolicited goods sent as aforesaid—

    (a) threatens to bring any legal proceedings; or

    (b) places or causes to be placed the name of any person on a list of defaulters or debtors or threatens to do so; or

    (c) invokes or causes to be invoked any other collection procedure or threatens to do so, shall be guilty of an offence and shall be liable on summary conviction to a fine not exceeding [level 5 on the standard scale].

3 Directory entries

[(1) A person ('the purchaser') shall not be liable to make any payment, and shall be entitled to recover any payment made by him, by way of charge for including or arranging for the inclusion in a directory of an entry relating to that person or his trade or business, unless—

    (a) there has been signed by the purchaser or on his behalf an order complying with this section,

    (b) there has been signed by the purchaser or on his behalf a note complying with this section of his agreement to the charge and before the note was signed, a copy of it was supplied, for retention by him, to him or a person acting on his behalf, ...

    (c) there has been transmitted by the purchaser or a person acting on his behalf an electronic communication which includes a statement that the purchaser agrees to the charge and the relevant condition is satisfied in relation to that communication, or

    (d) the charge arises under a contract in relation to which the conditions in section 3B(1) (renewed and extended contracts) are met.]

(2) A person shall be guilty of an offence punishable on summary conviction with a fine not exceeding £400 if, in a case where a payment in respect of a charge would [...] be recoverable from him in accordance with the terms of subsection (1) above, he demands payment, or asserts a present or prospective right to payment, of the charge or any part of it, without knowing or having reasonable cause to believe [that—

    (a) the entry to which the charge relates was ordered in accordance with this section,

    (b) a proper note of the agreement has been duly signed, or

    (c) the requirements set out in subsection (1)(c) or (d) above have been met.]

(3) For the purposes of [this section—

    (a) an order for an entry in a directory must be made by means of an order form or other stationery belonging to the purchaser, which may be sent electronically but which must bear his name and address (or one or more of his addresses); and

    (b) the note of a person s agreement to a charge must—

(i)   specify the particulars set out in Part 1 of the Schedule to the Regulatory Reform (Unsolicited Goods and Services Act 1971) (Directory Entries and Demands for Payment) Order 2005, and

(ii) give reasonable particulars of the entry in respect of which the charge would be payable.]

[(3A) In relation to an electronic communication which includes a statement that the purchaser agrees to a charge for including or arranging the inclusion in a directory of any entry, the relevant condition is that—

(a) before the electronic communication was transmitted the information referred to in subsection (3B) below was communicated to the purchaser, and

(b) the electronic communication can readily be produced and retained in a visible and legible form.

(3B) that information is—

(a) the following particulars—

(i)   the amount of the charge;

(ii)   the name of the directory or proposed directory;

(iii)   the name of the person producing the directory;

(iv)   the geographic address at which that person is established;

(v)   if the directory is or is to be available in printed form, the proposed date of publication of the directory or of the issue in which the entry is to be included;

(vi)   if the directory or the issue in which the entry is to be included is to be put on sale, the price at which it is to be offered for sale and the minimum number of copies which are to be available for sale;

(vii)   if the directory or the issue in which the entry is to be included is to be distributed free of charge (whether or not it is also to be put on sale), the minimum number of copies which are to be so distributed;

(viii) if the directory is or is to be available in a form other than in printed form, adequate details of how it may be accessed; and

(b) reasonable particulars of the entry in respect of which the charge would be payable.

(3C) In this section 'electronic communication' has the same meaning as in the Electronic Communications Act 2000.]

[3B   Renewed and extended contracts

(1) The conditions referred to in section 3(1)(d) above are met in relation to a contract ('the new contract') if—

(a) a person ('the purchaser') has entered into an earlier contract ('the earlier contract') for including or arranging for the inclusion in a particular issue or version of a directory ('the earlier directory') of an entry ('the earlier entry') relating to him or his trade or business;

(b) the purchaser was liable to make a payment by way of a charge arising under the earlier contract for including or arranging for the inclusion of the earlier entry in the earlier directory;

(c) the new contract is a contract for including or arranging for the inclusion in a later issue or version of a directory ('the later directory') of an entry ('the later entry') relating to the purchaser or his trade or business;

(d) the form, content and distribution of the later directory is materially the same as the form, content and distribution of the earlier directory;

(e) the form and content of the later entry is materially the same as the form and content of the earlier entry;

(f) if the later directory is published other than in electronic form—

(i)   the earlier directory was the last, or the last but one, issue or version of the directory to be published before the later directory, and

      (ii) the date of publication of the later directory is not more than 13 months after the date of publication of the earlier directory;

    (g) if the later directory is published in electronic form, the first date on which the new contract requires the later entry to be published is not more than the relevant period after the last date on which the earlier contract required the earlier entry to be published;

    (h) if it was a term of the earlier contract that the purchaser renew or extend the contract—

      (i)   before the start of the new contract the relevant publisher has given notice in writing to the purchaser containing the information set out in Part 3 of the Schedule to the Regulatory Reform (Unsolicited Goods and Services Act 1971) (Directory Entries and Demands for Payment) Order 2005; and

      (ii) the purchaser has not written to the relevant publisher withdrawing his agreement to the renewal or extension of the earlier contract within the period of 21 days starting when he receives the notice referred to in subparagraph (i); and

    (i) if the parties to the earlier contract and the new contract are different—

      (i)   the parties to both contracts have entered into a novation agreement in respect of the earlier contract; or

      (ii) the relevant publisher has given the purchaser the information set out in Part 4 of the Schedule to the Regulatory Reform (Unsolicited Goods and Services Act 1971) (Directory Entries and Demands for Payment) Order 2005.

(2) For the purposes of subsection (1)(d) and (e), the form, content or distribution of the later directory, or the form or content of the later entry, shall be taken to be materially the same as that of the earlier directory or the earlier entry (as the case may be), if a reasonable person in the position of the purchaser would—

    (a) view the two as being materially the same; or

    (b) view that of the later directory or the later entry as being an improvement on that of the earlier directory or the earlier entry.

(3) For the purposes of subsection (1)(g) 'the relevant period' means the period of 13 months or (if shorter) the period of time between the first and last dates on which the earlier contract required the earlier entry to be published.

(4) For the purposes of subsection (1)(h) and (i) 'the relevant publisher' is the person with whom the purchaser has entered into the new contract.

(5) The information referred to in subsection (1) (i) (ii) must be given to the purchaser prior to the conclusion of the new contract.]

4   Unsolicited publications

(1) A person shall be guilty of an offence if he sends or causes to be sent to another person any book, magazine or leaflet (or advertising material for any such publication) which he knows or ought reasonably to know is unsolicited and which describes or illustrates human sexual techniques.

(2) A person found guilty of an offence under this section shall be liable on summary conviction to a fine not exceeding [level 5 on the standard scale] for a first offence and to a fine not exceeding [level 5 on the standard scale] for any subsequent offence.

(3) A prosecution for an offence under this section shall not in England and Wales be instituted except by, or with the consent of, the Director of Public Prosecutions.

5   Offences by corporations

(1) Where an offence under this Act which has been committed by a body corporate is proved to have been committed with the consent or connivance of, or to be attributable to any neglect on the part of, any director, manager, secretary, or other similar officer of the body corporate, or of any person who was purporting to act in any such capacity, he as well as the body corporate shall be guilty of that offence and shall be liable to be proceeded against and punished accordingly.

(2) Where the affairs of a body corporate are managed by its members, this section shall apply in relation to the acts or defaults of a member in connection with his functions of management as if he were a director of the body corporate.

6 Interpretation

(1) In this Act, unless the context or subject matter otherwise requires,—

'acquire' includes hire;

'send' includes deliver, and 'sender' shall be construed accordingly;

'unsolicited' means, in relation to goods sent to any person, that they are sent without any prior request made by him or on his behalf.

[(2) For the purposes of this Act, any invoice or similar document stating the amount of any payment shall be regarded as asserting a right to the payment unless it complies with the conditions set out in Part 2 of the Schedule to the Regulatory Reform (Unsolicited Goods and Services Act 1971) (Directory Entries and Demands for Payment) Order 2005.]

[(3) Nothing in sections 3 or 3B shall affect the rights of any consumer under the Consumer Protection (Distance Selling) Regulations 2000.]

Defective Premises Act 1972

(1972, c. 35)

1 Duty to build dwellings properly

(1) A person taking on work for or in connection with the provision of a dwelling (whether the dwelling is provided by the erection or by the conversion or enlargement of a building) owes a duty—

(a) if the dwelling is provided to the order of any person, to that person; and

(b) without prejudice to paragraph (a) above, to every person who acquires an interest (whether legal or equitable) in the dwelling;

to see that the work which he takes on is done in a workmanlike or, as the case may be, professional manner, with proper materials and so that as regards that work the dwelling will be fit for habitation when completed.

(2) A person who takes on any such work for another on terms that he is to do it in accordance with instructions given by or on behalf of that other shall, to the extent to which he does it properly in accordance with those instructions, be treated for the purposes of this section as discharging the duty imposed on him by subsection (1) above except where he owes a duty to that other to warn him of any defects in the instructions and fails to discharge that duty.

(3) A person shall not be treated for the purposes of subsection (2) above as having given instructions for the doing of work merely because he has agreed to the work being done in a specified manner, with specified materials or to a specified design.

(4) A person who—

(a) in the course of a business which consists of or includes providing or arranging for the provision of dwellings or installations in dwellings; or

(b) in the exercise of a power of making such provision or arrangements conferred by or by virtue of any enactment;

arranges for another to take on work for or in connection with the provision of a dwelling shall be treated for the purposes of this section as included among the persons who have taken on the work.

(5) Any cause of action in respect of a breach of the duty imposed by this section shall be deemed, for the purposes of [the Limitation Act 1980], to have accrued at the time when the dwelling was completed, but if after that time a person who has done work for or in connection with the provision of the dwelling does further work to rectify the work he has already done, any such cause of action in respect of that further work shall be deemed for those purposes to have accrued at the time when the further work was finished.

2   Cases excluded from the remedy under section 1

(1) Where—

    (a) in connection with the provision of a dwelling or its first sale or letting for habitation any rights in respect of defects in the state of the dwelling are conferred by an approved scheme to which this section applies on a person having or acquiring an interest in the dwelling; and

    (b) it is stated in a document of a type approved for the purposes of this section that the requirements as to design or construction imposed by or under the scheme have, or appear to have, been substantially complied with in relation to the dwelling;

no action shall be brought by any person having or acquiring an interest in the dwelling for breach of the duty imposed by section 1 above in relation to the dwelling.

(2) A scheme to which this section applies—

    (a) may consist of any number of documents and any number of agreements or other transactions between any number of persons; but

    (b) must confer, by virtue of agreements entered into with persons having or acquiring an interest in the dwellings to which the scheme applies, rights on such persons in respect of defects in the state of the dwellings.

(3) In this section 'approved' means approved by the Secretary of State, and the power of the Secretary of State to approve a scheme or document for the purposes of this section shall be exercisable by order, except that any requirements as to construction or design imposed under a scheme to which this section applies may be approved by him without making any order or, if he thinks fit, by order.

(4) The Secretary of State—

    (a) may approve a scheme or document for the purposes of this section with or without limiting the duration of his approval; and

    (b) may by order revoke or vary a previous order under this section or, without such an order, revoke or vary a previous approval under this section given otherwise than by order.

(5) The production of a document purporting to be a copy of an approval given by the Secretary of State otherwise than by order and certified by an officer of the Secretary of State to be a true copy of the approval shall be conclusive evidence of the approval, and without proof of the handwriting or official position of the person purporting to sign the certificate.

(6) The power to make an order under this section shall be exercisable by statutory instrument which shall be subject to annulment in pursuance of a resolution by either House of Parliament.

(7) Where an interest in a dwelling is compulsorily acquired—

    (a) no action shall be brought by the acquiring authority for breach of the duty imposed by section 1 above in respect of the dwelling; and

    (b) if any work for or in connection with the provision of the dwelling was done otherwise than in the course of a business by the person in occupation of the dwelling at the time of the compulsory acquisition, the acquiring authority and not that person shall be treated as the person who took on the work and accordingly as owing that duty.

3   Duty of care with respect to work done on premises not abated by disposal of premises

(1) Where work of construction, repair, maintenance or demolition or any other work is done on or in relation to premises, any duty of care owed, because of the doing of the work, to persons who might reasonably be expected to be affected by defects in the state of the premises created by the doing of the work shall not be abated by the subsequent disposal of the premises by the person who owed the duty.

(2) This section does not apply—

    (a) in the case of premises which are let, where the relevant tenancy of the premises commenced, or the relevant tenancy agreement of the premises was entered into, before the commencement of this Act;

(b) in the case of premises disposed of in any other way, when the disposal of the premises was completed, or a contract for their disposal was entered into, before the commencement of this Act; or

(c) in either case, where the relevant transaction disposing of the premises is entered into in pursuance of an enforceable option by which the consideration for the disposal was fixed before the commencement of this Act.

4 Landlord's duty of care in virtue of obligation or right to repair premises demised

(1) Where premises are let under a tenancy which puts on the landlord an obligation to the tenant for the maintenance or repair of the premises the landlord owes to all persons who might reasonably be expected to be affected by defects in the state of the premises a duty to take such care as is reasonable in all the circumstances to see that they are reasonably safe from personal injury or from damage to their property caused by a relevant defect.

(2) The said duty is owed if the landlord knows (whether as the result of being notified by the tenant or otherwise) or if he ought in all the circumstances to have known of the relevant defect.

(3) In this section 'relevant defect' means a defect in the state of the premises existing at or after the material time and arising from, or continuing because of, an act or omission by the landlord which constituted or would if he had had notice of the defect, have constituted a failure by him to carry out his obligation to the tenant for the maintenance or repair of the premises; and for the purposes of the foregoing provision 'the material time' means—

(a) where the tenancy commenced before this Act, the commencement of this Act; and

(b) in all other cases, the earliest following times, that is to say—

(i)   the time when the tenancy commences;

(ii) the time when the tenancy agreement is entered into;

(iii) the time when possession is taken of the premises in contemplation of the letting.

(4) Where premises are let under a tenancy which expressly or impliedly gives the landlord the right to enter the premises to carry out any description of maintenance or repair of the premises, then, as from the time when he first is, or by notice or otherwise can put himself, in a position to exercise the right and so long as he is or can put himself in that position, he shall be treated for the purposes of subsections (1) to (3) above (but for no other purpose) as if he were under an obligation to the tenant for that description of maintenance or repair of the premises; but the landlord shall not owe the tenant any duty by virtue of this subsection in respect of any defect in the state of the premises arising from, or continuing because of, a failure to carry out an obligation expressly imposed on the tenant by the tenancy.

(5) For the purposes of this section obligations imposed or rights given by any enactment in virtue of a tenancy shall be treated as imposed or given by the tenancy.

(6) This section applies to a right of occupation given by contract or any enactment and not amounting to a tenancy as if the right were a tenancy, and 'tenancy' and cognate expressions shall be construed accordingly.

5 Application to Crown

This Act shall bind the Crown, but as regards the Crown s liability in tort shall not bind the Crown further than the Crown is made liable in tort by the Crown Proceedings Act 1947.

6 Supplemental

(1) In this Act: 'disposal', in relation to premises, includes a letting, and an assignment or surrender of a tenancy, of the premises and the creation by contract of any other right to occupy the premises, and 'dispose' shall be construed accordingly; 'personal injury' includes any disease and any impairment of a person's physical or mental condition...

(2) Any duty imposed by or enforceable by virtue of any provision of this Act is in addition to any duty a person may owe apart from that provision.

(3) Any term of an agreement which purports to exclude or restrict, or has the effect of excluding or restricting, the operation of any of the provisions of this Act, or any liability arising by virtue of any such provision, shall be void.

Supply of Goods (Implied Terms) Act 1973

(1973, c. 13)

8   Implied terms as to title

[(1) In every hire-purchase agreement, other than one to which subsection (2) below applies, there is—

(a) an implied term on the part of the creditor that he will have a right to sell the goods at the time when the property is to pass; and

(b) an implied term that—

(i)   the goods are free, and will remain free until the time when the property is to pass, from any charge or encumbrance not disclosed or known to the person to whom the goods are bailed or (in Scotland) hired before the agreement is made, and

(ii) that person will enjoy quiet possession of the goods except so far as it may be disturbed by any person entitled to the benefit of any charge or encumbrance so disclosed or known.

(2) In a hire-purchase agreement, in the case of which there appears from the agreement or is to be inferred from the circumstances of the agreement an intention that the creditor should transfer only such title as he or a third person may have, there is—

(a) an implied term that all charges or encumbrances known to the creditor and not known to the person to whom the goods are bailed or hired have been disclosed to that person before the agreement is made; and

(b) an implied term that neither—

(i)   the creditor; nor

(ii) in a case where the parties to the agreement intend that any title which may be transferred shall be only such title as a third person may have, that person; nor

(iii) anyone claiming through or under the creditor or that third person otherwise than under a charge or encumbrance disclosed or known to the person to whom the goods are bailed or hired, before the agreement is made;

will disturb the quiet possession of the person to whom the goods are bailed or hired.]

[(3) As regards England and Wales and Northern Ireland, the term implied by subsection (1)(a) above is a condition and the terms implied by subsections (1)(b), (2)(a) and (2)(b) above are warranties.]

9   Bailing or hiring by description

[(1) Where under a hire-purchase agreement goods are bailed or (in Scotland) hired by description, there is an implied term that the goods will correspond with the description, and if under the agreement the goods are bailed or hired by reference to a sample as well as a description, it is not sufficient that the bulk of the goods corresponds with the sample if the goods do not also correspond with the description.]

[(1A) As regards England and Wales and Northern Ireland, the term implied by subsection (1) above is a condition.]

[(2) Goods shall not be prevented from being bailed or hired by description by reason only that, being exposed for sale, bailment or hire, they are selected by the person to whom they are bailed or hired.]

10   Implied undertakings as to quality or fitness

[(1) Except as provided by this section and section 11 below and subject to the provisions of any other enactment, including any enactment of the Parliament of Northern Ireland or the Northern Ireland Assembly, there is no implied term as to the quality or fitness for any particular purpose of goods bailed or (in Scotland) hired under a hire-purchase agreement.]

[(2) Where the creditor bails or hires goods under a hire purchase agreement in the course of a business, there is an implied term that the goods supplied under the agreement are of satisfactory quality.

(2A) For the purposes of this Act, goods are of satisfactory quality if they meet the standard that a reasonable person would regard as satisfactory, taking account of any description of the goods, the price (if relevant) and all the other relevant circumstances.

(2B) For the purposes of this Act, the quality of goods includes their state and condition and the following (among others) are in appropriate cases aspects of the quality of goods—

    (a) fitness for all the purposes for which goods of the kind in question are commonly supplied,

    (b) appearance and finish,

    (c) freedom from minor defects,

    (d) safety, and

    (e) durability.

(2C) The term implied by subsection (2) above does not extend to any matter making the quality of goods unsatisfactory—

    (a) which is specifically drawn to the attention of the person to whom the goods are bailed or hired before the agreement is made,

    (b) where that person examines the goods before the agreement is made, which that examination ought to reveal, or

    (c) where the goods are bailed or hired by reference to a sample, which would have been apparent on a reasonable examination of the sample.]

[(2D) If the person to whom the goods are bailed or hired deals as consumer or, in Scotland, if the goods are hired to a person under a consumer contract, the relevant circumstances mentioned in subsection (2A) above include any public statements on the specific characteristics of the goods made about them by the creditor, the producer or his representative, particularly in advertising or on labelling.

(2E) A public statement is not by virtue of subsection (2D) above a relevant circumstance for the purposes of subsection (2A) above in the case of a contract of hire-purchase, if the creditor shows that—

    (a) at the time the contract was made, he was not, and could not reasonably have been, aware of the statement,

    (b) before the contract was made, the statement had been withdrawn in public or, to the extent that it contained anything which was incorrect or misleading, it had been corrected in public, or

    (c) the decision to acquire the goods could not have been influenced by the statement.

(2F) Subsections (2D) and (2E) above do not prevent any public statement from being a relevant circumstance for the purposes of subsection (2A) above (whether or not the person to whom the goods are bailed or hired deals as consumer or, in Scotland, whether or not the goods are hired to a person under a consumer contract) if the statement would have been such a circumstance apart from those subsections.]

[(3) Where the creditor bails or hires goods under a hire-purchase agreement in the course of a business and the person to whom the goods are bailed or hired, expressly or by implication, makes known—

    (a) to the creditor in the course of negotiations conducted by the creditor in relation to the making of the hire-purchase agreement, or

    (b) to a credit-broker in the course of negotiations conducted by that broker in relation to goods sold by him to the creditor before forming the subject matter of the hire-purchase agreement,

any particular purpose for which the goods are being bailed or hired, there is an implied term that the goods supplied under the agreement are reasonably fit for that purpose, whether or not that is a purpose for which such goods are commonly supplied, except where the circumstances show that the person to whom the goods are bailed or hired does not rely, or that it is unreasonable for him to rely, on the skill or judgment of the creditor or credit-broker.

(4) An implied term as to quality or fitness for a particular purpose may be annexed to a hire-purchase agreement by usage.

(5) The preceding provisions of this section apply to a hire-purchase agreement made by a person who in the course of a business is acting as agent for the creditor as they apply to an agreement made by the creditor in the course of a business, except where the creditor is not bailing or hiring in the course of a business and either the person to whom the goods are bailed or hired knows that fact or reasonable steps are taken to bring it to the notice of that person before the agreement is made.

(6) In subsection (3) above and this subsection—

    (a) 'credit-broker' means a person acting in the course of a business of credit brokerage;

    (b) 'credit brokerage' means the effecting of introductions of individuals desiring to obtain credit—

        (i)   to persons carrying on any business so far as it relates to the provision of credit, or

        (ii) to other persons engaged in credit brokerage.]

[(7) As regards England and Wales and Northern Ireland, the terms implied by subsections (2) and (3) above are conditions.]

[(8) In Scotland, 'consumer contract' in this section has the same meaning as in section 12A(3) below.]

11   Samples

[(1) Where under a hire-purchase agreement goods are bailed or (in Scotland) hired by reference to a sample, there is an implied term—

    (a) that the bulk will correspond with the sample in quality; and

    (b) that the person to whom the goods are bailed or hired will have a reasonable opportunity of comparing the bulk with the sample; and

    (c) that the goods will be free from any defect, making their quality unsatisfactory, which would not be apparent on reasonable examination of the sample.]

[(2) As regards England and Wales and Northern Ireland, the term implied by subsection (1) above is a condition.]

[11A   Modification of remedies for breach of statutory condition in non-consumer cases

(1) Where in the case of a hire purchase agreement—

    (a) the person to whom goods are bailed would, apart from this subsection, have the right to reject them by reason of a breach on the part of the creditor of a term implied by section 9, 10 or 11(1)(a) or (c) above, but

    (b) the breach is so slight that it would be unreasonable for him to reject them, then, if the person to whom the goods are bailed does not deal as consumer, the breach is not to be treated as a breach of condition but may be treated as a breach of warranty.

(2) This section applies unless a contrary intention appears in, or is to be implied from, the agreement.

(3) It is for the creditor to show—

    (a) that a breach fell within subsection (1)(b) above, and

    (b) that the person to whom the goods were bailed did not deal as consumer.

(4) The references in this section to dealing as consumer are to be construed in accordance with Part I of the Unfair Contract Terms Act 1977.

(5) This section does not apply to Scotland.]

[12   Exclusion of implied terms and conditions

(1) An express term does not negative a term implied by this Act unless inconsistent with it.]

[14   Special provisions as to conditional sale agreements

(1) Section 11(4) of the Sale of Goods Act 1979 (whereby in certain circumstances a breach of a condition in a contract of sale is treated only as a breach of warranty) shall not apply to a conditional sale agreement where the buyer deals as consumer within Part I of the Unfair Contract Terms Act 1977 ...

(2) In England and Wales and Northern Ireland a breach of a condition (whether express or implied) to be fulfilled by the seller under any such agreement shall be treated as a breach of warranty, and not as grounds for rejecting the goods and treating the agreement as repudiated, if (but only if) it would have fallen to be so treated had the condition been contained or implied in a corresponding hire-purchase agreement as a condition to be fulfilled by the creditor.]

15   Supplementary

[(1) In sections 8 to 14 above and this section—

'business' includes a profession and the activities of any government department (including a Northern Ireland department), [or local or public authority];

'buyer' and 'seller' includes a person to whom rights and duties under a conditional sale agreement have passed by assignment or operation of law;

'conditional sale agreement' means an agreement for the sale of goods under which the purchase price or part of it is payable by instalments, and the property in the goods is to remain in the seller (notwithstanding that the buyer is to be in possession of the goods) until such conditions as to the payment of instalments or otherwise as may be specified in the agreement are fulfilled;

['consumer sale' has the same meaning as in section 55 of the Sale of Goods Act 1979 (as set out in paragraph 11 of Schedule 1 to that Act)];

'creditor' means the person by whom the goods are bailed or (in Scotland) hired under a hire-purchase agreement or the person to whom his rights and duties under the agreement have passed by assignment or operation of law; and

'hire-purchase agreement' means an agreement, other than conditional sale agreement, under which—

(a) goods are bailed or (in Scotland) hired in return for periodical payments by the person to whom they are bailed or hired, and

(b) the property in the goods will pass to that person if the terms of the agreement are complied with and one or more of the following occurs—

(i)   the exercise of an option to purchase by that person,

(ii)   the doing of any other specified act by any party to the agreement,

(iii) the happening of any other specified event.

['producer' means the manufacturer of goods, the importer of goods into the European Economic Area or any person purporting to be a producer by placing his name, trade mark or other distinctive sign on the goods;]

(3) In section 14(2) above 'corresponding hire-purchase agreement' means, in relation to a conditional sale agreement, a hire-purchase agreement relating to the same goods as the conditional sale agreement and made between the same parties and at the same time and in the same circumstances and, as nearly as may be, in the same terms as the conditional sale agreement.

(4) Nothing in sections 8 to 13 above shall prejudice the operation of any other enactment including any enactment of the Parliament of Northern Ireland or the Northern Ireland Assembly or any rule of law whereby any term, other than one relating to quality or fitness, is to be implied in any hire-purchase agreement.]

Consumer Credit Act 1974

(1974, c. 39)

PART V

55 Disclosure of information

(1) Regulations may require specified information to be disclosed in the prescribed manner to the debtor or hirer before a regulated agreement is made.

[(2) If regulations under subsection (1) are not complied with, the agreement is enforceable against the debtor or hirer on an order of the court only (and for these purposes a retaking of goods or land to which the agreement relates is an enforcement of the agreement).]

[55A Pre-contractual explanations etc

(1) Before a regulated consumer credit agreement, other than an excluded agreement, is made, the creditor must—

    (a) provide the debtor with an adequate explanation of the matters referred to in subsection (2) in order to place him in a position enabling him to assess whether the agreement is adapted to his needs and his financial situation,

    (b) advise the debtor—

        (i)   to consider the information which is required to be disclosed under section 55(1), and

        (ii) where this information is disclosed in person to the debtor, that the debtor is able to take it away,

    (c) provide the debtor with an opportunity to ask questions about the agreement, and

    (d) advise the debtor how to ask the creditor for further information and explanation.

(2) The matters referred to in subsection (1)(a) are—

    (a) the features of the agreement which may make the credit to be provided under the agreement unsuitable for particular types of use,

    (b) how much the debtor will have to pay periodically and, where the amount can be determined, in total under the agreement,

    (c) the features of the agreement which may operate in a manner which would have a significant adverse effect on the debtor in a way which the debtor is unlikely to foresee,

    (d) the principal consequences for the debtor arising from a failure to make payments under the agreement at the times required by the agreement including legal proceedings and, where this is a possibility, repossession of the debtor's home, and

    (e) the effect of the exercise of any right to withdraw from the agreement and how and when this right may be exercised.

(3) The advice and explanation may be given orally or in writing except as provided in subsection (4).

(4) Where the explanation of the matters specified in paragraphs (a), (b) or (e) of subsection (2) is given orally or in person to a debtor, the explanation of the other matters specified in that paragraph, and the advice required to be given by subsection (1)(b), must be given orally to him.

(5) Subsections (1) to (4) do not apply to a creditor if a credit intermediary (see section 160A) has complied with those subsections in respect of the agreement.

(6) For the purposes of this section an agreement is an excluded agreement if it is—

    (a) an agreement under which the creditor provides the debtor with credit which exceeds £60,260, or

    (b) an agreement secured on land.]

56 Antecedent negotiations

(1) In this Act 'antecedent negotiations' means any negotiations with the debtor or hirer—

    (a) conducted by the creditor or owner in relation to the making of any regulated agreement, or

    (b) conducted by a credit-broker in relation to goods sold or proposed to be sold by the credit-broker to the creditor before forming the subject-matter of a debtor-creditor-supplier agreement within section 12(a), or

    (c) conducted by the supplier in relation to a transaction financed or proposed to be financed by a debtor-creditor-supplier agreement within section 12(b) or (c),

and 'negotiator' means the person by whom negotiations are so conducted with the debtor or hirer.

(2) Negotiations with the debtor in a case falling within subsection (1)(b) or (c) shall be deemed to be conducted by the negotiator in the capacity of agent of the creditor as well as in his actual capacity.

(3) An agreement is void if, and to the extent that, it purports in relation to an actual or prospective regulated agreement—

    (a) to provide that a person acting as, or on behalf of, a negotiator is to be treated as the agent of the debtor or hirer, or

    (b) to relieve a person from liability for acts or omissions of any person acting as, or on behalf of, a negotiator.

(4) For the purposes of this Act, antecedent negotiations shall be taken to begin when the negotiator and the debtor or hirer first enter into communication (including communication by advertisement), and to include any representations made by the negotiator to the debtor or hirer and any other dealings between them.

57 Withdrawal from prospective agreement

(1) The withdrawal of a party from a prospective regulated agreement shall operate to apply this Part to the agreement, any linked transaction and any other thing done in anticipation of the making of the agreement as it would apply if the agreement were made and then cancelled under section 69.

60 Form and content of agreements

(1) The Secretary of State shall make regulations as to the form and content of documents embodying regulated agreements, and the regulations shall contain such provisions as appear to him appropriate with a view to ensuring that the debtor or hirer is made aware of—

    (a) the rights and duties conferred or imposed on him by the agreement,

    (b) the amount and rate of the total charge for credit (in the case of a consumer credit agreement),

    (c) the protection and remedies available to him under this Act, and

    (d) any other matters which, in the opinion of the Secretary of State, it is desirable for him to know about in connection with the agreement.

65 Consequences of improper execution

(1) An improperly-executed regulated agreement is enforceable against the debtor or hirer on an order of the court only.

67 Cancellable agreements

[(1) Subject to subsection (2)] A regulated agreement may be cancelled by the debtor or hirer in accordance with this Part if the antecedent negotiations included oral representations made when in the presence of the debtor or hirer by an individual acting as, or on behalf of, the negotiator, unless—

    (a) the agreement is secured on land, or is a restricted-use credit agreement to finance the purchase of land or is an agreement for a bridging loan in connection with the purchase of land, or

    (b) the unexecuted agreement is signed by the debtor or hirer at premises at which any of the following is carrying on any business (whether on a permanent or temporary basis)—

        (i) the creditor or owner;

  (ii) any party to a linked transaction (other than the debtor or hirer or a relative of his);

  (iii) the negotiator in any antecedent negotiations.

[(2) This section does not apply where section 66A applies.]

68 Cooling-off period

The debtor or hirer may serve notice of cancellation of a cancellable agreement between his signing of the unexecuted agreement and—

  (a) the end of the fifth day following the day on which he received a copy under section 63(2) or a notice under section 64(1)(b), or

  (b) if (by virtue of regulations made under section 64(4)) section 64(1)(b) does not apply, the end of the fourteenth day following the day on which he signed the unexecuted agreement.

69 Notice of cancellation

(1) If within the period specified in section 68 the debtor or hirer under a cancellable agreement serves on—

  (a) the creditor or owner, or

  (b) the person specified in the notice under section 64(1), or

  (c) a person who (whether by virtue of subsection (6) or otherwise) is the agent of the creditor or owner,

a notice (a 'notice of cancellation') which, however expressed and whether or not conforming to the notice given under section 64(1), indicates the intention of the debtor or hirer to withdraw from the agreement, the notice shall operate—

  (i) to cancel the agreement, and any linked transaction, and

  (ii) to withdraw any offer by the debtor or hirer, or his relative, to enter into a linked transaction.

(4) Except as otherwise provided by or under this Act, an agreement or transaction cancelled under subsection (1) shall be treated as if it had never been entered into.

70 Cancellation: recovery of money paid by debtor or hirer

(1) On the cancellation of a regulated agreement, and of any linked transaction,—

  (a) any sum paid by the debtor or hirer, or his relative, under or in contemplation of the agreement or transaction, including any item in the total charge for credit, shall become repayable, and

  (b) any sum, including any item in the total charge for credit, which but for the cancellation is, or would or might become, payable by the debtor or hirer, or his relative, under the agreement or transaction shall cease to be, or shall not become, so payable, and

  (c) in the case of a debtor-creditor-supplier agreement falling within section 12(b), any sum paid on the debtor s behalf by the creditor to the supplier shall become repayable to the creditor.

(3) A sum repayable under subsection (1) is repayable by the person to whom it was originally paid, but in the case of a debtor-creditor-supplier agreement falling within section 12(b) the creditor and the supplier shall be under a joint and several liability to repay sums paid by the debtor, or his relative, under the agreement or under a linked transaction falling within section 19(1)(b) and accordingly, in such a case, the creditor shall be entitled, in accordance with rules of court, to have the supplier made a party to any proceedings brought against the creditor to recover any such sums.

(4) Subject to any agreement between them, the creditor shall be entitled to be indemnified by the supplier for loss suffered by the creditor in satisfying his liability under subsection (3), including costs reasonably incurred by him in defending proceedings instituted by the debtor.

71 Cancellation: repayment of credit

(1) Notwithstanding the cancellation of a regulated consumer credit agreement, other than a debtor-creditor-supplier agreement for restricted-use credit, the agreement shall continue in force so far as it relates to repayment of credit and payment of interest.

PART VI

75 Liability of creditor for breaches by supplier

(1) If the debtor under a debtor-creditor-supplier agreement falling within section 12(b) or (c) has, in relation to a transaction financed by the agreement, any claim against the supplier in respect of a misrepresentation or breach of contract, he shall have a like claim against the creditor, who, with the supplier, shall accordingly be jointly and severally liable to the debtor.

(2) Subject to any agreement between them, the creditor shall be entitled to be indemnified by the supplier for loss suffered by the creditor in satisfying his liability under subsection (1), including costs reasonably incurred by him in defending proceedings instituted by the debtor.

(3) Subsection (1) does not apply to a claim—
- (a) under a non-commercial agreement, or [. . .]
- (b) so far as the claim relates to any single item to which the supplier has attached a cash price not exceeding [£100] or more than [£30,000] [. . .]

(4) This section applies notwithstanding that the debtor, in entering into the transaction, exceeded the credit limit or otherwise contravened any term of the agreement.

(5) In an action brought against the creditor under subsection (1) he shall be entitled, in accordance with rules of court, to have the supplier made a party to the proceedings.

76 Duty to give notice before taking certain action

(1) The creditor or owner is not entitled to enforce a term of a regulated agreement by—
- (a) demanding earlier payment of any sum, or
- (b) recovering possession of any goods or land, or
- (c) treating any right conferred on the debtor or hirer by the agreement as terminated, restricted or deferred,

except by or after giving the debtor or hirer not less than seven days' notice of his intention to do so.

(2) Subsection (1) applies only where—
- (a) a period for the duration of the agreement is specified in the agreement, and
- (b) that period has not ended when the creditor or owner does an act mentioned in subsection (1),

but so applies notwithstanding that, under the agreement, any party is entitled to terminate it before the end of the period so specified.

(6) Subsection (1) does not apply to a right of enforcement arising by reason of any breach by the debtor or hirer of the regulated agreement.

PART VII

87 Need for default notice

(1) Service of a notice on the debtor or hirer in accordance with section 88 (a 'default notice') is necessary before the creditor or owner can become entitled, by reason of any breach by the debtor or hirer of a regulated agreement,—
- (a) to terminate the agreement, or
- (b) to demand earlier payment of any sum, or
- (c) to recover possession of any goods or land, or
- (d) to treat any right conferred on the debtor or hirer by the agreement as terminated, restricted or deferred, or
- (e) to enforce any security.

(2) Subsection (1) does not prevent the creditor from treating the right to draw upon any credit as restricted or deferred, and taking such steps as may be necessary to make the restriction or deferment effective.

(4) Regulations may provide that subsection (1) is not to apply to agreements described by the regulations.

88 Contents and effect of default notice

(1) The default notice must be in the prescribed form and specify—

(a) the nature of the alleged breach;

(b) if the breach is capable of remedy, what action is required to remedy it and the date before which that action is to be taken;

(c) if the breach is not capable of remedy, the sum (if any) required to be paid as compensation for the breach, and the date before which it is to be paid.

94 Right to complete payments ahead of time

(1) The debtor under a regulated consumer credit agreement is entitled at any time, by notice to the creditor and the payment to the creditor of all amounts payable by the debtor to him under the agreement [and any amount which the creditor claims under section 95A(2)] (less any rebate allowable under section 95), to discharge the debtor's indebtedness under the agreement.

96 Effect on linked transactions

(1) Where for any reason the indebtedness of the debtor under a regulated consumer credit agreement is discharged before the time fixed by the agreement, he, and any relative of his, shall at the same time be discharged from any liability under a linked transaction, other than a debt which has already become payable.

99 Right to terminate hire-purchase etc., agreements

(1) At any time before the final payment by the debtor under a regulated hire-purchase or regulated conditional sale agreement falls due, the debtor shall be entitled to terminate the agreement by giving notice to any person entitled or authorised to receive the sums payable under the agreement.

(2) Termination of an agreement under subsection (1) does not affect any liability under the agreement which has accrued before the termination.

(4) In the case of a conditional sale agreement relating to goods, where the property in the goods, having become vested in the debtor, is transferred to a person who does not become the debtor under the agreement, the debtor shall not thereafter be entitled to terminate the agreement under subsection (1).

100 Liability of debtor on termination of hire-purchase etc., agreement

(1) Where a regulated hire-purchase or regulated conditional sale agreement is terminated under section 99 the debtor shall be liable, unless the agreement provides for a smaller payment, or does not provide for any payment, to pay to the creditor the amount (if any) by which one-half of the total price exceeds the aggregate of the sums paid and the sums due in respect of the total price immediately before the termination.

(3) If in any action the court is satisfied that a sum less than the amount specified in subsection (1) would be equal to the loss sustained by the creditor in consequence of the termination of the agreement by the debtor, the court may make an order for the payment of that sum in lieu of the amount specified in subsection (1).

PART VIII

113 Act not to be evaded by use of security

(1) Where a security is provided in relation to an actual or prospective regulated agreement, the security shall not be enforced so as to benefit the creditor or owner, directly or indirectly, to an extent greater (whether as respects the amount of any payment or the time or manner of its being made) than would be the case if the security were not provided and any obligations of the debtor or hirer, or his relative, under or in relation to the agreement were carried out to the extent (if any) to which they would be enforced under this Act.

(2) In accordance with subsection (1), where a regulated agreement is enforceable on an order of the court or the [OFT] only, any security provided in relation to the agreement is enforceable (so

far as provided in relation to the agreement) where such an order has been made in relation to the agreement, but not otherwise.

(7) Where an indemnity [or guarantee] is given in a case where the debtor or hirer is a minor, or [an indemnity is given in a case where he] is otherwise not of full capacity, the reference in subsection (1) to the extent to which his obligations would be enforced shall be read in relation to the indemnity [or guarantee] as a reference to the extent to which [those obligations] would be enforced if he were of full capacity.

PART IX

127 Enforcement orders in cases of infringement

(1) In the case of an application for an enforcement order under—

[(za) section 55(2) (disclosure of information), or]

[(zb) section 61B(3) (duty to supply copy of overdraft agreement), or]

(a) section 65(1) (improperly executed agreements), ...

the court shall dismiss the application if, but (subject to subsections (3) and (4)) only if, it considers it just to do so having regard to—

    (i) prejudice caused to any person by the contravention in question, and the degree of culpability for it; and

    (ii) the powers conferred on the court by subsection (2) and sections 135 and 136.

(2) If it appears to the court just to do so, it may in an enforcement order reduce or discharge any sum payable by the debtor or hirer, or any surety, so as to compensate him for prejudice suffered as a result of the contravention in question.

129 Time orders

(1) [Subject to subsection (3) below,] If it appears to the court just to do so—

(a) on an application for an enforcement order;

(b) on an application made by a debtor or hirer under this paragraph after service on him of—

    (i) a default notice, or

    (ii) a notice under section 76(1) or 98(1);

[(ba) on an application made by a debtor or hirer under this paragraph after he has been given a notice under section 86B or 86C; or]

(c) in an action brought by a creditor or owner to enforce a regulated agreement or any security, or recover possession of any goods or land to which a regulated agreement relates,

the court may make an order under this section (a 'time order').

(2) A time order shall provide for one or both of the following, as the court considers just—

(a) the payment by the debtor or hirer or any surety of any sum owed under a regulated agreement or a security by such instalments, payable at such times, as the court, having regard to the means of the debtor or hirer and any surety, considers reasonable;

(b) the remedying by the debtor or hirer of any breach of a regulated agreement (other than non-payment of money) within such period as the court may specify.

132 Financial relief for hirer

(1) Where the owner under a regulated consumer hire agreement recovers possession of goods to which the agreement relates otherwise than by action, the hirer may apply to the court for an order that—

(a) the whole or part of any sum paid by the hirer to the owner in respect of the goods shall be repaid, and

(b) the obligation to pay the whole or part of any sum owed by the hirer to the owner in respect of the goods shall cease, and if it appears to the court just to do so, having regard to the extent of the enjoyment of the goods by the hirer, the court shall grant the application in full or in part.

[140A   Unfair relationships between creditors and debtors

(1) The court may make an order under section 140B in connection with a credit agreement if it determines that the relationship between the creditor and the debtor arising out of the agreement (or the agreement taken with any related agreement) is unfair to the debtor because of one or more of the following—

(a) any of the terms of the agreement or of any related agreement;

(b) the way in which the creditor has exercised or enforced any of his rights under the agreement or any related agreement;

(c) any other thing done (or not done) by, or on behalf of, the creditor (either before or after the making of the agreement or any related agreement).

(2) In deciding whether to make a determination under this section the court shall have regard to all matters it thinks relevant (including matters relating to the creditor and matters relating to the debtor).

(3) For the purposes of this section the court shall (except to the extent that it is not appropriate to do so) treat anything done (or not done) by, or on behalf of, or in relation to, an associate or a former associate of the creditor as if done (or not done) by, or on behalf of, or in relation to, the creditor.

(4) A determination may be made under this section in relation to a relationship notwithstanding that the relationship may have ended.

(5) An order under section 140B shall not be made in connection with a credit agreement which is an exempt agreement by virtue of section 16(6C).]

[140B   Powers of court in relation to unfair relationships

(1) An order under this section in connection with a credit agreement may do one or more of the following—

(a) require the creditor, or any associate or former associate of his, to repay (in whole or in part) any sum paid by the debtor or by a surety by virtue of the agreement or any related agreement (whether paid to the creditor, the associate or the former associate or to any other person);

(b) require the creditor, or any associate or former associate of his, to do or not to do (or to cease doing) anything specified in the order in connection with the agreement or any related agreement;

(c) reduce or discharge any sum payable by the debtor or by a surety by virtue of the agreement or any related agreement;

(d) direct the return to a surety of any property provided by him for the purposes of a security;

(e) otherwise set aside (in whole or in part) any duty imposed on the debtor or on a surety by virtue of the agreement or any related agreement;

(f) alter the terms of the agreement or of any related agreement;

(g) direct accounts to be taken, or (in Scotland) an accounting to be made, between any persons.

(2) An order under this section may be made in connection with a credit agreement only—

(a) on an application made by the debtor or by a surety;

(b) at the instance of the debtor or a surety in any proceedings in any court to which the debtor and the creditor are parties, being proceedings to enforce the agreement or any related agreement; or

(c) at the instance of the debtor or a surety in any other proceedings in any court where the amount paid or payable under the agreement or any related agreement is relevant.

(3) An order under this section may be made notwithstanding that its effect is to place on the creditor, or any associate or former associate of his, a burden in respect of an advantage enjoyed by another person.

(8) A party to any proceedings mentioned in subsection (2) shall be entitled, in accordance with rules of court, to have any person who might be the subject of an order under this section made a party to the proceedings.

(9) If, in any such proceedings, the debtor or a surety alleges that the relationship between the creditor and the debtor is unfair to the debtor, it is for the creditor to prove to the contrary.]

PART XI

162 Powers of entry and inspection

(1) A duly authorised officer of an enforcement authority, at all reasonable hours and on production, if required, of his credentials, may—

    (a) in order to ascertain whether a breach of any provision of or under this Act has been committed, inspect any goods and enter any premises (other than premises used only as a dwelling); ...

    (c) if he has reasonable cause to believe that a breach of any provision of or under this Act has been committed, seize and detain any goods in order to ascertain (by testing or otherwise) whether such a breach has been committed;

    (d) seize and detain any goods, [...] or documents which he has reason to believe may be required as evidence in proceedings for an offence under this Act;

    (e) for the purpose of exercising his powers under this subsection to seize goods, [...] or documents, but only if and to the extent that it is reasonably necessary for securing that the provisions of this Act and of any regulations made under it are duly observed, require any person having authority to do so to break open any container and, if that person does not comply, break it open himself.

(2) An officer seizing goods, [...] or documents in exercise of his powers under this section shall not do so without informing the person he seizes them from.

(4) An officer entering premises by virtue of this section may take such other persons and equipment with him as he thinks necessary; and on leaving premises entered by virtue of a warrant under subsection (3) shall, if they are unoccupied or the occupier is temporarily absent, leave them as effectively secured against trespassers as he found them.

(6) A person who is not a duly authorised officer of an enforcement authority, but purports to act as such under this section, commits an offence.

163 Compensation for loss

(1) Where, in exercising his powers under section 162, an officer of an enforcement authority seizes and detains goods and their owner suffers loss by reason of—

    (a) that seizure, or

    (b) the loss, damage or deterioration of the goods during detention,

then, unless the owner is convicted of an offence under this Act committed in relation to the goods, the authority shall compensate him for the loss so suffered.

165 Obstruction of authorised officers

(1) Any person who—

    (a) wilfully obstructs an officer of an enforcement authority acting in pursuance of this Act; or

    (b) wilfully fails to comply with any requirement properly made to him by such an officer under section 162; or

    (c) without reasonable cause fails to give such an officer (so acting) other assistance or information he may reasonably require in performing his functions under this Act,

commits an offence.

170   No further sanctions for breach of Act

(1) A breach of any requirement made (otherwise than by any court) by or under this Act shall incur no civil or criminal sanction as being such a breach, except to the extent (if any) expressly provided by or under this Act.

173   Contracting-out forbidden

(1) A term contained in a regulated agreement or linked transaction, or in any other agreement relating to an actual or prospective regulated agreement or linked transaction, is void if, and to the extent that, it is inconsistent with a provision for the protection of the debtor or hirer or his relative or any surety contained in this Act or in any regulation made under this Act.

(2) Where a provision specifies the duty or liability of the debtor or hirer or his relative or any surety in certain circumstances, a term is inconsistent with that provision if it purports to impose, directly or indirectly, an additional duty or liability on him in those circumstances.

(3) Notwithstanding subsection (1), a provision of this Act under which a thing may be done in relation to any person on an order of the court or the [OFT] only shall not be taken to prevent its being done at any time with that person's consent given at that time, but the refusal of such consent shall not give rise to any liability.

175   Duty of persons deemed to be agents

Where under this Act a person is deemed to receive a notice or payment as agent of the creditor or owner under a regulated agreement, he shall be deemed to be under a contractual duty to the creditor or owner to transmit the notice, or remit the payment, to him forthwith.

181   Power to alter monetary limits etc.

(1) The Secretary of State may by order made by statutory instrument amend, or further amend, any of the following provisions of this Act so as to reduce or increase a sum mentioned in that provision, namely, sections...75(3)(b)...

189   Definitions

(1) In this Act, unless the context otherwise requires—...

'representation' includes any condition or warranty, and any other statement or undertaking, whether oral or in writing;...

Health and Safety at Work Act 1974

(1974, c. 37)

2   General duties of employers to their employees

(1) It shall be the duty of every employer to ensure, so far as is reasonably practicable, the health, safety and welfare of work of all his employees.

3   General duties of employers and self-employed to persons other than their employees

(1) It shall be the duty of every employer to conduct his undertaking in such a way as to ensure, so far as is reasonably practicable, that persons not in his employment who may be affected thereby are not thereby exposed to risks to their health or safety.

(2) It shall be the duty of every self-employed person to conduct his undertaking in such a way as to ensure, so far as is reasonably practicable, that he and other persons (not being his employees) who may be affected thereby are not thereby exposed to risks to their health or safety.

(3) In such cases as may be prescribed, it shall be the duty of every employer and every self-employed person, in the prescribed circumstances and in the prescribed manner, to give to persons (not being his employees) who may be affected by the way in which he conducts his undertaking the prescribed information about such aspects of the way in which he conducts his undertaking as might affect their health or safety.

4   General duties of persons concerned with premises to persons other than their employees

(1) This section has effect for imposing on persons duties in relation to those who—

(a) are not their employees; but

(b) use non-domestic premises made available to them as a place of work or as a place where they may use plant or substances provided for their use there,

and applies to premises so made available and other non-domestic premises used in connection with them.

(2) It shall be the duty of each person who has, to any extent, control of premises to which this section applies or of the means of access thereto or egress therefrom or of any plant or substance in such premises to take such measures as it is reasonable for a person in his position to take to ensure, so far as is reasonably practicable, that the premises, all means of access thereto or egress therefrom available for use by persons using the premises, and any plant or substance in the premises or, as the case may be, provided for use there, is or are safe and without risks to health.

(3) Where a person has, by virtue of any contract or tenancy, an obligation of any extent in relation to—

(a) the maintenance or repair of any premises to which this section applies or any means of access thereto or egress therefrom; or

(b) the safety of or the absence of risks to health arising from plant or substances in any such premises;

that person shall be treated, for the purposes of subsection (2) above, as being a person who has control of the matters to which his obligation extends.

(4) Any reference in this section to a person having control of any premises or matter is a reference to a person having control of the premises or matter in connection with the carrying on by him of a trade, business or other undertaking (whether for profit or not).

17   Use of approved codes of practice in criminal proceedings

(1) A failure on the part of any person to observe any provision of an approved code of practice shall not of itself render him liable to any civil or criminal proceedings; but where in any criminal proceedings a party is alleged to have committed an offence by reason of a contravention of any requirement or prohibition imposed by or under any such provision as is mentioned in section 16(1) being a provision for which there was an approved code of practice at the time of the alleged contravention, the following subsection shall have effect with respect to that code in relation to those proceedings.

47   Civil liability

(1) Nothing in this Part shall be construed—

(a) as conferring a right of action in any civil proceedings in respect of any failure to comply with any duty imposed by sections 2 to 7 or any contravention of section 8; or

(b) as affecting the extent (if any) to which breach of a duty imposed by any of the existing statutory provisions is actionable; or

(c) as affecting the operation of section 12 of the Nuclear Installations Act 1965 (right to compensation by virtue of certain provisions of that Act).

(2) Breach of a duty imposed by health and safety regulations [...] shall, so far as it causes damages, be actionable except in so far as the regulations provide otherwise.

(3) No provision made by virtue of section 15(6)(b) shall afford a defence in any civil proceedings, whether brought by virtue of subsection (2) above or not; but as regards any duty imposed as mentioned in subsection (2) above health and safety regulations [...] may provide for any defence specified in the regulations to be available in any action for breach of that duty.

(4) Subsections (1)(a) and (2) above are without prejudice to any right of action which exists apart from the provisions of this Act, and subsection (3) above is without prejudice to any defence which may be available apart from the provisions of the regulations there mentioned.

(5) Any term of an agreement which purports to exclude or restrict the operation of subsection (2) above, or any liability arising by virtue of that subsection, shall be void, except in so far as health and safety regulations [...] provide otherwise.

(6) In this section 'damage' includes the death of, or injury to, any person (including any disease and any impairment of a person's physical or mental condition).

Rehabilitation of Offenders Act 1974

(1974, c. 53)

4 Effect of rehabilitation

(1) Subject to sections 7 and 8 below, a person who has become a rehabilitated person for the purposes of this Act in respect of a conviction shall be treated for all purposes in law as a person who has not committed or been charged with or prosecuted for or convicted of or sentenced for the offence or offences which were the subject of that conviction; ...

8 Defamation actions

(1) This section applies to any action for libel or slander begun after the commencement of this Act by a rehabilitated person and founded upon the publication of any matter imputing that the plaintiff has committed or been charged with or prosecuted for or convicted of or sentenced for an offence which was the subject of a spent conviction.

(2) Nothing in section 4(1) above shall affect an action to which this section applies where the publication complained of took place before the conviction in question became spent, and the following provisions of this section shall not apply in any such case.

(3) Subject to subsections (5) and (6) below, nothing in section 4(1) above shall prevent the defendant in an action to which this section applies from relying on any defence of justification or fair comment or of absolute or qualified privilege which is available to him, or restrict the matters he may establish in support of any such defence.

(4) Without prejudice to the generality of subsection (3) above, where in any such action malice is alleged against a defendant who is relying on a defence of qualified privilege, nothing in section 4(1) above shall restrict the matters he may establish in rebuttal of the allegation.

(5) A defendant in any such action shall not by virtue of subsection (3) above be entitled to rely upon the defence of justification if the publication is proved to have been made with malice.

(6) Subject to subsection (7) below a defendant in any such action shall not, by virtue of subsection (3) above, be entitled to rely on any matter or adduce or require any evidence for the purpose of establishing (whether under [section 14 of the Defamation Act 1996] or otherwise) the defence that the matter published constituted a fair and accurate report of judicial proceedings if it is proved that the publication contained a reference to evidence which was ruled to be inadmissible in the proceedings by virtue of section 4(1) above.

(7) Subsection (3) above shall apply without the qualifications imposed by subsection (6) above in relation to—

(a) any report of judicial proceedings contained in any bona fide series of law reports which does not form part of any other publication and consists solely of reports of proceedings in courts of law, and

(b) any report or account of judicial proceedings published for bona fide educational, scientific or professional purposes or given in the course of any lecture, class or discussion given or held for any of those purposes.

[(7A) Nothing in section 4(1) above shall restrict the evidence that may be adduced in mitigation of damages under section 13(2) of the Defamation Act 1996.]

Reservoirs Act 1975

(1975, c. 23)

Section 28

SCHEDULE 2

LIABILITY FOR DAMAGE AND INJURY

Where damage or injury is caused by the escape of water from a reservoir constructed after the year 1930 under statutory powers granted after July 1930, the fact that the reservoir was so constructed shall not exonerate the persons for the time being having the management and control of the reservoir from any indictment, action or other proceedings to which they would otherwise have been liable.

Congenital Disabilities (Civil Liability) Act 1976

(1976, c. 28)

1   Civil liability to child born disabled

(1) If a child is born disabled as the result of such an occurrence before its birth as is mentioned in subsection (2) below, and a person (other than the child's own mother) is under this section answerable to the child in respect of the occurrence, the child's disabilities are to be regarded as damage resulting from the wrongful act of that person and actionable accordingly at the suit of the child.

(2) An occurrence to which this section applies is one which—

(a) affected either parent of the child in his or her ability to have a normal, healthy child; or

(b) affected the mother during her pregnancy, or affected her or the child in the course of its birth, so that the child is born with disabilities which would not otherwise have been present.

(3) Subject to the following subsections, a person (here referred to as 'the defendant') is answerable to the child if he was liable in tort to the parent or would, if sued in due time, have been so; and it is no answer that there could not have been such liability because the parent suffered no actionable injury, if there was a breach of legal duty which, accompanied by injury, would have given rise to the liability.

(4) In the case of an occurrence preceding the time of conception, the defendant is not answerable to the child if at that time either or both of the parents knew the risk of their child being born disabled (that is to say, the particular risk created by the occurrence); but should it be the child's father who is the defendant, this subsection does not apply if he knew of the risk and the mother did not.

(5) The defendant is not answerable to the child, for anything he did or omitted to do when responsible in a professional capacity for treating or advising the parent, if he took reasonable care having due regard to then received professional opinion applicable to the particular class of case; but this does not mean that he is answerable only because he departed from received opinion.

(6) Liability to the child under this section may be treated as having been excluded or limited by contract made with the parent affected, to the same extent and subject to the same restrictions as liability in the parent's own case; and a contract term which could have been set up by the defendant in an action by the parent, so as to exclude or limit his liability to him or her, operates in the defendant's favour to the same, but no greater, extent in an action under this section by the child.

(7) If in the child's action under this section it is shown that the parent affected shared the responsibility for the child being born disabled, the damages are to be reduced to such extent as the court thinks just and equitable having regard to the extent of the parent's responsibility.

[1A   Extension of section 1 to cover infertility treatments

(1) In any case where—

    (a) a child carried by a woman as the result of the placing in her or an embryo or of sperm and eggs or her artificial insemination is born disabled,

    (b) the disability results from an act or omission in the course of the selection, or the keeping or use outside the body, of the embryo carried by her or of the gametes used to bring about the creation of the embryo, and

    (c) a person is under this section answerable to the child in respect of the act or omission,

the child's disabilities are to be regarded as damage resulting from the wrongful act of that person and actionable accordingly at the suit of the child.

(2) Subject to subsection (3) below and the applied provisions of section 1 of this Act, a person (here referred to as 'the defendant') is answerable to the child if he was liable in tort to one or both of the parents (here referred to as 'the parent or parents concerned') or would, if sued in due time, have been so; and it is no answer that there could not have been such liability because the parent or parents concerned suffered no actionable injury, if there was a breach of legal duty which, accompanied by injury, would have given rise to the liability.

(3) The defendant is not under this section answerable to the child if at the time the embryo, or the sperm and eggs, are placed in the woman or the time of her insemination (as the case may be) either or both of the parents knew the risk of their child being born disabled (that is to say, the particular risk created by the act or omission).

(4) Subsections (5) to (7) of section 1 of this Act apply for the purposes of this section as they apply for the purposes of that but as if references to the parent or the parent affected were references to the parent or parents concerned.

(4A) In the case of a child who has a parent by virtue of section 42 or 43 of the Human Fertilisation and Embryology Act 2008, the reference in subsection (4) to the child's father includes a reference to the woman who is a parent by virtue of that section.]

2   Liability of woman driving while pregnant

A woman driving a motor vehicle when she knows (or ought reasonably to know) herself to be pregnant is to be regarded as being under the same duty to take care for the safety of her unborn child as the law imposes on her with respect to the safety of other people; and if in consequence of her breach of that duty her child is born with disabilities which would not otherwise have been present, those disabilities are to be regarded as damage resulting from her wrongful act and actionable accordingly at the suit of the child.

3   Disabled birth due to radiation

(1) Section 1 of this Act does not affect the operation of the Nuclear Installations Act 1965 as to liability for, and compensation in respect of, injury or damage caused by occurrences involving nuclear matter or the emission of ionising radiations.

(2) For the avoidance of doubt anything which—

    (a) affects a man in his ability to have a normal, healthy child; or

    (b) affects a woman in that ability, or so affects her when she is pregnant that her child is born with disabilities which would not otherwise have been present,

is an injury for the purposes of that Act.

(3) If a child is born disabled as the result of an injury to either of its parents caused in breach of a duty imposed by any of sections 7 to 11 of that Act (nuclear site licensees and others to secure that nuclear incidents do not cause injury to persons, etc.), the child's disabilities are to be regarded under the subsequent provisions of that Act (compensation and other matters) as injuries caused on the same occasion, and by the same breach of duty, as was the injury to the parent.

(4) As respects compensation to the child, section 13(6) of that Act (contributory fault of person injured by radiation) is to be applied as if the reference there to fault were to the fault of the parent.

(5) Compensation is not payable in the child's case if the injury to the parent preceded the time of the child's conception and at that time either or both of the parents knew the risk of their child being born disabled (that is to say, the particular risk created by the injury).

4   Interpretation and other supplementary provisions

(1) References in this Act to a child being born disabled or with disabilities are to its being born with any deformity, disease or abnormality, including predisposition (whether or not susceptible or immediate prognosis) to physical or mental defect in the future.

(2) In this Act—

(a) 'born' means born alive (the moment of a child's birth being when it first has a life separate from its mother), and 'birth' has a corresponding meaning; and

(b) 'motor vehicle' means a mechanically propelled vehicle intended or adapted for use on roads.

[and references to embryos shall be construed in accordance with section 1(1) of the Human Fertilisation and Embryology Act 1990 and any regulations under section 1(6) of that Act.]

(3) Liability to a child under section 1 [1A] or 2 of this Act is to be regarded—

(a) as respects all its incidents and any matters arising or to arise out of it; and

(b) subject to any contrary context or intention, for the purpose of construing references in enactments and documents to personal or bodily injuries and cognate matters,

as liability for personal injuries sustained by the child immediately after its birth.

(4) No damages shall be recoverable under [any] of those sections in respect of any loss of expectation of life, nor shall any such loss be taken into account in the compensation payable in respect of a child under the Nuclear Installations Act 1965 as extended by section 3, unless (in either case) the child lives for at least 48 hours.

[(4A) In any case where a child carried by a woman as the result of the placing in her of an embryo or of sperm and eggs or her artificial insemination is born disabled, any reference in section 1 of this Act to a parent includes a reference to a person who would be a parent but for sections 27 to 29 of the Human Fertilisation and Embryology Act 1990 or sections 33 to 47 of the Human Fertilisation and Embryology Act 2008.]

(5) This Act applies in respect of births after (but not before) its passing, and in respect of any such birth it replaces any law in force before its passing, whereby a person could be liable to a child in respect of disabilities with which it might be born; but in section 1(3) of this Act the expression 'liable in tort' does not include any reference to liability by virtue of this Act or to liability by virtue of any such law.

5   Crown application

This Act binds the Crown.

Dangerous Wild Animals Act 1976

(1976, c. 38)

1   Licences

(1) Subject to section 5 of this Act, no person shall keep any dangerous wild animal except under the authority of a licence granted in accordance with the provisions of this Act by a local authority.

(3) A local authority shall not grant a licence under this Act unless it is satisfied that—

(a) it is not contrary to the public interest on the grounds of safety, nuisance or otherwise to grant the licence; ...

(e) all reasonable precautions will be taken at all such times to prevent and control the spread of infectious diseases; ...

4 Power to seize and to dispose of animals without compensation

(1) Where—

    (a) an animal is being kept contrary to section 1(1) of the Act, or

    (b) any condition of a licence under this Act is contravened or not complied with,

the local authority in whose area any animal concerned is for the time being may seize the animal, and either retain it in the authority's possession or destroy or otherwise dispose of it, and shall not be liable to pay compensation to any person in respect of the exercise of its powers under this subsection.

(2) A local authority which incurs any expenditure in exercising its powers under subsection (1)(a) of this section shall be entitled to recover the amount of the expenditure summarily as a civil debt from any person who was at the time of the seizure a keeper of the animal concerned.

(3) A local authority which incurs any expenditure in exercising its powers under subsection (1)(b) of this section shall be entitled to recover the amount of the expenditure summarily as a civil debt from the person to whom the licence concerned was granted.

Fatal Accidents Act 1976

(1976, c. 30)

1 Right of action for wrongful act causing death

[(1) If death is caused by any wrongful act, neglect or default which is such as would (if death had not ensued) have entitled the person injured to maintain an action and recover damages in respect thereof, the person who would have been liable if death had not ensued shall be liable to an action for damages, notwithstanding the death of the person injured.

(2) Subject to section 1A(2) below, every such action shall be for the benefit of the dependants of the person ('the deceased') whose death has been so caused.

(3) In this Act 'dependant' means—

    (a)   the wife or husband or former wife or husband of the deceased;

    [(aa)   the civil partner or former civil partner of the deceased;]

    (b)   any person who—

        (i)   was living with the deceased in the same household immediately before the date of the death; and

        (ii)   had been living with the deceased in the same household for at least two years before that date; and

        (iii)   was living during the whole of that period as the husband or wife or civil partner of the deceased;

    (c)   any parent or other ascendant of the deceased;

    (d)   any person who was treated by the deceased as his parent;

    (e)   any child or other descendant of the deceased;

    (f)   any person (not being a child of the deceased) who, in the case of any marriage to which the deceased was at any time a party, was treated by the deceased as a child of the family in relation to that marriage;

    [(fa)   any person (not being a child of the deceased) who, in the case of any civil partnership in which the deceased was at any time a civil partner, was treated by the deceased as a child of the family in relation to that civil partnership;]

    (g)   any person who is, or is the issue of, a brother, sister, uncle or aunt of the deceased.

(4) The reference to the former wife or husband of the deceased in subsection (3)(a) above includes a reference to a person whose marriage to the deceased has been annulled or declared void as well as a person whose marriage to the deceased has been dissolved.

[(4A) The reference to the former civil partner of the deceased in subsection (3)(aa) above includes a reference to a person whose civil partnership with the deceased has been annulled as well as a person whose civil partnership with the deceased has been dissolved.]

(5) In deducing any relationship for the purposes of subsection (3) above—

(a) any relationship by marriage or civil partnership shall be treated as a relationship of con-sanguinity, any relationship of the half blood as a relationship of the whole blood, and the stepchild of any person as his child, and

(b) an illegitimate person shall be treated as the legitimate child of his mother and reputed father.

(6) Any reference in this Act to injury includes any disease and any impairment of a person's physical or mental condition.]

[1A Bereavement

(1) An action under this Act may consist of or include a claim for damages for bereavement.

(2) A claim for damages for bereavement shall only be for the benefit—

(a) of the wife or husband [or civil partner] of the deceased; and

(b) where the deceased was a minor who was never married [or a civil partner]—

(i)　his parents, if he was legitimate; and

(ii)　of his mother, if he was illegitimate.

(3) Subject to subsection (5) below, the sum to be awarded as damages under this section shall be [£11,800].

(4) Where there is a claim for damages under this section for the benefit of both the parents of the deceased, the sum awarded shall be divided equally between them (subject to any deduction falling to be made in respect of costs not recovered from the defendant).

(5) The Lord Chancellor may by order made by statutory instrument, subject to annulment in pursuance of a resolution of either House of Parliament, amend this section by varying the sum for the time being specified in subsection (3) above.]

2 Persons entitled to bring the action

(1) The action shall be brought by and in the name of the executor or administrator of the deceased.

(2) If—

(a) there is no executor or administrator of the deceased, or

(b) no action is brought within six months after the death by and in the name of an executor or administrator of the deceased,

the action may be brought by and in the name of all or any of the persons for whose benefit an executor or administrator could have brought it.

(3) Not more than one action shall lie for and in respect of the same subject matter of complaint.

(4) The plaintiff in the action shall be required to deliver to the defendant or his solicitor full particulars of the persons for whom and on whose behalf the action is brought and of the nature of the claim in respect of which damages are sought to be recovered.

3 Assessment of damages

[(1) In the action such damages, other than damages for bereavement, may be awarded as are proportioned to the injury resulting from the death to the dependants respectively.

(2) After deducting the costs not recovered from the defendant any amount recovered otherwise than as damages for bereavement shall be divided among the dependants in such shares as may be directed.

(3) In an action under this Act where there fall to be assessed damages payable to a widow in respect of the death of her husband there shall not be taken into account the re-marriage of the widow or her prospects of re-marriage.

(4) In an action under this Act where there fall to be assessed damages payable to a person who is a dependant by virtue of section 1(3)(b) above in respect of the death of the person with whom the dependant was living as husband or wife [or civil partner] there shall be taken into account (together with any other matter that appears to the court to be relevant to the action) the fact that the dependant had no enforceable right to financial support by the deceased as a result of their liv-ing together.

(5) If the dependants have incurred funeral expenses in respect of the deceased, damages may be awarded in respect of those expenses.

(6) Money paid into court in satisfaction of a cause of action under this Act may be in one sum without specifying any person's share.]

4   Assessment of damages; disregard of benefits

[In assessing damages in respect of a person's death in an action under this Act, benefits which have accrued or will or may accrue to any person from his estate or otherwise as a result of his death shall be disregarded.]

5   Contributory negligence

Where any person dies as the result partly of his own fault and partly of the fault of any other person or persons, and accordingly if an action were brought for the benefit of the estate under the Law Reform (Miscellaneous Provisions) Act 1934 the damages recoverable would be reduced under section 1(1) of the Law Reform (Contributory Negligence) Act 1945, any damages recoverable in an action [...] under this Act shall be reduced to a proportionate extent.

Protection from Eviction Act 1977

(1977, c. 43)

1   Unlawful eviction and harassment of occupier

(1) In this section 'residential occupier', in relation to any premises, means a person occupying the premises as a residence, whether under a contract or by virtue of any enactment or rule of law giving him the right to remain in occupation or restricting the right of any other person to recover possession of the premises.

(2) If any person unlawfully deprives the residential occupier of any premises of his occupation of the premises or any part thereof, or attempts to do so, he shall be guilty of an offence unless he proves that he believed, and had reasonable cause to believe, that the residential occupier had ceased to reside in the premises.

(3) If any person with intent to cause the residential occupier of any premises—

    (a) to give up the occupation of the premises or any part thereof; or

    (b) to refrain from exercising any right or pursuing any remedy in respect of the premises or part thereof;

does acts [likely] to interfere with the peace or comfort of the residential occupier or members of his household, or persistently withdraws or withholds services reasonably required for the occupation of the premises as a residence, he shall be guilty of an offence.

[(3A) Subject to subsection (3B) below, the landlord of a residential occupier or an agent of the landlord shall be guilty of an offence if—

    (a) he does acts likely to interfere with the peace or comfort of the residential occupier or members of his household, or

    (b) he persistently withdraws or withholds services reasonably required for the occupation of the premises in question as a residence,

and (in either case) he knows, or has reasonable cause to believe, that that conduct is likely to cause the residential occupier to give up the occupation of the whole or part of the premises or to refrain from exercising any right or pursuing any remedy in respect of the whole or part of the premises.

(3B) A person shall not be guilty of an offence under subsection (3A) above if he proves that he had reasonable grounds for doing the acts or withdrawing or withholding the services in question.]

(5) Nothing in this section shall be taken to prejudice any liability or remedy to which a person guilty of an offence thereunder may be subject in civil proceedings.

2   Restriction on re-entry without due process of law

Where any premises are let as a dwelling on a lease which is subject to a right of re-entry or forfeiture it shall not be lawful to enforce that right otherwise than by proceedings in the court while any person is lawfully residing in the premises or part of them.

3   Prohibition of eviction without due process of law

(1)   Where any premises have been let as a dwelling under a tenancy which is [neither a statutorily protected tenancy nor an excluded tenancy] and—

(a)   the tenancy (in this section referred to as the former tenancy) has come to an end, but

(b)   the occupier continues to reside in the premises or part of them,

it shall not be lawful for the owner to enforce against the occupier, otherwise than by proceedings in the court, his right to recover possession of the premises.

(2)   In this section 'the occupier', in relation to any premises, means any person lawfully residing in the premises or part of them at the termination of the former tenancy.

Torts (Interference with Goods) Act 1977

(1977, c. 32)

1   Definition of 'wrongful interference with goods'

In this Act 'wrongful interference', or 'wrongful interference with goods', means—

(a)   conversion of goods (also called trover),

(b)   trespass to goods,

(c)   negligence so far as it results in damage to goods or to an interest in goods,

(d)   subject to section 2, any other tort so far as it results in damage to goods or to an interest in goods.

[and references in this Act (however worded) to proceedings for wrongful interference or to a claim or right to claim for wrongful interference shall include references to proceedings by virtue of Part I of the Consumer Protection Act 1987 or Part II of the Consumer Protection (Northern Ireland) Order 1987 (product liability) in respect of any damage to goods or to an interest in goods or, as the case may be, to a claim or right to claim by virtue of that Part in respect of any such damage.]

2   Abolition of detinue

(1)   Detinue is abolished.

(2)   An action lies in conversion for loss or destruction of goods which a bailee has allowed to happen in breach of his duty to his bailor (that is to say it lies in a case which is not otherwise conversion, but would have been detinue before detinue was abolished).

3   Forms of judgment where goods are detained

(1)   In proceedings for wrongful interference against a person who is in possession or in control of the goods relief may be given in accordance with this section, so far as appropriate.

(2)   The relief is—

(a)   an order for delivery of the goods, and for payment of any consequential damages, or

(b)   an order for delivery of the goods, but giving the defendant the alternative of paying damages by reference to the value of the goods, together in either alternative with payment of any consequential damages, or

(c)   damages.

(3)   Subject to rules of court—

(a)   relief shall be given under only one of paragraphs (a), (b) and (c) of subsection (2),

(b)   relief under paragraph (a) of subsection (2) is at the discretion of the court, and the claimant may choose between the others.

(4) If it is shown to the satisfaction of the court that an order under subsection (2)(a) had not been complied with, the court may—

    (a) revoke the order, or the relevant part of it, and

    (b) make an order for payment of damages by reference to the value of the goods.

(5) Where an order is made under subsection (2)(b) the defendant may satisfy the order by returning the goods at any time before execution of judgment, but without prejudice to liability to pay any consequential damages.

(6) An order for delivery of the goods under subsection (2)(a) or (b) may impose such conditions as may be determined by the court, or pursuant to rules of court, and in particular, where damages by reference to the value of the goods would not be the whole of the value of the goods, may require an allowance to be made by the claimant to reflect the difference.

For example, a bailor's action against the bailee may be one in which the measure of damages is not the full value of the goods, and then the court may order delivery of the goods, but require the bailor to pay the bailee a sum reflecting the difference.

(7) Where under subsection (1) or subsection (2) of section 6 an allowance is to be made in respect of an improvement of the goods, and an order is made under subsection (2)(a) or (b), the court may assess the allowance to be made in respect of the improvement, and by the order require, as a condition for delivery of the goods, that allowance to be made by the claimant.

(8) This section is without prejudice—

    (a) to the remedies afforded by section 133 of the Consumer Credit Act, or . . .

    (c) to any jurisdiction to afford ancillary or incidental relief.

4   Interlocutory relief where goods are detained

(1) In this section 'proceedings' means proceedings for wrongful interference.

(2) On the application of any person in accordance with rules of court, the High Court shall, in such circumstances as may be specified in the rules, have power to make an order providing for the delivery up of any goods which are or may become the subject matter of subsequent proceedings in the court, or as to which any question may arise in proceedings.

(3) Delivery shall be, as the order may provide, to the claimant or to a person appointed by the court for the purpose, and shall be on such terms and conditions as may be specified in the order.

5   Extinction of title on satisfaction of claim for damages

(1) Where damages for wrongful interference are, or would fall to be, assessed on the footing that the claimant is being compensated—

    (a) for the whole of his interest in the goods, or

    (b) for the whole of his interest in the goods subject to a reduction for contributory negligence,

payment of the assessed damages (under all heads), or as the case may be settlement of a claim for damages for the wrong (under all heads), extinguishes the claimant's title to that interest.

(2) In subsection (1) the reference to the settlement of the claim includes—

    (a) where the claim is made in court proceedings, and the defendant has paid a sum into court to meet the whole claim, the taking of that sum by the claimant, and

    (b) where the claim is made in court proceedings, and the proceedings are settled or compromised, the payment of what is due in accordance with the settlement or compromise, and

    (c) where the claim is made out of court and is settled or compromised, the payment of what is due in accordance with the settlement or compromise.

(3) It is hereby declared that subsection (1) does not apply where damages are assessed on the footing that the claimant is being compensated for the whole of his interest in the goods, but the damages paid are limited to some lesser amount by virtue of any enactment or rule of law.

(4) Where under section 7(3) the claimant accounts over to another person (the 'third party') so as to compensate (under all heads) the third party for the whole of his interest in the goods, the third party's title to that interest is extinguished.

(5) This section has effect subject to any agreement varying the respective rights of the parties to the agreement, and where the claim is made in court proceedings has effect subject to any order of the court.

6 Allowance for improvement of the goods

(1) If in proceedings for wrongful interference against a person (the 'improver') who has improved the goods, it is shown that the improver acted in the mistaken but honest belief that he had a good title to them, an allowance shall be made for the extent to which, at the time as at which the goods fall to be valued in assessing damages, the value of the goods is attributable to the improvement.

(2) If, in proceedings for wrongful interference against a person ('the purchaser') who has purported to purchase the goods—

  (a) from the improver, or
  (b) where after such a purported sale the goods passed by a further purported sale on one or more occasions, on any such occasion,

it is shown that the purchaser acted in good faith, an allowance shall be made on the principle set out in subsection (1).

For example, where a person in good faith buys a stolen car from the improver and is sued in conversion by the true owner the damages may be reduced to reflect the improvement, but if the person who bought the stolen car from the improver sues the improver for failure of consideration, and the improver acted in good faith, subsection (3) below will ordinarily make a comparable reduction in the damages he recovers from the improver.

(3) If in a case within subsection (2) the person purporting to sell the goods acted in good faith, then in proceedings by the purchaser for recovery of the purchase price because of failure of consideration, or in any other proceedings founded on that failure of consideration, an allowance shall, where appropriate, be made on the principle set out in subsection (1).

(4) This section applies, with the necessary modifications, to a purported bailment or other disposition of goods as it applies to a purported sale of goods.

7 Double liability

(1) In this section 'double liability' means the double liability of the wrongdoer which can arise—
  (a) where one of two or more rights of action for wrongful interference is founded on a possessory title, or
  (b) where the measure of damages in an action for wrongful interference founded on a proprietary title is or includes the entire value of the goods, although the interest is one of two or more interests in the goods.

(2) In proceedings to which any two or more claimants are parties, the relief shall be such as to avoid double liability of the wrongdoer as between those claimants.

(3) On satisfaction, in whole or in part, of any claim for an amount exceeding that recoverable if subsection (2) applied, the claimant is liable to account over to the other person having a right to claim to such extent as will avoid double liability.

(4) Where, as the result of enforcement of a double liability, any claimant is unjustly enriched to an extent, he shall be liable to reimburse the wrongdoer to that extent.

For example, if a converter of goods pays damages first to a finder of the goods, and then to the true owner, the finder is unjustly enriched unless he accounts over to the true owner under subsection (3); and then the true owner is unjustly enriched and becomes liable to reimburse the converter of the goods.

8 Competing rights to the goods

(1) The defendant in an action for wrongful interference shall be entitled to show, in accordance with rules of court, that a third party has a better right than the plaintiff as respects all or any part of the interest claimed by the plaintiff, or in right of which he sues, and any rule of law (sometimes called jus tertii) to the contrary is abolished.

(2)   Rules of court relating to proceedings for wrongful interference may—

    (a)   require the plaintiff to give particulars of his title,

    (b)   require the plaintiff to identify any person who, to his knowledge, has or claims any interest in the goods,

    (c)   authorise the defendant to apply for directions as to whether any person should be joined with a view to establishing whether he has a better right than the plaintiff, or has a claim as a result of which the defendant might be doubly liable,

    (d)   where a party fails to appear on an application within paragraph (c), or to comply with any direction given by the court on such an application, authorise the court to deprive him of any right of action against the defendant for the wrong either unconditionally, or subject to such terms or conditions as may be specified.

(3)   Subsection (2) is without prejudice to any other power of making rules of court.

9   Concurrent actions

(1)   This section applies where goods are the subject of two or more claims for wrongful interference (whether or not the claims are founded on the same wrongful act, and whether or not any of the claims relates also to other goods).

(2)   Where the goods are the subject of two or more claims under section 6 this section shall apply as if any claim under section 6(3) were a claim for wrongful interference.

(3)   If proceedings have been brought in a county court on one of those claims, county court rules may waive, or allow a court to waive, any limit (financial or territorial) on the jurisdiction of county courts in [the County Courts Act 1984] or the County Courts Act [(Northern Ireland) Order 1980] so as to allow another of those claims to be brought in the same county court.

(4)   If proceedings are brought on one of the claims in the High Court, and proceedings on any other are brought in a county court, whether prior to the High Court proceedings or not, the High Court may, on the application of the defendant, after notice has been given to the claimant in the county court proceedings—

    (a)   order that the county court proceedings be transferred to the High Court, and

    (b)   order security for costs or impose such other terms as the court thinks fit.

10   Co-owners

(1)   Co-ownership is no defence to an action founded on conversion or trespass to goods where the defendant without the authority of the other co-owner—

    (a)   destroys the goods, or disposes of the goods in a way giving a good title to the entire property in the goods, or otherwise does anything equivalent to the destruction of the other's interest in the goods, or

    (b)   purports to dispose of the goods in a way which would give a good title to the entire property in the goods if he was acting with the authority of all co-owners of the goods.

(2)   Subsection (1) shall not affect the law concerning execution or enforcement of judgments, or concerning any form of distress.

(3)   Subsection (1)(a) is by way of restatement of existing law so far as it relates to conversion.

11   Minor amendments

(1)   Contributory negligence is no defence in proceedings founded on conversion, or on intentional trespass to goods.

(2)   Receipt of goods by way of pledge is conversion if the delivery of the goods is conversion.

(3)   Denial of title is not of itself conversion.

12   Bailee's power of sale

(1)   This section applies to goods in the possession or under the control of a bailee where—

    (a)   the bailor is in breach of an obligation to take delivery of the goods or, if the terms of the bailment so provide, to give directions as to their delivery, or

    (b)   the bailee could impose such an obligation by giving notice to the bailor, but is unable to trace or communicate with the bailor, or

(c) the bailee can reasonably expect to be relieved of any duty to safeguard the goods on giving notice to the bailor, but is unable to trace or communicate with the bailor.

(2) In the cases of Part I of Schedule 1 to this Act a bailee may, for the purposes of subsection (1), impose an obligation on the bailor to take delivery of the goods, or as the case may be to give directions as to their delivery, and in those cases the said Part I sets out the method of notification.

(3) If the bailee—

(a) has in accordance with Part II of Schedule 1 to this Act given notice to the bailor of his intention to sell the goods under this subsection, or

(b) has failed to trace or communicate with the bailor with a view to giving him such a notice, after having taken reasonable steps for the purpose,

and is reasonably satisfied that the bailor owns the goods, he shall be entitled, as against the bailor, to sell the goods.

(4) Where subsection (3) applies but the bailor did not in fact own the goods, a sale under this section, or under section 13, shall not give a good title as against the owner, or as against a person claiming under the owner.

(5) A bailee exercising his powers under subsection (3) shall be liable to account to the bailor for the proceeds of sale, less any cost of sale, and—

(a) the account shall be taken on the footing that the bailee should have adopted the best method of sale reasonably available in the circumstances, and

(b) where subsection (3)(a) applies, any sum payable in respect of the goods by the bailor to the bailee which accrued due before the bailee gave notice of intention to sell the goods shall be deductible from the proceeds of sale.

(6) A sale duly made under this section gives a good title to the purchaser as against the bailor.

(7) In this section, section 13, and Schedule 1 to this Act,

(a) 'bailor' and 'bailee' include their respective successors in title, and

(b) references to what is payable, paid or due to the bailee in respect of the goods include references to what would be payable by the bailor to the bailee as a condition of delivery of the goods at the relevant time.

(8) This section, and Schedule 1 to this Act, have effect subject to the terms of the bailment.

(9) This section shall not apply where the goods were bailed before the commencement of this Act.

13   Sale authorised by the court

(1) If a bailee of the goods to which section 12 applies satisfies the court that he is entitled to sell the goods under section 12, or that he would be so entitled if he had given any notice required in accordance with Schedule 1 to this Act, the court—

(a) may authorise the sale of the goods subject to such terms and conditions, if any, as may be specified in the order, and

(b) may authorise the bailee to deduct from the proceeds of sale any costs of sale and any amount due from the bailor to the bailee in respect of the goods, and

(c) may direct the payment into court of the net proceeds of sale, less any amount deducted under paragraph (b), to be held to the credit of the bailor.

(2) A decision of the court authorising a sale under this section shall, subject to any right of appeal, be conclusive, as against the bailor, of the bailee's entitlement to sell the goods, and gives a good title to the purchaser as against the bailor.

(3) In this section 'the court' means the High Court or a county court, [and a county court shall have jurisdiction in the proceedings save that, in Northern Ireland, a county court shall only have jurisdiction in proceedings if the value of the goods does not exceed the county court limit mentioned in Article 10(1) of the County Courts (Northern Ireland) Order 1980.]

14   Interpretation

(1) In this Act, unless the context otherwise requires ...

'goods' includes all chattels personal other than things in action and money....

16 Extent and application to the Crown

(3) This Act shall bind the Crown, but as regards the Crown's liability in tort shall not bind the Crown further than the Crown is made liable in tort by the Crown Proceedings Act 1947.

Section 12

SCHEDULE 1

UNCOLLECTED GOODS

PART I POWER TO IMPOSE OBLIGATION TO COLLECT GOODS

1. (1) For the purposes of section 12(1) a bailee may, in the circumstances specified in this Part of this Schedule, by notice given to the bailor impose on him an obligation to take delivery of the goods.

(2) The notice shall be in writing, and may be given either—

(a) by delivering it to the bailor, or

(b) by leaving it at his proper address, or

(c) by post.

(3) The notice shall—

(a) specify the name and address of the bailee, and give sufficient particulars of the goods and the address or place where they are held, and

(b) state that the goods are ready for delivery to the bailor, or where combined with a notice terminating the contract of bailment, will be ready for delivery when the contract is terminated, and

(c) specify the amount, if any, which is payable by the bailor to the bailee in respect of the goods and which became due before the giving of the notice.

(4) Where the notice is sent by post it may be combined with a notice under Part II of this Schedule if the notice is sent by post in a way complying with paragraph 6(4).

(5) References in this Part of this Schedule to taking delivery of the goods include, where the terms of the bailment admit, references to giving directions as to their delivery.

(6) This Part of this Schedule is without prejudice to the provisions of any contract requiring the bailor to take delivery of the goods.

Goods accepted for repair or other treatment

2. If a bailee has accepted goods for repair or other treatment on the terms (expressed or implied) that they will be re-delivered to the bailor when the repair or other treatment has been carried out, the notice may be given at any time after the repair or other treatment has been carried out.

Goods accepted for valuation or appraisal

3. If a bailee has accepted goods in order to value or appraise them, the notice may be given at any time after the bailee has carried out the valuation or appraisal.

Storage, warehousing, etc.

4. (1) If a bailee is in possession of goods which he has held as custodian, and his obligation as custodian has come to an end, the notice may be given at any time after the ending of the obligation, or may be combined with any notice terminating his obligation as custodian.

(2) This paragraph shall not apply to goods held by a person as mercantile agent, that is to say by a person having in the customary course of his business as a mercantile agent authority either to sell goods or to consign goods for the purpose of sale, or to buy goods, or to raise money on the security of goods.

Supplemental

5. Paragraphs 2, 3 and 4 apply whether or not the bailor has paid any amount due to the bailee in respect of the goods, and whether or not the bailment is for reward, or in the course of business, or gratuitous.

PART II NOTICE OF INTENTION TO SELL GOODS

6. (1) A notice under section 12(3) shall—

   (a) specify the name and address of the bailee, and give sufficient particulars of the goods and the address or place where they are held, and

   (b) specify the date on or after which the bailee proposes to sell the goods, and

   (c) specify the amount, if any, which is payable by the bailor to the bailee in respect of the goods, and which became due before the giving of the notice.

(2) The period between giving of the notice and the date specified in the notice as that on or after which the bailee proposes to exercise the power of sale shall be such as will afford the bailor a reasonable opportunity of taking delivery of the goods.

(3) If any amount is payable in respect of the goods by the bailor to the bailee, and become due before giving of the notice, the said period shall be not less than three months.

(4) The notice shall be in writing and shall be sent by post in a registered letter, or by the recorded delivery service.

7. (1) The bailee shall not give a notice under section 12(3), or exercise his right to sell the goods pursuant to such a notice, at a time when he has notice that, because of a dispute concerning the goods, the bailor is questioning or refusing to pay all or any part of what the bailee claims to be due to him in respect of the goods.

(2) This paragraph shall be left out of account in determining under section 13(1) whether a bailee of goods is entitled to sell the goods under section 12, or would be so entitled if he had given any notice required in accordance with this Schedule.

Unfair Contract Terms Act 1977

(1977, c. 50)

PART I AMENDMENT OF THE LAW FOR ENGLAND AND WALES AND NORTHERN IRELAND

1 Scope of Part I

(1) For the purposes of this Part of this Act, 'negligence' means the breach—

   (a) of any obligation, arising from the express or implied terms of a contract, to take reasonable care or exercise reasonable skill in the performance of the contract;

   (b) of any common law duty to take reasonable care or exercise reasonable skill (but not any stricter duty);

   (c) of the common duty of care imposed by the Occupiers' Liability Act 1957 or the Occupier's Liability Act (Northern Ireland) 1957.

(2) This Part of this Act is subject to Part III; and in relation to contracts, the operation of sections 2 to 4 and 7 is subject to the exceptions made by Schedule I.

(3) In the case of both contract and tort, sections 2 to 7 apply (except where the contrary is stated in section 6(4)) only to business liability, that is liability for breach of obligations or duties arising—

   (a) from things done or to be done by a person in the course of a business (whether his own business or another's); or

   (b) from the occupation of premises used for business purposes of the occupier; and references to liability are to be read accordingly [but liability of an occupier of premises for breach of an obligation or duty towards a person obtaining access to the premises for recreational or educational purposes, being liability for loss or damage suffered by reason of the dangerous state of the premises, is not a business liability of the occupier unless granting that person such access for the purposes concerned falls within the business purposes of the occupier.]

(4) In relation to any breach of duty or obligation, it is immaterial for any purpose of this Part of this Act whether the breach was inadvertent or intentional, or whether liability for it arises directly or vicariously.

2 Negligence liability

(1) A person cannot by reference to any contract term or to a notice given to persons generally or to particular persons exclude or restrict his liability for death or personal injury resulting from negligence.

(2) In the case of other loss or damage, a person cannot so exclude or restrict his liability for negligence except in so far as the term or notice satisfies the requirement of reasonableness.

(3) Where a contract term or notice purports to exclude or restrict liability for negligence a person's agreement to or awareness of it is not of itself to be taken as indicating his voluntary acceptance of any risk.

3 Liability arising in contract

(1) This section applies as between contracting parties where one of them deals as consumer or on the other's written standard terms of business.

(2) As against that party, the other cannot by reference to any contract term—

    (a) when himself in breach of contract, exclude or restrict any liability of his in respect of the breach; or

    (b) claim to be entitled—

        (i) to render a contractual performance substantially different from that which was reasonably expected of him, or

        (ii) in respect of the whole or any part of his contractual obligation, to render no performance at all,

except in so far as (in any of the cases mentioned above in this subsection) the contract term satisfies the requirement of reasonableness.

4 Unreasonable indemnity clauses

(1) A person dealing as consumer cannot by reference to any contract term be made to indemnify another person (whether a party to the contract or not) in respect of liability that may be incurred by the other for negligence or breach of contract, except in so far as the contract term satisfies the requirement of reasonableness.

(2) This section applies whether the liability in question—

    (a) is directly that of the person to be indemnified or is incurred by him vicariously;

    (b) is to the person dealing as consumer or to someone else.

5 'Guarantee' of consumer goods

(1) In the case of goods of a type ordinarily supplied for private use or consumption, where loss or damage—

    (a) arises from the goods proving defective while in consumer use; and

    (b) results from the negligence of a person concerned in the manufacture or distribution of the goods,

liability for the loss or damage cannot be excluded or restricted by reference to any contract term or notice contained in or operating by reference to a guarantee of the goods.

(2) For these purposes—

    (a) goods are to be regarded as 'in consumer use' when a person is using them, or has them in his possession for use, otherwise than exclusively for the purposes of a business; and

    (b) anything in writing is a guarantee if it contains or purports to contain some promise or assurance (however worded or presented) that defects will be made good by complete or partial replacement, or by repair, monetary compensation or otherwise.

(3) This section does not apply as between the parties to a contract under or in pursuance of which possession or ownership of the goods passed.

6   Sale and hire-purchase

(1) Liability for breach of the obligations arising from—

    (a) [section 12 of the Sale of Goods Act 1979] (seller's implied undertakings as to title, etc.);

    (b) section 8 of the Supply of Goods (Implied Terms) Act 1973 (the corresponding thing in relation to hire-purchase),

cannot be excluded or restricted by reference to any contract term.

(2) As against a person dealing as consumer, liability for breach of the obligations arising from—

    (a) [section 13, 14 or 15 of the 1979 Act] (seller's implied undertakings as to conformity of goods with description or sample, or as to their quality or fitness for a particular purpose);

    (b) section 9, 10 or 11 of the 1973 Act (the corresponding things in relation to hire-purchase),

cannot be excluded or restricted by reference to any contract term.

(3) As against a person dealing otherwise than as consumer, the liability specified in subsection (2) above can be excluded or restricted by reference to a contract term, but only in so far as the term satisfies the requirement of reasonableness.

(4) The liabilities referred to in this section are not only the business liabilities defined by section 1(3), but include those arising under any contract of sale of goods or hire-purchase agreement.

7   Miscellaneous contracts under which goods pass

(1) Where the possession or ownership of goods passes under or in pursuance of a contract not governed by the law of sale of goods or hire-purchase, subsections (2) to (4) below apply as regards the effect (if any) to be given to contract terms excluding or restricting liability for breach of obligation arising by implication of law from the nature of the contract.

(2) As against a person dealing as consumer, liability in respect of the goods' correspondence with description or sample, or their quality or fitness for any particular purpose, cannot be excluded or restricted by reference to any such term.

(3) As against a person dealing otherwise than as consumer, that liability can be excluded or restricted by reference to such a term, but only in so far as the term satisfies the requirement of reasonableness.

[(3A) Liability for breach of the obligations arising under section 2 of the Supply of Goods and Services Act 1982 (implied terms about title etc. in certain contracts for the transfer of the property in goods) cannot be excluded or restricted by reference to any such term.]

(4) Liability in respect of—

    (a) the right to transfer ownership of the goods, or give possession; or

    (b) the assurance of quiet possession to a person taking goods in pursuance of the contract,

cannot [(in a case to which subsection (3A) above does not apply)] be excluded or restricted by reference to any such term except in so far as the term satisfies the requirement of reasonableness.

(5) This section does not apply in the case of goods passing on a redemption of trading stamps within the Trading Stamps Act 1964 or the Trading Stamps Act (Northern Ireland) 1965.

9   Effect of breach

(1) Where for reliance upon it a contract term has to satisfy the requirement of reasonableness, it may be found to do so and be given effect accordingly notwithstanding that the contract has been terminated either by breach or by a party electing to treat it as repudiated.

(2) Where on a breach the contract is nevertheless affirmed by a party entitled to treat it as repudiated, this does not of itself exclude the requirement of reasonableness in relation to any contract term.

10   Evasion by means of secondary contract

A person is not bound by any contract term prejudicing or taking away rights of his which arise under, or in connection with the performance of, another contract, so far as those rights extend to the enforcement of another's liability which this Part of this Act prevents that other from excluding or restricting.

11   The 'reasonableness' test

(1) In relation to a contract term, the requirement of reasonableness for the purposes of this Part of this Act, section 3 of the Misrepresentation Act 1967 and section 3 of the Misrepresentation Act (Northern Ireland) 1967 is that the term shall have been a fair and reasonable one to be included having regard to the circumstances which were, or ought reasonably to have been, known to or in the contemplation of the parties when the contract was made.

(2) In determining for the purposes of section 6 or 7 above whether a contract term satisfies the requirement of reasonableness, regard shall be had in particular to the matters specified in Schedule 2 to this Act; but this subsection does not prevent the court or arbitrator from holding, in accordance with any rule of law, that a term which purports to exclude or restrict any relevant liability is not a term of the contract.

(3) In relation to a notice (not being a notice having contractual effect), the requirement of reasonableness under this Act is that it should be fair and reasonable to allow reliance on it, having regard to all the circumstances obtaining when the liability arose or (but for the notice) would have arisen.

(4) Where by reference to a contract term or notice a person seeks to restrict liability to a specified sum of money, and the question arises (under this or any other Act) whether the term or notice satisfies the requirement of reasonableness, regard shall be had in particular (but without prejudice to subsection (2) above in the case of contract terms) to—

(a) the resources which he could expect to be available to him for the purpose of meeting the liability should it arise; and

(b) how far it was open to him to cover himself by insurance.

(5) It is for those claiming that a contract term or notice satisfies the requirement of reasonableness to show that it does.

12   'Dealing as consumer'

(1) A party to a contract 'deals as consumer' in relation to another party if—

(a) he neither makes the contract in the course of a business nor holds himself out as doing so; and

(b) the other party does make the contract in the course of a business; and

(c) in the case of a contract governed by the law of sale of goods or hire-purchase, or by section 7 of this Act, the goods passing under or in pursuance of the contract are of a type ordinarily supplied for private use or consumption.

[(1A) But if the first party mentioned in subsection (1) is an individual paragraph (c) of that section must be ignored.]

[(2) But the buyer is not in any circumstances to be regarded as dealing as consumer—

(a) if he is an individual and the goods are second hand goods sold at public auction at which individuals have the opportunity of attending the sale in person;

(b) if he is not an individual and the goods are sold by auction or by competitive tender.]

(3) Subject to this, it is for those claiming that a party does not deal as consumer to show that he does not.

13   Varieties of exemption clause

(1) To the extent that this Part of this Act prevents the exclusion or restriction of any liability it also prevents—

(a) making the liability or its enforcement subject to restrictive or onerous conditions;

(b) excluding or restricting any right or remedy in respect of the liability, or subjecting a person to any prejudice in consequence of his pursuing any such right or remedy;

(c) excluding or restricting rules of evidence or procedure;

and (to that extent) sections 2 and 5 to 7 also prevent excluding or restricting liability by reference to terms and notices which exclude or restrict the relevant obligation or duty.

(2) But an agreement in writing to submit present or future differences to arbitration is not to be treated under this Part of this Act as excluding or restricting any liability.

14 Interpretation of Part I

In this Part of the Act—

'business' includes a profession and the activities of any government department or local or public authority;

'goods' has the same meaning as in [the Sale of Goods Act 1979];

'hire-purchase agreement' has the same meaning as in the Consumer Credit Act 1974;

'negligence' has the meaning given by section 1(1);

'notice' includes an announcement, whether or not in writing, and any other communication or pretended communication; and

'personal injury' includes any disease and any impairment of physical or mental condition.

PART III PROVISIONS APPLYING TO WHOLE OF UNITED KINGDOM

26 International supply contracts

(1) The limits imposed by this Act on the extent to which a person may exclude or restrict liability by reference to a contract term do not apply to liability arising under such a contract as is described in subsection (3) below.

(2) The terms of such a contract are not subject to any requirement of reasonableness under section 3 or 4: and nothing in Part II of this Act shall require the incorporation of the terms of such a contract to be fair and reasonable for them to have effect.

(3) Subject to subsection (4), that description of contract is one whose characteristics are the following—

(a) either it is a contract of sale of goods or it is one under or in pursuance of which the possession or ownership of goods passes; and

(b) it is made by parties whose places of business (or, if they have none, habitual residences) are in the territories of different States (the Channel Islands and the Isle of Man being treated for this purpose as different States from the United Kingdom).

(4) A contract falls within subsection (3) above only if either—

(a) the goods in question are, at the time of the conclusion of the contract, in the course of carriage, or will be carried, from the territory of one State to the territory of another; or

(b) the acts constituting the offer and acceptance have been done in the territories of different States; or

(c) the contract provides for the goods to be delivered to the territory of a State other than that within whose territory those acts were done.

27 Choice of law clauses

(1) Where the [law applicable to] a contract is the law of any part of the United Kingdom only by choice of the parties (and apart from that choice would be the law of some country outside the United Kingdom) sections 2 to 7 and 16 to 21 of this Act do not operate as part [of the law applicable to the contract.]

(2) This Act has effect notwithstanding any contract term which applies or purports to apply the law of some country outside the United Kingdom, where (either or both)—

(a) the term appears to the court, or arbitrator or arbiter to have been imposed wholly or mainly for the purpose of enabling the party imposing it to evade the operation of this Act; or

(b) in the making of the contract one of the parties dealt as consumer, and he was then habitually resident in the United Kingdom, and the essential steps necessary for the making of the contract were taken there, whether by him or by others on his behalf.

(3) In the application of subsection (2) above to Scotland, for paragraph (b) there shall be substituted—

> '(b) the contract is a consumer contract as defined in Part II of this Act, and the consumer at the date when the contract was made was habitually resident in the United Kingdom, and the essential steps necessary for the making of the contract were taken there, whether by him or by others on his behalf.'.

28   Temporary provision for sea carriage of passengers
. . .

29   Saving for other relevant legislation

(1) Nothing in this Act removes or restricts the effect of, or prevents reliance upon, any contractual provision which—

(a) is authorised or required by the express terms or necessary implication of an enactment; or

(b) being made with a view to compliance with an international agreement to which the United Kingdom is a party, does not operate more restrictively than is contemplated by the agreement.

(2) A contract term is to be taken—

(a) for the purposes of Part I of this Act, as satisfying the requirement of reasonableness...

if it is incorporated or approved by, or incorporated pursuant to a decision or ruling of, a competent authority acting in the exercise of any statutory jurisdiction or function and is not a term in a contract to which the competent authority is itself a party.

(3) In this section—

'competent authority' means any court, arbitrator or arbiter, government department or public authority;

'enactment' means any legislation (including subordinate legislation) of the United Kingdom or Northern Ireland and any instrument having effect by virtue of such legislation; and

'statutory' means conferred by an enactment.

Section 1(2)   # SCHEDULE 1

SCOPE OF SECTIONS 2 TO 4 AND 7

1. Sections 2 to 4 of this Act do not extend to—

(a) any contract of insurance (including a contract to pay an annuity on human life);

(b) any contract so far as it relates to the creation or transfer of an interest in land, or to the termination of such an interest, whether by extinction, merger, surrender, forfeiture or otherwise;

(c) any contract so far as it relates to the creation or transfer of a right or interest in any patent, trade mark, copyright [or design right];

(d) any contract so far as it relates—

(i)   to the formation or dissolution of a company (which means any body corporate or unincorporated association and includes a partnership), or

(ii)   to its constitution or the rights or obligations of its corporators or members;

(e) any contract so far as it relates to the creation or transfer of securities or of any right or interest in securities.

2. Section 2(1) extends to—

(a) any contract of marine salvage or towage;

(b) any charterparty of a ship or hovercraft; and

(c) any contract for the carriage of goods by ship or hovercraft;

but subject to this sections 2 to 4 and 7 do not extend to any such contract except in favour of a person dealing as consumer.

3. Where goods are carried by ship or hovercraft in pursuance of a contract which either—

(a) specifies that as the means of carriage over part of the journey to be covered, or

(b) makes no provision as to the means of carriage and does not exclude that means,

then sections 2(2), 3 and 4 do not, except in favour of a person dealing as consumer, extend to the contract as it operates for and in relation to the carriage of the goods by that means.

4. Section 2(1) and (2) do not extend to a contract of employment, except in favour of the employee.

5. Section 2(1) does not affect the validity of any discharge and indemnity given by a person, on or in connection with an award to him of compensation for pneumoconiosis attributable to employment in the coal industry, in respect of any further claim arising from his contracting that disease.

Sections 11(2) and 24(2)   SCHEDULE 2

'GUIDELINES' FOR APPLICATION
OF REASONABLENESS TEST

The matters to which regard is to be had in particular for the purposes of sections 6(3), 7(3) and (4), 20 and 21 are any of the following which appear to be relevant—

(a) the strength of the bargaining positions of the parties relative to each other, taking into account (among other things) alternative means by which the customer's requirements could have been met;

(b) Whether the customer received an inducement to agree to the term, or in accepting it had an opportunity of entering into a similar contract with other persons, but without having to accept a similar term;

(c) whether the customer knew or ought reasonably to have known of the existence and extent of the term (having regard, among other things, to any custom of the trade and any previous course of dealing between the parties);

(d) where the term excludes or restricts any relevant liability if some condition is not complied with, whether it was reasonable at the time of the contract to expect that compliance with that condition would be practicable;

(e) whether the goods were manufactured, processed or adapted to the special order of the customer.

Civil Liability (Contribution) Act 1978

(1978, c. 47)

1 Entitlement to contribution

(1) Subject to the following provisions of this section, any person liable in respect of any damage suffered by another person may recover contribution from any other person liable in respect of the same damage (whether jointly with him or otherwise).

(2) A person shall be entitled to recover contribution by virtue of subsection (1) above notwithstanding that he has ceased to be liable in respect of the damage in question since the time when the damage occurred, provided that he was so liable immediately before he made or was ordered or agreed to make the payment in respect of which the contribution is sought.

(3) A person shall be liable to make contribution by virtue of subsection (1) above notwithstanding that he has ceased to be liable in respect of the damage in question since the time when the damage occurred, unless he ceased to be liable by virtue of the expiry of a period of limitation or prescription which extinguished the right on which the claim against him in respect of the damage was based.

(4) A person who has made or agreed to make any payment in bona fide settlement or compromise of any claim made against him in respect of any damage (including a payment into court which has been accepted) shall be entitled to recover contribution in accordance with this section without regard to whether or not he himself is or ever was liable in respect of the damage, provided, however, that he would have been liable assuming that the factual basis of the claim against him could be established.

(5) A judgment given in any action brought in any part of the United Kingdom by or on behalf of the person who suffered the damage in question against any person from whom contribution is sought under this section shall be conclusive in the proceedings for contribution as to any issue determined by that judgment in favour of the person from whom the contribution is sought.

(6) References in this section to a person's liability in respect of any damage are references to any such liability which has been or could be established in an action brought against him in England and Wales by or on behalf of the person who suffered the damage; but it is immaterial whether any issue arising in any such action was or would be determined (in accordance with the rules of private international law) by reference to the law of a country outside England and Wales.

2 Assessment of contribution

(1) Subject to subsection (3) below, in any proceedings for contribution under section 1 above the amount of the contribution recoverable from any person shall be such as may be found by the court to be just and equitable having regard to the extent of that person's responsibility for the damage in question.

(2) Subject to subsection (3) below, the court shall have power in any such proceedings to exempt any person from liability to make contribution or to direct that the contribution to be recovered from any person shall amount to a complete indemnity.

(3) Where the amount of the damages which have or might have been awarded in respect of the damage in question in any action brought in England and Wales by or on behalf of the person who suffered it against the person from whom the contribution is sought was or would have been subject to—

> (a) any limit imposed by or under any enactment or by any agreement made before the damage occurred;
> (b) any reduction by virtue of section 1 of the Law Reform (Contributory Negligence) Act 1945 or section 5 of the Fatal Accidents Act 1976; or
> (c) any corresponding limit or reduction under the law of a country outside England and Wales;

the person from whom the contribution is sought shall not by virtue of any contribution awarded under section 1 above be required to pay in respect of the damage a greater amount than the amount of those damages as so limited or reduced.

3 Proceedings against persons jointly liable for the same debt or damage

Judgment recovered against any person liable in respect of any debt or damage shall not be a bar to an action, or to the continuance of an action, against any other person who is (apart from any such bar) jointly liable with him in respect of the same debt or damage.

4 Successive actions against persons liable (jointly or otherwise) for the same damage

If more than one action is brought in respect of any damage by or on behalf of the person by whom it was suffered against persons liable in respect of the damage (whether jointly or otherwise) the plaintiff shall not be entitled to costs in any of those actions, other than that in which judgment is first given, unless the court is of the opinion that there was reasonable ground for bringing the action.

5 Application to the Crown

Without prejudice to section 4(1) of the Crown Proceedings Act 1947 (indemnity and contribution), this Act shall bind the Crown, but nothing in this Act shall be construed as in any way affecting

Her Majesty in Her private capacity (including in right of Her Duchy of Lancaster) or the Duchy of Cornwall.

6 Interpretation

(1) A person is liable in respect of any damage for the purposes of this Act if the person who suffered it (or anyone representing his estate or dependants) is entitled to recover compensation from him in respect of that damage (whatever the legal basis of his liability, whether tort, breach of contract, breach of trust or otherwise).

(2) References in this Act to an action brought by or on behalf of the person who suffered any damage include references to an action brought for the benefit of his estate or dependants.

(3) In this Act 'dependants' has the same meaning as in the Fatal Accidents Act 1976.

(4) In this Act, except in section 1(5) above, 'action' means an action brought in England and Wales.

7 Savings

(3) The right to recover contribution in accordance with section 1 above supersedes any right, other than an express contractual right, to recover contribution (as distinct from indemnity) otherwise than under this Act in corresponding circumstances; but nothing in this Act shall affect—

(a) any express or implied contractual or other right to indemnity; or

(b) any express contractual provision regulating or excluding contribution;

which would be enforceable apart from this Act (or render enforceable any agreement for indemnity or contribution which would not be enforceable apart from this Act).

State Immunity Act 1978

(1978, c. 33)

1 General immunity from jurisdiction

(1) A State is immune from the jurisdiction of the courts of the United Kingdom except as provided in the following provisions of this Part of this Act.

3 Commercial transactions and contracts to be performed in United Kingdom

(1) A State is not immune as respects proceedings relating to—

(a) a commercial transaction entered into by the State; or

(b) an obligation of the State which by virtue of a contract (whether a commercial transaction or not) falls to be performed wholly or partly in the United Kingdom.

5 Personal injuries and damage to property

A State is not immune as respects proceedings in respect of—

(a) death or personal injury; or

(b) damage to or loss of tangible property,

caused by an act or omission in the United Kingdom.

Customs and Excise Management Act 1979

(1979, c. 2)

[137A Recovery of overpaid excise duty

(1) Where a person pays to the Commissioners an amount by way of excise duty which is not due to them, the Commissioners are liable to repay that amount.

(2) The Commissioners shall not be required to make any such repayment unless a claim is made to them in such form, and supported by such documentary evidence, as may be prescribed by them by regulations; and regulations may make different provision for different cases.

(3) It is a defence to a claim for repayment that the repayment would unjustly enrich the claimant.

(4) The Commissioners shall not be liable, on a claim made under this section, to repay any amount paid to them more than three years before the making of the claim.

(5) Except as provided by this section the Commissioners are not liable to repay an amount paid to them by way of excise duty by reason of the fact that it was not duty due to them.]

Pneumoconiosis etc. (Workers' Compensation) Act 1979

(1979, c. 41)

1 Lump sum payments

(1) If, on a claim by a person who is disabled by a disease to which this Act applies, the Secretary of State is satisfied that the conditions of entitlement mentioned in section 2(1) below are fulfilled, he shall in accordance with this Act make to that person a payment of such amount as may be prescribed by regulations.

(2) If, on a claim by the dependant of a person who, immediately before he died, was disabled by a disease to which this Act applies, the Secretary of State is satisfied that the conditions of entitlement mentioned in section 2(2) below are fulfilled, he shall in accordance with this Act make to that dependant a payment of such amount as may be so prescribed.

(3) The diseases to which this Act applies are pneumoconiosis, byssinosis and diffuse mesothelioma [and any other disease which is specified by the Secretary of State for the purposes of this Act by order made by statutory instrument].

2 Conditions of entitlement

(1) In the case of a person who is disabled by a disease to which this Act applies, the conditions of entitlement are—

(a) that disablement benefit is payable to him in respect of the disease [or, subject to subsection (3A) below, would be payable to him in respect of it but for his disablement amounting to less than the appropriate percentage];

(b) that every relevant employer of his has ceased to carry on business; and

(c) that he has not brought any action, or compromised any claim, for damages in respect of the disablement.

(2) In the case of the dependant of a person who, immediately before he died, was disabled by a disease to which this Act applies, the conditions of entitlement are—

(a) that no payment under this Act has been made to the deceased in respect of the disease;

(b) that death benefit is payable to or in respect of the dependant by reason of the deceased's death as a result of the disease, or that disablement benefit was payable to the deceased in respect of the disease immediately before he died [or, subject to subsection (3A) below, would have been so payable to him—

(i)   but for his disablement amounting to less than the appropriate percentage; or

(ii) but for his not having claimed the benefit; or

(iii) but for his having died before he had suffered from the disease for the appropriate period];

(c) that every relevant employer of the deceased has ceased to carry on business; and

(d) that neither the deceased nor his personal representatives nor any relative of his has brought any action, or compromised any claim, for damages in respect of the disablement or death.

[(3A) No amount is payable under this Act in respect of disablement amounting to less than 1 per cent.]

(4) For the purposes of this section any action which has been dismissed otherwise than on the merits (as for example for want of prosecution or under any enactment relating to the limitation of actions) shall be disregarded.

5   Reconsideration of determinations

(1) Subject to subsection (2) below, the Secretary of State may reconsider a determination that a payment should not be made under this Act on the ground—

(a) that there has been a material change of circumstances since the determination was made; or

(b) that the determination was made in ignorance of, or was based on a mistake as to, some material fact;

and the Secretary of State may, on the ground set out in paragraph (b) above, reconsider a determination that such a payment should be made.

(4) If, whether fraudulently or otherwise, any person misrepresents or fails to disclose any material fact and in consequence of the misrepresentation or failure a payment is made under this Act, the person to whom the payment was made shall be liable to repay the amount of that payment to the Secretary of State unless he can show that the misrepresentation or failure occurred without his connivance or consent.

9   Financial provisions

(1) There shall be paid out of moneys provided by Parliament—

(a) any expenditure incurred by the Secretary of State in making payments under this Act . . .

Sale of Goods Act 1979

(1979, c. 54)

PART I   CONTRACTS TO WHICH ACT APPLIES

1   Contracts to which Act applies

(1) This Act applies to contracts of sale of goods made on or after (but not to those made before) 1 January 1894.

(2) In relation to contracts made on certain dates, this Act applies subject to the modification of certain of its sections as mentioned in Schedule 1 below.

(3) Any such modification is indicated in the section concerned by a reference to Schedule 1 below.

(4) Accordingly, where a section does not contain such a reference, this Act applies in relation to the contract concerned without such modification of the section.

PART II   FORMATION OF THE CONTRACT

Contract of sale

2   Contract of sale

(1) A contract of sale of goods is a contract by which the seller transfers or agrees to transfer the property in goods to the buyer for a money consideration, called the price.

(2) There may be a contract of sale between one part owner and another.

(3) A contract of sale may be absolute or conditional.

(4) Where under a contract of sale the property in the goods is transferred from the seller to the buyer the contract is called a sale.

(5) Where under a contract of sale the transfer of the property in the goods is to take place at a future time or subject to some condition later to be fulfilled the contract is called an agreement to sell.

(6) An agreement to sell becomes a sale when the time elapses or the conditions are fulfilled subject to which the property in the goods is to be transferred.

3   Capacity to buy and sell

(1) Capacity to buy and sell is regulated by the general law concerning capacity to contract and to transfer and acquire property.

(2) Where necessaries are sold and delivered to a minor or to a person who by reason of [. . .] drunkenness is incompetent to contract, he must pay a reasonable price for them.

(3) In subsection (2) above 'necessaries' means goods suitable to the condition in life of the minor or other person concerned and to his actual requirements at the time of the sale and delivery.

4   How contract of sale is made

(1) Subject to this and any other Act, a contract of sale may be made in writing (either with or without seal), or by word of mouth, or partly in writing and partly by word of mouth, or may be implied from the conduct of the parties.

(2) Nothing in this section affects the law relating to corporations.

5   Existing or future goods

(1) The goods which form the subject of a contract of sale may be either existing goods, owned or possessed by the seller, or goods to be manufactured or acquired by him after the making of the contract of sale, in this Act called future goods.

(2) There may be a contract for the sale of goods the acquisition of which by the seller depends on a contingency which may or may not happen.

(3) Where by a contract of sale the seller purports to effect a present sale of future goods, the contract operates as an agreement to sell the goods.

6   Goods which have perished

Where there is a contract for the sale of specific goods, and the goods without the knowledge of the seller have perished at the time when the contract is made, the contract is void.

7   Goods perishing before sale but after agreement to sell

Where there is an agreement to sell specific goods and subsequently the goods, without any fault on the part of the seller or buyer, perish before the risk passes to the buyer, the agreement is avoided.

8   Ascertainment of price

(1) The price in a contract of sale may be fixed by the contract, or may be left to be fixed in a manner agreed by the contract, or may be determined by the course of dealing between the parties.

(2) Where the price is not determined as mentioned in subsection (1) above the buyer must pay a reasonable price.

(3) What is a reasonable price is a question of fact dependent on the circumstances of each particular case.

9   Agreement to sell at valuation

(1) Where there is an agreement to sell goods on the terms that the price is to be fixed by the valuation of a third party, and he cannot or does not make the valuation, the agreement is avoided; but if the goods or any part of them have been delivered to and appropriated by the buyer he must pay a reasonable price for them.

(2) Where the third party is prevented from making the valuation by the fault of the seller or buyer, the party not at fault may maintain an action for damages against the party at fault.

[Implied terms etc.]

10   Stipulations about time

(1) Unless a different intention appears from the terms of the contract, stipulations as to time of payment are not of the essence of a contract of sale.

(2) Whether any other stipulation as to time is or is not of the essence of the contract depends on the terms of the contract.

(3) In a contract of sale 'month' prima facie means calendar month.

11 When condition to be treated as warranty

[(1) This section does not apply to Scotland.]

(2) Where a contract of sale is subject to a condition to be fulfilled by the seller, the buyer may waive the condition, or may elect to treat the breach of the condition as a breach of warranty and not as a ground for treating the contract as repudiated.

(3) Whether a stipulation in a contract of sale is a condition, the breach of which may give rise to a right to treat the contract as repudiated, or a warranty, the breach of which may give rise to a claim for damages but not to a right to reject the goods and treat the contract as repudiated, depends in each case on the construction of the contract; and a stipulation may be a condition, though called a warranty in the contract.

(4) [Subject to section 35A below] Where a contract of sale is not severable and the buyer has accepted the goods or part of them, the breach of a condition to be fulfilled by the seller can only be treated as a breach of warranty, and not as a ground for rejecting the goods and treating the contract as repudiated, unless there is an express or implied term of the contract to that effect.

(6) Nothing in this section affects a condition or warranty whose fulfilment is excused by law by reason of impossibility or otherwise.

(7) Paragraph 2 of Schedule 1 below applies in relation to a contract made before 22 April 1967 or (in the application of this Act to Northern Ireland) 28 July 1967.

12 Implied terms about title, etc.

(1) In a contract of sale, other than one to which subsection (3) below applies, there is an implied [term] on the part of the seller that in the case of a sale he has a right to sell the goods, and in the case of an agreement to sell he will have such a right at the time when the property is to pass.

(2) In a contract of sale, other than one to which subsection (3) below applies, there is also an implied [term] that—

  (a) the goods are free, and will remain free until the time when the property is to pass, from any charge or encumbrance not disclosed or known to the buyer before the contract is made, and

  (b) the buyer will enjoy quiet possession of the goods except so far as it may be disturbed by the owner or other person entitled to the benefit of any charge or encumbrance so disclosed or known.

(3) This subsection applies to a contract of sale in the case of which there appears from the contract or is to be inferred from its circumstances an intention that the seller should transfer only such title as he or a third person may have.

(4) In a contract to which subsection (3) above applies there is an implied [term] that all charges or encumbrances known to the seller and not known to the buyer have been disclosed to the buyer before the contract is made.

(5) In a contract to which subsection (3) above applies there is also an implied [term] that none of the following will disturb the buyer's quiet possession of the goods, namely—

  (a) the seller;

  (b) in a case where the parties to the contract intend that the seller should transfer only such title as a third person may have, that person;

  (c) anyone claiming through or under the seller or that third person otherwise than under a charge or encumbrance disclosed or known to the buyer before the contract is made.

[(5A) As regards England and Wales and Northern Ireland, the term implied by subsection (1) above is a condition and the terms implied by subsections (2), (4) and (5) above are warranties.]

(6) Paragraph 3 of Schedule 1 below applies in relation to a contract made before 18 May 1973.

13 Sale by description

(1) Where there is a contract for the sale of goods by description, there is an implied term that the goods will correspond with the description.

[(1A) As regards England and Wales and Northern Ireland, the term implied by subsection (1) above is a condition.]

(2) If the sale is by sample as well as by description it is not sufficient that the bulk of the goods corresponds with the sample if the goods do not also correspond with the description.

(3) A sale of goods is not prevented from being a sale by description by reason only that, being exposed for sale or hire, they are selected by the buyer.

(4) Paragraph 4 of Schedule 1 below applies in relation to a contract made before 18 May 1973.

14   Implied terms about quality or fitness

(1) Except as provided by this section and section 15 below and subject to any other enactment, there is no implied [term] about the quality or fitness for any particular purpose of goods supplied under a contract of sale.

[(2) Where the seller sells goods in the course of a business, there is an implied term that the goods supplied under the contract are of satisfactory quality.

(2A) For the purposes of this Act, goods are of satisfactory quality if they meet the standard that a reasonable person would regard as satisfactory, taking account of any description of the goods, the price (if relevant) and all the other relevant circumstances.

(2B) For the purposes of this Act, the quality of goods includes their state and condition and the following (among others) are in appropriate cases aspects of the quality of goods—

(a) fitness for all the purposes for which goods of the kind in question are commonly supplied,

(b) appearance and finish,

(c) freedom from minor defects,

(d) safety, and

(e) durability.

(2C) The term implied by subsection (2) above does not extend to any matter making the quality of goods unsatisfactory—

(a) which is specifically drawn to the buyer's attention before the contract is made,

(b) where the buyer examines the goods before the contract is made, which that examination ought to reveal, or

(c) in the case of a contract for sale by sample, which would have been apparent on a reasonable examination of the sample.]

[(2D) If the buyer deals as consumer or, in Scotland, if a contract of sale is a consumer contract, the relevant circumstances mentioned in subsection (2A) above include any public statements on the specific characteristics of the goods made about them by the seller, the producer or his representative, particularly in advertising or on labelling.

(2E) A public statement is not by virtue of subsection (2D) above a relevant circumstance for the purposes of subsection (2A) above in the case of a contract of sale, if the seller shows that—

(a) at the time the contract was made, he was not, and could not reasonably have been, aware of the statement,

(b) before the contract was made, the statement had been withdrawn in public or, to the extent that it contained anything which was incorrect or misleading, it had been corrected in public, or

(c) the decision to buy the goods could not have been influenced by the statement.

(2F) Subsections (2D) and (2E) above do not prevent any public statement from being a relevant circumstance for the purposes of subsection (2A) above (whether or not the buyer deals as consumer or, in Scotland, whether or not the contract of sale is a consumer contract) if the statement would have been such a circumstance apart from those subsections.]

(3) Where the seller sells goods in the course of a business and the buyer, expressly or by implication, makes known—

(a) to the seller, or

(b) where the purchase price or part of it is payable by instalments and the goods were previously sold by a credit-broker to the seller, to that credit-broker, any particular purpose for which the goods are being bought, there is an implied [term] that the goods supplied under the contract are reasonably fit for that purpose, whether or not that is a purpose for which such goods are commonly supplied, except where the circumstances show that the buyer does not rely, or that it is unreasonable for him to rely, on the skill or judgment of the seller or credit-broker.

(4) An implied [term] about quality or fitness for a particular purpose may be annexed to a contract of sale by usage.

(5) The preceding provisions of this section apply to a sale by a person who in the course of a business is acting as agent for another as they apply to a sale by a principal in the course of a business, except where that other is not selling in the course of a business and either the buyer knows that fact or reasonable steps are taken to bring it to the notice of the buyer before the contract is made.

[(6) As regards England and Wales and Northern Ireland, the terms implied by subsections (2) and (3) above are conditions.]

(7) Paragraph 5 of Schedule 1 below applies in relation to a contract made on or after 18 May 1973 and before the appointed day, and paragraph 6 in relation to one made before 18 May 1973.

(8) In subsection (7) above and paragraph 5 of Schedule 1 below references to the appointed day are to the day appointed for the purposes of those provisions by an order of the Secretary of State made by statutory instrument.

Sale by sample

15 Sale by sample

(1) A contract of sale is a contract for sale by sample where there is an express or implied [term] to that effect in the contract.

(2) In the case of a contract for sale by sample there is an implied [term]—

(a) that the bulk will correspond with the sample in quality;

[...]

(c) that the goods will be free from any defect, [making their quality unsatisfactory], which would not be apparent on reasonable examination of the sample.

[(3) As regards England and Wales and Northern Ireland, the term implied by subsection (2) above is a condition.]

(4) Paragraph 7 of Schedule 1 below applies in relation to a contract made before 18 May 1973.

Miscellaneous

[15A Modification of remedies for breach of condition in non-consumer cases

(1) Where in the case of a contract of sale—

(a) the buyer would, apart from this subsection, have the right to reject goods by reason of a breach on the part of the seller of a term implied by section 13, 14 or 15 above, but

(b) the breach is so slight that it would be unreasonable for him to reject them, then, if the buyer does not deal as consumer, the breach is not to be treated as a breach of condition but may be treated as a breach of warranty.

(2) This section applies unless a contrary intention appears in, or is to be implied from, the contract.

(3) It is for the seller to show that a breach fell within subsection (1)(b) above.

PART III EFFECTS OF THE CONTRACT

Transfer of property as between seller and buyer

16 Goods must be ascertained

[Subject to section (20A) below] Where there is a contract for the sale of unascertained goods no property in the goods is transferred to the buyer unless and until the goods are ascertained.

17   Property passes when intended to pass

(1) Where there is a contract for the sale of specific or ascertained goods the property in them is transferred to the buyer at such time as the parties to the contract intend it to be transferred.

(2) For the purpose of ascertaining the intention of the parties regard shall be had to the terms of the contract, the conduct of the parties and the circumstances of the case.

18   Rules for ascertaining intention

Unless a different intention appears, the following are rules for ascertaining the intention of the parties as to the time at which the property in the goods is to pass to the buyer.

Rule 1.—Where there is an unconditional contract for the sale of specific goods in a deliverable state the property in the goods passes to the buyer when the contract is made, and it is immaterial whether the time of payment or the time of delivery, or both, be postponed.

Rule 2.—Where there is a contract for the sale of specific goods and the seller is bound to do something to the goods for the purpose of putting them into a deliverable state, the property does not pass until the thing is done and the buyer has notice that it has been done.

Rule 3.—Where there is a contract for the sale of specific goods in a deliverable state but the seller is bound to weigh, measure, test, or do some other act or thing with reference to the goods for the purpose of ascertaining the price, the property does not pass until the act or thing is done and the buyer has notice that it has been done.

Rule 4.—When goods are delivered to the buyer on approval or on sale or return or other similar terms the property in the goods passes to the buyer—

> (a) when he signifies his approval or acceptance to the seller or does any other act adopting the transaction;
>
> (b) if he does not signify his approval or acceptance to the seller but retains the goods without giving notice of rejection, then, if a time has been fixed for the return of the goods, on the expiration of that time, and, if no time has been fixed, on the expiration of a reasonable time.

Rule 5.—(1) Where there is a contract for the sale of unascertained or future goods by description, and goods of that description and in a deliverable state are unconditionally appropriated to the contract, either by the seller with the assent of the buyer or by the buyer with the assent of the seller, the property in the goods then passes to the buyer; and the assent may be express or implied, and may be given either before or after the appropriation is made.

(2) Where, in pursuance of the contract, the seller delivers the goods to the buyer or to a carrier or other bailee or custodier (whether named by the buyer or not) for the purpose of transmission to the buyer, and does not reserve the right of disposal, he is to be taken to have unconditionally appropriated the goods to the contract.

[(3) Where there is a contract for the sale of a specified quantity of unascertained goods in a deliverable state forming part of a bulk which is identified either in the contract or by subsequent agreement between the parties and the bulk is reduced to (or to less than) that quantity, then, if the buyer under that contract is the only buyer to whom goods are then due out of the bulk—

> (a) the remaining goods are to be taken as appropriated to that contract at the time when the bulk is so reduced; and
>
> (b) the property in those goods then passes to that buyer.

(4) Paragraph (3) above applies also (with the necessary modifications) where a bulk is reduced to (or to less than) the aggregate of the quantities due to a single buyer under separate contracts relating to that bulk and he is the only buyer to whom goods are then due out of that bulk.]

19   Reservation of right of disposal

(1) Where there is a contract for the sale of specific goods or where goods are subsequently appropriated to the contract, the seller may, by the terms of the contract or appropriation, reserve the right of disposal of the goods until certain conditions are fulfilled; and in such a case, notwithstanding the delivery of the goods to the buyer, or to a carrier or other bailee or custodier for the purpose

of transmission to the buyer, the property in the goods does not pass to the buyer until the conditions imposed by the seller are fulfilled.

(2) Where goods are shipped, and by the bill of lading the goods are deliverable to the order of the seller or his agent, the seller is prima facie to be taken to reserve the right of disposal.

(3) Where the seller of goods draws on the buyer for the price, and transmits the bill of exchange and bill of lading to the buyer together to secure acceptance or payment of the bill of exchange, the buyer is bound to return the bill of lading if he does not honour the bill of exchange, and if he wrongfully retains the bill of lading the property in the goods does not pass to him.

20 [Passing of risk]

(1) Unless otherwise agreed, the goods remain at the seller's risk until the property in them is transferred to the buyer, but when the property in them is transferred to the buyer the goods are at the buyer's risk whether delivery has been made or not.

(2) But where delivery has been delayed through the fault of either buyer or seller the goods are at the risk of the party at fault as regards any loss which might not have occurred but for such fault.

(3) Nothing in this section affects the duties or liabilities of either seller or buyer as a bailee or custodier of the goods of the other party.

[(4) In a case where the buyer deals as consumer or, in Scotland, where there is a consumer contract in which the buyer is a consumer, subsections (1) to (3) above must be ignored and the goods remain at the seller's risk until they are delivered to the consumer.]

[20A Undivided shares in goods forming part of a bulk

(1) This section applies to a contract for the sale of a specified quantity of unascertained goods if the following conditions are met—

    (a) the goods or some of them form part of a bulk which is identified either in the contract or by subsequent agreement between the parties; and

    (b) the buyer has paid the price for some or all of the goods which are the subject of the contract and which form part of the bulk.

(2) Where this section applies, then (unless the parties agree otherwise), as soon as the conditions specified in paragraphs (a) and (b) of subsection (1) above are met or at such later time as the parties may agree—

    (a) property in an undivided share in the bulk is transferred to the buyer; and

    (b) the buyer becomes an owner in common of the bulk.

(3) Subject to subsection (4) below, for the purposes of this section, the undivided share of a buyer in a bulk at any time shall be such share as the quantity of goods paid for and due to the buyer out of the bulk bears to the quantity of goods in the bulk at that time.

(4) Where the aggregate of the undivided shares of buyers in a bulk determined under subsection (3) above would at any time exceed the whole of the bulk at that time, the undivided share in the bulk of each buyer shall be reduced proportionately so that the aggregate of the undivided shares is equal to the whole bulk.

(5) Where a buyer has paid the price for only some of the goods due to him out of a bulk, any delivery to the buyer out of the bulk shall, for the purposes of this section, be ascribed in the first place to the goods in respect of which payment has been made.

(6) For the purpose of this section payment of part of the price for any goods shall be treated as payment for a corresponding part of the goods.]

[20B Deemed consent by co-owner to dealings in bulk goods

(1) A person who has become an owner in common of a bulk by virtue of section 20A above shall be deemed to have consented to—

    (a) any delivery of goods out of the bulk to any other owner in common of the bulk, being goods which are due to him under his contract;

(b) any removal, dealing with, delivery or disposal of goods in the bulk by any other person who is an owner in common of the bulk in so far as the goods fall within that co-owner's undivided share in the bulk at the time of the removal, dealing, delivery or disposal.

(2) No cause of action shall accrue to anyone against a person by reason of that person having acted in accordance with paragraph (a) or (b) of subsection (1) above in reliance on any consent deemed to have been given under that subsection.

(3) Nothing in this section or section 20A above shall—

(a) impose an obligation on a buyer of goods out of a bulk to compensate any other buyer of goods out of that bulk for any shortfall in the goods received by that other buyer;

(b) affect any contractual arrangement between buyers of goods out of a bulk for adjustments between themselves; or

(c) affect the rights of any buyer under his contract.]

Transfer of title

21   Sale by person not the owner

(1) Subject to this Act, where goods are sold by a person who is not their owner, and who does not sell them under the authority or with the consent of the owner, the buyer acquires no better title to the goods than the seller had, unless the owner of the goods is by his conduct precluded from denying the seller's authority to sell.

(2) Nothing in this Act affects—

(a) the provisions of the Factors Acts or any enactment enabling the apparent owner of goods to dispose of them as if he were their true owner;

(b) the validity of any contract of sale under any special common law or statutory power of sale or under the order of a court of competent jurisdiction.

22   Market overt

[...]

23   Sale under voidable title

When the seller of goods has a voidable title to them, but his title has not been avoided at the time of the sale, the buyer acquires a good title to the goods, provided he buys them in good faith and without notice of the seller's defect of title.

24   Seller in possession after sale

Where a person having sold goods continues or is in possession of the goods, or of the documents of title to the goods, the delivery or transfer by that person, or by a mercantile agent acting for him, of the goods or documents of title under any sale, pledge, or other disposition thereof, to any person receiving the same in good faith and without notice of the previous sale, has the same effect as if the person making the delivery or transfer were expressly authorised by the owner of the goods to make the same.

25   Buyer in possession after sale

(1) Where a person having bought or agreed to buy goods obtains, with the consent of the seller, possession of the goods or the documents of title to the goods, the delivery or transfer by that person, or by a mercantile agent acting for him, of the goods or documents of title, under any sale, pledge, or other disposition thereof, to any person receiving the same in good faith and without notice of any lien or other right of the original seller in respect of the goods, has the same effect as if the person making the delivery or transfer were a mercantile agent in possession of the goods or documents of title with the consent of the owner.

(2) For the purposes of subsection (1) above—

(a) the buyer under a conditional sale agreement is to be taken not to be a person who has bought or agreed to buy goods, and

(b) 'conditional sale agreement' means an agreement for the sale of goods which is a consumer credit agreement within the meaning of the Consumer Credit Act 1974 under which the purchase price or part of it is payable by instalments, and the property in the goods is to remain in the seller (notwithstanding that the buyer is to be in possession of the goods) until such conditions as to the payment of instalments or otherwise as may be specified in the agreement are fulfilled.

(3) Paragraph 9 of Schedule 1 below applies in relation to a contract under which a person buys or agrees to buy goods and which is made before the appointed day.

(4) In subsection (3) above and paragraph 9 of Schedule 1 below references to the appointed day are to the day appointed for the purposes of those provisions by an order of the Secretary of State made by statutory instrument.

26   Supplementary to sections 24 and 25

In sections 24 and 25 above 'mercantile agent' means a mercantile agent having in the customary course of his business as such agent authority either—

(a) to sell goods, or

(b) to consign goods for the purpose of sale, or

(c) to buy goods, or

(d) to raise money on the security of goods.

PART IV PERFORMANCE OF THE CONTRACT

27   Duties of seller and buyer

It is the duty of the seller to deliver the goods, and of the buyer to accept and pay for them, in accordance with the terms of the contract of sale.

28   Payment and delivery are concurrent conditions

Unless otherwise agreed, delivery of the goods and payment of the price are concurrent conditions, that is to say, the seller must be ready and willing to give possession of the goods to the buyer in exchange for the price and the buyer must be ready and willing to pay the price in exchange for possession of the goods.

29   Rules about delivery

(1) Whether it is for the buyer to take possession of the goods or for the seller to send them to the buyer is a question depending in each case on the contract, express or implied, between the parties.

(2) Apart from any such contract, express or implied, the place of delivery is the seller's place of business if he has one, and if not, his residence; except that, if the contract is for the sale of specific goods, which to the knowledge of the parties when the contract is made are in some other place, then that place is the place of delivery.

(3) Where under the contract of sale the seller is bound to send the goods to the buyer, but no time for sending them is fixed, the seller is bound to send them within a reasonable time.

(4) Where the goods at the time of sale are in the possession of a third person, there is no delivery by seller to buyer unless and until the third person acknowledges to the buyer that he holds the goods on his behalf; but nothing in this section affects the operation of the issue or transfer of any document of title to goods.

(5) Demand or tender of delivery may be treated as ineffectual unless made at a reasonable hour; and what is a reasonable hour is a question of fact.

(6) Unless otherwise agreed, the expenses of and incidental to putting the goods into a deliverable state must be borne by the seller.

30   Delivery of wrong quantity

(1) Where the seller delivers to the buyer a quantity of goods less than he contracted to sell, the buyer may reject them, but if the buyer accepts the goods so delivered he must pay for them at the contract rate.

(2) Where the seller delivers to the buyer a quantity of goods larger than he contracted to sell, the buyer may accept the goods included in the contract and reject the rest, or he may reject the whole.

[(2A) A buyer who does not deal as consumer may not—

(a) where the seller delivers a quantity of goods less than he contracted to sell, reject the goods under subsection (1) above, or

(b) where the seller delivers a quantity of goods larger than he contracted to sell, reject the whole under subsection (2) above,

if the shortfall or, as the case may be, excess is so slight that it would be unreasonable for him to do so.

(2B) It is for the seller to show that a shortfall or excess fell within subsection (2A) above.

(2C) Subsections (2A) and (2B) above do not apply to Scotland.]

[(2D) Where the seller delivers a quantity of goods—

(a) less than he contracted to sell, the buyer shall not be entitled to reject the goods under subsection (1) above,

(b) larger than he contracted to sell, the buyer shall not be entitled to reject the whole under subsection (2) above,

unless the shortfall or excess is material.

(2E) Subsection (2D) above applies to Scotland only.]

(3) Where the seller delivers to the buyer a quantity of goods larger than he contracted to sell and the buyer accepts the whole of the goods so delivered he must pay for them at the contract rate.

(5) This section is subject to any usage of trade, special agreement, or course of dealing between the parties.

31   Instalment deliveries

(1) Unless otherwise agreed, the buyer of goods is not bound to accept delivery of them by instalments.

(2) Where there is a contract for the sale of goods to be delivered by stated instalments, which are to be separately paid for, and the seller makes defective deliveries in respect of one or more instalments, or the buyer neglects or refuses to take delivery of or pay for one or more instalments, it is a question in each case depending on the terms of the contract and the circumstances of the case whether the breach of contract is a repudiation of the whole contract or whether it is a severable breach giving rise to a claim for compensation but not to a right to treat the whole contract as repudiated.

32   Delivery to carrier

(1) Where, in pursuance of a contract of sale, the seller is authorised or required to send the goods to the buyer, delivery of the goods to a carrier (whether named by the buyer or not) for the purpose of transmission to the buyer is prima facie deemed to be delivery of the goods to the buyer.

(2) Unless otherwise authorised by the buyer, the seller must make such contact with the carrier on behalf of the buyer as may be reasonable having regard to the nature of the goods and the other circumstances of the case; and if the seller omits to do so, and the goods are lost or damaged in course of transit, the buyer may decline to treat the delivery to the carrier as a delivery to himself or may hold the seller responsible in damages.

(3) Unless otherwise agreed, where goods are sent by the seller to the buyer by a route involving sea transit, under circumstances in which it is usual to insure, the seller must give such notice to the buyer as may enable him to insure them during their sea transit, and if the seller fails to do so, the goods are at his risk during such sea transit.

[(4) In a case where the buyer deals as consumer or, in Scotland, where there is a consumer contract in which the buyer is a consumer, subsections (1) to (3) above must be ignored, but if in pursuance of a contract of sale the seller is authorised or required to send the goods to the buyer, delivery of the goods to the carrier is not delivery of the goods to the buyer.]

33   Risk where goods are delivered at distant place

Where the seller of goods agrees to deliver them at his own risk at a place other than that where they are when sold, the buyer must nevertheless (unless otherwise agreed) take any risk of deterioration in the goods necessarily incident to the course of transit.

34 Buyer's right of examining the goods

Unless otherwise agreed, when the seller tenders delivery of goods to the buyer, he is bound on request to afford the buyer a reasonable opportunity of examining the goods for the purpose of ascertaining whether they are in conformity with the contract [and, in the case of a contract for sale by sample, of comparing the bulk with the sample].

35 Acceptance

(1) The buyer is deemed to have accepted the goods [subject to subsection (2) below—
    (a) when he intimates to the seller that he has accepted them, or
    (b) when the goods have been delivered to him and he does any act in relation to them which is inconsistent with the ownership of the seller.

(2) Where goods are delivered to the buyer, and he has not previously examined them, he is not deemed to have accepted them under subsection (1) above until he has had a reasonable opportunity of examining them for the purpose—
    (a) of ascertaining whether they are in conformity with the contract, and
    (b) in the case of a contract for sale by sample, of comparing the bulk with the sample.

(3) Where the buyer deals as consumer or (in Scotland) the contract of sale is a consumer contract, the buyer cannot lose his right to rely on subsection (2) above by agreement, waiver or otherwise.

(4) The buyer is also deemed to have accepted the goods when after the lapse of a reasonable time he retains the goods without intimating to the seller that he has rejected them.

(5) The questions that are material in determining for the purposes of subsection (4) above whether a reasonable time has elapsed include whether the buyer has had a reasonable opportunity of examining the goods for the purpose mentioned in subsection (2) above.

(6) The buyer is not by virtue of this section deemed to have accepted the goods merely because—
    (a) he asks for, or agrees to, their repair by or under an arrangement with the seller, or
    (b) the goods are delivered to another under a sub-sale or other disposition.

(7) Where the contract is for the sale of goods making one or more commercial units, a buyer accepting any goods included in a unit is deemed to have accepted all the goods making the unit; and in this subsection 'commercial unit' means a unit division of which would materially impair the value of the goods or the character of the unit.]

[35A Right of partial rejection

(1) If the buyer—
    (a) has the right to reject the goods by reason of a breach on the part of the seller that affects some or all of them, but
    (b) accepts some of the goods, including, where there are any goods unaffected by the breach, all such goods,
he does not by accepting them lose his right to reject the rest.

(2) In the case of a buyer having the right to reject an instalment of goods, subsection (1) above applies as if references to the goods were references to the goods comprised in the instalment.

(3) For the purposes of subsection (1) above, goods are affected by a breach if by reason of the breach they are not in conformity with the contract.

(4) This section applies unless a contrary intention appears in, or is to be implied from, the contract.]

36 Buyer not bound to return rejected goods

Unless otherwise agreed, where goods are delivered to the buyer, and he refuses to accept them, having the right to do so, he is not bound to return them to the seller, but it is sufficient if he intimates to the seller that he refuses to accept them.

37 Buyer's liability for not taking delivery of goods

(1) When the seller is ready and willing to deliver the goods, and requests the buyer to take delivery, and the buyer does not within a reasonable time after such request take delivery of the goods, he

is liable to the seller for any loss occasioned by his neglect or refusal to take delivery, and also for a reasonable charge for the care and custody of the goods.

(2) Nothing in this section affects the rights of the seller where the neglect or refusal of the buyer to take delivery amounts to a repudiation of the contract.

PART V RIGHTS OF UNPAID SELLER AGAINST THE GOODS

Preliminary

38   Unpaid seller defined
(1) The seller of goods is an unpaid seller within the meaning of this Act—
  (a) when the whole of the price has not been paid or tendered;
  (b) when a bill of exchange or other negotiable instrument has been received as conditional payment, and the condition on which it was received has not been fulfilled by reason of the dishonour of the instrument or otherwise.

(2) In this Part of this Act 'seller' includes any person who is in the position of a seller, as, for instance, an agent of the seller to whom the bill of lading has been indorsed, or a consignor or agent who has himself paid (or is directly responsible for) the price.

39   Unpaid seller's rights
(1) Subject to this and any other Act, notwithstanding that the property in the goods may have passed to the buyer, the unpaid seller of goods, as such, has by implication of law—
  (a) a lien on the goods or right to retain them for the price while he is in possession of them;
  (b) in the case of the insolvency of the buyer, a right of stopping the goods in transit after he has parted with the possession of them;
  (c) a right of re-sale as limited by this Act.

(2) Where the property in goods has not passed to the buyer, the unpaid seller has (in addition to his other remedies) a right of withholding delivery similar to and coextensive with his rights of lien or retention and stoppage in transit where the property has passed to the buyer.

Unpaid seller's lien

41   Seller's lien
(1) Subject to this Act, the unpaid seller of goods who is in possession of them is entitled to retain possession of them until payment or tender of the price in the following cases:—
  (a) where the goods have been sold without any stipulation as to credit;
  (b) where the goods have been sold on credit but the term of credit has expired;
  (c) where the buyer becomes insolvent.

(2) The seller may exercise his lien or right of retention notwithstanding that he is in possession of the goods as agent or bailee or custodier for the buyer.

42   Part delivery
Where an unpaid seller has made part delivery of the goods, he may exercise his lien or right of retention on the remainder, unless such part delivery has been made under such circumstances as to show an agreement to waive the lien or right of retention.

43   Termination of lien
(1) The unpaid seller of goods loses his lien or right of retention in respect of them—
  (a) when he delivers the goods to a carrier or other bailee or custodier for the purpose of transmission to the buyer without reserving the right of disposal of the goods;
  (b) when the buyer or his agent lawfully obtains possession of the goods;
  (c) by waiver of the lien or right of retention.

(2) An unpaid seller of goods who has a lien or right of retention in respect of them does not lose his lien or right of retention by reason only that he has obtained judgment or decree for the price of the goods.

Stoppage in transit

44 Right of stoppage in transit

Subject to this Act, when the buyer of goods becomes insolvent the unpaid seller who has parted with the possession of the goods has the right of stopping them in transit, that is to say, he may resume possession of the goods as long as they are in course of transit, and may retain them until payment or tender of the price.

45 Duration of transit

(1) Goods are deemed to be in course of transit from the time when they are delivered to a carrier or other bailee or custodier for the purpose of transmission to the buyer, until the buyer or his agent in that behalf takes delivery of them from the carrier or other bailee or custodier.

(2) If the buyer or his agent in that behalf obtains delivery of the goods before their arrival at the appointed destination, the transit is at an end.

(3) If, after the arrival of the goods at the appointed destination, the carrier or other bailee or custodier acknowledges to the buyer or his agent that he holds the goods on his behalf and continues in possession of them as bailee or custodier for the buyer or his agent, the transit is at an end, and it is immaterial that a further destination for the goods may have been indicated by the buyer.

(4) If the goods are rejected by the buyer, and the carrier or other bailee or custodier continues in possession of them, the transit is not deemed to be at an end, even if the seller has refused to receive them back.

(5) When goods are delivered to a ship chartered by the buyer it is a question depending on the circumstances of the particular case whether they are in the possession of the master as a carrier or as agent to the buyer.

(6) Where the carrier or other bailee or custodier wrongfully refuses to deliver the goods to the buyer or his agent in that behalf, the transit is deemed to be at an end.

(7) Where part delivery of the goods has been made to the buyer or his agent in that behalf, the remainder of the goods may be stopped in transit, unless such part delivery has been made under such circumstances as to show an agreement to give up possession of the whole of the goods.

46 How stoppage in transit is effected

(1) The unpaid seller may exercise his right of stoppage in transit either by taking actual possession of the goods or by giving notice of his claim to the carrier or other bailee or custodier in whose possession the goods are.

(2) The notice may be given either to the person in actual possession of the goods or to his principal.

(3) If given to the principal, the notice is ineffective unless given at such time and under such circumstances that the principal, by the exercise of reasonable diligence, may communicate it to his servant or agent in time to prevent a delivery to the buyer.

(4) When notice of stoppage in transit is given by the seller to the carrier or other bailee or custodier in possession of the goods, he must re-deliver the goods to, or according to the directions of, the seller; and the expenses of the re-delivery must be borne by the seller.

Resale etc. by buyer

47 Effect of sub-sale etc. by buyer

(1) Subject to this Act, the unpaid seller's right of lien or retention or stoppage in transit is not affected by any sale or other disposition of the goods which the buyer may have made, unless the seller has assented to it.

(2) Where a document of title to goods has been lawfully transferred to any person as buyer or owner of the goods, and that person transfers the document to a person who takes it in good faith and for valuable consideration, then—

    (a) if the last-mentioned transfer was by way of sale the unpaid seller's right of lien or retention or stoppage in transit is defeated; and

    (b) if the last-mentioned transfer was made by way of pledge or other disposition for value, the unpaid seller's right of lien or retention of stoppage in transit can only be exercised subject to the rights of the transferee.

Rescission: and re-sale by seller

48   Rescission: and re-sale by seller

(1) Subject to this section, a contract of sale is not rescinded by the mere exercise by an unpaid seller of his right of lien or retention or stoppage in transit.

(2) Where an unpaid seller who has exercised his right of lien or retention or stoppage in transit re-sells the goods, the buyer acquires a good title to them as against the original buyer.

(3) Where the goods are of a perishable nature, or where the unpaid seller gives notice to the buyer of his intention to re-sell, and the buyer does not within a reasonable time pay or tender the price, the unpaid seller may re-sell the goods and recover from the original buyer damages for any loss occasioned by his breach of contract.

(4) Where the seller expressly reserves the right of re-sale in case the buyer should make default, and on the buyer making default re-sells the goods, the original contract of sale is rescinded but without prejudice to any claim the seller may have for damages.

[PART 5A ADDITIONAL RIGHTS OF BUYER IN CONSUMER CASES]

[48A   Introductory

(1) This section applies if—

    (a) the buyer deals as consumer or, in Scotland, there is a consumer contract in which the buyer is a consumer, and

    (b) the goods do not conform to the contract of sale at the time of delivery.

(2) If this section applies, the buyer has the right—

    (a) under and in accordance with section 48B below, to require the seller to repair or replace the goods, or

    (b) under and in accordance with section 48C below—

        (i)   to require the seller to reduce the purchase price of the goods to the buyer by an appropriate amount, or

        (ii) to rescind the contract with regard to the goods in question.

(3) For the purposes of subsection (1)(b) above goods which do not conform to the contract of sale at any time within the period of six months starting with the date on which the goods were delivered to the buyer must be taken not to have so conformed at that date.

(4) Subsection (3) above does not apply if—

    (a) it is established that the goods did so conform at that date;

    (b) its application is incompatible with the nature of the goods or the nature of the lack of conformity.]

[48B   Repair or replacement of the goods

(1) If section 48A above applies, the buyer may require the seller—

    (a) to repair the goods, or

    (b) to replace the goods.

(2) If the buyer requires the seller to repair or replace the goods, the seller must—

    (a) repair or, as the case may be, replace the goods within a reasonable time but without causing significant inconvenience to the buyer;

    (b) bear any necessary costs incurred in doing so (including in particular the cost of any labour, materials or postage).

(3) The buyer must not require the seller to repair or, as the case may be, replace the goods if that remedy is—

    (a) impossible, or

    (b) disproportionate in comparison to the other of those remedies, or

    (c) disproportionate in comparison to an appropriate reduction in the purchase price under paragraph (a), or rescission under paragraph (b), of section 48C(1) below.

(4) One remedy is disproportionate in comparison to the other if the one imposes costs on the seller which, in comparison to those imposed on him by the other, are unreasonable, taking into account—

    (a) the value which the goods would have if they conformed to the contract of sale,

    (b) the significance of the lack of conformity, and

    (c) whether the other remedy could be effected without significant inconvenience to the buyer.

(5) Any question as to what is a reasonable time or significant inconvenience is to be determined by reference to—

    (a) the nature of the goods, and

    (b) the purpose for which the goods were acquired.]

[48C Reduction of purchase price or rescission of contract

(1) If section 48A above applies, the buyer may—

    (a) require the seller to reduce the purchase price of the goods in question to the buyer by an appropriate amount, or

    (b) rescind the contract with regard to those goods,

if the condition in subsection (2) below is satisfied.

(2) The condition is that—

    (a) by virtue of section 48B(3) above the buyer may require neither repair nor replacement of the goods; or

    (b) the buyer has required the seller to repair or replace the goods, but the seller is in breach of the requirement of section 48B(2)(a) above to do so within a reasonable time and without significant inconvenience to the buyer.

(3) For the purposes of this Part, if the buyer rescinds the contract, any reimbursement to the buyer may be reduced to take account of the use he has had of the goods since they were delivered to him.]

[48D Relation to other remedies etc.

(1) If the buyer requires the seller to repair or replace the goods the buyer must not act under subsection (2) until he has given the seller a reasonable time in which to repair or replace (as the case may be) the goods.

(2) The buyer acts under this subsection if—

    (a) in England and Wales or Northern Ireland he rejects the goods and terminates the contract for breach of condition;

    (b) in Scotland he rejects any goods delivered under the contract and treats it as repudiated;

    (c) he requires the goods to be replaced or repaired (as the case may be).]

[48E Powers of the court

(1) In any proceedings in which a remedy is sought by virtue of this Part the court, in addition to any other power it has, may act under this section.

(2) On the application of the buyer the court may make an order requiring specific performance or, in Scotland, specific implement by the seller of any obligation imposed on him by virtue of section 48B above.

(3) Subsection (4) applies if—

    (a) the buyer requires the seller to give effect to a remedy under section 48B or 48C above or has claims to rescind under section 48C, but

    (b) the court decides that another remedy under section 48B or 48C is appropriate.

(4) The court may proceed—

    (a) as if the buyer had required the seller to give effect to the other remedy, or if the other remedy is rescission under section 48C

    (b) as if the buyer had claimed to rescind the contract under that section.

(5) If the buyer has claimed to rescind the contract the court may order that any reimbursement to the buyer is reduced to take account of the use he has had of the goods since they were delivered to him.

(6) The court may make an order under this section unconditionally or on such terms and conditions as to damages, payment of the price and otherwise as it thinks just.]

[48F   Conformity with the contract

For the purposes of this Part, goods do not conform to a contract of sale if there is, in relation to the goods, a breach of an express term of the contract or a term implied by section 13, 14 or 15 above.]

PART VI ACTIONS FOR BREACH OF THE CONTRACT

Seller's remedies

49   Action for price

(1) Where, under a contract of sale, the property in the goods has passed to the buyer and he wrongfully neglects or refuses to pay for the goods according to the terms of the contract, the seller may maintain an action against him for the price of the goods.

50   Damages for non-acceptance

(1) Where the buyer wrongfully neglects or refuses to accept and pay for the goods, the seller may maintain an action against him for damages for non-acceptance.

(2) The measure of damages is the estimated loss directly and naturally resulting, in the ordinary course of events, from the buyer's breach of contract.

(3) Where there is an available market for the goods in question the measure of damages is prima facie to be ascertained by the difference between the contract price and the market or current price at the time or times when the goods ought to have been accepted or (if no time was fixed for acceptance) at the time of the refusal to accept.

Buyer's remedies

51   Damages for non-delivery

(1) Where the seller wrongfully neglects or refuses to deliver the goods to the buyer, the buyer may maintain an action against the seller for damages for non-delivery.

(2) The measure of damages is the estimated loss directly and naturally resulting, in the ordinary course of events, from the seller's breach of contract.

(3) Where there is an available market for the goods in question the measure of damages is prima facie to be ascertained by the difference between the contract price and the market or current price of the goods at the time or times when they ought to have been delivered or (if no time was fixed) at the time of the refusal to deliver.

52   Specific performance

(1) In any action for breach of contract to deliver specific or ascertained goods the court may, if it thinks fit, on the plaintiff's application, by its judgment or decree direct that the contract shall be performed specifically, without giving the defendant the option of retaining the goods on payment of damages.

(3) The judgment or decree may be unconditional, or on such terms and conditions as to damages, payment of the price and otherwise as seem just to the court.

53 Remedy for breach of warranty

(1) Where there is a breach of warranty by the seller, or where the buyer elects (or is compelled) to treat any breach of a condition on the part of the seller as a breach of warranty, the buyer is not by reason only of such breach of warranty entitled to reject the goods; but he may—

(a) set up against the seller the breach of warranty in diminution or extinction of the price, or

(b) maintain an action against the seller for damages for the breach of warranty.

(2) The measure of damages for breach of warranty is the estimated loss directly and naturally resulting, in the ordinary course of events, from the breach of warranty.

(3) In the case of breach of warranty of quality such loss is prima facie the difference between the value of the goods at the time of delivery to the buyer and the value they would have had if they had fulfilled the warranty.

(4) The fact that the buyer has set up the breach of warranty in diminution or extinction of the price does not prevent him from maintaining an action for the same breach of warranty if he has suffered further damage.

[(5) This section does not apply to Scotland.]

Interest etc.

54 Interest, etc.

Nothing in this Act affects the right of the buyer or the seller to recover interest or special damages in any case where by law interest or special damages may be recoverable, or to recover money paid where the consideration for the payment of it has failed.

PART VII SUPPLEMENTARY

55 Exclusion of implied terms

(1) Where a right, duty or liability would arise under a contract of sale of goods by implication of law, it may (subject to the Unfair Contract Terms Act 1977) be negatived or varied by express agreement, or by the course of dealing between the parties, or by such usage as binds both parties to the contract.

(2) An express [term] does not negative a [term] implied by this Act unless inconsistent with it.

(3) Paragraph 11 of Schedule 1 below applies in relation to a contract made on or after 18 May 1973 and before 1 February 1978, and paragraph 12 in relation to one made before 18 May 1973.

56 Conflict of laws

Paragraph 13 of Schedule 1 below applies in relation to a contract made on or after 18 May 1973 and before 1 February 1978, so as to make provision about conflict of laws in relation to such a contract.

57 Auction sales

(1) Where goods are put up for sale by auction in lots, each lot is prima facie deemed to be the subject of a separate contract of sale.

(2) A sale by auction is complete when the auctioneer announces its completion by the fall of the hammer, or in other customary manner; and until the announcement is made any bidder may retract his bid.

(3) A sale by auction may be notified to be subject to a reserve or upset price, and a right to bid may also be reserved expressly by or on behalf of the seller.

(4) Where a sale by auction is not notified to be subject to a right to bid by or on behalf of the seller, it is not lawful for the seller to bid himself or to employ any person to bid at the sale, or for the auctioneer knowingly to take any bid from the seller or any such person.

(5) A sale contravening subsection (4) above may be treated as fraudulent by the buyer.

(6) Where, in respect of a sale by auction, a right to bid is expressly reserved (but not otherwise) the seller or any one person on his behalf may bid at the auction.

59   Reasonable time a question of fact

Where a reference is made in this Act to a reasonable time the question what is a reasonable time is a question of fact.

60   Rights etc. enforceable by action

Where a right, duty or liability is declared by this Act, it may (unless otherwise provided by this Act) be enforced by action.

61   Interpretation

(1) In this Act, unless the context or subject matter otherwise requires,—

'action' includes counterclaim and set-off, and in Scotland condescendence and claim and compensation;

['bulk' means a mass or collection of goods of the same kind which—

(a) is contained in a defined space or area; and

(b) is such that any goods in the bulk are interchangeable with any other goods therein of the same number or quantity;]

'business' includes a profession and the activities of any government department (including a Northern Ireland department) or local or public authority;

'buyer' means a person who buys or agrees to buy goods;

['consumer contract' has the same meaning as in section 25(1) of the Unfair Contract Terms Act 1977; and for the purposes of this Act the onus of proving that a contract is not to be regarded as a consumer contract shall lie on the seller]

'contract of sale' includes an agreement to sell as well as a sale;

'credit-broker' means a person acting in the course of a business of credit brokerage carried on by him, that is a business of effecting introductions of individuals desiring to obtain credit—

(a) to persons carrying on any business so far as it relates to the provision of credit, or

(b) to other persons engaged in credit brokerage;

'defendant' includes in Scotland defender, respondent, and claimant in a multiple poinding;

'delivery' means voluntary transfer of possession from one person to another; [except that in relation to sections 20A and 20B above it includes such appropriation of goods to the contract as results in property in the goods being transferred to the buyer;]

'document of title to goods' has the same meaning as it has in the Factors Acts;

'Factors Acts' means the Factors Act 1889, the Factors (Scotland) Act 1890, and any enactment amending or substituted for the same;

'fault' means wrongful act or default;

'future goods' means goods to be manufactured or acquired by the seller after the making of the contract of sale;

'goods' includes all personal chattels other than things in action and money, and in Scotland all corporeal moveables except money; and in particular 'goods' includes emblements, industrial growing crops, and things attached to or forming part of the land which are agreed to be severed before sale or under the contract of sale; [and includes an undivided share in goods;]

'plaintiff' includes pursuer, complainer, claimant in a multiplepoinding and defendant or defender counter-claiming;

['producer' means the manufacturer of goods, the importer of goods into the European Economic Area or any person purporting to be a producer by placing his name, trade mark or other distinctive sign on the goods;]

'property' means the general property in goods, and not merely a special property;

['repair' means, in cases where there is a lack of conformity in goods for the purposes of section 48F of this Act, to bring the goods into conformity with the contract;]

'sale' includes a bargain and sale as well as a sale and delivery;

'seller' means a person who sells or agrees to sell goods;

'specific goods' means goods identified and agreed on at the time a contract of sale is made; [and includes an undivided share, specified as a fraction or percentage, of goods identified and agreed on as aforesaid]

'warranty' (as regards England and Wales and Northern Ireland) means an agreement with reference to goods which are the subject of a contract of sale, but collateral to the main purpose of such contract, the breach of which gives rise to a claim for damages, but not to a right to reject the goods and treat the contract as repudiated.

(3) A thing is deemed to be done in good faith within the meaning of this Act when it is in fact done honestly, whether it is done negligently or not.

(4) A person is deemed to be insolvent within the meaning of this Act if he has either ceased to pay his debts in the ordinary course of business or he cannot pay his debts as they become due, [...]

(5) Goods are in a deliverable state within the meaning of this Act when they are in such a state that the buyer would under the contract be bound to take delivery of them.

[(5A) References in this Act to dealing as consumer are to be construed in accordance with Part I of the Unfair Contract Terms Act 1977; and, for the purposes of this Act, it is for a seller claiming that the buyer does not deal as consumer to show that he does not.]

(6) As regards the definition of 'business' in subsection (1) above, paragraph 14 of Schedule 1 below applies in relation to a contract made on or after 18 May 1973 and before 1 February 1978, and paragraph 15 in relation to one made before 18 May 1973.

62   Savings: rule of law etc.

(1) The rules in bankruptcy relating to contracts of sale apply to those contracts, notwithstanding anything in this Act.

(2) The rules of the common law, including the law merchant, except in so far as they are inconsistent with the provisions of this Act, and in particular the rules relating to the law of principal and agent and the effect of fraud, misrepresentation, duress or coercion, mistake, or other invalidating cause, apply to contracts for the sale of goods.

(3) Nothing in this Act or the Sale of Goods Act 1893 affects the enactments relating to bills of sale, or any enactment relating to the sale of goods which is not expressly repealed or amended by this Act or that.

(4) The provisions of this Act about contracts of sale do not apply to a transaction in the form of a contract of sale which is intended to operate by way of mortgage, pledge, charge, or other security.

Vaccine Damage Payments Act 1979

(1979, c. 17)

1   Payments to persons severely disabled by vaccination

(1) If, on consideration of a claim, the Secretary of State is satisfied—

(a) that a person is, or was immediately before his death, severely disabled as a result of vaccination against any of the diseases to which this Act applies; and

(b) that the conditions of entitlement which are applicable in accordance with section 2 below are fulfilled,

he shall in accordance with this Act make a payment of the relevant statutory sum to or for the benefit of that person or to his personal representatives.

[(1A) In subsection (1) above 'statutory sum' means [£30,000] or such other sum as is specified by the Secretary of State for the purposes of this Act by order made by statutory instrument with the consent of the Treasury; and the relevant statutory sum for the purposes of that subsection is the statutory sum at the time when a claim for payment is first made.]

(2) The diseases to which this Act applies are—

(a) diphtheria,

(b) tetanus,

    (c) whooping cough,

    (d) poliomyelitis,

    (e) measles,

    (f) rubella,

    (g) tuberculosis,

    (h) smallpox, and

    (i) any other disease which is specified by the Secretary of State for the purposes of this Act by order made by statutory instrument.

(3) Subject to section 2(3) below, this Act has effect with respect to a person who is severely disabled as a result of a vaccination given to his mother before he was born as if the vaccination had been given directly to him and, in such circumstances as may be prescribed by regulations under this Act, this Act has effect with respect to a person who is severely disabled as a result of contracting a disease through contact with a third person who was vaccinated against it as if the vaccination had been given to him and the disablement resulted from it.

For the purposes of this Act, a person is severely disabled if he suffers disablement to the extent of [60 per cent] or more, assessed as for the purposes of [section 103 of the Social Security Contributions and Benefits Act 1992 or section 103 of the Social Security Contributions and Benefits (Northern Ireland) Act 1992] (disablement gratuity and pension).

2   Conditions of entitlement

(1) Subject to the provisions of this section, the conditions of entitlement referred to in section 1(1)(b) above are—

    (a) that the vaccination in question was carried out—

        (i)   in the United Kingdom or the Isle of Man, and

        (ii) on or after 5 July 1948, and

        (iii) in the case of vaccination against smallpox, before 1st August 1971;

    (b) except in the case of vaccination against poliomyelitis or rubella, that the vaccination was carried out either at a time when the person to whom it was given was under the age of eighteen or at the time of an outbreak within the United Kingdom or the Isle of Man of the disease against which the vaccination was given; and

    (c) that the disabled person was over the age of two on the date when the claim was made or, if he died before that date, that he died after 9th May 1978 and was over the age of two when he died.

3   Determination of claims

(1) Any reference in this Act, other than section 7, to a claim is a reference to a claim for a payment under section 1(1) above which is made—

    (a) by or on behalf of the disabled person concerned or, as the case may be, by his personal representatives; and

    (b) in the manner prescribed by regulations under this Act; and

    [(c) on or before whichever is the later of—

        (i)   the date on which the disabled person attains the age of 21, or where he has died, the date on which he would have attained the age of 21; and

        (ii) the end of the period of six years beginning with the date of the vaccination to which the claim relates;] ...

6   Payments to or for the benefit of disabled persons

(1) Where a payment under section 1(1) above falls to be made in respect of a disabled person who is over eighteen and capable of managing his own affairs, the payment shall be made to him.

(2) Where such a payment falls to be made in respect of a disabled person who has died, the payment shall be made to his personal representatives.

(3) Where such a payment falls to be made in respect of any other disabled person, the payment shall be made for his benefit by paying it to such trustees as the Secretary of State may appoint to be

held by them upon such trusts or, in Scotland, for such purposes and upon such conditions as may be declared by the Secretary of State.

(4) The making of a claim for, or the receipt of, a payment under section 1(1) above does not prejudice the right of any person to institute or carry on proceedings in respect of disablement suffered as a result of vaccination against any disease to which this Act applies; but in any civil proceedings brought in respect of disablement resulting from vaccination against such a disease, the court shall treat a payment made to or in respect of the disabled person concerned under section 1(1) above as paid on account of any damages which the court awards in respect of such disablement.

12   Financial provisions

(4) There shall be paid out of moneys provided by Parliament—

(a) any expenditure incurred by the Secretary of State in making payments under section 1(1) above...

Highways Act 1980

(1980, c. 66)

41   Duty to maintain highways maintainable at public expense

(1) The authority who are for the time being the highway authority for a highway maintainable at the public expense are under a duty, subject to subsections (2) and (4) below, to maintain the highway.

[(1A) In particular, a highway authority are under a duty to ensure, so far as is reasonably practicable, that safe passage along a highway is not endangered by snow or ice.]

58   Special defence in action against a highway authority for damages for non-repair of highway

(1) In an action against a highway authority in respect of damage resulting from their failure to maintain a highway maintainable at the public expense it is a defence (without prejudice to any other defence or the application of the law relating to contributory negligence) to prove that the authority had taken such care as in all the circumstances was reasonably required to secure that the part of the highway to which the action relates was not dangerous for traffic.

102   Provision of works for protecting highways against hazards of nature

(1) The highway authority for a highway maintainable at the public expense may provide and maintain such barriers or other works as they consider necessary for the purpose of affording to the highway protection against snow, flood, landslide or other hazards of nature; and those works may be provided on the highway or on land which, or rights over which, has or have been acquired by the highway authority in the exercise of highway land acquisition powers for that purpose.

(3) A highway authority shall pay compensation to any person who suffers damage by reason of the execution by them under this section of any works on a highway.

[PART 8A RESTRICTION OF RIGHTS OVER HIGHWAY]

[129A   Gating orders

(1) A council may in accordance with this Part make an order under this section in relation to any relevant highway for which they are the highway authority.

(2) An order under this section is to be known as a 'gating order'.

(3) Before making a gating order in relation to a relevant highway the council must be satisfied that—

(a) premises adjoining or adjacent to the highway are affected by crime or anti-social behaviour;

(b) the existence of the highway is facilitating the persistent commission of criminal offences or anti-social behaviour; and

(c) it is in all the circumstances expedient to make the order for the purposes of reducing crime or anti-social behaviour.

(4) The circumstances referred to in subsection (3)(c) include—

(a) the likely effect of making the order on the occupiers of premises adjoining or adjacent to the highway;

(b) the likely effect of making the order on other persons in the locality; and

(c) in a case where the highway constitutes a through route, the availability of a reasonably convenient alternative route.]

[129B   Effect of gating orders

(1) A gating order restricts, to the extent specified in the order, the public right of way over the highway to which it relates.

(2) A gating order may in particular—

(a) restrict the public right of way at all times, or in respect of such times, days or periods as may be specified in the order;

(b) exclude persons of a description specified in the order from the effect of the restriction.

(3) A gating order may not be made so as to restrict the public right of way over a highway for the occupiers of premises adjoining or adjacent to the highway.

(4) A gating order may not be made so as to restrict the public right of way over a highway which is the only or principal means of access to any dwelling.

(5) In relation to a highway which is the only or principal means of access to any premises used for business or recreational purposes, a gating order may not be made so as to restrict the public right of way over the highway during periods when those premises are normally used for those purposes.

(6) A gating order may authorise the installation, operation and maintenance of a barrier or barriers for the purpose of enforcing the restriction provided for in the order.]

[129G   Interpretation

For the purposes of this Part—

'anti-social behaviour' means behaviour by a person which causes or is likely to cause harassment, alarm or distress to one or more other persons not of the same household as himself;]

165   Dangerous land adjoining street

(1) If, in or on any land adjoining a street, there is an unfenced or inadequately fenced source of danger to persons using the street, the local authority in whose area the street is situated may, by notice to the owner or occupier of that land, require him within such time as may be specified in the notice to execute such works of repair, protection, removal or enclosure as will obviate the danger.

(3) Subject to any order made on appeal, if a person on whom a notice is served under this section fails to comply with the notice within the time specified in it, the authority by whom the notice was served may execute such works as are necessary to comply with the notice and may recover the expenses reasonably incurred by them in so doing from that person.

Limitation Act 1980

(1980, c. 58)

PART I

1   Time limits under Part I subject to exclusion under Part II

(1) This Part of this Act gives the ordinary time limits for bringing actions of the various classes mentioned in the following provisions of this Part.

(2) The ordinary time limits given in this Part of this Act are subject to extension or exclusion in accordance with the provisions of Part II of this Act.

2   Time limit for actions founded on tort

An action founded on tort shall not be brought after the expiration of six years from the date on which the cause of action accrued.

3   Time limit in case of successive conversions and extinction of title of owner of converted goods

(1) Where any cause of action in respect of the conversion of a chattel has accrued to any person and, before he recovers possession of the chattel, a further conversion takes place, no action shall be brought in respect of the further conversion after the expiration of six years from the accrual of the cause of action in respect of the original conversion.

(2) Where any such cause of action has accrued to any person and the period prescribed for bringing that action has expired and he has not during that period recovered possession of the chattel, the title of that person to the chattel shall be extinguished.

4   Special time limit in case of theft

(1) The right of any person from whom a chattel is stolen to bring an action in respect of the theft shall not be subject to the time limits under sections 2 and 3(1) of this Act, but if his title to the chattel is extinguished under section 3(2) of this Act he may not bring an action in respect of a theft preceding the loss of his title, unless the theft in question preceded the conversion from which time began to run for the purposes of section 3(2).

(2) Subsection (1) above shall apply to any conversion related to the theft of a chattel as it applies to the theft of a chattel; and, except as provided below, every conversion following the theft of a chattel before the person from whom it is stolen recovers possession of it shall be regarded for the purposes of this section as related to the theft.

If any one purchases the stolen chattel in good faith neither the purchase nor any conversion following it shall be regarded as related to the theft.

(3) Any cause of action accruing in respect of the theft or any conversion related to the theft of a chattel to any person from whom the chattel is stolen shall be disregarded for the purpose of applying section 3(1) or (2) of this Act to his case.

(4) Where in any action brought in respect of the conversion of a chattel it is proved that the chattel was stolen from the plaintiff or anyone through whom he claims it shall be presumed that any conversion following the theft is related to the theft unless the contrary is shown.

(5) In this section 'theft' includes—
    (a) any conduct outside England and Wales which would be theft if committed in England and Wales; and
   [(b) obtaining any chattel (in England and Wales or elsewhere) by—
        (i) blackmail (within the meaning of section 21 of the Theft Act 1968), or
        (ii) fraud (within the meaning of the Fraud Act 2006);]
and references in this section to a chattel being 'stolen' shall be construed accordingly.

[4A   Time limit for actions for defamation or malicious falsehood

The time limit under section 2 of this Act shall not apply to an action for—
    (a) libel or slander, or
    (b) slander of title, slander of goods or other malicious falsehood,
but no such action shall be brought after the expiration of one year from the date on which the cause of action accrued.]

5   Time limit for actions founded on simple contract

An action founded on simple contract shall not be brought after the expiration of six years from the date on which the cause of action accrued.

6   Special time limit for actions in respect of certain loans

(1) Subject to subsection (3) below, section 5 of this Act shall not bar the right of action on a contract of loan to which this section applies.

(2) This section applies to any contract of loan which—

    (a) does not provide for repayment of the debt on or before a fixed or determinable date; and

    (b) does not effectively (whether or not it purports to do so) make the obligation to repay the debt conditional on a demand for repayment made by or on behalf of the creditor or on any other matter;

except where in connection with taking the loan the debtor enters into any collateral obligation to pay the amount of the debt or any part of it (as, for example, by delivering a promissory note as security for the debt) on terms which would exclude the application of this section to the contract of loan if they applied directly to repayment of the debt.

(3) Where a demand in writing for repayment of the debt under a contract of loan to which this section applies is made by or on behalf of the creditor (or, where there are joint creditors, by or on behalf of any one of them) section 5 of this Act shall thereupon apply as if the cause of action to recover the debt had accrued on the date on which the demand was made.

(4) In this section 'promissory note' has the same meaning as in the Bills of Exchange Act 1882.

8   Time limit for actions on a specialty

(1) An action upon a specialty shall not be brought after the expiration of twelve years from the date on which the cause of action accrued.

(2) Subsection (1) above shall not affect any action for which a shorter period of limitation is prescribed by any other provision of this Act.

9   Time limit for actions for sums recoverable by statute

(1) An action to recover any sum recoverable by virtue of any enactment shall not be brought after the expiration of six years from the date on which the cause of action accrued.

(2) Subsection (1) above shall not affect any action to which section 10 of this Act applies.

10   Special time limit for claiming contribution

(1) Where under section 1 of the Civil Liability (Contribution) Act 1978 any person becomes entitled to a right to recover contribution in respect of any damage from any other person, no action to recover contribution by virtue of that right shall be brought after the expiration of two years from the date on which that right accrued.

(2) For the purposes of this section the date on which a right to recover contribution in respect of any damage accrues to any person (referred to below in this section as 'the relevant date') shall be ascertained as provided in subsections (3) and (4) below.

(3) If the person in question is held liable in respect of that damage—

    (a) by a judgment given in any civil proceedings; or

    (b) by an award made on any arbitration;

the relevant date shall be the date on which the judgment is given, or the date of the award (as the case may be).

For the purposes of this subsection no account shall be taken of any judgment or award given or made on appeal in so far as it varies the amount of damages awarded against the person in question.

(4) If, in any case not within subsection (3) above, the person in question makes or agrees to make any payment to one or more persons in compensation for that damage (whether he admits any liability in respect of the damage or not), the relevant date shall be the earliest date on which the amount to be paid by him is agreed between him (or his representative) and the person (or each of the persons, as the case may be) to whom the payment is to be made.

(5) An action to recover contribution shall be one to which sections 28, 32 and 35 of this Act apply, but otherwise Parts II and III of this Act (except sections 34, 37 and 38) shall not apply for the purposes of this section.

11   Special time limit for actions in respect of personal injuries

(1) This section applies to any action for damages for negligence, nuisance or breach of duty (whether the duty exists by virtue of a contract or of provision made by or under a statute or independently of any contract or any such provision) where the damages claimed by the plaintiff for the

negligence, nuisance or breach of duty consist of or include damages in respect of personal injuries to the plaintiff or any other person.

[(1A) This section does not apply to any action brought for damages under section 3 of the Protection from Harassment Act 1997.]

(3) An action to which this section applies shall not be brought after the expiration of the period applicable in accordance with subsection (4) or (5) below.

(4) Except where subsection (5) below applies, the period applicable is three years from—

    (a) the date on which the cause of action accrued; or

    (b) the date of knowledge (if later) of the person injured.

(5) If the injured person dies before the expiration of the period mentioned in subsection (4) above, the period applicable as respects the cause of action surviving for the benefit of his estate by virtue of section 1 of the Law Reform (Miscellaneous Provisions) Act 1934 shall be three years from—

    (a) the date of death; or

    (b) the date of the personal representative's knowledge; whichever is the later.

[11A   Actions in respect of defective products

(1) This section shall apply to an action for damages by virtue of any provision of Part I of the Consumer Protection Act 1987.

[(1A) This section does not apply to any action brought for damages under section 3 of the Protection from Harassment Act 1977.]

(2) None of the time limits given in the preceding provisions of this Act shall apply to an action to which this section applies.

(3) An action to which this section applies shall not be brought after the expiration of the period of ten years from the relevant time, within the meaning of section 4 of the said Act of 1987; and this subsection shall operate to extinguish a right of action and shall do so whether or not that right of action had accrued, or time under the following provisions of this Act had begun to run, at the end of the said period of ten years.

(4) Subject to subsection (5) below, an action to which this section applies in which the damages claimed by the plaintiff consist of or include damages in respect of personal injuries to the plaintiff or any other person or loss of or damage to any property, shall not be brought after the expiration of the period of three years from whichever is the later of—

    (a) the date on which the cause of action accrued; and

    (b) the date of knowledge of the injured person or, in the case of loss of or damage to property, the date of knowledge of the plaintiff or (if earlier) of any person in whom his cause of action was previously vested.

(5) If in a case where the damages claimed by the plaintiff consist of or include damages in respect of personal injuries to the plaintiff or any other person the injured person died before the expiration of the period mentioned in subsection (4) above, the subsection shall have effect as respects the cause of action surviving for the benefit of his estate by virtue of section I of the Law Reform (Miscellaneous Provisions) Act 1934 as if for the reference to that period there were substituted a reference to the period of three years from whichever is the later of—

    (a) the date of death; and

    (b) the date of the personal representative's knowledge.

(6) For the purposes of this section 'personal representative' includes any person who is or has been a personal representative of the deceased, including an executor who has not proved the will (whether or not he has renounced probate) but not anyone appointed only as a special personal representative in relation to settled land; and regard shall be had to any knowledge acquired by any such person while a personal representative or previously.

(7) If there is more than one personal representative and their dates of knowledge are different, subsection (5)(b) above shall be read as referring to the earliest of those dates.

(8) Expressions used in this section or section 14 of this Act and in Part I of the Consumer Protection Act 1987 have the same meanings in this section or that section as in that Part; and section

1(1) of that Act (Part I to be construed as enacted for the purpose of complying with the product liability Directive) shall apply for the purpose of construing this section and the following provisions of this Act so far as they relate to an action by virtue of any provision of that Part as it applies for the purpose of construing that Part.]

12   Special time limit for actions under Fatal Accidents legislation

(1) An action under the Fatal Accidents Act 1976 shall not be brought if the death occurred when the person injured could no longer maintain an action and recover damages in respect of the injury (whether because of a time limit in this Act or in any other Act, or for any other reason).

Where any such action by the injured person would have been barred by the time limit in section 11 [or 11A] of this Act, no account shall be taken of the possibility of that time limit being overridden under section 33 of this Act.

(2) None of the time limits given in the preceding provisions of this Act shall apply to an action under the Fatal Accidents Act 1976, but no such action shall be brought after the expiration of three years from—

(a) the date of death; or

(b) the date of knowledge of the person for whose benefit the action is brought;

whichever is the later.

(3) An action under the Fatal Accidents Act 1976 shall be one to which sections 28, 33 and 35 of this Act apply, and the application to any such action of the time limit under subsection (2) above shall be subject to section 39; but otherwise Parts II and III of this Act shall not apply to any such action.

13   Operation of time limit under section 12 in relation to different dependants

(1) Where there is more than one person for whose benefit an action under the Fatal Accidents Act 1976 is brought, section 12(2)(b) of this Act shall be applied separately to each of them.

(2) Subject to subsection (3) below, if by virtue of subsection (1) above the action would be outside the time limit given by section 12(2) as regards one or more, but not all, of the persons for whose benefit it is brought, the court shall direct that any person as regards whom the action would be outside that limit shall be excluded from those for whom the action is brought.

(3) The court shall not give such a direction if it is shown that if the action were brought exclusively for the benefit of the person in question it would not be defeated by a defence of limitation (whether in consequence of section 28 of this Act or an agreement between the parties not to raise the defence, or otherwise).

14   Definition of date of knowledge for purposes of sections 11 and 12

(1) [Subject to subsection (1A) below,] In sections 11 and 12 of this Act references to a person's date of knowledge are references to the date on which he first had knowledge of the following facts—

(a) that the injury in question was significant; and

(b) that the injury was attributable in whole or in part to the act or omission which is alleged to constitute negligence, nuisance or breach of duty; and

(c) the identity of the defendant; and

(d) if it is alleged that the act or omission was that of a person other than the defendant, the identity of that person and the additional facts supporting the bringing of an action against the defendant;

and knowledge that any acts or omissions did or did not, as a matter of law, involve negligence, nuisance or breach of duty is irrelevant.

[(1A) In section 11A of this Act and in section 12 of this Act so far as that section applies to an action by virtue of section 6(1)(a) of the Consumer Protection Act 1987 (death caused by defective product) references to a person's date of knowledge are references to the date on which he first had knowledge of the following facts—

(a) such facts about the damage caused by the defect as would lead a reasonable person who had suffered such damage to consider it sufficiently serious to justify his instituting

proceedings for damages against a defendant who did not dispute liability and was able to satisfy a judgment; and
- (b) that the damage was wholly or partly attributable to the facts and circumstances alleged to constitute the defect; and
- (c) the identity of the defendant;

but, in determining the date on which a person first had such knowledge there shall be disregarded both the extent (if any) of that person's knowledge on any date of whether particular facts or circumstances would or would not, as a matter of law, constitute a defect and, in a case relating to loss of or damage to property, any knowledge which that person had on a date on which he had no right of action by virtue of Part of I of that Act in respect of the loss or damage.]

(2) For the purposes of this section an injury is significant if the person whose date of knowledge is in question would reasonably have considered it sufficiently serious to justify his instituting proceedings for damages against a defendant who did not dispute liability and was able to satisfy a judgment.

(3) For the purposes of this section a person's knowledge includes knowledge which he might reasonably have been expected to acquire—
- (a) from facts observable or ascertainable by him; or
- (b) from facts ascertainable by him with the help of medical or other appropriate expert advice which it is reasonable for him to seek;

but a person shall not be fixed under this subsection with knowledge of a fact ascertainable only with the help of expert advice so long as he has taken all reasonable steps to obtain (and, where appropriate, to act on) that advice.

[14A   Special time limit for negligence actions where facts relevant to cause of action are not known at date of accrual

(1) This section applies to any action for damages for negligence, other than one to which section 11 of this Act applies, where the starting date for reckoning the period of limitation under subsection (4)(b) below falls after the date on which the cause of action accrued.

(2) Section 2 of this Act shall not apply to an action to which this section applies.

(3) An action to which this section applies shall not be brought after the expiration of the period applicable in accordance with subsection (4) below.

(4) That period is either—
- (a) six years from the date on which the cause of action accrued; or
- (b) three years from the starting date as defined by subsection (5) below, if that period expires later than the period mentioned in paragraph (a) above.

(5) For the purposes of this section, the starting date for reckoning the period of limitation under subsection (4)(b) above is the earliest date on which the plaintiff or any person in whom the cause of action was vested before him first had both the knowledge required for bringing an action for damages in respect of the relevant damage and a right to bring such an action.

(6) In subsection (5) above 'the knowledge required for bringing an action for damages in respect of the relevant damage' means knowledge both—
- (a) of the material facts about the damage in respect of which damages are claimed; and
- (b) of the other facts relevant to the current action mentioned in subsection (8) below.

(7) For the purposes of subsection (6)(a) above, the material facts about the damage are such facts about the damage as would lead a reasonable person who had suffered such damage to consider it sufficiently serious to justify his instituting proceedings for damages against a defendant who did not dispute liability and was able to satisfy a judgment.

(8) The other facts referred to in subsection (6)(b) above are—
- (a) that the damage was attributable in whole or in part to the act or omission which is alleged to constitute negligence; and
- (b) the identity of the defendant; and

(c) if it is alleged that the act or omission was that of a person other than the defendant, the identity of that person and the additional facts supporting the bringing of an action against the defendant.

(9) Knowledge that any acts or omissions did or did not, as a matter of law, involve negligence is irrelevant for the purposes of subsection (5) above.

(10) For the purposes of this section a person's knowledge includes knowledge which he might reasonably have been expected to acquire—

(a) from facts observable or ascertainable by him; or

(b) from facts ascertainable by him with the help of appropriate expert advice which it is reasonable for him to seek;

but a person shall not be taken by virtue of this subsection to have knowledge of a fact ascertainable only with the help of expert advice so long as he has taken all reasonable steps to obtain (and, where appropriate, to act on) that advice.]

[14B   Overriding time limit for negligence actions not involving personal injuries

(1) An action for damages for negligence, other than one to which section 11 of this Act applies, shall not be brought after the expiration of fifteen years from the date (or, if more than one, from the last of the dates) on which there occurred any act or omission—

(a) which is alleged to constitute negligence; and

(b) to which the damage in respect of which damages are claimed is alleged to be attributable (in whole or in part).

(2) This section bars the right of action in a case to which subsection (1) above applies notwithstanding that—

(a) the cause of action has not yet accrued; or

(b) where section 14A of this Act applies to the action, the date which is for the purposes of that section the starting date for reckoning the period mentioned in subsection (4)(b) of that section has not yet occurred;

before the end of the period of limitation prescribed by this section.]

15   Time limit for actions to recover land

(1) No action shall be brought by any person to recover any land after the expiration of twelve years from the date on which the right of action accrued to him or, if it first accrued to some person through whom he claims, to that person.

(2) Subject to the following provisions of this section, where—

(a) the estate or interest claimed was an estate or interest in reversion or remainder or any other future estate or interest and the right of action to recover the land accrued on the date on which the estate or interest fell into possession by the determination of the preceding estate or interest; and

(b) the person entitled to the preceding estate or interest (not being a term of years absolute) was not in possession of the land on that date;

no action shall be brought by the person entitled to the succeeding estate or interest after the expiration of twelve years from the date on which the right of action accrued to the person entitled to the preceding estate or interest or six years from the date on which the right of action accrued to the person entitled to the succeeding estate or interest, whichever period last expires.

(3) Subsection (2) above shall not apply to any estate or interest which falls into possession on the determination of an entailed interest and which might have been barred by the person entitled to the entailed interest.

(4) No person shall bring an action to recover any estate or interest in land under an assurance taking effect after the right of action to recover the land had accrued to the person by whom the assurance was made or some person through whom he claimed or some person entitled to a preceding estate or interest, unless the action is brought within the period during which the person by whom the assurance was made could have brought such an action.

(5) Where any person is entitled to any estate or interest in land in possession and, while so entitled, is also entitled to any future estate or interest in that land, and his right to recover the estate or interest in possession is barred under this Act, no action shall be brought by that person, or by any person claiming through him, in respect of the future estate or interest, unless in the meantime possession of the land has been recovered by a person entitled to an intermediate estate or interest.

(6) Part I of Schedule 1 to this Act contains provisions for determining the date of accrual of rights of action to recover land in the cases there mentioned.

(7) Part II of that Schedule contains provisions modifying the provisions of this section in their application to actions brought by, or by a person claiming through, the Crown or any spiritual or eleemosynary corporation sole.

16   Time limit for redemption actions

When a mortgagee of land has been in possession of any of the mortgaged land for a period of twelve years, no action to redeem the land of which the mortgagee has been so in possession shall be brought after the end of that period by the mortgagor or any person claiming through him.

17   Extinction of title to land after expiration of time limit

Subject to—

(a) section 18 of this Act; [...]

at the expiration of the period prescribed by this Act for any person to bring an action to recover land (including a redemption action) the title of that person to the land shall be extinguished.

18   Settled land and land held on trust

(1) Subject to section 21(1) and (2) of this Act, the provisions of this Act shall apply to equitable interests in land, [...] as they apply to legal estates. Accordingly a right of action to recover the land shall, for the purposes of this Act but not otherwise, be treated as accruing to a person entitled in possession to such an equitable interest in the like manner and circumstances, and on the same date, as it would accrue if his interest were a legal estate in the land (and any relevant provision of Part I of Schedule 1 to this Act shall apply in any such case accordingly).

(2) Where the period prescribed by this Act has expired for the bringing of an action to recover land by a tenant for life or a statutory owner of settled land—

(a) his legal estate shall not be extinguished if and so long as the right of action to recover the land of any person entitled to a beneficial interest in the land either has not accrued or has not been barred by this Act; and

(b) the legal estate shall accordingly remain vested in the tenant for life or statutory owner and shall devolve in accordance with the Settled Land Act 1925;

but if and when every such right of action has been barred by this Act, his legal estate shall be extinguished.

(3) Where any land is held upon trust [...] and the period prescribed by this Act has expired for the bringing of an action to recover the land by the trustees, the estate of the trustees shall not be extinguished if and so long as the right of action to recover the land of any person entitled to a beneficial interest in the land [...] either has not accrued or has not been barred by this Act; but if and when every such right of action has been so barred the estate of the trustees shall be extinguished.

(4) Where—

(a) any settled land is vested in a statutory owner; or

(b) any land is held upon trust [...];

an action to recover the land may be brought by the statutory owner or trustees on behalf of any person entitled to a beneficial interest in possession in the land [...] whose right of action has not been barred by this Act, notwithstanding that the right of action of the statutory owner or trustees would apart from this provision have been barred by this Act.

19   Time limit for actions to recover rent

No action shall be brought, [and the power conferred by section 72(1) of the Tribunals, Courts and Enforcement Act 2007 shall not be exercisable], to recover arrears of rent, or damages in respect of arrears of rent, after the expiration of six years from the date on which the arrears became due.

[19A Actions for breach of commonhold duty

An action in respect of a right or duty of a kind referred to in section 37(1) of the Commonhold and Leasehold Reform Act 2002 (enforcement) shall not be brought after the expiration of six years from the date on which the cause of action accrued.]

20 Time limit for actions to recover money secured by a mortgage or charge or to recover proceeds of the sale of land

(1) No action shall be brought to recover—

(a) any principal sum of money secured by a mortgage or other charge on property (whether real or personal); or

(b) proceeds of the sale of land;

after the expiration of twelve years from the date on which the right to receive the money accrued.

(2) No foreclosure action in respect of mortgaged personal property shall be brought after the expiration of twelve years from the date on which the right to foreclose accrued.

But if the mortgagee was in possession of the mortgaged property after that date, the right to foreclose on the property which was in his possession shall not be treated as having accrued for the purposes of this subsection until the date on which his possession discontinued.

(3) The right to receive any principal sum of money secured by a mortgage or other charge and the right to foreclose on the property subject to the mortgage or charge shall not be treated as accruing so long as that property comprises any future interest or any life insurance policy which has not matured or been determined.

(4) Nothing in this section shall apply to a foreclosure action in respect of mortgaged land, but the provisions of this Act relating to actions to recover land shall apply to such an action.

(5) Subject to subsections (6) and (7) below, no action to recover arrears of interest payable in respect of any sum of money secured by a mortgage or other charge or payable in respect of proceeds of the sale of land, or to recover damages in respect of such arrears shall be brought after the expiration of six years from the date on which the interest became due.

(6) Where—

(a) a prior mortgagee or other incumbrancer has been in possession of the property charged; and

(b) an action is brought within one year of the discontinuance of that possession by the subsequent incumbrancer;

the subsequent incumbrancer may recover by that action all the arrears of interest which fell due during the period of possession by the prior incumbrancer or damages in respect of those arrears, notwithstanding that the period exceeded six years.

(7) Where—

(a) the property subject to the mortgage or charge comprises any future interest or life insurance policy; and

(b) it is a term of the mortgage or charge that arrears of interest shall be treated as part of the principal sum of money secured by the mortgage or charge;

interest shall not be treated as becoming due before the right to recover the principal sum of money has accrued or is treated as having accrued.

21 Time limit for actions in respect of trust property

(1) No period of limitation prescribed by this Act shall apply to an action by a beneficiary under a trust, being an action—

(a) in respect of any fraud or fraudulent breach of trust to which the trustee was a party or privy; or

(b) to recover from the trustee trust property or the proceeds of trust property in the possession of the trustee, or previously received by the trustee and converted to his use.

(2) Where a trustee who is also a beneficiary under the trust receives or retains trust property or its proceeds as his share on a distribution of trust property under the trust, his liability in any action brought by virtue of subsection (1)(b) above to recover that property or its proceeds after the expiration of the period of limitation prescribed by this Act for bringing an action to recover trust property shall be limited to the excess over his proper share.

This subsection only applies if the trustee acted honestly and reasonably in making the distribution.

(3) Subject to the preceding provisions of this section, an action by a beneficiary to recover trust property or in respect of any breach of trust, not being an action for which a period of limitation is prescribed by any other provision of this Act, shall not be brought after the expiration of six years from the date on which the right of action accrued. For the purposes of this subsection, the right of action shall not be treated as having accrued to any beneficiary entitled to a future interest in the trust property until the interest fell into possession.

(4) No beneficiary as against whom there would be a good defence under this Act shall derive any greater or other benefit from a judgment or order obtained by any other beneficiary than he could have obtained if he had brought the action and this Act had been pleaded in defence.

22   Time limit for actions claiming personal estate of a deceased person

Subject to section 21(1) and (2) of this Act—

    (a) no action in respect of any claim to the personal estate of a deceased person or to any share or interest in any such estate (whether under a will or on intestacy) shall be brought after the expiration of twelve years from the date on which the right to receive the share or interest accrued; and

    (b) no action to recover arrears of interest in respect of any legacy, or damages in respect of such arrears, shall be brought after the expiration of six years from the date on which the interest became due.

23   Time limit in respect of actions for an account

An action for an account shall not be brought after the expiration of any time limit under this Act which is applicable to the claim which is the basis of the duty to account.

24   Time limit for actions to enforce judgments

(1) An action shall not be brought upon any judgment after the expiration of six years from the date on which the judgment became enforceable.

(2) No arrears of interest in respect of any judgment debt shall be recovered after the expiration of six years from the date on which the interest became due.

26   Administration to date back to death

For the purposes of the provisions of this Act relating to actions for the recovery of land and advowsons an administrator of the estate of a deceased person shall be treated as claiming as if there had been no interval of time between the death of the deceased person and the grant of the letters of administration.

[27A   Actions for recovery of property obtained through unlawful conduct etc.

(1) None of the time limits given in the preceding provisions of this Act applies to any proceedings under Chapter 2 of Part 5 of the Proceeds of Crime Act 2002 (civil recovery of proceeds of unlawful conduct).

(2) Proceedings under that Chapter for a recovery order in respect of any recoverable property shall not be brought after the expiration of the period of [20 years] from the date on which the [relevant person's] cause of action accrued.

(3) Proceedings under that Chapter are brought when—

    (a)   a claim form is issued, or

    [(aa) an application is made for a property freezing order, or]

    (b)   an application is made for an interim receiving order, whichever is the [earliest].

    (4) The [relevant person's] cause of action accrues in respect of any recoverable property—

      (a) in the case of proceedings for a recovery order in respect of property obtained through unlawful conduct, when the property is so obtained,

      (b) in the case of proceedings for a recovery order in respect of any other recoverable property, when the property obtained through unlawful conduct which it represents is so obtained.

    (5) If—

      (a) a person would (but for the preceding provisions of this Act) have a cause of action in respect of the conversion of a chattel, and

      (b) proceedings are started under that Chapter for a recovery order in respect of the chattel,

section 3(2) of this Act does not prevent his asserting on an application under section 281 of that Act that the property belongs to him, or the court making a declaration in his favour under that section.

    (6) If the court makes such a declaration, his title to the chattel is to be treated as not having been extinguished by section 3(2) of this Act.

    (7) Expressions used in this section and Part 5 of that Act have the same meaning in this section as in that Part.]

    [(8) In this section 'relevant person' means—

      (a) the Serious Organised Crime Agency,

      (b) the Director of Public Prosecutions,

      (c) the Director of Revenue and Customs Prosecutions, or

      (d) the Director of the Serious Fraud Office.]

[27B　Actions for recovery of property for purposes of an external order

    (1) None of the time limits given in the preceding provisions of this Act applies to any proceedings under Chapter 2 of Part 5 of the Proceeds of Crime Act 2002 (External Requests and Orders) Order 2005 (civil proceedings for the realisation of property to give effect to an external order).

    (2) Proceedings under that Chapter for a recovery order in respect of any recoverable property shall not be brought after the expiration of the period of [20 years] from the date on which the [relevant person's] cause of action accrued.

    (3) Proceedings under that Chapter are brought when—

      (a) a claim form is issued, or

      (b) an application is made for a property freezing order, or

      (c) an application is made for an interim receiving order,

whichever is earliest.

    (4) The [relevant person's] cause of action accrues in respect of any recoverable property—

      (a) in the case of proceedings for a recovery order in respect of property obtained, or believed to have been obtained, as a result of or in connection with criminal conduct, when the property is so obtained,

      (b) in the case of proceedings for a recovery order in respect of any other recoverable property, when the property obtained, or believed to have been obtained, as a result of or in connection with criminal conduct which it represents is so obtained.

    (5) If—

      (a) a person would (but for the preceding provisions of this Act) have a cause of action in respect of the conversion of a chattel, and

      (b) proceedings are started under that Chapter for a recovery order in respect of the chattel,

section 3(2) of this Act does not prevent his asserting on an application under article 192 of that Order that the property belongs to him, or the court making a declaration in his favour under that article.

    (6) If the court makes such a declaration, his title to the chattel is to be treated as not having been extinguished by section 3(2) of this Act.

(7) In this section—

    (a) 'criminal conduct' is to be construed in accordance with section 447(8) of the Proceeds of Crime Act 2002, and

    (b) expressions used in this section which are also used in Part 5 of the Proceeds of Crime Act 2002 (External Requests and Orders) Order 2005 have the same meaning in this section as in that Part.]

[(8) In this section 'relevant person' means—

    (a) the Serious Organised Crime Agency,

    (b) the Director of Public Prosecutions,

    (c) the Director of Revenue and Customs Prosecutions, or

    (d) the Director of the Serious Fraud Office.]

[27C Actions for exploitation proceeds orders

(1) None of the time limits given in the preceding provisions of this Act applies to proceedings under Part 7 of the Coroners and Justice Act 2009 (criminal memoirs etc) for an exploitation proceeds order.

(2) Proceedings under that Part for such an order are not to be brought after the expiration of 6 years from the date on which the enforcement authority's cause of action accrued.

(3) Proceedings under that Part for such an order are brought when an application is made for the order.

(4) Where exploitation proceeds have been obtained by a person from a relevant offence, an enforcement authority's cause of action under that Part in respect of those proceeds accrues when the enforcement authority has actual knowledge that the proceeds have been obtained.

(5) Expressions used in this section and that Part have the same meaning in this section as in that Part.]

PART II

28 Extension of limitation period in case of disability

(1) Subject to the following provisions of this section, if on the date when any right of action accrued for which a period of limitation is prescribed by this Act, the person to whom it accrued was under a disability, the action may be brought at any time before the expiration of six years from the date when he ceased to be under a disability or died (whichever first occurred) notwithstanding that the period of limitation has expired.

(2) This section shall not affect any case where the right of action first accrued to some person (not under a disability) through whom the person under a disability claims.

(3) When a right of action which has accrued to a person under a disability accrues, on the death of that person while still under a disability, to another person under a disability, no further extension of time shall be allowed by reason of the disability of the second person.

[(4A) If the action is one to which section 4A of this Act applies, subsection (1) above shall have effect—

    (a) in the case of an action for libel or slander, as if for the words from 'at any time' to 'occurred)' there were substituted the words 'by him at any time before the expiration of one year from the date on which he ceased to be under a disability'; and

    (b) in the case of an action for slander of title, slander of goods or other malicious falsehood, as if for the words 'six years' there were substituted the words 'one year'.]

(5) If the action is one to which section 10 of this Act applies, subsection (1) above shall have effect as if for the words 'six years' there were substituted the words 'two years'.

(6) If the action is one to which section 11 or 12(2) of this Act applies, subsection (1) above shall have effect as if for the words 'six years' there were substituted the words 'three years'.

[(7) If the action is one to which section 11A of this Act applies or one by virtue of section 6(1)(a) of the Consumer Protection Act 1987 (death caused by defective product), subsection (1) above—

    (a) shall not apply to the time limit prescribed by subsection (3) of the said section 11A or to that time limit as applied by virtue of section 12(1) of this Act; and

    (b) in relation to any other time limit prescribed by this Act shall have effect as if for the words 'six years' there were substituted the words 'three years'.]

[28A   Extension for cases where the limitation period is the period under section 14A(4)(b)

(1) Subject to subsection (2) below, if in the case of any action for which a period of limitation is prescribed by section 14A of this Act—

    (a) the period applicable in accordance with subsection (4) of that section is the period mentioned in paragraph (b) of that subsection;

    (b) on the date which is for the purposes of that section the starting date for reckoning that period the person by reference to whose knowledge that date fell to be determined under subsection (5) of that section was under a disability; and

    (c) section 28 of this Act does not apply to the action;

the action may be brought at any time before the expiration of three years from the date when he ceased to be under a disability or died (whichever first occurred) notwithstanding that the period mentioned above has expired.

(2) An action may not be brought by virtue of subsection (1) above after the end of the period of limitation prescribed by section 14B of this Act.]

29   Fresh accrual of action on acknowledgment or part payment

(5) Subject to subsection (6) below, where any right of action has accrued to recover—

    (a) any debt or other liquidated pecuniary claim; or

    (b) any claim to the personal estate of a deceased person or to any share or interest in any such estate;

and the person liable or accountable for the claim acknowledges the claim or makes any payment in respect of it the right shall be treated as having accrued on and not before the date of the acknowledgment or payment.

(6) A payment of a part of the rent or interest due at any time shall not extend the period for claiming the remainder then due, but any payment of interest shall be treated as a payment in respect of the principal debt.

(7) Subject to subsection (6) above, a current period of limitation may be repeatedly extended under this section by further acknowledgments or payments, but a right of action, once barred by this Act shall not be revived by any subsequent acknowledgment or payment.

30   Formal provisions as to acknowledgments and part payments

(1) To be effective for the purposes of section 29 of this Act, an acknowledgment must be in writing and signed by the person making it.

(2) For the purposes of section 29, any acknowledgment or payment—

    (a) may be made by the agent of the person by whom it is required to be made under that section; and

    (b) shall be made to the person, or to an agent of the person, whose title or claim is being acknowledged or, as the case may be, in respect of whose claim the payment is being made.

31   Effect of acknowledgment or part payment on persons other than the maker or recipient

(6) An acknowledgment of any debt or other liquidated pecuniary claim shall bind the acknowledgor and his successors but not any other person.

(7) A payment made in respect of any debt or other liquidated pecuniary claim shall bind all persons liable in respect of the debt or claim.

(8) An acknowledgment by one of several personal representatives of any claim to the personal estate of a deceased person or to any share or interest in any such estate, or a payment by one of several personal representatives in respect of any such claim, shall bind the estate of the deceased person.

(9) In this section 'successor', in relation to any mortgagee or person liable in respect of any debt or claim, means his personal representatives and any other person on whom the rights under the mortgage or, as the case may be, the liability in respect of the debt or claim devolve (whether on death or bankruptcy or the disposition of property or the determination of a limited estate or interest in settled property or otherwise).

32 Postponement of limitation period in case of fraud, concealment or mistake

(1) Subject to [subsections (3) and (4A)] below, where in the case of any action for which a period of limitation is prescribed by this Act, either—

  (a) the action is based upon the fraud of the defendant; or
  (b) any fact relevant to the plaintiff's right of action has been deliberately concealed from him by the defendant; or
  (c) the action is for relief from the consequences of a mistake;

the period of limitation shall not begin to run until the plaintiff has discovered the fraud, concealment or mistake (as the case may be) or could with reasonable diligence have discovered it.

References in this subsection to the defendant include references to the defendant's agent and to any person through whom the defendant claims and his agent.

(2) For the purposes of subsection (1) above, deliberate commission of a breach of duty in circumstances in which it is unlikely to be discovered for some time amounts to deliberate concealment of the facts involved in that breach of duty.

(3) Nothing in this section shall enable any action—

  (a) to recover, or recover the value of, any property; or
  (b) to enforce any charge against, or set aside any transaction affecting, any property;

to be brought against the purchaser of the property or any person claiming through him in any case where the property has been purchased for valuable consideration by an innocent third party since the fraud or concealment or (as the case may be) the transaction in which the mistake was made took place.

(4) A purchaser is an innocent third party for the purposes of this section—

  (a) in the case of fraud or concealment of any fact relevant to the plaintiff's right of action, if he was not a party to the fraud or (as the case may be) to the concealment of that fact and did not at the time of the purchase know or have reason to believe that the fraud or concealment had taken place; and
  (b) in the case of mistake, if he did not at the time of the purchase know or have reason to believe that the mistake had been made.

[(4A) Subsection (1) above shall not apply in relation to the time limit prescribed by section 11A(3) of this Act or in relation to that time limit as applied by virtue of section 12(1) of this Act.]

[(5) Sections 14A and 14B of this Act shall not apply to any action to which subsection (1)(b) above applies (and accordingly the period of limitation referred to in that subsection, in any case to which either of those sections would otherwise apply, is the period applicable under section 23 of this Act).]

[32A Discretionary exclusion of time limit for actions for defamation or malicious falsehood

(1) If it appears to the court that it would be equitable to allow an action to proceed having regard to the degree to which—

  (a) the operation of section 4A of this Act prejudices the plaintiff or any person whom he represents, and
  (b) any decision of the court under this subsection would prejudice the defendant or any person whom he represents,

the court may direct that that section shall not apply to the action or shall not apply to any specified cause of action to which the action relates.

(2) In acting under this section the court shall have regard to all the circumstances of the case and in particular to—

    (a) the length of, and the reasons for, the delay on the part of the plaintiff;

    (b) where the reason or one of the reasons for the delay was that all or any of the facts relevant to the cause of action did not become known to the plaintiff until after the end of the period mentioned in section 4A—

        (i) the date on which any such facts did become known to him, and

        (ii) the extent to which he acted promptly and reasonably once he knew whether or not the facts in question might be capable of giving rise to an action; and

    (c) the extent to which, having regard to the delay, relevant evidence is likely—

        (i) to be unavailable, or

        (ii) to be less cogent than if the action had been brought within the period mentioned in section 4A.

(3) In the case of an action for slander of title, slander of goods or other malicious falsehood brought by a personal representative—

    (a) the references in subsection (2) above to the plaintiff shall be construed as including the deceased person to whom the cause of action accrued and any previous personal representative of that person; and

    (b) nothing in section 28(3) of this Act shall be construed as affecting the court's discretion under this section.

(4) In this section 'the court' means the court in which the action has been brought.]

33 Discretionary exclusion of time limit for actions in respect of personal injuries or death

(1) If it appears to the court that it would be equitable to allow an action to proceed having regard to the degree to which—

    (a) the provisions of section 11 [or 11A] or 12 of this Act prejudice the plaintiff or any person whom he represents; and

    (b) any decision of the court under this subsection would prejudice the defendant or any person whom he represents;

the court may direct that those provisions shall not apply to the action, or shall not apply to any specified cause of action to which the action relates.

[(1A) The court shall not under this section disapply—

    (a) subsection (3) of section 11A; or

    (b) where the damages claimed by the plaintiff are confined to damages for loss of or damage to any property, any other provision in its application to an action by virtue of Part I of the Consumer Protection Act 1987.]

(2) The court shall not under this section disapply section 12(1) except where the reason why the person injured could no longer maintain an action was because of the time limit in section 11 [or subsection (4) of section 11A].

If, for example, the person injured could at his death no longer maintain an action under the Fatal Accidents Act 1976 because of the time limit in Article 29 in Schedule 1 to the Carriage by Air Act 1961, the court has no power to direct that section 12(1) shall not apply.

(3) In acting under this section the court shall have regard to all the circumstances of the case and in particular to—

    (a) the length of, and the reasons for, the delay on the part of the plaintiff;

    (b) the extent to which, having regard to the delay, the evidence adduced or likely to be adduced by the plaintiff or the defendant is or is likely to be less cogent than if the action had been brought within the time allowed by section 11 [, by section 11A] or (as the case may be) by section 12;

    (c) the conduct of the defendant after the cause of action arose, including the extent (if any) to which he responded to requests reasonably made by the plaintiff for information or inspection for the purpose of ascertaining facts which were or might be relevant to the plaintiff's cause of action against the defendant;

(d) the duration of any disability of the plaintiff arising after the date of the accrual of the cause of action;

(e) the extent to which the plaintiff acted promptly and reasonably once he knew whether or not the act or omission of the defendant, to which the injury was attributable, might be capable at that time of giving rise to an action for damages;

(f) the steps, if any, taken by the plaintiff to obtain medical, legal or other expert advice and the nature of any such advice he may have received.

(4) In a case where the person injured died when, because of section 11 [or subsection (4) of section 11A], he could no longer maintain an action and recover damages in respect of the injury, the court shall have regard in particular to the length of, and the reasons for, the delay on the part of the deceased.

(5) In a case under subsection (4) above, or any other case where the time limit, or one of the time limits, depends on the date of knowledge of a person other than the plaintiff, subsection (3) above shall have effect with appropriate modifications, and shall have effect in particular as if references to the plaintiff included references to any person whose date of knowledge is or was relevant in determining a time limit.

(6) A direction by the court disapplying the provisions of section 12(1) shall operate to disapply the provisions to the same effect in section 1(1) of the Fatal Accidents Act 1976.

(7) In this section 'the court' means the court in which the action has been brought.

(8) References in this section to section 11 or 11A include references to that section as extended by any of the preceding provisions of this Part of this Act or by any provision of Part III of this Act.

35   New claims in pending actions; rules of court

(1) For the purposes of this Act, any new claim made in the course of any action shall be deemed to be a separate action and to have been commenced—

(a) in the case of a new claim made in or by way of third party proceedings, on the date on which those proceedings were commenced; and

(b) in the case of any other new claim, on the same date as the original action.

(2) In this section a new claim means any claim by way of set-off or counterclaim, and any claim involving either—

(a) the addition or substitution of a new cause of action; or

(b) the addition or substitution of a new party;

and 'third party proceedings' means any proceedings brought in the course of any action by any party to the action against a person not previously a party to the action, other than proceedings brought by joining any such person as defendant to any claim already made in the original action by the party bringing the proceedings.

(3) Except as provided by section 33 of this Act or by rules of court, neither the High Court nor any county court shall allow a new claim within subsection (1) (b) above, other than an original set-off or counterclaim, to be made in the course of any action after the expiry of any time limit under this Act which would affect a new action to enforce that claim.

For the purposes of this subsection, a claim is an original set-off or an original counterclaim if it is a claim made by way of set-off or (as the case may be) by way of counterclaim by a party who has not previously made any claim in the action.

(4) Rules of court may provide for allowing a new claim to which subsection (3) above applies to be made as there mentioned, but only if the conditions specified in subsection (5) below are satisfied, and subject to any further restrictions the rules may impose.

(5) The conditions referred to in subsection (4) above are the following—

(a) in the case of a claim involving a new cause of action, if the new cause of action arises out of the same facts or substantially the same facts as are already in issue on any claim previously made in the original action; and

(b) in the case of a claim involving a new party, if the addition or substitution of the new party is necessary for the determination of the original action.

(6) The addition or substitution of a new party shall not be regarded for the purposes of subsection (5)(b) above as necessary for the determination of the original action unless either—

(a) the new party is substituted for a party whose name was given in any claim made in the original action in mistake for the new party's name; or

(b) any claim already made in the original action cannot be maintained by or against an existing party unless the new party is joined or substituted as plaintiff or defendant in that action.

(7) Subject to subsection (4) above, rules of court may provide for allowing a party to any action to claim relief in a new capacity in respect of a new cause of action notwithstanding that he had no title to make that claim at the date of the commencement of the action.

This subsection shall not be taken as prejudicing the power of rules of court to provide for allowing a party to claim relief in a new capacity without adding or substituting a new cause of action.

(8) Subsections (3) to (7) above shall apply in relation to a new claim made in the course of third party proceedings as if those proceedings were the original action, and subject to such other modifications as may be prescribed by rules of court in any case or class of case.

PART III

36   Equitable jurisdiction and remedies

(1) The following time limits under this Act, that is to say—

(a)   the time limit under section 2 for actions founded on tort;

[(aa) the time limit under section 4A for actions for libel or slander;]

(b)   the time limit under section 5 for actions founded on simple contract;

(c)   the time limit under section 7 for actions to enforce awards where the submission is not by an instrument under seal;

(d)   the time limit under section 8 for actions on a specialty;

(e)   the time limit under section 9 for actions to recover a sum recoverable by virtue of any enactment; and

(f)   the time limit under section 24 for actions to enforce a judgment;

shall not apply to any claim for specific performance of a contract or for an injunction or for other equitable relief, except in so far as any such time limit may be applied by the court by analogy in like manner as the corresponding time limit under any enactment repealed by the Limitation Act 1939 was applied before 1st July 1940.

(2) Nothing in this Act shall affect any equitable jurisdiction to refuse relief on the ground of acquiescence or otherwise.

37   Application to the Crown and the Duke of Cornwall

(1) Except as otherwise expressly provided in this Act, and without prejudice to section 39, this Act shall apply to proceedings by or against the Crown in like manner as it applies to proceedings between subjects.

38   Interpretation

(1) In this Act, unless the context otherwise requires—...

'personal injuries' includes any disease and any impairment of a person's physical or mental condition, and 'injury' and cognate expressions shall be construed accordingly; ...

(2) For the purposes of this Act a person shall be treated as under a disability while he is an infant, or [lacks capacity (within the meaning of the mental capacity Act 2005) to conduct legal proceedings].

(3) For the purposes of subsection (2) above a person is of unsound mind if he is a person who, by reason of mental disorder [is incapable of managing and administering his property and affairs; and in this section 'mental disorder' has the same meaning as in the Mental Health Act 1983].

39   Saving for other limitation enactments

This Act shall not apply to any action or arbitration for which a period of limitation is prescribed by or under any other enactment (whether passed before or after the passing of this Act) or to any action or arbitration to which the Crown is a party and for which, if it were between subjects, a period of limitation would be prescribed by or under any such other enactment.

[Senior Courts Act 1981]

(1981, c. 54)

32   Orders for interim payment

(1) As regards proceedings pending in the High Court, provision may be made by rules of court for enabling the court, in such circumstances as may be prescribed, to make an order requiring a party to the proceedings to make an interim payment of such amount as may be specified in the order, with provision for the payment to be made to such other party to the proceedings as may be so specified or, if the order so provides, by paying it into court.

(2) Any rules of court which make provision in accordance with subsection (1) may include provision for enabling a party to any proceedings who, in pursuance of such an order, has made an interim payment to recover the whole or part of the amount of the payment in such circumstances, and from such other party to the proceedings, as may be determined in accordance with the rules.

(3) Any rules made by virtue of this section may include such incidental, supplementary and consequential provisions as the rule-making authority may consider necessary or expedient.

(4) Nothing in this section shall be construed as affecting the exercise of any power relating to costs, including any power to make rules of court relating to costs.

(5) In this section 'interim payment', in relation to a party to any proceedings, means a payment on account of any damages, debt or other sum (excluding any costs) which that party may be held liable to pay to or for the benefit of another party to the proceedings if a final judgment or order of the court in the proceedings is given or made in favour of that other party.

[32A   Orders for provisional damages for personal injuries

(1) This section applies to an action for damages for personal injuries in which there is proved or admitted to be a chance that at some definite or indefinite time in the future the injured person will, as a result of the act or omission which gave rise to the cause of action, develop some serious disease or suffer some serious deterioration in his physical or mental condition.

(2) Subject to subsection (4) below, as regards any action for damages to which this section applies in which a judgment is given in the High Court, provision may be made by rules of court for enabling the court, in such circumstances as may be prescribed, to award the injured person—

    (a) damages assessed on the assumption that the injured person will not develop the disease or suffer the deterioration in his condition; and

    (b) further damages at a future date if he develops the disease or suffers the deterioration.

(3) Any rules made by virtue of this section may include such incidental, supplementary and consequential provisions as the rule-making authority may consider necessary or expedient.

(4) Nothing in this section shall be construed—

    (a) as affecting the exercise of any power relating to costs, including any power to make rules of court relating to costs; or

    (b) as prejudicing any duty of the court under any enactment or rule of law to reduce or limit the total damages which would have been recoverable apart from any such duty.]

35   Provisions supplementary to ss. 33 and 34

(5) In sections [32A,] 33 and 34 and this section— ...

'personal injuries' includes any disease and any impairment of a person's physical or mental condition.

[35A   Powers of High Court to award interest on debts and damages

(1) Subject to rules of court, in proceedings (whenever instituted) before the High Court for the recovery of a debt or damages there may be included in any sum for which judgment is given simple interest, at such rate as the court thinks fit or as rules of court may provide, on all or any part of the debt or damages in respect of which judgment is given, or payment is made before judgment, for all or any part of the period between the date when the cause of action arose and—

(a) in the case of any sum paid before judgment, the date of the payment; and

(b) in the case of the sum for which judgment is given, the date of the judgment.

(2) In relation to a judgment given for damages for personal injuries or death which exceed £200 subsection (1) shall have effect—

(a) with the substitution of 'shall be included' for 'may be included'; and

(b) with the addition of 'unless the court is satisfied that there are special reasons to the contrary' after 'given', where first occurring.

(3) Subject to rules of court, where—

(a) there are proceedings (whenever instituted) before the High Court for the recovery of a debt; and

(b) the defendant pays the whole debt to the plaintiff (otherwise than in pursuance of a judgment in the proceedings),

the defendant shall be liable to pay the plaintiff simple interest at such rate as the court thinks fit or as rules of court may provide on all or any part of the debt for all or any part of the period between the date when the cause of action arose and the date of the payment.

(4) Interest in respect of a debt shall not be awarded under this section for a period during which, for whatever reason, interest on the debt already runs.

(5) Without prejudice to the generality of section 84, rules of court may provide for a rate of interest by reference to the rate specified in section 17 of the Judgments Act 1838 as that section has effect from time to time or by reference to a rate for which any other enactment provides.

(6) Interest under this section may be calculated at different rates in respect of different periods.

(7) In this section 'plaintiff' means the person seeking the debt or damages and 'defendant' means the person from whom the plaintiff seeks the debt or damages and 'personal injuries' includes any disease and any impairment of a person's physical or mental condition.]

49   Concurrent administration of law and equity

(1) Subject to the provisions of this or any other Act, every court exercising jurisdiction in England and Wales in any civil cause or matter shall continue to administer law and equity on the basis that, wherever there is any conflict or variance between the rules of equity and the rules of the common law with reference to the same matter, the rules of equity shall prevail.

50   Power to award damages as well as, or in substitution for, injunction or specific performance

Where the Court of Appeal or the High Court has jurisdiction to entertain an application for an injunction or specific performance, it may award damages in addition to, or in substitution for, an injunction or specific performance.

69   Trial by jury

(1) Where, on the application of any party to an action to be tried in the Queen's Bench Division, the court is satisfied that there is in issue—

(a) a charge of fraud against that party; or

(b) a claim in respect of libel, slander, malicious prosecution or false imprisonment; or

(c) any question or issue of a kind prescribed for the purposes of this paragraph,
the action shall be tried with a jury, unless the court is of opinion that the trial requires any prolonged examination of documents or accounts or any scientific or local investigation which cannot conveniently be made with a jury.

Administration of Justice Act 1982

(1982, c. 53)

1 Abolition of right to damages for loss of expectation of life
(1) In an action under the law of England and Wales or the law of Northern Ireland for damages for personal injuries—
   (a) no damages shall be recoverable in respect of any loss of expectation of life caused to the injured person by the injuries; but
   (b) if the injured person's expectation of life has been reduced by the injuries, the court, in assessing damages in respect of pain and suffering caused by the injuries, shall take account of any suffering caused or likely to be caused to him by awareness that his expectation of life has been so reduced.

(2) The reference in subsection (1)(a) above to damages in respect of loss of expectation of life does not include damages in respect of loss of income.

2 Abolition of actions for loss of services, etc.
No person shall be liable in tort under the law of England and Wales or the law of Northern Ireland—
   (a) to a husband on the ground only of having deprived him of the services or society of his wife;
   (b) to a parent (or person standing in the place of a parent) on the ground only of his having deprived him of the services of a child; or
   (c) on the ground only—
      (i) of having deprived another of the services of his menial servant;
      (ii) of having deprived another of the services of his female servant by raping or seducing her; or
      (iii) of enticement of a servant or harbouring a servant.

5 Maintenance at public expense to be taken into account in assessment of damages
In an action under the law of England and Wales or the law of Northern Ireland for damages for personal injuries (including any such action arising out of a contract) any saving to the injured person which is attributable to his maintenance wholly or partly at public expense in a hospital, nursing home or other institution shall be set off against any income lost by him as a result of his injuries.

Civil Aviation Act 1982

(1982, c. 16)

[38A Noise control schemes
(1) An aerodrome operator may establish and maintain a scheme (referred to in this section and sections 38B and 38C below as a 'noise control scheme') for the purpose of avoiding, limiting or mitigating the effect of noise connected with the taking off or landing of aircraft at the aerodrome.]

[38C Breaches of noise control schemes

(6) An aerodrome operator which receives penalties under a noise control scheme shall make payments equal to the amount of those penalties for purposes which appear to it to be likely to be of benefit to persons who live in the area in which the aerodrome is situated.]

76 Liability of aircraft in respect of trespass, nuisance and surface damage

(1) No action shall lie in respect of trespass or in respect of nuisance, by reason only of the flight of an aircraft over any property at a height above the ground which, having regard to wind, weather and all the circumstances of the case is reasonable, or the ordinary incidents of such flight, so long as the provisions of any Air Navigation Order and of any orders under section 62 above have been duly complied with and there has been no breach of section 81 below.

(2) Subject to subsection (3) below, where material loss or damage is caused to any person or property on land or water by, or by a person in, or an article, animal or person falling from, an aircraft while in flight, taking off or landing, then unless the loss or damage was caused or contributed to by the negligence of the person by whom it was suffered, damages in respect of the loss or damage shall be recoverable without proof of negligence or intention or other cause of action, as if the loss or damage had been caused by the wilful act, neglect, or default of the owner of the aircraft.

(3) Where material loss or damage is caused as aforesaid in circumstances in which—

(a) damages are recoverable in respect of the said loss or damage by virtue only of subsection (2) above, and

(b) a legal liability is created in some person other than the owner to pay damages in respect of the said loss or damage,

the owner shall be entitled to be indemnified by that other person against any claim in respect of the said loss or damage.

77 Nuisance caused by aircraft on aerodromes

(1) An Air Navigation Order may provide for regulating the conditions under which noise and vibration may be caused by aircraft on aerodromes and may provide that subsection (2) below shall apply to any aerodrome as respects which provision as to noise and vibration caused by aircraft is so made.

(2) No action shall lie in respect of nuisance by reason only of the noise and vibration caused by aircraft on an aerodrome to which this subsection applies by virtue of an Air Navigation Order, as long as the provisions of any such Order are duly complied with.

Forfeiture Act 1982

(1982, c. 34)

1 The 'forfeiture rule'

(1) In this Act, the 'forfeiture rule' means the rule of public policy which in certain circumstances precludes a person who has unlawfully killed another from acquiring a benefit in consequence of the killing...

2 Power to modify the rule

(1) Where a court determines that the forfeiture rule has precluded a person (in this section referred to as 'the offender') who has unlawfully killed another from acquiring any interest in property mentioned in subsection (4) below, the court may make an order under this section modifying the effect of that rule.

(2) The court shall not make an order under this section modifying the effect of the forfeiture rule in any case unless it is satisfied that, having regard to the conduct of the offender and of the deceased and to such other circumstances as appear to the court to be material, the justice of the case requires the effect of the rule to be so modified in that case.

(3) In any case where a person stands convicted of an offence of which unlawful killing is an element, the court shall not make an order under this section modifying the effect of the forfeiture rule in that case unless proceedings for the purpose are brought before the expiry of the period of three months beginning with his conviction.

(4) The interests in property referred to in subsection (1) above are—

  (a) any beneficial interest in property which (apart from the forfeiture rule) the offender would have acquired—

    (i)   under the deceased's will (including, as respects Scotland, any writing having testamentary effect) or the law relating to intestacy or by way of ius relicti, ius relictae or legitim;

    (ii) on the nomination of the deceased in accordance with the provisions of any enactment;

    (iii) as a donatio mortis causa made by the deceased; or

    (iv) under a special destination (whether relating to heritable or moveable property); or

  (b) any beneficial interest in property which (apart from the forfeiture rule) the offender would have acquired in consequence of the death of the deceased, being property which, before the death, was held on trust for any person.

(5) An order under this section may modify the effect of the forfeiture rule in respect of any interest in property to which the determination referred to in subsection (1) above relates and may do so in either or both of the following ways, that is—

  (a) where there is more than one such interest, by excluding the application of the rule in respect of any (but not all) of those interests; and

  (b) in the case of any such interest in property, by excluding the application of the rule in respect of part of the property.

(6) On the making of an order under this section, the forfeiture rule shall have effect for all purposes (including purposes relating to anything done before the order is made) subject to the modifications made by the order....

5 Exclusion of murderers

Nothing in this Act or in any order made under section 2 or referred to in section 3(1) of this Act [or in any decision made under section 4(1A) of this Act] shall affect the application of the forfeiture rule in the case of a person who stands convicted of murder.

Supply of Goods and Services Act 1982

(1982, c. 29)

PART I SUPPLY OF GOODS

Contracts for the transfer of property in goods

1 The contracts concerned

(1) In this Act [in its application to England and Wales and Northern Ireland] 'contract for the transfer of goods' means a contract under which one person transfers or agrees to transfer to another the property in goods, other than an excepted contract.

(2) For the purposes of this section an excepted contract means any of the following:—

  (a) a contract of sale of goods;

(b) a hire-purchase agreement;

[...]

(d) a transfer or agreement to transfer which is made by deed and for which there is no consideration other than the presumed consideration imported by the deed;

(e) a contract intended to operate by way of mortgage, pledge, charge or other security.

(3) For the purposes of this Act [in its application to England and Wales and Northern Ireland] a contract is a contract for the transfer of goods whether or not services are also provided or to be provided under the contract, and (subject to subsection (2) above) whatever is the nature of the consideration for the transfer or agreement to transfer.

2   Implied terms about title, etc.

(1) In a contract for the transfer of goods, other than one to which subsection (3) below applies, there is an implied condition on the part of the transferor that in the case of a transfer of the property in the goods he has a right to transfer the property and in the case of an agreement to transfer the property in the goods he will have such a right at the time when the property is to be transferred.

(2) In a contract for the transfer of goods, other than one to which subsection (3) below applies, there is also an implied warranty that—

(a) the goods are free, and will remain free until the time when the property is to be transferred, from any charge or encumbrance not disclosed or known to the transferee before the contract is made, and

(b) the transferee will enjoy quiet possession of the goods except so far as it may be disturbed by the owner or other person entitled to the benefit of any charge or encumbrance so disclosed or known.

(3) This subsection applies to a contract for the transfer of goods in the case of which there appears from the contract or is to be inferred from its circumstances an intention that the transferor should transfer only such title as he or a third person may have.

(4) In a contract to which subsection (3) above applies there is an implied warranty that all charges or encumbrances known to the transferor and not known to the transferee have been disclosed to the transferee before the contract is made.

(5) In a contract to which subsection (3) above applies there is also an implied warranty that none of the following will disturb the transferee's quiet possession of the goods, namely—

(a) the transferor;

(b) in a case where the parties to the contract intend that the transferor should transfer only such title as a third person may have, that person;

(c) anyone claiming through or under the transferor or that third person otherwise than under a charge or encumbrance disclosed or known to the transferee before the contract is made.

3   Implied terms where transfer is by description

(1) This section applies where, under a contract for the transfer of goods, the transferor transfers or agrees to transfer the property in the goods by description.

(2) In such case there is an implied condition that the goods will correspond with the description.

(3) If the transferor transfers or agrees to transfer the property in the goods by sample as well as by description it is not sufficient that the bulk of the goods corresponds with the sample if the goods do not also correspond with the description.

(4) A contract is not prevented from falling within subsection (1) above by reason only that, being exposed for supply, the goods are selected by the transferee.

4   Implied terms about quality or fitness

(1) Except as provided by this section and section 5 below and subject to the provision of any other enactment, there is no implied condition or warranty about the quality or fitness for any particular purpose of goods supplied under a contract for the transfer of goods.

[(2) Where, under such a contract, the transferor transfers the property in goods in the course of a business, there is an implied condition that the goods supplied under the contract are of satisfactory quality.

(2A) For the purposes of this section and section 5 below, goods are of satisfactory quality if they meet the standard that a reasonable person would regard as satisfactory, taking account of any description of the goods, the price (if relevant) and all the other relevant circumstances.]

[(2B) If the transferee deals as consumer, the relevant circumstances mentioned in subsection (2A) above include any public statements on the specific characteristics of the goods made about them by the transferor, the producer or his representative, particularly in advertising or on labelling.

(2C) A public statement is not by virtue of subsection (2B) above a relevant circumstance for the purposes of subsection (2A) above in the case of a contract for the transfer of goods, if the transferor shows that—

    (a) at the time the contract was made, he was not, and could not reasonably have been, aware of the statement,

    (b) before the contract was made, the statement had been withdrawn in public or, to the extent that it contained anything which was incorrect or misleading, it had been corrected in public, or

    (c) the decision to acquire the goods could not have been influenced by the statement.

(2D) Subsections (2B) and (2C) above do not prevent any public statement from being a relevant circumstance for the purposes of subsection (2A) above (whether or not the transferee deals as consumer) if the statement would have been such a circumstance apart from those subsections.]

[(3) The condition implied by subsection (2) above does not extend to any matter making the quality of goods unsatisfactory—

    (a) which is specifically drawn to the transferee's attention before the contract is made,

    (b) where the transferee examines the goods before the contract is made, which that examination ought to reveal, or

    (c) where the property in the goods is transferred by reference to a sample, which would have been apparent on a reasonable examination of the sample.]

(4) Subsection (5) below applies where, under a contract for the transfer of goods, the transferor transfers the property in goods in the course of a business and the transferee, expressly or by implication, makes known—

    (a) to the transferor, or

    (b) where the consideration or part of the consideration for the transfer is a sum payable by instalments and the goods were previously sold by a credit-broker to the transferor, to that credit-broker,

any particular purpose for which the goods are being acquired.

(5) In that case there is (subject to subsection (6) below) an implied condition that the goods supplied under the contract are reasonably fit for that purpose, whether or not that is a purpose for which such goods are commonly supplied.

(6) Subsection (5) above does not apply where the circumstances show that the transferee does not rely, or that it is unreasonable for him to rely, on the skill or judgment of the transferor or credit-broker.

(7) An implied condition or warranty about quality or fitness for a particular purpose may be annexed by usage to a contract for the transfer of goods.

(8) The preceding provisions of this section apply to a transfer by a person who in the course of a business is acting as agent for another as they apply to a transfer by a principal in the course of a business, except where that other is not transferring in the course of a business and either the transferee knows that fact or reasonable steps are taken to bring it to the transferee's notice before the contract concerned is made.

5   Implied terms where transfer is by sample

(1) This section applies where, under a contract for the transfer of goods, the transferor transfers or agrees to transfer the property in the goods by reference to a sample.

(2) In such a case there is an implied condition—

    (a) that the bulk will correspond with the sample in quality; and

    (b) that the transferee will have a reasonable opportunity of comparing the bulk with the sample; and

    (c) that the goods will be free from any defect, making their quality unsatisfactory, which would not be apparent on reasonable examination of the sample.

(4) For the purposes of this section a transferor transfers or agrees to transfer the property in goods by reference to a sample where there is an express or implied term to that effect in the contract concerned.

[5A   Modification of remedies for breach of statutory condition in non-consumer cases

(1) Where in the case of a contract for the transfer of goods—

    (a) the transferee would, apart from this subsection, have the right to treat the contract as repudiated by reason of a breach on the part of the transferor of a term implied by section 3, 4 or 5(2)(a) or (c) above, but

    (b) the breach is so slight that it would be unreasonable for him to do so,

then, if the transferee does not deal as consumer, the breach is not to be treated as a breach of condition but may be treated as a breach of warranty.

(2) This section applies unless a contrary intention appears in, or is to be implied from, the contract.

(3) It is for the transferor to show that a breach fell within subsection (1)(b) above.]

Contracts for the hire of goods

6   The contracts concerned

(1) In this Act [in its application to England and Wales and Northern Ireland] a 'contract for the hire of goods' means a contract under which one person bails or agrees to bail goods to another by way of hire, other than [a hire-purchase agreement].

(3) For the purposes of this Act [in its application to England and Wales and Northern Ireland] a contract is a contract for the hire of goods whether or not services are also provided or to be provided under the contract, and [...] whatever is the nature of the consideration for the bailment or agreement to bail by way of hire.

7   Implied terms about right to transfer possession, etc.

(1) In a contract for the hire of goods there is an implied condition on the part of the bailor that in the case of a bailment he has a right to transfer possession of the goods by way of hire for the period of the bailment and in the case of an agreement to bail he will have such a right at the time of the bailment.

(2) In a contract for the hire of goods there is also an implied warranty that the bailee will enjoy quiet possession of the goods for the period of the bailment except so far as the possession may be disturbed by the owner or other person entitled to the benefit of any charge or encumbrance disclosed or known to the bailee before the contract is made.

(3) The preceding provisions of this section do not affect the right of the bailor to repossess the goods under an express or implied term of the contract.

8   Implied terms where hire is by description

(1) This section applies where, under a contract for the hire of goods, the bailor bails or agrees to bail the goods by description.

(2) In such a case there is an implied condition that the goods will correspond with the description.

(3) If under the contract the bailor bails or agrees to bail the goods by reference to a sample as well as a description it is not sufficient that the bulk of the goods corresponds with the sample if the goods do not also correspond with the description.

(4) A contract is not prevented from falling within subsection (1) above by reason only that, being exposed for supply, the goods are selected by the bailee.

9   Implied terms about quality or fitness

(1) Except as provided by this section and section 10 below and subject to the provisions of any other enactment, there is no implied condition or warranty about the quality or fitness for any particular purpose of goods bailed under a contract for the hire of goods.

[(2) Where, under such a contract, the bailor bails goods in the course of a business, there is an implied condition that the goods supplied under the contract are of satisfactory quality.]

[(2A) For the purposes of this section and section 10 below, goods are of satisfactory quality if they meet the standard that a reasonable person would regard as satisfactory, taking account of any description of the goods, the consideration for the bailment (if relevant) and all the other relevant circumstances.]

[(2B) If the bailee deals as consumer, the relevant circumstances mentioned in subsection (2A) above include any public statements on the specific characteristics of the goods made about them by the bailor, the producer or his representative, particularly in advertising or on labelling.

(2C) A public statement is not by virtue of subsection (2B) above a relevant circumstance for the purposes of subsection (2A) above in the case of a contract for the hire of goods, if the bailor shows that—

(a) at the time the contract was made, he was not, and could not reasonably have been, aware of the statement,

(b) before the contract was made, the statement had been withdrawn in public or, to the extent that it contained anything which was incorrect or misleading, it had been corrected in public, or

(c) the decision to acquire the goods could not have been influenced by the statement.

(2D) Subsections (2B) and (2C) above do not prevent any public statement from being a relevant circumstance for the purposes of subsection (2A) above (whether or not the bailee deals as consumer) if the statement would have been such a circumstance apart from those subsections.]

[(3) The condition implied by subsection (2) above does not extend to any matter making the quality of goods unsatisfactory—

(a) which is specifically drawn to the bailee's attention before the contract is made,

(b) where the bailee examines the goods before the contract is made, which that examination ought to reveal, or

(c) where the goods are bailed by reference to a sample, which would have been apparent on a reasonable examination of the sample.]

(4) Subsection (5) below applies where, under a contract for the hire of goods, the bailor bails goods in the course of a business and the bailee, expressly or by implication, makes known—

(a) to the bailor in the course of negotiations conducted by him in relation to the making of the contract, or

(b) to a credit-broker in the course of negotiations conducted by that broker in relation to goods sold by him to the bailor before forming the subject matter of the contract,

any particular purpose for which the goods are being bailed.

(5) In that case there is (subject to subsection (6) below) an implied condition that the goods supplied under the contract are reasonably fit for that purpose, whether or not that is a purpose for which such goods are commonly supplied.

(6) Subsection (5) above does not apply where the circumstances show that the bailee does not rely, or that it is unreasonable for him to rely, on the skill or judgment of the bailor or credit-broker.

(7) An implied condition or warranty about quality or fitness for a particular purpose may be annexed by usage to a contract for the hire of goods.

(8) The preceding provisions of this section apply to a bailment by a person who in the course of a business is acting as agent for another as they apply to a bailment by a principal in the course of a business, except where that other is not bailing in the course of a business and either the bailee knows that fact or reasonable steps are taken to bring it to the bailee's notice before the contract concerned is made.

10   Implied terms where hire is by sample

(1) This section applies where, under a contract for the hire of goods, the bailor bails or agrees to bail the goods by reference to a sample.

(2) In such a case there is an implied condition—

(a) that the bulk will correspond with the sample in quality; and

(b) that the bailee will have a reasonable opportunity of comparing the bulk with the sample; and

(c) that the goods will be free from any defect, [making their quality unsatisfactory], which would not be apparent on reasonable examination of the sample.

(4) For the purposes of this section a bailor bails or agrees to bail goods by reference to a sample where there is an express or implied term to that effect in the contract concerned.

[10A   Modification of remedies for breach of statutory condition in non-consumer cases

(1) Where in the case of a contract for the hire of goods—

(a) the bailee would, apart from this subsection, have the right to treat the contract as repudiated by reason of a breach on the part of the bailor of a term implied by section 8, 9 or 10(2)(a) or (c) above, but

(b) the breach is so slight that it would be unreasonable for him to do so,

then, if the bailee does not deal as consumer, the breach is not to be treated as a breach of condition but may be treated as a breach of warranty.

(2) This section applies unless a contrary intention appears in, or is to be implied from, the contract.

(3) It is for the bailor to show that a breach fell within subsection (1)(b) above.]

Exclusion of implied terms, etc.

11   Exclusion of implied terms, etc.

(1) Where a right, duty or liability would arise under a contract for the transfer of goods or a contract for the hire of goods by implication of law, it may (subject to subsection (2) below and the 1977 Act) be negatived or varied by express agreement, or by the course of dealing between the parties, or by such usage as binds both parties to the contract.

(2) An express condition or warranty does not negative a condition or warranty implied by the preceding provisions of this Act unless inconsistent with it.

(3) Nothing in the preceding provisions of this Act prejudices the operation of any other enactment or any rule of law whereby any condition or warranty (other than one relating to quality or fitness) is to be implied in a contract for the transfer of goods or a contract for the hire of goods.

[PART 1B ADDITIONAL RIGHTS OF TRANSFEREE IN CONSUMER CASES]

[11M   Introductory

(1) This section applies if—

(a) the transferee deals as consumer or, in Scotland, there is a consumer contract in which the transferee is a consumer, and

(b) the goods do not conform to the contract for the transfer of goods at the time of delivery.

(2) If this section applies, the transferee has the right—

    (a) under and in accordance with section 11N below, to require the transferor to repair or replace the goods, or

    (b) under and in accordance with section 11P below—

        (i)   to require the transferor to reduce the amount to be paid for the transfer by the transferee by an appropriate amount, or

        (ii) to rescind the contract with regard to the goods in question.

(3) For the purposes of subsection (1)(b) above, goods which do not conform to the contract for the transfer of goods at any time within the period of six months starting with the date on which the goods were delivered to the transferee must be taken not to have so conformed at that date.

(4) Subsection (3) above does not apply if—

    (a) it is established that the goods did so conform at that date;

    (b) its application is incompatible with the nature of the goods or the nature of the lack of conformity.

(5) For the purposes of this section, 'consumer contract' has the same meaning as in section 11F(3) above.]

[11N   Repair or replacement of the goods

(1) If section 11M above applies, the transferee may require the transferor—

    (a) to repair the goods, or

    (b) to replace the goods.

(2) If the transferee requires the transferor to repair or replace the goods, the transferor must—

    (a) repair or, as the case may be, replace the goods within a reasonable time but without causing significant inconvenience to the transferee;

    (b) bear any necessary costs incurred in doing so (including in particular the cost of any labour, materials or postage).

(3) The transferee must not require the transferor to repair or, as the case may be, replace the goods if that remedy is—

    (a) impossible,

    (b) disproportionate in comparison to the other of those remedies, or

    (c) disproportionate in comparison to an appropriate reduction in the purchase price under paragraph (a), or rescission under paragraph (b), of section 11P(1) below.

(4) One remedy is disproportionate in comparison to the other if the one imposes costs on the transferor which, in comparison to those imposed on him by the other, are unreasonable, taking into account—

    (a) the value which the goods would have if they conformed to the contract for the transfer of goods,

    (b) the significance of the lack of conformity to the contract for the transfer of goods, and

    (c) whether the other remedy could be effected without significant inconvenience to the transferee.

(5) Any question as to what is a reasonable time or significant inconvenience is to be determined by reference to—

    (a) the nature of the goods, and

    (b) the purpose for which the goods were acquired.]

[11P   Reduction of purchase price or rescission of contract

(1) If section 11M above applies, the transferee may—

    (a) require the transferor to reduce the purchase price of the goods in question to the transferee by an appropriate amount, or

    (b) rescind the contract with regard to those goods,

if the condition in subsection (2) below is satisfied.

(2) The condition is that—

    (a) by virtue of section 11N(3) above the transferee may require neither repair nor replacement of the goods, or

    (b) the transferee has required the transferor to repair or replace the goods, but the transferor is in breach of the requirement of section 11N(2)(a) above to do so within a reasonable time and without significant inconvenience to the transferee.

(3) If the transferee rescinds the contract, any reimbursement to the transferee may be reduced to take account of the use he has had of the goods since they were delivered to him.]

[11Q   Relation to other remedies etc.

(1) If the transferee requires the transferor to repair or replace the goods the transferee must not act under subsection (2) until he has given the transferor a reasonable time in which to repair or replace (as the case may be) the goods.

(2) The transferee acts under this subsection if—

    (a) in England and Wales or Northern Ireland he rejects the goods and terminates the contract for breach of condition;

    (b) in Scotland he rejects any goods delivered under the contract and treats it as repudiated; or

    (c) he requires the goods to be replaced or repaired (as the case may be).]

[11R   Powers of the court

(1) In any proceedings in which a remedy is sought by virtue of this Part the court, in addition to any other power it has, may act under this section.

(2) On the application of the transferee the court may make an order requiring specific performance or, in Scotland, specific implement by the transferor of any obligation imposed on him by virtue of section 11N above.

(3) Subsection (4) applies if—

    (a) the transferee requires the transferor to give effect to a remedy under section 11N or 11P above or has claims to rescind under section 11P, but

    (b) the court decides that another remedy under section 11N or 11P is appropriate.

(4) The court may proceed—

    (a) as if the transferee had required the transferor to give effect to the other remedy, or if the other remedy is rescission under section 11P,

    (b) as if the transferee had claimed to rescind the contract under that section.

(5) If the transferee has claimed to rescind the contract the court may order that any reimbursement to the transferee is reduced to take account of the use he has had of the goods since they were delivered to him.

(6) The court may make an order under this section unconditionally or on such terms and conditions as to damages, payment of the price and otherwise as it thinks just.]

[11S   Conformity with the contract

(1) Goods do not conform to a contract for the supply or transfer of goods if—

    (a) there is, in relation to the goods, a breach of an express term of the contract or a term implied by section 3, 4 or 5 above or, in Scotland, by section 11C, 11D or 11E above, or

    (b) installation of the goods forms part of the contract for the transfer of goods, and the goods were installed by the transferor, or under his responsibility, in breach of the term implied by section 13 below or (in Scotland) in breach of any term implied by any rule of law as to the manner in which the installation is carried out.]

PART II SUPPLY OF SERVICES

12   The contracts concerned

(1) In this Act a 'contract for the supply of a service' means, subject to subsection (2) below, a contract under which a person ('the supplier') agrees to carry out a service.

(2) For the purposes of this Act, a contract of service or apprenticeship is not a contract for the supply of a service.

(3) Subject to subsection (2) above, a contract is a contract for the supply of a service for the purposes of this Act whether or not goods are also—

(a) transferred or to be transferred, or

(b) bailed or to be bailed by way of hire,

under the contract, and whatever is the nature of the consideration for which the service is to be carried out.

(4) The Secretary of State may by order provide that one or more of sections 13 to 15 below shall not apply to services of a description specified in the order, and such an order may make different provision for different circumstances.

(5) The power to make an order under subsection (4) above shall be exercisable by statutory instrument subject to annulment in pursuance of a resolution of either House of Parliament.

13   Implied term about care and skill

In a contract for the supply of a service where the supplier is acting in the course of a business, there is an implied term that the supplier will carry out the service with reasonable care and skill.

14   Implied term about time of performance

(1) Where, under a contract for the supply of a service by a supplier acting in the course of a business, the time for the service to be carried out is not fixed by the contract, left to be fixed in a manner agreed by the contract or determined by the course of dealing between the parties, there is an implied term that the supplier will carry out the service within a reasonable time.

(2) What is a reasonable time is a question of fact.

15   Implied term about consideration

(1) Where, under a contract for the supply of a service, the consideration for the service is not determined by the contract, left to be determined in a manner agreed by the contract or determined by the course of dealing between the parties, there is an implied term that the party contracting with the supplier will pay a reasonable charge.

(2) What is a reasonable charge is a question of fact.

16   Exclusion of implied terms, etc.

(1) Where a right, duty or liability would arise under a contract for the supply of a service by virtue of this Part of this Act, it may (subject to subsection (2) below and the 1977 Act) be negatived or varied by express agreement, or by the course of dealing between the parties, or by such usage as binds both parties to the contract.

(2) An express term does not negative a term implied by this Part of this Act unless inconsistent with it.

(3) Nothing in this Part of this Act prejudices—

(a) any rule of law which imposes on the supplier a duty stricter than that imposed by section 13 or 14 above; or

(b) subject to paragraph (a) above, any rule of law whereby any term not inconsistent with this Part of this Act is to be implied in a contract for the supply of a service.

(4) This Part of this Act has effect subject to any other enactment which defines or restricts the rights, duties or liabilities arising in connection with a service of any description.

PART III SUPPLEMENTARY

18   Interpretation: general

(1) In the preceding provisions of this Act and this section—

'bailee', in relation to a contract for the hire of goods means (depending on the context) a person to whom the goods are bailed under the contract, or a person to whom they are to be so bailed, or a person to whom the rights under the contract of either of those persons have passed;

'bailor', in relation to a contract for the hire of goods, means (depending on the context) a person who bails the goods under the contract, or a person who agrees to do so, or a person to whom the duties under the contract of either of those persons have passed;

'business' includes a profession and the activities of any government department or local or public authority;

'credit-broker' means a person acting in the course of a business of credit brokerage carried on by him;

'credit brokerage' means the effecting of introductions—

    (a) of individuals desiring to obtain credit to persons carrying on any business so far as it relates to the provision of credit; or

    (b) of individuals desiring to obtain goods on hire to persons carrying on a business which comprises or relates to the bailment [or as regards Scotland the hire] of goods under a contract for the hire of goods; or

    (c) of individuals desiring to obtain credit, or to obtain goods on hire, to other credit-brokers;

'enactment' means any legislation (including subordinate legislation) of the United Kingdom or Northern Ireland;

'goods' [includes all personal chattels, other than things in action and money, and as regards Scotland all corporeal moveables; and in particular 'goods' includes] emblements, industrial growing crops, and things attached to or forming part of the land which are agreed to be severed before the transfer [bailment or hire] concerned or under the contract concerned [...];

'hire-purchase agreement' has the same meaning as in the 1974 Act;

['producer' means the manufacturer of goods, the importer of goods into the European Economic Area or any person purporting to be a producer by placing his name, trade mark or other distinctive sign on the goods;]

'property', in relation to goods, means the general property in them and not merely a special property;

['repair' means, in cases where there is a lack of conformity in goods for the purposes of this Act, to bring the goods into conformity with the contract.]

'transferee', in relation to a contract for the transfer of goods, means (depending on the context) a person to whom the property in the goods is transferred under the contract, or a person to whom the property is to be so transferred, or a person to whom the rights under the contract of either of those persons have passed;

'transferor', in relation to a contract for the transfer of goods, means (depending on the context) a person who transfers the property in the goods under the contract, or a person who agrees to do so, or a person to whom the duties under the contract of either of those persons have passed.

(2) In subsection (1) above, in the definitions of bailee, bailor, transferee and transferor, a reference to rights or duties passing is to their passing by assignment, [assignation] operation of law or otherwise.

[(3) For the purposes of this Act, the quality of goods includes their state and condition and the following (among others) are in appropriate cases aspects of the quality of goods—

    (a) fitness for all the purposes for which goods of the kind in question are commonly supplied,

    (b) appearance and finish,

    (c) freedom from minor defects,

    (d) safety, and

    (e) durability.

(4) References to this Act to dealing as consumer are to be construed in accordance with Part I of the Unfair Contract Terms Act 1977; and, for the purposes of this Act, it is for the transferor or bailor claiming that the transferee or bailee does not deal as consumer to show that he does not.]

19 Interpretation: references to Acts

In this Act—

'the 1973 Act' means the Supply of Goods (Implied Terms) Act 1973;
'the 1974 Act' means the Consumer Credit Act 1974;
'the 1977 Act' means the Unfair Contract Terms Act 1977; and
'the 1979 Act' means the Sale of Goods Act 1979.

Building Act 1984

(1984, c. 55)

38 Civil liability

(1) Subject to this section—

(a) breach of a duty imposed by building regulations, so far as it causes damage, is actionable, except in so far as the regulations provide otherwise, and

(b) as regards such a duty, building regulations may provide for a prescribed defence to be available in an action for breach of that duty brought by virtue of this subsection.

(4) In this section, 'damage' includes the death of, or injury to, any person (including any disease and any impairment of a person's physical or mental condition).

Occupiers' Liability Act 1984

(1984, c. 3)

1 Duty of occupier to persons other than his visitors

(1) The rules enacted by this section shall have effect, in place of the rules of the common law, to determine—

(a) whether any duty is owed by a person as occupier of premises to persons other than his visitors in respect of any risk of their suffering injury on the premises by reason of any danger due to the state of the premises or to things done or omitted to be done on them; and

(b) if so, what that duty is.

(2) For the purposes of this section, the persons who are to be treated respectively as an occupier of any premises (which, for those purposes, include any fixed or movable structure) and as his visitors are—

(a) any person who owes in relation to the premises the duty referred to in section 2 of the Occupiers' Liability Act 1957 (the common duty of care), and

(b) those who are his visitors for the purposes of that duty.

(3) An occupier of premises owes a duty to another (not being his visitor) in respect of any such risk as is referred to in subsection (1) above if—

(a) he is aware of the danger or has reasonable grounds to believe that it exists;

(b) he knows or has reasonable grounds to believe that the other is in the vicinity of the danger concerned or that he may come into the vicinity of the danger (in either case, whether the other has lawful authority for being in that vicinity or not); and

(c) the risk is one against which, in all the circumstances of the case, he may reasonably be expected to offer the other some protection.

(4) Where, by virtue of this section, an occupier of premises owes a duty to another in respect of such a risk, the duty is to take such care as is reasonable in all the circumstances of the case to see that he does not suffer injury on the premises by reason of the danger concerned.

(5) Any duty owed by virtue of this section in respect of a risk may, in an appropriate case, be discharged by taking such steps as are reasonable in all the circumstances of the case to give warning of the danger concerned or to discourage persons from incurring the risk.

(6) No duty is owed by virtue of this section to any person in respect of risks willingly accepted as his by that person (the question whether a risk was so accepted to be decided on the same principles as in other cases in which one person owes a duty of care to another).

[(6A) At any time when the right conferred by section 2(1) of the Countryside and Rights of Way Act 2000 is exercisable in relation to land which is access land for the purposes of Part I of that Act, an occupier of the land owes (subject to subsection (6C) below) no duty by virtue of this section to any person in respect of—

    (a) a risk resulting from the existence of any natural feature of the landscape, or any river, stream, ditch or pond whether or not a natural feature, or

    (b) a risk of that person suffering injury when passing over, under or through any wall, fence or gate, except by proper use of the gate or of a stile.

[(6AA) Where the land is coastal margin for the purposes of Part 1 of that Act (including any land treated as coastal margin by virtue of section 16 of that Act), subsection (6A) has effect as if for paragraphs (a) and (b) of that subsection there were substituted "a risk resulting from the existence of any physical feature (whether of the landscape or otherwise)".]

(6B) For the purposes of subsection (6A) above, any plant, shrub or tree, of whatever origin, is to be regarded as a natural feature of the landscape.

(6C) Subsection (6A) does not prevent an occupier from owing a duty by virtue of this section in respect of any risk where the danger concerned is due to anything done by the occupier—

    (a) with the intention of creating that risk, or

    (b) being reckless as to whether that risk is created.]

(7) No duty is owed by virtue of this section to persons using the highway, and this section does not affect any duty owed to such persons.

(8) Where a person owes a duty by virtue of this section, he does not, by reason of any breach of the duty, incur any liability in respect of any loss of or damage to property.

(9) In this section—

'highway' means any part of a highway other than a ferry or waterway;

'injury' means anything resulting in death or personal injury, including any disease and any impairment of physical or mental condition; and

'movable structure' includes any vessel, vehicle or aircraft.

[**1A   Special considerations relating to access land**
In determining whether any, and if so what, duty is owed by virtue of section 1 by an occupier of land at any time when the right conferred by section 2(1) of the Countryside and Rights of Way Act 2000 is exercisable in relation to the land, regard is to be had, in particular, to—

    (a) the fact that the existence of that right ought not to place an undue burden (whether financial or otherwise) on the occupier,

    (b) the importance of maintaining the character of the countryside, including features of historic, traditional or archaeological interest, and

    (c) any relevant guidance given under section 20 of that Act.]

3   Application to Crown
Section 1 of this Act shall bind the Crown, but as regards the Crown's liability in tort shall not bind the Crown further than the Crown is made liable in tort by the Crown Proceedings Act 1947.

Police and Criminal Evidence Act 1984

(1984, c. 60)

17   Entry for purpose of arrest etc.
    (1) Subject to the following provisions of this section, and without prejudice to any other enactment, a constable may enter and search any premises for the purpose—

    (a) of executing—

        (i) a warrant of arrest issued in connection with or arising out of criminal proceedings; or

        (ii) a warrant of commitment issued under section 76 of the Magistrates' Courts Act 1980;

    (b) of arresting a person for an [indictable] offence; ...

    (e) of saving life or limb or preventing serious damage to property.

    (4) The power of search conferred by this section is only a power to search to the extent that is reasonably required for the purpose for which the power of entry is exercised.

    (5) Subject to subsection (6) below, all the rules of common law under which a constable has power to enter premises without a warrant are hereby abolished.

    (6) Nothing in subsection (5) above affects any power of entry to deal with or prevent a breach of the peace.

19   General power of seizure etc.

    (1) The powers conferred by subsections (2), (3) and (4) below are exercisable by a constable who is lawfully on any premises.

    (2) The constable may seize anything which is on the premises if he has reasonable grounds for believing—

    (a) that it has been obtained in consequence of the commission of an offence; and

    (b) that it is necessary to seize it in order to prevent it being concealed, lost, damaged, altered or destroyed.

22   Retention

    (1) Subject to subsection (4) below, anything which has been seized by a constable or taken away by a constable following a requirement made by virtue of section 19 or 20 above may be retained so long as is necessary in all the circumstances.

    (3) Nothing seized on the ground that it may be used—

    (a) to cause physical injury to any person;

    (b) to damage property;

    (c) to interfere with evidence; or

    (d) to assist in escape from police detention or lawful custody,

may be retained when the person from whom it was seized is no longer in police detention or the custody of a court or is in the custody of a court but has been released on bail.

[24   Arrest without warrant: constables

    (1) A constable may arrest without a warrant—

    (a) anyone who is about to commit an offence;

    (b) anyone who is in the act of committing an offence;

    (c) anyone whom he has reasonable grounds for suspecting to be about to commit an offence;

    (d) anyone whom he has reasonable grounds for suspecting to be committing an offence.

    (2) If a constable has reasonable grounds for suspecting that an offence has been committed, he may arrest without a warrant anyone whom he has reasonable grounds to suspect of being guilty of it.

    (3) If an offence has been committed, a constable may arrest without a warrant—

    (a) anyone who is guilty of the offence;

    (b) anyone whom he has reasonable grounds for suspecting to be guilty of it.

    (4) But the power of summary arrest conferred by subsection (1), (2) or (3) is exercisable only if the constable has reasonable grounds for believing that for any of the reasons mentioned in subsection (5) it is necessary to arrest the person in question.

    (5) The reasons are—

    (a) to enable the name of the person in question to be ascertained (in the case where the constable does not know, and cannot readily ascertain, the person's name, or has reasonable grounds for doubting whether a name given by the person as his name is his real name);

(b) correspondingly as regards the person's address;

(c) to prevent the person in question—

    (i)   causing physical injury to himself or any other person;

    (ii)   suffering physical injury;

    (iii)   causing loss of or damage to property;

    (iv)   committing an offence against public decency (subject to subsection (6)); or

    (v)   causing an unlawful obstruction of the highway;

(d) to protect a child or other vulnerable person from the person in question;

(e) to allow the prompt and effective investigation of the offence or of the conduct of the person in question;

(f) to prevent any prosecution for the offence from being hindered by the disappearance of the person in question.

(6) Subsection (5)(c)(iv) applies only where members of the public going about their normal business cannot reasonably be expected to avoid the person in question.]

[24A   Arrest without warrant: other persons

...]

[Section 24A provides 'A person other than a constable' with similar powers to those in s 24.]

32   Search upon arrest

(1) A constable may search an arrested person, in any case where the person to be searched has been arrested at a place other than a police station, if the constable has reasonable grounds for believing that the arrested person may present a danger to himself or others.

34   Limitations on police detention

(1) A person arrested for an offence shall not be kept in police detention except in accordance with the provisions of this Part of this Act.

(2) Subject to subsection (3) below, if at any time a custody officer—

(a) becomes aware, in relation to any person in police detention, that the grounds for the detention of that person have ceased to apply; and

(b) is not aware of any other grounds on which the continued detention of that person could be justified under the provisions of this Part of this Act,

it shall be the duty of the custody officer, subject to subsection (4) below, to order his immediate release from custody.

55   Intimate searches

(2) An officer may not authorise an intimate search of a person for anything unless he has reasonable grounds for believing that it cannot be found without his being intimately searched.

62   Intimate samples

(1) [Subject to section 63B below] An intimate sample may be taken from a person in police detention only—

(a) if a police officer of at least the rank of inspector authorises it to be taken; and

(b) if the appropriate consent is given.

[(1A) An intimate sample may be taken from a person who is not in police detention but from whom, in the course of the investigation of an offence, two or more intimate samples suitable for the same means of analysis have been taken which have proved insufficient—

(a) if a police officer of at least the rank of inspector authorises it to be taken; and

(b) if the appropriate consent is given.]

65   Part V—supplementary

[(1)] In this Part of this Act—...

['intimate sample' means—

(a) a sample of blood, semen or any other tissue fluid, urine or pubic hair;

(b) a dental impression;

(c) a swab taken from any part of a person's genitals (including pubic hair) or from a person's body orifice other than the mouth;]

Housing Act 1985

(1985, c. 68)

[**118   The right to acquire**

(1) A tenant of a registered social landlord who satisfies the conditions in section 16(1)(a) and (b) of the Housing Act 1996 has the right to acquire, that is to say, the right, in the circumstances and subject to the conditions and exceptions stated in the following provisions of this Part—

(a) if the dwelling-house is a house and the landlord owns the freehold, to acquire the freehold of the dwelling-house;

(b) if the landlord does not own the freehold or if the dwelling-house is a flat (whether or not the landlord owns the freehold), to be granted a lease of the dwelling-house.]

Landlord and Tenant Act 1985

(1985, c. 70)

8   Implied terms as to fitness for human habitation

(1) In a contract to which this section applies for the letting of a house for human habitation there is implied, notwithstanding any stipulation to the contrary—

(a) a condition that the house is fit for human habitation at the commencement of the tenancy, and

(b) an undertaking that the house will be kept by the landlord fit for human habitation during the tenancy.

(2) The landlord, or a person authorised by him in writing, may at reasonable times of the day, on giving 24 hours' notice in writing to the tenant or occupier, enter premises to which this section applies for the purpose of viewing their state and condition.

Insolvency Act 1986

(1986, c. 45)

238   Transactions at an undervalue (England and Wales)

(1) This section applies in the case of a company where—

[(a) the company enters administration,]

(b) the company goes into liquidation; and 'the office-holder' means the administrator or the liquidator, as the case may be.

(2) Where the company has at a relevant time (defined in section 240) entered into a transaction with any person at an undervalue, the office-holder may apply to the court for an order under this section.

(3) Subject as follows, the court shall, on such an application, make such order as it thinks fit for restoring the position to what it would have been if the company had not entered into that transaction.

(4) For the purposes of this section and section 241, a company enters into a transaction with a person at an undervalue if—

(a) the company makes a gift to that person or otherwise enters into a transaction with that person on terms that provide for the company to receive no consideration, or

(b) the company enters into a transaction with that person for a consideration the value of which, in money or money's worth, is significantly less than the value, in money or money's worth, of the consideration provided by the company.

(5) The court shall not make an order under this section in respect of a transaction at an undervalue if it is satisfied—

(a) that the company which entered into the transaction did so in good faith and for the purpose of carrying on its business, and

(b) that at the time it did so there were reasonable grounds for believing that the transaction would benefit the company.

Latent Damage Act 1986

(1986, c. 37)

1 Time limits for negligence actions in respect of latent damage not involving personal injuries

The following sections shall be inserted in the Limitation Act 1980 (referred to below in this Act as the 1980 Act)...

3 Accrual of cause of action to successive owners in respect of latent damage to property

(1) Subject to the following provisions of this section, where—

(a) a cause of action ('the original cause of action') has accrued to any person in respect of any negligence to which damage to any property in which he has an interest is attributable (in whole or in part); and

(b) another person acquires an interest in that property after the date on which the original cause of action accrued but before the material facts about the damage have become known to any person who, at the time when he first has knowledge of those facts, has any interest in the property;

a fresh cause of action in respect of that negligence shall accrue to that other person on the date on which he acquires his interest in the property.

(2) A cause of action accruing to any person by virtue of subsection (1) above—

(a) shall be treated as if based on breach of a duty of care at common law owed to the person to whom it accrues; and

(b) shall be treated for the purposes of section 14A of the 1980 Act (special time limit for negligence actions where facts relevant to cause of action are not known at date of accrual) as having accrued on the date on which the original cause of action accrued.

(3) Section 28 of the 1980 Act (extension of limitation period in case of disability) shall not apply in relation to any such cause of action.

(4) Subsection (1) above shall not apply in any case where the person acquiring an interest in the damaged property is either—

(a) a person in whom the original cause of action vests by operation of law; or

(b) a person in whom the interest in that property vests by virtue of any order made by a court under section 538 of the Companies Act 1985 (vesting of company property in liquidator).

[*The Companies Act 1985, s 538 has now been replaced by the Insolvency Act 1986, s 145.*]

(5) For the purposes of subsection (1)(b) above, the material facts about the damage are such facts about the damage as would lead a reasonable person who has an interest in the damaged

property at the time when those facts become known to him to consider it sufficiently serious to justify his instituting proceedings for damages against a defendant who did not dispute liability and was able to satisfy a judgment.

(6) For the purposes of this section a person's knowledge includes knowledge which he might reasonably have been expected to acquire—

(a) from facts observable or ascertainable by him; or

(b) from facts ascertained by him with the help of appropriate expert advice which it is reasonable for him to seek;

but a person shall not be taken by virtue of this subsection to have knowledge of a fact ascertainable by him only with the help of expert advice so long as he has taken all reasonable steps to obtain (and, where appropriate, to act on) that advice.

(7) This section shall bind the Crown, but as regards the Crown's liability in tort shall not bind the Crown further than the Crown is made liable in tort by the Crown Proceedings Act 1947.

Consumer Protection Act 1987

(1987, c. 43)

PART I PRODUCT LIABILITY

1 Purpose and construction of Part I

(1) This Part shall have effect for the purpose of making such provision as is necessary in order to comply with the product liability Directive and shall be construed accordingly.

(2) In this Part, except in so far as the context otherwise requires—

'agricultural produce' means any produce of the soil, of stock-farming or of fisheries;

'dependant' and 'relative' have the same meaning as they have in, respectively, the Fatal Accidents Act 1976 and the Damages (Scotland) Act 1976;

'producer', in relation to a product, means—

(a) the person who manufactured it;

(b) in the case of a substance which has not been manufactured but has been won or abstracted, the person who won or abstracted it;

(c) in the case of a product which has not been manufactured, won or abstracted but essential characteristics of which are attributable to an industrial or other process having been carried out (for example, in relation to agricultural produce), the person who carried out that process;

'product' means any goods or electricity and (subject to subsection (3) below) includes a product which is comprised in another product, whether by virtue of being a component part or raw material or otherwise; and

'the product liability Directive' means the Directive of the Council of the European Communities, dated 25th July 1985, (No. 85/374/EEC) on the approximation of the laws, regulations and administrative provisions of the member States concerning liability for defective products.

(3) For the purposes of this Part a person who supplies any product in which products are comprised, whether by virtue of being component parts or raw materials or otherwise, shall not be treated by reason only of his supply of that product as supplying any of the products so comprised.

2 Liability for defective products

(1) Subject to the following provisions of this Part, where any damage is caused wholly or partly by a defect in a product, every person to whom subsection (2) below applies shall be liable for the damage.

(2) This subsection applies to—

(a) the producer of the product;

(b) any person who, by putting his name on the product or using a trade mark or other distinguishing mark in relation to the product, has held himself out to be the producer of the product;

(c) any person who has imported the product into a member State from a place outside the member States in order, in the course of any business of his, to supply it to another.

(3) Subject as aforesaid, where any damage is caused wholly or partly by a defect in a product, any person who supplied the product (whether to the person who suffered the damage, to the producer of any product in which the product in question is comprised or to any other person) shall be liable for the damage if—

(a) the person who suffered the damage requests the supplier to identify one or more of the persons (whether still in existence or not) to whom subsection (2) above applies in relation to the product;

(b) that request is made within a reasonable period after the damage occurs and at a time when it is not reasonably practicable for the person making the request to identify all those persons; and

(c) the supplier fails, within a reasonable period after receiving the request, either to comply with the request or to identify the person who supplied the product to him.

(5) Where two or more persons are liable by virtue of this Part for the same damage, their liability shall be joint and several.

(6) This section shall be without prejudice to any liability arising otherwise than by virtue of this Part.

3 Meaning of 'defect'

(1) Subject to the following provisions of this section, there is a defect in a product for the purposes of this Part if the safety of the product is not such as persons generally are entitled to expect; and for those purposes 'safety', in relation to a product, shall include safety with respect to products comprised in that product and safety in the context of risks of damage to property, as well as in the context of risks of death or personal injury.

(2) In determining for the purposes of subsection (1) above what persons generally are entitled to expect in relation to a product all the circumstances shall be taken into account, including—

(a) the manner in which, and purposes for which, the product has been marketed, its get-up, the use of any mark in relation to the product and any instructions for, or warnings with respect to, doing or refraining from doing anything with or in relation to the product;

(b) what might reasonably be expected to be done with or in relation to the product; and

(c) the time when the product was supplied by its producer to another;

and nothing in this section shall require a defect to be inferred from the fact alone that the safety of a product which is supplied after that time is greater than the safety of the product in question.

4 Defences

(1) In any civil proceedings by virtue of this Part against any person ('the person proceeded against') in respect of a defect in a product it shall be a defence for him to show—

(a) that the defect is attributable to compliance with any requirement imposed by or under any enactment or with any Community obligation; or

(b) that the person proceeded against did not at any time supply the product to another; or

(c) that the following conditions are satisfied, that is to say—

(i) that the only supply of the product to another by the person proceeded against was otherwise than in the course of a business of that person's; and

(ii) that section 2(2) above does not apply to that person or applies to him by virtue only of things done otherwise than with a view to profit; or

(d) that the defect did not exist in the product at the relevant time; or

(e) that the state of scientific and technical knowledge at the relevant time was not such that a producer of products of the same description as the product in question might be expected to have discovered the defect if it had existed in his products while they were under his control; or

(f) that the defect—

    (i) constituted an defect in a product ('the subsequent product') in which the product in question had been comprised; and

    (ii) was wholly attributable to the design of the subsequent product or to compliance by the producer of the product in question with instructions given by the producer of the subsequent product.

(2) In this section 'the relevant time', in relation to electricity, means the time at which it was generated, being a time before it was transmitted or distributed, and in relation to any other product, means—

    (a) if the person proceeded against is a person to whom subsection (2) of section 2 above applies in relation to the product, the time when he supplied the product to another;

    (b) if that subsection does not apply to that person in relation to the product, the time when the product was last supplied by a person to whom that subsection does apply in relation to the product.

5   Damage giving rise to liability

(1) Subject to the following provisions of this section, in this Part 'damage' means death or personal injury or any loss of or damage to any property (including land).

(2) A person shall not be liable under section 2 above in respect of any defect in a product for the loss of or any damage to the product itself or for the loss of or any damage to the whole or any part of any product which has been supplied with the product in question comprised in it.

(3) A person shall not be liable under section 2 above for any loss of or damage to any property which, at the time it is lost or damaged, is not—

    (a) of a description of property ordinarily intended for private use, occupation or consumption; and

    (b) intended by the person suffering the loss or damage mainly for his own private use, occupation or consumption.

(4) No damages shall be awarded to any person by virtue of this Part in respect of any loss of or damage to any property if the amount which would fall to be so awarded to that person, apart from this subsection and any liability for interest, does not exceed £275.

(5) In determining for the purposes of this Part who has suffered any loss of or damage to property and when any such loss or damage occurred, the loss or damage shall be regarded as having occurred at the earliest time at which a person with an interest in the property had knowledge of the material facts about the loss or damage.

(6) For the purposes of subsection (5) above the material facts about any loss of or damage to any property are such facts about the loss or damage as would lead a reasonable person with an interest in the property to consider the loss or damage sufficiently serious to justify his instituting proceedings for damages against a defendant who did not dispute liability and was able to satisfy a judgment.

(7) For the purposes of subsection (5) above a person's knowledge includes knowledge which he might reasonably have been expected to acquire—

    (a) from facts observable or ascertainable by him; or

    (b) from facts ascertainable by him with the help of appropriate expert advice which it is reasonable for him to seek;

but a person shall not be taken by virtue of this subsection to have knowledge of a fact ascertainable by him only with the help of expert advice unless he has failed to take all reasonable steps to obtain (and, where appropriate, to act on) that advice.

6   Application of certain enactments etc.

(1) Any damage for which a person is liable under section 2 above shall be deemed to have been caused—

    (a) for the purposes of the Fatal Accidents Act 1976, by that person's wrongful act, neglect or default; ...

(2) Where—

    (a) a person's death is caused wholly or partly by a defect in a product, or a person dies after suffering damage which has been so caused;

    (b) a request such as mentioned in paragraph (a) of subsection (3) of section 2 above is made to a supplier of the product by that person's personal representatives or, in the case of a person whose death is caused wholly or partly by the defect, by any dependant or relative of that person; and

    (c) the conditions specified in paragraphs (b) and (c) of that subsection are satisfied in relation to that request,

this Part shall have effect for the purposes of the Law Reform (Miscellaneous Provisions) Act 1934, the Fatal Accidents Act 1976 and the Damages (Scotland) Act 1976 as if liability of the supplier to that person under that subsection did not depend on that person having requested the supplier to identify certain persons or on the said conditions having been satisfied in relation to a request made by that person.

(3) Section 1 of the Congenital Disabilities (Civil Liability) Act 1976 shall have effect for the purposes of this Part as if—

    (a) a person were answerable to a child in respect of an occurrence caused wholly or partly by a defect in a product if he is or has been liable under section 2 above in respect of any effect of the occurrence on a parent of the child, or would be so liable if the occurrence caused a parent of the child to suffer damage;

    (b) the provisions of this Part relating to liability under section 2 above applied in relation to liability by virtue of paragraph (a) above under the said section 1; and

    (c) subsection (6) of the said section 1 (exclusion of liability) were omitted.

(4) Where any damage is caused partly by a defect in a product and partly by the fault of the person suffering the damage, the Law Reform (Contributory Negligence) Act 1945 and section 5 of the Fatal Accidents Act 1976 (contributory negligence) shall have effect as if the defect were the fault of every person liable by virtue of this Part for the damage caused by the defect.

(5) In subsection (4) above 'fault' has the same meaning as in the said Act of 1945.

(6) Schedule 1 to this Act shall have effect for the purpose of amending the Limitation Act 1980 and the Prescription and Limitation (Scotland) Act 1973 in their application in relation to the bringing of actions by virtue of this Part.

(7) It is hereby declared that liability by virtue of this Part is to be treated as liability in tort for the purposes of any enactment conferring jurisdiction on any court with respect to any matter.

(8) Nothing in this Part shall prejudice the operation of section 12 of the Nuclear Installations Act 1965 (rights to compensation for certain breaches of duties confined to rights under that Act).

7 Prohibition on exclusions from liability

The liability of a person by virtue of this Part to a person who has suffered damage caused wholly or partly by a defect in a product, or to a dependant or relative of such a person, shall not be limited or excluded by any contract term, by any notice or by any other provision.

8 Power to modify Part I

(1) Her Majesty may by Order in Council make such modifications of this Part and of any other enactment (including an enactment contained in the following Parts of this Act, or in an Act passed after this Act) as appear to Her Majesty in Council to be necessary or expedient in consequence of any modification of the product liability Directive which is made at any time after the passing of this Act.

9 Application of Part I to Crown

(1) Subject to subsection (2) below, this Part shall bind the Crown.

(2) The Crown shall not, as regards the Crown's liability by virtue of this Part, be bound by this Part further than the Crown is made liable in tort or in reparation under the Crown Proceedings Act 1947, as that Act has effect from time to time.

PART II CONSUMER SAFETY

11 Safety regulations

(1) The Secretary of State may by regulations under this section ('safety regulations') make such provision as he considers appropriate [...] for the purpose of securing—

(a) that goods to which this section applies are safe;

(b) that goods to which this section applies which are unsafe, or would be unsafe in the hands of persons of a particular description, are not made available to persons generally or, as the case may be, to persons of that description; and

(c) that appropriate information is, and inappropriate information is not, provided in relation to goods to which this section applies.

12 Offences against the safety regulations

(1) Where safety regulations prohibit a person from supplying or offering or agreeing to supply any goods or from exposing or possessing any goods for supply, that person shall be guilty of an offence if he contravenes the prohibition.

(2) Where safety regulations require a person who makes or processes any goods in the course of carrying on a business—

(a) to carry out a particular test or use a particular procedure in connection with the making or processing of the goods with a view to ascertaining whether the goods satisfy any requirements of such regulations; or

(b) to deal or not to deal in a particular way with a quantity of the goods of which the whole or part does not satisfy such a test or does not satisfy standards connected with such a procedure,

that person shall be guilty of an offence if he does not comply with the requirement.

(3) If a person contravenes a provision of safety regulations which prohibits or requires the provision, by means of a mark or otherwise, of information of a particular kind in relation to goods, he shall be guilty of an offence.

(4) Where safety regulations require any person to give information to another for the purpose of enabling that other to exercise any function, that person shall be guilty of an offence if—

(a) he fails without reasonable cause to comply with the requirement; or

(b) in giving the information which is required of him—

(i)   he makes any statement which he knows is false in a material particular; or

(ii) he recklessly makes any statement which is false in a material particular.

PART IV ENFORCEMENT OF PARTS II AND III

29 Powers of search etc.

(1) Subject to the following provisions of this Part, a duly authorised officer of an enforcement authority may at any reasonable hour and on production, if required, of his credentials exercise any of the powers conferred by the following provisions of this section.

(2) The officer may, for the purpose of ascertaining whether there has been any contravention of any safety provision [...], inspect any goods and enter any premises other than premises occupied only as a person's residence.

(3) The officer may, for the purpose of ascertaining whether there has been any contravention of any safety provision, examine any procedure (including any arrangements for carrying out a test) connected with the production of any goods.

(4) If the officer has reasonable grounds for suspecting that any goods are manufactured or imported goods which have not been supplied in the United Kingdom since they were manufactured or imported he may—

(a) for the purpose of ascertaining whether there has been any contravention of any safety provision in relation to the goods, require any person carrying on a business, or employed in connection with the business, to produce any records relating to the business;

(b) for the purpose of ascertaining (by testing or otherwise) whether there has been any such contravention, seize and detain the goods;

(c) take copies of, or of any entry in, any records produced by virtue of paragraph (a) above.

(5) If the officer has reasonable grounds for suspecting that there has been a contravention in relation to any goods of any safety provision [...], he may—

(a) for the purpose of ascertaining whether there has been any such contravention, require any person carrying on a business, or employed in connection with a business, to produce any records relating to the business;

(b) for the purpose of ascertaining (by testing or otherwise) whether there has been any such contravention, seize and detain the goods;

(c) take copies of, or of any entry in, any records produced by virtue of paragraph (a) above.

(6) The officer may seize and detain—

(a) any goods or records which he has reasonable grounds for believing may be required as evidence in proceedings for an offence in respect of a contravention of any safety provision [...].

(b) any goods which he has reasonable grounds for suspecting may be liable to be forfeited under section 16 or 17 above.

(7) If and to the extent that it is reasonably necessary to do so to prevent a contravention of any safety provision [...], the officer may, for the purpose of exercising his power under subsection (4), (5) or (6) above to seize any goods or records—

(a) require any person having authority to do so to open any container or to open any vending machine; and

(b) himself open or break open any such container or machine where a requirement made under paragraph (a) above in relation to the container or machine has not been complied with.

30   Provisions supplemental to s. 29

(1) An officer seizing any goods or records under section 29 above shall inform the following persons that the goods or records have been so seized, that is to say—

(a) the person from whom they are seized; and

(b) in the case of imported goods seized on any premises under the control of the Commissioners of Customs and Excise, the importer of those goods (within the meaning of the Customs and Excise Management Act 1979).

(2) If a justice of the peace—

(a) is satisfied by any written information on oath that there are reasonable grounds for believing either—

(i) that any goods or records which any officer has power to inspect under section 29 above are on any premises and that their inspection is likely to disclose evidence that there has been a contravention of any safety provision [...]; or

(ii) that such a contravention has taken place, is taking place or is about to take place on any premises; and

(b) is also satisfied by any such information either—

(i) that admission to the premises has been or is likely to be refused and that notice of intention to apply for a warrant under this subsection has been given to the occupier; or

(ii) that an application for admission, or the giving of such a notice, would defeat the object of the entry or that the premises are unoccupied or that the occupier is temporarily absent and it might defeat the object of the entry to await his return,

the justice may by warrant under his hand, which shall continue in force for a period of one month, authorise any officer of an enforcement authority to enter the premises, if need be by force.

(3) An officer entering any premises by virtue of section 29 above or a warrant under subsection (2) above may take with him such other persons and such equipment as may appear to him necessary.

(4) On leaving any premises which a person is authorised to enter by a warrant under subsection (2) above, that person shall, if the premises are unoccupied or the occupier is temporarily absent, leave the premises as effectively secured against trespassers as he found them.

(6) Where any goods seized by an officer under section 29 above are submitted to a test, the officer shall inform the persons mentioned in subsection (1) above of the result of the test and, if—

    (a) proceedings are brought for an offence in respect of a contravention in relation to the goods of any safety provision [...] or for the forfeiture of the goods under section 16 or 17 above, or a suspension notice is served in respect of any goods; and

    (b) the officer is requested to do so and it is practicable to comply with the request,

the officer shall allow any person who is a party to the proceedings or, as the case may be, has an interest in the goods to which the notice relates to have the goods tested.

(7) The Secretary of State may by regulations provide that any test of goods seized under section 29 above by an officer of an enforcement authority shall—

    (a) be carried out at the expense of the authority in a manner and by a person prescribed by or determined under the regulations; or

    (b) be carried out either as mentioned in paragraph (a) above or by the authority in a manner prescribed by the regulations.

32   Obstruction of authorised officer

(1) Any person who—

    (a) intentionally obstructs any officer of an enforcement authority who is acting in pursuance of any provision of this Part or any customs officer who is so acting; or

    (b) intentionally fails to comply with any requirement made of him by any officer of any enforcement authority under any provision of this Part; or

    (c) without reasonable cause fails to give any officer of an enforcement authority who is so acting any other assistance or information which the officer may reasonably require of him for the purposes of the exercise of the officer's functions under any provision of this Part,

shall be guilty of an offence and liable on summary conviction to a fine not exceeding level 5 on the standard scale.

(2) A person shall be guilty of an offence if, in giving any information which is required of him by virtue of subsection (1)(c) above—

    (a) he makes any statement which he knows is false in a material particular; or

    (b) he recklessly makes a statement which is false in a material particular.

(3) A person guilty of an offence under subsection (2) above shall be liable—

    (a) on conviction on indictment, to a fine;

    (b) on summary conviction, to a fine not exceeding the statutory maximum.

33   Appeals against detention of goods

(1) Any person having an interest in any goods which are for the time being detained under any provision of this Part by an enforcement authority or by an officer of such an authority may apply for an order requiring the goods to be released to him or to another person.

(2) An application under this section may be made—

    (a) to any magistrates' court in which proceedings have been brought in England and Wales or Northern Ireland—

        (i)   for an offence in respect of a contravention in relation to the goods of any safety provision [...]; or

        (ii)   for the forfeiture of the goods under section 16 above;

    (b) where no such proceedings have been so brought, by way of complaint to a magistrates' court...

(3) On an application under this section to a magistrates' court..., an order requiring goods to be released shall be made only if the court... is satisfied—

(a) that proceedings—

(i)   for an offence in respect of a contravention in relation to the goods of any safety provision [...]; or

(ii) for the forfeiture of the goods under section 16 or 17 above, have not been brought or, having been brought, have been concluded without the goods being forfeited; and

(b) where no such proceedings have been brought, that more than six months have elapsed since the goods were seized.

(4) Any person aggrieved by an order made under this section by a magistrates' court in England and Wales or Northern Ireland, or by a decision of such a court not to make such an order, may appeal against that order or decision—

(a) in England and Wales, to the Crown Court;

(b) in Northern Ireland, to the county court;

and an order so made may contain such provision as appears to the court to be appropriate for delaying the coming into force of the order pending the making and determination of any appeal (including any application under section 111 of the Magistrates' Courts Act 1980 or Article 146 of the Magistrates' Courts (Northern Ireland) Order 1981 (statement of case)).

34   Compensation for seizure and detention

(1) Where an officer of an enforcement authority exercises any power under section 29 above to seize and detain goods, the enforcement authority shall be liable to pay compensation to any person having an interest in the goods in respect of any loss or damage caused by reason of the exercise of the power if—

(a) there has been no contravention in relation to the goods of any safety provision [...]; and

(b) the exercise of the power is not attributable to any neglect or default by that person.

(2) Any disputed question as to the right to or the amount of any compensation payable under this section shall be determined by arbitration...

PART V MISCELLANEOUS AND SUPPLEMENTAL

39   Defence of due diligence

(1) Subject to the following provisions of this section, in proceedings against any person for an offence to which this section applies it shall be a defence for that person to show that he took all reasonable steps and exercised all due diligence to avoid committing the offence.

41   Civil proceedings

(1) An obligation imposed by safety regulations shall be a duty owed to any person who may be affected by a contravention of the obligation and, subject to any provision to the contrary in the regulations and to the defences and other incidents applying to actions for breach of statutory duty, a contravention of any such obligation shall be actionable accordingly.

(2) This Act shall not be construed as conferring any other right of action in civil proceedings, apart from the right conferred by virtue of Part I of this Act, in respect of any loss or damage suffered in consequence of a contravention of a safety provision [...].

(3) Subject to any provision to the contrary in the agreement itself, an agreement shall not be void or unenforceable by reason only of a contravention of a safety provision [...].

(4) Liability by virtue of subsection (1) above shall not be limited or excluded by any contract term, by any notice or (subject to the power contained in subsection (1) above to limit or exclude it in safety regulations) by any other provision.

(5) Nothing in subsection (1) above shall prejudice the operation of section 12 of the Nuclear Installations Act 1965 (rights to compensation for certain breaches of duties confined to rights under that Act).

(6) In this section 'damage' includes personal injury and death.

45 Interpretation

(1) In this Act, except in so far as the context otherwise requires—

...

'business' includes a trade or profession and the activities of a professional or trade association or of a local authority or other public authority;

'conditional sale agreement', 'credit-sale agreement' and 'hire-purchase agreement' have the same meanings as in the Consumer Credit Act 1974 but as if in the definitions in that Act 'goods' had the same meaning as in this Act;

...

'goods' includes substances, growing crops and things comprised in land by virtue of being attached to it and any ship, aircraft or vehicle;

'information' includes accounts, estimates and returns;

...

'personal injury' includes any disease and any other impairment of a person's physical or mental condition;

'premises' includes any place and any ship, aircraft or vehicle;

'safety provision' means [...] any provision of safety regulations, a prohibition notice or a suspension notice;

'safety regulations' means regulations under section 11 above;

...

'substance' means any natural or artificial substance, whether in solid, liquid or gaseous form or in the form of a vapour, and includes substances that are comprised in or mixed with other goods;

'supply' and cognate expressions shall be construed in accordance with section 46 below;

Minors' Contracts Act 1987

(1987, c. 13)

2 Guarantees

Where—

(a) a guarantee is given in respect of an obligation of a party to a contract made after the commencement of this Act, and

(b) the obligation is unenforceable against him (or he repudiates the contract)

(c) because he was a minor when the contract was made,

the guarantee shall not for that reason alone be unenforceable against the guarantor.

3 Restitution

(1) Where—

(a) a person ('the plaintiff') has after the commencement of this Act entered into a contract with another ('the defendant'), and

(b) the contract is unenforceable against the defendant (or he repudiates it) because he was a minor when the contract was made,

the court may, if it is just and equitable to do so, require the defendant to transfer to the plaintiff any property acquired by the defendant under the contract, or any property representing it.

(2) Nothing in this section shall be taken to prejudice any other remedy available to the plaintiff.

Copyright, Designs and Patents Act 1988

(1988, c. 48)

96 Infringement actionable by copyright owner

(1) An infringement of copyright is actionable by the copyright owner.

(2) In an action for infringement of copyright all such relief by way of damages, injunctions, accounts or otherwise is available to the plaintiff as is available in respect of the infringement of any other property right.

97 Provisions as to damages in infringement action

(1) Where in an action for infringement of copyright it is shown that at the time of the infringement the defendant did not know, and had no reason to believe, that copyright subsisted in the work to which the action relates, the plaintiff is not entitled to damages against him, but without prejudice to any other remedy.

(2) The court may in an action for infringement of copyright having regard to all the circumstances, and in particular to—

(a) the flagrancy of the infringement, and

(b) any benefit accruing to the defendant by reason of the infringement,

award such additional damages as the justice of the case may require.

229 Rights and remedies of design right owner

(1) An infringement of design right is actionable by the design right owner.

(2) In an action for infringement of design right all such relief by way of damages, injunctions, accounts or otherwise is available to the plaintiff as is available in respect of the infringement of any other property right.

(3) The court may in an action for infringement of design right, having regard to all the circumstances and in particular to—

(a) the flagrancy of the infringement, and

(b) any benefit accruing to the defendant by reason of the infringement,

award such additional damages as the justice of the case may require.

253 Remedy for groundless threats of infringement proceedings.

(1) Where a person threatens another person with proceedings for infringement of design right, a person aggrieved by the threats may bring an action against him claiming—

(a) a declaration to the effect that the threats are unjustifiable;

(b) an injunction against the continuance of the threats;

(c) damages in respect of any loss which he has sustained by the threats.

(2) If the plaintiff proves that the threats were made and that he is a person aggrieved by them, he is entitled to the relief claimed unless the defendant shows that the acts in respect of which proceedings were threatened did constitute, or if done would have constituted, an infringement of the design right concerned.

(3) Proceedings may not be brought under this section in respect of a threat to bring proceedings for an infringement alleged to consist of making or importing anything.

(4) Mere notification that a design is protected by design right does not constitute a threat of proceedings for the purposes of this section.

Housing Act 1988

(1988, c. 50)

16   Access for repairs

It shall be an implied term of every assured tenancy that the tenant shall afford to the landlord access to the dwelling-house let on the tenancy and all reasonable facilities for executing therein any repairs which the landlord is entitled to execute.

27   Damages for unlawful eviction

(1) This section applies if, at any time after 9th June 1988, a landlord (in this section referred to as 'the landlord in default') or any person acting on behalf of the landlord in default unlawfully deprives the residential occupier of any premises of his occupation of the whole or part of the premises.

(2) This section also applies if, at any time after 9th June 1988, a landlord (in this section referred to as 'the landlord in default') or any person acting on behalf of the landlord in default—

> (a) attempts unlawfully to deprive the residential occupier of any premises of his occupation of the whole or part of the premises, or
>
> (b) knowing or having reasonable cause to believe that the conduct is likely to cause the residential occupier of any premises—
>
> > (i) to give up his occupation of the premises or any part thereof, or
> >
> > (ii) to refrain from exercising any right or pursuing any remedy in respect of the premises or any part thereof,

does acts likely to interfere with the peace or comfort of the residential occupier or members of his household, or persistently withdraws or withholds services reasonably required for the occupation of the premises as a residence, and, as a result, the residential occupier gives up his occupation of the premises as a residence.

(3) Subject to the following provisions of this section, where this section applies, the landlord in default shall, by virtue of this section, be liable to pay to the former residential occupier, in respect of his loss of the right to occupy the premises in question as his residence, damages assessed on the basis set out in section 28 below.

(4) Any liability arising by virtue of subsection (3) above—

> (a) shall be in the nature of a liability in tort; and
>
> (b) subject to subsection (5) below, shall be in addition to any liability arising apart from this section (whether in tort, contract or otherwise).

(5) Nothing in this section affects the right of a residential occupier to enforce any liability which arises apart from this section in respect of his loss of the right to occupy premises as his residence; but damages shall not be awarded both in respect of such a liability and in respect of a liability arising by virtue of this section on account of the same loss.

(6) No liability shall arise by virtue of subsection (3) above if—

> (a) before the date on which proceedings to enforce the liability are finally disposed of, the former residential occupier is reinstated in the premises in question in such circumstances that he becomes again the residential occupier of them; or
>
> (b) at the request of the former residential occupier, a court makes an order (whether in the nature of an injunction or otherwise) as a result of which he is reinstated as mentioned in paragraph (a) above;

and, for the purposes of paragraph (a) above, proceedings to enforce a liability are finally disposed of on the earliest date by which the proceedings (including any proceedings on or in consequence of an appeal) have been determined and any time for appealing or further appealing has expired, except that if any appeal is abandoned, the proceedings shall be taken to be disposed of on the date of the abandonment.

(7) If, in proceedings to enforce a liability arising by virtue of subsection (3) above, it appears to the court—

    (a) that, prior to the event which gave rise to the liability, the conduct of the former residential occupier or any person living with him in the premises concerned was such that it is reasonable to mitigate the damages for which the landlord in default would otherwise be liable, or

    (b) that, before the proceedings were begun, the landlord in default offered to reinstate the former residential occupier in the premises in question and either it was unreasonable of the former residential occupier to refuse that offer or, if he had obtained alternative accommodation before the offer was made, it would have been unreasonable of him to refuse that offer if he had not obtained that accommodation,

the court may reduce the amount of damages which would otherwise be payable to such amount as it thinks appropriate.

(8) In proceedings to enforce a liability arising by virtue of subsection (3) above, it shall be a defence for the defendant to prove that he believed, and had reasonable cause to believe—

    (b) that, where the liability would otherwise arise by virtue only of the doing of acts or the withdrawal or withholding of services, he had reasonable grounds for doing the acts or withdrawing or withholding the services in question.

28   The measure of damages

(1) The basis for the assessment of damages referred to in section 27(3) above is the difference in value, determined as at the time immediately before the residential occupier ceased to occupy the premises in question as his residence, between—

    (a) the value of the interest of the landlord in default determined on the assumption that the residential occupier continues to have the same right to occupy the premises as before that time; and

    (b) the value of that interest determined on the assumption that the residential occupier has ceased to have that right.

(3) For the purposes of the valuations referred to in subsection (1) above, it shall be assumed—

    (a) that the landlord in default is selling his interest on the open market to a willing buyer;

    (b) that neither the residential occupier nor any member of his family wishes to buy; and

    (c) that it is unlawful to carry out any substantial development of any of the land in which the landlord's interest subsists or to demolish the whole or part of any building on that land.

Road Traffic Act 1988

(1988, c. 52)

38   The Highway Code

(7) A failure on the part of a person to observe a provision of the Highway Code shall not of itself render that person liable to criminal proceedings of any kind but any such failure may in any proceedings (whether civil or criminal, and including proceedings for an offence under the Traffic Acts, the Public Passenger Vehicles Act 1981 or sections 18 to 23 of the Transport Act 1985) be relied upon by any party to the proceedings as tending to establish or negative any liability which is in question in those proceedings.

143   Users of motor vehicles to be insured or secured against third-party risks

(1) Subject to the provisions of this Part of this Act—

    (a) a person must not use a motor vehicle on a road [or other public place] unless there is in force in relation to the use of the vehicle by that person such a policy of insurance or such a security in respect of third party risks as complies with the requirements of this Part of this Act, and

(b) a person must not cause or permit any other person to use a motor vehicle on a road [or other public place] unless there is in force in relation to the use of the vehicle by that other person such a policy of insurance or such a security in respect of third party risks as complies with the requirements of this Part of this Act.

(2) If a person acts in contravention of subsection (1) above he is guilty of an offence.

(3) A person charged with using a motor vehicle in contravention of this section shall not be convicted if he proves—

(a) that the vehicle did not belong to him and was not in his possession under a contract of hiring or of loan,

(b) that he was using the vehicle in the course of his employment, and

(c) that he neither knew nor had reason to believe that there was not in force in relation to the vehicle such a policy of insurance or security as is mentioned in subsection (1) above.

(4) This Part of this Act does not apply to invalid carriages.

144   Exceptions from requirement of third-party insurance or security

(1) Section 143 of this Act does not apply to a vehicle owned by a person who has deposited and keeps deposited with the Accountant General of the [Senior Courts] the sum of [£500,000], at a time when the vehicle is being driven under the owner's control.

[(1A) The Secretary of State may by order made by statutory instrument substitute a greater sum for the sum for the time being specified in subsection (1) above.]

(2) Section 143 does not apply—

(a) to a vehicle owned—

(i) by the council of a county or county district in England and Wales [the Broads Authority], the Common Council of the City of London, the council of a London borough [a National Park Authority], the Inner London Education Authority [the London Fire and Emergency Planning Authority, an authority established for an area in England by an order under section 207 of the Local Government and Public Involvement in Health Act 2007 (joint waste authorities)], [, a joint authority (other than a police authority) established by Part 4 of the Local Government Act 1985, an economic prosperity board established under section 88 of the Local Democracy, Economic Development and Construction Act 2009 or a combined authority established under section 103 of that Act,]

(ii) by a [council constituted under section 2 of the Local Government etc. (Scotland) Act 1994] in Scotland, or

(iii) by a joint board or committee in England or Wales, or joint committee in Scotland, which is so constituted as to include among its members representatives of any such council,

at a time when the vehicle is being driven under the owner's control,

(b) to a vehicle owned by a police authority [or the Receiver for the Metropolitan Police district], at a time when it is being driven under the owner's control, or to a vehicle at a time when it is being driven for police purposes by or under the direction of a constable, or by a person employed by a police authority, or employed by the Receiver,

(c) to a vehicle at a time when it is being driven on a journey to or from any place undertaken for salvage purposes pursuant to the Merchant Shipping Act 1995,

[(da) to a vehicle owned by a health service body, as defined in section 60(7) of the National Health Service and Community Care Act 1990 by a Primary Care Trust established under section 18 of the National Health Service Act 2006 or by a Local Health Board established under section 11 of the National Health Service (Wales) Act 2006, at a time when the vehicle is being driven under the owner's control, (db) to an ambulance owned by a National Health Service trust established under section 25 of the National Health Service Act 2006, section 18 of the National Health Service (Wales) Act 2006 or the National Health Service (Scotland) Act 1978, at a time when a vehicle is being driven under the owner's control,

(dc) to an ambulance owned by an NHS foundation trust, at a time when the vehicle is being driven under the owner's control,]

(e) to a vehicle which is made available by the Secretary of State or the Welsh Ministers to any person, body or local authority in pursuance of [section 12 or 80 of the National Health Service (Wales) Act 2006, or section 10 or 38 of the National Health Service (Wales) Act 2006] at a time when it is being used in accordance with the terms on which it is so made available.

145   Requirements in respect of policies of insurance

(1) In order to comply with the requirements of this Part of this Act, a policy of insurance must satisfy the following conditions.

(2) The policy must be issued by an authorised insurer.

(3) Subject to subsection (4) below, the policy—

(a)   must insure such person, persons or classes of persons as may be specified in the policy in respect of any liability which may be incurred by him or them in respect of the death of or bodily injury to any person or damage to property caused by, or arising out of, the use of the vehicle on a road [or other public place] in Great Britain, and

[(aa) must, in the case of a vehicle normally based in the territory of another member State, insure him or them in respect of any civil liability which may be incurred by him or them as a result of an event related to the use of the vehicle in Great Britain if,—

(i)   according to the law of that territory, he or they would be required to be insured in respect of a civil liability which would arise under that law as a result of that event if the place where the vehicle was used when the event occurred were in that territory, and

(ii)   the cover required by that law would be higher than that required by paragraph (a) above, and]

(b)   must[, in the case of a vehicle normally based in Great Britain,] insure him or them in respect of any liability which may be incurred by him or them in respect of the use of the vehicle and of any trailer, whether or not coupled, in the territory other than Great Britain and Gibraltar of each of the member States of the Communities according to

[(i)   the law on compulsory insurance against civil liability in respect of the use of vehicles of the State in whose territory the event giving rise to the liability occurred; or

(ii)   if it would give higher cover, the law which would be applicable under this Part of this Act if the place where the vehicle was used when that event occurred were in Great Britain; and]

(c)   must also insure him or them in respect of any liability which may be incurred by him or them under the provisions of this Part of this Act relating to payment for emergency treatment.

(4) The policy shall not, by virtue of subsection (3)(a) above, be required—

(a) to cover liability in respect of the death, arising out of and in the course of his employment, of a person in the employment of a person insured by the policy or of bodily injury sustained by such a person arising out of and in the course of his employment, or

(b) to provide insurance of more than [£1,000,000] in respect of all such liabilities as may be incurred in respect of damage to property caused by, or arising out of, any one accident involving the vehicle, or

(c) to cover liability in respect of damage to the vehicle, or

(d) to cover liability in respect of damage to goods carried for hire or reward in or on the vehicle or in or on any trailer (whether or not coupled) drawn by the vehicle, or

    (e) to cover any liability of a person in respect of damage to property in his custody or under his control, or

    (f) to cover any contractual liability.

[(4A) In the case of a person—

    (a) carried in or upon a vehicle, or

    (b) entering or getting on to, or alighting from, a vehicle,

the provisions of paragraph (a) of subsection (4) above do not apply unless cover in respect of the liability referred to in that paragraph is in fact provided pursuant to a requirement of the Employers' Liability (Compulsory Insurance) Act 1969.]

148 Avoidance of certain exceptions to policies or securities

(1) Where a certificate of insurance or certificate of security has been delivered under section 147 of this Act to the person by whom a policy has been effected or to whom a security has been given, so much of the policy or security as purports to restrict—

    (a) the insurance of the persons insured by the policy, or

    (b) the operation of the security,

(as the case may be) by reference to any of the matters mentioned in subsection (2) below shall, as respects such liabilities as are required to be covered by a policy under section 145 of this Act, be of no effect.

(2) Those matters are—

    (a) the age or physical or mental condition of persons driving the vehicle,

    (b) the condition of the vehicle,

    (c) the number of persons that the vehicle carries,

    (d) the weight or physical characteristics of the goods that the vehicle carries,

    (e) the time at which or the areas within which the vehicle is used,

    (f) the horsepower or cylinder capacity or value of the vehicle,

    (g) the carrying on the vehicle of any particular apparatus, or

    (h) the carrying on the vehicle of any particular means of identification other than any means of identification required to be carried by or under [the Vehicles Excise and Registration Act 1994].

(3) Nothing in subsection (1) above requires an insurer or the giver of a security to pay any sum in respect of the liability of any person otherwise than in or towards the discharge of that liability.

(4) Any sum paid by an insurer or the giver of a security in or towards the discharge of any liability of any person which is covered by the policy or security by virtue only of subsection (1) above is recoverable by the insurer or giver of the security from that person.

(5) A condition in a policy or security issued or given for the purposes of this Part of this Act providing—

    (a) that no liability shall arise under the policy or security, or

    (b) that any liability so arising shall cease,

in the event of some specified thing being done or omitted to be done after the happening of the event giving rise to a claim under the policy or security, shall be of no effect in connection with such liabilities as are required to be covered by a policy under section 145 of this Act.

(6) Nothing in subsection (5) above shall be taken to render void any provision in a policy or security requiring the person insured or secured to pay to the insurer or the giver of the security any sums which the latter may have become liable to pay under the policy or security and which have been applied to the satisfaction of the claims of third parties.

(7) Notwithstanding anything in any enactment, a person issuing a policy of insurance under section 145 of this Act shall be liable to indemnify the persons or classes of persons specified in the policy in respect of any liability which the policy purports to cover in the case of those persons or classes of persons.

149   Avoidance of certain agreements as to liability towards passengers

(1) This section applies where a person uses a motor vehicle in circumstances such that under section 143 of this Act there is required to be in force in relation to his use of it such a policy of insurance or such a security in respect of third-party risks as complies with the requirements of this Part of this Act.

(2) If any other person is carried in or upon the vehicle when the user is so using it, any antecedent agreement or understanding between them (whether intended to be legally binding or not) shall be of no effect so far as it purports or might be held—

> (a) to negative or restrict any such liability of the user in respect of persons carried in or upon the vehicle as is required by section 145 of this Act to be covered by a policy of insurance, or
>
> (b) to impose any conditions with respect to the enforcement of any such liability of the user.

(3) The fact that a person so carried has willingly accepted as his the risk of negligence on the part of the user shall not be treated as negativing any such liability of the user.

(4) For the purposes of this section—

> (a) references to a person being carried in or upon a vehicle include references to a person entering or getting on to, or alighting from, the vehicle, and
>
> (b) the reference to an antecedent agreement is to one made at any time before the liability arose.

151   Duty of insurers of persons giving security to satisfy judgment against persons insured or secured against third-party risks

(1) This section applies where, after a certificate of insurance or certificate of security has been delivered under section 147 of this Act to the person by whom a policy has been effected or to whom a security has been given, a judgment to which this subsection applies is obtained.

(2) Subsection (1) above applies to judgments relating to a liability with respect to any matter where liability with respect to that matter is required to be covered by a policy of insurance under section 145 of this Act and either—

> (a) it is a liability covered by the terms of the policy or security to which the certificate relates, and the judgment is obtained against any person who is insured by the policy or whose liability is covered by the security, as the case may be, or
>
> (b) it is a liability, other than an excluded liability, which would be so covered if the policy insured all persons or, as the case may be, the security covered the liability of all persons, and the judgment is obtained against any person other than one who is insured by the policy or, as the case may be, whose liability is covered by the security.

(3) In deciding for the purposes of subsection (2) above whether a liability is or would be covered by the terms of a policy or security, so much of the policy or security as purports to restrict, as the case may be, the insurance of the persons insured by the policy or the operation of the security by reference to the holding by the driver of the vehicle of a licence authorising him to drive it shall be treated as of no effect.

(4) In subsection (2)(b) above 'excluded liability' means a liability in respect of the death of, or bodily injury to, or damage to the property of any person who, at the time of the use which gave rise to the liability, was allowing himself to be carried in or upon the vehicle and knew or had reason to believe that the vehicle had been stolen or unlawfully taken, not being a person who—

> (a) did not know and had no reason to believe that the vehicle had been stolen or unlawfully taken until after the commencement of his journey, and
>
> (b) could not reasonably have been expected to have alighted from the vehicle.

In this subsection the reference to a person being carried in or upon a vehicle includes a reference to a person entering or getting on to, or alighting from, the vehicle.

(5) Notwithstanding that the insurer may be entitled to avoid or cancel, or may have avoided or cancelled, the policy or security, he must, subject to the provisions of this section, pay to the persons entitled to the benefit of the judgment—

(a) as regards liability in respect of death or bodily injury, any sum payable under the judgment in respect of the liability, together with any sum which, by virtue of any enactment relating to interest on judgments, is payable in respect of interest on that sum,

(b) as regards liability in respect of damage to property, any sum required to be paid under subsection (6) below, and

(c) any amount payable in respect of costs.

(6) This subsection requires—

(a) where the total of any amounts paid, payable or likely to be payable under the policy or security in respect of damage to property caused by, or arising out of, the accident in question does not exceed [£1,000,000], the payment of any sum payable under the judgment in respect of the liability, together with any sum which, by virtue of any enactment relating to interest on judgments, is payable in respect of interest on that sum,

(b) where that total exceeds [£1,000,000], the payment of either—

(i) such proportion of any sum payable under the judgment in respect of the liability as [£1,000,000] bears to that total, together with the same proportion of any sum which, by virtue of any enactment relating to interest on judgments, is payable in respect of interest on that sum, or

(ii) the difference between the total of any amounts already paid under the policy or security in respect of such damage and [£1,000,000], together with such proportion of any sum which, by virtue of any enactment relating to interest on judgments, is payable in respect of interest on any sum payable under the judgment in respect of the liability as the difference bears to that sum,

whichever is the less, unless not less than [£1,000,000] has already been paid under the policy or security in respect of such damage (in which case nothing is payable).

(7) Where an insurer becomes liable under this section to pay an amount in respect of a liability of a person who is insured by a policy or whose liability is covered by a security, he is entitled to recover from that person—

(a) that amount, in a case where he became liable to pay it by virtue only of subsection (3) above, or

(b) in a case where that amount exceeds the amount for which he would, apart from the provisions of this section, be liable under the policy or security in respect of that liability, the excess.

(8) Where an insurer becomes liable under this section to pay an amount in respect of a liability of a person who is not insured by a policy or whose liability is not covered by a security, he is entitled to recover the amount from that person or from any person who—

(a) is insured by the policy, or whose liability is covered by the security, by the terms of which the liability would be covered if the policy insured all persons or, as the case may be, the security covered the liability of all persons, and

(b) caused or permitted the use of the vehicle which gave rise to the liability.

(9) In this section—

(a) 'insurer' includes a person giving a security,

(c) 'liability covered by the terms of the policy or security' means a liability which is covered by the policy or security or which would be so covered but for the fact that the insurer is entitled to avoid or cancel, or has avoided or cancelled, the policy or security.

153   Bankruptcy, etc., of insured or secured persons not to affect claims by third parties

(1) Where, after a certificate of insurance or certificate of security has been delivered under section 147 of this Act to the person by whom a policy has been effected or to whom a security has been given, any of the events mentioned in subsection (2) below happens, the happening of that event shall, notwithstanding anything in the Third Parties (Rights Against Insurers) Act 1930, not affect

any such liability of that person as is required to be covered by a policy of insurance under section 145 of this Act.

(2) In the case of the person by whom the policy was effected or to whom the security was given, the events referred to in subsection (1) above are—

(a) that he becomes bankrupt or makes a composition or arrangement with his creditors or that his estate is sequestrated or he grants a trust deed for his creditors,

(b) that he dies and—

    (i)   his estate falls to be administered in accordance with an order under section 421 of the Insolvency Act 1986,

    (ii)   an award of sequestration of his estate is made, or

    (iii)   a judicial factor is appointed to administer his estate under section 11A of the Judicial Factors (Scotland) Act 1889,

(c) that if that person is a company—

    (i)   a winding-up order [. . .] is made with respect of the company [or the company enters administration],

    (ii)   a resolution for a voluntary winding-up is passed with respect to the company,

    (iii)   a receiver or manager of the company's business or undertaking is duly appointed, or

    (iv)   possession is taken, by or on behalf of the holders of any debentures secured by a floating charge, of any property comprised in or subject to the charge.

(3) Nothing in subsection (1) above affects any rights conferred by the Third Parties (Rights Against Insurers) Act 1930 on the person to whom the liability was incurred, being rights so conferred against the person by whom the policy was issued or the security was given.

157   Payment for hospital treatment of traffic casualties

(1) Subject to subsection (2) below, where—

(a) a payment, other than a payment under section 158 of this Act, is made (whether or not with an admission of liability) in respect of the death of, or bodily injury to, any person arising out of the use of a motor vehicle on a road or in a place to which the public have a right of access, and

(b) the payment is made—

    (i)   by an authorised insurer, the payment being made under or in consequence of a policy issued under section 145 of this Act, or

    (ii)   by the owner of a vehicle in relation to the use of which a security under this Part of this Act is in force, or

    (iii)   by the owner of a vehicle who has made a deposit under this Part of this Act, and

(c) the person who has so died or been bodily injured has to the knowledge of the insurer or owner, as the case may be, received treatment at a hospital, whether as an in-patient or as an out-patient, in respect of the injury so arising,

the insurer or owner must pay the expenses reasonably incurred by the hospital in affording the treatment, after deducting from the expenses any moneys actually received in payment of a specific charge for the treatment, not being moneys received under any contributory scheme.

(2) The amount to be paid shall not exceed [£2,949.00] for each person treated as an inpatient or [£295.00] for each person treated as an out-patient.

(3) For the purposes of this section 'expenses reasonably incurred' means—

(a) in relation to a person who receives treatment at a hospital as an in-patient, an amount for each day he is maintained in the hospital representing the average daily cost, for each in-patient, of the maintenance of the hospital and the staff of the hospital and the maintenance and treatment of the in-patients in the hospital, and

(b) in relation to a person who receives treatment at a hospital as an out-patient, reasonable expenses actually incurred.

158 Payment for emergency treatment of traffic casualties

(1) Subsection (2) below applies where—

    (a) medical or surgical treatment or examination is immediately required as a result of bodily injury (including fatal injury) to a person caused by, or arising out of, the use of a motor vehicle on a road and

    (b) the treatment or examination so required (in this Part of this Act referred to as 'emergency treatment') is effected by a legally qualified medical practitioner.

(2) The person who was using the vehicle at the time of the event out of which the bodily injury arose must, on a claim being made in accordance with the provisions of section 159 of this Act, pay to the practitioner (or, where emergency treatment is effected by more than one practitioner, to the practitioner by whom it is first effected)—

    (a) a fee of [£21.30] in respect of each person in whose case the emergency treatment is effected by him, and

    (b) a sum, in respect of any distance in excess of two miles which he must cover in order—

        (i)   to proceed from the place from which he is summoned to the place where the emergency treatment is carried out by him, and

        (ii) to return to the first mentioned place, equal to [41 pence] for every complete mile and additional part of a mile of that distance.

(3) Where emergency treatment is first effected in a hospital, the provisions of subsections (1) and (2) above with respect to payment of a fee shall, so far as applicable, but subject (as regards the recipient of a payment) to the provisions of section 159 of this Act, have effect with the substitution of references to the hospital for references to a legally qualified medical practitioner.

(4) Liability incurred under this section by the person using a vehicle shall, where the event out of which it arose was caused by the wrongful act of another person, be treated for the purposes of any claim to recover damage by reason of that wrongful act as damage sustained by the person using the vehicle.

159 Supplementary provisions as to payments for treatment

(2) A claim for a payment under section 158 of this Act may be made at the time when the emergency treatment is effected, by oral request to the person who was using the vehicle, and if not so made must be made by request in writing served on him within seven days from the day on which the emergency treatment was effected.

(4) A payment made under section 158 of this Act shall operate as a discharge, to the extent of the amount paid, of any liability of the person who was using the vehicle, or of any other person, to pay any sum in respect of the expenses of remuneration of the practitioner or hospital concerned of or for effecting the emergency treatment.

Road Traffic (Consequential Provisions) Act 1988

(1988, c. 54)

7 Saving for law of nuisance

Nothing in the Road Traffic Acts authorises a person to use on a road a vehicle so constructed or used as to cause a public or private nuisance...or affects the liability, whether under statute or common law, of the driver or owner so using a vehicle.

Employment Act 1989

(1989, c. 38)

11   Exemption of Sikhs from requirements as to wearing of safety helmets on construction sites

(1) Any requirement to wear a safety helmet which (apart from this section) would, by virtue of any statutory provision or rule of law, be imposed on a Sikh who is on a construction site shall not apply to him at any time when he is wearing a turban.

(2) Accordingly, where—

(a) a Sikh who is on a construction site is for the time being wearing a turban, and

(b) (apart from this section) any associated requirement would, by virtue of any statutory provision or rule of law, be imposed—

(i)   on the Sikh, or

(ii) on the other person,

in connection with the wearing by the Sikh of a safety helmet, that requirement shall not apply to the Sikh or (as the case may be) to that other person.

(4) It is hereby declared that, where a person does not comply with any requirement, being a requirement which for the time being does not apply to him by virtue of subsection (1) or (2)—

(a) he shall not be liable in tort to any person in respect of any injury, loss or damage caused by his failure to comply with that requirement...

(5) If a Sikh who is on a construction site—

(a) does not comply with any requirement to wear a safety helmet, being a requirement which for the time being does not apply to him by virtue of subsection (1), and

(b) in consequence of any act or omission of some other person sustains any injury, loss or damage which is to any extent attributable to the fact that he is not wearing a safety helmet in compliance with the requirement,

that other person shall, if liable to the Sikh in tort (or, in Scotland, in an action for reparation), be so liable only to the extent that injury, loss or damage would have been sustained by the Sikh even if he had been wearing a safety helmet in compliance with the requirement.

(6) Where—

(a) the act or omission referred to in subsection (5) causes the death of the Sikh, and

(b) the Sikh would have sustained some injury (other than loss of life) in consequence of the act or omission even if he had been wearing a safety helmet in compliance with the requirement in question,

the amount of any damages which, by virtue of that subsection, are recoverable in tort (or, in Scotland, in an action for reparation) in respect of that injury shall not exceed the amount of any damages which would (apart from that subsection) be so recoverable in respect of the Sikh's death.

(7) In this section—

'injury' includes loss of life, any impairment of a person's physical or mental condition and any disease; ...

Law of Property (Miscellaneous Provisions) Act 1989

(1989, c. 34)

1   Deeds and their execution

(1) Any rule of law which—

(a) restricts the substances on which a deed may be written;

(b) requires a seal for the valid execution of an instrument as a deed by an individual; or

(c) requires authority by one person to another to deliver an instrument as a deed on his behalf to be given by deed,

is abolished.

(2) An instrument shall not be a deed unless—

(a) it makes it clear on its face that it is intended to be a deed by the person making it or, as the case may be, by the parties to it (whether by describing itself as a deed or expressing itself to be executed or signed as a deed or otherwise); and

(b) it is validly executed as a deed

[(i) by that person or a person authorised to execute it in the name or on behalf of that person, or

(ii) by one or more of those parties or a person authorised to execute it in the name or on behalf of one of more of those parties.]

[(2A) For the purposes of subsection (2)(a) above, an instrument shall not be taken to make it clear on its face that it is intended to be a deed merely because it is executed under seal.]

(3) An instrument is validly executed as a deed by an individual if, and only if—

(a) it is signed—

(i) by him in the presence of a witness who attests the signature; of

(ii) at his direction and in his presence and the presence of two witnesses who each attest the signature; and

(b) it is delivered as a deed [...].

(4) In subsections (2) and (3) above 'sign', in relation to an instrument, includes

[(a) an individual signing the name of the person or party on whose behalf he executes the instrument; and

(b) making one's mark on the instrument,

and 'signature' is to be construed accordingly.]

[(4A) Subsection (3) above applies in the case of an instrument executed by an individual in the name or on behalf of another person whether or not that person is also an individual.]

(5) Where [a relevant lawyer, or an agent or employee of a relevant lawyer], in the course of or in connection with a transaction [...], purports to deliver an instrument as a deed on behalf of a party to the instrument, it shall be conclusively presumed in favour of a purchaser that he is authorised so to deliver the instrument.

(6) In subsection (5) above—

['purchaser' has the same meaning] as in the Law of Property Act 1925;]

['relevant lawyer' means a person who, for the purposes of the Legal Services Act 2007, is an authorised person in relation to an activity which constitutes a reserved instrument activity (within the meaning of that Act);].

(7) Where an instrument under seal that constitutes a deed is required for the purposes of an Act passed before this section comes into force, this section shall have effect as to signing, sealing or delivery of an instrument by an individual in place of any provision of that Act as to signing, sealing or delivery.

(10) The references in this section to the execution of a deed by an individual do not include execution by a corporation sole and the reference in subsection (7) above to signing, sealing or delivery by an individual does not include signing, sealing or delivery by such a corporation.

(11) Nothing in this section applies in relation to instruments delivered as deeds before this section comes into force.

2   Contracts for sale etc. of land to be made by signed writing

(1) A contract for the sale or other disposition of an interest in land can only be made in writing and only by incorporating all the terms which the parties have expressly agreed in one document or, where contracts are exchanged, in each.

(2) The terms may be incorporated in a document either by being set out in it or by reference to some other document.

(3) The document incorporating the terms or, where contracts are exchanged, one of the documents incorporating them (but not necessarily the same one) must be signed by or on behalf of each party to the contract.

(4) Where a contract for the sale or other disposition of an interest in land satisfies the conditions of this section by reason only of the rectification of one or more documents in pursuance of an order of a court, the contract shall come into being, or be deemed to have come into being, at such time as may be specified in the order.

(5) This section does not apply in relation to—

    (a) a contract to grant such a lease as is mentioned in section 54(2) of the Law of Property Act 1925 (short leases);

    (b) a contract made in the course of a public auction; or

    [(c) a contract regulated under the Financial Services and Markets Act 2000, other than a regulated mortgage contract, a regulated home reversion plan or a regulated home purchase plan;]

and nothing in this section affects the creation or operation of resulting, implied or constructive trusts.

(6) In this section—

'disposition' has the same meaning as in the Law of Property Act 1925;

'interest in land' means any estate, interest or charge in or over land [. . .]

['regulated mortgage contract', 'regulated home reversion plan' and 'regulated home purchase plan' must be read with—

    (a) section 22 of the Financial Services and Markets Act 2000,

    (b) any relevant order under that section, and

    (c) Schedule 2 to that Act.]

(7) Nothing in this section shall apply in relation to contracts made before this section comes into force.

(8) Section 40 of the Law of Property Act 1925 (which is superseded by this section) shall cease to have effect.

3 Abolition of rule in *Brian v Fothergill*

The rule of law known as the rule in *Brian v Fothergill* is abolished in relation to contracts made after this section comes into force.

Broadcasting Act 1990

(1990, c. 42)

166 Defamatory material

(1) For the purposes of the law of libel and slander [. . .] the publication of words in the course of any programme included in a programme service shall be treated as publication in permanent form.

(2) Subsection (1) above shall apply for the purposes of section 3 of each of the Defamation Acts (slander of title etc.) as it applies for the purposes of the law of libel and slander.

    . . .

(4) In this section 'the Defamation Acts' means the Defamation Act 1952 and the Defamation Act (Northern Ireland) 1955.

Section 203(1)   **SCHEDULE 20**

MINOR AND CONSEQUENTIAL AMENDMENTS

Parliamentary Papers Act 1840 (c. 9)

1. Section 3 (protection in respect of proceedings for printing extracts from or abstracts of parliamentary papers) shall have effect as if the reference to printing included a reference to including in a programme service.

Courts and Legal Services Act 1990

(1990, c. 41)

8   Powers of Court of Appeal to award damages

(1) In this section 'case' means any case where the Court of Appeal has power to order a new trial on the ground that damages awarded by a jury are excessive or inadequate.

(2) Rules of court may provide for the Court of Appeal, in such classes of case as may be specified in the rules, to have power, in place of ordering a new trial, to substitute for the sum awarded by the jury such sum as appears to the court to be proper.

61   Right of barrister to enter into contract for the provision of his services

(1) Any rule of law which prevents a barrister from entering into a contract for the provision of his services as a barrister is hereby abolished.

(2) Nothing in subsection (1) prevents the General Council of the Bar from making rules (however described) which prohibit barristers from entering into contracts or restrict their right to do so.

Environmental Protection Act 1990

(1990, c. 43)

PART II WASTE ON LAND

33   Prohibition on unauthorised or harmful deposit, treatment or disposal etc. of waste

. . .

34   Duty of care etc. as respects waste

(1) Subject to subsection (2) below, it shall be the duty of any person who imports, produces, carries, keeps, treats or disposes of controlled waste or, as a broker, has control of such waste, to take all such measures applicable to him in that capacity as are reasonable in the circumstances—

    (a)   to prevent any contravention by any other person of section 33 above;

  [(aa) to prevent any contravention by any person of regulation 12 of the 2007 Regulations or of an environmental permit;]

    (b)   to prevent the escape of the waste from his control or that of any other person;

    (c)   on the transfer of the waste, to secure—

        (i)   that the transfer is only to an authorised person or to a person for authorised transport purposes; and

       (ii) that there is transferred such a written description of the waste as will enable other persons to avoid a contravention of that section [or regulation 12 of the

2007 Regulations, or a contravention of a condition of an environmental permit] and to comply with the duty under this subsection as respects the escape of waste.

(2) The duty imposed by subsection (1) above does not apply to an occupier of domestic property as respects the household waste produced on the property.

(6) Any person who fails to comply with the duty imposed by subsection (1) above or with any requirement imposed under subsection (5) above shall be liable—

(a) on summary conviction, to a fine not exceeding the statutory maximum; and

(b) on conviction on indictment, to a fine.

(7) The Secretary of State shall, after consultation with such persons or bodies as appear to him representative of the interests concerned, prepare and issue a code of practice for the purpose of providing to persons practical guidance on how to discharge the duty imposed on them by subsection (1) above.

[58B Litigation funding agreements

(1) A litigation funding agreement which satisfies all of the conditions applicable to it by virtue of this section shall not be unenforceable by reason only of its being a litigation funding agreement.]

73 Appeals and other provisions relating to legal proceedings and civil liability

(6) Where any damage is caused by waste which has been deposited in or on land, any person who deposited it, or knowingly caused or knowingly permitted it to be deposited, in either case so as to commit an offence under section 33(1) or 63(2) above, is liable for the damage except where the damage—

(a) was due wholly to the fault of the person who suffered it; or

(b) was suffered by a person who voluntarily accepted the risk of the damage being caused;

but without prejudice to any liability arising otherwise than under this subsection.

(7) The matters which may be proved by way of defence under section 33(7) above may be proved also by way of defence to an action brought under subsection (6) above.

(8) In subsection (6) above—

'damage' includes the death of, or injury to, any person (including any disease and any impairment of physical or mental condition); and

'fault' has the same meaning as in the Law Reform (Contributory Negligence) Act 1945.

(9) For the purposes of the following enactments—

(a) the Fatal Accidents Act 1976;

(b) the Law Reform (Contributory Negligence) Act 1945; and

(c) the Limitation Act 1980; ...

[PART IIA CONTAMINATED LAND]

[78A Preliminary

(2) 'Contaminated land' is any land which appears to the local authority in whose area it is situated to be in such a condition, by reason of substances in, on or under the land, that—

(a) significant harm is being caused or there is a significant possibility of such harm being caused; or

(b) [significant pollution of controlled waters is being caused or there is a significant possibility of such pollution being caused];

and, in determining whether any land appears to be such land, a local authority shall, subject to subsection (5) below, act in accordance with guidance issued by the Secretary of State in accordance with section 78YA below with respect to the manner in which that determination is to be made.

(7) 'Remediation' means—

(a) the doing of anything for the purpose of assessing the condition of—

(i) the contaminated land in question;

    (ii)   any controlled waters affected by that land; or

    (iii) any land adjoining or adjacent to that land;

  (b) the doing of any works, the carrying out of any operations or the taking of any steps in relation to any such land or waters for the purpose—

    (i)   of preventing or minimising, or remedying or mitigating the effects of, any significant harm, or any pollution of controlled waters, by reason of which the contaminated land is such land; or

    (ii) of restoring the land or waters to their former state; or

  (c) the making of subsequent inspections from time to time for the purpose of keeping under review the condition of the land or waters;

and cognate expressions shall be construed accordingly.]

[78E   Duty of enforcing authority to require remediation of contaminated land etc.

  (1) In any case where—

  (a) any land has been designated as a special site by virtue of section 78C(7) or 78D(6) above, or

  (b) a local authority has identified any contaminated land (other than a special site) in its area,

the enforcing authority shall, in accordance with such procedure as may be prescribed and subject to the following provisions of this Part, serve on each person who is an appropriate person a notice (in this Part referred to as a 'remediation notice') specifying what that person is to do by way of remediation and the periods within which he is required to do each of the things so specified.]

[78K   Liability in respect of contaminating substances which escape to other land

  (1) A person who has caused or knowingly permitted any substances to be in, on or under any land shall also be taken for the purposes of this Part to have caused or, as the case may be, knowingly permitted those substances to be in, on or under any other land to which they appear to have escaped.

  (2) Subsections (3) and (4) below apply in any case where it appears that any substances are or have been in, on or under any land (in this section referred to as 'land') as a result of their escape, whether directly or indirectly, from other land in, on or under which a person caused or knowingly permitted them to be.

  (3) Where this subsection applies, no remediation notice shall require a person—

  (a) who is the owner or occupier of land A, and

  (b) who has not caused or knowingly permitted the substances in question to be in, on or under that land,

to do anything by way of remediation to any land or waters (other than land or waters of which he is the owner or occupier) in consequence of land A appearing to be in such a condition, by reason of the presence of those substances in, on or under it, that significant harm [, or significant pollution of controlled waters,] is being caused, or there is a significant possibility of such harm [or pollution] being caused, or that pollution of controlled waters is being, or is likely to be caused.

  (4) Where this subsection applies, no remediation notice shall require a person—

  (a) who is the owner or occupier of land A, and

  (b) who has not caused or knowingly permitted the substances in question to be in, on or under that land,

to do anything by way of remediation in consequence of any further land in, on or under which those substances or any of them appear to be or to have been present as a result of their escape from land ('land B') appearing to be in such a condition, by reason of the presence of those substances in, on or under it, that significant harm [, or significant pollution of controlled waters,] is being caused, or there is a significant possibility of such harm [or pollution] being caused, or that pollution of controlled waters is being, or is likely to be caused, unless he is also the owner or occupier of land B.

(5) In any case where—

    (a) a person ('person A') has caused or knowingly permitted any substances to be in, on, or under any land,

    (b) another person ('person B') who has not caused or knowingly permitted those substances to be in, on or under that land becomes the owner or occupier of that land, and

    (c) the substances, or any of the substances, mentioned in paragraph (a) above appear to have escaped to other land,

no remediation notice shall require person B to do anything by way of remediation to that other land in consequence of the apparent acts or omissions of person A, except to the extent that person B caused or knowingly permitted the escape.

(6) Nothing in subsection (3), (4) or (5) above prevents the enforcing authority from doing anything by way of remediation under section 78N below which it could have done apart from that subsection, but the authority shall not be entitled under section 78P below to recover from any person any part of the cost incurred by the authority in doing by way of remediation anything which it is precluded by subsection (3), (4) or (5) above from requiring that person to do.

(7) in this section, 'appear' means appear to the enforcing authority, and cognate expressions shall be construed accordingly.]

[78M   Offences of not complying with a remediation notice

(1) If a person on whom an enforcing authority serves a remediation notice fails, without reasonable excuse, to comply with any of the requirements of the notice, he shall be guilty of an offence.]

[78N   Powers of the enforcing authority to carry out remediation

(1) Where this section applies, the enforcing authority shall itself have power, in a case falling within paragraph (a) or (b) of section 78E(1) above, to do what is appropriate by way of remediation to the relevant land or waters.]

[78P   Recovery of, and security for, the cost of remediation by the enforcing authority

(1) Where, by virtue of section 78N(3)(a), (c), (e) or (f) above, the enforcing authority does any particular thing by way of remediation, it shall be entitled, subject to sections 78J(7) and 78K(6) above, to recover the reasonable cost incurred in doing it from the appropriate person or, if there are two or more appropriate persons in relation to the thing in question, from those persons in proportions determined pursuant to section 78F(7) above.

(2) In deciding whether to recover the cost, and, if so, how much of the cost, which it is entitled to recover under subsection (1) above, the enforcing authority shall have regard—

    (a) to any hardship which the recovery may cause to the person from whom the cost is recoverable; and

    (b) to any guidance issued by the Secretary of State for the purposes of this subsection.

(3) Subsection (4) below shall apply in any case where—

    (a) any cost is recoverable under subsection (1) above from a person—

        (i)   who is the owner of any premises which consist of or include the contaminated land in question; and

        (ii) who caused or knowingly permitted the substances, or any of the substances, by reason of which the land is contaminated and to be in, on or under the land; and

    (b) the enforcing authority serves a notice under this subsection (in this Part referred to as a 'charging notice') on that person.

(4) Where this subsection applies—

    (a) the cost shall carry interest, at such reasonable rate as the enforcing authority may determine, from the date of service of the notice until the whole amount is paid; and

    (b) subject to the following provisions of this section, the cost and accrued interest shall be a charge on the premises mentioned in subsection (3)(a)(i) above.]

PART III STATUTORY NUISANCES AND CLEAN AIR

79 Statutory nuisances and inspections therefor

(1) [Subject to subsections (1A) to (6A) below], the following matters constitute 'statutory nuisances' for the purposes of this Part, that is to say—

    (a)   any premises in such a state as to be prejudicial to health or a nuisance;

    (b)   smoke emitted from premises so as to be prejudicial to health or a nuisance;

    (c)   fumes or gases emitted from premises so as to be prejudicial to health or a nuisance;

    (d)   any dust, steam, smell or other effluvia arising on industrial, trade or business premises and being prejudicial to health or a nuisance;

    (e)   any accumulation or deposit which is prejudicial to health or a nuisance;

    (f)   any animal kept in such a place or manner as to be prejudicial to health or a nuisance;

  [(fa) any insects emanating from relevant industrial, trade or business premises and being prejudicial to health or a nuisance;]

  [(fb) artificial light emitted from premises so as to be prejudicial to health or a nuisance;]

    (g)   noise emitted from premises so as to be prejudicial to health or a nuisance;

  [(ga) noise that is prejudicial to health or a nuisance and is emitted from or caused by a vehicle, machinery or equipment in a street or, in Scotland, road;]

    (h)   any other matter declared by any enactment to be a statutory nuisance;

and it shall be the duty of every local authority to cause its area to be inspected from time to time to detect any statutory nuisances which ought to be dealt with under section 80 below or sections 80 and 80A below and, where a complaint of a statutory nuisance is made to it by a person living within its area, to take such steps as are reasonably practicable to investigate the complaint.

[(1A) No matter shall constitute a statutory nuisance to the extent that it consists of, or is caused by, any land being in a contaminated state.]

80 Summary proceedings for statutory nuisances

(1) [Subject to subsection (2A)] Where a local authority is satisfied that a statutory nuisance exists, or is likely to occur or recur, in the area of the authority, the local authority shall serve a notice ('an abatement notice') imposing all or any of the following requirements—

    (a) requiring the abatement of the nuisance or prohibiting or restricting its occurrence or recurrence;

    (b) requiring the execution of such works, and the taking of such other steps, as may be necessary for any of those purposes,

and the notice shall specify the time or times within which the requirements of the notice are to be complied with.

(2) [Subject to section 80A(1) below, the abatement notice] shall be served—

    (a) except in a case falling within paragraph (b) or (c) below, on the person responsible for the nuisance;

    (b) where the nuisance arises from any defect of a structural character, on the owner of the premises;

    (c) where the person responsible for the nuisance cannot be found or the nuisance has not yet occurred, on the owner or occupier of the premises.

[(2A) Where a local authority is satisfied that a statutory nuisance falling within paragraph (g) of section 79(1) above exists, or is likely to occur or recur, in the area of the authority, the authority shall—

    (a) serve an abatement notice in respect of the nuisance in accordance with subsections (1) and (2) above; or

    (b) take such other steps as it thinks appropriate for the purpose of persuading the appropriate person to abate the nuisance or prohibit or restrict its occurrence or recurrence.

(2B) If a local authority has taken steps under subsection (2A)(b) above and either of the conditions in subsection (2C) below is satisfied, the authority shall serve an abatement notice in respect of the nuisance.

(2C) The conditions are—

    (a) that the authority is satisfied at any time before the end of the relevant period that the steps taken will not be successful in persuading the appropriate person to abate the nuisance or prohibit or restrict its occurrence or recurrence;

    (b) that the authority is satisfied at the end of the relevant period that the nuisance continues to exist, or continues to be likely to occur or recur, in the area of the authority.

(2D) The relevant period is the period of seven days starting with the day on which the authority was first satisfied that the nuisance existed, or was likely to occur or recur.

(2E) The appropriate person is the person on whom the authority would otherwise be required under subsection (2A)(a) above to serve an abatement notice in respect of the nuisance.]

(3) [A person served with an abatement notice] may appeal against the notice to a magistrates' court [or, in Scotland, the sheriff] within the period of twenty-one days beginning with the date on which he was served with the notice.

(4) If a person on whom an abatement notice is served, without reasonable excuse, contravenes or fails to comply with any requirement or prohibition imposed by the notice, he shall be guilty of an offence.

(7) Subject to subsection (8) below, in any proceedings for an offence under subsection (4) above in respect of a statutory nuisance it shall be a defence to prove that the best practicable means were used to prevent, or to counteract the effects of, the nuisance.

(8) The defence under subsection (7) above is not available—

    (a)   in the case of a nuisance falling within paragraph (a), (d), (e), (f)[, (fa)] or (g) of section 79(1) above except where the nuisance arises on industrial, trade or business premises;

    [(aza) in the case of a nuisance falling within paragraph (fb) of section 79(1) above except where—

        (i)   the artificial light is emitted from industrial, trade or business premises, or

        (ii) the artificial light (not being light to which sub-paragraph (i) applies) is emitted by lights used for the purpose only of illuminating an outdoor relevant sports facility;]

    [(aa) in the case of a nuisance falling within paragraph (ga) o section 79(1) above except where the noise is emitted from or caused by a vehicle, machinery or equipment being used for industrial, trade or business purposes;]

    (b)   in the case of a nuisance falling within paragraph (b) of section 79(1) above except where the smoke is emitted from a chimney; and

    (c)   in the case of a nuisance falling within paragraph (c) or (h) of section 79(1) above.

[80A Abatement notice in respect of noise in street
    ...]

82 Summary proceedings by person aggrieved by statutory nuisances

(1) A magistrates' court may act under this section on a complaint [or, in Scotland, the sheriff may act under this section on a summary application,] made by any person on the ground that he is aggrieved by the existence of a statutory nuisance.

(2) If the magistrates' court [or, in Scotland, the sheriff] is satisfied that the alleged nuisance exists, or that although abated it is likely to recur on the same premises [or, in the case of a nuisance within section 79(1)(ga) above, in the same street or, in Scotland, road], the court [or the sheriff] shall make an order for either or both of the following purposes—

    (a) requiring the defendant [or, in Scotland, the defender] to abate the nuisance, within a time specified in the order, and to execute any work necessary for that purpose;

    (b) prohibiting a recurrence of the nuisance, and requiring the defendant [or defender], within a time specified in the order, to execute any works necessary to prevent the recurrence, and[, in England and Wales,] may also impose on the defendant a fine not exceeding level 5 on the standard scale.

(3) If the magistrates' court [or the sheriff] is satisfied that the alleged nuisance exists and is such as, in the opinion of the court [or the sheriff], to render premises unfit for human habitation, an order under subsection (2) above may prohibit the use of the premises for human habitation until the premises are, to the satisfaction of the court, rendered fit for that purpose.

(4) Proceedings for an order under subsection (2) above shall be brought—

    (a) except in a case falling within [paragraph (b), (c) or (d) below], against the person responsible for the nuisance;

    (b) where the nuisance arises from any defect of a structural character, against the owner of the premises;

    (c) where the person responsible for the nuisance cannot be found, against the owner or occupier of the premises.

    [(d) in the case of a statutory nuisance within section 79(1)(ga) above caused by noise emitted from or caused by an unattended vehicle or unattended machinery or equipment, against the person responsible for the vehicle, machinery or equipment.]

(5) [Subject to subsection (5A) below, where] more than one person is responsible for a statutory nuisance, subsections (1) to (4) above shall apply to each of those persons whether or not what any one of them is responsible for would by itself amount to a nuisance.

[(5A) In relation to a statutory nuisance within section 79(1)(ga) above for which more than one person is responsible (whether or not what any one of those persons is responsible for would by itself amount to such a nuisance), subsection (4)(a) above shall apply with the substitution of 'each person responsible for the nuisance who can be found' for 'the person responsible for the nuisance'.

(5B) In relation to a statutory nuisance within section 79(1)(ga) above caused by noise emitted from or caused by an unattended vehicle or unattended machinery or equipment for which more than one person is responsible, subsection (4)(d) above shall apply with the substitution of 'any person' for 'the person'.]

(8) A person who, without reasonable excuse, contravenes any requirement or prohibition imposed by an order under subsection (2) above shall be guilty of an offence and liable on summary conviction to a fine not exceeding level 5 on the standard scale together with a further fine of an amount equal to one-tenth of that level for each day on which the offence continues after the conviction.

(9) Subject to subsection (1) below, in any proceedings for an offence under subsection (8) above in respect of a statutory nuisance it shall be a defence to prove that the best practicable means were used to prevent, or to counteract the effects of, the nuisance.

(10) The defence under subsection (9) above is not available—

    (a) in the case of a nuisance falling within paragraph (a), (d), (e), (f) [, (fa)] or (g) of section 79(1) above except where the nuisance arises on industrial, trade or business premises;

    [(aza) in the case of a nuisance falling within paragraph (fb) of section 79(1) above except where—

      (i) the artificial light is emitted from industrial, trade or business premises, or

      (ii) the artificial light (not being light to which sub-paragraph (i) applies) is emitted by lights used for the purpose only of illuminating an outdoor relevant sports facility;]

    [(aa) in the case of a nuisance falling within paragraph (ga) of section 79(1) above except where the noise is emitted from or caused by a vehicle, machinery or equipment being used for industrial, trade or business purposes;]

    (b) in the case of a nuisance falling within paragraph (b) of section 79(1) above except where the smoke is emitted from a chimney; and

    (c) in the case of a nuisance falling within paragraph (c) or (h) or section 79(1) above; and

    (d) in the case of a nuisance which is such as to render the premises unfit for human habitation.

(11) If a person is convicted of an offence under subsection (8) above, a magistrates' court [or the sheriff] may, after giving the local authority in whose area the nuisance has occurred an opportunity of being heard, direct the authority to do anything which the person convicted was required to do by the order to which the conviction relates.

(12) Where on the hearing of proceedings for an order under subsection (2) above it is proved that the alleged nuisance existed at the date of the making of the complaint [or summary application], then, whether or not at the date of the hearing it still exists or is likely to recur, the court [or the sheriff] shall order the [defendant or defender (or defendants or defenders)] in such proportions as appears fair and reasonable) to pay to the person bringing the proceedings such amount as the court [or the sheriff] considers reasonably sufficient to compensate him for any expenses properly incurred by him in the proceedings.

(13) If it appears to the magistrates' court [or the sheriff] that neither the person responsible for the nuisance nor the owner or occupier of the premises [or (as the case may be) the person responsible for the vehicle, machinery or equipment] can be found the court [or the sheriff] may, after giving the local authority in whose area the nuisance has occurred an opportunity of being heard, direct the authority to do anything which the court [or the sheriff] would have ordered that person to do.

Food Safety Act 1990

(1990, c. 16)

44   Protection of officers acting in good faith

(1) An officer of a food authority is not personally liable in respect of any act done by him—

  (a) in the execution or purported execution of this Act; and

  (b) within the scope of his employment,

if he did that act in the honest belief that his duty under this Act required or entitled him to do it.

(2) Nothing in subsection (1) above shall be construed as relieving any food authority from any liability in respect of the acts of their officers.

(3) Where an action has been brought against an officer of a food authority in respect of an act done by him—

  (a) in the execution or purported execution of this Act; but

  (b) outside the scope of his employment,

the authority may indemnify him against the whole or a part of any damages which he has been ordered to pay or any costs which he may have incurred if they are satisfied that he honestly believed that the act complained of was within the scope of his employment.

Water Industry Act 1991

(1991, c. 56)

209   Civil liability of undertakers for escapes of water etc.

(1) Where an escape of water, however caused, from a pipe vested in a water undertaker causes loss or damage, the undertaker shall be liable, except as otherwise provided in this section, for the loss or damage.

(2) A water undertaker shall not incur any liability under subsection (1) above if the escape was due wholly to the fault of the person who sustained the loss or damage or of any servant, agent or contractor of his.

(3) A water undertaker shall not incur any liability under subsection (1) above in respect of any loss or damage for which the undertaker would not be liable apart from that subsection and which is sustained—

(a) by [the Environment Agency], a relevant undertaker or any statutory undertakers, within the meaning of section 336(1) of the Town and Country Planning Act 1990;

(b) by any public gas supplier within the meaning of Part I of the Gas Act 1986 or the holder of a licence under section 6(1) of the Electricity Act 1989;

(c) by any highway authority; or

(d) by any person on whom a right to compensation is conferred by section 82 of the New Roads and Street Works Act 1991.

(4) The Law Reform (Contributory Negligence) Act 1945, the Fatal Accidents Act 1976 and the Limitation Act 1980 shall apply in relation to any loss or damage for which a water undertaker is liable under this section, but which is not due to the undertaker's fault, as if it were due to its fault.

(5) Nothing in subsection (1) above affects any entitlement which a water undertaker may have to recover contribution under the Civil Liability (Contribution) Act 1978; and for the purposes of that Act, any loss for which a water undertaker is liable under that subsection shall be treated as if it were damage.

(6) Where a water undertaker is liable under any enactment or agreement passed or made before April 1, 1982, to make any payment in respect of any loss or damage the undertaker shall not incur liability under subsection (1) above in respect of the same loss or damage.

(7) In this section 'fault' has the same meaning as in the Law Reform (Contributory Negligence) Act 1945.

Water Resources Act 1991

(1991, c. 57)

[Restoration and improvement works for controlled waters]

[161 Anti-pollution works and operations

(1) This section applies where it appears to the Agency that any poisonous, noxious or polluting matter or any waste matter is or has been present in, or is likely to enter, any controlled waters.

(2) In a case where the matter appears to be or to have been present in the controlled waters, the Agency shall be entitled to carry out works and operations for any of the following purposes—

(a) removing or disposing of the matter;

(b) remedying or mitigating any pollution caused by its presence in the waters; or

(c) restoring (so far as it is reasonably practicable to do so) the waters, including any flora and fauna dependent on the aquatic environment of the waters, to their state immediately before the matter became present in the waters.

(3) In a case where the matter appears to be likely to enter the controlled waters, the Agency shall be entitled to carry out works and operations for the purpose of preventing it from doing so.

(4) The Agency shall be entitled to carry out investigations for the purpose of establishing any of the following—

(a) the nature of the matter,

(b) the source of the matter;

(c) the nature and effects of any pollution caused or likely to be caused by the presence of the matter; and

(d) the identity of any responsible persons.

(5) Without prejudice to the power of the Agency to carry out those investigations, the powers conferred by subsection (2) or (3) shall only be exercisable in a case where—

(a) the Agency considers it necessary to carry out forthwith any works or operations falling within that subsection; or

(b) it appears to the Agency, after reasonable enquiry, that no responsible person can be found on whom to serve a works notice.

(6) In this section "responsible person" means a person who has caused or knowingly permitted the matter—

    (a) to be present in the controlled waters; or

    (b) to be at a place from which it was likely, in the opinion of the Agency, to enter the controlled waters.]

[161ZA   Other works and operations in respect of harm to controlled waters

(1) This section applies where it appears to the Agency that any controlled waters are being or have been harmed, or are likely to be harmed, by any event, process or other source of potential harm (and it is immaterial whether the source of potential harm has been identified).

(2) In this section "harm" means any adverse impact on the condition of any hydromorphological quality element affecting the controlled waters that would be likely to prevent the achievement of the environmental objectives applicable to the controlled waters (whether by itself or in combination with other factors), other than an adverse impact caused by the entry into or presence in those waters of any poisonous, noxious or polluting matter or waste matter.

(3) In subsection (2) "environmental objectives" and "hydromorphological quality element" have the same meaning as in the Water Framework Directive.

(4) The Agency shall be entitled to carry out works and operations for any of the following purposes (so far as it is reasonably practicable to achieve them)—

    (a) removing the source of potential harm;

    (b) preventing any harm or further harm being caused to the controlled waters;

    (c) in a case where the controlled waters are being or have been harmed—

        (i)   remedying or mitigating the effects of the harm;

        (ii) restoring the waters, including any flora and fauna dependent on the aquatic environment of the waters, to their state immediately before any harm was caused.

(5) The Agency shall be entitled to carry out investigations for the purpose of establishing any of the following—

    (a) the source of any harm or potential harm to the controlled waters;

    (b) the nature and effects of any harm caused or likely to be caused to those waters; and

    (c) the identity of any responsible persons.

(6) Without prejudice to the power of the Agency to carry out those investigations, the powers conferred by subsection (4) shall only be exercisable in a case where—

    (a) the Agency considers it necessary to carry out forthwith any works or operations falling within that subsection; or

    (b) it appears to the Agency, after reasonable enquiry, that no responsible person can be found on whom to serve a works notice.

(7) In this section "responsible person" means a person who has caused or knowingly permitted—

    (a) any harm to be caused to the controlled waters; or

    (b) a source of potential harm to exist that is likely, in the opinion of the Agency, to cause harm to the controlled waters.]

[161ZB   Works and operations for improving controlled waters

(1) This section applies where it appears to the Agency that—

    (a) the condition of any hydromorphological quality element affecting any controlled waters is unsatisfactory; and

    (b) it is possible to improve the hydromorphological quality element by carrying out works or operations.

(2) For the purposes of this section the condition of a hydromorphological quality element affecting the controlled waters is unsatisfactory if (whether by itself or in combination with other factors) if it is likely to prevent the waters from achieving the applicable environmental objectives.

(3) In this section "environmental objectives" and "hydromorphological quality element" have the same meaning as in the Water Framework Directive.

(4)　The Agency shall be entitled to carry out works and operations for the purpose of improving the condition of the hydromorphological quality element in question with a view to achieving (or contributing to the achievement of) the applicable environmental objectives.

(5)　The Agency shall be entitled to carry out investigations for the purpose of establishing why the condition of the hydromorphological quality element in question is unsatisfactory.

(6)　Without prejudice to the power of the Agency to carry out those investigations, the powers conferred by subsection (4) shall only be exercisable if it appears to the Agency that it is unable to secure that the necessary works or operations are carried out by exercising its powers under section 161 or 161ZA or by serving a works notice on any responsible person.]

[161ZC　Sections 161 to 161ZB: supplementary

(1)　Nothing in sections 161 to 161ZB shall entitle the Agency to impede or prevent the making of any discharge in pursuance of [an environmental permit].

(2)　Where the Agency carries out any works, operations or investigations under any of the powers conferred by section 161 or 161ZA it shall, subject to subsection (3), be entitled to recover the expenses reasonably incurred in doing so from any responsible person (within the meaning of the section conferring the powers in question).

(6)　Nothing in sections 161, 161ZA and 161ZB—

>　(a)　derogates from any right of action or other remedy (whether civil or criminal) in proceedings instituted otherwise than under any of those sections; or

>　(b)　affects any restriction imposed by or under any other enactment, whether public local or private.

(7)　In this section—

"expenses" includes costs; . . .

"works notice" means a notice under section 161A.

(8)　In sections 161, 161ZA and 161ZB and this section "controlled waters" has the same meaning as in Part 3 of this Act and in sections 161ZA and 161ZB, and "Water Framework Directive" has the same meaning as in section 93(7) of this Act.]

[161A　Notices requiring persons to carry out works and operations

(1)　Where it appears to the Agency that—

>　(a)　any poisonous, noxious or polluting matter or any waste matter is or has been present in, or is likely to enter, any controlled waters (so that section 161 applies), or

>　(b)　any controlled waters are being or have been harmed, or are likely to be harmed, by any event, process or other source of potential harm (so that section 161ZA applies),

the Agency shall be entitled to serve a works notice on any responsible person.

(2)　In this section "responsible person" has the same meaning as in section 161 or 161ZA) (as the case may be).

(3)　For the purposes of this section a works notice is a notice requiring the person on whom it is served to carry out such works or operations as may be specified in the notice.

(4)　The works or operations that may be so specified are works or operations which may be carried out under section 161(2) or (3) or section 161ZA(4) (as the case may be).

(5)　Where the Agency has carried out any such investigations as are mentioned in sections 161(4) or 161ZA(5) and serves a works notice on a responsible person in connection with the matters to which the investigations relate it shall (unless the notice is quashed or withdrawn) be entitled to recover from that person the costs or expenses reasonably incurred in carrying out those investigations.

(6)　The appropriate national authority may, if it thinks fit in relation to any person, give directions to the Agency as to whether or how it should exercise its powers under this section or section 161AA.]

[161B　Grant of, and compensation for, rights of entry etc.

. . .]

[161D   Consequences of not complying with a works notice

(1) If a person on whom the Agency serves a works notice fails to comply with any of the requirements of the notice, he shall be guilty of an offence.]

208   Civil liability of the [Agency] for escapes of water etc.

(1) Where an escape of water, however caused, from a pipe vested in the [Agency] causes loss or damage, the [Agency] shall be liable, except as otherwise provided in this section, for the loss or damage.

(2) The [Agency] shall not incur any liability under subsection (1) above if the escape was due wholly to the fault of the person who sustained the loss or damage or of any servant, agent or contractor of his.

(3) The [Agency] shall not incur any liability under subsection (1) above in respect of any loss or damage for which the [Agency] would not be liable apart from that subsection and which is sustained—

(a) by any water undertaker or sewerage undertaker or by any statutory undertakers, within the meaning of section 336(1) of the Town and Country Planning Act 1990;

(b) by any public gas supplier within the meaning of Part I of the Gas Act 1986 or the holder of a licence under section 6(1) of the Electricity Act 1989;

(c) by any highway authority; or

(d) by any person on whom a right to compensation is conferred by section 82 of the New Roads and Street Works Act 1991.

(4) The Law Reform (Contributory Negligence) Act 1945, the Fatal Accidents Act 1976 and the Limitation Act 1980 shall apply in relation to any loss or damage for which the [Agency] is liable under this section, but which is not due to the [Agency's] fault, as if it were due to its fault.

(5) Nothing in subsection (1) above affects any entitlement which the [Agency] may have to recover contribution under the Civil Liability (Contribution) Act 1978; and for the purposes of that Act, any loss for which the Authority is liable under that subsection shall be treated as if it were damage.

(6) Where the [Agency] is liable under any enactment or agreement passed or made before April 1, 1982, to make any payment in respect of any loss or damage the [Agency] shall not incur liability under subsection (1) above in respect of the same loss or damage.

(7) In this section 'fault' has the same meaning as in the Law Reform (Contributory Negligence) Act 1945.

221   General interpretation

(1) In this Act, except in so far as the context otherwise requires—

. . .

['the Agency' means the Environment Agency;] . . .

Access to Neighbouring Land Act 1992

(1992, c. 23)

1   Access orders

(1) A person—

(a) who, for the purpose of carrying out works to any land (the 'dominant land'), desires to enter upon any adjoining or adjacent land (the 'servient land'), and

(b) who needs, but does not have, the consent of some other person to that entry, may make an application to the court for an order under this section ('an access order') against that other person.

(2) On an application under this section, the court shall make an access order if, and only if, it is satisfied—

    (a) that the works are reasonably necessary for the preservation of the whole or any part of the dominant land; and

    (b) that they cannot be carried out, or would be substantially more difficult to carry out, without entry upon the servient land;

but this subsection is subject to subsection (3) below.

(3) The court shall not make an access order in any case where it is satisfied that, were it to make such an order—

    (a) the respondent or any other person would suffer interference with, or disturbance of, his use or enjoyment of the servient land, or

    (b) the respondent, or any other person (whether of full age or capacity or not) in occupation of the whole or any part of the servient land, would suffer hardship,

to such a degree by reason of the entry (notwithstanding any requirement of this Act or any term or condition that may be imposed under it) that it would be unreasonable to make the order.

(4) Where the court is satisfied on an application under this section that it is reasonably necessary to carry out any basic preservation works to the dominant land, those works shall be taken for the purposes of this Act to be reasonably necessary for the preservation of the land; and in this subsection 'basic preservation works' means any of the following, that is to say—

    (a) the maintenance, repair or renewal of any part of a building or other structure comprised in, or situate on, the dominant land;

    (b) the clearance, repair or renewal of any drain, sewer, pipe or cable so comprised or situate;

    (c) the treatment, cutting back, felling, removal or replacement of any hedge, tree, shrub or other growing thing which is so comprised and which is, or is in danger of becoming, damaged, diseased, dangerous, insecurely rooted or dead;

    (d) the filling in, or clearance, of any ditch so comprised;

but this subsection is without prejudice to the generality of the works which may, apart from it, be regarded by the court as reasonably necessary for the preservation of any land.

(5) If the court considers it fair and reasonable in all the circumstances of the case, works may be regarded for the purposes of this Act as being reasonably necessary for the preservation of any land (or, for the purposes of subsection (4) above, as being basic preservation works which it is reasonably necessary to carry out to any land) notwithstanding that the works incidentally involve—

    (a) the making of some alteration, adjustment or improvement to the land, or

    (b) the demolition of the whole or any part of a building or structure comprised in or situate upon the land.

(6) Where any works are reasonably necessary for the preservation of the whole or any part of the dominant land, the doing to the dominant land of anything which is requisite for, incidental to, or consequential on, the carrying out of those works shall be treated for the purposes of this Act as the carrying out of works which are reasonably necessary for the preservation of that land; and references in this Act to works, or to the carrying out of works, shall be construed accordingly.

(7) Without prejudice to the generality of subsection (6) above, if it is reasonably necessary for a person to inspect the dominant land—

    (a) for the purpose of ascertaining whether any works may be reasonably necessary for the preservation of the whole or any part of that land,

    (b) for the purpose of making any map or plan, or ascertaining the course of any drain, sewer, pipe or cable, in preparation for, or otherwise in connection with, the carrying out of works which are so reasonably necessary, or

    (c) otherwise in connection with the carrying out of any such works,

the making of such an inspection shall be taken for the purposes of this Act to be the carrying out to the dominant land of works which are reasonably necessary for the preservation of that land; and references in this Act to works, or to the carrying out of works, shall be construed accordingly.

2   Terms and conditions of access orders

(1) An access order shall specify—

    (a) the works to the dominant land that may be carried out by entering upon the servient land in pursuance of the order;

    (b) the particular area of servient land that may be entered upon by virtue of the order for the purpose of carrying out those works to the dominant land; and

    (c) the date on which, or the period during which, the land may be so entered upon;

and in the following provisions of this Act any reference to the servient land is a reference to the area specified in the order in pursuance of paragraph (b) above.

(2) An access order may impose upon the applicant or the respondent such terms and conditions as appear to the court to be reasonably necessary for the purpose of avoiding or restricting—

    (a) any loss, damage, or injury which might otherwise be caused to the respondent or any other person by reason of the entry authorised by the order; or

    (b) any inconvenience or loss of privacy that might otherwise be so caused to the respondent or any other person.

(3) Without prejudice to the generality of subsection (2) above, the terms and conditions which may be imposed under that subsection include provisions with respect to—

    (a) the manner in which the specified works are to be carried out;

    (b) the days on which, and the hours between which, the work involved may be executed;

    (c) the persons who may undertake the carrying out of the specified works or enter upon the servient land under or by virtue of the order;

    (d) the taking of any such precautions by the applicant as may be specified in the order.

(4) An access order may also impose terms and conditions—

    (a) requiring the applicant to pay, or to secure that such person connected with him as may be specified in the order pays, compensation for—

        (i) any loss, damage or injury, or

        (ii) any substantial loss of privacy or other substantial inconvenience,

    which will, or might, be caused to the respondent or any other person by reason of the entry authorised by the order;

    (b) requiring the applicant to secure that he, or such person connected with him as may be specified in the order, is insured against any such risks as may be so specified;

    (c) requiring such a record to be made of the condition of the servient land, or of such part of it as may be so specified, as the court may consider expedient with a view to facilitating the determination of any question that may arise concerning damage to that land.

(5) An access order may include provision requiring the applicant to pay the respondent such sum by way of consideration for the privilege of entering the servient land in pursuance of the order as appears to the court to be fair and reasonable having regard to all the circumstances of the case, including in particular—

    (a) the likely financial advantage of the order to the applicant and any persons connected with him; and

    (b) the degree of inconvenience likely to be caused to the respondent or any other person by the entry;

but no payment shall be ordered under this subsection if and to the extent that the works which the applicant desires to carry out by means of the entry are works to residential land.

(6) For the purposes of subsection (5)(a) above, the likely financial advantage of an access order to the applicant and any persons connected with him shall in all cases be taken to be a sum of money equal to the greater of the following amounts, that is to say—

    (a) the amount (if any) by which so much of any likely increase in the value of any land—

        (i) which consists of or includes the dominant land, and

        (ii) which is owned or occupied by the same person as the dominant land, as may reasonably be regarded as attributable to the carrying out of the specified works exceeds the likely cost of carrying out those works with the benefit of the access order; and

(b) the difference (if it would have been possible to carry out the specified works without entering upon the servient land) between—

(i) the likely cost of carrying out those works without entering upon the servient land; and

(ii) the likely cost of carrying them out with the benefit of the access order.

(7) For the purposes of subsection (5) above, 'residential land' means so much of any land as consists of—

(a) a dwelling or part of a dwelling;

(b) a garden, yard, private garage or outbuilding which is used and enjoyed wholly or mainly with a dwelling; or

(c) in the case of a building which includes one or more dwellings, any part of the building which is used and enjoyed wholly or mainly with those dwellings or any of them.

(8) The persons who are to be regarded for the purposes of this section as 'connected with' the applicant are—

(a) the owner of any estate or interest in, or right over, the whole or any part of the dominant land;

(b) the occupier of the whole or any part of the dominant land; and

(c) any person whom the applicant may authorise under section 3(7) below to exercise the power of entry conferred by the access order.

(9) The court may make provision—

(a) for the reimbursement by the applicant of any expenses reasonably incurred by the respondent in connection with the application which are not otherwise recoverable as costs;

(b) for the giving of security by the applicant for any sum that might become payable to the respondent or any other person by virtue of this section or section 3 below.

3 Effect of access order

(1) An access order requires the respondent, so far as he has power to do so, to permit the applicant or any of his associates to do anything which the applicant or associate is authorised or required to do under or by virtue of the order or this section.

(2) Except as otherwise provided by or under this Act, an access order authorises the applicant or any of his associates, without the consent of the respondent,—

(a) to enter upon the servient land for the purpose of carrying out the specified works;

(b) to bring on to that land, leave there during the period permitted by the order and, before the end of that period, remove, such materials, plant and equipment as are reasonably necessary for the carrying out of those works; and

(c) to bring on to that land any waste arising from the carrying out of those works, if it is reasonably necessary to do so in the course of removing it from the dominant land; but nothing in this Act or in any access order shall authorise the applicant or any of his associates to leave anything in, on or over the servient land (otherwise than in discharge of their duty to make good that land) after their entry for the purpose of carrying out works to the dominant land ceases to be authorised under or by virtue of the order.

(3) An access order requires the applicant—

(a) to secure that any waste arising from the carrying out of the specified works is removed from the servient land forthwith;

(b) to secure that, before the entry ceases to be authorised under or by virtue of the order, the servient land is, so far as reasonably practicable, made good; and

(c) to indemnify the respondent against any damage which may be caused to the servient land or any goods by the applicant or any of his associates which would not have been so caused had the order not been made;

but this subsection is subject to subsections (4) and (5) below.

(4) In making an access order, the court may vary or exclude, in whole or in part,—

(a) any authorisation that would otherwise be conferred by subsection 2(b) or (c) above; or

(b) any requirement that would otherwise be imposed by subsection (3) above.

(5) Without prejudice to the generality of subsection (4) above, if the court is satisfied that it is reasonably necessary for any such waste as may arise from the carrying out of the specified works to be left on the servient land for some period before removal, the access order may, in place of subsection (3)(a) above, include provision—

(a) authorising the waste to be left on that land for such period as may be permitted by the order; and

(b) requiring the applicant to secure that the waste is removed before the end of that period.

(6) Where the applicant or any of his associates is authorised or required under or by virtue of an access order or this section to enter, or do any other thing, upon the servient land, he shall not (as respects that access order) be taken to be a trespasser from the beginning on account of his, or any other person's, subsequent conduct.

(7) For the purposes of this section, the applicant's 'associates' are such number of persons (whether or not servants or agents of his) whom he may reasonably authorise under this subsection to exercise the power of entry conferred by the access order as may be reasonably necessary for carrying out the specified works.

4   Persons bound by access order, unidentified persons and bar on contracting out

(1) In addition to the respondent, an access order shall, subject to the provisions of the Land Charges Act 1972 and the [Land Registration Act 2002], be binding on—

(a) any of his successors in title to the servient land; and

(b) any person who has an estate or interest in, or right over, the whole or any part of the servient land which was created after the making of the order and who derives his title to that estate, interest or right under the respondent;

and references to the respondent shall be construed accordingly.

(2) If and to the extent that the court considers it just and equitable to allow him to do so, a person on whom an access order becomes binding by virtue of subsection (1)(a) or (b) above shall be entitled, as respects anything falling to be done after the order becomes binding on him, to enforce the order or any of its terms or conditions as if he were the respondent, and references to the respondent shall be construed accordingly.

(3) Rules of court may—

(a) provide a procedure which may be followed where the applicant does not know, and cannot reasonably ascertain, the name of any person whom he desires to make respondent to the application; and

(b) make provision enabling such an applicant to make such a person respondent by description instead of by name;

and in this subsection 'applicant' includes a person who proposes to make an application for an access order.

(4) Any agreement, whenever made, shall be void if and to the extent that it would, apart from this subsection, prevent a person from applying for an access order or restrict his right to do so.

6   Variation of orders and damages for breach

(1) Where an access order or an order under this subsection has been made, the court may, on the application of any party to the proceedings in which the order was made or of any other person on whom the order is binding—

(a) discharge or vary the order or any of its terms or conditions;

(b) suspend any of its terms or conditions; or

(c) revive any term or condition suspended under paragraph (b) above;

and in the application of subsections (1) and (2) of section 4 above in relation to an access order, any order under this subsection which relates to the access order shall be treated for the purposes of those subsections as included in the access order.

(2) If any person contravenes or fails to comply with any requirement, term or condition imposed upon him by or under this Act, the court may, without prejudice to any other remedy available, make an order for the payment of damages by him to any other person affected by the contravention or failure who makes an application for relief under this subsection.

Carriage of Goods by Sea Act 1992

(1992, c. 50)

1 Shipping documents etc. to which Act applies

(1) This Act applies to the following documents, that is to say—
   (a) any bill of lading;
   (b) any sea waybill; and
   (c) any ship's delivery order.

(2) References in this Act to a bill of lading—
   (a) do not include references to a document which is incapable of transfer either by indorsement or, as a bearer bill, by delivery without indorsement; but
   (b) subject to that, do include references to a received for shipment bill of lading.

(3) References in this Act to a sea waybill are references to any document which is not a bill of lading but—
   (a) is such a receipt for goods as contains or evidences a contract for the carriage of goods by sea; and
   (b) identifies the person to whom delivery of the goods is to be made by the carrier in accordance with that contract.

(4) References in this Act to a ship's delivery order are references to any document which is neither a bill of lading nor a sea waybill but contains an undertaking which—
   (a) is given under or for the purposes of a contract for the carriage by sea of the goods to which the document relates, or of goods which include those goods; and
   (b) is an undertaking by the carrier to a person identified in the document to deliver the goods to which the document relates to that person.

(5) The Secretary of State may by regulations make provision for the application of this Act to cases where an electronic communications network or any other information technology is used for effecting transactions corresponding to—
   (a) the issue of a document to which this Act applies;
   (b) the indorsement, delivery or other transfer of such a document; or
   (c) the doing of anything else in relation to such a document.

(6) Regulations under subsection (5) above may—
   (a) make such modifications of the following provisions of this Act as the Secretary of State considers appropriate in connection with the application of this Act to any case mentioned in that subsection; and
   (b) contain supplemental, incidental, consequential and transitional provision; and the power to make regulations under that subsection shall be exercisable by statutory instrument subject to annulment in pursuance of a resolution of either House of Parliament.

2 Rights under shipping documents

(1) Subject to the following provisions of this section, a person who becomes—
   (a) the lawful holder of a bill of lading;
   (b) the person who (without being an original party to the contract of carriage) is the person to whom delivery of the goods to which a sea waybill relates is to be made by the carrier in accordance with that contract; or

(c) the person to whom delivery of the goods to which a ship's delivery order relates is to be made in accordance with the undertaking contained in the order,

shall (by virtue of becoming the holder of the bill or, as the case may be, the person to whom delivery is to be made) have transferred to and vested in him all rights of suit under the contract of carriage as if he had been a party to that contract.

(2) Where, when a person becomes the lawful holder of a bill of lading, possession of the bill no longer gives a right (as against the carrier) to possession of the goods to which the bill relates, that person shall not have any rights transferred to him by virtue of subsection (1) above unless he becomes the holder of the bill—

(a) by virtue of a transaction effected in pursuance of any contractual or other arrangements made before the time when such a right to possession ceased to attach to possession of the bill; or

(b) as a result of the rejection to that person by another person of goods or documents delivered to the other person in pursuance of any such arrangements.

(3) The rights vested in any person by virtue of the operation of subsection (1) above in relation to a ship's delivery order—

(a) shall be so vested subject to the terms of the order; and

(b) where the goods to which the order relates form a part only of the goods to which the contract of carriage relates, shall be confined to rights in respect of the goods to which the order relates.

(4) Where, in the case of any document to which this Act applies—

(a) a person with any interest or right in or in relation to goods to which the document relates sustains loss or damage in consequence of a breach of the contract of carriage; but

(b) subsection (1) above operates in relation to that document so that rights of suit in respect of that breach are vested in another person,

the other person shall be entitled to exercise those rights for the benefit of the person who sustained the loss or damage to the same extent as they could have been exercised if they had been vested in the person for whose benefit they are exercised.

(5) Where rights are transferred by virtue of the operation of subsection (1) above in relation to any document, the transfer for which that subsection provides shall extinguish any entitlement to those rights which derives—

(a) where that document is a bill of lading, from a person's having been an original party to the contract of carriage; or

(b) in the case of any document to which this Act applies, from the previous operation of that subsection in relation to that document;

but the operation of that subsection shall be without prejudice to any rights which derive from a person's having been an original party to the contract contained in, or evidenced by, a sea waybill and, in relation to a ship's delivery order, shall be without prejudice to any rights deriving otherwise than from the previous operation of that subsection in relation to that order.

3   Liabilities under shipping documents

(1) Where subsection (1) of section 2 of this Act operates in relation to any document to which this Act applies and the person in whom rights are vested by virtue of that subsection—

(a) takes or demands delivery from the carrier of any of the goods to which the document relates;

(b) makes a claim under the contract of carriage against the carrier in respect of any of those goods; or

(c) is a person who, at a time before those rights were vested in him, took or demanded delivery from the carrier of any of those goods,

that person shall (by virtue of taking or demanding delivery or making the claim or, in a case falling within paragraph (c) above, of having the rights vested in him) become subject to the same liabilities under that contract as if he had been a party to that contract.

(2) Where the goods to which a ship's delivery order relates form a part only of the goods to which the contract of carriage relates, the liabilities to which any person is subject by virtue of the operation of this section in relation to that order shall exclude liabilities in respect of any goods to which the order does not relate.

(3) This section, so far as it imposes liabilities under any contract on any person, shall be without prejudice to the liabilities under the contract of any person as an original party to the contract.

4   Representations in bills of lading

A bill of lading which—

> (a) represents goods to have been shipped on board a vessel or to have been received for shipment on board a vessel; and
>
> (b) has been signed by the master of the vessel or by a person who was not the master but had the express, implied or apparent authority of the carrier to sign bills of lading,

shall, in favour of a person who has become the lawful holder of the bill, be conclusive evidence against the carrier of the shipment of the goods or, as the case may be, of their receipt for shipment.

5   Interpretation etc.

(1) In this Act—

'bill of lading', 'sea way bill' and 'ship's delivery order' shall be construed in accordance with section 1 above;

'the contract of carriage'—

> (a) in relation to a bill of lading or sea waybill, means the contract contained in or evidenced by that bill or waybill; and
>
> (b) in relation to a ship's delivery order, means the contract under or for the purposes of which the undertaking contained in the order is given;

'holder', in relation to a bill of lading, shall be construed in accordance with subsection (2) below;

'information technology' includes any computer or other technology by means of which information or other matter may be recorded or communicated without being reduced to documentary form;

[...].

(2) References in this Act to the holder of a bill of lading are references to any of the following persons, that is to say—

> (a) a person with possession of the bill who, by virtue of being the person identified in the bill, is the consignee of the goods to which the bill relates;
>
> (b) a person with possession of the bill as a result of the completion, by delivery of the bill, of any indorsement of the bill or, in the case of a bearer bill, of any other transfer of the bill;
>
> (c) a person with possession of the bill as a result of any transaction by virtue of which he would have become a holder falling within paragraph (a) or (b) above had not the transaction been effected at a time when possession of the bill no longer gave a right (as against the carrier) to possession of the goods to which the bill relates;

and a person shall be regarded for the purposes of this Act as having become the lawful holder of a bill of lading wherever he has become the holder of the bill in good faith.

(3) References in this Act to a person's being identified in a document include references to his being identified by a description which allows for the identity of the person in question to be varied, in accordance with the terms of the document, after its issue; and the reference in section 1(3)(b) of this Act to a document's identifying a person shall be construed accordingly.

(4) Without prejudice to sections 2(2) and 4 above, nothing in this Act shall preclude its operation in relation to a case where the goods to which a document relates—

> (a) cease to exist after the issue of the document; or
>
> (b) cannot be identified (whether because they are mixed with other goods or for any other reason);

and references in this Act to the goods to which a document relates shall be construed accordingly.

(5) The preceding provisions of this Act shall have effect without prejudice to the application, in relation to any case, of the rules (the Hague-Visby Rules) which for the time being have the force of law by virtue of section 1 of the Carriage of Goods by Sea Act 1971.

Social Security Contributions and Benefits Act 1992

(1992, c. 4)

94   Right to industrial injuries benefit

(1) Industrial injuries benefit shall be payable where an employed earner suffers personal injury caused after 4 July 1948 by accident arising out of and in the course of his employment, being employed earner's employment.

(3) For the purposes of industrial injuries benefit an accident arising in the course of an employed earner's employment shall be taken, in the absence of evidence to the contrary, also to have arisen out of that employment.

97   Accidents in course of illegal employments

(1) Subsection (2) below has effect in any case where—
  (a) a claim is made for industrial injuries benefit in respect of an accident, or of a prescribed disease or injury; or
  (b) an application is made under section 29 of the Social Security Act 1998 for a declaration that an accident was an industrial accident, or for a corresponding declaration as to a prescribed disease or injury.

(2) The Secretary of State may direct that the relevant employment shall, in relation to that accident, disease or injury, be treated as having been employed earner's employment notwithstanding that by reason of a contravention of, or non-compliance with, some provision contained in or having effect under an enactment passed for the protection of employed persons or any class of employed persons, either—
  (a) the contract purporting to govern the employment was void; or
  (b) the employed person was not lawfully employed in the relevant employment at the time when, or in the place where, the accident happened or the disease or injury was contracted or received.

(3) In subsection (2) above 'relevant employment' means—
  (a) in relation to an accident, the employment out of and in the course of which the accident arises; and
  (b) in relation to a prescribed disease or injury, the employment to the nature of which the disease or injury is due.

98   Earner acting in breach of regulations, etc.

An accident shall be taken to arise out of and in the course of an employed earner's employment, notwithstanding that he is at the time of the accident acting in contravention of any statutory or other regulations applicable to his employment, or of any orders given by or on behalf of his employer, or that he is acting without instructions from his employer, if—
  (a) the accident would have been taken so to have arisen had the act not been done in contravention of any such regulations or orders, or without such instructions, as the case may be; and
  (b) the act is done for the purposes of and in connection with the employer's trade or business.

100   Accidents happening while meeting emergency

An accident happening to an employed earner in or about any premises at which he is for the time being employed for the purposes of his employer's trade or business shall be taken to arise out of and in the course of his employment if it happens while he is taking steps, on an actual or supposed emergency at those premises, to rescue, succour or protect persons who are, or are thought to be or possibly to be, injured or imperilled, or to avert or minimise serious damage to property.

101   Accident caused by another's misconduct etc.

An accident happening after 19 December 1961 shall be treated for the purposes of industrial injuries benefit, where it would not apart from this section be so treated, as arising out of an employed earner's employment if—

    (a) the accident arises in the course of the employment; and

    (b) the accident either is caused—

        (i)   by another person's misconduct, skylarking or negligence, or

        (ii) by steps taken in consequence of any such misconduct, skylarking or negligence, or

        (iii) by the behaviour or presence of an animal (including a bird, fish or insect), or is caused by or consists in the employed earner being struck by any object or by lightning; and

    (c) the employed earner did not directly or indirectly induce or contribute to the happening of the accident by his conduct outside the employment or by any act not incidental to the employment.

174   References to Acts

In this Act—

    'the Administration Act' means the Social Security Administration Act 1992;

Trade Union and Labour Relations (Consolidation) Act 1992

(1992, c. 52)

1   Meaning of 'trade union'

In this Act a 'trade union' means an organisation (whether temporary or permanent)—

    (a) which consists wholly or mainly of workers of one or more descriptions and whose principal purposes include the regulation of relations between workers of that description or those descriptions and employers or employers' associations; or . . .

10   Quasi-corporate status of trade unions

    (1) A trade union is not a body corporate but—

    (a) it is capable of making contracts;

    (b) it is capable of suing and being sued in its own name, whether in proceedings relating to property or founded on contract or tort or any other cause of action; and

    (c) proceedings for an offence alleged to have been committed by it or on its behalf may be brought against it in its own name.

11   Exclusion of common law rules as to restraint of trade

    (1) The purposes of a trade union are not, by reason only that they are in restraint of trade, unlawful so as—

    (a) to make any member of the trade union liable to criminal proceedings for conspiracy or otherwise, or

    (b) to make any agreement or trust void or voidable.

    (2) No rule of a trade union is unlawful or unenforceable by reason only that it is in restraint of trade.

20   Liability of trade union in certain proceedings in tort

    (1) Where proceedings in tort are brought against a trade union—

    (a) on the ground that an act—

        (i)   induces another person to break a contract or interferes or induces another person to interfere with its performance, or

(ii) consists in threatening that a contract (whether one to which the union is a party or not) will be broken or its performance interfered with, or that the union will induce another person to break a contract or interfere with its performance, or

(b) in respect of an agreement or combination by two or more persons to do or to procure the doing of an act which, if it were done without any such agreement or combination, would be actionable in tort on such a ground,

then, for the purpose of determining in those proceedings whether the union is liable in respect of the act in question, that act shall be taken to have been done by the union if, but only if, it is to be taken to have been authorised or endorsed by the trade union in accordance with the following provisions.

(5) Where for the purposes of any proceedings an act is by virtue of this section taken to have been done by a trade union, nothing in this section shall affect the liability of any other person, in those or any other proceedings, in respect of that act.

(6) In proceedings arising out of an act which is by virtue of this section taken to have been done by a trade union, the power of the court to grant an injunction or interdict includes power to require the union to take such steps as the court considers appropriate for ensuring—

(a) that there is no, or no further, inducement of persons to take part or to continue to take part in industrial action, and

(b) that no person engages in any conduct after the granting of the injunction or interdict by virtue of having been induced before it was granted to take part or to continue to take part in industrial action.

The provisions of subsections (2) to (4) above apply in relation to proceedings for failure to comply with any such injunction or interdict as they apply in relation to the original proceedings.

22   Limit on damages awarded against trade unions in actions in tort

(1) This section applies to any proceedings in tort brought against a trade union, except—

(a) proceedings for personal injury as a result of negligence, nuisance or breach of duty;

(b) proceedings for breach of duty in connection with the ownership, occupation, possession, control or use of property;

(c) proceedings brought by virtue of Part I of the Consumer Protection Act 1987 (product liability).

In any proceedings in tort to which this section applies the amount which may be awarded against the union by way of damages shall not exceed the following limit—

Number of members of union	Maximum award of damages
Less than 5,000	£10,000
5,000 or more but less than 25,000	£50,000
25,000 or more but less than 100,000	£125,000
100,000 or more	£250,000

(3) The Secretary of State may by order amend subsection (2) so as to vary any of the sums specified...

127   Corporate or quasi-corporate status of employers' associations

(1) An employers' association may be either a body corporate or an unincorporated association.

(2) Where an employers' association is unincorporated—

(a) it is capable of making contracts;

(b) it is capable of suing and being sued in its own name, whether in proceedings relating to property or founded on contract or tort or any other cause of action; and

(c) proceedings for an offence alleged to have been committed by it or on its behalf may be brought against it in its own name.

128   Exclusion of common law rules as to restraint of trade

(1) The purposes of an unincorporated employers' association and, so far as they relate to the regulation of relations between employers and workers or trade unions, the purposes of an employers' association which is a body corporate are not, by reason only that they are in restraint of trade, unlawful so as—

(a) to make any member of the association liable to criminal proceedings for conspiracy or otherwise, or

(b) to make any agreement or trust void or voidable.

(2) No rule of an unincorporated employers' association or, so far as it relates to the regulation of relations between employers and workers or trade unions, of an employers' association which is a body corporate, is unlawful or unenforceable by reason only that it is in restraint of trade.

137   Refusal of employment on grounds related to union membership

(1) It is unlawful to refuse a person employment—

(a) because he is, or is not, a member of a trade union, or

(b) because he is unwilling to accept a requirement—

(i)   to take steps to become or cease to be, or to remain or not to become, a member of a trade union, or

(ii) to make payments or suffer deductions in the event of his not being a member of a trade union.

(2) A person who is thus unlawfully refused employment has a right of complaint to an [employment tribunal].

138   Refusal of service of employment agency on grounds related to union membership

. . .

140   Remedies

(1) Where the [employment tribunal] finds that a complaint under section 137 or 138 is well-founded, it shall make a declaration to that effect and may make such of the following as it considers just and equitable—

(a) an order requiring the respondent to pay compensation to the complainant of such amount as the tribunal may determine;

(b) a recommendation that the respondent take within a specified period action appearing to the tribunal to be practicable for the purpose of obviating or reducing the adverse effect on the complainant of any conduct to which the complaint relates.

(2) Compensation shall be assessed on the same basis as damages for breach of statutory duty and may include compensation for injury to feelings.

(3) If the respondent fails without reasonable justification to comply with a recommendation to take action, the tribunal may increase its award of compensation or, if it has not made such an award, make one.

(4) The total amount of compensation shall not exceed the limit for the time being imposed by [section 124(1) of the Employment Rights Act 1996] (limit on compensation for unfair dismissal).

142   Awards against third parties

(1) If in proceedings on a complaint under section 137 or 138 either the complainant or the respondent claims that the respondent was induced to act in the manner complained of by pressure which a trade union or other person exercised on him by calling, organising, procuring or financing a strike or other industrial action, or by threatening to do so, the complainant or the respondent may request the [employment tribunal] to direct that the person who he claims exercised the pressure be joined or sisted as a party to the proceedings.

(3) Where a person has been so joined or sisted as a party to the proceedings and the tribunal—
  (a) finds that the complaint is well-founded,
  (b) makes an award of compensation, and
  (c) also finds that the claim in subsection (1) above is well-founded,

it may order that the compensation shall be paid by the person joined instead of by the respondent, or partly by that person and partly by the respondent, as the tribunal may consider just and equitable in the circumstances.

143   Interpretation and other supplementary provisions

(4) The remedy of a person for conduct which is unlawful by virtue of section 137 or 138 is by way of a complaint to an [employment tribunal] in accordance with this Part, and not otherwise.

No other legal liability arises by reason that conduct is unlawful by virtue of either of those sections.

144   Union membership requirement in contract for goods or services void

A term or condition of a contract for the supply of goods or services is void in so far as it purports to require that the whole, or some part, of the work done for the purposes of the contract is done only by persons who are, or are not, members of trade unions or of a particular trade union.

145   Refusal to deal on union membership grounds prohibited

(1) A person shall not refuse to deal with a supplier or prospective supplier of goods or services on union membership grounds.

'Refuse to deal' and 'union membership grounds' shall be construed as follows.

(2) A person refuses to deal with a person if, where he maintains (in whatever form) a list of approved suppliers of goods or services, or of persons from whom tenders for the supply of goods or services may be invited, he fails to include the name of that person in that list.

He does so on union membership grounds if the grounds, or one of the grounds, for failing to include his name is that if that person were to enter into a contract with him for the supply of goods or services, work to be done for the purposes of the contract would, or would be likely to, be done by persons who were, or who were not, members of trade unions or of a particular trade union.

(3) A person refuses to deal with a person if, in relation to a proposed contract for the supply of goods or services—
  (a) he excludes that person from the group of persons from whom tenders for the supply of the goods or services are invited, or
  (b) he fails to permit that person to submit such a tender, or
  (c) he otherwise determines not to enter into a contract with that person for the supply of the goods or services.

He does so on union membership grounds if the ground, or one of the grounds, on which he does so is that if the proposed contract were entered into with that person, work to be done for the purposes of the contract would, or would be likely to, be done by persons who were, or who were not, members of trade unions or of a particular trade union.

(4) A person refuses to deal with a person if he terminates a contract with him for the supply of goods or services.

He does so on union membership grounds if the ground, or one of the grounds, on which he does so is that work done, or to be done, for the purposes of the contract has been, or is likely to be, done by persons who are or are not members of trade unions or of a particular trade union.

(5) The obligation to comply with this section is a duty owed to the person with whom there is a refusal to deal and to any other person who may be adversely affected by its contravention; and a breach of the duty is actionable accordingly (subject to the defences and other incidents applying to actions for breach of statutory duty).

166   Consequences of failure to comply with order

(1) If on the application of an employee an [employment tribunal] is satisfied that the employer has not complied with the terms of an order for the reinstatement or re-engagement of the employee under section 163(4) or (5), the tribunal shall—

(a) make an order for the continuation of the employee's contract of employment, and

(b) order the employer to pay the employee such compensation as the tribunal considers just and equitable in all the circumstances having regard—

   (i) to the infringement of the employee's right to be reinstated or re-engaged in pursuance of the order, and

   (ii) to any loss suffered by the employee in consequence of the non-compliance.

(3) If on the application of an employee an [employment tribunal] is satisfied that the employer has not complied with the terms of an order for the continuation of a contract of employment, the following provisions apply.

(4) If the non-compliance consists of a failure to pay an amount by way of pay specified in the order, the tribunal shall determine the amount owed by the employer on the date of the determination.

If on that date the tribunal also determines the employee's complaint that he has been unfairly dismissed, it shall specify that amount separately from any other sum awarded to the employee.

(5) In any other case, the tribunal shall order the employer to pay the employee such compensation as the tribunal considers just and equitable in all the circumstances having regard to any loss suffered by the employee in consequence of the non-compliance.

178   Collective agreements and collective bargaining

(1) In this Act 'collective agreement' means any agreement or arrangement made by or on behalf of one or more trade unions and one or more employers or employers' associations and relating to one or more of the matters specified below; and 'collective bargaining' means negotiations relating to or connected with one or more of those matters.

(2) The matters referred to above are—

(a) terms and conditions of employment, or the physical conditions in which any workers are required to work;

(b) engagement or non-engagement, or termination or suspension of employment or the duties of employment, of one or more workers;

(c) allocation of work or the duties of employment between workers or groups of workers;

(d) matters of discipline;

(e) a worker's membership or non-membership of a trade union;

(f) facilities for officials of trade unions; and

(g) machinery for negotiation or consultation, and other procedures, relating to any of the above matters, including the recognition by employers or employers' associations of the right of a trade union to represent workers in such negotiation or consultation or in the carrying out of such procedures.

179   Whether agreement intended to be a legally enforceable contract

(1) A collective agreement shall be conclusively presumed not to have been intended by the parties to be a legally enforceable contract unless the agreement—

(a) is in writing, and

(b) contains a provision which (however expressed) states that the parties intend that the agreement shall be a legally enforceable contract.

(2) A collective agreement which does satisfy those conditions shall be conclusively presumed to have been intended by the parties to be a legally enforceable contract.

(3) If a collective agreement is in writing and contains a provision which (however expressed) states that the parties intend that one or more parts of the agreement specified in that provision, but not the whole of the agreement, shall be a legally enforceable contract, then—

(a) the specified part or parts shall be conclusively presumed to have been intended by the parties to be a legally enforceable contract, and

(b) the remainder of the agreement shall be conclusively presumed not to have been intended by the parties to be such a contract.

(4) A part of a collective agreement which by virtue of subsection (3)(b) is not a legally enforceable contract may be referred to for the purpose of interpreting a part of the agreement which is such a contract.

180   Effect of provisions restricting right to take industrial action

(1) Any terms of a collective agreement which prohibit or restrict the right of workers to engage in a strike or other industrial action, or have the effect of prohibiting or restricting that right, shall not form part of any contract between a worker and the person for whom he works unless the following conditions are met.

(2) The conditions are that the collective agreement—

    (a) is in writing,

    (b) contains a provision expressly stating that those terms shall or may be incorporated in such a contract,

    (c) is reasonably accessible at his place of work to the worker to whom it applies and is available for him to consult during working hours, and

    (d) is one where each trade union which is a party to the agreement is an independent trade union;

and that the contract with the worker expressly or impliedly incorporates those terms in the contract.

(3) The above provisions have effect notwithstanding anything in section 179 and notwithstanding any provision to the contrary in any agreement (including a collective agreement or a contract with any worker).

186   Recognition requirement in contract for goods or services void

A term or condition of a contract for the supply of goods or services is void in so far as it purports to require a party to the contract—

    (a) to recognise one or more trade unions (whether or not named in the contract) for the purpose of negotiating on behalf of workers, or any class of worker, employed by him, or

    (b) to negotiate or consult with, or with an official of, one or more trade unions (whether or not so named).

187   Refusal to deal on grounds of union exclusion prohibited

(1) A person shall not refuse to deal with a supplier or prospective supplier of goods or services if the ground or one of the grounds for his action is that the person against whom it is taken does not, or is not likely to—

    (a) recognise one or more trade unions for the purpose of negotiating on behalf of workers, or any class of worker, employed by him, or

    (b) negotiate or consult with, or with an official of, one or more trade unions.

(2) A person refuses to deal with a person if—

    (a) where he maintains (in whatever form) a list of approved suppliers of goods or services, or of persons from whom tenders for the supply of goods or services may be invited, he fails to include the name of that person in that list; or

    (b) in relation to a proposed contract for the supply of goods or services—

        (i)   he excludes that person from the group of persons from whom tenders for the supply of the goods or services are invited, or

        (ii) he fails to permit that person to submit such a tender; or

        [(iii)] he otherwise determines not to enter into a contract with that person for the supply of the goods or services. [or

    (c) he terminates a contract with that person for the supply of goods or services.]

(3) The obligation to comply with this section is a duty owed to the person with whom there is a refusal to deal and to any other person who may be adversely affected by its contravention; and a

breach of the duty is actionable accordingly (subject to the defences and other incidents applying to actions for breach of statutory duty).

219 Protection from certain tort liabilities

(1) An act done by a person in contemplation or furtherance of a trade dispute is not actionable in tort on the ground only—

(a) that it induces another person to break a contract or interferes or induces another person to interfere with its performance, or

(b) that it consists in his threatening that a contract (whether one to which he is a party or not) will be broken or its performance interfered with, or that he will induce another person to break a contract or interfere with its performance.

(2) An agreement or combination by two or more persons to do or procure the doing of an act in contemplation or furtherance of a trade dispute is not actionable in tort if the act is one which if done without any such agreement or combination would not be actionable in tort.

(3) Nothing in subsections (1) and (2) prevents an act done in the course of picketing from being actionable in tort unless it is done in the course of attendance declared lawful by section 220 (peaceful picketing).

(4) Subsections (1) and (2) have effect subject to sections 222 to 225 (action excluded from protection) [and to sections 226 (requirement of ballot before action by trade union) and 234A (requirement of notice to employer of industrial action); and in those sections 'not protected' means excluded from the protection afforded by this section or, where the expression is used with reference to a particular person, excluded from that protection as respects that person.]

220 Peaceful picketing

(1) It is lawful for a person in contemplation or furtherance of a trade dispute to attend—

(a) at or near his own place of work, or

(b) if he is an official of a trade union, at or near the place of work of a member of the union whom he is accompanying and whom he represents,

for the purpose only of peacefully obtaining or communicating information, or peacefully persuading any person to work or abstain from working.

(2) If a person works or normally works—

(a) otherwise than at any one place, or

(b) at a place the location of which is such that attendance there for a purpose mentioned in subsection (1) is impracticable,

his place of work for the purposes of that subsection shall be any premises of his employer from which he works or from which his work is administered.

221 Restrictions on grant of injunctions and interdicts

(1) Where—

(a) an application for an injunction or interdict is made to a court in the absence of the party against whom it is sought or any representative of his, and

(b) he claims, or in the opinion of the court would be likely to claim, that he acted in contemplation or furtherance of a trade dispute,

the court shall not grant the injunction or interdict unless satisfied that all steps which in the circumstances were reasonable have been taken with a view to securing that notice of the application and an opportunity of being heard with respect to the application have been given to him.

(2) Where—

(a) an application for an interlocutory injunction is made to a court pending the trial of an action, and

(b) the party against whom it is sought claims that he acted in contemplation or furtherance of a trade dispute,

the court shall, in exercising its discretion whether or not to grant the injunction, have regard to the likelihood of that party's succeeding at the trial of the action in establishing any matter which would afford a defence to the action under section 219 (protection from certain tort liabilities) or section 220 (peaceful picketing).

This subsection does not extend to Scotland.

222   Action to enforce trade union membership

(1) An act is not protected if the reason, or one of the reasons, for which it is done is the fact or belief that a particular employer—

    (a) is employing, has employed or might employ a person who is not a member of a trade union, or

    (b) is failing, has failed or might fail to discriminate against such a person.

(2) For the purposes of subsection (1)(b) an employer discriminates against a person if, but only if, he ensures that his conduct in relation to—

    (a) persons, or persons of any description, employed by him, or who apply to be, or are, considered by him for employment, or

    (b) that provision of employment for such persons, is different, in some or all cases, according to whether or not they are members of a trade union, and is more favourable to those who are.

(3) An act is not protected if it constitutes, or is one of a number of acts which together constitute, an inducement or attempted inducement of a person—

    (a) to incorporate in a contract to which that person is a party, or a proposed contract to which he intends to be a party, a term or condition which is or would be void by virtue of section 144 (union membership requirement in contract for goods or services), or

    (b) to contravene section 145 (refusal to deal with person on grounds relating to union membership).

224   Secondary action

(1) An Act is not protected if one of the facts relied on for the purpose of establishing liability is that there has been secondary action which is not lawful picketing.

(2) There is secondary action in relation to a trade dispute when, and only when, a person—

    (a) induces another to break a contract of employment or interferes or induces another to interfere with its performance, or

    (b) threatens that a contract of employment under which he or another is employed will be broken or its performance interfered with, or that he will induce another to break a contract of employment or to interfere with its performance,

and the employer under the contract of employment is not the employer party to the dispute.

(3) Lawful picketing means acts done in the course of such attendance as is declared lawful by section 220 (peaceful picketing)—

    (a) by a worker employed (or, in the case of a worker not in employment, last employed) by the employer party to the dispute, or

    (b) by a trade union official whose attendance is lawful by virtue of subsection (1)(b) of that section.

(4) For the purposes of this section an employer shall not be treated as party to a dispute between another employer and workers of that employer; and where more than one employer is in dispute with his workers, the dispute between each employer and his workers shall be treated as a separate dispute.

In this subsection 'worker' has the same meaning as in section 244 (meaning of 'trade dispute').

(5) An act in contemplation or furtherance of a trade dispute which is primary action in relation to that dispute may not be relied on as secondary action in relation to another trade dispute.

Primary action means such action as is mentioned in paragraph (a) or (b) of subsection (2) where the employer under the contract of employment is the employer party to the dispute.

(6) In this section 'contract of employment' includes any contract under which one person personally does work or performs services for another, and related expressions shall be construed accordingly.

225 Pressure to impose union recognition requirement

(1) An act is not protected if it constitutes, or is one of a number of acts which together constitute, an inducement or attempted inducement of a person—

    (a) to incorporate in a contract to which that person is a party, or a proposed contract to which he intends to be a party, a term or condition which is or would be void by virtue of section 186 (recognition requirement in contract for goods or services), or

    (b) to contravene section 187 (refusal to deal with person on grounds of union exclusion).

(2) An act is not protected if—

    (a) it interferes with the supply (whether or not under a contract) of goods or services, or can reasonably be expected to have that effect, and

    (b) one of the facts relied upon for the purpose of establishing liability is that a person has—

        (i) induced another to break a contract of employment or interfered or induced another to interfere with its performance, or

        (ii) threatened that a contract of employment under which he or another is employed will be broken or its performance interfered with, or that he will induce another to break a contract of employment or to interfere with its performance, and

    (c) the reason, or one of the reasons, for doing the act is the fact or belief that the supplier (not being the employer under the contract of employment mentioned in paragraph (b)) does not, or might not—

        (i) recognise one or more trade unions for the purpose of negotiating on behalf of workers, or any class of worker, employed by him, or

        (ii) negotiate or consult with, or with an official of, one or more trade unions.

226 Requirement of ballot before action by trade union

(1) An act done by a trade union to induce a person to take part, or continue to take part, in industrial action[—

    (a) is not protected unless the industrial action has the support of a ballot, and

    (b) where section 226A falls to be complied with in relation to the person's employer, is not protected as respects the employer unless the trade union has complied with section 226A in relation to him.]

236 No compulsion to work

No court shall, whether by way of—

    (a) an order for specific performance or specific implement of a contract of employment, or

    (b) an injunction or interdict restraining a breach or threatened breach of such a contract,

compel an employee to do any work or attend at any place for the doing of any work.

237 Dismissal of those taking part in unofficial industrial action

(1) An employee has no right to complain of unfair dismissal if at the time of dismissal he was taking part in an unofficial strike or other unofficial industrial action.

(2) A strike or other industrial action is unofficial in relation to an employee unless—

    (a) he is a member of a trade union and the action is authorised or endorsed by that union, or

    (b) he is not a member of a trade union but there are among those taking part in the industrial action members of a trade union by which the action has been authorised or endorsed.

Provided that, a strike or other industrial action shall not be regarded as unofficial if none of those taking part in it are members of a trade union.

240 Breach of contract involving injury to persons or property

(1) A person commits an offence who wilfully and maliciously breaks a contract of service or hiring, knowing or having reasonable cause to believe that the probable consequences of his so doing, either alone or in combination with others, will be—

    (a) to endanger human life or cause serious bodily injury, or

    (b) to expose valuable property, whether real or personal, to destruction or serious injury.

(2) Subsection (1) applies equally whether the offence is committed from malice conceived against the person endangered or injured or, as the case may be, the owner of the property destroyed or injured, or otherwise.

(4) This section does not apply to seamen.

241   Intimidation or annoyance by violence or otherwise

(1) A person commits an offence who, with a view to compelling another person to abstain from doing or to do any act which that person has a legal right to do or abstain from doing, wrongfully and without legal authority—

(a) uses violence to or intimidates that person or his [spouse or civil partner] or children, or injures his property,

(b) persistently follows that person about from place to place,

(c) hides any tools, clothes or other property owned or used by that person, or deprives him of or hinders him in the use thereof,

(d) watches or besets the house or other place where that person resides, works, carries on business or happens to be, or the approach to any such house or place, or

(e) follows that person with two or more other persons in a disorderly manner in or through any street or road.

244   Meaning of 'trade dispute' in Part V [ss 219–246]

(1) In this Part a 'trade dispute' means a dispute between workers and their employer which relates wholly or mainly to one or more of the following—

(a) terms and conditions of employment, or the physical conditions in which any workers are required to work;

(b) engagement or non-engagement, or termination or suspension of employment or the duties of employment, of one or more workers;

(c) allocation of work or the duties of employment between workers or groups of workers;

(d) matters of discipline;

(e) a worker's membership or non-membership of a trade union;

(f) facilities for officials of trade unions; and

(g) machinery for negotiation or consultation, and other procedures, relating to any of the above matters, including the recognition by employers or employers' associations of the right of a trade union to represent workers in such negotiation or consultation or in the carrying out of such procedures.

245   Crown employees and contracts

Where a person holds any office or employment under the Crown on terms which do not constitute a contract of employment between that person and the Crown, those terms shall nevertheless be deemed to constitute such a contract for the purposes of—

(a) the law relating to liability in tort of a person who commits an act which—

(i) induces another person to break a contract, interferes with the performance of a contract or induces another person to interfere with its performance, or

(ii) consists in a threat that a contract will be broken or its performance interfered with, or that any person will be induced to break a contract or interfere with its performance, and

(b) the provisions of this or any other Act which refer (whether in relation to contracts generally or only in relation to contracts of employment) to such an act.

273   Crown employment

(1) The provisions of this Act have effect (except as mentioned below) in relation to Crown employment and persons in Crown employment as in relation to other employment and other workers or employees.

(5) Sections 137 to 143 (rights in relation to trade union membership: access to employment) apply in relation to Crown employment otherwise than under a contract only where the terms of employment correspond to those of a contract of employment.

288   Restriction on contracting out

(1) Any provision in an agreement (whether a contract of employment or not) is void in so far as it purports—

    (a) to exclude or limit the operation of any provision of this Act, or

    (b) to preclude a person from bringing—

        (i) proceedings before an [employment tribunal] or the Central Arbitration Committee under any provision of this Act, [...]

[(2A) Subsection (1) does not apply to an agreement to refrain from instituting or continuing any proceedings, other than excepted proceedings, specified in subsection 1(b) of that section before an industrial tribunal if the conditions regulating compromise agreements under this Act are satisfied in relation to the agreement.

(2B) The conditions regulating compromise agreements under this Act are that—

    (a) the agreement must be in writing;

    (b) the agreement must relate to the particular proceedings;

    (c) the complainant must have received advice from a relevant independent adviser as to the terms and effect of the proposed agreement and in particular its effect on his ability to pursue his rights before an industrial tribunal;

    (d) there must be in force, when the adviser gives the advice, a contract of insurance, or an indemnity provided for members of a profession or professional body covering the risk of a claim by the complainant in respect of loss arising in consequence of the advice;

    (e) the agreement must identify the adviser; and

    (f) the agreement must state that the conditions regulating compromise agreements under this Act are satisfied.]

Railways Act 1993

(1993, c. 43)

122   Statutory authority as a defence to actions in nuisance etc.

(1) Subject to the following provisions of this section—

    (a) any person shall have authority—

        (i) to use, or to cause or permit any agent or independent contractor of his to use, rolling stock on any track, or

        (ii) to use, or to cause or permit any agent or independent contractor of his to use, any land comprised in a network, station or light maintenance depot for or in connection with the provision of network services, station services in light maintenance services, and

    (b) any person who is the owner or occupier of any land shall have authority to authorise, consent to or acquiesce in—

        (i) the use by another of rolling stock on any track comprised in that land, or

        (ii) the use by another of that land for or in connection with the provision of network services, station services or light maintenance services,

if and so long as the qualifying conditions are satisfied in the particular case.

(3) The authority conferred by this section is conferred only for the purpose of providing a defence of statutory authority—

    (a) in England and Wales—

        (i) in any proceedings, whether civil or criminal, in nuisance; or

(ii) in any civil proceedings, other than proceedings for breach of statutory duty, in respect of the escape of things from land;

(4) Nothing in this section shall be construed as excluding a defence of statutory authority otherwise available under or by virtue of any enactment.

Criminal Justice and Public Order Act 1994

(1994, c. 33)

60 Powers to stop and search in anticipation of violence

[(1) If a police officer of or above the rank of inspector reasonably believes—

(a) that incidents involving serious violence may take place in any locality in his police area, and that it is expedient to give an authorisation under this section to prevent their occurrence, or

(b) that persons are carrying dangerous instruments or offensive weapons in any locality in his police area without good reason,

he may give an authorisation that the powers conferred by this section shall be exercisable at any place within that locality for a specified period not exceeding 24 hours.]

(5) A constable may, in the exercise of [the powers conferred by subsection (4) above], stop any person or vehicle and make any search he thinks fit whether or not he has any grounds for suspecting that the person or vehicle is carrying weapons or articles of that kind.

(6) If in the course of a search under this section a constable discovers a dangerous instrument or an article which he has reasonable grounds for suspecting to be an offensive weapon, he may seize it.

61 Power to remove trespassers on land

(1) If the senior police officer present at the scene reasonably believes that two or more persons are trespassing on land and are present there with the common purpose of residing there for any period, that reasonable steps have been taken by or on behalf of the occupier to ask them to leave and—

(a) that any of those persons has caused damage to the land or to property on the land or used threatening, abusive or insulting words or behaviour towards the occupier, a member of his family or an employee or agent of his, or

(b) that those persons have between them six or more vehicles on the land,

he may direct those persons, or any of them, to leave the land and to remove any vehicles or other property they have with them on the land.

(4) If a person knowing that a direction under subsection (1) above has been given which applies to him—

(a) fails to leave the land as soon as reasonably practicable, or

(b) having left again enters the land as a trespasser within the period of three months beginning with the day on which the direction was given, he commits an offence...

62 Supplementary powers of seizure

(1) If a direction has been given under section 61 and a constable reasonably suspects that any person to whom the direction applies has, without reasonable excuse—

(a) failed to remove any vehicle on the land which appears to the constable to belong to him or to be in his possession or under his control; or

(b) entered the land as a trespasser with a vehicle within the period of three months beginning with the day on which the direction was given,

the constable may seize and remove that vehicle.

63 Powers to remove persons attending or preparing for a rave

(1) This section applies to a gathering on land in the open air of [20] or more persons (whether or not trespassers) at which amplified music is played during the night (with or without intermissions)

and is such as, by reason of its loudness and duration and the time at which it is played, is likely to cause serious distress to the inhabitants of the locality; and for this purpose—

(a) such a gathering continues during intermissions in the music and where the gathering extends over several days, throughout the period during which amplified music is played at night (with or without intermissions); and

(b) 'music' includes sounds wholly or predominantly characterised by the emission of a succession of repetitive beats.

[(1A) This section also applies to a gathering if—

(a) it is a gathering on land of 20 or more persons who are trespassing on the land; and

(b) it would be a gathering of a kind mentioned in subsection (1) above if it took place on land in the open air.]

(2) If, as respects any land [...], a police officer of at least the rank of superintendent reasonably believes that—

(a) two or more persons are making preparations for the holding there of a gathering to which this section applies,

(b) ten or more persons are waiting for such a gathering to begin there, or

(c) ten or more persons are attending such a gathering which is in progress,

he may give a direction that those persons and any other persons who come to prepare or wait for or to attend the gathering are to leave the land and remove any vehicles or other property which they have with them on the land.

(6) If a person knowing that a direction has been given which applies to him—

(a) fails to leave the land as soon as reasonably practicable, or

(b) having left again enters the land within the period of 7 days beginning with the day on which the direction was given,

he commits an offence...

64 Supplementary powers of entry and seizure

(4) If a direction has been given under section 63 and a constable reasonably suspects that any person to whom the direction applies has, without reasonable excuse—

(a) failed to remove any vehicle or sound equipment on the land which appears to the constable to belong to him or to be in his possession or under his control; or

(b) entered the land as a trespasser with a vehicle or sound equipment within the period of 7 days beginning with the day on which the direction was given,

the constable may seize and remove that vehicle or sound equipment.

65 Raves: power to stop persons from proceeding

(1) If a constable in uniform reasonably believes that a person is on his way to a gathering to which section 63 applies in relation to which a direction under section 63(2) is in force, he may, subject to subsections (2) and (3) below—

(a) stop that person, and

(b) direct him not to proceed in the direction of the gathering.

(2) The power conferred by subsection (1) above may only be exercised at a place within 5 miles of the boundary of the site of the gathering.

66 Power of court to forfeit sound equipment

(1) Where a person is convicted of an offence under section 63 in relation to a gathering to which that section applies and the court is satisfied that any sound equipment which has been seized from him under section 64(4), or which was in his possession or under his control at the relevant time, has been used at the gathering the court may make an order for forfeiture under this subsection in respect of that property.

(2) The court may make an order under subsection (1) above whether or not it also deals with the offender in respect of the offence in any other way and without regard to any restrictions on forfeiture in any enactment.

(3) In considering whether to make an order under subsection (1) above in respect of any property a court shall have regard—

    (a) to the value of the property; and

    (b) to the likely financial and other effects on the offender of the making of the order (taken together with any other order that the court contemplates making).

(4) An order under subsection (1) above shall operate to deprive the offender of his rights, if any, in the property to which it relates, and the property shall (if not already in their possession) be taken into the possession of the police.

(5) Except in a case to which subsection (6) below applies, where any property has been forfeited under subsection (1) above, a magistrates' court may, on application by a claimant of the property, other than the offender from whom it was forfeited under subsection (1) above, make an order for delivery of the property to the applicant if it appears to the court that he is the owner of the property.

(7) No application shall be made under subsection (5), or by virtue of subsection (6), above by any claimant of the property after the expiration of 6 months from the date on which an order under subsection (1) above was made in respect of the property.

(8) No such application shall succeed unless the claimant satisfies the court either that he had not consented to the offender having possession of the property or that he did not know, and had no reason to suspect, that the property was likely to be used at a gathering to which section 63 applies.

68   Offence of aggravated trespass

(1) A person commits the offence of aggravated trespass if he trespasses on land [...] and, in relation to any lawful activity which persons are engaging in or are about to engage in on that or adjoining land [...], does there anything which is intended by him to have the effect—

    (a) of intimidating those persons or any of them so as to deter them or any of them from engaging in that activity,

    (b) of obstructing that activity, or

    (c) of disrupting that activity.

[(1A) The reference in subsection (1) above to trespass includes, in Scotland, the exercise of access rights (within the meaning of the Land Reform (Scotland) Act 2003 (asp 2) up to the point when they cease to be exercisable by virtue of the commission of the offence under that subsection.]

(2) Activity on any occasion on the part of a person or persons on land is 'lawful' for the purposes of this section if he or they may engage in the activity on the land on that occasion without committing an offence or trespassing on the land.

69   Powers to remove persons committing or participating in aggravated trespass

(1) If the senior police officer present at the scene reasonably believes—

    (a) that a person is committing, has committed or intends to commit the offence of aggravated trespass on land [...]; or

    (b) that two or more persons are trespassing on land [...] and are present there with the common purpose of intimidating persons so as to deter them from engaging in a lawful activity or of obstructing or disrupting a lawful activity,

he may direct that person or (as the case may be) those persons (or any of them) to leave the land.

(3) If a person knowing that a direction under subsection (1) above has been given which applies to him—

    (a) fails to leave the land as soon as practicable, or

    (b) having left again enters the land as a trespasser within the period of [51 weeks] beginning with the day on which the direction was given,

he commits an offence . . .

Value Added Tax Act 1994

(1994, c. 23)

80 **[Credit for, or repayment of, overstated or overpaid VAT]**
  [(1) Where a person—
  (a) has accounted to the Commissioners for VAT for a prescribed accounting period (whenever ended), and
  (b) in doing so, has brought into account as output tax an amount that was not output tax due,
the Commissioners shall be liable to credit the person with that amount.
  (1A) Where the Commissioners—
  (a) have assessed a person to VAT for a prescribed accounting period (whenever ended), and
  (b) in doing so, have brought into account as output tax an amount that was not output tax due,
they shall be liable to credit the person with that amount.
  (1B) Where a person has for a prescribed accounting period (whenever ended) paid to the Commissioners an amount by way of VAT that was not VAT due to them, otherwise than as a result of—
  (a) an amount that was not output tax due being brought into account as output tax, or
  (b) an amount of input tax allowable under section 26 not being brought into account,
the Commissioners shall be liable to repay to that person the amount so paid.]
  (2) The Commissioners shall only be liable to [credit or] repay an amount under this section on a claim being made for the purpose.
  [(2A) Where—
  (a) as a result of a claim under this section by virtue of subsection (1) or (1A) above an amount falls to be credited to a person, and
  (b) after setting any sums against it under or by virtue of this Act, some or all of that amount remains to his credit,
the Commissioners shall be liable to pay (or repay) to him so much of that amount as so remains.]
  (3) It shall be a defence, in relation to a claim [under this section by virtue of subsection (1) or (1A) above, that the crediting] of an amount would unjustly enrich the claimant.]
  [(3A) Subsection (3B) below applies for the purposes of subsection (3) above where—
  (a) an amount would (apart from subsection (3) above) fall to be credited under subsection (1) or (1A) above to any person ('the taxpayer'), and
  (b) the whole or a part of the amount brought into account as mentioned in paragraph (b) of that subsection has, for practical purposes, been borne by a person other than the taxpayer.
  (3B) Where, in a case to which this subsection applies, loss or damage has been or may be incurred by the taxpayer as a result of mistaken assumptions made in his case about the operation of any VAT provisions, that loss or damage shall be disregarded, except to the extent of the quantified amount, in the making of any determination—
  (a) of whether or to what extent the crediting of an amount to the taxpayer would enrich him; or
  (b) of whether or to what extent any enrichment of the taxpayer would be unjust.
  (3C) In subsection (3B) above—
  'the quantified amount' means the amount (if any) which is shown by the taxpayer to constitute the amount that would appropriately compensate him for loss or damage shown by him to have resulted, for any business carried on by him, from the making of the mistaken assumptions; and
  'VAT provisions' means the provisions of—
  (a) any enactment, subordinate legislation or Community legislation (whether or not still in force) which relates to VAT or to any matter connected with VAT; or

(b) any notice published by the Commissioners under or for the purposes of any such enactment or subordinate legislation.

(4) The Commissioners shall not be liable on a claim under this section—

(a) to credit an amount to a person under subsection (1) or (1A) above, or

(b) to repay an amount to a person under subsection (1B) above,

if the claim is made more than 4 years after the relevant date.

(4A) Where—

(a) an amount has been credited under subsection (1) or (1A) above to any person at any time on or after 26th May 2005, and

(b) the amount so credited exceeded the amount which the Commissioners were liable at that time to credit to that person,

the Commissioners may, to the best of their judgement, assess the excess credited to that person and notify it to him.

(4AA) An assessment under subsection (4A) shall not be made more than 2 years after the later of:

(a) the end of the prescribed accounting period in which the amount was credited to the person, and

(b) the time when evidence of facts sufficient in the opinion of the Commissioners to justify the making of the assessment comes to the knowledge of the Commissioners.

(4C) Subsections (3) to (8) of section 78A apply in the case of an assessment under subsection (4A) above as they apply in the case of an assessment under section 78A(1).

(6) A claim under this section shall be made in such form and manner and shall be supported by such documentary evidence as the Commissioners prescribe by regulations; and regulations under this subsection may make different provision for different cases.

(7) Except as provided by this section, the Commissioners shall not be liable to repay an amount accounted for or paid to them by way of VAT that was not VAT due to them.]

[80A   Arrangements for reimbursing customers

(1) The Commissioners may by regulations make provision for reimbursement arrangements made by any person to be disregarded for the purposes of section 80(3) except where the arrangements—

(a) contain such provision as may be required by the regulations; and

(b) are supported by such undertakings to comply with the provisions of the arrangements as may be required by the regulations to be given to the Commissioners.

(2) In this section 'reimbursement arrangements' means any arrangements for the purposes of a claim under section 80 which—

(a) are made by any person for the purpose of securing that he is not unjustly enriched by the [crediting] of any amount in pursuance of the claim; and

(b) provide for the reimbursement of persons who have for practical purposes borne the whole or any part of [the amount bought into account as mentioned in paragraph (b) of subsection (1) or (1A) of that section].

(3) Without prejudice to the generality of subsection (1) above, the provision that may be required by regulations under this section to be contained in reimbursement arrangements includes—

(a) provision requiring a reimbursement for which the arrangements provide to be made within such period after the crediting of that amount to which it relates as may be specified in the regulations;

[(b) provision for cases where an amount is credited but an equal amount is not reimbursed in accordance with the arrangements;]

(c) provision requiring interest paid by the Commissioners on any amount [paid (or repaid)] by them to be treated in the same way as that amount for the purposes of any requirement under the arrangements to make reimbursement or to repay the Commissioners;

(d) provision requiring such records relating to the carrying out of the arrangements as may be described in the regulations to be kept and produced to the Commissioners, or to an officer of theirs.

(4) Regulations under this section may impose obligations on such persons as may be specified in the regulations—

(a) [to make the repayments, or give the notifications, to the Commissioners that they are required to make or give] in pursuance of any provisions contained in any reimbursement arrangements by virtue of subsection (3)(b) or (c) above;

(e) to comply with any requirements contained in any such arrangements by virtue of subsection (3)(d) above.

(5) Regulations under this section may make provision for the form and manner in which, and the times at which, undertakings are to be given to the Commissioners in accordance with the regulations; and any such provision may allow for those matters to be determined by the Commissioners in accordance with the regulations.

(6) Regulations under this section may—

(a) contain any such incidental, supplementary, consequential or transitional provision as appears to the Commissioners to be necessary or expedient; and

(b) make different provision for different circumstances.

(7) Regulations under this section may have effect (irrespective of when the claim for [credit] was made) for the purposes of [the crediting of any amount] by the Commissioners after the time when the regulations are made; and, accordingly, such regulations may apply to arrangements made before that time.]

Criminal Injuries Compensation Act 1995

(1995, c. 53)

1   The Criminal Injuries Compensation Scheme

(1) The Secretary of State shall make arrangements for the payment of compensation to, or in respect of, persons who have sustained one or more criminal injuries.

(2) Any such arrangements shall include the making of a scheme providing, in particular, for—

(a) the circumstances in which awards may be made; and

(b) the categories of person to whom awards may be made.

(3) The scheme shall be known as the Criminal Injuries Compensation Scheme.

(4) In this Act—

'award' means an award of compensation made in accordance with the provisions of the Scheme;

'claim officer' means a person appointed by the Secretary of State under section 3(4)(b);

'compensation' means compensation payable under an award;

'criminal injury', 'loss of earnings' and 'special expenses' have such meaning as may be specified;

'the Scheme' means the Criminal Injuries Compensation Scheme;

'Scheme manager' means a person appointed by the Secretary of State to have overall responsibility for managing the provisions of the Scheme (other than those to which section 5(2) applies); and

'specified' means specified by the Scheme.

2   Basis on which compensation is to be calculated

(1) The amount of compensation payable under an award shall be determined in accordance with the provisions of the Scheme.

(2) Provision shall be made for—

(a) a standard amount of compensation, determined by reference to the nature of the injury;

(b) in such cases as may be specified, an additional amount of compensation calculated with respect to loss of earnings;

     (c) in such cases as may be specified, an additional amount of compensation calculated with respect to special expenses; and

     (d) in cases of fatal injury, such additional amounts as may be specified or otherwise determined in accordance with the Scheme.

  (3) Provision shall be made for the standard amount to be determined—

     (a) in accordance with a table ('the Tariff') prepared by the Secretary of State as part of the Scheme and such other provisions of the Scheme as may be relevant; or

     (b) where no provision is made in the Tariff with respect to the injury in question, in accordance with such provisions of the Scheme as may be relevant.

  (4) The Tariff shall show, in respect of each description of injury mentioned in the Tariff, the standard amount of compensation payable in respect of that description of injury.

  (5) An injury may be described in the Tariff in such a way, including by reference to the nature of the injury, its severity or the circumstances in which it was sustained, as the Secretary of State considers appropriate.

  (6) The Secretary of State may at any time alter the Tariff—

     (a) by adding to the descriptions of injury mentioned there;

     (b) by removing a description of injury;

     (c) by increasing or reducing the amount shown as the standard amount of compensation payable in respect of a particular description of injury; or

     (d) in such other way as he considers appropriate.

  (7) The Scheme may—

     (a) provide for amounts of compensation not to exceed such maximum amounts as may be specified;

     (b) include such transitional provision with respect to any alteration of its provisions relating to compensation as the Secretary of State considers appropriate.

3   Claims and awards

  (1) The Scheme may, in particular, include provision—

     (a) as to the circumstances in which an award may be withheld or the amount of compensation reduced;

     (b) for an award to be made subject to conditions;

     (c) for the whole or any part of any compensation to be repayable in specified circumstances;

     (d) for compensation to be held subject to trusts, in such cases as may be determined in accordance with the Scheme;

     (e) requiring claims under the Scheme to be made within such periods as may be specified by the Scheme; and

     (f) imposing other time limits.

  (2) Where, in accordance with any provision of the Scheme, it falls to one person to satisfy another as to any matter, the standard of proof required shall be that applicable in civil proceedings.

  (3) Where, in accordance with any provision of the Scheme made by virtue of subsection (1)(c), any amount falls to be repaid it shall be recoverable as a debt due to the Crown.

  (4) The Scheme shall include provision for claims for compensation to be determined and awards and payments of compensation to be made—

     (a) if a Scheme manager has been appointed, by persons appointed for the purpose by the Scheme manager; but

     (b) otherwise by persons ('claims officers') appointed for the purpose by the Secretary of State.

  (5) A claims officer—

     (a) shall be appointed on such terms and conditions as the Secretary of State considers appropriate; but

     (b) shall not be regarded as having been appointed to exercise functions of the Secretary of State or to act on his behalf.

(6) No decision taken by a claims officer shall be regarded as having been taken by, or on behalf of, the Secretary of State.

(7) If a Scheme manager has been appointed—

(a) he shall not be regarded as exercising functions of the Secretary of State or as acting on his behalf; and

(b) no decision taken by him or by any person appointed by him shall be regarded as having been taken by, or on behalf of, the Secretary of State.

7 Inalienability of awards

(1) Every assignment (or, in Scotland, assignation) of, or charge on, an award and every agreement to assign or charge an award shall be void.

(2) On the bankruptcy of a person in whose favour an award is made (or, in Scotland, on the sequestration of such a person's estate), the award shall not pass to any trustee or other person acting on behalf of his creditors.

[7A Recovery of compensation from offenders: general

(1) The Secretary of State may, by regulations made by statutory instrument, make provision for the recovery from an appropriate person of an amount equal to all or part of the compensation paid in respect of a criminal injury.

(2) An appropriate person is a person who has been convicted of an offence in respect of the criminal injury.

(3) The amount recoverable from a person under the regulations must be determined by reference only to the extent to which the criminal injury is directly attributable to an offence of which he has been convicted.

(4) The regulations may confer functions in respect of recovery on—

(a) claims officers;

(b) if a Scheme manager has been appointed, persons appointed by the Scheme manager under section 3(4)(a).

(5) The regulations may not authorise the recovery of an amount in respect of compensation from a person to the extent that the compensation has been repaid in accordance with the Scheme.]

[7B Recovery notices

(1) If, under regulations made under section 7A(1), an amount has been determined as recoverable from a person, he must be given a notice (a 'recovery notice') in accordance with the regulations which—

(a) requires him to pay that amount, and

(b) contains the information mentioned in subsection (2).

(2) The information is—

(a) the reasons for the determination that an amount is recoverable from the person;

(b) the basis on which the amount has been determined;

(c) the way in which and the date before which the amount is required to be paid;

(d) the means by which the amount may be recovered if it is not paid in accordance with the notice;

(e) the grounds on which and the procedure by means of which he may seek a review if he objects to—

(i)   the determination that an amount is recoverable from him;

(ii) the amount determined as recoverable from him.

(3) The Secretary of State may by order made by statutory instrument amend subsection (2) by—

(a) adding information;

(b) omitting information;

(c) changing the description of information.]

[7C   Review of recovery determinations

(1) Regulations under section 7A(1) shall include provision for the review, in such circumstances as may be prescribed by the regulations, of—

    (a) a determination that an amount is recoverable from a person;

    (b) the amount determined as recoverable from a person.

(2) A person from whom an amount has been determined as recoverable under the regulations may seek such a review only on the grounds—

    (a) that he has not been convicted of an offence to which the injury is directly attributable;

    (b) that the compensation paid was not determined in accordance with the Scheme;

    (c) that the amount determined as recoverable from him was not determined in accordance with the regulations.

(3) Any such review must be conducted by a person other than the person who made the determination under review.

(4) The person conducting any such review may—

    (a) set aside the determination that the amount is recoverable;

    (b) reduce the amount determined as recoverable;

    (c) increase the amount determined as recoverable;

    (d) determine to take no action under paragraphs (a) to (c).

(5) But the person conducting any such review may increase the amount determined as recoverable if (but only if) it appears to that person that the interests of justice require the amount to be increased.]

[7D   Recovery proceedings

(1) An amount determined as recoverable from a person under regulations under section 7A(1) is recoverable from him as a debt due to the Crown if (but only if)—

    (a) he has been given a recovery notice in accordance with the regulations which complies with the requirements of section 7B, and

    (b) he has failed to pay the amount in accordance with the notice.

(2) In any proceedings for the recovery of the amount from a person, it is a defence for the person to show—

    (a) that he has not been convicted of an offence to which the injury is directly attributable;

    (b) that the compensation paid was not determined in accordance with the Scheme; or

    (c) that the amount determined as recoverable from him was not determined in accordance with regulations under section 7A.

(3) In any such proceedings, except for the purposes of subsection (2)(b), no question may be raised or finding made as to the amount that was, or ought to have been, the subject of an award.

(4) For the purposes of section 9 of the Limitation Act 1980 (time limit for actions for sums recoverable by statute to run from date on which cause of action accrued) the cause of action to recover that amount shall be taken to have accrued—

    (a) on the date on which the compensation was paid; or

    (b) if later, on the date on which a person from whom an amount is sought to be recovered was convicted of an offence to which the injury is directly attributable.

(5) If that person is convicted of more than one such offence and the convictions are made on different dates, the reference in subsection (4)(b) to the date on which he was convicted of such an offence shall be taken to be a reference to the earlier or earliest (as the case may be) of the dates on which he was convicted of such an offence.]

9   Financial provisions

(1) The Secretary of State may pay such remuneration, allowances or gratuities to or in respect of claims officers and other persons appointed by him under this Act [...] as he considers appropriate.

(4) Sums required for the payment of compensation in accordance with the Scheme shall be provided by the Secretary of State out of money provided by Parliament.

(5) Where a Scheme manager has been appointed, the Secretary of State may make such payments to him, in respect of the discharge of his functions in relation to the Scheme, as the Secretary of State considers appropriate.

(6) Any expenses incurred by the Secretary of State under this Act shall be paid out of money provided by Parliament.

[(6A) Any expenses incurred by the Secretary of State under subsection (6) above as regards Scotland shall be reimbursed to the Secretary of State by the Scottish Minister.]

(7) Any sums received by the Secretary of State under any provision of the Scheme made by virtue of section 3(1)(c) [, or by virtue of regulations made under section 7A(1),] shall be paid by him into the Consolidated Fund.

Landlord and Tenant (Covenants) Act 1995

(1995, c. 30)

3 Transmission of benefit and burden of covenants

(1) The benefit and burden of all landlord and tenant covenants of a tenancy—

  (a) shall be annexed and incident to the whole, and to each and every part, of the premises demised by the tenancy and of the reversion in them, and

  (b) shall in accordance with this section pass on an assignment of the whole or any part of those premises or of the reversion in them.

(2) Where the assignment is by the tenant under the tenancy, then as from the assignment the assignee—

  (a) becomes bound by the tenant covenants of the tenancy except to the extent that—

    (i) immediately before the assignment they did not bind the assignor, or

    (ii) they fall to be complied with in relation to any demised premises not comprised in the assignment; and

  (b) becomes entitled to the benefit of the landlord covenants of the tenancy except to the extent that they fall to be complied with in relation to any such premises.

(3) Where the assignment is by the landlord under the tenancy, then as from the assignment the assignee—

  (a) becomes bound by the landlord covenants of the tenancy except to the extent that—

    (i) immediately before the assignment they did not bind the assignor, or

    (ii) they fall to be complied with in relation to any demised premises not comprised in the assignment; and

  (b) becomes entitled to the benefit of the tenant covenants of the tenancy except to the extent that they fall to be complied with in relation to any such premises.

(4) In determining for the purposes of subsection (2) or (3) whether any covenant bound the assignor immediately before the assignment, any waiver or release of the covenant (in whatever terms) is expressed to be personal to the assignor shall be disregarded.

(5) Any landlord or tenant covenant of a tenancy which is restrictive of the user of land shall, as well as being capable of enforcement against an assignee, be capable of being enforced against any other person who is the owner or occupier of any demised premises to which the covenant relates, even though there is no express provision in the tenancy to that effect.

(6) Nothing in this section shall operate—

  (a) in the case of a covenant which (in whatever terms) is expressed to be personal to any person, to make the covenant enforceable by or (as the case may be) against any other person; or

  (b) to make a covenant enforceable against any person if, apart from this section, it would not be enforceable against him by reason of its not having been registered under the [Land Registration Act 2002] or the Land Charges Act 1972.

(7) To the extent that there remains in force any rule of law by virtue of which the burden of a covenant whose subject matter is not in existence at the time when it is made does not run with the land affected unless the covenantor covenants on behalf of himself and his assigns, that rule of law is hereby abolished in relation to tenancies.

5   Tenant released from covenants on assignment of tenancy

(1) This section applies where a tenant assigns premises demised to him under a tenancy.

(2) If the tenant assigns the whole of the premises demised to him, he—

(a) is released from the tenant covenants of the tenancy, and

(b) ceases to be entitled to the benefit of the landlord covenants of the tenancy, as from the assignment.

(3) If the tenant assigns part only of the premises demised to him, then as from the assignment he—

(a) is released from the tenant covenants of the tenancy, and

(b) ceases to be entitled to the benefit of the landlord covenants of the tenancy, only to the extent that those covenants fall to be complied with in relation to that part of the demised premises.

(4) This section applies as mentioned in subsection (1) whether or not the tenant is tenant of the whole of the premises comprised in the tenancy.

13   Covenants binding two or more persons

(1) Where in consequence of this Act two or more persons are bound by the same covenant, they are so bound both jointly and severally.

(2) Subject to section 24(2), where by virtue of this Act—

(a) two or more persons are bound jointly and severally by the same covenant, and

(b) any of the persons so bound is released from the covenant, the release does not extend to any other of those persons.

(3) For the purpose of providing for contribution between persons who, by virtue of this Act, are bound jointly and severally by a covenant, the Civil Liability (Contribution) Act 1978 shall have effect as if—

(a) liability to a person under a covenant were liability in respect of damage suffered by that person;

(b) references to damage accordingly include a breach of a covenant of a tenancy; and

(c) section 7(2) of that Act were omitted.

23   Effects of becoming subject to liability under, or entitled to benefit of, covenant etc.

(1) Where as a result of an assignment a person becomes by virtue of this Act, bound by or entitled to the benefit of a covenant, he shall not by virtue of this Act have any liability or rights under the covenant in relation to any time falling before the assignment.

(2) Subsection (1) does not preclude any such rights being expressly assigned to the person in question.

(3) Where as a result of an assignment a person becomes, by virtue of this Act, entitled to a right of re-entry contained in a tenancy, that right shall be exercisable in relation to any breach of a covenant of the tenancy occurring before the assignment as in relation to one occurring thereafter, unless by reason of any waiver or release it was not so exercisable immediately before the assignment.

24   Effects of release from liability under, or loss of benefit of, covenant

(1) Any release of a person from a covenant by virtue of this Act does not affect any liability of his arising from a breach of the covenant occurring before the release.

(4) Where by virtue of this Act a person ceases to be entitled to the benefit of a covenant, this does not affect any rights of his arising from a breach of the covenant occurring before he ceases to be so entitled.

25 Agreement void if it restricts operation of the Act

(1) Any agreement relating to a tenancy is void to the extent that—

    (a) it would apart from this section have effect to exclude, modify or otherwise frustrate the operation of any provision of this Act, or

    (b) it provides for—

        (i) the termination or surrender of the tenancy, or

        (ii) the imposition on the tenant of any penalty, disability or liability, in the event of the operation of any provision of this Act, or

    (c) it provides for any of the matters referred to in paragraph (b)(i) or (ii) and does so (whether expressly or otherwise) in connection with, or in consequence of, the operation of any provision of this Act.

Merchant Shipping Act 1995

(1995, c. 21)

92 Duty of ship to assist the other in case of collision

(1) In every case of collision between two ships, it shall be the duty of the master of each ship, if and so far as he can do so without danger to his own ship, crew and passengers (if any)—

    (a) to render to the other ship, its master, crew and passengers (if any) such assistance as may be practicable, and may be necessary to save them from any danger caused by the collision, and to stay by the other ship until he has ascertained that it has no need of further assistance; and

    (b) to give to the master of the other ship the name of his own ship and also the names of the ports from which it comes and to which it is bound.

(2) The duties imposed on the master of a ship by subsection (1) above apply to the masters of United Kingdom ships and to the masters of foreign ships when in United Kingdom waters.

(3) The failure of the master of a ship to comply with the provisions of this section shall not raise any presumption of law that the collision was caused by his wrongful act, neglect, or default.

(4) If the master fails without reasonable excuse to comply with this section, he shall—

    (a) in the case of a failure to comply with subsection (1)(a) above, be liable—

        (i) on summary conviction, to a fine not exceeding £50,000 or imprisonment for a term not exceeding six months or both;

        (ii) on conviction on indictment, to a fine or imprisonment for a term not exceeding two years or both; and

    (b) in the case of a failure to comply with subsection (1)(b) above, be liable—

        (i) on summary conviction, to a fine not exceeding the statutory maximum;

        (ii) on conviction on indictment, to a fine;

and in either case if he is a certified officer, an inquiry into his conduct may be held, and his certificate cancelled or suspended.

93 Duty to assist ships, etc. in distress

(1) The master of a ship, on receiving at sea a signal of distress [from an aircraft] or information from any source that [an] aircraft is in distress, shall proceed with all speed to the assistance of the persons in distress (informing them if possible that he is doing so) unless he is unable, or in the special circumstances of the case considers it unreasonable or unnecessary, to do so, or unless he is released from this duty under subsection (4) or (5) below.

234 Power to pass over adjoining land

(1) In circumstances where this section applies by virtue of section 231 in relation to any vessel, all persons may, subject to subsections (3) and (4) below, for the purpose of—

    (a) rendering assistance to the vessel,

    (b) saving the lives of shipwrecked persons, or

    (c) saving the cargo or equipment of the vessel,

pass and repass over any adjoining land without being subject to interruption by the owner or occupier and deposit on the land any cargo or other article recovered from the vessel.

    (2) The right of passage conferred by subsection (1) above is a right of passage with or without vehicles.

    (3) No right of passage is conferred by subsection (1) above where there is some public road equally convenient.

    (4) The rights conferred by subsection (1) above shall be so exercised as to do as little damage as possible.

    (5) Any damage sustained by an owner or occupier of land in consequence of the exercise of the right conferred by this section shall be a charge on the vessel, cargo or articles in respect of or by which the damage is caused.

    (6) Any amount payable in respect of such damage shall, in case of dispute, be determined and shall, in default of payment, be recoverable in the same manner as the amount of salvage is determined and recoverable under this Part.

    (7) If the owner or occupier of any land—

        (a) impedes or hinders any person in the exercise of the rights conferred by this section;

        (b) impedes or hinders the deposit on the land of any cargo or other article recovered from the vessel; or

        (c) prevents or attempts to prevent any cargo or other article recovered from the vessel from remaining deposited on the land for a reasonable time until it can be removed to a safe place of public deposit;

he shall be liable, on summary conviction, to a fine not exceeding level 3 on the standard scale.

Arbitration Act 1996

(1996, c. 23)

8   Whether agreement discharged by death of a party

    (1) Unless otherwise agreed by the parties, an arbitration agreement is not discharged by the death of a party and may be enforced by or against the personal representatives of that party.

    (2) Subsection (1) does not affect the operation of any enactment or rule of law by virtue of which a substantive right or obligation is extinguished by death.

29   Immunity of arbitrator

    (1) An arbitrator is not liable for anything done or omitted in the discharge or purported discharge of his functions as arbitrator unless the act or omission is shown to have been in bad faith.

40   General duty of parties

    (1) The parties shall do all things necessary for the proper and expeditious conduct of the arbitral proceedings.

87   Effectiveness of agreement to exclude court's jurisdiction

    (1) In the case of a domestic arbitration agreement any agreement to exclude the jurisdiction of the court under—

        (a) section 45 (determination of preliminary point of law), or

        (b) section 69 (challenging the award: appeal on point of law),

is not effective unless entered into after the commencement of the arbitral proceedings in which the question arises or the award is made.

89 Application of unfair terms regulations to consumer arbitration agreements

(1) The following sections extend the application of the Unfair Terms in Consumer Contracts Regulations 1994 in relation to a term which constitutes an arbitration agreement.

For this purpose 'arbitration agreement' means an agreement to submit to arbitration present or future disputes or differences (whether or not contractual).

90 Regulations apply where consumer is a legal person

The Regulations apply where the consumer is a legal person as they apply where the consumer is a natural person.

91 Arbitration agreement unfair where modest amount sought

(1) A term which constitutes an arbitration agreement is unfair for the purposes of the Regulations so far as it relates to a claim for a pecuniary remedy which does not exceed the amount specified by order for the purposes of this section.

Damages Act 1996

(1996, c. 48)

1 Assumed rate of return on investment of damages

(1) In determining the return to be expected from the investment of a sum awarded as general damages for future pecuniary loss in an action for personal injury the court shall, subject to and in accordance with rules of court made for the purposes of this section, take into account such rate of return as may from time to time be prescribed by an order made by the Lord Chancellor.

(2) Subsection (1) above shall not however prevent the court taking a different rate of return into account if any party to the proceedings shows that it is more appropriate in the case in question.

(3) An order under subsection (1) above may prescribe different rates of return for different classes of case.

(4) Before making an order under subsection (1) above the Lord Chancellor shall consult the Government Actuary and the Treasury; and any order under that subsection shall be made by statutory instrument subject to annulment in pursuance of a resolution of either House of Parliament.

[(5) In the application of this section to Scotland—
- (a) for the reference to the Lord Chancellor in subsections (1) and (4) there is substituted a reference to the Scottish Ministers; and
- (b) in subsection (4)—
- (c) 'and the Treasury' is omitted; and
- (d) for 'either House of Parliament' there is substituted 'the Scottish Parliament'.]

[2 Periodical payments

(1) A court awarding damages for future pecuniary loss in respect of personal injury—
- (a) may order that the damages are wholly or partly to take the form of periodical payments, and
- (b) shall consider whether to make that order.

(2) A court awarding other damages in respect of personal injury may, if the parties consent, order that the damages are wholly or partly to take the form of periodical payments.

(3) A court may not make an order for periodical payments unless satisfied that the continuity of payment under the order is reasonably secure.

(4) For the purpose of subsection (3) the continuity of payment under an order is reasonably secure if—
- (a) it is protected by a guarantee given under section 6 of or the Schedule to this Act,
- (b) it is protected by a scheme under section 213 of the Financial Services and Markets Act 2000 (compensation) (whether or not as modified by section 4 of this Act), or

(c) the source of payment is a government or health service body.

(5) An order for periodical payments may include provision—

(a) requiring the party responsible for the payments to use a method (selected or to be selected by him) under which the continuity of payment is reasonably secure by virtue of subsection (4);

(b) about how the payments are to be made, if not by a method under which the continuity of payment is reasonably secure by virtue of subsection (4);

(c) requiring the party responsible for the payments to take specified action to secure continuity of payment, where continuity is not reasonably secure by virtue of subsection (4);

(d) enabling a party to apply for a variation of provision included under paragraph (b), or (c).

(6) Where a person has a right to receive payments under an order for periodical payments, or where an arrangement is entered into in satisfaction of an order which gives a person a right to receive periodical payments, that person's right under the order or arrangement may not be assigned or charged without the approval of the court which made the order; and—

(a) a court shall not approve an assignment or charge unless satisfied that special circumstances make it necessary, and

(b) a purported assignment or charge, or agreement to assign or charge, is void unless approved by the court.

(7) Where an order is made for periodical payments, an alteration of the method by which the payments are made shall be treated as a breach of the order (whether or not the method was specified under subsection (5)(b)) unless—

(a) the court which made the order declares its satisfaction that the continuity of payment under the new method is reasonably secure,

(b) the new method is protected by a guarantee given under section 6 of or the Schedule to this Act,

(c) the new method is protected by a scheme under section 213 of the Financial Services and Markets Act 2000 (compensation) (whether or not as modified by section 4 of this Act), or

(d) the source of payment under the new method is a government or health service body.

(8) An order for periodical payments shall be treated as providing for the amount of payments to vary by reference to the retail prices index (within the meaning of section 833(2) of the Income and Corporation Taxes Act 1988) at such times, and in such a manner, as may be determined by or in accordance with Civil Procedure Rules.

(9) But an order for periodical payments may include provision—

(a) disapplying subsection (8), or

(b) modifying the effect of subsection (8).]

[2A   Periodical payments: supplementary

(1) Civil Procedure Rules may require a court to take specified matters into account in considering—

(a) whether to order periodical payments;

(b) the security of the continuity of payment;

(c) whether to approve an assignment or charge.

(2) For the purposes of section 2(4)(c) and (7)(d) 'government or health service body' means a body designated as a government body or a health service body by order made by the Lord Chancellor.

(3) An order under subsection (2)—

(a) shall be made by statutory instrument, and

(b) shall be subject to annulment in pursuance of a resolution of either House of Parliament.

(4) Section 2(6) is without prejudice to a person's power to assign a right to the scheme manager established under section 212 of the Financial Services and Markets Act 2000.

(5) In section 2 'damages' includes an interim payment which a court orders a defendant to make to a claimant.

(6) In the application of this section and section 2 to Northern Ireland—

(a) a reference to Civil Procedure Rules shall be taken as a reference to rules of court, and

(b) a reference to a claimant shall be taken as a reference to a plaintiff.

(7) Section 2 is without prejudice to any power exercisable apart from that section.]

[2B Variation of orders and settlements

(1) The Lord Chancellor may by order enable a court which has made an order for periodical payments to vary the order in specified circumstances (otherwise than in accordance with section 2(5)(d)).

(2) The Lord Chancellor may by order enable a court in specified circumstances to vary the terms on which a claim or action for damages for personal injury is settled by agreement between the parties if the agreement—

(a) provides for periodical payments, and

(b) expressly permits a party to apply to a court for variation in those circumstances.

(3) An order under this section may make provision—

(a) which operates wholly or partly by reference to a condition or other term of the court's order or of the agreement;

(b) about the nature of an order which may be made by a court on a variation;

(c) about the matters to be taken into account on considering variation;

(d) of a kind that could be made by Civil Procedure Rules or, in relation to Northern Ireland, rules of court (and which may be expressed to be with or without prejudice to the power to make those rules).

(4) An order under this section may apply (with or without modification) or amend an enactment about provisional or further damages.

(5) An order under this section shall be subject to any order under section 1 of the Courts and Legal Services Act 1990 (allocation between High Court and county courts).

(6) An order under this section—

(a) shall be made by statutory instrument,

(b) may not be made unless the Lord Chancellor has consulted such persons as he thinks appropriate,

(c) may not be made unless a draft has been laid before and approved by resolution of each House of Parliament, and

(d) may include transitional, consequential or incidental provision.

(7) In subsection (4)—

'provisional damages' means damages awarded by virtue of subsection (2)(a) of section 32A of the Supreme Court Act 1981 or section 51 of the County Courts Act 1984 (or, in relation to Northern Ireland, paragraph 10(2)(a) of Schedule 6 to the Administration of Justice Act 1982), and

'further damages' means damages awarded by virtue of subsection (2)(b) of either of those sections (or, in relation to Northern Ireland, paragraph 10(2)(b) of Schedule 6 to the Administration of Justice Act 1982).]

3 Provisional damages and fatal accident claims

(1) This section applies where a person—

(a) is awarded provisional damages; and

(b) subsequently dies as a result of the act or omission which gave rise to the cause of action for which the damages were awarded.

(2) The award of the provisional damages shall not operate as a bar to an action in respect of that person's death under the Fatal Accidents Act 1976.

(3) Such part (if any) of—

(a) the provisional damages; and

(b) any further damages awarded to the person in question before his death, as was intended to compensate him for pecuniary loss in a period which in the event falls after his death, shall be taken into account in assessing the amount of any loss of support suffered by the person or persons for whose benefit the action under the Fatal Accidents Act 1976 is brought.

(4) No award of further damages made in respect of that person after his death shall include any amount for loss of income in respect of any period after his death.

(5) In this section 'provisional damages' means damages awarded by virtue of subsection (2)(a) of section 32A of the [Senior Courts Act 1981] or section 51 of the County Courts Act 1984 and 'further damages' means damages awarded by virtue of subsection (2)(b) of either of those sections.

(6) Subsection (2) above applies whether the award of provisional damages was before or after the coming into force of that subsection; and subsections (3) and (4) apply to any award of damages under the 1976 Act or, as the case may be, further damages after the coming into force of those subsections.

(7) In the application of this section to Northern Ireland—

(a) for references to the Fatal Accidents Act 1976 there shall be substituted references to the Fatal Accidents (Northern Ireland) Order 1977;

(b) for the reference to subsection (2)(a) and (b) of section 32A of the [Senior Courts Act 1981] and section 51 of the County Courts Act 1984 there shall be substituted a reference to paragraph 10(2)(a) and (b) of Schedule 6 to the Administration of Justice Act 1982.

[4   Enhanced protection for periodical payments

(1) Subsection (2) applies where—

(a) a person has a right to receive periodical payments, and

(b) his right is protected by a scheme under section 213 of the Financial Services and Markets Act 2000 (compensation), but only as to part of the payments.

(2) The protection provided by the scheme shall extend by virtue of this section to the whole of the payments.

(3) Subsection (4) applies where—

(a) one person ('the claimant') has a right to receive periodical payments from another person ('the defendant'),

(b) a third person ('the insurer') is required by or in pursuance of an arrangement entered into with the defendant (whether or not together with other persons and whether before or after the creation of the claimant's right) to make payments in satisfaction of the claimant's right or for the purpose of enabling it to be satisfied, and

(c) the claimant's right to receive the payments would be wholly or partly protected by a scheme under section 213 of the Financial Services and Markets Act 2000 if it arose from an arrangement of the same kind as that mentioned in paragraph (b) but made between the claimant and the insurer.

(4) For the purposes of the scheme under section 213 of that Act—

(a) the claimant shall be treated as having a right to receive the payments from the insurer under an arrangement of the same kind as that mentioned in subsection (3)(b),

(b) the protection under the scheme in respect of those payments shall extend by virtue of this section to the whole of the payments, and

(c) no person other than the claimant shall be entitled to protection under the scheme in respect of the payments.

(5) In this section 'periodical payments' means periodical payments made pursuant to—

(a) an order of a court in so far as it is made in reliance on section 2 above (including an order as varied), or

(b) an agreement in so far as it settles a claim or action for damages in respect of personal injury (including an agreement as varied).

(6) In subsection (5)(b) the reference to an agreement in so far as it settles a claim or action for damages in respect of personal injury includes a reference to an undertaking given by the Motor Insurers' Bureau (being the company of that name incorporated on 14th June 1946 under the

Companies Act 1929), or an Article 75 insurer under the Bureau's Articles of Association, in relation to a claim or action in respect of personal injury.]

6 Guarantees for public sector settlements

(1) This section applies where—

 (a) a claim or action for damages for personal injury is settled [on terms whereby the damages are to consist wholly or partly of periodical payments]; or

 (b) a court awarding damages for personal injury makes an order incorporating such terms.

(2) If it appears to a Minister of the Crown that the payments are to be made by a body in relation to which he has, by virtue of this section, power to do so, he may guarantee the payments to be made under the agreement or order.

(3) The bodies in relation to which a Minister may give such a guarantee shall, subject to subsection (4) below, be such bodies as are designated in relation to the relevant government department by guidelines agreed upon between that department and the Treasury.

(4) A guarantee purporting to be given by a Minister under this section shall not be invalidated by any failure on his part to act in accordance with such guidelines as are mentioned in subsection (3) above.

(5) A guarantee under this section shall be given on such terms as the Minister concerned may determine but those terms shall in every case require the body in question to reimburse the Minister, with interest, for any sums paid by him in fulfilment of the guarantee.

(6) Any sums required by a Minister for fulfilling a guarantee under this section shall be defrayed out of money provided by Parliament and any sums received by him by way of reimbursement or interest shall be paid into the Consolidated Fund.

(7) A Minister who has given one or more guarantees under this section shall, as soon as possible after the end of each financial year, lay before each House of Parliament a statement showing what liabilities are outstanding in respect of the guarantees in that year, what sums have been paid in that year in fulfilment of the guarantees and what sums (including interest) have been recovered in that year in respect of the guarantees or are still owing.

(8) In this section 'government department' means any department of Her Majesty's government in the United Kingdom and for the purposes of this section a government department is a relevant department in relation to a Minister if he has responsibilities in respect of that department.

[(8A) In the application of subsection (3) above to Scotland, for the words from 'guidelines' to the end there shall be substituted 'the Minister'.]

[(8B) In the application of this section to Scotland, 'relevant government department' shall be read as if it was a reference to any part of the Scottish Administration and subsection (8) shall cease to have effect.]

(9) The Schedule to this Act has effect for conferring corresponding powers on Northern Ireland departments.

7 Interpretation

(1) Subject to subsection (2) below, in this Act 'personal injury' includes any disease and any impairment of a person's physical or mental condition and references to a claim or action for personal injury include references to such a claim or action brought by virtue of the Law Reform (Miscellaneous Provisions) Act 1934 and to a claim or action brought by virtue of the Fatal Accidents Act 1976.

Defamation Act 1996

(1996, c. 31)

Responsibility for publication

1 Responsibility for publication

(1) In defamation proceedings a person has a defence if he shows that—

 (a) he was not the author, editor or publisher of the statement complained of,

(b) he took reasonable care in relation to its publication, and

(c) he did not know, and had no reason to believe, that what he did caused or contributed to the publication of a defamatory statement.

(2) For this purpose 'author', 'editor' and 'publisher' have the following meanings, which are further explained in subsection (3)—

'author' means the originator of the statement, but does not include a person who did not intend that his statement be published at all;

'editor' means a person having editorial or equivalent responsibility for the content of the statement or the decision to publish it; and

'publisher' means a commercial publisher, that is, a person whose business is issuing material to the public, or a section of the public, who issues material containing the statement in the course of that business.

(3) A person shall not be considered the author, editor or publisher of a statement if he is only involved—

(a) in printing, producing, distributing or selling printed material containing the statement;

(b) in processing, making copies of, distributing, exhibiting or selling a film or sound recording (as defined in Part I of the Copyright, Designs and Patents Act 1988) containing the statement;

(c) in processing, making copies of, distributing or selling any electronic medium in or on which the statement is recorded, or in operating or providing any equipment, system or service by means of which the statement is retrieved, copied, distributed or made available in electronic form;

(d) as the broadcaster of a live programme containing the statement in circumstances in which he has no effective control over the maker of the statement;

(e) as the operator of or provider of access to a communications system by means of which the statement is transmitted, or made available, by a person over whom he has no effective control.

In a case not within paragraphs (a) to (e) the court may have regard to those provisions by way of analogy in deciding whether a person is to be considered the author, editor or publisher of a statement.

(4) Employees or agents of an author, editor or publisher are in the same position as their employer or principal to the extent that they are responsible for the content of the statement or the decision to publish it.

(5) In determining for the purposes of this section whether a person took reasonable care, or had reason to believe that what he did caused or contributed to the publication of a defamatory statement, regard shall be had to—

(a) the extent of his responsibility for the content of the statement or the decision to publish it,

(b) the nature or circumstances of the publication, and

(c) the previous conduct or character of the author, editor or publisher.

(6) This section does not apply to any cause of action which arose before the section came into force.

Offer to make amends

2   Offer to make amends

(1) A person who has published a statement alleged to be defamatory of another may offer to make amends under this section.

(2) The offer may be in relation to the statement generally or in relation to a specific defamatory meaning which the person making the offer accepts that the statement conveys ('a qualified offer').

(3) An offer to make amends—

(a) must be in writing,

(b) must be expressed to be an offer to make amends under section 2 of the Defamation Act 1996, and

(c) must state whether it is a qualified offer and, if so, set out the defamatory meaning in relation to which it is made.

(4) An offer to make amends under this section is an offer—

(a) to make a suitable correction of the statement complained of and a sufficient apology to the aggrieved party,

(b) to publish the correction and apology in a manner that is reasonable and practicable in the circumstances, and

(c) to pay the aggrieved party such compensation (if any), and such costs, as may be agreed or determined to be payable.

The fact that the offer is accompanied by an offer to take specific steps does not affect the fact that an offer to make amends under this section is an offer to do all the things mentioned in paragraphs (a) to (c).

(5) An offer to make amends under this section may not be made by a person after serving a defence in defamation proceedings brought against him by the aggrieved party in respect of the publication in question.

(6) An offer to make amends under this section may be withdrawn before it is accepted; and a renewal of an offer which has been withdrawn shall be treated as a new offer.

3 Accepting an offer to make amends

(1) If an offer to make amends under section 2 is accepted by the aggrieved party, the following provisions apply.

(2) The party accepting the offer may not bring or continue defamation proceedings in respect of the publication concerned against the person making the offer, but he is entitled to enforce the offer to make amends, as follows.

(3) If the parties agree on the steps to be taken in fulfilment of the offer, the aggrieved party may apply to the court for an order that the other party fulfil his offer by taking the steps agreed.

(4) If the parties do not agree on the steps to be taken by way of correction, apology and publication, the party who made the offer may take such steps as he thinks appropriate, and may in particular—

(a) make the correction and apology by a statement in open court in terms approved by the court, and

(b) give an undertaking to the court as to the manner of their publication.

(5) If the parties do not agree on the amount to be paid by way of compensation, it shall be determined by the court on the same principles as damages in defamation proceedings.

The court shall take account of any steps taken in fulfilment of the offer and (so far as not agreed between the parties) of the suitability of the correction, the sufficiency of the apology and whether the manner of their publication was reasonable in the circumstances, and may reduce or increase the amount of compensation accordingly.

(6) If the parties do not agree on the amount to be paid by way of costs, it shall be determined by the court on the same principles as costs awarded in court proceedings.

(7) The acceptance of an offer by one person to make amends does not affect any cause of action against another person in respect of the same publication, subject as follows.

(8) In England and Wales or Northern Ireland, for the purposes of the Civil Liability (Contribution) Act 1978—

(a) the amount of compensation paid under the offer shall be treated as paid in bona fide settlement or compromise of the claim; and

(b) where another person is liable in respect of the same damage (whether jointly or otherwise), the person whose offer to make amends was accepted is not required to pay by virtue of any contribution under section 1 of that Act a greater amount than the amount of the compensation payable in pursuance of the offer.

(9) In Scotland—

    (a) subsection (2) of section 3 of the Law Reform (Miscellaneous Provisions) (Scotland) Act 1940 (right of one joint wrongdoer as respects another to recover contribution towards damages) applies in relation to compensation paid under an offer to make amends as it applies in relation to damages in an action to which that section applies; and

    (b) where another person is liable in respect of the same damage (whether jointly or otherwise), the person whose offer to make amends was accepted is not required to pay by virtue of any contribution under section 3(2) of that Act a greater amount than the amount of compensation payable in pursuance of the offer.

(10) Proceedings under this section shall be heard and determined without a jury.

4 Failure to accept offer to make amends

(1) If an offer to make amends under section 2, duly made and not withdrawn, is not accepted by the aggrieved party, the following provisions apply.

(2) The fact that the offer was made is a defence (subject to subsection (3)) to defamation proceedings in respect of the publication in question by that party against the person making the offer.

A qualified offer is only a defence in respect of the meaning to which the offer related.

(3) There is no such defence if the person by whom the offer was made knew or had reason to believe that the statement complained of—

    (a) referred to the aggrieved party or was likely to be understood as referring to him, and

    (b) was both false and defamatory of that party;

but it shall be presumed until the contrary is shown that he did not know and had no reason to believe that was the case.

(4) The person who made the offer need not rely on it by way of defence, but if he does he may not rely on any other defence.

If the offer was a qualified offer, this applies only in respect of the meaning to which the offer related.

(5) The offer may be relied on in mitigation of damages whether or not it was relied on as a defence.

The meaning of a statement

7 Ruling on the meaning of a statement

In defamation proceedings the court shall not be asked to rule whether a statement is arguably capable, as opposed to capable, of bearing a particular meaning or meanings attributed to it.

Summary disposal of claim

8 Summary disposal of claim

(1) In defamation proceedings the court may dispose summarily of the plaintiffs claim in accordance with the following provisions.

(2) The court may dismiss the plaintiff's claim if it appears to the court that it has no realistic prospect of success and there is no reason why it should be tried.

(3) The court may give judgment for the plaintiff and grant him summary relief (see section 9) if it appears to the court that there is no defence to the claim which has a realistic prospect of success, and that there is no other reason why the claim should be tried.

Unless the plaintiff asks for summary relief, the court shall not act under this subsection unless it is satisfied that summary relief will adequately compensate him for the wrong he has suffered.

(4) In considering whether a claim should be tried the court shall have regard to—

    (a) whether all the persons who are or might be defendants in respect of the publication complained of are before the court;

    (b) whether summary disposal of the claim against another defendant would be inappropriate;

    (c) the extent to which there is a conflict of evidence;

(d) the seriousness of the alleged wrong (as regards the content of the statement and the extent of publication); and

(e) whether it is justifiable in the circumstances to proceed to a full trial.

(5) Proceedings under this section shall be heard and determined without a jury.

9 Meaning of summary relief

(1) For the purposes of section 8 (summary disposal of claim) 'summary relief' means such of the following as may be appropriate—

(a) a declaration that the statement was false and defamatory of the plaintiff;

(b) an order that the defendant publish or cause to be published a suitable correction and apology;

(c) damages not exceeding £10,000 or such other amount as may be prescribed by order of the Lord Chancellor;

(d) an order restraining the defendant from publishing or further publishing the matter complained of.

(2) The content of any correction and apology, and the time, manner, form and place of publication, shall be for the parties to agree.

If they cannot agree on the content, the court may direct the defendant to publish or cause to be published a summary of the court's judgment agreed by the parties or settled by the court in accordance with rules of court.

If they cannot agree on the time, manner, form or place of publication, the court may direct the defendant to take such reasonable and practicable steps as the court considers appropriate.

[(2A) The Lord Chancellor must consult the Lord Chief Justice of England and Wales before making any order under subsection (1)(c) in relation to England and Wales.

(2B) The Lord Chancellor must consult the Lord Chief Justice of Northern Ireland before making any order under subsection (1)(c) in relation to Northern Ireland.

(2C) The Lord Chief Justice may nominate a judicial office holder (as defined in section 109(4) of the Constitutional Reform Act 2005) to exercise his functions under this section.

(2D) The Lord Chief Justice of Northern Ireland may nominate any of the following to exercise his functions under this section—

(a) the holder of one of the offices listed in Schedule 1 to the Justice (Northern Ireland) Act 2002;

(b) a Lord Justice of Appeal (as defined in section 88 of that Act).]

(3) Any order under subsection (1)(c) shall be made by statutory instrument which shall be subject to annulment in pursuance of a resolution of either House of Parliament.

10 Summary disposal: rules of court

(1) Provision may be made by rules of court as to the summary disposal of the plaintiff's claim in defamation proceedings.

(2) Without prejudice to the generality of that power, provision may be made—

(a) authorising a party to apply for summary disposal at any stage of the proceedings;

(b) authorising the court at any stage of the proceedings—

(i) to treat any application, pleading or other step in the proceedings as an application for summary disposal, or

(ii) to make an order for summary disposal without any such application;

(c) as to the time for serving pleadings or taking any other step in the proceedings in a case where there are proceedings for summary disposal;

(d) requiring the parties to identify any question of law or construction which the court is to be asked to determine in the proceedings;

(e) as to the nature of any hearing on the question of summary disposal, and in particular—

(i) authorising the court to order affidavits or witness statements to be prepared for use as evidence at the hearing, and

(ii) requiring the leave of the court for the calling of oral evidence, or the introduction of new evidence, at the hearing;

(f) authorising the court to require a defendant to elect, at or before the hearing, whether or not to make an offer to make amends under section 2.

Evidence concerning proceedings in Parliament

13   Evidence concerning proceedings in Parliament

(1) Where the conduct of a person in or in relation to proceedings in Parliament is in issue in defamation proceedings, he may waive for the purposes of those proceedings, so far as concerns him, the protection of any enactment or rule of law which prevents proceedings in Parliament being impeached or questioned in any court or place out of Parliament.

(2) Where a person waives that protection—

(a) any such enactment or rule of law shall not apply to prevent evidence being given, questions being asked or statements, submissions, comments or findings being made about his conduct, and

(b) none of those things shall be regarded as infringing the privilege of either House of Parliament.

(3) The waiver by one person of that protection does not affect its operation in relation to another person who has not waived it.

(4) Nothing in this section affects any enactment or rule of law so far as it protects a person (including a person who has waived the protection referred to above) from legal liability for words spoken or things done in the course of, or for the purposes of or incidental to, any proceedings in Parliament.

(5) Without prejudice to the generality of subsection (4), that subsection applies to—

(a) the giving of evidence before either House or a committee;

(b) the presentation or submission of a document to either House or a committee;

(c) the preparation of a document for the purposes of or incidental to the transacting of any such business;

(d) the formulation, making or publication of a document, including a report, by or pursuant to an order of either House or a committee; and

(e) any communication with the Parliamentary Commissioner for Standards or any person having functions in connection with the registration of Members' interests.

In this subsection 'a committee' means a committee of either House or a joint committee of both Houses of Parliament.

Statutory privilege

14   Reports of court proceedings absolutely privileged

(1) A fair and accurate report of proceedings in public before a court to which this section applies, if published contemporaneously with the proceedings, is absolutely privileged.

(2) A report of proceedings which by an order of the court, or as a consequence of any statutory provision, is required to be postponed shall be treated as published contemporaneously if it is published as soon as practicable after publication is permitted.

(3) This section applies to—

(a) any court in the United Kingdom,

(b) the European Court of Justice or any court attached to that court,

(c) the European Court of Human Rights, and

(d) any international criminal tribunal established by the Security Council of the United Nations or by an international agreement to which the United Kingdom is a party.

In paragraph (a) 'court' includes any tribunal or body exercising the judicial power of the State.

15   Reports, etc. protected by qualified privilege

(1) The publication of any report or other statement mentioned in Schedule 1 to this Act is privileged unless the publication is shown to be made with malice, subject as follows.

(2) In defamation proceedings in respect of the publication of a report or other statement mentioned in Part II of that Schedule, there is no defence under this section if the plaintiff shows that the defendant—

(a) was requested by him to publish in a suitable manner a reasonable letter or statement by way of explanation or contradiction, and

(b) refused or neglected to do so.

For this purpose 'in a suitable manner' means in the same manner as the publication complained of or in a manner that is adequate and reasonable in the circumstances.

(3) This section does not apply to the publication to the public, or a section of the public, of matter which is not of public concern and the publication of which is not for the public benefit.

(4) Nothing in this section shall be construed—

(a) as protecting the publication of matter the publication of which is prohibited by law, or

(b) as limiting or abridging any privilege subsisting apart from this section.

Supplementary provisions

17 Interpretation

(1) In this Act—

'publication' and 'publish', in relation to a statement, have the meaning they have for the purposes of the law of defamation generally, but 'publisher' is specially defined for the purposes of section 1;

'statement' means words, pictures, visual images, gestures or any other method of signifying meaning; and

'statutory provision' means—

(a)   a provision contained in an Act or in subordinate legislation within the meaning of the Interpretation Act 1978

[(aa) a provision contained in an Act of the Scottish Parliament or in an instrument made under such an Act], or

(b)   a statutory provision within the meaning given by section 1(f) of the Interpretation Act (Northern Ireland) 1954.

Section 15

SCHEDULE 1

QUALIFIED PRIVILEGE

PART I STATEMENTS HAVING QUALIFIED PRIVILEGE WITHOUT EXPLANATION OR CONTRADICTION

1. A fair and accurate report of proceedings in public of a legislature anywhere in the world.

2. A fair and accurate report of proceedings in public before a court anywhere in the world.

3. A fair and accurate report of proceedings in public of a person appointed to hold a public inquiry by a government or legislature anywhere in the world.

4. A fair and accurate report of proceedings in public anywhere in the world of an international organisation or an international conference.

5. A fair and accurate copy of or extract from any register or other document required by law to be open to public inspection.

6. A notice or advertisement published by or on the authority of a court, or of a judge or officer of a court, anywhere in the world.

7. A fair and accurate copy of or extract from matter published by or on the authority of a government or legislature anywhere in the world.

8. A fair and accurate copy of or extract from matter published anywhere in the world by an international organisation or an international conference.

PART II STATEMENTS PRIVILEGED SUBJECT TO EXPLANATION OR CONTRADICTION

9.—(1) A fair and accurate copy of or extract from a notice or other matter issued for the information of the public by or on behalf of—

(a) a legislature in any member State or the European Parliament;

(b) the government of any member State, or any authority performing governmental functions in any member State or part of a member State, or the European Commission;

(c) an international organisation or international conference.

(2) In this paragraph 'governmental functions' includes police functions.

10. A fair and accurate copy of or extract from a document made available by a court in any member State or the European Court of Justice (or any court attached to that court), or by a judge or officer of any such court.

11.—(1) A fair and accurate report of proceedings at any public meeting or sitting in the United Kingdom of—

(a) a local authority [, local authority committee or in the case of a local authority which are operating executive arrangements the executive of that authority or a committee of that executive];

(b) a justice or justices of the peace acting otherwise than as a court exercising judicial authority;

(c) a commission, tribunal, committee or person appointed for the purposes of any inquiry by any statutory provision, by Her Majesty or by a Minister of the Crown [a member of the Scottish Executive, the Welsh Ministers or the Counsel General to the Welsh Assembly Government] or a Northern Ireland Department;

(d) a person appointed by a local authority to hold a local inquiry in pursuance of any statutory provision;

(e) any other tribunal, board, committee or body constituted by or under, and exercising functions under, any statutory provision.

[(1A) In the case of a local authority which are operating executive arrangements, a fair and accurate record of any decision made by any member of the executive where that record is required to be made and available for public inspection by virtue of section 22 of the Local Government Act 2000 or of any provision in regulations made under that section.]

(2) [In sub-paragraphs (1)(a) and (1A)—

'executive' and 'executive arrangements' have the same meaning as in Part II of the Local Government Act 2000;]

'local authority' means—

(a) in relation to England and Wales, a principal council within the meaning of the Local Government Act 1972, any body falling within any paragraph of section 100J(1) of that Act or an authority or body to which the Public Bodies (Admission to Meetings) Act 1960 applies,

(b) in relation to Scotland, a council constituted under section 2 of the Local Government etc. (Scotland) Act 1994 or an authority or body to which the Public Bodies (Admission to Meetings) Act 1960 applies,

(c) in relation to Northern Ireland, any authority or body to which sections 23 to 27 of the Local Government Act (Northern Ireland) 1972 apply; and

'local authority committee' means any committee of a local authority or of local authorities, and includes—

(a) any committee or sub-committee in relation to which sections 100A to 100D of the Local Government Act 1972 apply by virtue of section 100E of that Act (whether or not also by virtue of section 100J of that Act), and

(b) any committee or sub-committee in relation to which sections 50A to 50D of the Local Government (Scotland) Act 1973 apply by virtue of section 50E of that Act.

(3) A fair and accurate report of any corresponding proceedings in any of the Channel Islands or the Isle of Man or in another member State.

12.—(1) A fair and accurate report of proceedings at any public meeting held in a member State.

(2) In this paragraph a 'public meeting' means a meeting bona fide and lawfully held for a lawful purpose and for the furtherance or discussion of a matter of public concern, whether admission to the meeting is general or restricted.

13.—(1) A fair and accurate report of proceedings at a general meeting of a UK public company.

(2) A fair and accurate copy of or extract from any document circulated to members of a UK public company—

(a) by or with the authority of the board of directors of the company,

(b) by the auditors of the company, or

(c) by any member of the company in pursuance of a right conferred by any statutory provision.

(3) A fair and accurate copy or extract from any document circulated to members of a UK public company which relates to the appointment, resignation, retirement or dismissal of directors of the company.

(4) In this paragraph 'UK public company' means—

(a) a public company within the meaning of [section 4(2) of the Companies Act 2006], or

(b) a body corporate incorporated by or registered under any other statutory provision, or by Royal Charter, or formed in pursuance of letters patent.

(5) A fair and accurate report of proceedings at any corresponding meeting of, or copy of or extract from any corresponding document circulated to members of, a public company formed under the law of any of the Channel Islands or the Isle of Man or of another member State.

14. A fair and accurate report of any finding or decision of any of the following descriptions of association, formed in the United Kingdom or another member State, or of any committee or governing body of such an association—

(a) an association formed for the purpose of promoting or encouraging the exercise of or interest in any art, science, religion or learning, and empowered by its constitution to exercise control over or adjudicate on matters of interest or concern to the association, or the actions or conduct of any person subject to such control or adjudication;

(b) an association formed for the purpose of promoting or safeguarding the interests of any trade, business, industry or profession, or of the persons carrying on or engaged in any trade, business, industry or profession, and empowered by its constitution to exercise control over or adjudicate upon matters connected with that trade, business, industry or profession, or the actions or conduct of those persons;

(c) an association formed for the purpose of promoting or safeguarding the interests of a game, sport or pastime to the playing or exercise of which members of the public are invited or admitted, and empowered by its constitution to exercise control over or adjudicate upon persons connected with or taking part in the game, sport or pastime;

(d) an association formed for the purpose of promoting charitable objects or other objects beneficial to the community and empowered by its constitution to exercise control over or to adjudicate on matters of interest or concern to the association, or the actions or conduct of any person subject to such control or adjudication.

15.—(1) A fair and accurate report of, or copy of or extract from, any adjudication, report, statement or notice issued by a body, officer or other person designated for the purposes of this paragraph—

(a) for England and Wales or Northern Ireland, by order of the Lord Chancellor, and

(b) for Scotland, by order of the Secretary of State.

(2) An order under this paragraph shall be made by statutory instrument which shall be subject to annulment in pursuance of a resolution of either House of Parliament.

PART III SUPPLEMENTARY PROVISIONS

16.—(1) In this Schedule—

'court' includes any tribunal or body exercising the judicial power of the State;

'international conference' means a conference attended by representatives of two or more governments;

'international organisation' means an organisation of which two or more governments are members, and includes any committee or other subordinate body of such an organisation; and

'legislature' includes a local legislature.

(2) References in this Schedule to a member State include any European dependent territory of a member State.

(3) In paragraphs 2 and 6 'court' includes—

(a) the European Court of Justice (or any court attached to that court) and the Court of Auditors of the European Communities,

(b) the European Court of Human Rights,

(c) any international criminal tribunal established by the Security Council of the United Nations or by an international agreement to which the United Kingdom is a party, and

(d) the International Court of Justice and any other judicial or arbitral tribunal deciding matters in dispute between States.

(4) In paragraphs 1, 3 and 7 'legislature' includes the European Parliament.

17.—(1) Provision may be made by order identifying—

(a) for the purposes of paragraph 11, the corresponding proceedings referred to in sub-paragraph (3);

(b) for the purposes of paragraph 13, the corresponding meetings and documents referred to in sub-paragraph (5).

(2) An order under this paragraph may be made—

(a) for England and Wales or Northern Ireland, by the Lord Chancellor, and

(b) for Scotland, by the Secretary of State.

(3) An order under this paragraph shall be made by statutory instrument which shall be subject to annulment in pursuance of a resolution of either House of Parliament.

Police Act 1996

(1996, c. 16)

88   Liability for wrongful acts of constables

(1) The chief officer of police for a police area shall be liable in respect of any unlawful conduct of constables under his direction and control in the performance or purported performance of their functions in like manner as a master is liable in respect of [any unlawful conduct of] his servants in the course of their employment, and accordingly shall [, in the case of a tort,] be treated for all purposes as a joint tortfeasor.

(2) There shall be paid out of the police fund—

(a) any damages or costs awarded against the chief officer of police in any proceedings brought against him by virtue of this section and any costs incurred by him in any such proceedings so far as not recovered by him in the proceedings; and

(b) any sum required in connection with the settlement of any claim made against the chief officer of police by virtue of this section, if the settlement is approved by the police authority.

(4) A police authority may, in such cases and to such extent as appear to it to be appropriate, pay out of the police fund—

    (a) any damages or costs awarded against a person to whom this subsection applies in proceedings for [any unlawful conduct of] that person,

    (b) any costs incurred and not recovered by such a person in such proceedings, and

    (c) any sum required in connection with the settlement of a claim that has or might have given rise to such proceedings.

Local Government (Contracts) Act 1997

(1997, c. 65)

1   Functions to include power to enter into contracts

(1) Every statutory provision conferring or imposing a function on a local authority confers power on the local authority to enter into a contract with another person for the provision or making available of assets or services, or both, (whether or not together with goods), for the purposes of, or in connection with, the discharge of the function by the local authority.

2   Certified contracts to be intra vires

(1) Where a local authority has entered into a contract, the contract shall, if it is a certified contract, have effect (and be deemed always to have had effect) as if the local authority had had power to enter into it (and had exercised that power properly in entering into it).

(2) For the purposes of this Act a contract entered into by a local authority is a certified contract if (and, subject to subsections (3) and (4), only if) the certification requirements have been satisfied by the local authority with respect to the contract and they were so satisfied before the end of the certification period.

Protection from Harassment Act 1997

(1997, c. 40)

1   Prohibition of harassment

(1) A person must not pursue a course of conduct—

    (a) which amounts to harassment of another, and

    (b) which he knows or ought to know amounts to harassment of the other.

[(1A) A person must not pursue a course of conduct—

    (a) which involves harassment of two or more persons, and

    (b) which he knows or ought to know involves harassment of those persons, and

    (c) by which he intends to persuade any person (whether or not one of those mentioned above)—

        (i)   not to do something that he is entitled or required to do, or

        (ii) to do something that he is not under any obligation to do.]

(2) For the purposes of this section, the person whose course of conduct is in question ought to know that it amounts to or involves harassment of another if a reasonable person in possession of the same information would think the course of conduct amounted to [or involved] harassment of the other.

(3) Subsection (1) [or (1A)] does not apply to a course of conduct if the person who pursued it shows—

    (a) that it was pursued for the purpose of presenting or detecting crime,

    (b) that it was pursued under any enactment or rule of law or to comply with any condition or requirement imposed by any person under any enactment, or

    (c) that in the particular circumstances the pursuit of the course of conduct was reasonable.

2 Offence of harassment

(1) A person who pursues a course of conduct in breach of [section 1 or (1A)] is guilty of an offence.

3 Civil remedy

(1) An actual or apprehended breach of [section 1(1)] may be the subject of a claim in civil proceedings by the person who is or may be the victim of the course of conduct in question.

(2) On such a claim, damages may be awarded for (among other things) any anxiety caused by the harassment and any financial loss resulting from the harassment.

(3) Where—

    (a) in such proceedings the High Court or a county court grants an injunction for the purpose of restraining the defendant from pursuing any conduct which amounts to harassment, and

    (b) the plaintiff considers that the defendant has done anything which he is prohibited from doing by the injunction,

the plaintiff may apply for the issue of a warrant for the arrest of the defendant.

(5) The judge or district judge to whom an application under subsection (3) is made may only issue a warrant if—

    (a) the application is substantiated on oath, and

    (b) the judge or district judge has reasonable grounds for believing that the defendant has done anything which he is prohibited from doing by the injunction.

(6) Where—

    (a) the High Court or a county court grants an injunction for the purpose mentioned in subsection (3)(a), and

    (b) without reasonable excuse the defendant does anything which he is prohibited from doing by the injunction,

he is guilty of an offence.

[3A Injunctions to protect persons from harassment within section 1(1A)

(1) This section applies where there is an actual or apprehended breach of section 1(1A) by any person ('the relevant person').

(2) In such a case—

    (a) any person who is or may be a victim of the course of conduct in question, or

    (b) any person who is or may be a person falling within section 1(1A)(c),

may apply to the High Court or a county court for an injunction restraining the relevant person from pursuing any conduct which amounts to harassment in relation to any person or persons mentioned or described in the injunction.]

4 Putting people in fear of violence

(1) A person whose course of conduct causes another to fear, on at least two occasions, that violence will be used against him is guilty of an offence if he knows or ought to know that his course of conduct will cause the other so to fear on each of those occasions.

(2) For the purposes of this section, the person whose course of conduct is in question ought to know that it will cause another to fear that violence will be used against him on any occasion if a reasonable person in possession of the same information would think the course of conduct would cause the other so to fear on that occasion.

(3) It is a defence for a person charged with an offence under this section to show that—

    (a) his course of conduct was pursued for the purpose of preventing or detecting crime,

    (b) his course of conduct was pursued under any enactment or rule of law or to comply with any condition or requirement imposed by any person under any enactment, or

    (c) the pursuit of his course of conduct was reasonable for the protection of himself or another or for the protection of his or another's property.

5   Restraining orders [on conviction]

(1) A court sentencing or otherwise dealing with a person ('the defendant') convicted of an offence [...] may (as well as sentencing him or dealing with him in any other way) make an order under this section.

(2) The order may, for the purpose of protecting the victim [or victims] of the offence, or any other person mentioned in the order, from [...] conduct which—

(a) amounts to harassment, or

(b) will cause a fear of violence,

prohibit the defendant from doing anything described in the order.

(5) If without reasonable excuse the defendant does anything which he is prohibited from doing by an order under this section, he is guilty of an offence.

[5A   Restraining orders on acquittal

(1) A court before which a person ('the defendant') is acquitted of an offence may, if it considers it necessary to do so to protect a person from harassment by the defendant, make an order prohibiting the defendant from doing anything described in the order.]

7   Interpretation of this group of sections

(1) This section applies for the interpretation of [sections 1 to 5A].

(2) References to harassing a person include alarming the person or causing the person distress.

[(3) A 'course of conduct' must involve—

(a) in the case of conduct in relation to a single person (see section 1(1)), conduct on at least two occasions in relation to that person, or

(b) in the case of conduct in relation to two or more persons (see section 1(1A)), conduct on at least one occasion in relation to each of those persons.]

[(3A) A person's conduct on any occasion shall be taken, if aided, abetted, counselled or procured by another—

(a) to be conduct on that occasion of the other (as well as conduct of the person whose conduct it is); and

(b) to be conduct in relation to which the other's knowledge and purpose, and what he ought to have known, are the same as they were in relation to what was contemplated or reasonably foreseeable at the time of the aiding, abetting, counselling or procuring.]

(4) 'Conduct' includes speech.

[(5) References to a person, in the context of the harassment of a person, are references to a person who is an individual.]

12   National security, etc.

(1) If the Secretary of State certifies that in his opinion anything done by a specified person on a specified occasion related to—

(a) national security,

(b) the economic well-being of the United Kingdom, or

(c) the prevention or detection of serious crime,

and was done on behalf of the Crown, the certificate is conclusive evidence that this Act does not apply to any conduct of that person on that occasion.

Social Security (Recovery of Benefits) Act 1997

(1997, c. 27)

1   Cases in which this Act applies

(1) This Act applies in cases where—

(a) a person makes a payment (whether on his own behalf or not) to or in respect of any other person in consequence of any accident, injury or disease suffered by the other, and

(b) any listed benefits have been, or are likely to be, paid to or for the other during the relevant period in respect of the accident, injury or disease.

(2) The reference above to a payment in consequence of any accident, injury or disease is to a payment made—

(a) by or on behalf of a person who is, or is alleged to be, liable to any extent in respect of the accident, injury or disease, or

(b) in pursuance of a compensation scheme for motor accidents;

but does not include a payment mentioned in Part I of Schedule 1.

(3) Subsection (1)(a) applies to a payment made—

(a) voluntarily, or in pursuance of a court order or an agreement, or otherwise, and

(b) in the United Kingdom or elsewhere.

(4) In a case where this Act applies—

(a) the 'injured person' is the person who suffered the accident, injury or disease,

(b) the 'compensation payment' is the payment within subsection (1)(a), and

(c) 'recoverable benefit' is any listed benefit which has been or is likely to be paid as mentioned in subsection (1)(b).

[1A Lump sum payments: regulation-making power

(1) The Secretary of State may by regulations make provision about the recovery of the amount of a payment to which subsection (2) applies (a "lump sum payment") where—

(a) a compensation payment in consequence of a disease is made to or in respect of a person ("P") to whom, or in respect of whom, a lump sum payment has been, or is likely to be, made, and

(b) the compensation payment is made in consequence of the same disease as the lump sum payment.

(2) This subsection applies to—

(a) a payment made in accordance with the Pneumoconiosis etc. (Workers' Compensation) Act 1979 ("the 1979 Act"),

(b) a payment made in accordance with Part 4 of the Child Maintenance and Other Payments Act 2008, and

(c) an extra-statutory payment (within the meaning given by subsection (5)(d) below).

(3) Regulations under this section may, in particular—

(a) make provision about the recovery of the amount of a lump sum payment made to or in respect of a dependant of P;

(b) make provision enabling the recovery of the amount of a lump sum payment from a compensation payment (including provision enabling the recovery of an amount which reduces the compensation payment to nil);

(c) enable the amount of a lump sum payment made before commencement to be recovered from a compensation payment made after commencement;

(d) make provision about certificates in respect of lump sum payments;

(e) apply any provision of this Act, with or without modifications.

(4) References in subsection (1) to a payment made in consequence of a disease—

(a) are references to a payment made by or on behalf of a person who is, or is alleged to be, liable to any extent in respect of the disease, but

(b) do not include references to a payment mentioned in Part 1 of Schedule 1.

(5) In this section—

(a) "commencement" means the date on which this section comes into force,

(b) "compensation payment" means a payment within section 1(1)(a) above,

(c) "dependant" has the meaning given by section 3 of the 1979 Act, and

(d) "extra-statutory payment" means a payment made by the Secretary of State to or in respect of a person following the rejection by the Secretary of State of a claim under the 1979 Act.]

2   Compensation payments to which this Act applies

This Act applies in relation to compensation payments made on or after the day on which this section comes into force, unless they are made in pursuance of a court order or agreement made before that day.

3   'The relevant period'

(1) In relation to a person ('the claimant') who has suffered any accident, injury or disease, 'the relevant period' has the meaning given by the following subsections.

(2) Subject to subsection (4), if it is a case of accident or injury, the relevant period is the period of five years immediately following the day on which the accident or injury in question occurred.

(3) Subject to subsection (4), if it is a case of disease, the relevant period is the period of five years beginning with the date on which the claimant first claims a listed benefit in consequence of the disease.

(4) If at any time before the end of the period referred to in subsection (2) or (3)—

(a) a person makes a compensation payment in final discharge of any claim made by or in respect of the claimant and arising out of the accident, injury or disease, or

(b) an agreement is made under which an earlier compensation payment is treated as having been made in final discharge of any such claim,

the relevant period ends at that time.

4   Applications for certificates of recoverable benefits

(1) Before a person ('the compensator') makes a compensation payment he must apply to the Secretary of State for a certificate of recoverable benefits.

...

5   Information contained in certificates

(1) A certificate of recoverable benefits must specify, for each recoverable benefit—

(a) the amount which has been or is likely to have been paid on or before a specified date, and

(b) if the benefit is paid or likely to be paid after the specified date, the rate and period for which, and the intervals at which, it is or is likely to be so paid.

(2) In a case where the relevant period has ended before the day on which the Secretary of State receives the application for the certificate, the date specified in the certificate for the purposes of subsection (1) must be the day on which the relevant period ended.

(3) In any other case, the date specified for those purposes must not be earlier than the day on which the Secretary of State received the application.

(4) The Secretary of State may estimate, in such manner as he thinks fit, any of the amounts, rates or periods specified in the certificate.

(5) Where the Secretary of State issues a certificate of recoverable benefits, he must provide the information contained in the certificate to—

(a) the person who appears to him to be the injured person, or

(b) any person who he thinks will receive a compensation payment in respect of the injured person.

(6) A person to whom a certificate of recoverable benefits is issued or who is provided with information under subsection (5) is entitled to particulars of the manner in which any amount, rate or period specified in the certificate has been determined, if he applies to the Secretary of State for those particulars.

6   Liability to pay Secretary of State amount of benefits

(1) A person who makes a compensation payment in any case is liable to pay to the Secretary of State an amount equal to the total amount of the recoverable benefits.

(2) The liability referred to in subsection (1) arises immediately before the compensation payment or, if there is more than one, the first of them is made.

(3) No amount becomes payable under this section before the end of the period of 14 days following the day on which the liability arises.

(4) Subject to subsection (3), an amount becomes payable under this section at the end of the period of 14 days beginning with the day on which a certificate of recoverable benefits is first issued showing that the amount of recoverable benefit to which it relates has been or is likely to have been paid before a specified date.

7 Recovery of payments due under section 6

(1) This section applies where a person has made a compensation payment but—

    (a) has not applied for a certificate of recoverable benefits, or

    (b) has not made a payment to the Secretary of State under section 6 before the end of the period allowed under that section.

(2) The Secretary of State may—

    (a) issue the person who made the compensation payment with a certificate of recoverable benefits, if none has been issued, or

    (b) issue him with a copy of the certificate of recoverable benefits or (if more than one has been issued) the most recent one,

and (in either case) issue him with a demand that payment of any amount due under section 6 be made immediately.

(3) The Secretary of State may, in accordance with subsections (4) and (5), recover the amount for which a demand for payment is made under subsection (2) from the person who made the compensation payment.

(4) If the person who made the compensation payment resides or carries on business in England and Wales and a county court so orders, any amount recoverable under subsection (3) is recoverable [under section 85 of the County Courts Act 1984] or otherwise as if it were payable under an order of that court.

(5) If the person who made the payment resides or carries on business in Scotland, any amount recoverable under subsection (3) may be enforced in like manner as an extract registered decree arbitral bearing a warrant for execution issued by the sheriff court of any sheriffdom in Scotland.

(6) A document bearing a certificate which—

    (a) is signed by a person authorised to do so by the Secretary of State, and

    (b) states that the document, apart from the certificate, is a record of the amount recoverable under subsection (3),

is conclusive evidence that that amount is so recoverable.

(7) A certificate under subsection (6) purporting to be signed by a person authorised to do so by the Secretary of State is to be treated as so signed unless the contrary is proved.

8 Reduction of compensation payment

(1) This section applies in a case where, in relation to any head of compensation listed in column 1 of Schedule 2—

    (a) any of the compensation payment is attributable to the head, and

    (b) any recoverable benefit is shown against that head in column 2 of the Schedule.

(2) In such a case, any claim of a person to receive the compensation payment is to be treated for all purposes as discharged if—

    (a) he is paid the amount (if any) of the compensation payment calculated in accordance with this section, and

    (b) if the amount of the compensation payment so calculated is nil, he is given a statement saying so by the person who (apart from this section) would have paid the gross amount of the compensation payment.

(3) For each head of compensation listed in column 1 of the Schedule for which paragraphs (a) and (b) of subsection (1) are met, so much of the gross amount of the compensation payment as is attributable to that head is to be reduced (to nil, if necessary) by deducting the amount of the recoverable benefit or, as the case may be, the aggregate amount of the recoverable benefits shown against it.

(4) Subsection (3) is to have effect as if a requirement to reduce a payment by deducting an amount which exceeds the payment were a requirement to reduce that payment to nil.

(5) The amount of the compensation payment calculated in accordance with this section is—

    (a) the gross amount of the compensation payment, less

    (b) the sum of the reductions made under subsection (3),

(and, accordingly, the amount may be nil).

9   Section 8: supplementary

(1) A person who makes a compensation payment calculated in accordance with section 8 must inform the person to whom the payment is made—

    (a) that the payment has been so calculated, and

    (b) of the date for payment by reference to which the calculation has been made.

(2) If the amount of a compensation payment calculated in accordance with section 8 is nil, a person giving a statement saying so is to be treated for the purposes of this Act as making a payment within section 1(1)(a) on the day on which he gives the statement.

(3) Where a person—

    (a) makes a compensation payment calculated in accordance with section 8, and

    (b) if the amount of the compensation payment so calculated is nil, gives a statement saying so,

he is to be treated, for the purpose of determining any rights and liabilities in respect of contribution or indemnity, as having paid the gross amount of the compensation payment.

(4) For the purposes of this Act—

    (a) the gross amount of the compensation payment is the amount of the compensation payment apart from section 8, and

    (b) the amount of any recoverable benefit is the amount determined in accordance with the certificate of recoverable benefits.

10   Review of certificates of recoverable benefits

[(1) Any certificate of recoverable benefits may be reviewed by the Secretary of State—

    (a) either within the prescribed period or in prescribed cases or circumstances; and

    (b) either on an application made for the purpose or on his own initiative.]

(2) On a review under this section the Secretary of State may either—

    (a) confirm the certificate, or

    (b) (subject to subsection (3)) issue a fresh certificate containing such variations as he considers appropriate, [or

    (c) revoke the certificate.].

(3) The Secretary of State may not vary the certificate so as to increase the total amount of the recoverable benefits unless it appears to him that the variation is required as a result of the person who applied for the certificate supplying him with incorrect or insufficient information.

11   Appeals against certificates of recoverable benefits

(1) An appeal against a certificate of recoverable benefits may be made on the ground—

    (a) that any amount, rate or period specified in the certificate is incorrect, or

    (b) that listed benefits which have been, or are likely to be, paid otherwise than in respect of the accident, injury or disease in question have been brought into account [or

    (c) that listed benefits which have not been, and are not likely to be, paid to the injured person during the relevant period have been brought into account, or

    (d) that the payment on the basis of which the certificate was issued is not a payment within section 1(1)(a)].

(2) An appeal under this section may be made by—

    (a) the person who applied for the certificate of recoverable benefits, or

 [(aa) (in a case where that certificate was issued under section 7(2)(a)) the person to whom it was so issued, or]

    (b) (in a case where the amount of the compensation payment has been calculated under section 8) the injured person or other person to whom the payment is made.

(3) No appeal may be made under this section until—

(a) the claim giving rise to the compensation payment has been finally disposed of, and

(b) the liability under section 6 has been discharged.

(4) For the purposes of subsection (3)(a), if an award of damages in respect of a claim has been made under or by virtue of—

(a) section 32A(2)(a) of [the Senior Courts Act 1981],

(b) section 12(2)(a) of the Administration of Justice Act 1982, or

(c) section 51(2)(a) of the County Courts Act 1984,

(orders for provisional damages in personal injury cases), the claim is to be treated as having been finally disposed of.

(5) Regulations may make provision—

(a) as to the manner in which, and the time within which, appeals under this section may be made,

(b) [...] and

(c) for the purpose of enabling any such appeal to be treated as an application for review under section 10.

12   Reference of questions to [First-tier Tribunal]

[(1) The Secretary of State must refer an appeal under section 11 to the First-tier Tribunal.]

(3) In determining any appeal under section 11, the tribunal must take into account any decision of a court relating to the same, or any similar, issue arising in connection with the accident, injury or disease in question.

(4) On [an appeal under section 11 the First-tier Tribunal] may either—

(a) confirm the amounts, rates and periods specified in the certificate of recoverable benefits, or

(b) specify any variations which are to be made on the issue of a fresh certificate under sub-section (5) [or

(c) declare that the certificate of recoverable benefits is to be revoked.].

(5) When the Secretary of State has received the decision of the tribunal on the appeal under section 11, he must in accordance with that decision either—

(a) confirm the certificate against which the appeal was brought, or

(b) issue a fresh certificate [or

(c) revoke the certificate.].

(7) Regulations [...] may (among other things) provide for the non-disclosure of medical advice or medical evidence given or submitted following a reference under subsection (1).

13   Appeal to [Upper Tribunal]

(1) An appeal may be made to a Commissioner against any decision of [an appeal tribunal] under section 12 on the ground that the decision was erroneous in point of law.

(2) An appeal [to the Upper Tribunal under section 11 of the Tribunals, Courts and Enforcement Act 2007 which arises from any decision of the First-Tier Tribunal made under section 12 of this Act] may be made by—

(a)   the Secretary of State,

(b)   the person who applied for the certificate of recoverable benefits, [...]

[(bb) (in a case where that certificate was issued under section 7(2)(a)) the person to whom it was so issued, or]

(c)   (in a case where the amount of the compensation payment has been calculated in accordance with section 8) the injured person or other person to whom the payment is made.

14   Reviews and appeals: supplementary

(1) This section applies in cases where a fresh certificate of recoverable benefits is issued as a result of a review under section 10 or an appeal under section 11.

(2) If—

    (a) a person has made one or more payments to the Secretary of State under section 6, and

    (b) in consequence of the review or appeal, it appears that the total amount paid is more than the amount that ought to have been paid,

regulations may provide for the Secretary of State to pay the difference to that person, or to the person to whom the compensation payment is made, or partly to one and partly to the other.

(3) If—

    (a) a person has made one or more payments to the Secretary of State under section 6, and

    (b) in consequence of the review or appeal, it appears that the total amount paid is less than the amount that ought to have been paid,

regulations may provide for that person to pay the difference to the Secretary of State.

(4) Regulations under this section may provide—

    (a) for the re-calculation in accordance with section 8 of the amount of any compensation payment,

    (b) for giving credit for amounts already paid, and

    (c) for the payment by any person of any balance or the recovery from any person of any excess,

and may provide for any matter by modifying this Act.

15   Court orders

(1) This section applies where a court makes an order for a compensation payment to be made in any case, unless the order is made with the consent of the injured person and the person by whom the payment is to be made.

(2) The court must, in the case of each head of compensation listed in column 1 of Schedule 2 to which any of the compensation payment is attributable, specify in the order the amount of the compensation payment which is attributable to that head.

16   Payments into court

(1) Regulations may make provision (including provision modifying this Act) for any case in which a payment into court is made.

(2) The regulations may (among other things) provide—

    (a) for the making of a payment into court to be treated in prescribed circumstances as the making of a compensation payment,

    (b) for application for, and issue of, certificates of recoverable benefits, and

    (c) for the relevant period to be treated as ending on a date determined in accordance with the regulations.

(3) Rules of court may make provision governing practice and procedure in such cases.

(4) This section does not extend to Scotland.

17   Benefits irrelevant to assessment of damages

In assessing damages in respect of any accident, injury or disease, the amount of any listed benefits paid or likely to be paid is to be disregarded.

18   Lump sum and periodical payments

(1) Regulations may make provision (including provision modifying this Act) for any case in which two or more compensation payments in the form of lump sums are made by the same person to or in respect of the injured person in consequence of the same accident, injury or disease.

(2) The regulations may (among other things) provide—

    (a) for the re-calculation in accordance with section 8 of the amount of any compensation payment,

    (b) for giving credit for amounts already paid, and

    (c) for the payment by any person of any balance or the recovery from any person of any excess.

(3) For the purposes of subsection (2), the regulations may provide for the gross amounts of the compensation payments to be aggregated and for—

    (a) the aggregate amount to be taken to be the gross amount of the compensation payment for the purposes of section 8,

    (b) so much of the aggregate amount as is attributable to a head of compensation listed in column 1 of Schedule 2 to be taken to be the part of the gross amount which is attributable to that head;

and for the amount of any recoverable benefit shown against any head in column 2 of that Schedule to be taken to be the amount determined in accordance with the most recent certificate of recoverable benefits.

(4) Regulations may make provision (including provision modifying this Act) for any case in which, in final settlement of the injured person's claim, an agreement is entered into for the making of—

    (a) periodical compensation payments (whether of an income or capital nature), or

    (b) periodical compensation payments and lump sum compensation payments.

(5) Regulations made by virtue of subsection (4) may (among other things) provide—

    (a) for the relevant period to be treated as ending at a prescribed time,

    (b) for the person who is to make the payments under the agreement to be treated for the purposes of this Act as if he had made a single compensation payment on a prescribed date.

(6) A periodical payment may be a compensation payment for the purposes of this section even though it is a small payment (as defined in Part II of Schedule 1).

19   Payments by more than one person

(1) Regulations may make provision (including provision modifying this Act) for any case in which two or more persons ('the compensators') make compensation payments to or in respect of the same injured person in consequence of the same accident, injury or disease.

(2) In such a case, the sum of the liabilities of the compensators under section 6 is not to exceed the total amount of the recoverable benefits, and the regulations may provide for determining the respective liabilities under that section of each of the compensators.

(3) The regulations may (among other things) provide in the case of each compensator—

    (a) for determining or re-determining the part of the recoverable benefits which may be taken into account in his case,

    (b) for calculating or re-calculating in accordance with section 8 the amount of any compensation payment,

    (c) for giving credit for amounts already paid, and

    (d) for the payment by any person of any balance or the recovery from any person of any excess.

20   Amounts overpaid under section 6

(1) Regulations may make provision (including provision modifying this Act) for cases where a person has paid to the Secretary of State under section 6 any amount ('the amount of the overpayment') which he was not liable to pay.

(2) The regulations may provide—

    (a) for the Secretary of State to pay the amount of the overpayment to that person, or to the person to whom the compensation payment is made, or partly to one and partly to the other, or

    (b) for the receipt by the Secretary of State of the amount of the overpayment to be treated as the recovery of that amount.

(3) Regulations made by virtue of subsection (2)(b) are to have effect in spite of anything in section 71 of the Social Security Administration Act 1992 (overpayments—general).

(4) The regulations may also (among other things) provide—

    (a) for the re-calculation in accordance with section 8 of the amount of any compensation payment,

    (b) for giving credit for amounts already paid, and

    (c) for the payment by any person of any balance or the recovery from any person of any excess.

(5) This section does not apply in a case where section 14 applies.

21   Compensation payments to be disregarded

(1) If, when a compensation payment is made, the first and second conditions are met, the payment is to be disregarded for the purposes of sections 6 and 8.

(2) The first condition is that the person making the payment—

    (a) has made an application for a certificate of recoverable benefits which complies with subsection (3), and

    (b) has in his possession a written acknowledgement of the receipt of his application.

(3) An application complies with this subsection if it—

    (a) accurately states the prescribed particulars relating to the injured person and the accident, injury or disease in question, and

    (b) specifies the name and address of the person to whom the certificate is to be sent.

(4) The second condition is that the Secretary of State has not sent the certificate to the person, at the address, specified in the application, before the end of the period allowed under section 4.

(5) In any case where—

    (a) by virtue of subsection (1), a compensation payment is disregarded for the purposes of sections 6 and 8, but

    (b) the person who made the compensation payment nevertheless makes a payment to the Secretary of State for which (but for subsection (1)) he would be liable under section 6,

subsection (1) is to cease to apply in relation to the compensation payment.

(6) If, in the opinion of the Secretary of State, circumstances have arisen which adversely affect normal methods of communication—

    (a) he may by order provide that subsection (1) is not to apply during a specified period not exceeding three months, and

    (b) he may continue any such order in force for further periods not exceeding three months at a time.

22   Liability of insurers

(1) If a compensation payment is made in a case where—

    (a) a person is liable to any extent in respect of the accident, injury or disease, and

    (b) the liability is covered to any extent by a policy of insurance,

the policy is also to be treated as covering any liability of that person under section 6.

(2) Liability imposed on the insurer by subsection (1) cannot be excluded or restricted.

(3) For that purpose excluding or restricting liability includes—

    (a) making the liability or its enforcement subject to restrictive or onerous conditions,

    (b) excluding or restricting any right or remedy in respect of the liability, or subjecting a person to any prejudice in consequence of his pursuing any such right or remedy, or

    (c) excluding or restricting rules of evidence or procedure.

(4) Regulations may in prescribed cases limit the amount of the liability imposed on the insurer by subsection (1).

(5) This section applies to policies of insurance issued before (as well as those issued after) its coming into force.

(6) References in this section to policies of insurance and their issue include references to contracts of insurance and their making.

23   Provision of information

(1) Where compensation is sought in respect of any accident, injury or disease suffered by any person ('the injured person'), the following persons must give the Secretary of State the prescribed information about the injured person—

    (a) anyone who is, or is alleged to be, liable in respect of the accident, injury or disease, and

    (b) anyone acting on behalf of such a person.

(2) A person who receives or claims a listed benefit which is or is likely to be paid in respect of an accident, injury or disease suffered by him, must give the Secretary of State the prescribed information about the accident, injury or disease.

(3) Where a person who has received a listed benefit dies, the duty in subsection (2) is imposed on his personal representative.

(4) Any person who makes a payment (whether on his own behalf or not)—

(a) in consequence of, or

(b) which is referable to any costs (in Scotland, expenses) incurred by reason of, any accident, injury or disease, or any damage to property, must, if the Secretary of State requests him in writing to do so, give the Secretary of State such particulars relating to the size and composition of the payment as are specified in the request.

(5) The employer of a person who suffers or has suffered an accident, injury or disease, and anyone who has been the employer of such a person at any time during the relevant period, must give the Secretary of State the prescribed information about the payment of statutory sick pay in respect of that person.

(6) In subsection (5) 'employer' has the same meaning as it has in Part XI of the Social Security Contributions and Benefits Act 1992.

(7) A person who is required to give information under this section must do so in the prescribed manner, at the prescribed place and within the prescribed time.

(8) Section 1 does not apply in relation to this section.

28   The Crown

This Act applies to the Crown.

29   General interpretation

In this Act—

'benefit' means any benefit under the Social Security Contributions and Benefits Act 1992, a job-seeker's allowance[, an employment and support allowance] or mobility allowance,

'compensation scheme for motor accidents' means any scheme or arrangement under which funds are available for the payment of compensation in respect of motor accidents caused, or alleged to have been caused, by uninsured or unidentified persons,

'listed benefit' means a benefit listed in column 2 of Schedule 2,

'payment' means payment in money or money's worth, and related expressions are to be interpreted accordingly,

'prescribed' means prescribed by regulations, and

'regulations' means regulations made by the Secretary of State.

30   Regulations and orders

(3) Regulations under section 20, under section 24 amending the list of benefits in column 2 of Schedule 2 or under paragraph 9 of Schedule 1 may not be made without the consent of the Treasury.

(4) Subsections (4), (5), (6) and (9) of section 189 of the Social Security Administration Act 1992 (regulations and orders—general) apply for the purposes of this Act as they apply for the purposes of that.

31   Financial arrangements

(1) There are to be paid out of the National Insurance Fund any expenses of the Secretary of State in making payments under section 14 or 20 to the extent that he estimates that those payments relate to sums paid out of that Fund.

(2) There are to be paid out of money provided by Parliament—

(a) any expenses of the Secretary of State in making payments under section 14 or 20 to the extent that he estimates that those payments relate to sums paid out of the Consolidated Fund, and

(b) (subject to subsection (1)) any other expenses of the Secretary of State incurred in consequence of this Act.

(3) Any sums paid to the Secretary of State under section 6 or 14 are to be paid—

(a) into the Consolidated Fund, to the extent that the Secretary of State estimates that the sums relate to payments out of money provided by Parliament, and

(b) into the National Insurance Fund, to the extent that he estimates that they relate to payments out of that Fund.

32   Power to make transitional, consequential etc. provisions

(1) Regulations may make such transitional and consequential provisions, and such savings, as the Secretary of State considers necessary or expedient in preparation for, in connection with, or in consequence of—

(a) the coming into force of any provision of this Act, or

(b) the operation of any enactment repealed or amended by a provision of this Act during any period when the repeal or amendment is not wholly in force.

(2) Regulations under this section may (among other things) provide—

(a) for compensation payments in relation to which, by virtue of section 2, this Act does not apply to be treated as payments in relation to which this Act applies,

(b) for compensation payments in relation to which, by virtue of section 2, this Act applies to be treated as payments in relation to which this Act does not apply, and

(c) for the modification of any enactment contained in this Act or referred to in subsection (1)(b) in its application to any compensation payment.

Section 1   SCHEDULE 1

COMPENSATION PAYMENTS

PART I EXEMPTED PAYMENTS

1. Any small payment (defined in Part II of this Schedule).

2. Any payment made to or for the injured person under [section 130 of the Powers of Criminal Courts (Sentencing) Act 2000] or section 249 of the Criminal Procedure (Scotland) Act 1995 (compensation orders against convicted persons).

3. Any payment made in the exercise of a discretion out of property held subject to a trust in a case where no more than 50 per cent. by value of the capital contributed to the trust was directly or indirectly provided by persons who are, or are alleged to be, liable in respect of—

(a) the accident, injury or disease suffered by the injured person, or

(b) the same or any connected accident, injury or disease suffered by another.

4. Any payment made out of property held for the purposes of any prescribed trust (whether the payment also falls within paragraph 3 or not).

5. [(1)] Any payment made to the injured person by an [insurer] under the terms of any contract of insurance entered into between the injured person and the company before—

(a) the date on which the injured person first claims a listed benefit in consequence of the disease in question, or

(b) the occurrence of the accident or injury in question.

6. Any redundancy payment falling to be taken into account in the assessment of damages in respect of an accident, injury or disease.

7. So much of any payment as is referable to costs.

8. Any prescribed payment.

PART II POWER TO DISREGARD SMALL PAYMENTS

9.—(1) Regulations may make provision for compensation payments to be disregarded for the purposes of sections 6 and 8 in prescribed cases where the amount of the compensation payment, or the aggregate amount of two or more connected compensation payments, does not exceed the prescribed sum.

(2) A compensation payment disregarded by virtue of this paragraph is referred to in paragraph 1 as a 'small payment'.

(3) For the purposes of this paragraph—

    (a) two or more compensation payments are 'connected' if each is made to or in respect of the same injured person and in respect of the same accident, injury or disease, and

    (b) any reference to a compensation payment is a reference to a payment which would be such a payment apart from paragraph 1.

Section 8   # SCHEDULE 2

CALCULATION OF COMPENSATION PAYMENT

(1) *Head of compensation*	(2) *Benefit*
1. Compensation for earnings lost during the relevant period	[...]
	Disablement pension payable under section 103 of the 1992 Act
	Incapacity benefit
	Income support
	Invalidity pension and allowance
	Jobseeker's allowance
	Reduced earnings allowance
	Severe disablement allowance
	Sickness benefit
	Statutory sick pay
	Unemployability supplement
	Unemployment benefit
2. Compensation for cost of care incurred during the relevant period	Attendance allowance
	Care component of disability living allowance
	Disablement pension increase payable under section 104 or 105 of the 1992 Act
	[Employment and support allowance]
3. Compensation for loss of mobility during the relevant period	Mobility allowance
	Mobility component of disability living allowance

Notes

1.—(1) References to incapacity benefit, invalidity pension and allowance, severe disablement allowance, sickness benefit and unemployment benefit also include any income support paid with each of those benefits on the same instrument of payment or paid concurrently with each of those benefits by means of an instrument for benefit payment.

    (2) For the purpose of this Note, income support includes personal expenses addition, special transitional additions and transitional addition as defined in the Income Support (Transitional) Regulations 1987.

2. Any reference to statutory sick pay—

    (a) includes only 80 per cent. of payments made between 6 April 1991 and 5 April 1994, and

    (b) does not include payments made on or after 6 April 1994.

3. In this Schedule "the 1992 Act" means the Social Security Contributions and Benefits Act 1992.

Data Protection Act 1998

(1998, c. 29)

10 Right to prevent processing likely to cause damage or distress

(1) Subject to subsection (2), an individual is entitled at any time by notice in writing to a data controller to require the data controller at the end of such period as is reasonable in the circumstances to cease, or not to begin, processing, or processing for a specified purpose or in a specified manner, any personal data in respect of which he is the data subject, on the ground that, for specified reasons—

    (a) the processing of those data or their processing for that purpose or in that manner is causing or is likely to cause substantial damage or substantial distress to him or to another, and

    (b) that damage or distress is or would be unwarranted.

(2) Subsection (1) does not apply—

    (a) in a case where any of the conditions in paragraphs 1 to 4 of Schedule 2 is met, or

    (b) on such other cases as may be prescribed by the [Secretary of State] by order.

(3) The data controller must within twenty-one days of receiving a notice under subsection (1) ('the data subject notice') give the individual who gave it a written notice—

    (a) stating that he has complied or intends to comply with the data subject notice, or

    (b) stating his reasons for regarding the data subject notice as to any extent unjustified and the extent (if any) to which he has complied or intends to comply with it.

(4) If a court is satisfied, on the application of any person who has given a notice under subsection (1) which appears to the court to be justified (or to be justified to any extent), that the data controller in question has failed to comply with the notice, the court may order him to take such steps for complying with the notice (or for complying with it to that extent) as the court thinks fit.

(5) The failure by a data subject to exercise the right conferred by subsection (1) or section 11(1) does not affect any other right conferred on him by this Part.

13 Compensation for failure to comply with certain requirements

(1) An individual who suffers damage by reason of any contravention by a data controller of any of the requirements of this Act is entitled to compensation from the data controller for that damage.

(2) An individual who suffers distress by reason of any contravention by a data controller of any of the requirements of this Act is entitled to compensation from the data controller for that distress if—

    (a) the individual also suffers damage by reason of the contravention, or

    (b) the contravention relates to the processing of personal data for the special purposes.

(3) On proceedings brought against a person by virtue of this section it is a defence to prove that he had taken such care as in all the circumstances was reasonably required to comply with the requirement concerned.

57 Avoidance of certain contractual terms relating to health records

(1) Any term or condition of a contract is void in so far as it purports to require an individual—

    (a) to supply any other person with a record to which this section applies, or with a copy of such a record or a part of such a record, or

    (b) to produce to any other person such a record, copy or part.

(2) This section applies to any record which—

    (a) has been or is to be obtained by a data subject in the exercise of the right conferred by section 7, and

    (b) consists of the information contained in any health record as defined by section 68(2).

Human Rights Act 1998

(1998, c. 42)

Introduction

1   The Convention Rights

(1) In this Act 'the Convention rights' means the rights and fundamental freedoms set out in—

    (a) Articles 2 to 12 and 14 of the Convention,

    (b) Articles 1 to 3 of the First Protocol, and

    (c) [Article 1 of the Thirteenth Protocol,]

as read with Articles 16 to 18 of the Convention.

(2) Those Articles are to have effect for the purposes of this Act subject to any designated derogation or reservation (as to which see sections 14 and 15).

(3) The Articles are set out in Schedule 1.

(4) The [Secretary of State] may by order make such amendments to this Act as he considers appropriate to reflect the effect, in relation to the United Kingdom, of a protocol.

(5) In subsection (4) 'protocol' means a protocol to the Convention—

    (a) which the United Kingdom has ratified; or

    (b) which the United Kingdom has signed with a view to ratification.

(6) No amendment may be made by an order under subsection (4) so as to come into force before the protocol concerned is in force in relation to the United Kingdom.

2   Interpretation of Convention rights

(1) A court or tribunal determining a question which has arisen in connection with a Convention right must take into account any—

    (a) judgment, decision, declaration or advisory opinion of the European Court of Human Rights,

    (b) opinion of the Commission given in a report adopted under Article 31 of the Convention,

    (c) decision of the Commission in connection with Article 26 or 27(2) of the Convention, or

    (d) decision of the Committee of Ministers taken under Article 46 of the Convention,

whenever made or given, so far as, in the opinion of the court or tribunal, it is relevant to the proceedings in which that question has arisen.

(2) Evidence of any judgment, decision, declaration or opinion of which account may have to be taken under this section is to be given in proceedings before any court or tribunal in such manner as may be provided by rules.

(3) In this section 'rules' means rules of court or, in the case of proceedings before a tribunal, rules made for the purposes of this section—

    (a) by [the Lord Chancellor or] the Secretary of State, in relation to any proceedings outside Scotland;

    (b) by the Secretary of State, in relation to proceedings in Scotland; or

    (c) by a Northern Ireland department, in relation to proceedings before a tribunal in Northern Ireland—

        (i)   which deals with transferred matters; and

        (ii)   for which no rules made under paragraph (a) are in force.

Legislation

3   Interpretation of legislation

(1) So far as it is possible to do so, primary legislation and subordinate legislation must be read and given effect in a way which is compatible with the Convention rights.

(2) This section—

    (a) applies to primary legislation and subordinate legislation whenever enacted;

(b) does not affect the validity, continuing operation or enforcement of any incompatible primary legislation; and

(c) does not affect the validity, continuing operation or enforcement of any incompatible subordinate legislation if (disregarding any possibility of revocation) primary legislation prevents removal of the incompatibility.

4   Declaration of incompatibility

(1) Subsection (2) applies in any proceedings in which a court determines whether a provision of primary legislation is compatible with a Convention right.

(2) If the court is satisfied that the provision is incompatible with a Convention right, it may make a declaration of that incompatibility.

(3) Subsection (4) applies in any proceedings in which a court determines whether a provision of subordinate legislation, made in the exercise of a power conferred by primary legislation, is compatible with a Convention right.

(4) If the court is satisfied—

(a) that the provision is incompatible with a Convention right, and

(b) that (disregarding any possibility of revocation) the primary legislation concerned prevents removal of the incompatibility,

it may make a declaration of that incompatibility.

(5) In this section 'court' means—

(a) the [Supreme Court];

(b) the Judicial Committee of the Privy Council;

(c) the [Courts Martial Appeal Court];

(d) in Scotland, the High Court of Justiciary sitting otherwise than as a trial court or the Court of Session;

(e) in England and Wales or Northern Ireland, the High Court or the Court of Appeal

[(f) the Court of Protection, in any matter being dealt with by the President of the Family Division, the Vice-Chancellor or a puisne judge of the High Court.]

(6) A declaration under this section ('a declaration of incompatibility')—

(a) does not affect the validity, continuing operation or enforcement of the provision in respect of which it is given; and

(b) is not binding on the parties to the proceedings in which it is made.

5   Right of Crown to intervene

(1) Where a court is considering whether to make a declaration of incompatibility, the Crown is entitled to notice in accordance with rules of court.

(2) In any case to which subsection (1) applies—

(a) a Minister of the Crown (or a person nominated by him),

(b) a member of the Scottish Executive,

(c) a Northern Ireland Minister,

(d) a Northern Ireland department,

is entitled, on giving notice in accordance with rules of court, to be joined as a party to the proceedings.

(3) Notice under subsection (2) may be given at any time during the proceedings.

(4) A person who has been made a party to criminal proceedings (other than in Scotland) as the result of a notice under subsection (2) may, with leave, appeal to the [Supreme Court] against any declaration of incompatibility made in the proceedings.

(5) In subsection (4)—

'criminal proceedings' includes all proceedings before the [Courts Martial Appeal Court]; and

'leave' means leave granted by the court making the declaration of incompatibility or by the [Supreme Court].

Public authorities

6 Acts of public authorities

(1) It is unlawful for a public authority to act in a way which is incompatible with a Convention right.

(2) Subsection (1) does not apply to an act if—

(a) as the result of one or more provisions of primary legislation, the authority could not have acted differently; or

(b) in the case of one or more provisions of, or made under, primary legislation which cannot be read or given effect in a way which is compatible with the Convention rights, the authority was acting so as to give effect to or enforce those provisions.

(3) In this section 'public authority' includes—

(a) a court or tribunal, and

(b) any person certain of whose functions are functions of a public nature,

but does not include either House of Parliament or a person exercising functions in connection with proceedings in Parliament.

(5) In relation to a particular act, a person is not a public authority by virtue only of subsection (3)(b) if the nature of the act is private.

(6) 'An act' includes a failure to act but does not include a failure to—

(a) introduce in, or lay before, Parliament a proposal for legislation; or

(b) make any primary legislation or remedial order.

7 Proceedings

(1) A person who claims that a public authority has acted (or proposes to act) in a way which is made unlawful by section 6(1) may—

(a) bring proceedings against the authority under this Act in the appropriate court or tribunal, or

(b) rely on the Convention right or rights concerned in any legal proceedings,

but only if he is (or would be) a victim of the unlawful act.

(2) In subsection (1)(a) 'appropriate court or tribunal' means such court or tribunal as may be determined in accordance with rules; and proceedings against an authority include a counterclaim or similar proceedings.

(3) If the proceedings are brought on an application for judicial review, the applicant is to be taken to have a sufficient interest in relation to the unlawful act only if he is, or would be, a victim of that act.

(4) If the proceedings are made by way of a petition for judicial review in Scotland, the applicant shall be taken to have title and interest to sue in relation to the unlawful act only if he is, or would be, a victim of that act.

(5) Proceedings under subsection (1)(a) must be brought before the end of—

(a) the period of one year beginning with the date on which the act complained of took place; or

(b) such longer period as the court or tribunal considers equitable having regard to all the circumstances,

but that is subject to any rule imposing a stricter time limit in relation to the procedure in question.

(6) In subsection (1)(b) 'legal proceedings' includes—

(a) proceedings brought by or at the instigation of a public authority; and

(b) an appeal against the decision of a court or tribunal.

(7) For the purposes of this section, a person is a victim of an unlawful act only if he would be a victim for the purposes of Article 34 of the Convention if proceedings were brought in the European Court of Human Rights in respect of that act.

(8) Nothing in this Act creates a criminal offence.

(9) In this section 'rules' means—

    (a) in relation to proceedings before a court or tribunal outside Scotland, rules made by [the Lord Chancellor or] the Secretary of State for the purposes of this section or rules of court,

    (b) in relation to proceedings before a court or tribunal in Scotland, rules made by the Secretary of State for those purposes,

    (c) in relation to proceedings before a tribunal in Northern Ireland—

        (i) which deals with transferred matters; and

        (ii) for which no rules made under paragraph (a) are in force,

    rules made by a Northern Ireland department for those purposes,

and includes provision made by order under section 1 of the Courts and Legal Services Act 1990.

(10) In making rules, regard must be had to section 9.

(11) The Minister who has power to make rules in relation to a particular tribunal may, to the extent he considers it necessary to ensure that the tribunal can provide an appropriate remedy in relation to an act (or proposed act) of a public authority which is (or would be) unlawful as a result of section 6(1), by order add to—

    (a) the relief or remedies which the tribunal may grant; or

    (b) the grounds on which it may grant any of them.

(12) An order made under subsection (11) may contain such incidental, supplemental, consequential or transitional provision as the Minister making it considers appropriate.

(13) 'The Minister' includes the Northern Ireland department concerned.

8 Judicial remedies

(1) In relation to any act (or proposed act) of a public authority which the court finds is (or would be) unlawful, it may grant such relief or remedy, or make such order, within its powers as it considers just and appropriate.

(2) But damages may be awarded only by a court which has power to award damages, or to order the payment of compensation, in civil proceedings.

(3) No award of damages is to be made unless, taking account of all the circumstances of the case, including—

    (a) any other relief or remedy granted, or order made, in relation to the act in question (by that or any other court), and

    (b) the consequences of any decision (of that or any other court) in respect of that act,

the court is satisfied that the award is necessary to afford just satisfaction to the person in whose favour it is made.

(4) In determining—

    (a) whether to award damages, or

    (b) the amount of an award,

the court must take into account the principles applied by the European Court of Human Rights in relation to the award of compensation under Article 41 of the Convention.

(5) A public authority against which damages are awarded is to be treated—

    (a) in Scotland, for the purposes of section 3 of the Law Reform (Miscellaneous Provisions) (Scotland) Act 1940 as if the award were made in an action of damages in which the authority has been found liable in respect of loss or damage to the person to whom the award is made;

    (b) for the purposes of the Civil Liability (Contribution) Act 1978 as liable in respect of damage suffered by the person to whom the award is made.

(6) In this section—

'court' includes a tribunal;

'damages' means damages for an unlawful act of a public authority; and

'unlawful' means unlawful under section 6(1).

9   Judicial acts

(1) Proceedings under section 7(1)(a) in respect of a judicial act may be brought only—

(a) by exercising a right of appeal;

(b) on an application (in Scotland a petition) for judicial review; or

(c) in such other forum as may be prescribed by rules.

(2) That does not affect any rule of law which prevents a court from being the subject of judicial review.

(3) In proceedings under this Act in respect of a judicial act done in good faith, damages may not be awarded otherwise than to compensate a person to the extent required by Article 5(5) of the Convention.

(4) An award of damages permitted by subsection (3) is to be made against the Crown; but no award may be made unless the appropriate person, if not a party to the proceedings, is joined.

(5) In this section—

'appropriate person' means the Minister responsible for the court concerned, or a person or government department nominated by him;

'court' includes a tribunal;

'judge' includes a member of a tribunal, a justice of the peace [or, in Northern Ireland, a lay magistrate] and a clerk or other officer entitled to exercise the jurisdiction of a court;

'judicial act' means a judicial act of a court and includes an act done on the instructions, or on behalf, of a judge; and

'rules' has the same meaning as in section 7(9).

Remedial action

10   Power to take remedial action

(1) This section applies if—

(a) a provision of legislation has been declared under section 4 to be incompatible with a Convention right and, if an appeal lies—

(i) all persons who may appeal have stated in writing that they do not intend to do so;

(ii) the time for bringing an appeal has expired and no appeal has been brought within that time; or

(iii) an appeal brought within that time has been determined or abandoned; or

(b) it appears to a Minister of the Crown or Her Majesty in Council that, having regard to a finding of the European Court of Human Rights made after the coming into force of this section in proceedings against the United Kingdom, a provision of legislation is incompatible with an obligation of the United Kingdom arising from the Convention.

(2) If a Minister of the Crown considers that there are compelling reasons for proceeding under this section, he may by order make such amendments to the legislation as he considers necessary to remove the incompatibility.

(3) If, in the case of subordinate legislation, a Minister of the Crown considers—

(a) that it is necessary to amend the primary legislation under which the subordinate legislation in question was made, in order to enable the incompatibility to be removed, and

(b) that there are compelling reasons for proceeding under this section,

he may by order make such amendments to the primary legislation as he considers necessary.

(4) This section also applies where the provision in question is in subordinate legislation and has been quashed, or declared invalid, by reason of incompatibility with a Convention right and the Minister proposes to proceed under paragraph 2(b) of Schedule 2.

(5) If the legislation is an Order in Council, the power conferred by subsection (2) or (3) is exercisable by Her Majesty in Council.

(6) In this section 'legislation' does not include a Measure of the Church Assembly or of the General Synod of the Church of England.

(7) Schedule 2 makes further provision about remedial orders.

Other rights and proceedings

11 Safeguard for existing human rights

A person's reliance on a Convention right does not restrict—

    (a) any other right or freedom conferred on him by or under any law having effect in any part of the United Kingdom; or

    (b) his right to make any claim or bring any proceedings which he could make or bring apart from sections 7 to 9.

12 Freedom of expression

(1) This section applies if a court is considering whether to grant any relief which, if granted, might affect the exercise of the Convention right to freedom of expression.

(2) If the person against whom the application for relief is made ('the respondent') is neither present nor represented, no such relief is to be granted unless the court is satisfied—

    (a) that the applicant has taken all practicable steps to notify the respondent; or

    (b) that there are compelling reasons why the respondent should not be notified.

(3) No such relief is to be granted so as to restrain publication before trial unless the court is satisfied that the applicant is likely to establish that publication should not be allowed.

(4) The court must have particular regard to the importance of the Convention right to freedom of expression and, where the proceedings relate to material which the respondent claims, or which appears to the court, to be journalistic, literary or artistic material (or to conduct connected with such material), to—

    (a) the extent to which—

        (i)   the material has, or is about to, become available to the public; or

        (ii) it is, or would be, in the public interest for the material to be published;

    (b) any relevant privacy code.

(5) In this section—

'court' includes a tribunal; and

'relief' includes any remedy or order (other than in criminal proceedings).

13 Freedom of thought, conscience and religion

(1) If a court's determination of any question arising under this Act might affect the exercise by a religious organisation (itself or its members collectively) of the Convention right to freedom of thought, conscience and religion, it must have particular regard to the importance of that right.

(2) In this section 'court' includes a tribunal.

Parliamentary procedure

19 Statements of compatibility

(1) A Minister of the Crown in charge of a Bill in either House of Parliament must, before Second Reading of the Bill—

    (a) make a statement to the effect that in his view the provisions of the Bill are compatible with the Convention rights ('a statement of compatibility'); or

    (b) make a statement to the effect that although he is unable to make a statement of compatibility the government nevertheless wishes the House to proceed with the Bill.

(2) The statement must be in writing and be published in such manner as the Minister making it considers appropriate.

Supplemental

21 Interpretation, etc.

(1) In this Act—

'amend' includes repeal and apply (with or without modifications);

'the appropriate Minister' means the Minister of the Crown having charge of the appropriate authorised government department (within the meaning of the Crown Proceedings Act 1947);

'the Commission' means the European Commission of Human Rights;

'the Convention' means the Convention for the Protection of Human Rights and Fundamental Freedoms, agreed by the Council of Europe at Rome on 4th November 1950 as it has effect for the time being in relation to the United Kingdom;

'declaration of incompatibility' means a declaration under section 4;

'Minister of the Crown' has the same meaning as in the Ministers of the Crown Act 1975;

'Northern Ireland Minister' includes the First Minister and the deputy First Minister in Northern Ireland;

'primary legislation' means any—

    (a) public general Act;

    (b) local and personal Act;

    (c) private Act;

    (d) Measure of the Church Assembly;

    (e) Measure of the General Synod of the Church of England;

    (f) Order in Council—

        (i)   made in exercise of Her Majesty's Royal Prerogative;

        (ii) made under section 38(1)(a) of the Northern Ireland Constitution Act 1973 or the corresponding provision of the Northern Ireland Act 1998; or

        (iii) amending an Act of a kind mentioned in paragraph (a), (b) or (c);

and includes an order or other instrument made under primary legislation (otherwise than by the [Welsh Ministers, the First Minister for Wales, the Counsel General to the Welsh Assembly Government,] a member of the Scottish Executive, a Northern Ireland Minister or a Northern Ireland department) to the extent to which it operates to bring one or more provisions of that legislation into force or amends any primary legislation;

'the First Protocol' means the protocol to the Convention agreed at Paris on 20th March 1952;

'the Eleventh Protocol' means the protocol to the Convention (restructuring the control machinery established by the Convention) agreed at Strasbourg on 11th May 1994;

['the Thirteenth Protocol' means the protocol to the Convention (concerning the abolition of the death penalty in all circumstances) agreed at Vilnius on 3rd May 2002;]

'remedial order' means an order under section 10;

'subordinate legislation' means any—

    (a) Order in Council other than one—

        (i)   made in exercise of Her Majesty's Royal Prerogative;

        (ii) made under section 38(1)(a) of the Northern Ireland Constitution Act 1973 or the corresponding provision of the Northern Ireland Act 1998; or

        (iii) amending an Act of a kind mentioned in the definition of primary legislation;

    (b) Act of the Scottish Parliament;

    [(ba) Measure of the National Assembly for Wales;

    (bb) Act of the National Assembly for Wales;]

    (c) Act of the Parliament of Northern Ireland;

    (d) Measure of the Assembly established under section 1 of the Northern Ireland Assembly Act 1973;

    (e) Act of the Northern Ireland Assembly;

    (f) order, rules, regulations, scheme, warrant, byelaw or other instrument made under primary legislation (except to the extent to which it operates to bring one or more provisions of that legislation into force or amends any primary legislation);

    (g) order, rules, regulations, scheme, warrant, byelaw or other instrument made under legislation mentioned in paragraph (b), (c), (d) or (e) or made under an Order in Council applying only to Northern Ireland;

    (h) order, rules, regulations, scheme, warrant, byelaw or other instrument made by a member of the Scottish Executive, [Welsh Ministers, the First Minister for Wales, the Counsel General to the Welsh Assembly Government,] a Northern Ireland Minister or a Northern Ireland department in exercise of prerogative or other executive functions of Her Majesty which are exercisable by such a person on behalf of Her Majesty;

'transferred matters' has the same meaning as in the Northern Ireland Act 1998; and

'tribunal' means any tribunal in which legal proceedings may be brought.

(2) The references in paragraphs (b) and (c) of section 2(1) to Articles are to Articles of the Convention as they had effect immediately before the coming into force of the Eleventh Protocol.

(3) The reference in paragraph (d) of section 2(1) to Article 46 includes a reference to Articles 32 and 54 of the Convention as they had effect immediately before the coming into force of the Eleventh Protocol.

(4) The references in section 2(1) to a report or decision of the Commission or a decision of the Committee of Ministers include references to a report or decision made as provided by paragraphs 3, 4 and 6 of Article 5 of the Eleventh Protocol (transitional provisions).

(5) Any liability under the Army Act 1955, the Air Force Act 1955 or the Naval Discipline Act 1957 to suffer death for an offence is replaced by a liability to imprisonment for life or any less punishment authorised by those Acts; and those Acts shall accordingly have effect with the necessary modifications.

22   Short title, commencement, application and extent

(5) This Act binds the Crown.

(6) This Act extends to Northern Ireland.

Section 1(3)

SCHEDULE 1

THE ARTICLES

PART I THE CONVENTION

Rights and freedoms

Article 2   Right to life

1. Everyone's right to life shall be protected by law. No one shall be deprived of his life intentionally save in the execution of a sentence of a court following his conviction of a crime for which this penalty is provided by law.

2. Deprivation of life shall not be regarded as inflicted in contravention of this Article when it results from the use of force which is no more than absolutely necessary:

    (a) in defence of any person from unlawful violence;

    (b) in order to effect a lawful arrest or to prevent the escape of a person lawfully detained;

    (c) in action lawfully taken for the purpose of quelling a riot or insurrection.

Article 3   Prohibition of torture

No one shall be subjected to torture or to inhuman or degrading treatment or punishment.

Article 4   Prohibition of slavery and forced labour

1. No one shall be held in slavery or servitude.

2. No one shall be required to perform forced or compulsory labour.

3. For the purpose of this Article the term 'forced or compulsory labour' shall not include:

    (a) any work required to be done in the ordinary course of detention imposed according to the provisions of Article 5 of this Convention or during conditional release from such detention;

    (b) any service of a military character or, in case of conscientious objectors in countries where they are recognised, service exacted instead of compulsory military service;

(c) any service exacted in case of an emergency or calamity threatening the life or well-being of the community;

(d) any work or service which forms part of normal civic obligations.

Article 5   Right to liberty and security

1. Everyone has the right to liberty and security of person. No one shall be deprived of his liberty save in the following cases and in accordance with a procedure prescribed by law:

(a) the lawful detention of a person after conviction by a competent court;

(b) the lawful arrest or detention of a person for non-compliance with the lawful order of a court or in order to secure the fulfilment of any obligation prescribed by law;

(c) the lawful arrest or detention of a person effected for the purpose of bringing him before the competent legal authority on reasonable suspicion of having committed an offence or when it is reasonably considered necessary to prevent his committing an offence or fleeing after having done so;

(d) the detention of a minor by lawful order for the purpose of educational supervision or his lawful detention for the purpose of bringing him before the competent legal authority.

(e) the lawful detention of persons for the prevention of the spreading of infectious diseases, of persons of unsound mind, alcoholics or drug addicts or vagrants;

(f) the lawful arrest or detention of a person to prevent his effecting an unauthorised entry into the country or of a person against whom action is being taken with a view to deportation or extradition.

2. Everyone who is arrested shall be informed promptly, in a language which he understands, of the reasons for his arrest and of any charge against him.

3. Everyone arrested or detained in accordance with the provisions of paragraph 1(c) of this Article shall be brought promptly before a judge or other officer authorised by law to exercise judicial power and shall be entitled to trial within a reasonable time or to release pending trial. Release may be conditioned by guarantees to appear for trial.

4. Everyone who is deprived of his liberty by arrest or detention shall be entitled to take proceedings by which the lawfulness of his detention shall be decided speedily by a court and his release ordered if the detention is not lawful.

5. Everyone who has been the victim of arrest or detention in contravention of the provisions of this Article shall have an enforceable right to compensation.

Article 6   Right to a fair trial

1. In the determination of his civil rights and obligations or of any criminal charge against him, everyone is entitled to a fair and public hearing within a reasonable time by an independent and impartial tribunal established by law. Judgment shall be pronounced publicly but the press and public may be excluded from all or part of the trial in the interest of morals, public order or national security in a democratic society, where the interests of juveniles or the protection of the private life of the parties so require, or to the extent strictly necessary in the opinion of the court in special circumstances where publicity would prejudice the interests of justice.

2. Everyone charged with a criminal offence shall be presumed innocent until proved guilty according to law.

3. Everyone charged with a criminal offence has the following minimum rights:

(a) to be informed promptly, in a language which he understands and in detail, of the nature and cause of the accusation against him;

(b) to have adequate time and facilities for the preparation of his defence;

(c) to defend himself in person or through legal assistance of his own choosing or, if he has not sufficient means to pay for legal assistance, to be given it free when the interests of justice so require;

(d) to examine or have examined witnesses against him and to obtain the attendance and examination of witnesses on his behalf under the same conditions as witnesses against him;

(e) to have the free assistance of an interpreter if he cannot understand or speak the language used in court.

Article 7   No punishment without law

1. No one shall be held guilty of any criminal offence on account of any act or omission which did not constitute a criminal offence under national or international law at the time when it was committed. Nor shall a heavier penalty be imposed than the one that was applicable at the time the criminal offence was committed.

2. This Article shall not prejudice the trial and punishment of any person for any act or omission which, at the time when it was committed, was criminal according to the general principles of law recognised by civilised nations.

Article 8   Right to respect for private and family life

1. Everyone has the right to respect for his private and family life, his home and his correspondence.

2. There shall be no interference by a public authority with the exercise of this right except such as is in accordance with the law and is necessary in a democratic society in the interests of national security, public safety or the economic well-being of the country, for the prevention of disorder or crime, for the protection of health or morals, or for the protection of the rights and freedoms of others.

Article 9   Freedom of thought, conscience and religion

1. Everyone has the right to freedom of thought, conscience and religion; this right includes freedom to change his religion or belief and freedom, either alone or in community with others and in public or private, to manifest his religion or belief, in worship, teaching, practice and observance.

2. Freedom to manifest one's religion or beliefs shall be subject only to such limitations as are prescribed by law and are necessary in a democratic society in the interests of public safety, for the protection of public order, health or morals, or for the protection of the rights and freedoms of others.

Article 10   Freedom of expression

1. Everyone has the right to freedom of expression. This right shall include freedom to hold opinions and to receive and impart information and ideas without interference by public authority and regardless of frontiers. This Article shall not prevent States from requiring the licensing of broadcasting, television or cinema enterprises.

2. The exercise of these freedoms, since it carries with it duties and responsibilities, may be subject to such formalities, conditions, restrictions or penalties as are prescribed by law and are necessary in a democratic society, in the interests of national security, territorial integrity or public safety, for the prevention of disorder or crime, for the protection of health or morals, for the protection of the reputation or rights of others, for preventing the disclosure of information received in confidence, or for maintaining the authority and impartiality of the judiciary.

Article 11   Freedom of assembly and association

1. Everyone has the right to freedom of peaceful assembly and to freedom of association with others, including the right to form and to join trade unions for the protection of his interests.

2. No restrictions shall be placed on the exercise of these rights other than such as are prescribed by law and are necessary in a democratic society in the interests of national security or public safety, for the prevention of disorder or crime, for the protection of health or morals or for the protection of the rights and freedoms of others. This Article shall not prevent the imposition of lawful restrictions on the exercise of these rights by members of the armed forces, of the police or of the administration of the State.

Article 12   Right to marry

Men and women of marriageable age have the right to marry and to found a family, according to the national laws governing the exercise of this right.

Article 14   Prohibition of discrimination

The enjoyment of the rights and freedoms set forth in this Convention shall be secured without discrimination on any ground such as sex, race, colour, language, religion, political or other opinion, national or social origin, association with a national minority, property, birth or other status.

Article 16   Restrictions on political activity of aliens

Nothing in Articles 10, 11 and 14 shall be regarded as preventing the High Contracting Parties from imposing restrictions on the political activity of aliens.

Article 17   Prohibition of abuse of rights

Nothing in this Convention may be interpreted as implying for any State, group or person any right to engage in any activity or perform any act aimed at the destruction of any of the rights and freedoms set forth herein or at their limitation to a greater extent than is provided for in the Convention.

Article 18   Limitation on use of restrictions on rights

The restrictions permitted under this Convention to the said rights and freedoms shall not be applied for any purpose other than those for which they have been prescribed.

PART II THE FIRST PROTOCOL

Article 1   Protection of property

Every natural or legal person is entitled to the peaceful enjoyment of his possessions. No one shall be deprived of his possessions except in the public interest and subject to the conditions provided for by law and by the general principles of international law.

   The preceding provisions shall not, however, in any way impair the right of a State to enforce such laws as it deems necessary to control the use of property in accordance with the general interest or to secure the payment of taxes or other contributions or penalties.

Article 2   Right to education

No person shall be denied the right to education. In the exercise of any functions which it assumes in relation to education and to teaching, the State shall respect the right of parents to ensure such education and teaching in conformity with their own religious and philosophical convictions.

Article 3   Right to free elections

The High Contracting Parties undertake to hold free elections at reasonable intervals by secret ballot, under conditions which will ensure the free expression of the opinion of the people in the choice of the legislature.

[PART 3 ARTICLE 1 OF THE THIRTEENTH PROTOCOL

Abolition of the death penalty

The death penalty shall be abolished. No one shall be condemned to such penalty or executed.]

Late Payment of Commercial Debts (Interest) Act 1998

(1998, c. 20)

PART I STATUTORY INTEREST ON QUALIFYING DEBTS

1   Statutory interest

   (1) It is an implied term in a contract to which this Act applies that any qualifying debt created by the contract carries simple interest subject to and in accordance with this Part.

(2) Interest carried under that implied term (in this Act referred to as 'statutory interest') shall be treated, for the purposes of any rule of law or enactment (other than this Act) relating to interest on debts, in the same way as interest carried under an express contract term.

(3) This Part has effect subject to Part II (which in certain circumstances permits contract terms to oust or vary the right to statutory interest that would otherwise be conferred by virtue of the term implied by subsection (1)).

2   Contracts to which Act applies

(1) This Act applies to a contract for the supply of goods or services where the purchaser and the supplier are each acting in the course of a business, other than an excepted contract.

(2) In this Act 'contract for the supply of goods or services' means—

(a) a contract of sale of goods; or

(b) a contract (other than a contract of sale of goods) by which a person does any, or any combination, of the things mentioned in subsection (3) for a consideration that is (or includes) a money consideration.

(3) Those things are—

(a) transferring or agreeing to transfer to another the property in goods;

(b) bailing or agreeing to bail goods to another by way of hire or, in Scotland, hiring or agreeing to hire goods to another; and

(c) agreeing to carry out a service.

(4) For the avoidance of doubt a contract of service or apprenticeship is not a contract for the supply of goods or services.

(5) The following are excepted contracts—

(a) a consumer credit agreement;

(b) a contract intended to operate by way of mortgage, pledge, charge or other security; and

[...]

(7) In this section—

'business' includes a profession and the activities of any government department or local or public authority;

'consumer credit agreement' has the same meaning as in the Consumer Credit Act 1974;

'contract of sale of goods' and 'goods' have the same meaning as in the Sale of Goods Act 1979;

['government department' includes any part of the Scottish Administration;]

'property in goods' means the general property in them and not merely a special property.

3   Qualifying debts

(1) A debt created by virtue of an obligation under a contract to which this Act applies to pay the whole or any part of the contract price is a 'qualifying debt' for the purposes of this Act, unless (when created) the whole of the debt is prevented from carrying statutory interest by this section.

(2) A debt does not carry statutory interest if or to the extent that it consists of a sum to which a right to interest or to charge interest applies by virtue of any enactment (other than section 1 of this Act).

This subsection does not prevent a sum from carrying statutory interest by reason of the fact that a court, arbitrator or arbiter would, apart from this Act, have power to award interest on it.

(3) A debt does not carry (and shall be treated as never having carried) statutory interest if or to the extent that a right to demand interest on it, which exists by virtue of any rule of law, is exercised.

4   Period for which statutory interest runs

(1) Statutory interest runs in relation to a qualifying debt in accordance with this section (unless section 5 applies).

(2) Statutory interest starts to run on the day after the relevant day for the debt, at the rate prevailing under section 6 at the end of the relevant day.

(3) Where the supplier and the purchaser agree a date for payment of the debt (that is, the day on which the debt is to be created by the contract), that is the relevant day unless the debt relates to an obligation to make an advance payment.

A date so agreed may be a fixed one or may depend on the happening of an event or the failure of an event to happen.

(4) Where the debt relates to an obligation to make an advance payment, the relevant day is the day on which the debt is treated by section 11 as having been created.

(5) In any other case, the relevant day is the last day of the period of 30 days beginning with—

   (a) the day on which the obligation of the supplier to which the debt relates is performed; or
   (b) the day on which the purchaser has notice of the amount of the debt or (where the amount is unascertained) the sum which the supplier claims is the amount of the debt, whichever is the later.

(6) Where the debt is created by virtue of an obligation to pay a sum due in respect of a period of hire of goods, subsection (5)(a) has effect as if it referred to the last day of that period.

(7) Statutory interest ceases to run when the interest would cease to run if it were carried under an express contract term.

(8) In this section 'advance payment' has the same meaning as in section 11.

5   Remission of statutory interest

(1) This section applies where, by reason of any conduct of the supplier, the interests of justice require that statutory interest should be remitted in whole or part in respect of a period for which it would otherwise run in relation to a qualifying debt.

(2) If the interests of justice require that the supplier should receive no statutory interest for a period, statutory interest shall not run for that period.

(3) If the interests of justice require that the supplier should receive statutory interest at a reduced rate for a period, statutory interest shall run at such rate as meets the justice of the case for that period.

(4) Remission of statutory interest under this section may be required—

   (a) by reason of conduct at any time (whether before or after the time at which the debt is created); and
   (b) for the whole period for which statutory interest would otherwise run or for one or more parts of that period.

(5) In this section 'conduct' includes any act or omission.

[5A   Compensation arising out of late payment

(1) Once statutory interest begins to run in relation to a qualifying debt, the supplier shall be entitled to a fixed sum (in addition to the statutory interest on the debt).

(2) That sum shall be—

   (a) for a debt less than £1,000, the sum of £40;
   (b) for a debt of £1,000 or more, but less than £10,000, the sum of £70;
   (c) for a debt of £10,000 or more, the sum of £100.

(3) The obligation to pay an additional fixed sum under this section in respect of a qualifying debt shall be treated as part of the term implied by section 1(1) in the contract creating the debt.]

6   Rate of statutory interest

(1) The Secretary of State shall by order made with the consent of the Treasury set the rate of statutory interest by prescribing—

   (a) a formula for calculating the rate of statutory interest; or
   (b) the rate of statutory interest.

(2) Before making such an order the Secretary of State shall, among other things, consider the extent to which it may be desirable to set the rate so as to—

   (a) protect suppliers whose financial position makes them particularly vulnerable if their qualifying debts are paid late; and
   (b) deter generally the late payment of qualifying debts.

PART II CONTRACT TERMS RELATING
TO LATE PAYMENT OF QUALIFYING DEBTS

7 Purpose of Part II

(1) This Part deals with the extent to which the parties to a contract to which this Act applies may by reference to contract terms oust or vary the right to statutory interest that would otherwise apply when a qualifying debt created by the contract (in this Part referred to as 'the debt') is not paid.

(2) This Part applies to contract terms agreed before the debt is created; after that time the parties are free to agree terms dealing with the debt.

(3) This Part has effect without prejudice to any other ground which may affect the validity of a contract term.

8 Circumstances where statutory interest may be ousted or varied

(1) Any contract terms are void to the extent that they purport to exclude the right to statutory interest in relation to the debt, unless there is a substantial contractual remedy for late payment of the debt.

(2) Where the parties agree a contractual remedy for late payment of the debt that is a substantial remedy, statutory interest is not carried by the debt (unless they agree otherwise).

(3) The parties may not agree to vary the right to statutory interest in relation to the debt unless either the right to statutory interest as varied or the overall remedy for late payment of the debt is a substantial remedy.

(4) Any contract terms are void to the extent that they purport to—

(a) confer a contractual right to interest that is not a substantial remedy for late payment of the debt, or

(b) vary the right to statutory interest so as to provide for a right to statutory interest that is not a substantial remedy for late payment of the debt,

unless the overall remedy for late payment of the debt is a substantial remedy.

(5) Subject to this section, the parties are free to agree contract terms which deal with the consequences of late payment of the debt.

9 Meaning of 'substantial remedy'

(1) A remedy for the late payment of the debt shall be regarded as a substantial remedy unless—

(a) the remedy is insufficient either for the purpose of compensating the supplier for late payment or for deterring late payment; and

(b) it would not be fair or reasonable to allow the remedy to be relied on to oust or (as the case may be) to vary the right to statutory interest that would otherwise apply in relation to the debt.

(2) In determining whether a remedy is not a substantial remedy, regard shall be had to all the relevant circumstances at the time the terms in question are agreed.

(3) In determining whether subsection (1)(b) applies, regard shall be had (without prejudice to the generality of subsection (2)) to the following matters—

(a) the benefits of commercial certainty;

(b) the strength of the bargaining positions of the parties relative to each other;

(c) whether the term was imposed by one party to the detriment of the other (whether by the use of standard terms or otherwise); and

(d) whether the supplier received an inducement to agree to the term.

10 Interpretation of Part II

(1) In this Part—

'contract term' means a term of the contract creating the debt or any other contract term binding the parties (or either of them);

'contractual remedy' means a contractual right to interest or any contractual remedy other than interest;

'contractual right to interest' includes a reference to a contractual right to charge interest;

'overall remedy', in relation to the late payment of the debt, means any combination of a contractual right to interest, a varied right to statutory interest or a contractual remedy other than interest;

'substantial remedy' shall be construed in accordance with section 9.

(2) In this Part a reference (however worded) to contract terms which vary the right to statutory interest is a reference to terms altering in any way the effect of Part I in relation to the debt (for example by postponing the time at which interest starts to run or by imposing conditions on the right to interest).

(3) In this Part a reference to late payment of the debt is a reference to late payment of the sum due when the debt is created (excluding any part of that sum which is prevented from carrying statutory interest by section 3).

PART III GENERAL AND SUPPLEMENTARY

11   Treatment of advance payments of the contract price

(1) A qualifying debt created by virtue of an obligation to make an advance payment shall be treated for the purposes of this Act as if it was created on the day mentioned in subsection (3), (4) or (5) (as the case may be).

(2) In this section 'advance payment' means a payment falling due before the obligation of the supplier to which the whole contract price relates ('the supplier's obligation') is performed, other than a payment of a part of the contract price that is due in respect of any part performance of that obligation and payable on or after the day on which that part performance is completed.

(3) Where the advance payment is the whole contract price, the debt shall be treated as created on the day on which the supplier's obligation is performed.

(4) Where the advance payment is a part of the contract price, but the sum is not due in respect of any part performance of the supplier's obligation, the debt shall be treated as created on the day on which the supplier's obligation is performed.

(5) Where the advance payment is a part of the contract price due in respect of any part performance of the supplier's obligation, but is payable before that part performance is completed, the debt shall be treated as created on the day on which the relevant part performance is completed.

(6) Where the debt is created by virtue of an obligation to pay a sum due in respect of a period of hire of goods, this section has effect as if—

    (a) references to the day on which the supplier's obligation is performed were references to the last day of that period; and

    (b) references to part performance of that obligation were references to part of that period.

(7) For the purposes of this section an obligation to pay the whole outstanding balance of the contract price shall be regarded as an obligation to pay the whole contract price and not as an obligation to pay a part of the contract price.

13   Assignments, etc.

(1) The operation of this Act in relation to a qualifying debt is not affected by—

    (a) any change in the identity of the parties to the contract creating the debt; or

    (b) the passing of the right to be paid the debt, or the duty to pay it (in whole or in part) to a person other than the person who is the original creditor or the original debtor when the debt is created.

(2) Any reference in this Act to the supplier or the purchaser is a reference to the person who is for the time being the supplier or the purchaser or, in relation to a time after the debt in question has been created, the person who is for the time being the creditor or the debtor, as the case may be.

(3) Where the right to be paid part of a debt passes to a person other than the person who is the original creditor when the debt is created, any reference in this Act to a debt shall be construed as (or, if the context so requires, as including) a reference to part of a debt.

(4) A reference in this section to the identity of the parties to a contract changing, or to a right or duty passing, is a reference to it changing or passing by assignment or assignation, by operation of law or otherwise.

14   Contract terms relating to the date for payment of the contract price

(1) This section applies to any contract term which purports to have the effect of postponing the time at which a qualifying debt would otherwise be created by a contract to which this Act applies.

(2) Sections 3(2)(b) and 17(1)(b) of the Unfair Contract Terms Act 1977 (no reliance to be placed on certain contract terms) shall apply in cases where such a contract term is not contained in written standard terms of the purchaser as well as in cases where the term is contained in such standard terms.

(3) In this section 'contract term' has the same meaning as in section 10(1).

15   Orders and regulations

(1) Any power to make an order or regulations under this Act is exercisable by statutory instrument.

(2) Any statutory instrument containing an order or regulations under this Act, other than an order under section 17(2), shall be subject to annulment in pursuance of a resolution of either House of Parliament.

16   Interpretation

(1) In this Act—

'contract for the supply of goods or services' has the meaning given in section 2(2);

'contract price' means the price in a contract of sale of goods or the money consideration referred to in section 2(2)(b) in any other contract for the supply of goods or services;

'purchaser' means (subject to section 13(2)) the buyer in a contract of sale or the person who contracts with the supplier in any other contract for the supply of goods or services;

'qualifying debt' means a debt falling within section 3(1);

'statutory interest' means interest carried by virtue of the term implied by section 1(1); and

'supplier' means (subject to section 13(2)) the seller in a contract of sale of goods or the person who does one or more of the things mentioned in section 2(3) in any other contract for the supply of goods or services.

(2) In this Act any reference (however worded) to an agreement or to contract terms includes a reference to both express and implied terms (including terms established by a course of dealing or by such usage as binds the parties).

17   Short title, commencement and extent

(5) This Act extends to Northern Ireland.

National Minimum Wage Act 1998

(1998, c. 39)

1   Workers to be paid at least the national minimum wage

(1) A person who qualifies for the national minimum wage shall be remunerated by his employer in respect of his work in any pay reference period at a rate which is not less than the national minimum wage.

Contracts (Rights of Third Parties) Act 1999

(1999, c. 31)

1　Right of third party to enforce contractual term

(1)　Subject to the provisions of this Act, a person who is not a party to a contract (a 'third party') may in his own right enforce a term of the contract if—

    (a)　the contract expressly provides that he may, or

    (b)　subject to subsection (2), the term purports to confer a benefit on him.

(2)　Subsection (1)(b) does not apply if on a proper construction of the contract it appears that the parties did not intend the term to be enforceable by the third party.

(3)　The third party must be expressly identified in the contract by name, as a member of a class or as answering a particular description but need not be in existence when the contract is entered into.

(4)　This section does not confer a right on a third party to enforce a term of a contract otherwise than subject to and in accordance with any other relevant terms of the contract.

(5)　For the purpose of exercising his right to enforce a term of the contract, there shall be available to the third party any remedy that would have been available to him in an action for breach of contract if he had been a party to the contract (and the rules relating to damages, injunctions, specific performance and other relief shall apply accordingly).

(6)　Where a term of a contract excludes or limits liability in relation to any matter references in this Act to the third party enforcing the term shall be construed as references to his availing himself of the exclusion or limitation.

(7)　In this Act, in relation to a term of a contract which is enforceable by a third party—

'the promisor' means the party to the contract against whom the term is enforceable by the third party, and

'the promisee' means the party to the contract by whom the term is enforceable against the promisor.

2　Variation and rescission of contract

(1)　Subject to the provisions of this section, where a third party has a right under section 1 to enforce a term of the contract, the parties to the contract may not, by agreement, rescind the contract, or vary it in such a way as to extinguish or alter his entitlement under that right, without his consent if—

    (a)　the third party has communicated his assent to the term to the promisor,

    (b)　the promisor is aware that the third party has relied on the term, or

    (c)　the promisor can reasonably be expected to have foreseen that the third party would rely on the term and the third party has in fact relied on it.

(2)　The assent referred to in subsection (1)(a)—

    (a)　may be by words or conduct, and

    (b)　if sent to the promisor by post or other means, shall not be regarded as communicated to the promisor until received by him.

(3)　Subsection (1) is subject to any express term of the contract under which—

    (a)　the parties to the contract may by agreement rescind or vary the contract without the consent of the third party, or

    (b)　the consent of the third party is required in circumstances specified in the contract instead of those set out in subsection (1)(a) to (c).

(4)　Where the consent of a third party is required under subsection (1) or (3), the court or arbitral tribunal may, on the application of the parties to the contract, dispense with his consent if satisfied—

    (a)　that his consent cannot be obtained because his whereabouts cannot reasonably be ascertained, or

    (b)　that he is mentally incapable of giving his consent.

(5)　The court or arbitral tribunal may, on the application of the parties to a contract, dispense with any consent that may be required under subsection (1)(c) if satisfied that it cannot reasonably be ascertained whether or not the third party has in fact relied on the term.

(6) If the court or arbitral tribunal dispenses with a third party's consent, it may impose such conditions as it thinks fit, including a condition requiring the payment of compensation to the third party.

(7) The jurisdiction conferred on the court by subsections (4) to (6) is exercisable by both the High Court and a county court.

3 Defences etc. available to promisor

(1) Subsections (2) to (5) apply where, in reliance on section 1, proceedings for the enforcement of a term of a contract are brought by a third party.

(2) The promisor shall have available to him by way of defence or set-off any matter that—

    (a) arises from or in connection with the contract and is relevant to the term, and

    (b) would have been available to him by way of defence or set-off if the proceedings had been brought by the promisee.

(3) The promisor shall also have available to him by way of defence or set-off any matter if—

    (a) an express term of the contract provides for it to be available to him in proceedings brought by the third party, and

    (b) it would have been available to him by way of defence or set-off if the proceedings had been brought by the promisee.

(4) The promisor shall also have available to him—

    (a) by way of defence or set-off any matter, and

    (b) by way of counterclaim any matter not arising from the contract, that would have been available to him by way of defence or set-off or, as the case maybe, by way of counterclaim against the third party if the third party had been a party to the contract.

(5) Subsections (2) and (4) are subject to any express term of the contract as to the matters that are not to be available to the promisor by way of defence, set-off or counterclaim.

(6) Where in any proceedings brought against him a third party seeks in reliance on section 1 to enforce a term of a contract (including, in particular, a term purporting to exclude or limit liability), he may not do so if he could not have done so (whether by reason of any particular circumstances relating to him or otherwise) had he been a party to the contract.

4 Enforcement of contract by promisee

Section 1 does not affect any right of the promisee to enforce any term of the contract.

5 Protection of promisor from double liability

Where under section 1 a term of a contract is enforceable by a third party, and the promisee has recovered from the promisor a sum in respect of—

    (a) the third party's loss in respect of the term, or

    (b) the expense to the promisee of making good to the third party the default of the promisor,

then, in any proceedings brought in reliance on that section by the third party, the court or arbitral tribunal shall reduce any award to the third party to such extent as it thinks appropriate to take account of the sum recovered by the promisee.

6 Exceptions

(1) Section 1 confers no rights on a third party in the case of a contract on a bill of exchange, promissory note or other negotiable instrument.

(2) Section 1 confers no rights on a third party in the case of any contract binding on a company and its members under [section 33 of the Companies Act 2006 (effect of company's constitution)].

[(2A) Section 1 confers no rights on a third party in the case of any incorporation document of a limited liability partnership or any agreement (express or implied) between the members of a limited liability partnership, or between a limited liability partnership and its members, that determines the mutual rights and duties of the members and their rights and duties in relation to the limited liability partnership.]

(3) Section 1 confers no right on a third party to enforce—

    (a) any term of a contract of employment against an employee,

     (b) any term of a worker's contract against a worker (including a home worker), or

     (c) any term of a relevant contract against an agency worker.

  (4) In subsection (3)—

     (a) 'contract of employment', 'employee', 'worker's contract', and 'worker' have the meaning given by section 54 of the National Minimum Wage Act 1998,

     (b) 'home worker' has the meaning given by section 35(2) of that Act,

     (c) 'agency worker' has the same meaning as in section 34(1) of that Act, and

     (d) 'relevant contract' means a contract entered into, in a case where section 34 of that Act applies, by the agency worker as respects work falling within subsection (1)(a) of that section.

  (5) Section 1 confers no rights on a third party in the case of—

     (a) a contract for the carriage of goods by sea, or

     (b) a contract for the carriage of goods by rail or road, or for the carriage of cargo by air, which is subject to the rules of the appropriate international transport convention,

except that a third party may in reliance on that section avail himself of an exclusion or limitation of liability in such a contract.

  (6) In subsection (5) 'contract for the carriage of goods by sea' means a contract of carriage—

     (a) contained in or evidenced by a bill of lading, sea waybill or a corresponding electronic transaction, or

     (b) under or for the purposes of which there is given an undertaking which is contained in a ship's delivery order or a corresponding electronic transaction.

  (7) For the purposes of subsection (6)—

     (a) 'bill of lading', 'sea waybill' and 'ship's delivery order' have the same meaning as in the Carriage of Goods by Sea Act 1992, and

     (b) a corresponding electronic transaction is a transaction within section 1(5) of that Act which corresponds to the issue, indorsement, delivery or transfer of a bill of lading, sea waybill or ship's delivery order.

  (8) In subsection (5) 'the appropriate international transport convention' means—

     (a) in relation to a contract for the carriage of goods by rail, the Convention which has the force of law in the United Kingdom under [regulation 3 of the Railways (Convention on International Carriage by Rail) Regulations 2005],

     (b) in relation to a contract for the carriage of goods by road, the Convention which has the force of law in the United Kingdom under section 1 of the Carriage of Goods by Road Act 1965, and

     (c) in relation to a contract for the carriage of cargo by air—

       (i) the Convention which has the force of law in the United Kingdom under section 1 of the Carriage by Air Act 1961, or

       (ii) the Convention which has the force of law under section 1 of the Carriage by Air (Supplementary Provisions) Act 1962, or

       (iii) either of the amended Conventions set out in Part B of Schedule 2 or 3 to the Carriage by Air Acts (Application of Provisions) Order 1967.

7 Supplementary provisions relating to third party

  (1) Section 1 does not affect any right or remedy of a third party that exists or is available apart from this Act.

  (2) Section 2(2) of the Unfair Contract Terms Act 1977 (restriction on exclusion etc. of liability for negligence) shall not apply where the negligence consists of the breach of an obligation arising from a term of a contract and the person seeking to enforce it is a third party acting in reliance on section 1.

  (3) In sections 5 and 8 of the Limitation Act 1980 the references to an action founded on a simple contract and an action upon a specialty shall respectively include references to an action brought in reliance on section 1 relating to a simple contract and an action brought in reliance on that section relating to a specialty.

(4) A third party shall not, by virtue of section 1(5) or 3(4) or (6), be treated as a party to the contract for the purposes of any other Act (or any instrument made under any other Act).

8   Arbitration provisions

(1) Where—

    (a) a right under section 1 to enforce a term ('the substantive term') is subject to a term providing for the submission of disputes to arbitration ('the arbitration agreement'), and

    (b) the arbitration agreement is an agreement in writing for the purposes of Part I of the Arbitration Act 1996,

the third party shall be treated for the purposes of that Act as a party to the arbitration agreement as regards disputes between himself and the promisor relating to the enforcement of the substantive term by the third party.

(2) Where—

    (a) a third party has a right under section 1 to enforce a term providing for one or more descriptions of dispute between the third party and the promisor to be submitted to arbitration ('the arbitration agreement'),

    (b) the arbitration agreement is an agreement in writing for the purposes of Part I of the Arbitration Act 1996, and

    (c) the third party does not fall to be treated under subsection (1) as a party to the arbitration agreement,

the third party shall, if he exercises the right, be treated for the purposes of that Act as a party to the arbitration agreement in relation to the matter with respect to which the right is exercised, and be treated as having been so immediately before the exercise of the right.

9   Northern Ireland

(1) In its application to Northern Ireland, this Act has effect with the modifications specified in subsections (2) and (3).

(3) In section 7, for subsection (3) there is substituted—

'(3) In Articles 4(a) and 15 of the Limitation (Northern Ireland) Order 1989, the references to an action founded on a simple contract and an action upon an instrument under seal shall respectively include references to an action brought in reliance on section 1 relating to a simple contract and an action brought in reliance on that section relating to a contract under seal.'.

10   Short title, commencement and extent

(1) This Act may be cited as the Contracts (Rights of Third Parties) Act 1999.

(2) This Act comes into force on the day on which it is passed but, subject to subsection (3), does not apply in relation to a contract entered into before the end of the period of six months beginning with that day.

(3) The restriction in subsection (2) does not apply in relation to a contract which—

    (a) is entered into on or after the day on which this Act is passed, and

    (b) expressly provides for the application of this Act.

(4) This Act extends as follows—

    (a) section 9 extends to Northern Ireland only;

    (b) the remaining provisions extend to England and Wales and Northern Ireland only.

EXPLANATORY NOTES

1. These explanatory notes ... have been prepared by the Lord Chancellor's Department in order to assist the reader in understanding the Act. They do not form part of the Act and have not been endorsed by Parliament.

Section 3:   Defences etc. available to promisor

15. *Section 3* enables the promisor, in a claim by the third party, to rely on any defence or set-off arising out of the contract and relevant to the term being enforced, which would have been

available to him had the claim been by the promisee. He may also rely on any defence or set-off, or make any counterclaim, where this would have been possible had the third party been a party to the contract.

16. *Subsection (2)* can be illustrated as follows—

(I)   a third party can no more enforce a void, discharged or unenforceable contract than a promisee could;

(II) P1 (the promisor) and P2 (the promisee) contract that P2 will sell goods to P1, who will pay the contract price to P3 (the third party). In breach of contract, P2 delivers goods that are not of the standard contracted for. In an action for the price by P3 (just as in an action for the price by P2) P1 is entitled to reduce or extinguish the price by reason of the damages for breach of contract.

17. *Subsection (3)* can be illustrated as follows—

P1 and P2 contract that P1 will pay P3 if P2 transfers his car to P1. P2 owes P1 money under a wholly unrelated contract. P1 and P2 agree to an express term in the contract which provides that P1 can raise against a claim by P3 any matter which would have given P1 a defence or set-off to a claim by P2.

18. *Subsection (4)* makes it clear that the promisor also has available any defence or setoff, and any counterclaim not arising from the contract, which is specific to the third party. It can be illustrated as follows.

(I)   P1 contracts with P2 to pay P3 £1000. P3 already owes P1 £600. P1 has a set-off to P3's claim so that P1 is only bound to pay P3 £400.

(II) P3 induced P1 to enter into the contract with P2 by misrepresentation, but P2 has no actual or constructive notice of that misrepresentation. P1 may have a defence (or a counterclaim for damages) against P3 which would not have been available had the action been brought by P2.

19. *Subsection (5)* makes subsections (2) and (4) subject to any express term of the contract which narrows the defences or set-offs available under section 3(2) or narrows the defences, set-offs or counterclaims available under section 3(4). For example—

(I)   in relation to subsection (2), P2 agrees with P1 to purchase a painting, the painting to be delivered to P3, who is expressly given a right to enforce the delivery obligation. P2 owes P1 considerable sums for other art works purchased. P2 wishes to ensure that P3's right is not affected. P1 and P2 expressly agree that P1 may not raise against P3 defences and set-offs that would have been available to P1 in an action by P2.

(II) in relation to subsection (4), P1 agrees with P2 to pay £5000 to P3 if P2 will transfer a number of cases of wine to P1. P3 is in dispute with P1 over a prior contract and P1 alleges that P3 owes P1 money. P2 is concerned that P1 may seek to withhold part of the £5000 payable to P3 by raising a set-off or counterclaim against P3 in relation to the prior contract. Consequently P1 and P2 include an express term that P1 may raise no defences, set-offs or counterclaims of any nature whatever against a claim by P3 to enforce P1's obligation to pay the £5000.

20. *Subsection (6)* ensures that an analogous approach to that set out in subsections (2) to (5) applies where the proceedings are brought against the third party and he seeks to avail himself of, for example, an exclusion section.

Countryside and Rights of Way Act 2000

(2000, c. 37)

1   Principal definitions for Part I

(1) In this Part 'access land' means any land which—

(a)   is shown as open country on a map in conclusive form issued by the appropriate coun-tryside body for the purposes of this Part,

(b)   is shown on such a map as registered common land,

(c)   is registered common land in any area outside Inner London for which no such map relating to registered common land has been issued,

(d)   is situated more than 600 metres above sea level in any area for which no such map relating to open country has been issued,

[(da) is coastal margin, or]

(e)   is dedicated for the purposes of this Part under section 16,

but does not (in any of those cases) include excepted land or land which is treated by section 15(1) as being accessible to the public apart from this Act.

2   Rights of public in relation to access land

(1) Any person is entitled by virtue of this subsection to enter and remain on any access land for the purposes of open-air recreation, if and so long as—

(a) he does so without breaking or damaging any wall, fence, hedge, stile or gate, and

(b) he observes the general restrictions in Schedule 2 and any other restrictions imposed in relation to the land under Chapter II.

(2) Subsection (1) has effect subject to subsections (3) and (4) and to the provisions of Chapter II.

(3) Subsection (1) does not entitle a person to enter or be on any land, or do anything on any land, in contravention of any [relevant statutory prohibition].

[(3A) In subsection (3) "relevant statutory prohibition" means—

(a) in the case of land which is coastal margin, a prohibition contained in or having effect under any enactment, and

(b) in any other case, a prohibition contained in or having effect under any enactment other than an enactment contained in a local or private Act.]

(4) If a person becomes a trespasser on any access land by failing to comply with—

(a) subsection (1)(a),

(b) the general restrictions in Schedule 2, or

(c) any other restrictions imposed in relation to the land under Chapter II, he may not, within 72 hours after leaving that land, exercise his right under subsection (1) to enter that land again or to enter other land in the same ownership.

12   Effect of right of access on rights and liabilities of owners

(1) The operation of section 2(1) in relation to any access land does not increase the liability, under any enactment not contained in this Act or under any rule of law, of a person interested in the access land or any adjoining land in respect of the state of the land or of things done or omitted to be done on the land.

(2) Any restriction arising under a covenant or otherwise as to the use of any access land shall have effect subject to the provisions of this Part, and any liability of a person interested in any access land in respect of such a restriction is limited accordingly.

(3) For the purposes of any enactment or rule of law as to the circumstances in which the dedication of a highway or the grant of an easement may be presumed, or may be established by prescription, the use by the public or by any person of a way across land in the exercise of the right conferred by section 2(1) is to be disregarded.

(4) The use of any land by the inhabitants of any locality for the purposes of open-air recreation in the exercise of the right conferred by section 2(1) is to be disregarded in determining whether the land has become a town or village green.

Finance Act 2000

(2000, c. 17)

Section 30

SCHEDULE 6

CLIMATE CHANGE LEVY

142 Adjustment of contracts

(1) Sub-paragraph (2) applies in the case of a contract for the supply of a taxable commodity if—

(a) the contract is entered into before 1 April 2001 (whether before or after the passing of this Act) or at a time when supplies such as are provided for by the contract are not taxable supplies, but

(b) supplies falling to be made under the contract will be, or become or will become, taxable supplies.

(2) The supplier of the commodity may unilaterally vary the contract by adjusting the price chargeable for any supply made under the contract if he does so for the purpose of passing on, to the person liable to pay for the supply, the burden (or any part of the burden) of the levy for which the supplier is liable to account on the supply.

(3) Sub-paragraph (4) applies in the case of a contract for the supply of a taxable commodity if it provides (whether as a result of a variation under sub-paragraph (2) or otherwise) for the passing on, to the person liable to pay for the supply, of the burden (or any part of the burden) of any levy for which the supplier is liable to account on the supply.

(a) any change in the rate at which levy is charged on the supply;

(b) levy ceasing to be chargeable on the supply.

(5) The powers conferred by this paragraph are in addition to any contractual powers.

Financial Services and Markets Act 2000

(2000, c. 8)

19 The general prohibition

(1) No person may carry on a regulated activity in the United Kingdom, or purport to do so, unless he is—

(a) an authorised person; or

(b) an exempt person.

(2) The prohibition is referred to in this Act as the general prohibition.

26 Agreements made by unauthorised persons

(1) An agreement made by a person in the course of carrying on a regulated activity in contravention of the general prohibition is unenforceable against the other party.

(2) The other party is entitled to recover—

(a) any money or other property paid or transferred by him under the agreement; and

(b) compensation for any loss sustained by him as a result of having parted with it.

(3) 'Agreement' means an agreement—

(a) made after this section comes into force; and

(b) the making or performance of which constitutes, or is part of, the regulated activity in question.

27 Agreements made through unauthorised persons

(1) An agreement made by an authorised person ('the provider')—

(a) in the course of carrying on a regulated activity (not in contravention of the general prohibition), but

(b) in consequence of something said or done by another person ('the third party') in the course of a regulated activity carried on by the third party in contravention of the general prohibition,

is unenforceable against the other party.

(2) The other party is entitled to recover—

(a) any money or other property paid or transferred by him under the agreement; and

(b) compensation for any loss sustained by him as a result of having parted with it.

(3) 'Agreement' means an agreement—

(a) made after this section comes into force; and

(b) the making or performance of which constitutes, or is part of, the regulated activity in question carried on by the provider.

71   Actions for damages

(1) A contravention of section 56(6) or 59(1) or (2) is actionable at the suit of a private person who suffers loss as a result of the contravention, subject to the defences and other incidents applying to actions for breach of statutory duty.

(2) In prescribed cases, a contravention of that kind which would be actionable at the suit of a private person is actionable at the suit of a person who is not a private person, subject to the defences and other incidents applying to actions for breach of statutory duty.

80   General duty of disclosure in listing particulars

(1) Listing particulars submitted to the competent authority under section 79 must contain all such information as investors and their professional advisers would reasonably require, and reasonably expect to find there, for the purpose of making an informed assessment of—

(a) the assets and liabilities, financial position, profits and losses, and prospects of the issuer of the securities; and

(b) the rights attaching to the securities.

90   [Compensation for statements in listing particulars or prospectus]

(1) Any person responsible for listing particulars is liable to pay compensation to a person who has—

(a) acquired securities to which the particulars apply; and

(b) suffered loss in respect of them as a result of—

(i)   any untrue or misleading statement in the particulars; or

(ii)   the omission from the particulars of any matter required to be included by section 80 or 81.

(2) Subsection (1) is subject to exemptions provided by Schedule 10.

(3) If listing particulars are required to include information about the absence of a particular matter, the omission from the particulars of that information is to be treated as a statement in the listing particulars that there is no such matter.

(4) Any person who fails to comply with section 81 is liable to pay compensation to any person who has—

(a) acquired securities of the kind in question; and

(b) suffered loss in respect of them as a result of the failure.

(5) Subsection (4) is subject to exemptions provided by Schedule 10.

(6) This section does not affect any liability which may be incurred apart from this section.

(7) References in this section to the acquisition by a person of securities include references to his contracting to acquire them or any interest in them.

(8) No person shall, by reason of being a promoter of a company or otherwise, incur any liability for failing to disclose information which he would not be required to disclose in listing particulars in respect of a company's securities—

(a) if he were responsible for those particulars; or

(b) if he is responsible for them, which he is entitled to omit by virtue of section 82.

(9) The reference in subsection (8) to a person incurring liability includes a reference to any other person being entitled as against that person to be granted any civil remedy or to rescind or repudiate an agreement.

[(12) A person is not to be subject to civil liability solely on the basis of a summary in a prospectus unless the summary is misleading, inaccurate or inconsistent when read with the rest of the prospectus; and, in this subsection, a summary includes any translation of it.]

102   Exemption from liability in damages

(1) Neither the competent authority nor any person who is, or is acting as, a member, officer or member of staff of the competent authority is to be liable in damages for anything done or omitted in the discharge, or purported discharge, of the authority's functions.

(2) Subsection (1) does not apply—

    (a) if the act or omission is shown to have been in bad faith; or

    (b) so as to prevent an award of damages made in respect of an act or omission on the ground that the act or omission was unlawful as a result of section 6(1) of the Human Rights Act 1998.

131   Effect on transactions

The imposition of a penalty under this Part does not make any transaction void or unenforceable.

139   Miscellaneous ancillary matters

(2) An institution with which an account is kept in pursuance of rules relating to the handling of clients' money does not incur any liability as constructive trustee if money is wrongfully paid from the account, unless the institution permits the payment—

    (a) with knowledge that it is wrongful; or

    (b) having deliberately failed to make enquiries in circumstances in which a reasonable and honest person would have done so.

(3) In the application of subsection (1) to Scotland, the reference to money being held on trust is to be read as a reference to its being held as agent for the person who is entitled to call for it to be paid over to him or to be paid on his direction or to have it otherwise credited to him.

(4) Rules may—

    (a) confer rights on persons to rescind agreements with, or withdraw offers to, authorised persons within a specified period; and

    (b) make provision, in respect of authorised persons and persons exercising those rights, for the restitution of property and the making or recovery of payments where those rights are exercised.

150   Actions for damages

(1) A contravention by an authorised person of a rule is actionable at the suit of a private person who suffers loss as a result of the contravention, subject to the defences and other incidents applying to actions for breach of statutory duty.

213   The compensation scheme

(1) The Authority must by rules establish a scheme for compensating persons in cases where relevant persons are unable, or are likely to be unable, to satisfy claims against them.

(2) The rules are to be known as the Financial Services Compensation Scheme (but are referred to in this Act as 'the compensation scheme').

(3) The compensation scheme must, in particular, provide for the scheme manager—

    (a) to assess and pay compensation, in accordance with the scheme, to claimants in respect of claims made in connection with regulated activities carried on (whether or not with permission) by relevant persons; and

    (b) to have power to impose levies on authorised persons, or any class of authorised person, for the purpose of meeting its expenses (including in particular expenses incurred, or expected to be incurred, in paying compensation, borrowing or insuring risks).

(4) The compensation scheme may provide for the scheme manager to have power to impose levies on authorised persons, or any class of authorised person, for the purpose of recovering the cost (whenever incurred) of establishing the scheme.

(5) In making any provision of the scheme by virtue of subsection (3)(b), the Authority must take account of the desirability of ensuring that the amount of the levies imposed on a particular class of authorised person reflects, so far as practicable, the amount of the claims made, or likely to be made, in respect of that class of person.

(6) An amount payable to the scheme manager as a result of any provision of the scheme made by virtue of subsection (3)(b) or (4) may be recovered as a debt due to the scheme manager.

222 Statutory immunity

(1) Neither the scheme manager nor any person who is, or is acting as, its board member, officer[, scheme agent] or member of staff is to be liable in damages for anything done or omitted in the discharge, or purported discharge, of the scheme manager's functions.

(2) Subsection (1) does not apply—

> (a) if the act or omission is shown to have been in bad faith; or
> (b) so as to prevent an award of damages made in respect of an act or omission on the ground that the act or omission was unlawful as a result of section 6(1) of the Human Rights Act 1998.

291 Liability in relation to recognised body's regulatory functions

(1) A recognised body and its officers and staff [and an Operator and its officers and staff] are not to be liable in damages for anything done or omitted in the discharge of the recognised body's [or the Operator's] regulatory functions unless it is shown that the act or omission was in bad faith.

(2) But subsection (1) does not prevent an award of damages made in respect of an act or omission on the ground that the act or omission was unlawful as a result of section 6(1) of the Human Rights Act 1998.

380 Injunctions

(3) If, on the application of the authority or the Secretary of State, the court is satisfied that any person may have—

> (a) contravened a relevant requirement, or
> (b) been knowingly concerned in the contravention of such a requirement,

it may make an order restraining (or in Scotland an interdict prohibiting) him from disposing of, or otherwise dealing with, any assets of his which it is satisfied he is reasonably likely to dispose of or otherwise deal with.

381 Injunctions in cases of market abuse

(3) Subsection (4) applies if, on the application of the Authority, the court is satisfied that any person—

> (a) may be engaged in market abuse; or
> (b) may have been engaged in market abuse.

(4) The court make an order restraining (or in Scotland an interdict prohibiting) the person concerned from disposing of, or otherwise dealing with, any assets of his which it is satisfied that he is reasonably likely to dispose of, or otherwise deal with.

382 Restitution orders

(1) The court may, on the application of the Authority or the Secretary of State, make an order under subsection (2) if it is satisfied that a person has contravened a relevant requirement, or been knowingly concerned in the contravention of such a requirement, and—

> (a) that profits have accrued to him as a result of the contravention; or
> (b) that one or more persons have suffered loss or been otherwise adversely affected as a result of the contravention.

(2) The court may order the person concerned to pay to the Authority such sum as appears to the court to be just having regard—

    (a) in a case within paragraph (a) of subsection (1), to the profits appearing to the court to have accrued;

    (b) in a case within paragraph (b) of that subsection, to the extent of the loss or other adverse effect;

    (c) in a case within both of those paragraphs, to the profits appearing to the court to have accrued and to the extent of the loss or other adverse effect.

(3) Any amount paid to the Authority in pursuance of an order under subsection (2) must be paid by it to such qualifying person or distributed by it among such qualifying persons as the court may direct.

(4) On an application under subsection (1) the court may require the person concerned to supply it with such accounts or other information as it may require for any one or more of the following purposes—

    (a) establishing whether any and, if so, what profits have accrued to him as mentioned in paragraph (a) of that subsection;

    (b) establishing whether any person or persons have suffered any loss or adverse effect as mentioned in paragraph (b) of that subsection and, if so, the extent of that loss or adverse effect; and

    (c) determining how any amounts are to be paid or distributed under subsection (3).

(5) The court may require any accounts or other information supplied under subsection (4) to be verified in such manner as it may direct.

(6) The jurisdiction conferred by this section is exercisable by the High Court and the Court of Session.

(7) Nothing in this section affects the right of any person other than the Authority or the Secretary of State to bring proceedings in respect of the matters to which this section applies.

(8) 'Qualifying person' means a person appearing to the court to be someone—

    (a) to whom the profits mentioned in subsection (1)(a) are attributable; or

    (b) who has suffered the loss or adverse effect mentioned in subsection (1)(b).

(9) 'Relevant requirement'—

    (a) in relation to an application by the Authority, means a requirement—

        (i) which is imposed by or under this Act; or

        (ii) which is imposed by or under any other Act and whose contravention constitutes an offence which the Authority has power to prosecute under this Act;

    (b) in relation to an application by the Secretary of State, means a requirement which is imposed by or under this Act and whose contravention constitutes an offence which the Secretary of State has power to prosecute under this Act.

(10) In the application of subsection (9) to Scotland—

    (a) in paragraph (a)(ii) for 'which the Authority has power to prosecute under this Act' substitute 'mentioned in paragraph (a) or (b) of section 402(1); and

    (b) in paragraph (b) omit 'which the Secretary of State has power to prosecute under this Act'.

383 Restitution orders in cases of market abuse

(1) The court may, on the application of the Authority, make an order under subsection (4) if it is satisfied that a person ('the person concerned')—

    (a) has engaged in market abuse, or

    (b) by taking or refraining from taking any action has required or encouraged another person or persons to engage in behaviour which, if engaged in by the person concerned, would amount to market abuse,

and the condition mentioned in subsection (2) is fulfilled.

(2) The condition is—

    (a) that profits have accrued to the person concerned as a result; or

(b) that one or more persons have suffered loss or been otherwise adversely affected as a result.

(3) But the court may not make an order under subsection (4) if it is satisfied that—

(a) the person concerned believed, on reasonable grounds, that his behaviour did not fall within paragraph (a) or (b) of subsection (1); or

(b) he took all reasonable precautions and exercised all due diligence to avoid behaving in a way which fell within paragraph (a) or (b) of subsection (1).

(4) The court may order the person concerned to pay to the Authority such sum as appears to the court to be just having regard—

(a) in a case within paragraph (a) of subsection (2), to the profits appearing to the court to have accrued;

(b) in a case within paragraph (b) of that subsection, to the extent of the loss or other adverse effect;

(c) in a case within both of those paragraphs, to the profits appearing to the court to have accrued and to the extent of the loss or other adverse effect.

(5) Any amount paid to the Authority in pursuance of an order under subsection (4) must be paid by it to such qualifying person or distributed by it among such qualifying persons as the court may direct.

(6) On an application under subsection (1) the court may require the person concerned to supply it with such accounts or other information as it may require for any one or more of the following purposes—

(a) establishing whether any and, if so, what profits have accrued to him as mentioned in subsection (2)(a);

(b) establishing whether any person or persons have suffered any loss or adverse effect as mentioned in subsection (2)(b) and, if so, the extent of that loss or adverse effect; and

(c) determining how any amounts are to be paid or distributed under subsection (5).

(7) The court may require any accounts or other information supplied under subsection (6) to be verified in such manner as it may direct.

(8) The jurisdiction conferred by this section is exercisable by the High Court and the Court of Session.

(9) Nothing in this section affects the right of any person other than the Authority to bring proceedings in respect of the matters to which this section applies.

(10) 'Qualifying person' means a person appearing to the court to be someone—

(a) to whom the profits mentioned in paragraph (a) of subsection (2) are attributable; or

(b) who has suffered the loss or adverse effect mentioned in paragraph (b) of that subsection.

384 Power of Authority to require restitution

(1) The Authority may exercise the power in subsection (5) if it is satisfied that an authorised person ('the person concerned') has contravened a relevant requirement, or been knowingly concerned in the contravention of such a requirement, and—

(a) that profits have accrued to him as a result of the contravention; or

(b) that one or more persons have suffered loss or been otherwise adversely affected as a result of the contravention.

(2) The Authority may exercise the power in subsection (5) if it is satisfied that a person ('the person concerned')—

(a) has engaged in market abuse, or

(b) by taking or refraining from taking any action has required or encouraged another person or persons to engage in behaviour which, if engaged in by the person concerned, would amount to market abuse,

and the condition mentioned in subsection (3) is fulfilled.

(3) The condition is—

(a) that profits have accrued to the person concerned as a result of the market abuse; or

(b) that one or more persons have suffered loss or been otherwise adversely affected as a result of the market abuse.

(4) But the Authority may not exercise that power as a result of subsection (2) if, having considered any representations made to it in response to a warning notice, there are reasonable grounds for it to be satisfied that—

 (a) the person concerned believed, on reasonable grounds, that his behaviour did not fall within paragraph (a) or (b) of that subsection; or

 (b) he took all reasonable precautions and exercised all due diligence to avoid behaving in a way which fell within paragraph (a) or (b) of that subsection.

(5) The power referred to in subsections (1) and (2) is a power to require the person concerned, in accordance with such arrangements as the Authority considers appropriate, to pay to the appropriate person or distribute among the appropriate persons such amount as appears to the Authority to be just having regard—

 (a) in a case within paragraph (a) of subsection (1) or (3), to the profits appearing to the Authority to have accrued;

 (b) in a case within paragraph (b) of subsection (1) or (3), to the extent of the loss or other adverse effect;

 (c) in a case within paragraphs (a) and (b) of subsection (1) or (3), to the profits appearing to the Authority to have accrued and to the extent of the loss or other adverse effect.

(6) 'Appropriate person' means a person appearing to the Authority to be someone—

 (a) to whom the profits mentioned in paragraph (a) of subsection (1) or (3) are attributable; or

 (b) who has suffered the loss or adverse effect mentioned in paragraph (b) of subsection (1) or (3).

(7) 'Relevant requirement' means—

 (a) a requirement imposed by or under this Act; and

 (b) a requirement which is imposed by or under any other Act and whose contravention constitutes an offence in relation to which this Act confers power to prosecute on the Authority.

(8) In the application of subsection (7) to Scotland, in paragraph (b) for 'in relation to which this Act confers power to prosecute on the Authority' substitute 'mentioned in paragraph (a) or (b) of section 402(1)'.

385   Warning notices

(1) If the Authority proposes to exercise the power under section 384(5) in relation to a person, it must give him a warning notice.

(2) A warning notice under this section must specify the amount which the Authority proposes to require the person concerned to pay or distribute as mentioned in section 384(5).

386   Decision notices

(1) If the Authority decides to exercise the power under section 384(5), it must give a decision notice to the person in relation to whom the power is exercised.

(2) The decision notice must—

 (a) state the amount that he is to pay or distribute as mentioned in section 384(5);

 (b) identify the person or persons to whom that amount is to be paid or among whom that amount is to be distributed; and

 (c) state the arrangements in accordance with which the payment or distribution is to be made.

(3) If the Authority decides to exercise the power under section 384(5), the person in relation to whom it is exercised may refer the matter to the Tribunal.

Freedom of Information Act 2000

(2000, c. 36)

56   No action against public authority

(1) This Act does not confer any right of action in civil proceedings in respect of any failure to comply with any duty imposed by or under this Act.

79   Defamation

Where any information communicated by a public authority to a person ('the applicant') under section 1 was supplied to the public authority by a third person, the publication to the applicant of any defamatory matter contained in the information shall be privileged unless the publication is shown to have been made with malice.

Postal Services Act 2000

(2000, c. 26)

89   Schemes as to terms and conditions for provision of a universal postal service

. . .

90   Exclusion of liability

(1) No proceedings in tort shall lie or, in Scotland, be competent against a universal service provider in respect of loss or damage suffered by any person in connection with the provision of a universal postal service because of—

    (a) anything done or omitted to be done in relation to any postal packet in the course of transmission by post, or

    (b) any omission to carry out arrangements for the collection of anything to be conveyed by post.

(2) No officer, servant, employee, agent or sub-contractor of a universal service provider shall be subject, except at the suit or instance of the provider, to any civil liability for—

    (a) any loss or damage in the case of which liability of the provider is excluded by subsection (1), or

    (b) any loss of, or damage to, an inland packet to which section 91 applies.

(3) No person engaged in or about the conveyance of postal packets and no officer, servant, employee, agent or sub-contractor of any such person shall be subject, except at the suit or instance of the universal service provider concerned, to any civil liability for—

    (a) any loss or damage in the case of which liability of the provider is excluded by subsection (1), or

    (b) any loss of, or damage to, an inland packet to which section 91 applies.

(5) This section is subject to section 91.

91   Limited liability for registered inland packets

(1) Proceedings shall lie or, in Scotland, be competent against a universal service provider under this section, but not otherwise, in respect of relevant loss of, or relevant damage to, an inland packet in respect of which the universal service provider accepts liability under this section in pursuance of a scheme made under section 89.

(2) The references in subsection (1) to relevant loss or damage are to loss or damage so far as it is due to any wrongful act of, or any neglect or default by, an officer, servant, employee, agent or sub-contractor of the universal service provider while performing or purporting to perform in that capacity his functions in relation to the receipt, conveyance, delivery or other dealing with the packet.

(3) No proceedings shall lie or, in Scotland, be competent under this section in relation to a packet unless they are begun within the period of twelve months starting with the day on which the packet was posted.

Powers of Criminal Courts (Sentencing) Act 2000

(2000, c. 6)

73 Reparation orders

(1) Where a child or young person (that is to say, any person aged under 18) is convicted of an offence other than one for which the sentence is fixed by law, the court by or before which he is convicted may make an order requiring him to make reparation specified in the order—

    (a) to a person or persons so specified; or

    (b) to the community at large;

and any person so specified must be a person identified by the court as a victim of the offence or a person otherwise affected by it.

(3) In this section and section 74 below 'make reparation', in relation to an offender, means make reparation for the offence otherwise than by the payment of compensation; and the requirements that may be specified in a reparation order are subject to section 74(1) to (3).

130 Compensation orders against convicted persons

(1) A court by or before which a person is convicted of an offence, instead of or in addition to dealing with him in any other way, may, on application or otherwise, make an order (in this Act referred to as a 'compensation order') requiring him—

    (a) to pay compensation for any personal injury, loss or damage resulting from that offence or any other offence which is taken into consideration by the court in determining sentence; or

    (b) to make payments for funeral expenses or bereavement in respect of a death resulting from any such offence, other than a death due to an accident arising out of the presence of a motor vehicle on a road;

but this is subject to the following provisions of this section and to section 131 below.

(3) A court shall give reasons, on passing sentence, if it does not make a compensation order in a case where this section empowers it to do so.

(4) Compensation under subsection (1) above shall be of such amount as the court considers appropriate, having regard to any evidence and to any representations that are made by or on behalf of the accused or the prosecutor.

(5) In the case of an offence under the Theft Act 1968 [or Fraud Act 2006], where the property in question is recovered, any damage to the property occurring while it was out of the owner's possession shall be treated for the purposes of subsection (1) above as having resulted from the offence, however and by whomever the damage was caused.

(6) A compensation order may only be made in respect of injury, loss or damage (other than loss suffered by a person's dependants in consequence of his death) which was due to an accident arising out of the presence of a motor vehicle on a road, if

    (a) it is in respect of damage which is treated by subsection (5) above as resulting from an offence under the Theft Act 1968 [or Fraud Act 2006]; or

    (b) it is in respect of injury, loss or damage as respects which—

        (i)   the offender is uninsured in relation to the use of the vehicle; and

        (ii) compensation is not payable under any arrangements to which the Secretary of State is a party.

(7) Where a compensation order is made in respect of injury, loss or damage due to an accident arising out of the presence of a motor vehicle on a road, the amount to be paid may include an amount

representing the whole or part of any loss of or reduction in preferential rates of insurance attribut-able to the accident.

(8) A vehicle the use of which is exempted from insurance by section 144 of the Road Traffic Act 1988 is not uninsured for the purposes of subsection (6) above.

(9) A compensation order in respect of funeral expenses may be made for the benefit of anyone who incurred the expenses.

(10) A compensation order in respect of bereavement may be made only for the benefit of a person for whose benefit a claim for damages for bereavement could be made under section 1A of the Fatal Accidents Act 1976; and the amount of compensation in respect of bereavement shall not exceed the amount for the time being specified in section 1A(3) of that Act.

(11) In determining whether to make a compensation order against any person, and in deter-mining the amount to be paid by any person under such an order, the court shall have regard to his means so far as they appear or are known to the court.

(12) Where the court considers—

(a) that it would be appropriate both to impose a fine and to make a compensation order, but

(b) that the offender has insufficient means to pay both an appropriate fine and appropriate compensation,

the court shall give preference to compensation (though it may impose a fine as well).

134 Effect of compensation order on subsequent award of damages in civil proceedings

(1) This section shall have effect where a compensation order, or a service compensation order [...], has been made in favour of any person in respect of any injury, loss or damage and a claim by him in civil proceedings for damages in respect of the injury, loss or damage subsequently falls to be determined.

(2) The damages in the civil proceedings shall be assessed without regard to the order [...], but the plaintiff may only recover an amount equal to the aggregate of the following—

(a) any amount by which they exceed the compensation; and

(b) a sum equal to any portion of the compensation which he fails to recover,

and may not enforce the judgment, so far as it relates to a sum such as is mentioned in paragraph (b) above, without the leave of the court.

[(3) In this section 'service compensation order' means a service compensation order under the Armed Forces Act 2006.]

137 Power to order parent or guardian to pay fine, costs or [compensation or surcharge]

(1) Where—

(a) a child or young person (that is to say, any person aged under 18) is convicted of any offence for the commission of which a fine or costs may be imposed or a compensation order may be made, and

(b) the court is of the opinion that the case would best be met by the imposition of a fine or costs or the making of such an order, whether with or without any other punishment,

the court shall order that the fine, compensation or costs awarded be paid by the parent or guard-ian of the child or young person instead of by the child or young person himself, unless the court is satisfied—

(i)   that the parent or guardian cannot be found; or

(ii) that it would be unreasonable to make an order for payment, having regard to the circumstances of the case.

(3) In the case of a young person aged 16 or over, subsections (1) to (2) above shall have effect as if, instead of imposing a duty, they conferred a power to make such an order as is mentioned in those subsections.

143   Powers to deprive offender of property used etc. for purposes of crime

...

145   Application of proceeds of forfeited property

(1) Where a court makes an order under section 143 above in a case where—

   (a) the offender has been convicted of an offence which has resulted in a person suffering personal injury, loss or damage, or

   (b) any such offence is taken into consideration by the court in determining sentence,

the court may also make an order that any proceeds which arise from the disposal of the property and which do not exceed a sum specified by the court shall be paid to that person.

(2) The court may make an order under this section only if it is satisfied that but for the inadequacy of the offender's means it would have made a compensation order under which the offender would have been required to pay compensation of an amount not less than the specified amount.

148   Restitution orders

(1) This section applies where goods have been stolen, and either—

   (a) a person is convicted of any offence with reference to the theft (whether or not the stealing is the gist of his offence); or

   (b) a person is convicted of any other offence, but such an offence as is mentioned in paragraph (a) above is taken into consideration in determining his sentence.

(2) Where this section applies, the court by or before which the offender is convicted may on the conviction (whether or not the passing of sentence is in other respects deferred) exercise any of the following powers—

   (a) the court may order anyone having possession or control of the stolen goods to restore them to any person entitled to recover them from him; or

   (b) on the application of a person entitled to recover from the person convicted any other goods directly or indirectly representing the stolen goods (as being the proceeds of any disposal or realisation of the whole or part of them or of goods so representing them), the court may order those other goods to be delivered or transferred to the applicant; or

   (c) the court may order that a sum not exceeding the value of the stolen goods shall be paid, out of any money of the person convicted which was taken out of his possession on his apprehension, to any person who, if those goods were in the possession of the person convicted, would be entitled to recover them from him;

and in this subsection 'the stolen goods' means the goods referred to in subsection (1) above.

(3) Where the court has power on a person's conviction to make an order against him both under paragraph (b) and under paragraph (c) of subsection (2) above with reference to the stealing of the same goods, the court may make orders under both paragraphs provided that the person in whose favour the orders are made does not thereby recover more than the value of those goods.

(4) Where the court on a person's conviction makes an order under subsection (2)(a) above for the restoration of any goods, and it appears to the court that the person convicted—

   (a) has sold the goods to a person acting in good faith, or

   (b) has borrowed money on the security of them from a person so acting,

the court may order that there shall be paid to the purchaser or lender, out of any money of the person convicted which was taken out of his possession on his apprehension, a sum not exceeding the amount paid for the purchase by the purchaser or, as the case may be, the amount owed to the lender in respect of the loan.

(10) In this section and section 149 below, 'goods', except in so far as the context otherwise requires, includes money and every other description of property (within the meaning of the Theft Act 1968) except land, and includes things severed from the land by stealing.

(11) An order may be made under this section in respect of money owed by the Crown.

149   Restitution orders: supplementary

(1) The following provisions of this section shall have effect with respect to section 148 above.

(2) The powers conferred by subsections (2)(c) and (4) of that section shall be exercisable without any application being made in that behalf or on the application of any person appearing to the court to be interested in the property concerned.

Enterprise Act 2002

(2002, c. 40)

1   The Office of Fair Trading

(1) There shall be a body corporate to be known as the Office of Fair Trading (in this Act referred to as 'the OFT').

108   Defamation

For the purposes of the law relating to defamation, absolute privilege attaches to any advice, guidance, notice or direction given, or decision or report made, by the OFT, [OFCOM,] the Commission or the Secretary of State in the exercise of any of their functions under this Part [ss 22–130].

173   Defamation: Part 4 [ss 131–184]

For the purposes of the law relating to defamation, absolute privilege attaches to any advice, guidance, notice or direction given, or decision or report made, by the OFT, by the Secretary of State, by the appropriate Minister (other than the Secretary of State acting alone) or by the Commission in the exercise of any of their functions under this Part.

Proceeds of Crime Act 2002

(2002, c. 29)

7   Recoverable amount

(1) The recoverable amount for the purposes of section 6 is an amount equal to the defendant's benefit from the conduct concerned.

304   Property obtained through unlawful conduct

(1) Property obtained through unlawful conduct is recoverable property.

(2) But if property obtained through unlawful conduct has been disposed of (since it was so obtained), it is recoverable property only if it is held by a person into whose hands it may be followed.

(3) Recoverable property obtained through unlawful conduct may be followed into the hands of a person obtaining it on a disposal by—

    (a) the person who through the conduct obtained the property, or

    (b) a person into whose hands it may (by virtue of this subsection) be followed.

305   Tracing property, etc.

(1) Where property obtained through unlawful conduct ('the original property') is or has been recoverable, property which represents the original property is also recoverable property.

(2) If a person enters into a transaction by which—

    (a) he disposes of recoverable property, whether the original property or property which (by virtue of this Chapter) represents the original property, and

    (b) he obtains other property in place of it,

the other property represents the original property.

(3) If a person disposes of recoverable property which represents the original property, the property may be followed into the hands of the person who obtains it (and it continues to represent the original property).

306 Mixing property

(1) Subsection (2) applies if a person's recoverable property is mixed with other property (whether his property or another's).

(2) The portion of the mixed property which is attributable to the recoverable property represents the property obtained through unlawful conduct.

(3) Recoverable property is mixed with other property if (for example) it is used—

    (a) to increase funds held in a bank account,

    (b) in part payment for the acquisition of an asset,

    (c) for the restoration or improvement of land,

    (d) by a person holding a leasehold interest in the property to acquire the freehold.

307 Recoverable property: accruing profits

(1) This section applies where a person who has recoverable property obtains further property consisting of profits accruing in respect of the recoverable property.

(2) The further property is to be treated as representing the property obtained through unlawful conduct.

Anti-social Behaviour Act 2003

(2003, c. 38)

PART 1 PREMISES WHERE DRUGS USED UNLAWFULLY

9 Exemption from liability for certain damages

(1) A constable is not liable for relevant damages in respect of anything done or omitted to be done by him in the performance or purported performance of his functions under this Part.

(2) A chief officer of police is not liable for relevant damages in respect of anything done or omitted to be done by a constable under his direction or control in the performance or purported performance of the constable's functions under this Part.

(3) Subsections (1) and (2) do not apply—

    (a) if the act or omission is shown to have been in bad faith;

    (b) so as to prevent an award of damages made in respect of an act or omission on the ground that the act or omission was unlawful by virtue of section 6(1) of the Human Rights Act 1998 (c. 42).

(4) This section does not affect any other exemption from liability for damages (whether at common law or otherwise).

(5) Relevant damages are damages in proceedings for judicial review or for the tort of negligence or misfeasance in public duty.

10 Compensation

(1) This section applies to any person who incurs financial loss in consequence of—

    (a) the issue of a closure notice, or

    (b) a closure order having effect.

(4) On an application under this section the court may order the payment of compensation out of central funds if it is satisfied—

    (a) that the person had no connection with the use of the premises as mentioned in section 1(1),

    (b) if the person is the owner or occupier of the premises, that he took reasonable steps to prevent the use,

(c) that the person has incurred financial loss as mentioned in subsection (1), and

(d) having regard to all the circumstances it is appropriate to order payment of compensation in respect of that loss.

[PART 1A PREMISES ASSOCIATED WITH PERSISTENT DISORDER OR NUISANCE]

[11A   Part 1A closure notice

(1) This section applies to premises if a police officer not below the rank of superintendent ("the authorising officer") or the local authority has reasonable grounds for believing—

(a) that at any time during the relevant period a person has engaged in anti-social behaviour on the premises, and

(b) that the use of the premises is associated with significant and persistent disorder or persistent serious nuisance to members of the public.

(2) The authorising officer may authorise the issue of a Part 1A closure notice in respect of the premises if the officer is satisfied—

(a) that the local authority has been consulted; and

(b) that reasonable steps have been taken to establish the identity of any person who lives on the premises or who has control of or responsibility for, or an interest in, the premises.]

PART 4 DISPERSAL OF GROUPS ETC.

30   Dispersal of groups and removal of persons under 16 to their place of residence

(1) This section applies where a relevant officer has reasonable grounds for believing—

(a) that any members of the public have been intimidated, harassed, alarmed or distressed as a result of the presence or behaviour of groups of two or more persons in public places in any locality in his police area (the 'relevant locality'), and

(b) that anti-social behaviour is a significant and persistent problem in the relevant locality.

(3) Subsection (4) applies if a constable in uniform has reasonable grounds for believing that the presence or behaviour of a group of two or more persons in any public place in the relevant locality has resulted, or is likely to result, in any members of the public being intimidated, harassed, alarmed or distressed.

(4) The constable may give one or more of the following directions, namely—

(a) a direction requiring the persons in the group to disperse (either immediately or by such time as he may specify and in such way as he may specify),

(b) a direction requiring any of those persons whose place of residence is not within the relevant locality to leave the relevant locality or any part of the relevant locality (either immediately or by such time as he may specify and in such way as he may specify), and

(c) a direction prohibiting any of those persons whose place of residence is not within the relevant locality from returning to the relevant locality or any part of the relevant locality for such period (not exceeding 24 hours) from the giving of the direction as he may specify;

but this subsection is subject to subsection (5).

(5) A direction under subsection (4) may not be given in respect of a group of persons—

(a) who are engaged in conduct which is lawful under section 220 of the Trade Union and Labour Relations (Consolidation) Act 1992, or

(b) who are taking part in a public procession of the kind mentioned in section 11(1) of the Public Order Act 1986 in respect of which—

(i)   written notice has been given in accordance with section 11 of that Act, or

(ii) such notice is not required to be given as provided by subsections (1) and (2) of that section.

36 Interpretation

In this Part—

'anti-social behaviour' means behaviour by a person which causes or is likely to cause harassment, alarm or distress to one or more other persons not of the same household as the person,

. . .

'public place' means—

(a) any highway, and

(b) any place to which at the material time the public or any section of the public has access, on payment or otherwise, as of right or by virtue of express or implied permission,

. . .

PART 6 THE ENVIRONMENT

40 Closure of noisy premises

(1) The chief executive officer of the relevant local authority may make a closure order in relation to premises to which this section applies if he reasonably believes that—

(a) a public nuisance is being caused by noise coming from the premises, and

(b) the closure of the premises is necessary to prevent that nuisance.

(2) This section applies to premises if—

(a) a premises licence has effect in respect of them, or

(b) a temporary event notice has effect in respect of them.

(3) In this section 'closure order' means an order which requires specified premises to be kept closed during a specified period which—

(a) does not exceed 24 hours, and

(b) begins when a manager of the premises receives written notice of the order.

(4) A person commits an offence if without reasonable excuse he permits premises to be open in contravention of a closure order.

PART 8 HIGH HEDGES

65 Complaints to which this Part applies

(1) This Part applies to a complaint which—

(a) is made for the purposes of this Part by an owner or occupier of a domestic property; and

(b) alleges that his reasonable enjoyment of that property is being adversely affected by the height of a high hedge situated on land owned or occupied by another person.

(2) This Part also applies to a complaint which—

(a) is made for the purposes of this Part by an owner of a domestic property that is for the time being unoccupied, and

(b) alleges that the reasonable enjoyment of that property by a prospective occupier of that property would be adversely affected by the height of a high hedge situated on land owned or occupied by another person,

as it applies to a complaint falling within subsection (1).

(4) This Part does not apply to complaints about the effect of the roots of a high hedge.

66 High hedges

(1) In this Part 'high hedge' means so much of a barrier to light or access as—

(a) is formed wholly or predominantly by a line of two or more evergreens; and

(b) rises to a height of more than two metres above ground level.

(2) For the purposes of subsection (1) a line of evergreens is not to be regarded as forming a barrier to light or access if the existence of gaps significantly affects its overall effect as such a barrier at heights of more than two metres above ground level.

68 Procedure for dealing with complaints

(1) This section has effect where a complaint to which this Part applies—

    (a) is made to the relevant authority; and

    (b) is accompanied by such fee (if any) as the authority may determine.

(2) If the authority consider—

    (a) that the complainant has not taken all reasonable steps to resolve the matters complained of without proceeding by way of such a complaint to the authority, or

    (b) that the complaint is frivolous or vexatious,

the authority may decide that the complaint should not be proceeded with.

(3) If the authority do not so decide, they must decide—

    (a) whether the height of the high hedge specified in the complaint is adversely affecting the complainant's reasonable enjoyment of the domestic property so specified; and

    (b) if so, what action (if any) should be taken in relation to that hedge, in pursuance of a remedial notice under section 69, with a view to remedying the adverse effect or preventing its recurrence.

(4) If the authority decide under subsection (3) that action should be taken as mentioned in paragraph (b) of that subsection, they must as soon as is reasonably practicable—

    (a) issue a remedial notice under section 69 implementing their decision;

    (b) send a copy of that notice to the following persons, namely—

        (i) every complainant; and

        (ii) every owner and every occupier of the neighbouring land; and

    (c) notify each of those persons of the reasons for their decision.

(5) If the authority—

    (a) decide that the complaint should not be proceeded with, or

    (b) decide either or both of the issues specified in subsection (3) otherwise than in the complainant's favour,

they must as soon as is reasonably practicable notify the appropriate person or persons of any such decision and of their reasons for it.

69 Remedial notices

(1) For the purposes of this Part a remedial notice is a notice—

    (a) issued by the relevant authority in respect of a complaint to which this Part applies; and

    (b) stating the matters mentioned in subsection (2).

(2) Those matters are—

    (a) that a complaint has been made to the authority under this Part about a high hedge specified in the notice which is situated on land so specified;

    (b) that the authority have decided that the height of that hedge is adversely affecting the complainant's reasonable enjoyment of the domestic property specified in the notice;

    (c) the initial action that must be taken in relation to that hedge before the end of the compliance period;

    (d) any preventative action that they consider must be taken in relation to that hedge at times following the end of that period while the hedge remains on the land; and

    (e) the consequences under sections 75 and 77 of a failure to comply with the notice.

(3) The action specified in a remedial notice is not to require or involve—

    (a) a reduction in the height of the hedge to less than two metres above ground level; or

    (b) the removal of the hedge.

(6) 'The compliance period' in the case of a remedial notice is such reasonable period as is specified in the notice for the purposes of subsection (2)(c) as the period within which the action so specified is to be taken; and that period shall begin with the operative date of the notice.

(8) While a remedial notice has effect, the notice—

    (a) shall be a local land charge; and

(b) shall be binding on every person who is for the time being an owner or occupier of the land specified in the notice as the land where the hedge in question is situated.

(9) In this Part—

'initial action' means remedial action or preventative action, or both;

'remedial action' means action to remedy the adverse effect of the height of the hedge on the complainant's reasonable enjoyment of the domestic property in respect of which the complaint was made; and

'preventative action' means action to prevent the recurrence of the adverse effect.

75 Offences

(1) Where—

(a) a remedial notice requires the taking of any action, and

(b) that action is not taken in accordance with that notice within the compliance period or (as the case may be) by the subsequent time by which it is required to be taken,

every person who, at a relevant time, is an owner or occupier of the neighbouring land is guilty of an offence and shall be liable, on summary conviction, to a fine not exceeding level 3 on the standard scale.

(3) In proceedings against a person for an offence under subsection (1) it shall be a defence for him to show that he did everything he could be expected to do to secure compliance with the notice.

76 Power to require occupier to permit action to be taken by owner

Section 289 of the Public Health Act 1936 (c. 49) (power of court to require occupier to permit work to be done by owner) shall apply with any necessary modifications for the purpose of giving an owner of land to which a remedial notice relates the right, as against all other persons interested in the land, to comply with the notice.

77 Action by relevant authority

(1) This section applies where—

(a) a remedial notice requires the taking of any action; and

(b) that action is not taken in accordance with that notice within the compliance period or (as the case may be) after the end of that period when it is required to be taken by the notice.

(2) Where this section applies—

(a) a person authorised by the relevant authority may enter the neighbouring land and take the required action; and

(b) the relevant authority may recover any expenses reasonably incurred by that person in doing so from any person who is an owner or occupier of the land.

(3) Expenses recoverable under this section shall be a local land charge and binding on successive owners of the land and on successive occupiers of it.

(4) Where expenses are recoverable under this section from two or more persons, those persons shall be jointly and severally liable for the expenses.

(5) A person shall not enter land in the exercise of a power conferred by this section unless at least 7 days' notice of the intended entry has been given to every occupier of the land.

(6) A person authorised under this section to enter land—

(a) shall, if so required, produce evidence of his authority before entering; and

(b) shall produce such evidence if required to do so at any time while he remains on the land.

(7) A person who enters land in the exercise of a power conferred by this section may—

(a) use a vehicle to enter the land;

(b) take with him such other persons as may be necessary;

(c) take with him equipment and materials needed for the purpose of taking the required action.

(8) If, in the exercise of a power conferred by this section, a person enters land which is unoccupied or from which all of the persons occupying the land are temporarily absent, he must on his departure leave it as effectively secured against unauthorised entry as he found it.

(9) A person who wilfully obstructs a person acting in the exercise of powers under this section to enter land and take action on that land is guilty of an offence and shall be liable, on summary conviction, to a fine not exceeding level 3 on the standard scale.

Criminal Justice Act 2003

(2003, c. 44)

329   Civil proceedings for trespass to the person brought by offender

(1) This section applies where—

   (a) a person ('the claimant') claims that another person ('the defendant') did an act amounting to trespass to the claimant's person, and

   (b) the claimant has been convicted in the United Kingdom of an imprisonable offence committed on the same occasion as that on which the act is alleged to have been done.

(2) Civil proceedings relating to the claim may be brought only with the permission of the court.

(3) The court may give permission for the proceedings to be brought only if there is evidence that either—

   (a) the condition in subsection (5) is not met, or

   (b) in all the circumstances, the defendant's act was grossly disproportionate.

(4) If the court gives permission and the proceedings are brought, it is a defence for the defendant to prove both—

   (a) that the condition in subsection (5) is met, and

   (b) that, in all the circumstances, his act was not grossly disproportionate.

(5) The condition referred to in subsection (3)(a) and (4)(a) is that the defendant did the act only because—

   (a) he believed that the claimant—

      (i)   was about to commit an offence,

      (ii) was in the course of committing an offence, or

      (iii) had committed an offence immediately beforehand; and

   (b) he believed that the act was necessary to—

      (i)   defend himself or another person,

      (ii) protect or recover property,

      (iii) prevent the commission or continuation of an offence, or

      (iv) apprehend, or secure the conviction, of the claimant after he had committed an offence;

or was necessary to assist in achieving any of those things.

(6) Subsection (4) is without prejudice to any other defence.

(8) In this section—

   (a) the reference to trespass to the person is a reference to—

      (i)   assault,

      (ii) battery, or

      (iii) false imprisonment;

   (b) references to a defendant's belief are to his honest belief, whether or not the belief was also reasonable;

   (c) 'court' means the High Court or a county court; and

   (d) 'imprisonable offence' means an offence which, in the case of a person aged 18 or over, is punishable by imprisonment.

Health and Social Care (Community Health and Standards) Act 2003

(2003, c. 43)

PART 3 RECOVERY OF NHS CHARGES

NHS charges

150 Liability to pay NHS charges

(1) This section applies if—

    (a) a person makes a compensation payment to or in respect of any other person (the 'injured person') in consequence of any injury, whether physical or psychological, suffered by the injured person, and

    (b) the injured person has—

        (i)   received NHS treatment at a health service hospital as a result of the injury,

        (ii) been provided with NHS ambulance services as a result of the injury for the purpose of taking him to a health service hospital for NHS treatment (unless he was dead on arrival at that hospital), or

        (iii) received treatment as mentioned in sub-paragraph (i) and been provided with ambulance services as mentioned in sub-paragraph (ii).

(2) The person making the compensation payment is liable to pay the relevant NHS charges—

    (a) in respect of—

        (i)   the treatment, in so far as received at a hospital in England or Wales,

        (ii) the ambulance services, in so far as provided to take the injured person to such a hospital,

    to the Secretary of State,

    (b) in respect of—

        (i)   the treatment, in so far as received at a hospital in Scotland,

        (ii) the ambulance services, in so far as provided to take the injured person to such a hospital,

    to the Scottish Ministers.

(3) 'Compensation payment' means a payment, including a payment in money's worth, made—

    (a) by or on behalf of a person who is, or is alleged to be, liable to any extent in respect of the injury, or

    (b) in pursuance of a compensation scheme for motor accidents,

but does not include a payment mentioned in Schedule 10.

(4) Subsection (1)(a) applies—

    (a) to a payment made—

        (i)   voluntarily, or in pursuance of a court order or an agreement, or otherwise, and

        (ii) in the United Kingdom or elsewhere, and

    (b) if more than one payment is made, to each payment.

(5) 'Injury' does not include any disease.

(6) Nothing in subsection (5) prevents this Part from applying to—

    (a) treatment received as a result of any disease suffered by the injured person, or

    (b) ambulance services provided as a result of any disease suffered by him,

if the disease in question is attributable to the injury suffered by the injured person (and accordingly that treatment is received or those services are provided as a result of the injury).

(11) 'Compensation scheme for motor accidents' means any scheme or arrangement under which funds are available for the payment of compensation in respect of motor accidents caused, or alleged to have been caused, by uninsured or unidentified persons.

(14) For the purpose of this Part, it is irrelevant whether a compensation payment is made with or without an admission of liability.

Certificates of NHS charges

151   Applications for certificates of NHS charges
(1) Before a person makes a compensation payment in consequence of any injury suffered by an injured person, he may apply for a certificate to the Secretary of State, the Scottish Ministers or both, according to whether he believes the relevant NHS charges payable by him (if any) would be due to the Secretary of State, the Scottish Ministers or both.

153   Information contained in certificates
(1) A certificate must specify the amount (or amounts) for which the person to whom it is issued is liable under section 150 (2).

(2) The amount (or amounts) to be specified is (or are) to be that (or those) set out in, or determined in accordance with, regulations, reduced if applicable in accordance with subsection (3) or regulations under subsection (10).

(3) If a certificate relates to a claim made by or on behalf of an injured person—

   (a) in respect of which a court in England and Wales or Scotland has ordered a reduction of damages in accordance with section 1 of the Law Reform (Contributory Negligence) Act 1945,

   ...

   (d) in respect of which an officer of a court in England and Wales or Northern Ireland has entered or sealed an agreed judgement or order which specifies—

     (i) that the damages are to be reduced to reflect the injured person's share in the responsibility for the injury in question, and

     (ii) the amount or proportion by which they are to be so reduced,

     ...

   (f) in respect of which a document has been made under any provision of the law of a country other than England and Wales, Scotland or Northern Ireland—

     (i) which appears to the Secretary of State to correspond to an agreed judgement or order entered or sealed by an officer of a court in England and Wales, and

     (ii) which specifies the matters mentioned in paragraph (d)(i) and (ii), or

     ...

the amount (or amounts) specified in the certificate is (or are) to be that (or those) which would be so specified apart from this subsection, reduced by the same proportion as the reduction of damages.

(4) If a certificate relates to an injured person who has not received NHS treatment at a health service hospital or been provided with NHS ambulance services as a result of the injury, it must indicate that no amount is payable to the Secretary of State or the Scottish Ministers (as the case may be) by reference to that certificate.

155   Recovery of NHS charges
(1) This section applies if a person has made a compensation payment and either—

   (a) subsection (7) of section 151 applies but he has not applied for a certificate as required by that subsection, or

   (b) he has not made payment, in full, of any amount due under section 150(2) by the end of the period allowed under section 154.

(2) The Secretary of State, the Scottish Ministers or both, according to the circumstances of the case, may—

   (a) in a case within subsection (1)(a), issue the person who made the compensation payment with a certificate, and

   (b) in a case within subsection (1)(b), issue him with a copy of the certificate or (if more than one has been issued) the most recent one,

and, in either case, issue him with a demand that payment of any amount due under section 150(2) be made immediately.

   (6) The Secretary of State or the Scottish Ministers may recover the amount for which a demand for payment is made under subsection (2) from the person who made the compensation payment.

Payments to hospitals or ambulance trusts

162 Payment of NHS charges to hospitals or ambulance trusts

   (1) If the Secretary of State receives or the Scottish Ministers receive a payment of relevant NHS charges under section 150(2)—

   (a) if the payment relates only to NHS treatment received at a health service hospital, he or they must pay the amount received to the responsible body of the health service hospital,

   (b) if the payment relates only to the provision of NHS ambulance services, he or they must pay the amount received to the relevant ambulance trust,

   (c) if the payment relates to NHS treatment received at more than one health service hospital, he or they must divide the amount received among the responsible bodies of the hospitals concerned in such manner as he considers or they consider appropriate,

   (d) if the payment relates to NHS treatment received at one or more health service hospitals and the provision of NHS ambulance services, he or they must divide the amount received among the responsible body or bodies of the hospital or hospitals and any relevant ambulance trusts concerned in such manner as he considers or they consider appropriate.

   (2) Subsection (1) does not apply to any amount received by the Secretary of State or the Scottish Ministers under section 150(2) which he is or they are required to repay in accordance with regulations under section 153(2).

   (4) Any amounts received under this section by the responsible bodies of the health service hospitals concerned must be used for the purposes of providing goods and services for the benefit of patients receiving NHS treatment at those hospitals.

   (5) Any amounts received under this section by the relevant ambulance trusts concerned must be used for the purposes of NHS ambulance services.

Miscellaneous and general

163 Regulations governing lump sums, periodical payments etc.

   (1) Regulations may make provision (including provision modifying this Part)—

   (a) for cases to which section 150(2) applies in which two or more compensation payments in the form of lump sums are made by the same person in respect of the same injury,

   (b) for cases to which section 150(2) applies in which an agreement is entered into for the making of—

     (i) periodical compensation payments (whether of an income or capital nature), or

     (ii) periodical compensation payments and lump sum compensation payments,

   (c) for cases in which the compensation payment to which section 150(2) applies is an interim payment of damages which a court orders to be repaid.

   (2) Regulations made by virtue of subsection (1)(a) may (among other things) provide—

   (a) for giving credit for amounts already paid, and

   (b) for the payment by any person of any balance or the recovery from any person of any excess.

   (3) Regulations may make provision modifying the application of this Part in relation to cases in which a payment into court is made and, in particular, may provide—

   (a) for the making of a payment into court to be treated in prescribed circumstances as the making of a compensation payment,

   (b) for application for, and issue of, certificates.

164 Liability of insurers

(1) If a compensation payment is made in a case where—

    (a) a person is liable to any extent in respect of the injury, and

    (b) the liability is covered to any extent by a policy of insurance,

the policy is also to be treated as covering any liability of that person under section 150(2).

(2) Liability imposed on the insurer by subsection (1) cannot be excluded or restricted.

(3) For that purpose excluding or restricting liability includes—

    (a) making the liability or its enforcement subject to restrictive or onerous conditions,

    (b) excluding or restricting any right or remedy in respect of the liability, or subjecting a person to any prejudice in consequence of his pursuing any such right or remedy, or

    (c) excluding or restricting rules of evidence or procedure.

(4) Regulations may in prescribed cases limit the amount of the liability imposed on the insurer by subsection (1).

(5) This section applies in relation to policies of insurance issued before (as well as those issued after) the date on which it comes into force.

(6) References in this section to policies of insurance and their issue include references to contracts of insurance and their making.

165 Power to apply Part 3 to treatment at non-health service hospitals

. . .

166 The Crown

This Part binds the Crown.

Civil Partnership Act 2004

(2004, c. 33)

1 Civil partnership

(1) A civil partnership is a relationship between two people of the same sex ('civil partners')—

    (a) which is formed when they register as civil partners of each other— . . . or

    (b) which they are treated under Chapter 2 of Part 5 as having formed (at the time determined under that Chapter) by virtue of having registered an overseas relationship.

69 Actions in tort between civil partners

(1) This section applies if an action in tort is brought by one civil partner against the other during the subsistence of the civil partnership.

(2) The court may stay the proceedings if it appears—

    (a) that no substantial benefit would accrue to either civil partner from the continuation of the proceedings, or

    (b) that the question or questions in issue could more conveniently be disposed of on an application under section 66.

73 Civil partnership agreements unenforceable

(1) A civil partnership agreement does not under the law of England and Wales have effect as a contract giving rise to legal rights.

(2) No action lies in England and Wales for breach of a civil partnership agreement, whatever the law applicable to the agreement.

(3) In this section and section 74 'civil partnership agreement' means an agreement between two people—

    (a) to register as civil partners of each other— . . .

Gambling Act 2005

(2005, c. 19)

335   Enforceability of gambling contracts

(1) The fact that a contract relates to gambling shall not prevent its enforcement.

(2) Subsection (1) is without prejudice to any rule of law preventing the enforcement of a contract on the grounds of unlawfulness (other than a rule relating specifically to gambling).

336   Power of Gambling Commission to void bet

(1) The Commission may make an order under this subsection in relation to a bet accepted by or through the holder of—

    (a) a general betting operating licence,

    (b) a pool betting operating licence, or

    (c) a betting intermediary operating licence.

(2) Where the Commission makes an order under subsection (1) in relation to a bet—

    (a) any contract or other arrangement in relation to the bet is void, and

    (b) any money paid in relation to the bet (whether by way of stake, winnings, commission or otherwise) shall be repaid to the person who paid it, and repayment may be enforced as a debt due to that person.

(3) The Commission may make an order under subsection (1) in relation to a bet only if satisfied that the bet was substantially unfair.

(4) In considering whether a bet was unfair the Commission shall, in particular, take account of any of the following that applies—

    (a) the fact that either party to the bet supplied insufficient, false or misleading information in connection with it,

    (b) the fact that either party to the bet believed or ought to have believed that a race, competition or other event or process to which the bet related was or would be conducted in contravention of industry rules,

    (c) the fact that either party to the bet believed or ought to have believed that an offence under section 42 had been or was likely to be committed in respect of anything to which the bet related, and

    (d) the fact that either party to the bet was convicted of an offence under section 42 in relation to the bet.

(5) An order under subsection (1) may be made in relation to a bet only during the period of six months beginning with the day on which the result of the bet is determined.

(6) But subsection (5) shall not apply to an order made taking account of the fact that a party to the bet was convicted of an offence under section 42 in relation to it.

337   Section 336: supplementary

(1) Where the Commission makes an order under section 336(1) in relation to a bet a party to the bet or to any contract or other arrangement in relation to the bet may appeal to the [First-tier Tribunal]; ...

(2) The Commission may make an order under section 336(1) in relation to the whole, or any part or aspect of, a betting transaction.

(3) An order under section 336(1) may make incidental provision; in particular, an order may make provision about—

    (a) the consequences of the order for bets connected with the bet which becomes void under the order;

    (b) the consequences of the order for other parts or aspects of a betting transaction one part or aspect of which becomes void under the order.

(7) In section 336(4)(b) 'industry rules' means rules established by an organisation having, by virtue of an agreement, instrument or enactment, responsibility for the conduct of races, competitions or other events or processes.

338 Interim moratorium

(1) Where the Commission has reason to suspect that it may wish to make an order under section 336(1) in relation to a bet, the Commission may make an order under this subsection in relation to the bet.

(2) While an order under subsection (1) has effect in relation to a bet, an obligation to pay money in relation to the bet (whether by way of stake, winnings, commission or otherwise) shall have no effect.

(3) An order under subsection (1) shall have effect for the period of 14 days beginning with the day on which the order is made (subject to extension under subsection (4) and without prejudice to the making of a new order).

Mental Capacity Act 2005

(2005, c. 9)

PART 1 PERSONS WHO LACK CAPACITY

The principles

1 The principles

(1) The following principles apply for the purposes of this Act.

(2) A person must be assumed to have capacity unless it is established that he lacks capacity.

(3) A person is not to be treated as unable to make a decision unless all practicable steps to help him to do so have been taken without success.

(4) A person is not to be treated as unable to make a decision merely because he makes an unwise decision.

(5) An act done, or decision made, under this Act for or on behalf of a person who lacks capacity must be done, or made, in his best interests.

(6) Before the act is done, or the decision is made, regard must be had to whether the purpose for which it is needed can be as effectively achieved in a way that is less restrictive of the person's rights and freedom of action.

Preliminary

2 People who lack capacity

(1) For the purposes of this Act, a person lacks capacity in relation to a matter if at the material time he is unable to make a decision for himself in relation to the matter because of an impairment of, or a disturbance in the functioning of, the mind or brain.

(2) It does not matter whether the impairment or disturbance is permanent or temporary.

(3) A lack of capacity cannot be established merely by reference to—

    (a) a person's age or appearance, or

    (b) a condition of his, or an aspect of his behaviour, which might lead others to make unjustified assumptions about his capacity.

(4) In proceedings under this Act or any other enactment, any question whether a person lacks capacity within the meaning of this Act must be decided on the balance of probabilities.

(5) No power which a person ('D') may exercise under this Act—

    (a) in relation to a person who lacks capacity, or

    (b) where D reasonably thinks that a person lacks capacity,

is exercisable in relation to a person under 16.

(6) Subsection (5) is subject to section 18(3).

3   Inability to make decisions

(1) For the purposes of section 2, a person is unable to make a decision for himself if he is unable—

    (a) to understand the information relevant to the decision,

    (b) to retain that information,

    (c) to use or weigh that information as part of the process of making the decision, or

    (d) to communicate his decision (whether by talking, using sign language or any other means).

(2) A person is not to be regarded as unable to understand the information relevant to a decision if he is able to understand an explanation of it given to him in a way that is appropriate to his circumstances (using simple language, visual aids or any other means).

(3) The fact that a person is able to retain the information relevant to a decision for a short period only does not prevent him from being regarded as able to make the decision.

(4) The information relevant to a decision includes information about the reasonably foreseeable consequences of—

    (a) deciding one way or another, or

    (b) failing to make the decision.

4   Best interests

(1) In determining for the purposes of this Act what is in a person's best interests, the person making the determination must not make it merely on the basis of—

    (a) the person's age or appearance, or

    (b) a condition of his, or an aspect of his behaviour, which might lead others to make unjustified assumptions about what might be in his best interests.

(2) The person making the determination must consider all the relevant circumstances and, in particular, take the following steps.

(3) He must consider—

    (a) whether it is likely that the person will at some time have capacity in relation to the matter in question, and

    (b) if it appears likely that he will, when that is likely to be.

(4) He must, so far as reasonably practicable, permit and encourage the person to participate, or to improve his ability to participate, as fully as possible in any act done for him and any decision affecting him.

(5) Where the determination relates to life-sustaining treatment he must not, in considering whether the treatment is in the best interests of the person concerned, be motivated by a desire to bring about his death.

(6) He must consider, so far as is reasonably ascertainable—

    (a) the person's past and present wishes and feelings (and, in particular, any relevant written statement made by him when he had capacity),

    (b) the beliefs and values that would be likely to influence his decision if he had capacity, and

    (c) the other factors that he would be likely to consider if he were able to do so.

(7) He must take into account, if it is practicable and appropriate to consult them, the views of—

    (a) anyone named by the person as someone to be consulted on the matter in question or on matters of that kind,

    (b) anyone engaged in caring for the person or interested in his welfare,

    (c) any donee of a lasting power of attorney granted by the person, and

    (d) any deputy appointed for the person by the court,

as to what would be in the person's best interests and, in particular, as to the matters mentioned in subsection (6).

(8) The duties imposed by subsections (1) to (7) also apply in relation to the exercise of any powers which—

    (a) are exercisable under a lasting power of attorney, or

(b) are exercisable by a person under this Act where he reasonably believes that another person lacks capacity.

(9) In the case of an act done, or a decision made, by a person other than the court, there is sufficient compliance with this section if (having complied with the requirements of subsections (1) to (7)) he reasonably believes that what he does or decides is in the best interests of the person concerned.

(10) 'Life-sustaining treatment' means treatment which in the view of a person providing health care for the person concerned is necessary to sustain life.

(11) 'Relevant circumstances' are those—

(a) of which the person making the determination is aware, and

(b) which it would be reasonable to regard as relevant.

[4A   Restriction on deprivation of liberty

(1) This Act does not authorise any person ('D') to deprive any other person ('P') of his liberty.

(2) But that is subject to—

(a) the following provisions of this section, and

(a) section 4B.

(3) D may deprive P of his liberty if, by doing so, D is giving effect to a relevant decision of the court.

(4) A relevant decision of the court is a decision made by an order under section 16(2)(a) in relation to a matter concerning P's personal welfare.

(5) D may deprive P of his liberty if the deprivation is authorised by Schedule A1 (hospital and care home residents: deprivation of liberty).]

[4B Deprivation of liberty necessary for life-sustaining treatment etc

(1) If the following conditions are met, D is authorised to deprive P of his liberty while a decision as respects any relevant issue is sought from the court.

(2) The first condition is that there is a question about whether D is authorised to deprive P of his liberty under section 4A.

(3) The second condition is that the deprivation of liberty—

(a) is wholly or partly for the purpose of—

(i)   giving P life-sustaining treatment, or

(ii) doing any vital act, or

(b) consists wholly or partly of—

(i)   giving P life-sustaining treatment, or

(ii) doing any vital act.

(4) The third condition is that the deprivation of liberty is necessary in order to—

(a) give the life-sustaining treatment, or

(a) do the vital act.

(5) A vital act is any act which the person doing it reasonably believes to be necessary to prevent a serious deterioration in P's condition.]

5   Acts in connection with care or treatment

(1) If a person ('D') does an act in connection with the care or treatment of another person ('P'), the act is one to which this section applies if—

(a) before doing the act, D takes reasonable steps to establish whether P lacks capacity in relation to the matter in question, and

(b) when doing the act, D reasonably believes—

(i)   that P lacks capacity in relation to the matter, and

(ii) that it will be in P's best interests for the act to be done.

(2) D does not incur any liability in relation to the act that he would not have incurred if P—

(a) had had capacity to consent in relation to the matter, and

(b) had consented to D's doing the act.

(3) Nothing in this section excludes a person's civil liability for loss or damage, or his criminal liability, resulting from his negligence in doing the act.

(4) Nothing in this section affects the operation of sections 24 to 26 (advance decisions to refuse treatment).

6 Section 5 acts: limitations

(1) If D does an act that is intended to restrain P, it is not an act to which section 5 applies unless two further conditions are satisfied.

(2) The first condition is that D reasonably believes that it is necessary to do the act in order to prevent harm to P.

(3) The second is that the act is a proportionate response to—

(a) the likelihood of P's suffering harm, and

(b) the seriousness of that harm.

(4) For the purposes of this section D restrains P if he—

(a) uses, or threatens to use, force to secure the doing of an act which P resists, or

(b) restricts P's liberty of movement, whether or not P resists.

(6) Section 5 does not authorise a person to do an act which conflicts with a decision made, within the scope of his authority and in accordance with this Part, by—

(a) a donee of a lasting power of attorney granted by P, or

(b) a deputy appointed for P by the court.

(7) But nothing in subsection (6) stops a person—

(a) providing life-sustaining treatment, or

(b) doing any act which he reasonably believes to be necessary to prevent a serious deterioration in P's condition,

while a decision as respects any relevant issue is sought from the court.

7 Payment for necessary goods and services

(1) If necessary goods or services are supplied to a person who lacks capacity to contract for the supply, he must pay a reasonable price for them.

(2) 'Necessary' means suitable to a person's condition in life and to his actual requirements at the time when the goods or services are supplied.

8 Expenditure

(1) If an act to which section 5 applies involves expenditure, it is lawful for D—

(a) to pledge P's credit for the purpose of the expenditure, and

(b) to apply money in P's possession for meeting the expenditure.

(2) If the expenditure is borne for P by D, it is lawful for D—

(a) to reimburse himself out of money in P's possession, or

(b) to be otherwise indemnified by P.

(3) Subsections (1) and (2) do not affect any power under which (apart from those subsections) a person—

(a) has lawful control of P's money or other property, and

(b) has power to spend money for P's benefit.

Advance decisions to refuse treatment

24 Advance decisions to refuse treatment: general

(1) 'Advance decision' means a decision made by a person ('P'), after he has reached 18 and when he has capacity to do so, that if—

(a) at a later time and in such circumstances as he may specify, a specified treatment is proposed to be carried out or continued by a person providing health care for him, and

(b) at that time he lacks capacity to consent to the carrying out or continuation of the treatment,

the specified treatment is not to be carried out or continued.

(2) For the purposes of subsection (1)(a), a decision may be regarded as specifying a treatment or circumstances even though expressed in layman's terms.

(3) P may withdraw or alter an advance decision at any time when he has capacity to do so.

(4) A withdrawal (including a partial withdrawal) need not be in writing.

(5) An alteration of an advance decision need not be in writing (unless section 25(5) applies in relation to the decision resulting from the alteration).

25   Validity and applicability of advance decisions

(1) An advance decision does not affect the liability which a person may incur for carrying out or continuing a treatment in relation to P unless the decision is at the material time—

   (a) valid, and
   (b) applicable to the treatment.

(2) An advance decision is not valid if P—

   (a) has withdrawn the decision at a time when he had capacity to do so,
   (b) has, under a lasting power of attorney created after the advance decision was made, conferred authority on the donee (or, if more than one, any of them) to give or refuse consent to the treatment to which the advance decision relates, or
   (c) has done anything else clearly inconsistent with the advance decision remaining his fixed decision.

(3) An advance decision is not applicable to the treatment in question if at the material time P has capacity to give or refuse consent to it.

(4) An advance decision is not applicable to the treatment in question if—

   (a) that treatment is not the treatment specified in the advance decision,
   (b) any circumstances specified in the advance decision are absent, or
   (c) there are reasonable grounds for believing that circumstances exist which P did not anticipate at the time of the advance decision and which would have affected his decision had he anticipated them.

(5) An advance decision is not applicable to life-sustaining treatment unless—

   (a) the decision is verified by a statement by P to the effect that it is to apply to that treatment even if life is at risk, and
   (b) the decision and statement comply with subsection (6).

(6) A decision or statement complies with this subsection only if—

   (a) it is in writing,
   (b) it is signed by P or by another person in P's presence and by P's direction,
   (c) the signature is made or acknowledged by P in the presence of a witness, and
   (d) the witness signs it, or acknowledges his signature, in P's presence.

(7) The existence of any lasting power of attorney other than one of a description mentioned in subsection (2)(b) does not prevent the advance decision from being regarded as valid and applicable.

26   Effect of advance decisions

(1) If P has made an advance decision which is—

   (a) valid, and
   (b) applicable to a treatment,

the decision has effect as if he had made it, and had had capacity to make it, at the time when the question arises whether the treatment should be carried out or continued.

(2) A person does not incur liability for carrying out or continuing the treatment unless, at the time, he is satisfied that an advance decision exists which is valid and applicable to the treatment.

(3) A person does not incur liability for the consequences of withholding or withdrawing a treatment from P if, at the time, he reasonably believes that an advance decision exists which is valid and applicable to the treatment.

(4) The court may make a declaration as to whether an advance decision—
  (a) exists;
  (b) is valid;
  (c) is applicable to a treatment.
(5) Nothing in an apparent advance decision stops a person—
  (a) providing life-sustaining treatment, or
  (b) doing any act he reasonably believes to be necessary to prevent a serious deterioration in P's condition,
while a decision as respects any relevant issue is sought from the court.

Excluded decisions

27 Family relationships etc.

(1) Nothing in this Act permits a decision on any of the following matters to be made on behalf of a person—
  (a) ...
  (b) consenting to have sexual relations, ...

28 Mental Health Act matters

(1) Nothing in this Act authorises anyone—
  (a) to give a patient medical treatment for mental disorder, or
  (b) to consent to a patient's being given medical treatment for mental disorder,
if, at the time when it is proposed to treat the patient, his treatment is regulated by Part 4 of the Mental Health Act.

Research

30 Research

(1) Intrusive research carried out on, or in relation to, a person who lacks capacity to consent to it is unlawful unless it is carried out—
  (a) as part of a research project which is for the time being approved by the appropriate body for the purposes of this Act in accordance with section 31, and
  (b) in accordance with sections 32 and 33.
(2) Research is intrusive if it is of a kind that would be unlawful if it was carried out—
  (a) on or in relation to a person who had capacity to consent to it, but
  (b) without his consent.
(3) A clinical trial which is subject to the provisions of clinical trials regulations is not to be treated as research for the purposes of this section.
(4) 'Appropriate body', in relation to a research project, means the person, committee or other body specified in regulations made by the appropriate authority as the appropriate body in relation to a project of the kind in question.
(5) 'Clinical trials regulations' means—
  (a) the Medicines for Human Use (Clinical Trials) Regulations 2004 (S.I. 2004/1031) and any other regulations replacing those regulations or amending them, and
  (b) any other regulations relating to clinical trials and designated by the Secretary of State as clinical trials regulations for the purposes of this section.
(6) In this section, section 32 and section 34, 'appropriate authority' means—
  (a) in relation to the carrying out of research in England, the Secretary of State, and
  (b) in relation to the carrying out of research in Wales, the National Assembly for Wales.

31 Requirements for approval

(1) The appropriate body may not approve a research project for the purposes of this Act unless satisfied that the following requirements will be met in relation to research carried out as

part of the project on, or in relation to, a person who lacks capacity to consent to taking part in the project ('P').

(2) The research must be connected with—

    (a) an impairing condition affecting P, or

    (b) its treatment.

(3) 'Impairing condition' means a condition which is (or may be) attributable to, or which causes or contributes to (or may cause or contribute to), the impairment of, or disturbance in the functioning of, the mind or brain.

(4) There must be reasonable grounds for believing that research of comparable effectiveness cannot be carried out if the project has to be confined to, or relate only to, persons who have capacity to consent to taking part in it.

(5) The research must—

    (a) have the potential to benefit P without imposing on P a burden that is disproportionate to the potential benefit to P, or

    (b) be intended to provide knowledge of the causes or treatment of, or of the care of persons affected by, the same or a similar condition.

(6) If the research falls within paragraph (b) of subsection (5) but not within paragraph (a), there must be reasonable grounds for believing—

    (a) that the risk to P from taking part in the project is likely to be negligible, and

    (b) that anything done to, or in relation to, P will not—

        (i) interfere with P's freedom of action or privacy in a significant way, or

        (ii) be unduly invasive or restrictive.

(7) There must be reasonable arrangements in place for ensuring that the requirements of sections 32 and 33 will be met.

32 Consulting carers etc.

(1) This section applies if a person ('R')—

    (a) is conducting an approved research project, and

    (b) wishes to carry out research, as part of the project, on or in relation to a person ('P') who lacks capacity to consent to taking part in the project.

(2) R must take reasonable steps to identify a person who—

    (a) otherwise than in a professional capacity or for remuneration, is engaged in caring for P or is interested in P's welfare, and

    (b) is prepared to be consulted by R under this section.

(3) If R is unable to identify such a person he must, in accordance with guidance issued by the appropriate authority, nominate a person who—

    (a) is prepared to be consulted by R under this section, but

    (b) has no connection with the project.

(4) R must provide the person identified under subsection (2), or nominated under subsection (3), with information about the project and ask him—

    (a) for advice as to whether P should take part in the project, and

    (b) what, in his opinion, P's wishes and feelings about taking part in the project would be likely to be if P had capacity in relation to the matter.

(5) If, at any time, the person consulted advises R that in his opinion P's wishes and feelings would be likely to lead him to decline to take part in the project (or to wish to withdraw from it) if he had capacity in relation to the matter, R must ensure—

    (a) if P is not already taking part in the project, that he does not take part in it;

    (b) if P is taking part in the project, that he is withdrawn from it.

(6) But subsection (5)(b) does not require treatment that P has been receiving as part of the project to be discontinued if R has reasonable grounds for believing that there would be a significant risk to P's health if it were discontinued.

(7) The fact that a person is the donee of a lasting power of attorney given by P, or is P's deputy, does not prevent him from being the person consulted under this section.

(8) Subsection (9) applies if treatment is being, or is about to be, provided for P as a matter of urgency and R considers that, having regard to the nature of the research and of the particular circumstances of the case—

    (a) it is also necessary to take action for the purposes of the research as a matter of urgency, but

    (b) it is not reasonably practicable to consult under the previous provisions of this section.

(9) R may take the action if—

    (a) he has the agreement of a registered medical practitioner who is not involved in the organisation or conduct of the research project, or

    (b) where it is not reasonably practicable in the time available to obtain that agreement, he acts in accordance with a procedure approved by the appropriate body at the time when the research project was approved under section 31.

(10) But R may not continue to act in reliance on subsection (9) if he has reasonable grounds for believing that it is no longer necessary to take the action as a matter of urgency.

33   Additional safeguards

(1) This section applies in relation to a person who is taking part in an approved research project even though he lacks capacity to consent to taking part.

(2) Nothing may be done to, or in relation to, him in the course of the research—

    (a) to which he appears to object (whether by showing signs of resistance or otherwise) except where what is being done is intended to protect him from harm or to reduce or prevent pain or discomfort, or

    (b) which would be contrary to—

        (i)   an advance decision of his which has effect, or

        (ii) any other form of statement made by him and not subsequently withdrawn, of which R is aware.

(3) The interests of the person must be assumed to outweigh those of science and society.

(4) If he indicates (in any way) that he wishes to be withdrawn from the project he must be withdrawn without delay.

(5) P must be withdrawn from the project, without delay, if at any time the person conducting the research has reasonable grounds for believing that one or more of the requirements set out in section 31(2) to (7) is no longer met in relation to research being carried out on, or in relation to, P.

(6) But neither subsection (4) nor subsection (5) requires treatment that P has been receiving as part of the project to be discontinued if R has reasonable grounds for believing that there would be a significant risk to P's health if it were discontinued.

34   Loss of capacity during research project

(1) This section applies where a person ('P')—

    (a) has consented to take part in a research project begun before the commencement of section 30, but

    (b) before the conclusion of the project, loses capacity to consent to continue to take part in it.

(2) The appropriate authority may by regulations provide that, despite P's loss of capacity, research of a prescribed kind may be carried out on, or in relation to, P if—

    (a) the project satisfies prescribed requirements,

    (b) any information or material relating to P which is used in the research is of a prescribed description and was obtained before P's loss of capacity, and

    (c) the person conducting the project takes in relation to P such steps as may be prescribed for the purpose of protecting him.

(3) The regulations may, in particular,—

    (a) make provision about when, for the purposes of the regulations, a project is to be treated as having begun;

    (b) include provision similar to any made by section 31, 32 or 33.

Independent mental capacity advocate service

35 Appointment of independent mental capacity advocates

(1) The appropriate authority must make such arrangements as it considers reasonable to enable persons ('independent mental capacity advocates') to be available to represent and support persons to whom acts or decisions proposed under sections 37, 38 and 39 relate [or persons who fall within section 39A, 39C or 39D].

36 Functions of independent mental capacity advocates

(1) The appropriate authority may make regulations as to the functions of independent mental capacity advocates.

37 Provision of serious medical treatment by NHS body

(1) This section applies if an NHS body—

(a) is proposing to provide, or secure the provision of, serious medical treatment for a person ('P') who lacks capacity to consent to the treatment, and

(b) is satisfied that there is no person, other than one engaged in providing care or treatment for P in a professional capacity or for remuneration, whom it would be appropriate to consult in determining what would be in P's best interests.

(2) But this section does not apply if P's treatment is regulated by Part 4 of the Mental Health Act.

(3) Before the treatment is provided, the NHS body must instruct an independent mental capacity advocate to represent P.

(4) If the treatment needs to be provided as a matter of urgency, it may be provided even though the NHS body has not been able to comply with subsection (3).

(5) The NHS body must, in providing or securing the provision of treatment for P, take into account any information given, or submissions made, by the independent mental capacity advocate.

(6) 'Serious medical treatment' means treatment which involves providing, withholding or withdrawing treatment of a kind prescribed by regulations made by the appropriate authority.

Miscellaneous and supplementary

42 Codes of practice

(1) The Lord Chancellor must prepare and issue one or more codes of practice—

(a) for the guidance of persons assessing whether a person has capacity in relation to any matter,

(b) for the guidance of persons acting in connection with the care or treatment of another person (see section 5),

(c) for the guidance of donees of lasting powers of attorney,

(d) for the guidance of deputies appointed by the court,

(e) for the guidance of persons carrying out research in reliance on any provision made by or under this Act (and otherwise with respect to sections 30 to 34),

(f) for the guidance of independent mental capacity advocates,

[(fa) for the guidance of persons exercising functions under Schedule A1,

(fb) for the guidance of representatives appointed under Part 10 of Schedule A1,]

(g) with respect to the provisions of sections 24 to 26 (advance decisions and apparent advance decisions), and

(h) with respect to such other matters concerned with this Act as he thinks fit.

(4) It is the duty of a person to have regard to any relevant code if he is acting in relation to a person who lacks capacity and is doing so in one or more of the following ways—

(a) as the donee of a lasting power of attorney,

(b) as a deputy appointed by the court,

(c) as a person carrying out research in reliance on any provision made by or under this Act (see sections 30 to 34),

(d)   as an independent mental capacity advocate,
[(da) in the exercise of functions under Schedule A1,
(db) as a representative appointed under Part 10 of Schedule A1,]
(e)   in a professional capacity,
(f)   for remuneration.
(5) If it appears to a court or tribunal conducting any criminal or civil proceedings that—
(a) a provision of a code, or
(b) a failure to comply with a code,
is relevant to a question arising in the proceedings, the provision or failure must be taken into account in deciding the question.

Companies Act 2006

(2006, c. 46)

17   A company's constitution
Unless the context otherwise requires, references in the Companies Acts to a company's constitution include—
(a) the company's articles, and
(b) any resolutions and agreements to which Chapter 3 applies (see section 29).

33   Effect of company's constitution
(1) The provisions of a company's constitution bind the company and its members to the same extent as if there were covenants on the part of the company and of each member to observe those provisions.
(2) Money payable by a member to the company under its constitution is a debt due from him to the company.
In England and Wales and Northern Ireland it is of the nature of an ordinary contract debt.

39   A company's capacity
(1) The validity of an act done by a company shall not be called into question on the ground of lack of capacity by reason of anything in the company's constitution.

40   Power of directors to bind the company
(1) In favour of a person dealing with a company in good faith, the power of the directors to bind the company, or authorise others to do so, is deemed to be free of any limitation under the company's constitution.
(2) For this purpose—
(a) a person 'deals with' a company if he is a party to any transaction or other act to which the company is a party,
(b) a person dealing with a company—
(i)   is not bound to enquire as to any limitation on the powers of the directors to bind the company or authorise others to do so,
(ii)   is presumed to have acted in good faith unless the contrary is proved, and
(iii) is not to be regarded as acting in bad faith by reason only of his knowing that an act is beyond the powers of the directors under the company's constitution.

41   Constitutional limitations: transactions involving directors or their associates
(1) This section applies to a transaction if or to the extent that its validity depends on section 40 (power of directors deemed to be free of limitations under company's constitution in favour of person dealing with company in good faith).

Nothing in this section shall be read as excluding the operation of any other enactment or rule of law by virtue of which the transaction may be called in question or any liability to the company may arise.

(2) Where—

(a) a company enters into such a transaction, and

(b) the parties to the transaction include—

 (i) a director of the company or of its holding company, or

 (ii) a person connected with any such director,

the transaction is voidable at the instance of the company.

(3) Whether or not it is avoided, any such party to the transaction as is mentioned in subsection (2)(b)(i) or (ii), and any director of the company who authorised the transaction, is liable—

(a) to account to the company for any gain he has made directly or indirectly by the transaction, and

(b) to indemnify the company for any loss or damage resulting from the transaction.

(4) The transaction ceases to be voidable if—

(a) restitution of any money or other asset which was the subject matter of the transaction is no longer possible, or

(b) the company is indemnified for any loss or damage resulting from the transaction, or

(c) rights acquired bona fide for value and without actual notice of the directors' exceeding their powers by a person who is not party to the transaction would be affected by the avoidance, or

(d) the transaction is affirmed by the company.

(5) A person other than a director of the company is not liable under subsection (3) if he shows that at the time the transaction was entered into he did not know that the directors were exceeding their powers.

(6) Nothing in the preceding provisions of this section affects the rights of any party to the transaction not within subsection (2)(b)(i) or (ii).

But the court may, on the application of the company or any such party, make an order affirming, severing or setting aside the transaction on such terms as appear to the court to be just.

(7) In this section—

(a) 'transaction' includes any act; and

(b) the reference to a person connected with a director has the same meaning as in Part 10 (company directors).

43 Company contracts

(1) Under the law of England and Wales or Northern Ireland a contract may be made—

(a) by a company, by writing under its common seal, or

(b) on behalf of a company, by a person acting under its authority, express or implied.

(2) Any formalities required by law in the case of a contract made by an individual also apply, unless a contrary intention appears, to a contract made by or on behalf of a company.

51 Pre-incorporation contracts, deeds and obligations

(1) A contract that purports to be made by or on behalf of a company at a time when the company has not been formed has effect, subject to any agreement to the contrary, as one made with the person purporting to act for the company or as agent for it, and he is personally liable on the contract accordingly.

(2) Subsection (1) applies—

(a) to the making of a deed under the law of England and Wales or Northern Ireland, and

(b) to the undertaking of an obligation under the law of Scotland,

as it applies to the making of a contract.

83 Civil consequences of failure to make required disclosure

(1) This section applies to any legal proceedings brought by a company to which section 82 applies (requirement to disclose company name etc) to enforce a right arising out of a contract made

in the course of a business in respect of which the company was, at the time the contract was made, in breach of regulations under that section.

(2) The proceedings shall be dismissed if the defendant (in Scotland, the defender) to the proceedings shows—

>(a) that he has a claim against the claimant (pursuer) arising out of the contract that he has been unable to pursue by reason of the latter's breach of the regulations, or

>(b) that he has suffered some financial loss in connection with the contract by reason of the claimant's (pursuer's) breach of the regulations,

unless the court before which the proceedings are brought is satisfied that it is just and equitable to permit the proceedings to continue.

(3) This section does not affect the right of any person to enforce such rights as he may have against another person in any proceedings brought by that person.

170   Scope and nature of general duties

(1) The general duties specified in sections 171 to 177 are owed by a director of a company to the company.

(3) The general duties are based on certain common law rules and equitable principles as they apply in relation to directors and have effect in place of those rules and principles as regards the duties owed to a company by a director.

(4) The general duties shall be interpreted and applied in the same way as common law rules or equitable principles, and regard shall be had to the corresponding common law rules and equitable principles in interpreting and applying the general duties.

174   Duty to exercise reasonable care, skill and diligence

(1) A director of a company must exercise reasonable care, skill and diligence.

(2) This means the care, skill and diligence that would be exercised by a reasonably diligent person with—

>(a) the general knowledge, skill and experience that may reasonably be expected of a person carrying out the functions carried out by the director in relation to the company, and

>(b) the general knowledge, skill and experience that the director has.

176   Duty not to accept benefits from third parties

(1) A director of a company must not accept a benefit from a third party conferred by reason of—

>(a) his being a director, or

>(b) his doing (or not doing) anything as director.

178   Civil consequences of breach of general duties

(1) The consequences of breach (or threatened breach) of sections 171 to 177 are the same as would apply if the corresponding common law rule or equitable principle applied.

(2) The duties in those sections (with the exception of section 174 (duty to exercise reasonable care, skill and diligence)) are, accordingly, enforceable in the same way as any other fiduciary duty owed to a company by its directors.

189   Directors' long-term service contracts: civil consequences of contravention

If a company agrees to provision in contravention of section 188 (directors' long-term service contracts: requirement of members' approval)—

>(a) the provision is void, to the extent of the contravention, and

>(b) the contract is deemed to contain a term entitling the company to terminate it at any time by the giving of reasonable notice.

195   Property transactions: civil consequences of contravention

(1) This section applies where a company enters into an arrangement in contravention of section 190 (requirement of members' approval for substantial property transactions).

(2) The arrangement, and any transaction entered into in pursuance of the arrangement (whether by the company or any other person), is voidable at the instance of the company, unless—

    (a) restitution of any money or other asset that was the subject matter of the arrangement or transaction is no longer possible,

    (b) the company has been indemnified in pursuance of this section by any other persons for the loss or damage suffered by it, or

    (c) rights acquired in good faith, for value and without actual notice of the contravention by a person who is not a party to the arrangement or transaction would be affected by the avoidance.

(3) Whether or not the arrangement or any such transaction has been avoided, each of the persons specified in subsection (4) is liable—

    (a) to account to the company for any gain that he has made directly or indirectly by the arrangement or transaction, and

    (b) (jointly and severally with any other person so liable under this section) to indemnify the company for any loss or damage resulting from the arrangement or transaction.

(4) The persons so liable are—

    (a) any director of the company or of its holding company with whom the company entered into the arrangement in contravention of section 190,

    (b) any person with whom the company entered into the arrangement in contravention of that section who is connected with a director of the company or of its holding company,

    (c) the director of the company or of its holding company with whom any such person is connected, and

    (d) any other director of the company who authorised the arrangement or any transaction entered into in pursuance of such an arrangement.

(5) Subsections (3) and (4) are subject to the following two subsections.

(6) In the case of an arrangement entered into by a company in contravention of section 190 with a person connected with a director of the company or of its holding company, that director is not liable by virtue of subsection (4)(c) if he shows that he took all reasonable steps to secure the company's compliance with that section.

(7) In any case—

    (a) a person so connected is not liable by virtue of subsection (4)(b), and

    (b) a director is not liable by virtue of subsection (4)(d),

if he shows that, at the time the arrangement was entered into, he did not know the relevant circumstances constituting the contravention.

(8) Nothing in this section shall be read as excluding the operation of any other enactment or rule of law by virtue of which the arrangement or transaction may be called in question or any liability to the company may arise.

196 Property transactions: effect of subsequent affirmation

Where a transaction or arrangement is entered into by a company in contravention of section 190 (requirement of members' approval) but, within a reasonable period, it is affirmed—

    (a) in the case of a contravention of subsection (1) of that section, by resolution of the members of the company, and

    (b) in the case of a contravention of subsection (2) of that section, by resolution of the members of the holding company,

the transaction or arrangement may no longer be avoided under section 195.

222 Payments made without approval: civil consequences

(1) If a payment is made in contravention of section 217 (payment by company)—

    (a) it is held by the recipient on trust for the company making the payment, and

    (b) any director who authorised the payment is jointly and severally liable to indemnify the company that made the payment for any loss resulting from it.

(2) If a payment is made in contravention of section 218 (payment in connection with transfer of undertaking etc), it is held by the recipient on trust for the company whose undertaking or property is or is proposed to be transferred.

(3) If a payment is made in contravention of section 219 (payment in connection with share transfer)—

    (a) it is held by the recipient on trust for persons who have sold their shares as a result of the offer made, and

    (b) the expenses incurred by the recipient in distributing that sum amongst those persons shall be borne by him and not retained out of that sum.

(4) If a payment is in contravention of section 217 and section 218, subsection (2) of this section applies rather than subsection (1).

(5) If a payment is in contravention of section 217 and section 219, subsection (3) of this section applies rather than subsection (1), unless the court directs otherwise.

232   Provisions protecting directors from liability

(1) Any provision that purports to exempt a director of a company (to any extent) from any liability that would otherwise attach to him in connection with any negligence, default, breach of duty or breach of trust in relation to the company is void.

(2) Any provision by which a company directly or indirectly provides an indemnity (to any extent) for a director of the company, or of an associated company, against any liability attaching to him in connection with any negligence, default, breach of duty or breach of trust in relation to the company of which he is a director is void, except as permitted by—

    (a) section 233 (provision of insurance),

    (b) section 234 (qualifying third party indemnity provision), or

    (c) section 235 (qualifying pension scheme indemnity provision).

463   Liability for false or misleading statements in reports

(1) The reports to which this section applies are—

    (a) the directors' report,

    (b) the directors' remuneration report, and

    (c) a summary financial statement so far as it is derived from either of those reports.

(2) A director of a company is liable to compensate the company for any loss suffered by it as a result of—

    (a) any untrue or misleading statement in a report to which this section applies, or

    (b) the omission from a report to which this section applies of anything required to be included in it.

(3) He is so liable only if—

    (a) he knew the statement to be untrue or misleading or was reckless as to whether it was untrue or misleading, or

    (b) he knew the omission to be dishonest concealment of a material fact.

(4) No person shall be subject to any liability to a person other than the company resulting from reliance, by that person or another, on information in a report to which this section applies.

(5) The reference in subsection (4) to a person being subject to a liability includes a reference to another person being entitled as against him to be granted any civil remedy or to rescind or repudiate an agreement.

(6) This section does not affect—

    (a) liability for a civil penalty, or

    (b) liability for a criminal offence.

532   Voidness of provisions protecting auditors from liability

(1) This section applies to any provision—

    (a) for exempting an auditor of a company (to any extent) from any liability that would otherwise attach to him in connection with any negligence, default, breach of duty or breach of trust in relation to the company occurring in the course of the audit of accounts, or

  (b) by which a company directly or indirectly provides an indemnity (to any extent) for an auditor of the company, or of an associated company, against any liability attaching to him in connection with any negligence, default, breach of duty or breach of trust in relation to the company of which he is auditor occurring in the course of the audit of accounts.

  (2) Any such provision is void, except as permitted by—

  (a) section 533 (indemnity for costs of successfully defending proceedings), or

  (b) sections 534 to 536 (liability limitation agreements).

534 Liability limitation agreements

  (1) A 'liability limitation agreement' is an agreement that purports to limit the amount of a liability owed to a company by its auditor in respect of any negligence, default, breach of duty or breach of trust, occurring in the course of the audit of accounts, of which the auditor may be guilty in relation to the company.

537 Effect of liability limitation agreement

  (1) A liability limitation agreement is not effective to limit the auditor's liability to less than such amount as is fair and reasonable in all the circumstances of the case having regard (in particular) to—

  (a) the auditor's responsibilities under this Part,

  (b) the nature and purpose of the auditor's contractual obligations to the company, and

  (c) the professional standards expected of him.

  (2) A liability limitation agreement that purports to limit the auditor's liability to less than the amount mentioned in subsection (1) shall have effect as if it limited his liability to that amount.

  (3) In determining what is fair and reasonable in all the circumstances of the case no account is to be taken of—

  (a) matters arising after the loss or damage in question has been incurred, or

  (b) matters (whenever arising) affecting the possibility of recovering compensation from other persons liable in respect of the same loss or damage.

655 Shares no bar to damages against company

A person is not debarred from obtaining damages or other compensation from a company by reason only of his holding or having held shares in the company or any right to apply or subscribe for shares or to be included in the company's register of members in respect of shares.

847 Consequences of unlawful distribution

  (1) This section applies where a distribution, or part of one, made by a company to one of its members is made in contravention of this Part.

  (2) If at the time of the distribution the member knows or has reasonable grounds for believing that it is so made, he is liable—

  (a) to repay it (or that part of it, as the case may be) to the company, or

  (b) in the case of a distribution made otherwise than in cash, to pay the company a sum equal to the value of the distribution (or part) at that time.

  (3) This is without prejudice to any obligation imposed apart from this section on a member of a company to repay a distribution unlawfully made to him.

942 The Panel

  (1) The body known as the Panel on Takeovers and Mergers ('the Panel') is to have the functions conferred on it by or under this Chapter.

954 Compensation

  (1) Rules may confer power on the Panel to order a person to pay such compensation as it thinks just and reasonable if he is in breach of a rule the effect of which is to require the payment of money.

(2) Rules made by virtue of this section may include provision for the payment of interest (including compound interest).

956   No action for breach of statutory duty etc.

(1) Contravention of a rule-based requirement or a disclosure requirement does not give rise to any right of action for breach of statutory duty.

(2) Contravention of a rule-based requirement does not make any transaction void or unenforceable or (subject to any provision made by rules) affect the validity of any other thing.

1218   Exemption from liability for damages

(1) No person within subsection (2) is to be liable in damages for anything done or omitted in the discharge or purported discharge of functions to which this subsection applies.

(2) The persons within this subsection are—

    (a) any recognised supervisory body,

    (b) any officer or employee of a recognised supervisory body, and

    (c) any member of the governing body of a recognised supervisory body.

Compensation Act 2006

(2006, c. 29)

PART 1   STANDARD OF CARE

1   Deterrent effect of potential liability

A court considering a claim in negligence or breach of statutory duty may, in determining whether the defendant should have taken particular steps to meet a standard of care (whether by taking precautions against a risk or otherwise), have regard to whether a requirement to take those steps might—

    (a) prevent a desirable activity from being undertaken at all, to a particular extent or in a particular way, or

    (b) discourage persons from undertaking functions in connection with a desirable activity.

2   Apologies, offers of treatment or other redress

An apology, an offer of treatment or other redress, shall not of itself amount to an admission of negligence or breach of statutory duty.

3   Mesothelioma: damages

(1) This section applies where—

    (a) a person ('the responsible person') has negligently or in breach of statutory duty caused or permitted another person ('the victim') to be exposed to asbestos,

    (b) the victim has contracted mesothelioma as a result of exposure to asbestos,

    (c) because of the nature of mesothelioma and the state of medical science, it is not possible to determine with certainty whether it was the exposure mentioned in paragraph (a) or another exposure which caused the victim to become ill, and

    (d) the responsible person is liable in tort, by virtue of the exposure mentioned in paragraph (a), in connection with damage caused to the victim by the disease (whether by reason of having materially increased a risk or for any other reason).

(2) The responsible person shall be liable—

    (a) in respect of the whole of the damage caused to the victim by the disease (irrespective of whether the victim was also exposed to asbestos—

        (i)   other than by the responsible person, whether or not in circumstances in which another person has liability in tort, or

        (ii)   by the responsible person in circumstances in which he has no liability in tort), and

    (b) jointly and severally with any other responsible person.

(3) Subsection (2) does not prevent—

    (a) one responsible person from claiming a contribution from another, or

    (b) a finding of contributory negligence.

(4) In determining the extent of contributions of different responsible persons in accordance with subsection (3)(a), a court shall have regard to the relative lengths of the periods of exposure for which each was responsible; but this subsection shall not apply—

    (a) if or to the extent that responsible persons agree to apportion responsibility amongst themselves on some other basis, or

    (b) if or to the extent that the court thinks that another basis for determining contributions is more appropriate in the circumstances of a particular case.

(5) In subsection (1) the reference to causing or permitting a person to be exposed to asbestos includes a reference to failing to protect a person from exposure to asbestos.

(6) In the application of this section to Scotland—

    (a) a reference to tort shall be taken as a reference to delict, and

    (b) a reference to a court shall be taken to include a reference to a jury.

(7) The Treasury may make regulations about the provision of compensation to a responsible person where—

    (a) he claims, or would claim, a contribution from another responsible person in accordance with subsection (3)(a), but

    (b) he is unable or likely to be unable to obtain the contribution, because an insurer of the other responsible person is unable or likely to be unable to satisfy the claim for a contribution.

(8) The regulations may, in particular—

    (a) replicate or apply (with or without modification) a provision of the Financial Services Compensation Scheme;

    (b) replicate or apply (with or without modification) a transitional compensation provision;

    (c) provide for a specified person to assess and pay compensation;

    (d) provide for expenses incurred (including the payment of compensation) to be met out of levies collected in accordance with section 213(3)(b) of the Financial Services and Markets Act 2000 (c. 8) (the Financial Services Compensation Scheme);

    (e) modify the effect of a transitional compensation provision;

    (f) enable the Financial Services Authority to amend the Financial Services Compensation Scheme;

    (g) modify the Financial Services and Markets Act 2000 in its application to an amendment pursuant to paragraph (f);

    (h) make, or require the making of, provision for the making of a claim by a responsible person for compensation whether or not he has already satisfied claims in tort against him;

    (i) make, or require the making of, provision which has effect in relation to claims for contributions made on or after the date on which this Act is passed.

(9) Provision made by virtue of subsection (8)(a) shall cease to have effect when the Financial Services Compensation Scheme is amended by the Financial Services Authority by virtue of subsection (8)(f).

(10) In subsections (7) and (8)—

    (a) a reference to a responsible person includes a reference to an insurer of a responsible person, and

    (b) 'transitional compensation provision' means a provision of an enactment which is made under the Financial Services and Markets Act 2000 and—

        (i) preserves the effect of the Policyholders Protection Act 1975 (c. 75), or

        (ii) applies the Financial Services Compensation Scheme in relation to matters arising before its establishment.

(11) Regulations under subsection (7)—

    (a) may include consequential or incidental provision,

(b) may make provision which has effect generally or only in relation to specified cases or circumstances,

(c) may make different provision for different cases or circumstances,

(d) shall be made by statutory instrument, and

(e) may not be made unless a draft has been laid before and approved by resolution of each House of Parliament.

PART 2 CLAIMS MANAGEMENT SERVICES

4   Provision of regulated claims management services

(1) A person may not provide regulated claims management services unless—

(a) he is an authorised person,

(b) he is an exempt person,

(c) the requirement for authorisation has been waived in relation to him in accordance with regulations under section 9, or

(d) he is an individual acting otherwise than in the course of a business.

Government of Wales Act 2006

(2006, c. 32)

1   The Assembly

(1) There is to be an Assembly for Wales to be known as the National Assembly for Wales or Cynulliad Cenedlaethol Cymru (referred to in this Act as 'the Assembly').

42   Defamation

(1) For the purposes of the law of defamation—

(a) any statement made in Assembly proceedings, and

(b) the publication under the authority of the Assembly of any statement, is absolutely privileged.

(2) The Welsh Ministers may by regulations make provision for and in connection with establishing in any legal proceedings that any statement or publication is absolutely privileged by virtue of subsection (1).

(3) No regulations are to be made under subsection (2) unless a draft of the statutory instrument containing them has been laid before, and approved by a resolution of, the Assembly.

(4) In this section 'statement' has the same meaning as in the Defamation Act 1996 (c. 31).

130   Payments in by mistake

Where a sum is paid into the Welsh Consolidated Fund which should not or need not have been paid into the Fund, the Auditor General may grant an approval to draw a payment equal to the amount of that sum out of the Fund.

National Health Service Act 2006

(2006, c. 41)

9   NHS contracts

(1) In this Act, an NHS contract is an arrangement under which one health service body ('the commissioner') arranges for the provision to it by another health service body ('the provider') of goods or services which it reasonably requires for the purposes of its functions.

(5) Whether or not an arrangement which constitutes an NHS contract would apart from this subsection be a contract in law, it must not be regarded for any purpose as giving rise to contractual rights or liabilities.

(6) But if any dispute arises with respect to such an arrangement, either party may refer the matter to the Secretary of State for determination under this section

(7) If, in the course of negotiations intending to lead to an arrangement which will be an NHS contract, it appears to a health service body—

    (a) that the terms proposed by another health service body are unfair by reason that the other is seeking to take advantage of its position as the only, or the only practicable, provider of the goods or services concerned or by reason of any other unequal bargaining position as between the prospective parties to the proposed arrangement, or

    (b) that for any other reason arising out of the relative bargaining position of the prospective parties any of the terms of the proposed arrangement cannot be agreed,

that health service body may refer the terms of the proposed arrangement to the Secretary of State for determination under this section.

(8) Where a reference is made to the Secretary of State under subsection (6) or (7), he may determine the matter himself or appoint a person to consider and determine it in accordance with regulations.

NHS Redress Act 2006

(2006, c. 44)

England

1 Power to establish redress scheme

(1) The Secretary of State may by regulations establish a scheme for the purpose of enabling redress to be provided without recourse to civil proceedings in circumstances in which this section applies.

(2) This section applies where under the law of England and Wales qualifying liability in tort on the part of a body or other person mentioned in subsection (3) arises in connection with the provision, as part of the health service in England, of qualifying services.

(3) The bodies and other persons referred to are—

    (a) the Secretary of State,

    (b) a Primary Care Trust,

    (c) a designated Strategic Health Authority, and

    (d) a body or other person providing, or arranging for the provision of, services whose provision is the subject of arrangements with a body or other person mentioned in paragraph (a), (b) or (c).

(4) The reference in subsection (2) to qualifying liability in tort is to liability in tort owed—

    (a) in respect of or consequent upon personal injury or loss arising out of or in connection with breach of a duty of care owed to any person in connection with the diagnosis of illness, or the care or treatment of any patient, and

    (b) in consequence of any act or omission by a health care professional.

(5) For the purposes of subsection (2), services are qualifying services if—

    (a) they are provided in a hospital (in England or elsewhere), or

    (b) they are of such other description (including a description involving provision outside England) as the Secretary of State may specify by regulations.

(6) Regulations under subsection (5)(b) may not specify services of any of the following descriptions—

    (a) primary dental services,

    (b) primary medical services,

    (c) services provided under section 38 of the National Health Service Act 1977 (c. 49) (general ophthalmic services),

(d) services provided under [section 126 of the National Health Service Act 2006] (arrangements for pharmaceutical services) or by virtue of [section 127] of that Act (arrangements for additional pharmaceutical services), and

(e) services of a kind which may be provided under [section 126 of that Act, or by virtue of section 127 of that Act, which are provided under Schedule 12 to that Act (local pharmaceutical services schemes) or under section 134 of that Act (local pharmaceutical services pilot schemes).]

(7) The references in subsection (6) to primary dental services and primary medical services are to primary dental services and primary medical services under [the National Health Service Act 2006], except that the Secretary of State may by regulations provide that services of a description specified in the regulations are not to be regarded as primary dental services or primary medical services for the purposes of that subsection.

(8) Regulations under subsection (5)(b) or (7) may, in particular, describe services by reference to the manner or circumstances in which they are provided.

(9) In subsection (3)(d), the reference to a person providing services does not include a person providing services under a contract of employment.

(10) In subsection (4), the reference to a health care professional is to a member of a profession (whether or not regulated by, or by virtue of, any enactment) which is concerned (wholly or partly) with the physical or mental health of individuals.

(11) In this section, 'hospital' has the same meaning as in [the National Health Service Act 2006].

2   Application of scheme

(1) Subject to subsection (2), a scheme may make such provision defining its application as the Secretary of State thinks fit.

(2) A scheme must provide that it does not apply in relation to a liability that is or has been the subject of civil proceedings.

3   Redress under scheme

(1) Subject to subsections (2) and (5), a scheme may make such provision as the Secretary of State thinks fit about redress under the scheme.

(2) A scheme must provide for redress ordinarily to comprise—

(a) the making of an offer of compensation in satisfaction of any right to bring civil proceedings in respect of the liability concerned,

(b) the giving of an explanation,

(c) the giving of an apology, and

(d) the giving of a report on the action which has been, or will be, taken to prevent similar cases arising,

but may specify circumstances in which one or more of those forms of redress is not required.

(3) A scheme may, in particular—

(a) make provision for the compensation that may be offered to take the form of entry into a contract to provide care or treatment or of financial compensation, or both;

(b) make provision about the circumstances in which different forms of compensation may be offered.

(4) A scheme that provides for financial compensation to be offered may, in particular—

(a) make provision about the matters in respect of which financial compensation may be offered;

(b) make provision with respect to the assessment of the amount of any financial compensation.

(5) A scheme that provides for financial compensation to be offered—

(a) may specify an upper limit on the amount of financial compensation that may be included in an offer under the scheme;

(b) if it does not specify a limit under paragraph (a), must specify an upper limit on the amount of financial compensation that may be included in such an offer in respect of pain and suffering;

(c) may not specify any other limit on what may be included in such an offer by way of financial compensation.

6　Proceedings under scheme

(1) Subject to subsections (3) to (6), a scheme may make such provision as the Secretary of State thinks fit about proceedings under the scheme.

(2) A scheme may, in particular, make provision—

(a) about the investigation of cases under the scheme (including provision for the overseeing of the investigation by an individual of a specified description);

(b) about the making of decisions about the application of the scheme;

(c) for time limits in relation to acceptance of an offer of compensation under the scheme;

(d) about the form and content of settlement agreements under the scheme;

(e) for settlement agreements under the scheme to be subject in cases of a specified description to approval by a court;

(f) about the termination of proceedings under the scheme.

(3) A scheme must—

(a) make provision for the findings of an investigation of a case under the scheme to be recorded in a report, and

(b) subject to subsection (4), make provision for a copy of the report to be provided on request to the individual seeking redress.

(4) A scheme may provide that no copy of an investigation report need be provided—

(a) before an offer is made under the scheme or proceedings under the scheme are terminated, or

(b) in such other circumstances as may be specified.

(5) A scheme must provide for a settlement agreement under the scheme to include a waiver of the right to bring civil proceedings in respect of the liability to which the settlement relates.

(6) A scheme must provide for the termination of proceedings under the scheme if the liability to which the proceedings relate becomes the subject of civil proceedings.

7　Suspension of limitation period

(1) A scheme must make provision for the period during which a liability is the subject of proceedings under the scheme to be disregarded for the purposes of calculating whether any relevant limitation period has expired.

(2) In subsection (1), the reference to any relevant limitation period is to any period of time for the bringing of civil proceedings in respect of the liability which is prescribed by or under the Limitation Act 1980 (c. 58) or any other enactment.

(3) A scheme may define for the purposes of provision in pursuance of subsection (1) when liability is the subject of proceedings under the scheme.

8　Legal advice etc.

(1) Subject to subsections (2) and (4), a scheme may make such provision as the Secretary of State thinks fit—

(a) for the provision of legal advice without charge to individuals seeking redress under the scheme;

(b) for the provision in connection with proceedings under the scheme of other services, including the services of medical experts.

(2) A scheme must make such provision as the Secretary of State considers appropriate in order to secure that individuals to whom an offer under the scheme is made have access to legal advice without charge in relation to—

(a) the offer, and

(b) any settlement agreement.

(3) Provision under subsection (1)(a) or (2) about who may provide the legal advice may operate by reference to whether a potential provider is included in a list prepared by a specified person.

(4) A scheme that makes provision for the provision of the services of medical experts must provide for such experts to be instructed jointly by the scheme authority and the individual seeking redress under the scheme.

9 Assistance for individuals seeking redress under scheme

(1) It is the duty of the Secretary of State to arrange, to such extent as he considers necessary to meet all reasonable requirements, for the provision of assistance (by way of representation or otherwise) to individuals seeking, or intending to seek, redress under a scheme.

(2) The Secretary of State may make such other arrangements as he thinks fit for the provision of assistance to individuals in connection with cases which are the subject of proceedings under a scheme.

(3) The Secretary of State may make payments to any person in pursuance of arrangements under this section.

(4) In making arrangements under this section, the Secretary of State must have regard to the principle that the provision of services under the arrangements in connection with a particular case should, so far as practicable, be independent of any person to whose conduct the case relates or who is involved in dealing with the case.

10 Scheme members

(1) Subject to subsection (3), a scheme may make such provision as the Secretary of State thinks fit—

(a) about membership of the scheme on the part of any body or other person to whose liability the scheme applies, and

(b) about the functions of members in connection with the scheme.

11 Scheme authority

(1) A scheme must make provision for a specified Special Health Authority (in this Act referred to as 'the scheme authority') to have such functions in connection with the scheme as the Secretary of State thinks fit.

12 General duty to promote resolution under scheme

A scheme must include provision requiring the scheme authority and the members of the scheme, in carrying out their functions under the scheme, to have regard in particular to the desirability of redress being provided without recourse to civil proceedings.

13 Duties of co-operation

(1) The scheme authority under a scheme and [the Care Quality Commission] must co-operate with each other where it appears to them that it is appropriate to do so for the efficient and effective discharge of their respective functions.

(2) The scheme authority under a scheme and the National Patient Safety Agency must co-operate with each other where it appears to them that it is appropriate to do so for the efficient and effective discharge of their respective functions.

14 Complaints

(1) The Secretary of State may by regulations make provision about the handling and consideration of complaints made under the regulations about maladministration by any body or other person—

(a) in the exercise of functions under a scheme,

(b) in the exercise of other functions relating to proceedings under a scheme, or

(c) in connection with a settlement agreement entered into under a scheme.

Corporate Manslaughter and Corporate Homicide Act 2007

(2007, c. 19)

1   The offence

(1) An organisation to which this section applies is guilty of an offence if the way in which its activities are managed or organised—

    (a) causes a person's death, and

    (b) amounts to a gross breach of a relevant duty of care owed by the organisation to the deceased.

(2) The organisations to which this section applies are—

    (a) a corporation;

    (b) a department or other body listed in Schedule 1;

    (c) a police force;

    (d) a partnership, or a trade union or employers' association, that is an employer.

(3) An organisation is guilty of an offence under this section only if the way in which its activities are managed or organised by its senior management is a substantial element in the breach referred to in subsection (1).

(4) For the purposes of this Act—

    (a) 'relevant duty of care' has the meaning given by section 2, read with sections 3 to 7;

    (b) a breach of a duty of care by an organisation is a 'gross' breach if the conduct alleged to amount to a breach of that duty falls far below what can reasonably be expected of the organisation in the circumstances;

    (c) 'senior management', in relation to an organisation, means the persons who play significant roles in—

        (i)   the making of decisions about how the whole or a substantial part of its activities are to be managed or organised, or

        (ii) the actual managing or organising of the whole or a substantial part of those activities.

(5) The offence under this section is called—

    (a) corporate manslaughter, in so far as it is an offence under the law of England and Wales or Northern Ireland;

    (b) corporate homicide, in so far as it is an offence under the law of Scotland.

(6) An organisation that is guilty of corporate manslaughter or corporate homicide is liable on conviction on indictment to a fine.

2   Meaning of 'relevant duty of care'

(1) A 'relevant duty of care', in relation to an organisation, means any of the following duties owed by it under the law of negligence—

    (a) a duty owed to its employees or to other persons working for the organisation or performing services for it;

    (b) a duty owed as occupier of premises;

    (c) a duty owed in connection with—

        (i)   the supply by the organisation of goods or services (whether for consideration or not),

        (ii)   the carrying on by the organisation of any construction or maintenance operations,

        (iii) the carrying on by the organisation of any other activity on a commercial basis, or

        (iv)   the use or keeping by the organisation of any plant, vehicle or other thing;

    (d) a duty owed to a person who, by reason of being a person within subsection (2), is someone for whose safety the organisation is responsible.

(2) A person is within this subsection if—

    (a) he is detained at a custodial institution or in a custody area at a court or police station;

    (b) he is detained at a removal centre or short-term holding facility;

(c) he is being transported in a vehicle, or being held in any premises, in pursuance of prison escort arrangements or immigration escort arrangements;

(d) he is living in secure accommodation in which he has been placed;

(e) he is a detained patient.

(3) Subsection (1) is subject to sections 3 to 7.

(4) A reference in subsection (1) to a duty owed under the law of negligence includes a reference to a duty that would be owed under the law of negligence but for any statutory provision under which liability is imposed in place of liability under that law.

(5) For the purposes of this Act, whether a particular organisation owes a duty of care to a particular individual is a question of law.

The judge must make any findings of fact necessary to decide that question.

(6) For the purposes of this Act there is to be disregarded—

(a) any rule of the common law that has the effect of preventing a duty of care from being owed by one person to another by reason of the fact that they are jointly engaged in unlawful conduct;

(b) any such rule that has the effect of preventing a duty of care from being owed to a person by reason of his acceptance of a risk of harm.

(7) In this section—

. . .

'the law of negligence' includes—

(a) in relation to England and Wales, the Occupiers' Liability Act 1957 (c. 31), the Defective Premises Act 1972 (c. 35) and the Occupiers' Liability Act 1984 (c. 3);

(b) in relation to Scotland, the Occupiers' Liability (Scotland) Act 1960 (c. 30);

(c) in relation to Northern Ireland, the Occupiers' Liability Act (Northern Ireland) 1957 (c. 25), the Defective Premises (Northern Ireland) Order 1975 (S.I. 1975/1039 (N.I. 9)), the Occupiers' Liability (Northern Ireland) Order 1987 (S.I. 1987/1280 (N.I. 15)) and the Defective Premises (Landlord's Liability) Act (Northern Ireland) 2001 (c. 10);

. . .

3   Public policy decisions, exclusively public functions and statutory inspections

(1) Any duty of care owed by a public authority in respect of a decision as to matters of public policy (including in particular the allocation of public resources or the weighing of competing public interests) is not a 'relevant duty of care'.

(2) Any duty of care owed in respect of things done in the exercise of an exclusively public function is not a 'relevant duty of care' unless it falls within section 2(1)(a), (b) or (d).

(3) Any duty of care owed by a public authority in respect of inspections carried out in the exercise of a statutory function is not a 'relevant duty of care' unless it falls within section 2(1)(a) or (b).

(4) In this section—

'exclusively public function' means a function that falls within the prerogative of the Crown or is, by its nature, exercisable only with authority conferred—

(a) by the exercise of that prerogative, or

(b) by or under a statutory provision;

'statutory function' means a function conferred by or under a statutory provision.

4   Military activities

. . .

5   Policing and law enforcement

(1) Any duty of care owed by a public authority in respect of—

(a) operations within subsection (2),

(b) activities carried on in preparation for, or directly in support of, such operations, or

(c) training of a hazardous nature, or training carried out in a hazardous way, which it is considered needs to be carried out, or carried out in that way, in order to improve or maintain the effectiveness of officers or employees of the public authority with respect to such operations,

is not a 'relevant duty of care'.

   (2) Operations are within this subsection if—

      (a) they are operations for dealing with terrorism, civil unrest or serious disorder,

      (b) they involve the carrying on of policing or law-enforcement activities, and

      (c) officers or employees of the public authority in question come under attack, or face the threat of attack or violent resistance, in the course of the operations.

   (3) Any duty of care owed by a public authority in respect of other policing or law-enforcement activities is not a 'relevant duty of care' unless it falls within section 2(1)(a), (b) or (d).

6 Emergencies

   (1) Any duty of care owed by an organisation within subsection (2) in respect of the way in which it responds to emergency circumstances is not a 'relevant duty of care' unless it falls within section 2(1)(a) or (b).

   (2) The organisations within this subsection are—

      (a) a fire and rescue authority in England and Wales;

      (b) a fire and rescue authority or joint fire and rescue board in Scotland;

      (c) the Northern Ireland Fire and Rescue Service Board;

      (d) any other organisation providing a service of responding to emergency circumstances either—

         (i)   in pursuance of arrangements made with an organisation within paragraph (a), (b) or (c), or

         (ii) (if not in pursuance of such arrangements) otherwise than on a commercial basis;

      (e) a relevant NHS body;

      (f) an organisation providing ambulance services in pursuance of arrangements—

         (i)   made by, or at the request of, a relevant NHS body, or

         (ii) made with the Secretary of State or with the Welsh Ministers;

      (g) an organisation providing services for the transport of organs, blood, equipment or personnel in pursuance of arrangements of the kind mentioned in paragraph (f);

      (h) an organisation providing a rescue service;

      (i) the armed forces.

   (3) For the purposes of subsection (1), the way in which an organisation responds to emergency circumstances does not include the way in which—

      (a) medical treatment is carried out, or

      (b) decisions within subsection (4) are made.

   (7) In this section—

'emergency circumstances' means circumstances that are present or imminent and—

      (a) are causing, or are likely to cause, serious harm or a worsening of such harm, or

      (b) are likely to cause the death of a person; ...

. . .

'serious harm' means—

      (a) serious injury to or the serious illness (including mental illness) of a person;

      (b) serious harm to the environment (including the life and health of plants and animals);

      (c) serious harm to any building or other property.

   (8) A reference in this section to emergency circumstances includes a reference to circumstances that are believed to be emergency circumstances.

7 Child-protection and probation functions

   (1) A duty of care to which this section applies is not a 'relevant duty of care' unless it falls within section 2(1)(a), (b) or (d).

8 Factors for jury

(1) This section applies where—

(a) it is established that an organisation owed a relevant duty of care to a person, and

(b) it falls to the jury to decide whether there was a gross breach of that duty.

(2) The jury must consider whether the evidence shows that the organisation failed to comply with any health and safety legislation that relates to the alleged breach, and if so—

(a) how serious that failure was;

(b) how much of a risk of death it posed.

(3) The jury may also—

(a) consider the extent to which the evidence shows that there were attitudes, policies, systems or accepted practices within the organisation that were likely to have encouraged any such failure as is mentioned in subsection (2), or to have produced tolerance of it;

(b) have regard to any health and safety guidance that relates to the alleged breach.

(4) This section does not prevent the jury from having regard to any other matters they consider relevant.

(5) In this section 'health and safety guidance' means any code, guidance, manual or similar publication that is concerned with health and safety matters and is made or issued (under a statutory provision or otherwise) by an authority responsible for the enforcement of any health and safety legislation.

9 Power to order breach etc to be remedied

. . .

11 Application to Crown bodies

(1) An organisation that is a servant or agent of the Crown is not immune from prosecution under this Act for that reason.

Income Tax Act 2007

(2007, c. 3)

762 [and 781] Tracing value

(1) This section applies if it is necessary to determine the extent to which the value of any property or right is derived from any other property or right for the purposes of this Chapter.

(2) Value may be traced through any number of companies, partnerships and trusts.

(3) The property held by a company, partnership or trust must be attributed to the shareholders, partners or beneficiaries at each stage in such manner as is appropriate in the circumstances.

Legal Services Act 2007

(2007, c. 29)

131 Acts and omissions by employees etc

(1) For the purposes of this Part and the ombudsman scheme, any act or omission by a person in the course of the person's employment is to be treated as also an act or omission by the person's employer, whether or not it was done with the employer's knowledge or approval.

154 Protection from defamation claims

For the purposes of the law of defamation—

(a) proceedings in relation to a complaint under the ombudsman scheme are to be treated as if they were proceedings before a court, and

(b) the publication of any matter by the OLC ['the Office for Legal Complaints'] under this Part is absolutely privileged.

176 Duties of regulated persons

(1) A person who is a regulated person in relation to an approved regulator has a duty to comply with the regulatory arrangements of the approved regulator as they apply to that person.

Tribunals, Courts and Enforcement Act 2007

(2007, c. 15)

62 Enforcement by taking control of goods

(1) Schedule 12 applies where an enactment, writ or warrant confers power to use the procedure in that Schedule (taking control of goods and selling them to recover a sum of money).

(2) The power conferred by a writ or warrant of control to recover a sum of money, and any power conferred by a writ or warrant of possession or delivery to take control of goods and sell them to recover a sum of money, is exercisable only by using that procedure.

63 Enforcement agents

(1) This section and section 64 apply for the purposes of Schedule 12.

(2) An individual may act as an enforcement agent only if one of these applies—

    (a) he acts under a certificate under section 64;

    (b) he is exempt;

    (c) he acts in the presence and under the direction of a person to whom paragraph (a) or (b) applies.

(3) An individual is exempt if he acts in the course of his duty as one of these—

    (a) a constable;

    (b) an officer of Revenue and Customs;

    (c) a person appointed under section 2(1) of the Courts Act 2003 (c. 39) (court officers and staff).

65 Common law rules replaced

(1) This Chapter replaces the common law rules about the exercise of the powers which under it become powers to use the procedure in Schedule 12.

(2) The rules replaced include—

    (a) rules distinguishing between an illegal, an irregular and an excessive exercise of a power;

    (b) rules that would entitle a person to bring proceedings of a kind for which paragraph 66 of Schedule 12 provides (remedies available to the debtor);

    (c) rules of replevin;

    (d) rules about rescuing goods.

85 Contracts for similar rights to be void

(1) A provision of a contract is void to the extent that it would do any of these—

    (a) confer a right to seize or otherwise take control of goods to recover amounts within subsection (2);

    (b) confer a right to sell goods to recover amounts within subsection (2);

    (c) modify the effect of section 72(1), except in accordance with subsection (3).

(2) The amounts are any amounts payable—

    (a) as rent;

    (b) under a lease (other than as rent);

    (c) under an agreement collateral to a lease;

    (d) under an instrument creating a rentcharge;

    (e) in respect of breach of a covenant or condition in a lease, in an agreement collateral to a lease or in an instrument creating a rentcharge;

    (f) under an indemnity in respect of a payment within paragraphs (a) to (e).

(3) A provision of a contract is not void under subsection (1)(c) to the extent that it prevents or restricts the exercise of CRAR [*commercial rent arrears recovery*].

89 Application to the Crown

(1) This Part binds the Crown.

(2) But the procedure in Schedule 12 may not be used—

    (a) to recover debts due from the Crown,

    (b) to take control of or sell goods of the Crown (including goods owned by the Crown jointly or in common with another person), or

    (c) to enter premises occupied by the Crown.

Dormant Bank and Building Society Accounts Act 2008

(2008, c. 31)

1 Transfer of balances to reclaim fund

(1) This section applies where—

    (a) a bank or building society transfers to an authorised reclaim fund the balance of a dormant account that a person ("the customer") holds with it, and

    (b) the reclaim fund consents to the transfer.

(2) After the transfer—

    (a) the customer no longer has any right against the bank or building society to payment of the balance, but

    (b) the customer has against the reclaim fund whatever right to payment of the balance the customer would have against the bank or building society if the transfer had not happened.

4 Effect of balance transfer on membership rights

(1) This section applies where a person ("the member") holds a share in a building society represented by an account with the society, and either—

    (a) a transfer is made to a reclaim fund with the result that section 1 applies in relation to the account, or

    (b) transfers are made to a reclaim fund and one or more charities with the result that section 2 applies in relation to the account.

(2) After the transfer or transfers the member is to be treated as having whatever share in the building society the member would have if the transfer or transfers had not happened (and accordingly as having whatever rights, including distribution rights, a holder of that share would have as such).

5 Functions etc. of a reclaim fund

(1) A "reclaim fund" is a company the objects of which are restricted by its articles of association to the following—

    (a) the meeting of repayment claims;

    (b) the management of dormant account funds in such a way as to enable the company to meet whatever repayment claims it is prudent to anticipate;

    (c) the transfer of money to the body or bodies for the time being specified in section 16(1), subject to the need for the company—

        (i) to have access at any given time to enough money to meet whatever repayment claims it is prudent to anticipate,

        (ii) to comply with any requirement with regard to its financial resources that is imposed on it by or under any enactment, and

        (iii) to defray its expenses;

    (d) objects that are incidental or conducive to, or otherwise connected with, any of the above (including in particular the prudent investment of dormant account funds).

10 "Dormant"

(1) An account is "dormant" at a particular time if—

 (a) the account has been open throughout the period of 15 years ending at that time, but

 (b) during that period no transactions have been carried out in relation to the account by or on the instructions of the holder of the account.

Banking Act 2009

(2009, c. 1)

191 Directions

(1) The Bank of England may give directions to the operator of a recognised inter-bank payment system.

(2) A direction may—

 (a) require or prohibit the taking of specified action in the operation of the system;

 (b) set standards to be met in the operation of the system.

(3) Before giving a direction the Bank must notify the Treasury.

(4) The Treasury may by order confer immunity from liability in damages in respect of action or inaction in accordance with a direction.

(5) An immunity does not extend to action or inaction—

 (a) in bad faith, or

 (b) in contravention of section 6(1) of the Human Rights Act 1998.

(6) An order—

 (a) shall be made by statutory instrument, and

 (b) shall be subject to annulment in pursuance of a resolution of either House of Parliament.

244 Immunity

(1) The Bank of England has immunity in its capacity as a monetary authority.

(2) In this section—

 (a) a reference to the Bank of England is a reference to the Bank and anyone who acts or purports to act as a director, officer, servant or agent of the Bank,

 (b) "immunity" means immunity from liability in damages in respect of action or inaction, and

(3) The immunity does not extend to action or inaction—

 (a) in bad faith, or

 (b) in contravention of section 6(1) of the Human Rights Act 1998.

Equality Act 2010

(2010, c. 15)

PART 2 EQUALITY: KEY CONCEPTS

4 The protected characteristics

The following characteristics are protected characteristics—

age;

disability;

gender reassignment;

marriage and civil partnership;

pregnancy and maternity;

race;

religion or belief;

sex;

sexual orientation.

13   Direct discrimination

(1) A person (A) discriminates against another (B) if, because of a protected characteristic, A treats B less favourably than A treats or would treat others.

26   Harassment

(1) A person (A) harasses another (B) if—

    (a) A engages in unwanted conduct related to a relevant protected characteristic, and

    (b) the conduct has the purpose or effect of—

        (i)   violating B's dignity, or

        (ii) creating an intimidating, hostile, degrading, humiliating or offensive environment for B.

27   Victimisation

(1) A person (A) victimises another person (B) if A subjects B to a detriment because—

    (a) B does a protected act, or

    (b) A believes that B has done, or may do, a protected act.

(2) Each of the following is a protected act—

    (a) bringing proceedings under this Act;

    (b) giving evidence or information in connection with proceedings under this Act;

    (c) doing any other thing for the purposes of or in connection with this Act;

    (d) making an allegation (whether or not express) that A or another person has contravened this Act.

(3) Giving false evidence or information, or making a false allegation, is not a protected act if the evidence or information is given, or the allegation is made, in bad faith.

(4) This section applies only where the person subjected to a detriment is an individual.

(5) The reference to contravening this Act includes a reference to committing a breach of an equality clause or rule.

PART 3   SERVICES AND PUBLIC FUNCTIONS

28   Application of this Part

(1) This Part does not apply to the protected characteristic of—

    (a) age, so far as relating to persons who have not attained the age of 18;

    (b) marriage and civil partnership.

(2) This Part does not apply to discrimination, harassment or victimisation—

    (a) that is prohibited by Part 4 (premises), 5 (work) or 6 (education), or

    (b) that would be so prohibited but for an express exception.

(3) This Part does not apply to—

    (a) a breach of an equality clause or rule;

    (b) anything that would be a breach of an equality clause or rule but for section 69 or Part 2 of Schedule 7;

    (c) a breach of a non-discrimination rule.

29   Provision of services, etc.

(1) A person (a "service-provider") concerned with the provision of a service to the public or a section of the public (for payment or not) must not discriminate against a person requiring the service by not providing the person with the service.

(2) A service-provider (A) must not, in providing the service, discriminate against a person (B)—

    (a) as to the terms on which A provides the service to B;

    (b) by terminating the provision of the service to B;

(c) by subjecting B to any other detriment.

(3) A service-provider must not, in relation to the provision of the service, harass—

    (a) a person requiring the service, or

    (b) a person to whom the service-provider provides the service.

(4) A service-provider must not victimise a person requiring the service by not providing the person with the service.

(5) A service-provider (A) must not, in providing the service, victimise a person (B)—

    (a) as to the terms on which A provides the service to B;

    (b) by terminating the provision of the service to B;

    (c) by subjecting B to any other detriment.

(6) A person must not, in the exercise of a public function that is not the provision of a service to the public or a section of the public, do anything that constitutes discrimination, harassment or victimisation.

(8) In the application of section 26 for the purposes of subsection (3), and subsection (6) as it relates to harassment, neither of the following is a relevant protected characteristic—

    (a) religion or belief;

    (b) sexual orientation.

31 Interpretation and exceptions

(1) This section applies for the purposes of this Part.

(2) A reference to the provision of a service includes a reference to the provision of goods or facilities.

PART 4 PREMISES

32 Application of this Part

(1) This Part does not apply to the following protected characteristics—

    (a) age;

    (b) marriage and civil partnership.

33 Disposals, etc.

(1) A person (A) who has the right to dispose of premises must not discriminate against another (B)—

    (a) as to the terms on which A offers to dispose of the premises to B;

    (b) by not disposing of the premises to B;

    (c) in A's treatment of B with respect to things done in relation to persons seeking premises.

PART 5 WORK

39 Employees and applicants

(1) An employer (A) must not discriminate against a person (B)—

    (a) in the arrangements A makes for deciding to whom to offer employment;

    (b) as to the terms on which A offers B employment;

    (c) by not offering B employment.

(2) An employer (A) must not discriminate against an employee of A's (B)—

    (a) as to B's terms of employment;

    (b) in the way A affords B access, or by not affording B access, to opportunities for promotion, transfer or training or for receiving any other benefit, facility or service;

    (c) by dismissing B;

    (d) by subjecting B to any other detriment.

66 Sex equality clause

(1) If the terms of A's work do not (by whatever means) include a sex equality clause, they are to be treated as including one.

(2) A sex equality clause is a provision that has the following effect—

(a) if a term of A's is less favourable to A than a corresponding term of B's is to B, A's term is modified so as not to be less favourable;

(b) if A does not have a term which corresponds to a term of B's that benefits B, A's terms are modified so as to include such a term.

PART 9 ENFORCEMENT

114   Jurisdiction

(1) A county court or, in Scotland, the sheriff has jurisdiction to determine a claim relating to—

(a) a contravention of Part 3 (services and public functions);

(b) a contravention of Part 4 (premises);

(c) a contravention of Part 6 (education);

(d) a contravention of Part 7 (associations);

(e) a contravention of section 108, 111 or 112 that relates to Part 3, 4, 6 or 7.

119   Remedies

(1) This section applies if a county court or the sheriff finds that there has been a contravention of a provision referred to in section 114(1).

(2) The county court has power to grant any remedy which could be granted by the High Court—

(a) in proceedings in tort;

(b) on a claim for judicial review.

(4) An award of damages may include compensation for injured feelings (whether or not it includes compensation on any other basis).

(7) The county court or sheriff must not grant a remedy other than an award of damages or the making of a declaration unless satisfied that no criminal matter would be prejudiced by doing so.

PART 10   CONTRACTS ETC.

142   Unenforceable terms

(1) A term of a contract is unenforceable against a person in so far as it constitutes, promotes or provides for treatment of that or another person that is of a description prohibited by this Act.

(2) A relevant non-contractual term is unenforceable against a person in so far as it constitutes, promotes or provides for treatment of that or another person that is of a description prohibited by this Act, in so far as this Act relates to disability.

(3) A relevant non-contractual term is a term which—

(a) is a term of an agreement that is not a contract, and

(b) relates to the provision of an employment service within section 56(2)(a) to (e) or to the provision under a group insurance arrangement of facilities by way of insurance.

143   Removal or modification of unenforceable terms

(1) A county court or the sheriff may, on an application by a person who has an interest in a contract or other agreement which includes a term that is unenforceable as a result of section 142, make an order for the term to be removed or modified.

(2) An order under this section must not be made unless every person who would be affected by it—

(a) has been given notice of the application (except where notice is dispensed with in accordance with rules of court), and

(b) has been afforded an opportunity to make representations to the county court or sheriff.

(3) An order under this section may include provision in respect of a period before the making of the order.

144   Contracting out

(1) A term of a contract is unenforceable by a person in whose favour it would operate in so far as it purports to exclude or limit a provision of or made under this Act.

(2) A relevant non-contractual term (as defined by section 142) is unenforceable by a person in whose favour it would operate in so far as it purports to exclude or limit a provision of or made under this Act, in so far as the provision relates to disability.

(3) This section does not apply to a contract which settles a claim within section 114 [*Civil courts: Jurisdiction*].

(4) This section does not apply to a contract which settles a complaint within section 120 [*Employment Tribunals: Jurisdiction*] if the contract—

    (a) is made with the assistance of a conciliation officer, or

    (b) is a qualifying compromise contract.

(5) A contract within subsection (4) includes a contract which settles a complaint relating to a breach of an equality clause or rule or of a non-discrimination rule.

(6) A contract within subsection (4) includes an agreement by the parties to a dispute to submit the dispute to arbitration if—

    (a) the dispute is covered by a scheme having effect by virtue of an order under section 212A of the Trade Union and Labour Relations (Consolidation) Act 1992, and

    (b) the agreement is to submit the dispute to arbitration in accordance with the scheme.

145   Void and unenforceable terms

(1) A term of a collective agreement is void in so far as it constitutes, promotes or provides for treatment of a description prohibited by this Act.

(2) A rule of an undertaking is unenforceable against a person in so far as it constitutes, promotes or provides for treatment of the person that is of a description prohibited by this Act.

146   Declaration in respect of void term, etc.

(1) A qualifying person (P) may make a complaint to an employment tribunal that a term is void, or that a rule is unenforceable, as a result of section 145.

(2) But subsection (1) applies only if—

    (a) the term or rule may in the future have effect in relation to P, and

    (b) where the complaint alleges that the term or rule provides for treatment of a description prohibited by this Act, P may in the future be subjected to treatment that would (if P were subjected to it in present circumstances) be of that description.

PART 16 GENERAL AND MISCELLANEOUS

212   General interpretation

(2) A reference (however expressed) to an act includes a reference to an omission.

(3) A reference (however expressed) to an omission includes (unless there is express provision to the contrary) a reference to—

    (a) a deliberate omission to do something;

    (b) a refusal to do it;

    (c) a failure to do it.

Third Parties (Rights against Insurers) Act 2010

(2010, c. 10)

1   Rights against insurer of insolvent person etc

(1) This section applies if—

    (a) a relevant person incurs a liability against which that person is insured under a contract of insurance, or

       (b) a person who is subject to such a liability becomes a relevant person.

    (2) The rights of the relevant person under the contract against the insurer in respect of the liability are transferred to and vest in the person to whom the liability is or was incurred (the "third party").

    (3) The third party may bring proceedings to enforce the rights against the insurer without having established the relevant person's liability; but the third party may not enforce those rights without having established that liability.

    (4) For the purposes of this Act, a liability is established only if its existence and amount are established; and, for that purpose, "establish" means establish—

       (a) by virtue of a declaration under section 2 . . .,

       (b) by a judgment or decree,

       (c) by an award in arbitral proceedings or by an arbitration, or

       (d) by an enforceable agreement.

    (5) In this Act—

       (a) references to an "insured" are to a person who incurs or who is subject to a liability to a third party against which that person is insured under a contract of insurance;

       (b) references to a "relevant person" are to a person within sections 4 to 7;

       (c) references to a "third party" are to be construed in accordance with subsection (2);

       (d) references to "transferred rights" are to rights under a contract of insurance which are transferred under this section.

2   Establishing liability in England and Wales and Northern Ireland

    (1) This section applies where a person (P)—

       (a) claims to have rights under a contract of insurance by virtue of a transfer under section 1, but

       (b) has not yet established the insured's liability which is insured under that contract.

    (2) P may bring proceedings against the insurer for either or both of the following—

       (a) a declaration as to the insured's liability to P;

       (b) a declaration as to the insurer's potential liability to P.

    (3) In such proceedings P is entitled, subject to any defence on which the insurer may rely, to a declaration under subsection (2)(a) or (b) on proof of the insured's liability to P or (as the case may be) the insurer's potential liability to P.

    (4) Where proceedings are brought under subsection (2)(a) the insurer may rely on any defence on which the insured could rely if those proceedings were proceedings brought against the insured in respect of the insured's liability to P.

    (5) Subsection (4) is subject to section 12(1).

    (6) Where the court makes a declaration under this section, the effect of which is that the insurer is liable to P, the court may give the appropriate judgment against the insurer.

    (9) When bringing proceedings under subsection (2)(a), P may also make the insured a defendant to those proceedings.

    (10) If (but only if) the insured is a defendant to proceedings under this section (whether by virtue of subsection (9) or otherwise), a declaration under subsection (2) binds the insured as well as the insurer.

    (11) In this section, references to the insurer's potential liability to P are references to the insurer's liability in respect of the insured's liability to P, if established.

4   Individuals

    (1) An individual is a relevant person if any of the following is in force in respect of that individual in England and Wales—

       (a) a deed of arrangement registered in accordance with the Deeds of Arrangement Act 1914,

       (b) an administration order made under Part 6 of the County Courts Act 1984,

       (c) an enforcement restriction order made under Part 6A of that Act,

       (d) subject to subsection (4), a debt relief order made under Part 7A of the Insolvency Act 1986,

    (e) a voluntary arrangement approved in accordance with Part 8 of that Act, or

    (f) a bankruptcy order made under Part 9 of that Act.

(4) If an individual is a relevant person by virtue of subsection (1)(d), that person is a relevant person for the purposes of section 1(1)(b) only.

6 Corporate bodies etc

(1) A body corporate or an unincorporated body is a relevant person if—

    (a) a compromise or arrangement between the body and its creditors (or a class of them) is in force, having been sanctioned in accordance with section 899 of the Companies Act 2006, or

    (b) the body has been dissolved under section 1000, 1001 or 1003 of that Act, and the body has not been—

        (i)   restored to the register by virtue of section 1025 of that Act, or

        (ii) ordered to be restored to the register by virtue of section 1031 of that Act.

(2) A body corporate or an unincorporated body is a relevant person if, in England and Wales . . .—

    (a) a voluntary arrangement approved in accordance with Part 1 of the Insolvency Act 1986 is in force in respect of it,

    (b) an administration order made under Part 2 of that Act is in force in respect of it,

    (c) there is a person appointed in accordance with Part 3 of that Act who is acting as receiver or manager of the body's property (or there would be such a person so acting but for a temporary vacancy),

    (d) the body is, or is being, wound up voluntarily in accordance with Chapter 2 of Part 4 of that Act,

    (e) there is a person appointed under section 135 of that Act who is acting as provisional liquidator in respect of the body (or there would be such a person so acting but for a temporary vacancy), or

    (f) the body is, or is being, wound up by the court following the making of a winding-up order under Chapter 6 of Part 4 of that Act or Part 5 of that Act.

(5) A body within subsection (1)(a) is not a relevant person in relation to a liability that is transferred to another body by the order sanctioning the compromise or arrangement.

(6) Where a body is a relevant person by virtue of subsection (1)(a), section 1 has effect to transfer rights only to a person on whom the compromise or arrangement is binding.

(9) In this section—

    (a) a reference to a person appointed in accordance with Part 3 of the Insolvency Act 1986 includes a reference to a person appointed under section 101 of the Law of Property Act 1925;

    (b) a reference to a receiver or manager of a body's property includes a reference to a receiver or manager of part only of the property and to a receiver only of the income arising from the property or from part of it;

    (c) for the purposes of subsection (3) "body corporate or unincorporated body" includes any entity, other than a trust, the estate of which may be sequestrated under section 6 of the Bankruptcy (Scotland) Act 1985; . . .

8 Limit on rights transferred

Where the liability of an insured to a third party is less than the liability of the insurer to the insured (ignoring the effect of section 1), no rights are transferred under that section in respect of the difference.

10 Insurer's right of set off

(1) This section applies if—

    (a) rights of an insured under a contract of insurance have been transferred to a third party under section 1,

    (b) the insured is under a liability to the insurer under the contract ("the insured's liability"), and

(c) if there had been no transfer, the insurer would have been entitled to set off the amount of the insured's liability against the amount of the insurer's own liability to the insured.

(2) The insurer is entitled to set off the amount of the insured's liability against the amount of the insurer's own liability to the third party in relation to the transferred rights.

14   Effect of transfer on insured's liability

(1) Where rights in respect of an insured's liability to a third party are transferred under section 1, the third party may enforce that liability against the insured only to the extent (if any) that it exceeds the amount recoverable from the insurer by virtue of the transfer.

(2) Subsection (3) applies if a transfer of rights under section 1 occurs because the insured person is a relevant person by virtue of—

(a) section 4(1)(a) or (e), (2)(b) or (3)(b) or (c),

(b) section 6(1)(a), (2)(a), (3)(c) or (4)(a), or

(c) section 7(1)(b).

(3) If the liability is subject to the arrangement, trust deed or compromise by virtue of which the insured is a relevant person, the liability is to be treated as subject to that arrangement, trust deed or compromise only to the extent that the liability exceeds the amount recoverable from the insurer by virtue of the transfer.

(6) For the purposes of this section the amount recoverable from the insurer does not include any amount that the third party is unable to recover as a result of—

(a) a shortage of assets on the insurer's part, in a case where the insurer is a relevant person, or

(b) a limit set by the contract of insurance on the fund available to meet claims in respect of a particular description of liability of the insured.

16   Voluntarily-incurred liabilities

It is irrelevant for the purposes of section 1 whether or not the liability of the insured is or was incurred voluntarily.

17   Avoidance

(1) A contract of insurance to which this section applies is of no effect in so far as it purports, whether directly or indirectly, to avoid or terminate the contract or alter the rights of the parties under it in the event of the insured—

(a) becoming a relevant person, or

(b) dying insolvent (within the meaning given by section 5(2)).

(2) A contract of insurance is one to which this section applies if the insured's rights under it are capable of being transferred under section 1.

Damages (Scotland) Act 2011

(2011, asp 7)

1   Damages to injured person whose expectation of life is diminished

(1) This section applies to an action for damages in respect of personal injuries suffered by a pursuer whose date of death is expected to be earlier than had the injuries not been suffered.

(2) In assessing the amount of damages by way of solatium the court is, if the pursuer—

(a) was at any time,

(b) is, or

(c) is likely to become,

aware of the reduced expectation of life, to have regard to the extent to which the pursuer, in consequence of that awareness, has suffered or is likely to suffer.

(3 Subject to subsection (2), no damages by way of solatium are recoverable by the pursuer in respect of loss of expectation of life.

(4) In making an award of damages by way of solatium, the court is not required to ascribe specifically any part of the award to loss of expectation of life.

(5) In assessing the amount of any patrimonial loss in respect of the period after the date of decree the court is to assume that the pursuer will live until the date when death would have been expected had the injuries not been suffered (the "notional date of death").

(6) Such part of that amount as is attributable to the period between the expected date of death and the notional date of death (the "lost period") is to be assessed as follows—

    (a) the court is to estimate what (if anything) the pursuer would have earned during the lost period through the pursuer's own labour or own gainful activity had the injuries not been suffered,

    (b) the court may, if it thinks fit, add to the amount so estimated (whether or not that amount is nil) an amount equivalent to all or part of what it estimates the pursuer would have received by way of relevant benefits during the lost period had the injuries not been suffered, and

    (c) the court is then to deduct, from the total amount obtained by virtue of paragraphs (a) and (b), 25% of that amount (to represent what would have been the pursuer's living expenses during the lost period had the injuries not been suffered).

(7) But, if satisfied that it is necessary to do so for the purpose of avoiding a manifestly and materially unfair result, the court may apply a different percentage to that specified in subsection (6)(c).

(8) In paragraph (b) of subsection (6), "relevant benefits" means benefits in money or money's worth other than benefits—

    (a) derived from the pursuer's own estate, or

    (b) consisting of such earnings as are mentioned in paragraph (a) of that subsection.

2   Transmission of deceased's rights to executor

(1) There are transmissible to a deceased person's executor ("E") the like rights to damages, including a right to damages for non-patrimonial loss, in respect of injuries suffered by the deceased ("A") and vested in A immediately before A's death, being—

    (a) personal injuries, or

    (b) injuries which, though not personal injuries, are—

        (i)   injuries to name or reputation, or

        (ii)   injuries resulting from harassment actionable under section 8 of the Protection from Harassment Act 1997.

(2) The "like rights" mentioned in subsection (1) do not include any right to damages by way of compensation for patrimonial loss attributable to any period after the date of death; and in determining the amount of damages for non-patrimonial loss payable to E by virtue of this section, the only period to which the court is to have regard is that ending immediately before A's death.

(3) In so far as a right to damages vested in A comprises a right to damages for non-patrimonial loss in respect of such injuries as are mentioned in sub-paragraph (i) of subsection (1)(b), that right is transmissible to E only if an action to enforce the right is brought by A and is not concluded before A's death.

(4) For the purposes of subsection (3) an action is not to be taken to be concluded—

    (a) while an appeal is competent, or

    (b) before any appeal taken is disposed of.

3   Application of sections 4 to 6

Sections 4 to 6 apply where a person ("A") dies in consequence of suffering personal injuries as the result of the act or omission of another person ("B") and the act or omission—

    (a) gives rise to liability to pay damages to A (or to A's executor), or

    (b) would have given rise to such liability but for A's death.

4   Sums of damages payable to relatives

(1) B is liable under this subsection to pay—

(a) to any relative of A who is a member of A's immediate family, such sums of damages as are mentioned in paragraphs (a) and (b) of subsection (3),

(b) to any other relative of A, such sum of damages as is mentioned in paragraph (a) of that subsection.

(2) But, except as provided for in section 5, no such liability arises if the liability to pay damages to A (or to A's executor) in respect of the act or omission—

(a) is excluded or discharged, whether by antecedent agreement or otherwise, by A before A's death, or

(b) is excluded by virtue of an enactment.

(3) The sums of damages are—

(a) such sum as will compensate for any loss of support which as a result of the act or omission is sustained, or is likely to be sustained, by the relative after the date of A's death together with any reasonable expenses incurred by the relative in connection with A's funeral, and

(b) such sum, if any, as the court thinks just by way of compensation for all or any of the following—

(i)   distress and anxiety endured by the relative in contemplation of the suffering of A before A's death,

(ii) grief and sorrow of the relative caused by A's death,

(iii) the loss of such non-patrimonial benefit as the relative might have been expected to derive from A's society and guidance if A had not died.

(4) The court, in making an award under paragraph (b) of subsection (3) is not required to ascribe any part of the award specifically to any of the sub-paragraphs of that paragraph.

(5) For the purpose of subsection (1)(a)—

(a) a relative of A is a member of A's immediate family if the relative falls within any of paragraphs (a) to (d) of the definition of "relative" in section 14(1),

(b) paragraphs (a)(i) and (b) of section 14(2) are to be disregarded.

5   Discharge of liability to pay damages: exception for mesothelioma

(1) This section applies where—

(a) the liability to pay damages to A (or to A's executor) is discharged, whether by antecedent agreement or otherwise, by A before A's death,

(b) the personal injury in consequence of which A died is mesothelioma, and

(c) the discharge and the death each occurred on or after 20th December 2006.

(2) Liability arises under section 4(1) but is limited to the payment of such sum of damages as is mentioned in paragraph (b) of section 4(3).

6   Relative's loss of personal services

(1) A relative entitled to damages under paragraph (a) of section 4(3) is entitled to include, as a head of damages under that paragraph, a reasonable sum in respect of the loss to the relative of A's personal services as a result of the act or omission.

(2) In subsection (1), "personal services" has the same meaning as in section 9(1) of the Administration of Justice Act 1982 (damages in respect of inability of injured person to render such services).

7   Assessment of compensation for loss of support

(1) Such part of an award under paragraph (a) of section 4(3) as consists of a sum in compensation for loss of support is to be assessed applying the following paragraphs—

(a) the total amount to be available to support A's relatives is an amount equivalent to 75% of A's net income,

(b) in the case of any other relative than—

(i)   a person described in paragraph (a) of the definition of "relative" in section 14(1), or

    (ii) a dependent child,

the relative is not to be awarded more in compensation for loss of support than the actual amount of that loss,

  (c) if—

    (i)   no such other relative is awarded a sum in compensation for loss of support, the total amount mentioned in paragraph (a) is to be taken to be spent by A in supporting such of A's relatives as are mentioned in sub-paragraphs (i) and (ii) of paragraph (b),

    (ii) any such other relative is awarded a sum in compensation for loss of support, the total amount mentioned in paragraph (a) is, after deduction of the amount of the sum so awarded, to be taken to be spent by A in supporting such of A's relatives as are mentioned in those sub-paragraphs, and

  (d) any multiplier applied by the court—

    (i)   is to run from the date of the interlocutor awarding damages, and

    (ii) is to apply only in respect of future loss of support.

(2) But, if satisfied that it is necessary to do so for the purpose of avoiding a manifestly and materially unfair result, the court may apply a different percentage to that specified in subsection (1)(a).

(3) In subsection (1)(b)(ii), "dependent child" means a child who as at the date of A's death—

  (a) has not attained the age of 18 years, and

  (b) is owed an obligation of aliment by A.

8 Further provision as regards relative's entitlement to damages

(1) Subject to subsection (3), in assessing for the purposes of section 4 or 6 the amount of any loss of support sustained by a relative of A no account is to be taken of—

  (a) any patrimonial gain or advantage which has accrued or will or may accrue to the relative, by way of succession or settlement, from A or from any other person, or

  (b) any insurance money, benefit, pension or gratuity which has been, or will or may be, paid as a result of A's death.

(2) In subsection (1)—

"benefit" means benefit under the Social Security Contributions and Benefits Act 1992 (c.4) or the Social Security Contributions and Benefits (Northern Ireland) Act 1992 (c.7) and any payment by a friendly society or trade union for the relief or maintenance of a member's dependants,

"insurance money" includes a return of premiums, and

"pension" includes a return of contributions and any payment of a lump sum in respect of a person's employment.

(3) Where A has been awarded a provisional award of damages under section 12(2) of the Administration of Justice Act 1982, the making of that award does not prevent liability from arising under section 4(1); but in assessing for the purposes of section 4 or 6 the amount of any loss of support sustained by a relative the court is to take into account such part of the provisional award relating to future patrimonial loss as was intended to compensate A for a period beyond the date on which A died.

(4) In order to establish loss of support for the purposes of section 4 or 6, it is not essential for a relative to show that A was, or might have become, subject to a duty in law to provide support for, or contribute to the support of, the relative; but if any such fact is established it may be taken into account in determining whether, and if so to what extent, A would (had A not died) have been likely to provide, or contribute to, such support.

(5) Except as provided for in this Act or in any other enactment, no person is entitled by reason of relationship to damages in respect of the death of another person.

(6) In subsection (5), "damages" includes damages by way of solatium.

9 Transmission of relative's rights to executor

(1) This section applies where liability to pay damages to a relative ("R") has arisen under section 4 or 6 but R dies.

(2) If the right to damages is vested in R immediately before R's death that right is transmissible to R's executor ("E"); but in determining the amount of damages payable to E by virtue of this section, the only period to which the court is to have regard is the period ending immediately before R's death.

(3) In a case where—

(a) section 5 applies, and

(b) R died before 27th April 2007,

any right of R to damages under that section is to be taken, for the purposes of subsection (2), to have vested in R on A's death.

10 Enforcement by executor of rights transmitted under section 2 or 9

(1) Where a right is transmitted by virtue of section 2 or 9, the executor in question is entitled—

(a) to bring an action to enforce it, or

(b) if an action to enforce it was brought by the deceased but not concluded before the date of death, to be sisted as pursuer in that action.

(2) For the purposes of subsection (1)(b) an action is not to be taken to be concluded—

(a) while an appeal is competent, or

(b) before any appeal taken is disposed of.

11 Executor's claim not excluded by relative's claim etc

(1) A claim made by virtue of this Act by a deceased's executor is not excluded by a claim so made by a relative of the deceased (or by such a relative's executor).

(2) Nor is a claim so made by a such a relative (or by such a relative's executor) excluded by a claim so made by the deceased's executor.

12 Limitation of total amount of liability

(1) This section applies to an action directed against a defender ("B") in which, following the death of a person ("A") from personal injuries, damages are claimed—

(a) in respect of those injuries, by A's executor, or

(b) in respect of A's death, by any relative of A or by the executor of any relative of A.

(2) If it is shown that the liability arising in relation to B from the personal injuries in question—

(a) had before A's death, by antecedent agreement or otherwise, been limited to damages of a specified or ascertainable amount, or

(b) is so limited by virtue of an enactment,

nothing in this Act makes B liable to pay damages exceeding that amount.

(3) Accordingly, where there are two or more pursuers, any damages to which they would (but for this section) respectively be entitled under this Act are, if necessary, to be reduced pro rata.

(4) And where two or more actions are conjoined the conjoined actions are to be treated, for the purposes of this section, as if they were a single action.

14 Interpretation

(1) In this Act, unless the context otherwise requires—

"personal injuries" means—

(a) any disease, and

(b) any impairment of a person's physical or mental condition, and

"relative", in relation to a person who has died, means a person who—

(a) immediately before the death is the deceased's spouse or civil partner or is living with the deceased as if married to, or in civil partnership with, the deceased,

(b) is a parent or child of the deceased, accepted the deceased as a child of the person's family or was accepted by the deceased as a child of the deceased's family,

(c) is the brother or sister of the deceased or was brought up in the same household as the deceased and accepted as a child of the family in which the deceased was a child,

(d) is a grandparent or grandchild of the deceased, accepted the deceased as a grandchild of the person or was accepted by the deceased as a grandchild of the deceased,

(e) is an ascendant or descendant of the deceased (other than a parent or grandparent or a child or grandchild of the deceased),

(f) is an uncle or aunt of the deceased,

(g) is a child or other issue of—

    (i) a brother or sister of the deceased, or

    (ii) an uncle or aunt of the deceased, or

(h) is a former spouse or civil partner of the deceased having become so by virtue of divorce or (as the case may be) dissolution of the partnership.

(2) In deducing a relationship for the purposes of the definition of "relative" in subsection (1)—

(a) any relationship—

    (i) by affinity is to be treated as a relationship by consanguinity,

    (ii) of the half blood is to be treated as a relationship of the whole blood,

(b) a stepchild of a person is to be treated as the person's child.

(3) In any enactment passed or made before this Act, unless the context otherwise requires, any reference to——

(a) solatium in respect of the death of any person (however expressed), or

(b) a loss of society award,

is to be construed as a reference to an award under paragraph (b) of section 4(3).

Part II

Proposed Statutes

(Draft) Negligence (Psychiatric Illness) Bill

(Law Com. No. 249)

An Act to amend and clarify the law relating to liability in negligence for psychiatric illness.   [1998]

New duties of care

1 Close tie: duty of care

(1) Subsection (2) imposes a duty of care for the purposes of the tort of negligence, and that subsection has effect subject to (and only to) subsections (3) to (6).

(2) A person (the defendant) owes a duty to take reasonable care to avoid causing another person (the plaintiff) to suffer a recognisable psychiatric illness as a result of the death, injury or imperilment of a third person (the immediate victim) if it is reasonably foreseeable that the defendant's act or omission might cause the plaintiff to suffer such an illness.

(3) The defendant must be taken not to have owed the duty unless—

    (a) his act or omission caused the death, injury or imperilment of the immediate victim, and

    (b) the plaintiff and the immediate victim had a close tie of love and affection immediately before the act or omission occurred or immediately before the onset of the plaintiff's illness (or both).

(4) The duty is not imposed if the court is satisfied that its imposition would not be just and reasonable—

    (a) because of any factor by virtue of which the defendant owed no duty of care to the immediate victim,

    (b) because the immediate victim voluntarily accepted the risk that the defendant's act or omission might cause his death, injury or imperilment, or

    (c) because the plaintiff was involved in conduct which is illegal or contrary to public policy.

(5) The duty is not imposed if the plaintiff—

    (a) voluntarily accepted the risk of suffering the illness, or

    (b) excluded the duty.

(6) The duty is not imposed if a provision which is contained in or made under another enactment, or which has the force of law by virtue of another enactment, regulates the defendant's duty to the plaintiff as regards the act or omission in place of the common law rules of the tort of negligence.

2 Close tie: duty of care if defendant is victim

(1) Subsection (2) imposes a duty of care for the purposes of the tort of negligence, and that subsection has effect subject to (and only to) subsections (3) to (6).

(2) A person (the defendant) owes a duty to take reasonable care to avoid causing another person (the plaintiff) to suffer a recognisable psychiatric illness as a result of the death, injury or imperilment of the defendant if it is reasonably foreseeable that the defendant's act or omission might cause the plaintiff to suffer such an illness.

(3) The defendant must be taken not to have owed the duty unless—

    (a) his act or omission caused his death, injury or imperilment, and

    (b) the plaintiff and the defendant had a close tie of love and affection immediately before the act or omission occurred or immediately before the onset of the plaintiff's illness (or both).

(4) The duty is not imposed if the court is satisfied that its imposition would not be just and reasonable—

    (a) because the defendant chose to cause his death, injury or imperilment, or

    (b) because the plaintiff was involved in conduct which is illegal or contrary to public policy.

(5) The duty is not imposed if the plaintiff—

    (a) voluntarily accepted the risk of suffering the illness, or

    (b) excluded the duty.

(6) The duty is not imposed if a provision which is contained in or made under another enactment, or which has the force of law by virtue of another enactment, regulates the defendant's duty to the plaintiff as regards the act or omission in place of the common law rules of the tort of negligence.

3 Meaning of close tie

(1) Subsections (2) to (5) have effect to determine whether for the purposes of section 1 the plaintiff and the immediate victim had a close tie of love and affection at a particular time.

(2) If at the time concerned the plaintiff fell within any of the categories listed in subsection (4) he and the immediate victim must be conclusively taken to have had a close tie of love and affection at that time.

(3) Otherwise it is for the plaintiff to show that he and the immediate victim had a close tie of love and affection at the time concerned.

(4) The categories are—

    (a) the immediate victim's spouse;

    (b) either parent of the immediate victim;

    (c) any child of the immediate victim;

    (d) any brother or sister of the immediate victim;

    (e) the immediate victim's cohabitant.

(5) The plaintiff was the immediate victim's cohabitant at the time concerned if and only if—

    (a) though not married to each other, they lived together as man and wife for a period of at least two years immediately before the time concerned, or

    (b) though of the same gender, they had a relationship equivalent to that described in paragraph (a) for such a period.

(6) Subsections (2) to (5) also have effect to determine whether for the purposes of section 2 the plaintiff and the defendant had a close tie of love and affection at a particular time, reading references in those subsections to the immediate victim as references to the defendant.

Common law duty of care

4 Close tie: abolition of common law duty

The common law duty of care under the tort of negligence is abolished to the extent that (apart from this section)—

    (a) it would arise in respect of a recognisable psychiatric illness suffered by a person (A) as a result of the death, injury or imperilment of another (B),

    (b) it would depend on the existence of a close tie of love and affection between A and B, and

    (c) it would be imposed on the person (whether B or a third person) causing the death, injury or imperilment.

5   Removal of certain restrictions

(1) This section amends and clarifies the law relating to a claim which—

    (a) Is founded on the common law duty of care under the tort of negligence, and

    (b) is made in respect of a recognisable psychiatric illness.

(2) It is not a condition of the claim's success that the illness was induced by a shock.

(3) The court may allow the claim even if the illness results from the defendant causing his own death, injury or imperilment.

(Draft) Unfair Contract Terms Bill

(Law Com. No. 292; Scot. Law Com. No. 199)

A Bill to limit the exclusion or restriction of civil liability by contract terms or notices; to limit the effect of unfair terms in consumer and small business contracts; to make provision about the protection of the collective interests of consumers; and for connected purposes. [2005]

PART 1 BUSINESS LIABILITY FOR NEGLIGENCE

1   Business liability for negligence

(1) Business liability for death or personal injury resulting from negligence cannot be excluded or restricted by a contract term or a notice.

(2) Business liability for other loss or damage resulting from negligence cannot be excluded or restricted by a contract term or a notice unless the term or notice is fair and reasonable.

(3) 'Business liability' means liability arising from—

    (a) anything that was or should have been done for purposes related to a business, or

    (b) the occupation of premises used for purposes related to the occupier's business.

(4) The reference in subsection (3)(a) to anything done for purposes related to a business includes anything done by an employee of that business within the scope of his employment.

(5) 'Negligence' means the breach of—

    (a) an obligation to take reasonable care or exercise reasonable skill in the performance of a contract where the obligation arises from an express or implied term of the contract,

    (b) a common law duty to take reasonable care or exercise reasonable skill,

    (c) the common duty of care imposed by the Occupiers' Liability Act 1957 (c. 31) or the Occupiers' Liability Act (Northern Ireland) 1957 (c. 25 NI), or

    (d) the duty of reasonable care imposed by section 2(1) of the Occupiers' Liability (Scotland) Act 1960 (c. 30).

(6) It does not matter—

    (a) whether a breach of obligation or duty was, or was not, inadvertent, or

    (b) whether liability for it arises directly or vicariously.

2   Exceptions to section 1

(1) Section 1 does not prevent an employee from excluding or restricting his liability for negligence to his employer.

(2) Section 1 does not apply to the business liability of an occupier of premises to a person who obtains access to the premises for recreational or educational purposes if—

    (a) that person suffers loss or damage because of the dangerous state of the premises, and

    (b) allowing that person access to those premises for those purposes is not within the purposes of the occupier's business.

(3) Subsection (2) does not extend to Scotland.

3 Voluntary acceptance of risk

The defence that a person voluntarily accepted a risk cannot be used against him just because he agreed to or knew about a contract term, or a notice, appearing to exclude or restrict business liability for negligence in the case in question.

PART 2 CONSUMER CONTRACTS

Contracts in general

4 Terms of no effect unless fair and reasonable

(1) If a term of a consumer contract is detrimental to the consumer, the business cannot rely on the term unless the term is fair and reasonable.

(2) But subsection (1) does not apply to a term which defines the main subject-matter of a consumer contract, if the definition is—

(a) transparent, and

(b) substantially the same as the definition the consumer reasonably expected.

(3) Nor does subsection (1) apply to a term in so far as it sets the price payable under a consumer contract, if the price is—

(a) transparent,

(b) payable in circumstances substantially the same as those the consumer reasonably expected, and

(c) calculated in a way substantially the same as the way the consumer reasonably expected.

(4) Nor does subsection (1) apply to a term which—

(a) is transparent, and

(b) leads to substantially the same result as would be produced as a matter of law if the term were not included.

(5) The reference to the price payable under a consumer contract does not include any amount, payment of which would be incidental or ancillary to the main purpose of the contract.

(6) 'Price' includes remuneration.

Sale or supply of goods

5 Sale or supply to consumer

(1) This section applies to a consumer contract for the sale or supply of goods to the consumer.

(2) In the case of a contract for the sale of the goods, the business cannot rely on a term of the contract to exclude or restrict liability arising under any of the following sections of the 1979 Act—

(a) section 12 (implied term that seller entitled to sell),

(b) section 13 (implied term that goods match description),

(c) section 14 (implied term that goods satisfactory and fit for the purpose),

(d) section 15 (implied term that goods match sample).

(3) In the case of a contract for the hire-purchase of the goods, the business cannot rely on a term of the contract to exclude or restrict liability arising under any of the following sections of the 1973 Act—

(a) section 8 (implied term that supplier entitled to supply),

(b) section 9 (implied term that goods match description),

(c) section 10 (implied term that goods satisfactory and fit for the purpose),

(d) section 11 (implied term that goods match sample).

(4) In the case of any other contract for the transfer of property in the goods, the business cannot rely on a term of the contract to exclude or restrict liability arising under any of the following sections of the 1982 Act—

(a) section 2 or 11B (implied term that supplier entitled to supply),

(b) section 3 or 11C (implied term that goods match description),

(c) section 4 or 11D (implied term that goods satisfactory and fit for the purpose),

(d) section 5 or 11E (implied term that goods match sample).

(5) In the case of a contract for the hire of the goods, the business cannot rely on a term of the contract to exclude or restrict liability arising under any of the following sections of the 1982 Act—

(a) section 8 or 11I (implied term that goods match description),

(b) section 9 or 11J (implied term that goods satisfactory and fit for the purpose),

(c) section 10 or 11K (implied term that goods match sample).

(6) Subsection (2)(b) to (d) does not apply if the contract is—

(a) for the sale of second-hand goods, and

(b) made at a public auction which the consumer had the opportunity to attend in person.

6   Sale or supply to business

(1) This section applies to a consumer contract for the sale or supply of goods to the business.

(2) In the case of a contract for the sale of the goods, the consumer cannot rely on a term of the contract to exclude or restrict liability—

(a) arising under section 12 of the 1979 Act (implied term that seller entitled to sell), or

(b) unless the term is fair and reasonable, arising under either of the following sections of that Act—

(i) section 13 (implied term that goods match description),

(ii) section 15 (implied term that goods match sample).

(3) In the case of a contract for the hire-purchase of the goods, the consumer cannot rely on a term of the contract to exclude or restrict liability—

(a) arising under section 8 of the 1973 Act (implied term that supplier entitled to supply), or

(b) unless the term is fair and reasonable, arising under either of the following sections of that Act—

(i) section 9 (implied term that goods match description),

(ii) section 11 (implied term that goods match sample).

Supplemental

7   Regulation and enforcement

Schedule 1 confers functions on the OFT and regulators in relation to—

(a) consumer contract terms,

(b) terms drawn up or proposed for use as consumer contract terms,

(c) terms which a trade association recommends for use as consumer contract terms, and

(d) notices relating to the rights conferred or duties imposed by consumer contracts.

8   Ambiguity

(1) If it is reasonable to read a written term of a consumer contract in two (or more) ways, the term is to be read in whichever of those ways it is reasonable to think the more (or the most) favourable to the consumer.

(2) This section does not apply in relation to proceedings under Schedule 1 (regulation and enforcement of consumer contract terms, etc.).

PART 3   NON-CONSUMER CONTRACTS

Business contracts

9   Written standard terms

(1) This section applies where one party to a business contract ('A') deals on the written standard terms of business of the other ('B').

(2) Unless the term is fair and reasonable, B cannot rely on any of those terms to exclude or restrict its liability to A for breach of the contract.

(3) Unless the term is fair and reasonable, B cannot rely on any of those terms to claim that it has the right—

    (a) to carry out its obligations under the contract in a way substantially different from the way in which A reasonably expected them to be carried out, or

    (b) not to carry out all or part of those obligations.

10 Sale or supply of goods

(1) In the case of a business contract for the sale of goods, the seller cannot rely on a term of the contract to exclude or restrict liability arising under section 12 of the 1979 Act (implied term that seller entitled to sell).

(2) In the case of a business contract for the hire-purchase of goods, the supplier cannot rely on a term of the contract to exclude or restrict liability arising under section 8 of the 1973 Act (implied term that supplier entitled to supply).

(3) In the case of any other business contract for the transfer of property in goods, the supplier cannot rely on a term of the contract to exclude or restrict liability arising under section 2 or 11B of the 1982 Act (implied term that supplier entitled to supply).

Small business contracts

11 Non-negotiated terms

(1) This section applies where there is a small business contract and—

    (a) the terms on which one party ('A') deals include a term which the other party ('B') put forward during the negotiation of the contract as one of its written standard terms of business,

    (b) the substance of the term was not, as a result of negotiation, changed in favour of A, and

    (c) at the time the contract is made, A is a small business.

(2) If that term is detrimental to A, B cannot rely on the term unless the term is fair and reasonable.

(3) But subsection (2) does not apply to a term which defines the main subject-matter of a small business contract, if the definition is—

    (a) transparent, and

    (b) substantially the same as the definition A reasonably expected.

(4) Nor does subsection (2) apply to a term in so far as it sets the price payable under a small business contract, if the price is—

    (a) transparent,

    (b) payable in circumstances substantially the same as those A reasonably expected, and

    (c) calculated in a way substantially the same as the way A reasonably expected.

(5) Nor does subsection (2) apply to a term which—

    (a) is transparent, and

    (b) leads to substantially the same result as would be produced as a matter of law if the term were not included.

(6) The reference to the price payable under a small business contract does not include any amount, payment of which would be incidental or ancillary to the main purpose of the contract.

(7) 'Price' includes remuneration.

Employment contracts

12 Written standard terms

(1) This section applies in relation to an employment contract under which an individual ('the employee') is employed by a business on its written standard terms of employment.

(2) Unless the term is fair and reasonable, the business cannot rely on any of those terms to exclude or restrict its liability for breach of the contract.

(3) Unless the term is fair and reasonable, the business cannot rely on any of those terms to claim it has the right—

(a) to carry out its obligations under the contract in a way substantially different from the way in which the employee reasonably expected them to be carried out, or

(b) not to carry out all or part of those obligations.

Private contracts

13   Sale or supply of goods

(1) This section applies if neither party to a contract for the sale or supply of goods enters into it for purposes related to a business of his.

(2) In the case of a contract for the sale of the goods, the seller cannot rely on a term of the contract to exclude or restrict liability—

(a) arising under section 12 of the 1979 Act (implied term that seller entitled to sell), or

(b) unless the term is fair and reasonable, arising under either of the following sections of that Act—

(i)   section 13 (implied term that goods match description),

(ii) section 15 (implied term that goods match sample).

(3) In the case of a contract for the hire-purchase of the goods, the supplier cannot rely on a term of the contract to exclude or restrict liability—

(a) arising under section 8 of the 1973 Act (implied term that supplier entitled to supply), or

(b) unless the term is fair and reasonable, arising under either of the following sections of that Act—

(i)   section 9 (implied term that goods match description),

(ii) section 11 (implied term that goods match sample).

PART 4 THE 'FAIR AND REASONABLE' TEST

The test

14   The test

(1) Whether a contract term is fair and reasonable is to be determined by taking into account—

(a) the extent to which the term is transparent, and

(b) the substance and effect of the term, and all the circumstances existing at the time it was agreed.

(2) Whether a notice is fair and reasonable is to be determined by taking into account—

(a) the extent to which the notice is transparent, and

(b) the substance and effect of the notice, and all the circumstances existing at the time when the liability arose (or, but for the notice, would have arisen).

(3) 'Transparent' means—

(a) expressed in reasonably plain language,

(b) legible,

(c) presented clearly, and

(d) readily available to any person likely to be affected by the contract term or notice in question.

(4) Matters relating to the substance and effect of a contract term, and to all the circumstances existing at the time it was agreed, include the following—

(a) the other terms of the contract,

(b) the terms of any other contract on which the contract depends,

(c) the balance of the parties' interests,

(d) the risks to the party adversely affected by the term,

(e) the possibility and probability of insurance,

(f) other ways in which the interests of the party adversely affected by the term might have been protected,

    (g) the extent to which the term (whether alone or with others) differs from what would have been the case in its absence,

    (h) the knowledge and understanding of the party adversely affected by the term,

    (i) the strength of the parties' bargaining positions,

    (j) the nature of the goods or services to which the contract relates.

(5) Subsection (4) applies, with any necessary modifications, in relation to a notice as it applies in relation to a contract term.

(6) Schedule 2 contains an indicative and non-exhaustive list of consumer contract terms and small business contract terms which may be regarded as not being fair and reasonable.

(7) The Secretary of State may by order amend Schedule 2 so as to add, modify or omit an entry.

Burden of proof

15 Business liability for negligence

It is for a person wishing to rely on a contract term or a notice which purports to exclude or restrict liability of the kind mentioned in section 1(2) (business liability for negligence other than in case of death or personal injury) to prove that the term or notice is fair and reasonable.

16 Consumer contracts

(1) If an issue is raised as to whether a term in a consumer contract is fair and reasonable, it is for the business to prove that it is.

(2) But in proceedings under Schedule 1 (regulation and enforcement of consumer contracts) it is for a person claiming that a term in a consumer contract, or a notice, is not fair and reasonable to prove that it is not.

(3) It is for a person wishing to rely on a contract not being a consumer contract to prove that it is not.

17 Business contracts

(1) It is for a person wishing to rely on a term of a business contract to prove that the term is fair and reasonable.

(2) But in relation to a term to which section 11(2) (non-negotiated terms in small business contracts) applies, it is for a person claiming that the term is not fair and reasonable to prove that it is not.

. . .

PART 6 MISCELLANEOUS AND SUPPLEMENTARY

Miscellaneous

21 Unfairness issue raised by court

A court may, in proceedings before it, raise an issue about whether a contract term or a notice is fair and reasonable even if none of the parties to the proceedings has raised the issue or indicated that it intends to raise it.

22 Exceptions

Schedule 3 sets out types of contract, and of contract term, to which this Act does not apply or to which specified provisions of this Act do not apply.

23 Secondary contracts

(1) A term of a contract ('the secondary contract') which reduces the rights or remedies, or increases the obligations, of a person under another contract ('the main contract') is subject to the provisions of this Act that would apply to the term if it were in the main contract.

(2) It does not matter for the purposes of this section whether the parties to the secondary contract are the same as the parties to the main contract.

(3) This section does not apply if the secondary contract is a settlement of a claim arising under the main contract.

24   Effect of unfair term on contract

Where a contract term cannot be relied on by a person as a result of this Act, the contract continues, so far as practicable, to have effect in every other respect.

Interpretation, etc.

25   Preliminary

Sections 26 to 32 define or otherwise explain expressions for the purposes of this Act.

26   'Consumer contract' and 'business contract'

    (1) 'Consumer contract' means a contract (other than one of employment) between—

        (a) an individual ('the consumer') who enters into it wholly or mainly for purposes unrelated to a business of his, and

        (b) a person ('the business') who enters into it wholly or mainly for purposes related to his business.

    (2) 'Business contract' means a contract between two persons, each of whom enters into it wholly or mainly for purposes related to his business.

27   'Small business'

    (1) 'Small business' means a person in whose business the number of employees does not exceed—

        (a) nine, or

        (b) where the Secretary of State specifies by order another number for the purposes of this section, that number.

    (2) But a person is not a small business if adding the number of employees in his business to the number of employees in any other business of his, or in any business of an associated person, gives a total exceeding the number which for the time being applies for the purposes of subsection (1).

    (3) A reference to the number of employees in a business is to the number calculated according to Schedule 4.

28   'Associated person'

    (1) For the purposes of this Act, two persons are associated if—

        (a) one controls the other, or

        (b) both are controlled by the same person.

    (2) A person ('A') controls a body corporate ('B') if A can secure that B's affairs are conducted according to A's wishes, directions or instructions.

    (3) The reference in subsection (2) to wishes, directions or instructions does not include advice given in a professional capacity.

    (4) Subsection (2) applies, with any necessary modifications, in relation to an unincorporated association (other than a partnership) as it applies in relation to a body corporate.

    (5) A person controls a partnership if he has the right to a share of more than half the assets or income of the partnership.

    (6) For the purposes of this section, one person does not control another just because he grants that other person a right to supply goods or services.

29   'Small business contract'

    (1) 'Small business contract' means a business contract—

        (a) to which at least one of the parties is, at the time the contract is made, a small business, and

        (b) which does not come within any of four exceptions.

    (2) The first exception is that the price payable under the contract exceeds £500,000.

    (3) The second is that—

    (a) the transaction provided for by the contract forms part of a larger transaction, or part of a scheme or arrangement, and

    (b) the total price payable in respect of the larger transaction, or the scheme or arrangement, exceeds £500,000.

(4) The third is that—

    (a) a person agrees to carry on a regulated activity under the contract, and

    (b) he is an authorised person or, in relation to that activity, an exempt person.

(5) The fourth is that the contract is a series contract.

(6) A contract is a series contract if—

    (a) the transaction provided for by the contract forms part of a series, and

    (b) during the period of two years ending with the date of the contract, the total price payable under contracts providing for transactions in the series exceeds £500,000.

(7) A contract is also a series contract if, at the time the contract was made, both parties intended that—

    (a) the transaction provided for by the contract would form part of a series, and

    (b) the total price payable under contracts providing for transactions in the series and made during any period of two years, would exceed £500,000.

(8) Where a contract is a series contract, every subsequent contract providing for a transaction in the series is a series contract.

(9) The Secretary of State may by order vary the amount specified in subsections (2), (3), (6) and (7).

(10) 'Authorised person', 'exempt person' and 'regulated activity' have the same meaning as in the Financial Services and Markets Act 2000 (c. 8).

30 'Excluding or restricting liability'

(1) A reference to excluding or restricting a liability includes—

    (a) making a right or remedy in respect of the liability subject to a restrictive or onerous condition;

    (b) excluding or restricting a right or remedy in respect of the liability;

    (c) putting a person at a disadvantage if he pursues a right or remedy in respect of the liability;

    (d) excluding or restricting rules of evidence or procedure.

(2) A reference in Part 1 or section 5, 6, 10 or 13 to excluding or restricting a liability includes preventing an obligation or duty arising or limiting its extent.

(3) A written agreement to submit current or future differences to arbitration is not to be regarded as excluding or restricting the liability in question.

31 'Hire-purchase' and 'hire'

(1) A reference to a contract for the hire-purchase of goods is to a hire-purchase agreement within the meaning of the Consumer Credit Act 1974 (c. 39).

(2) A reference to a contract for the hire of goods is to be read with the 1982 Act.

32 General interpretation

(1) In this Act—

'the 1973 Act' means the Supply of Goods (Implied Terms) Act 1973 (c. 13),

'the 1979 Act' means the Sale of Goods Act 1979 (c. 54),

'the 1982 Act' means the Supply of Goods and Services Act 1982 (c. 29),

'associated person' has the meaning given in section 28,

'business contract' has the meaning given in section 26(2),

'business liability' has the meaning given in section 1(3) and (4),

'consumer', in relation to a party to a consumer contract, has the meaning given by section 26(1)(a),

'consumer contract' has the meaning given in section 26(1),

'court' means—

   (a) in England and Wales and Northern Ireland, the High Court or a county court, and

   (b) in Scotland, the Court of Session or a sheriff,

and, except in Schedule 1, includes a tribunal, arbitrator or arbiter,

'enactment' includes—

   (a) a provision of, or of an instrument made under, an Act of the Scottish Parliament or Northern Ireland legislation, and

   (b) a provision of subordinate legislation (within the meaning of the Interpretation Act 1978 (c. 30)),

'fair and reasonable', in relation to a contract term or a notice, has the meaning given in section 14,

'goods' has the same meaning as in the 1979 Act,

'injunction' includes interim injunction,

'interdict' includes interim interdict,

'negligence' has the meaning given in section 1(5),

'notice' includes an announcement, whether or not in writing, and any other communication,

'the OFT' means the Office of Fair Trading,

'personal injury' includes any disease and any impairment of physical or mental condition,

'public authority' has the same meaning as in section 6 of the Human Rights Act 1998 (c. 42),

'regulator' has the meaning given in paragraph 10 of Schedule 1,

'small business' has the meaning given in section 27,

'small business contract' has the meaning given in section 29,

'statutory' means conferred by an enactment,

'supplier', in relation to a contract for the hire-purchase of goods or a contract for the hire of goods, means the person by whom goods are bailed or (in Scotland) hired to another person under the contract, and

'transparent' has the meaning given in section 14(3).

   (2) A reference to a business includes a profession and the activities of a public authority.

   (3) A reference to excluding or restricting liability is to be read with section 30.

   (4) A reference to a contract for the hire-purchase or hire of goods is to be read with section 31.

Final provisions

33 Orders

   (1) Any power of the Secretary of State to make an order under this Act is exercisable by statutory instrument.

   (2) A statutory instrument containing an order under this Act, other than one containing an order under section 35 (commencement), is subject to annulment in pursuance of a resolution of either House of Parliament.

34 Consequential amendments and repeals, etc.

   (1) Schedule 5 contains minor and consequential amendments.

   (2) Schedule 6 contains repeals and revocations.

35 Short title, commencement and extent

   (1) This Act may be cited as the Unfair Contract Terms Act 2005.

   (2) The preceding provisions come into force on such day as the Secretary of State may by order appoint.

   (3) Different days may be appointed for different provisions.

   (4) No provision of this Act applies in relation to a contract term agreed before the commencement of the provision (except in so far as the term has been varied after that commencement).

   (5) An amendment, repeal or revocation contained in Schedule 5 or 6 has the same extent as the enactment to which it relates.

   (6) This Act extends to Northern Ireland.

Section 7

SCHEDULE 1

CONSUMER CONTRACT TERMS, ETC.: REGULATION AND ENFORCEMENT

1   Cases where this Schedule applies

(1) This Schedule applies to a complaint about—

    (a) a consumer contract term,

    (b) a term drawn up or proposed for use as a consumer contract term, or

    (c) a term which a trade association recommends for use as a consumer contract term.

(2) This Schedule also applies to a complaint about—

    (a) a notice relating to the rights conferred or duties imposed by a consumer contract on the parties, or

    (b) any other notice purporting to exclude or restrict liability for negligence.

2   Consideration of complaints

(1) If the OFT receives a complaint to which this Schedule applies, it must consider the complaint unless—

    (a) it thinks that the complaint is frivolous or vexatious,

    (b) it is notified by a regulator that that regulator intends to consider the complaint, or

    (c) in the case of a complaint under paragraph 1(2)(b), it thinks that sub-paragraph (2) applies in relation to the notice.

(2) This sub-paragraph applies in relation to a notice which—

    (a) does not exclude or restrict business liability for negligence, or

    (b) excludes or restricts such liability only in relation to a person who, at the time when the liability arises, is acting for purposes related to a business.

(3) If the regulator intends to consider a complaint to which this Schedule applies, it must—

    (a) notify the OFT that it intends to consider the complaint, and

    (b) consider the complaint.

3   Application for injunction or interdict

(1) The OFT (or a regulator) may apply for an injunction or interdict against such persons as it considers appropriate if it thinks that the term or notice to which the complaint relates comes within this paragraph.

(2) A term or notice comes within this paragraph if it purports to exclude or restrict liability of the kind mentioned in—

    (a) section 1(1) (business liability for death or personal injury resulting from negligence), or

    (b) section 5 (implied terms in supply of goods to consumer).

(3) A term or notice also comes within this paragraph if it—

    (a) is drawn up for general use, and

    (b) is not fair and reasonable.

(4) A term also comes within this paragraph if—

    (a) however it is expressed, it is in its effect a term of a kind which the business usually seeks to include in the kind of consumer contract in question, and

    (b) it is not fair and reasonable.

(5) A term which comes within paragraph 1(b) or (c) (but not within paragraph 1(a)) is to be treated for the purposes of section 14 (the 'fair and reasonable' test) as if it were a contract term.

4   Notification of application

(1) If a regulator intends to make an application under paragraph 3—

    (a) it must notify the OFT of its intention, and

    (b) it may make the application only if this paragraph applies.

(2) This paragraph applies if—

    (a) the period of 14 days beginning with the date of the notification to the OFT has ended, or

    (b) before the end of that period, the OFT allows the regulator to make the application.

(3) Where the OFT (or a regulator), having considered a complaint to which this Schedule applies, decides not to make an application under paragraph 3 in response to the complaint, it must give its reasons to the person who made the complaint.

5 Determination of application

(1) On an application under paragraph 3, the court may grant an injunction or interdict on such conditions, and against such of the respondents, as it thinks appropriate.

(2) The injunction or interdict may include provision about—

    (a) a term or notice to which the application relates;

    (b) any consumer contract term, or any notice, of a similar kind or like effect.

(3) It is not a defence to show that, because of a rule of law, a term to which the application relates is not, or could not be, an enforceable contract term.

(4) If a regulator makes the application, it must notify the OFT of—

    (a) the outcome of the application, and

    (b) if an injunction or interdict is granted, the conditions on which, and the identity of any person against whom, it is granted.

6 Undertakings

(1) The OFT (or a regulator) may accept from a relevant person an undertaking that he will comply with such conditions about the use of specified terms or notices, or of terms or notices of a specified kind, as he and the OFT (or the regulator) may agree.

(2) If a regulator accepts an undertaking under this paragraph, it must notify the OFT of—

    (a) the conditions on which the undertaking is accepted, and

    (b) the identity of the person who gave it.

(3) 'Relevant person', in relation to the OFT or a regulator, means a person against whom it has applied, or thinks it is entitled to apply, for an injunction or interdict under paragraph 3.

(4) 'Specified', in relation to an undertaking, means specified in the undertaking.

7 Power to obtain information

(1) The OFT (or a regulator which is a public authority) may, for a purpose mentioned in sub-paragraph (2)(a) or (b), give notice to a person requiring him to provide it with specified information.

(2) The purposes are—

    (a) to facilitate the exercise of the OFT's (or the regulator's) functions for the purposes of this Schedule,

    (b) to find out whether a person has complied, or is complying, with—

        (i) an injunction or interdict granted under paragraph 5 on an application by the OFT (or the regulator), or

        (ii) an undertaking accepted by it under paragraph 6.

(3) The notice must—

    (a) be in writing,

    (b) specify the purpose for which the information is required, and

    (c) specify how and when the notice is to be complied with.

(4) The notice may require the production of specified documents or documents of a specified description.

(5) The OFT (or the regulator) may take copies of any documents produced in compliance with the notice.

(6) The notice may be varied or revoked by a subsequent notice under this paragraph.

(7) The notice may not require a person to provide information or produce documents which he would be entitled to refuse to provide or produce—

    (a) in proceedings in the High Court, on the grounds of legal professional privilege;

(b) in proceedings in the Court of Session, on the grounds of confidentiality of communication.

(8) 'Specified', in relation to a notice under this paragraph, means specified in the notice.

8   Notices under paragraph 7: enforcement

(1) If the OFT (or the regulator) thinks that a person (a 'defaulter') has failed, or is failing, to comply with a notice given under paragraph 7, it may apply to the court for an order under this paragraph (a 'compliance order').

(2) If the court thinks that the defaulter has failed to comply with the notice, it may make a compliance order.

(3) A compliance order—
(a) must specify such things as the court thinks it reasonable for the defaulter to do to ensure compliance with the notice;
(b) must require the defaulter to do those things;
(c) may require the defaulter to pay some or all of the costs or expenses of the application for the order ('the application costs').

(4) If the defaulter is a company or association, the court may, when acting under sub-paragraph (3)(c), require payment of some or all of the application costs by an officer of the company or association whom the court thinks responsible for the failure.

(5) If a regulator applies for a compliance order, it must notify the OFT of—
(a) the outcome of the application, and
(b) if the order is made, the conditions on which, and the identity of any person against whom, it is made.

(6) 'Officer'—
(a) in relation to a company, means a director, manager, secretary or other similar officer of the company,
(b) in relation to a partnership, means a partner,
(c) in relation to any other association, means an officer of the association or a member of its governing body.

9   Publication, information and advice

(1) The OFT must arrange to publish details of any—
(a) application it makes for an injunction or interdict under paragraph 3;
(b) injunction or interdict granted on an application by it under paragraph 3;
(c) injunction or interdict notified to it under paragraph 5(4)(b);
(d) undertaking it accepts under paragraph 6(1);
(e) undertaking notified to it under paragraph 6(2);
(f) application it makes for a compliance order under paragraph 8(1);
(g) compliance order made under paragraph 8(2);
(h) compliance order notified to it under paragraph 8(5)(b).

(2) Sub-paragraph (3) applies where a person tells the OFT about a term or notice and asks the OFT whether that term or notice, or one of a similar kind or like effect, is or has been the subject of an injunction, interdict or undertaking under this Schedule.

(3) The OFT must reply; and if it replies that the term or notice, or one of a similar kind or like effect, is or has been the subject of an injunction, interdict or undertaking under this Schedule, the OFT must give the person—
(a) a copy of the injunction or interdict or details of the undertaking, and
(b) if the person giving the undertaking has agreed to amend the term or notice concerned, a copy of the amendments.

(4) The OFT may arrange to publish advice and information about the provisions of this Act.

(5) A reference to an injunction or interdict under this Schedule is to an injunction or interdict—
(a) granted on an application by the OFT under paragraph 3, or
(b) notified to it under paragraph 5(4)(b).

(6) A reference to an undertaking under this Schedule is to an undertaking—
  (a) accepted by the OFT under paragraph 6(1), or
  (b) notified to it under paragraph 6(2).

10   Meaning of 'regulator'

(1) For the purposes of this Schedule, 'regulator' means—
  (a) the Financial Services Authority,
  (b) the Office of Communications,
  (c) the Information Commissioner,
  (d) the Gas and Electricity Markets Authority,
  (e) the Water Services Regulation Authority,
  (f) the Office of Rail Regulation,
  (g) the Northern Ireland Authority for Energy Regulation,
  (h) the Department of Enterprise, Trade and Investment in Northern Ireland,
  (i) a local weights and measures authority in Great Britain, or
  (j) a body designated as a regulator under sub-paragraph (3).

(2) The Secretary of State may by order amend sub-paragraph (1) so as to add, modify or omit an entry.

(3) Where the Secretary of State thinks that a body which is not a public authority represents the interests of consumers (or consumers of a particular description), he may by order designate the body as a regulator.

(4) The Secretary of State may cancel the designation if he thinks that the body has failed, or is likely to fail, to comply with a duty imposed on it under this Act.

(5) The Secretary of State must publish (and may from time to time vary) other criteria to be applied by him in deciding whether to make or cancel a designation under this paragraph.

11   The Financial Services Authority

Any function that the Financial Services Authority has under this Act is to be regarded, for the purposes of the Financial Services and Markets Act 2000 (c. 8), as a function that it has under that Act.

Section 14(6)   **SCHEDULE 2**

CONTRACT TERMS WHICH MAY BE REGARDED AS NOT FAIR AND REASONABLE

PART 1 INTRODUCTION

1—(1) A term of a consumer contract or small business contract may be regarded as not being fair and reasonable if it—
  (a) has the object or effect of a term listed in Part 2, and
  (b) does not come within an exception mentioned in Part 3.

(2) In this Schedule—
  (a) in relation to a consumer contract, 'A' means the consumer and 'B' means the business, and
  (b) in relation to a small business contract, 'A' and 'B' mean, respectively, the persons referred to as A and B in section 11.

PART 2 LIST OF TERMS

2 A term excluding or restricting liability to A for breach of contract.

3 A term imposing obligations on A in circumstances where B's obligation to perform depends on the satisfaction of a condition wholly within B's control.

4 A term entitling B, if A exercises a right to cancel the contract or if B terminates the contract as a result of A's breach, to keep sums that A has paid, the amount of which is unreasonable.

5 A term requiring A, when in breach of contract, to pay B a sum significantly above the likely loss to B.

6 A term entitling B to cancel the contract without incurring liability, unless there is also a term entitling A to cancel it without incurring liability.

7 A term entitling B, if A exercises a right to cancel the contract, to keep sums A has paid in respect of services which B has yet to supply.

8 A term in a fixed-term contract or a contract of indefinite duration entitling B to terminate the contract without giving A reasonable advance notice (except in an urgent case).

9 A term—

    (a) providing for a contract of fixed duration to be renewed unless A indicates otherwise, and

    (b) requiring A to give that indication a disproportionately long time before the contract is due to expire.

10 A term binding A to terms with which A did not have an opportunity to become familiar before the contract was made.

11 A term entitling B, without a good reason which is specified in the contract, to vary the terms of the contract.

12 A term entitling B, without a good reason, to vary the characteristics of the goods or services concerned.

13 A term requiring A to pay whatever price is set for the goods at the time of delivery (including a case where the price is set by reference to a list price), unless there is also a term entitling A to cancel the contract if that price is higher than the price indicated to A when the contract was made.

14 A term entitling B to increase the price specified in the contract, unless there is also a term entitling A to cancel the contract if the business does increase the price.

15 A term giving B the exclusive right (and, accordingly, excluding any power of a court) to determine—

    (a) whether the goods or services supplied match the definition of them given in the contract, or

    (b) the meaning of any term in the contract.

16 A term excluding or restricting B's liability for statements or promises made by B's employees or agents, or making B's liability for statements or promises subject to formalities.

17 A term requiring A to carry out its obligations in full (in particular, to pay the whole of the price specified in the contract) in circumstances where B has failed to carry out its obligations in full.

18 A term entitling B to transfer its obligations without A's consent.

19 A term entitling B to transfer its rights in circumstances where A's position might be weakened as a result.

20 A term excluding or restricting A's right—

    (a) to bring or defend any action or other legal proceedings, or

    (b) to exercise other legal remedies.

21 A term restricting the evidence on which A may rely.

PART 3 EXCEPTIONS

22 Financial services contracts

(1) Sub-paragraph (2) applies where a term in a financial services contract of indefinite duration provides that B may terminate the contract—

    (a) by giving A relatively short advance notice, or

    (b) if B has a good reason for terminating the contract, without giving A any advance notice.

(2) Paragraph 8 (termination without reasonable notice) does not apply to the term if the contract also provides that B must immediately inform A of the termination.

(3) Sub-paragraph (4) applies where a term in a financial services contract of indefinite duration provides that B may vary the interest rate or other charges payable under it—

  (a) by giving A relatively short advance notice, or

  (b) if B has a good reason for making the variation, without giving A any advance notice.

(4) Paragraph 11 (variation without good reason) does not apply to a term if the contract also provides that—

  (a) B must as soon as practicable inform A of the variation, and

  (b) A may then cancel the contract, without incurring liability.

(5) 'Financial services contract' means a contract for the supply by B of financial services to A.

23   Contracts of indefinite duration

Paragraph 11 (variation without good reason) does not apply to a term in a contract of indefinite duration if the contract also provides that—

  (a) B must give reasonable notice of the variation, and

  (b) A may then cancel the contract, without incurring liability.

24   Contracts for sale of securities, foreign currency, etc.

(1) None of the following paragraphs applies to a contract term if sub-paragraph (2) or (3) applies—

  (a) paragraph 8 (termination without reasonable notice),

  (b) paragraph 11 (variation without good reason),

  (c) paragraph 13 (determination of price at time of delivery),

  (d) paragraph 14 (increase in price).

(2) This sub-paragraph applies if the contract is for the transfer of securities, financial instruments or anything else, the price of which is linked to—

  (a) fluctuations in prices quoted on a stock exchange, or

  (b) a financial index or market rate that B does not control.

(3) This sub-paragraph applies if the contract is for the sale of foreign currency (and, for this purpose, that includes foreign currency in the form of traveller's cheques or international money orders).

25   Price index clauses

Neither paragraph 13 nor paragraph 14 (determination of price at time of delivery or increase in price) applies to a contract term if—

  (a) the term provides for the price of the goods or services to be varied by reference to an index of prices, and

  (b) the contract specifies how a change to the index is to affect the price.

Section 22   ## SCHEDULE 3

EXCEPTIONS

1   Legal requirements

(1) This Act does not apply to a contract term—

  (a) required by an enactment or a rule of law,

  (b) required or authorised by a provision in an international convention to which the United Kingdom or the European Community is a party, or

  (c) required by, or incorporated as a result of a decision or ruling of, a competent authority acting in the exercise of its statutory jurisdiction or any of its functions.

(2) Sub-paragraph 1(c) does not apply if the competent authority is itself a party to the contract.

(3) 'Competent authority' means a public authority other than a local authority.

2   Settlements of claims

(1) This Act does not apply to a contract term in so far as it is, or forms part of—

(a) a settlement of a claim in tort;

(b) a discharge or indemnity given by a person in consideration of the receipt by him of compensation in settlement of any claim which he has.

(2) In sub-paragraph (1)—

(a) paragraph (a) does not extend to Scotland, and

(b) paragraph (b) extends only to Scotland.

3 Insurance

The following sections do not apply to an insurance contract (including a contract to pay an annuity on human life)—

(a) section 1 (exclusion of business liability for negligence),

(b) section 9 (exclusion of liability for breach of business contract where one party deals on written standard terms of the other),

(c) section 11 (non-negotiated terms in small business contracts),

(d) section 12 (exclusion of employer's liability under employment contract).

4 Land

The following sections do not apply to a contract term in so far as it relates to the creation, transfer, variation or termination of an interest or real right in land—

(a) section 1 (exclusion of business liability for negligence),

(b) section 9 (exclusion of liability for breach of business contract where one party deals on written standard terms of the other),

(c) section 11 (non-negotiated terms in small business contracts).

5 Intellectual property

Nor do those sections apply to a contract term in so far as it relates to the creation, transfer, variation or termination of a right or interest in any patent, trade mark, copyright or design right, registered design, technical or commercial information or other intellectual property.

6 Company formation, etc.

Nor do those sections apply to a contract term in so far as it relates to—

(a) the formation or dissolution of a body corporate or unincorporated association (including a partnership),

(b) its constitution, or

(c) the rights and obligations of its members.

7 Securities

Nor do those sections apply to a contract term in so far as it relates to the creation or transfer of securities or of a right or interest in securities.

8 International supply contracts

The following provisions do not apply to a business contract for the supply of goods where the supply is to be made to a place outside the United Kingdom—

(a) section 1(2) (business liability for negligence other than in case of death or personal injury),

(b) sections 9 to 11 (unfair terms in business contracts),

(c) sections 19 and 20 (choice of law in business contracts).

Shipping

9—(1) Section 1(2) does not apply to a shipping contract unless it is also a consumer contract.

(2) Sections 9 and 11 do not apply to a shipping contract.

(3) 'Shipping contract' means—

(a) a contract of marine salvage or towage,

(b) a charterparty of a ship or hovercraft, or

(c) a contract for the carriage of goods by ship or hovercraft.

10—(1) This paragraph applies where goods are carried by ship or hovercraft under a contract which—

    (a) specifies that as the means of transport for part of the journey, or

    (b) does not specify a means of transport but does not exclude that one.

(2) Section 1(2) does not apply to the contract, unless it is also a consumer contract, in so far as it relates to the carriage of the goods by that means of transport.

(3) Sections 9 and 11 do not apply to the contract in so far as it relates to the carriage of the goods by that means of transport.

Section 27

SCHEDULE 4

CALCULATING THE NUMBER OF EMPLOYEES IN A BUSINESS

1   Introduction

(1) This Schedule sets out how to calculate the number of employees that a party to a business contract, or an associated person, has in its business.

(2) 'The business period' means a continuous period for which—

    (a) the party to the business contract has been carrying on the business to which the contract relates, or

    (b) an associated person has been carrying on business.

2   Calculation for established business

Where the business period is at least twelve months ending on the last day of the month immediately before the month including the contract date—

    (a) work out how many full-time employees there are in the business on the last day of each of the twelve months ending with the last complete month before the contract date,

    (b) add together the numbers for those twelve days, and

    (c)   divide the total by twelve.

Calculation for new business

3   Where the business period is at least one complete month ending on the last day of the month immediately before the month including the contract date (but paragraph 2 does not apply)—

    (a) work out how many full-time employees there are in the business on the last day of each complete month,

    (b) add together the numbers for those days, and

    (c) divide the total by the number of complete months.

4   Where the business period is less than one complete month, but more than one day, before the contract date—

    (a) work out how many full-time employees there are in the business on each day,

    (b) add together the numbers for those days, and

    (c) divide that total by the number of days.

5   Where the party to the contract enters into it on the first day on which it carries on the business to which the contract relates, or an associated person has been carrying on business for only one day, work out how many full-time employees there are in the business on the day in question.

6   The number of full-time employees in a business

(1) This paragraph sets out how to work out how many full-time employees there are in a business.

(2) An employee who works for at least 35 hours a week for a business counts as one full-time employee.

(3) An employee who works for under 35 hours a week for a business (a 'part-time employee') counts as a fraction of one full-time employee, with the fraction being calculated as—

$$\frac{A}{B}$$

where A and B are defined as follows.

(4) A is the number of hours a week which the part-time employee works for the business.

(5) B is—

    (a) the number of hours a week which a full-time employee of the same description as the part-time employee works for the business, or

    (b) if there are no full-time employees of that description, 35 hours a week.

(6) The number of hours a week which an employee works for a business is—

    (a) the number of hours a week which he is contractually required to work for the business, or

    (b) if he ordinarily works for a longer period than that, or his contract does not specify for how many hours a week he is to work, the number of hours a week he ordinarily works for the business,

but does not include any meal break, or rest period, exceeding 15 minutes.

Interpretation

7 'Contract date', in relation to a business contract, means the date on which the contract is made.

8 'Employee'—

    (a) in relation to any business, means an individual who works in the business under a contract of employment or a contract for services;

    (b) in relation to a business carried on by a partnership (or other unincorporated association), includes a partner (or member);

    (c) in relation to a business carried on by only one individual, includes that individual.

Defamation Bill

A Bill to amend the law of defamation; and for connected purposes.   [2010]

Defences

1 Responsible publication on matters of public interest

(1) Any defendant in an action for defamation has a defence if the defendant shows that—

    (a) the words or matters complained of were published for the purposes of, or otherwise in connection with, the discussion of a matter of public interest; and

    (b) the defendant acted responsibly in making the publication.

(2) Subsection (1) applies irrespective of whether the publication contains statements of fact or inferences or opinions.

(3) The court when deciding for the purposes of subsection (1)(b) whether the defendant has acted responsibly must have regard to all the circumstances of the case.

(4) Those circumstances may include (among other things)—

    (a) the nature of the publication and its context;

    (b) the nature and seriousness of anything alleged about the claimant;

    (c) what information the defendant had before publication;

    (d) what steps (if any) were taken by the defendant to verify what was published;

    (e) if appropriate, whether the defendant gave the claimant an opportunity to comment before publication;

    (f) whether there were factors supporting urgent publication;

    (g) the extent of the defendant's compliance with any relevant code of conduct or other relevant guidelines; or

    (h) whether subsection (5) applies.

(5) Where a publication reports accurately and impartially on a pre-existing matter (for example, that there is a dispute between two parties), a defendant may be regarded as acting responsibly to the extent that the court is satisfied that it is in the public interest for the existence of that matter, and anything reported in connection with it, to be the subject of a report or series of reports.

(6) In determining for the purposes of subsection (5) whether publication is in the public interest, the court may disregard any question as to the truth of anything reported in connection with a pre-existing matter.

2   Honest opinion

In an action for defamation, the defence known before the commencement of this section as the defence of fair comment is, after commencement, to be known as the defence of honest opinion.

3   Establishing a defence of honest opinion

(1) A defendant has a defence of honest opinion in an action for defamation if the defendant shows that Conditions 1 to 4 are satisfied (subject to subsections (7) and (8)).

(2) Condition 1 is that the words or matters complained of relate to a matter of public interest.

(3) Condition 2 is that, in the circumstances in which the words or matters are published, an ordinary person would reasonably consider those words or matters to be an opinion.

(4) Condition 3 is that, at the time of publication, there existed—

(a) one or more facts;

(b) any material that falls within section 1 (responsible publication on matters of public interest);

(c) any material that falls within section 6, 7 or 8 (statutory privilege); or

(d) any material that is otherwise protected by privilege.

(5) Condition 4 is that an honest person could form the opinion on the basis of the facts or material shown by the defendant in satisfying Condition 3.

(6) In relation to the facts or material relied on by the defendant as providing a basis for the opinion, no account is to be taken of—

(a) anything that the defendant does not show, provided that the defendant shows that Condition 4 is satisfied on the basis of what is shown;

(b) whether the defendant first learned of the facts or material before or after publication; or

(c) whether the facts or material were or were not included (by reference or otherwise) in the publication.

(7) There is no defence of honest opinion if the claimant shows that the defendant did not in fact hold the opinion.

(8) Where the defendant was not the author ("A") of the words or matters complained of, there is no defence of honest opinion if the claimant shows that—

(a) the defendant knew that A did not in fact hold the opinion; or

(b) the defendant had reason to believe that A did not in fact hold the opinion and published without determining whether or not A did hold it.

4   Truth

In an action for defamation, the defence known before the commencement of this section as the defence of justification is, after commencement, to be known as the defence of truth.

5   Establishing a defence of truth

(1) A defendant has a defence of truth in an action for defamation if the words or matters complained of are substantially true.

(2) For these purposes, the defendant may show either that—

(a) the meaning (or meanings) alleged by the claimant are substantially true; or

(b) the words or matters complained of have a less serious meaning (or meanings) and each such meaning is substantially true.

(3) A defence of justification does not fail only because a particular meaning alleged by the claimant is not shown as being substantially true, if that meaning would not materially injure the

claimant's reputation having regard to the truth of what the defendant has shown to be substantially true.

(4) Where—

    (a) the words or matters complained of make two or more distinct allegations; and

    (b) the truth of every allegation is not shown;

a defence of justification does not fail only because of paragraph (b) if anything not shown to be true does not materially injure the claimant's reputation having regard to the truth of the remaining allegations.

Statutory privilege

6 Reports of court proceedings protected by absolute privilege

(1) A fair and accurate report of proceedings in public before a court to which this section applies, if published contemporaneously with the proceedings, is absolutely privileged.

(2) A report of proceedings which by an order of the court, or as a consequence of any statutory provision, is required to be postponed is to be treated as published contemporaneously if it is published as soon as practicable after publication is permitted.

(3) This section applies to—

    (a) any court in the United Kingdom;

    (b) the European Court of Justice or any court attached to that court;

    (c) the European Court of Human Rights;

    (d) any international criminal tribunal established by the Security Council of the United Nations or by an international agreement to which the United Kingdom is a party;

    (e) any court established under the law of a country or territory outside the United Kingdom;

    (f) the Inter-American Court of Human Rights;

    (g) the African Court of Human and People's Rights;

    (h) the International Court of Justice; and

    (i) any other judicial or arbitral tribunal deciding matters in dispute between States.

In paragraph (a) "court" includes any tribunal or body exercising the judicial power of the State.

7 Reports etc of certain Parliamentary matters protected by absolute privilege

(1) The following are absolutely privileged—

    (a) a fair and accurate report of proceedings in Parliament;

    (b) a fair and accurate report of anything published by or on the authority of Parliament; and

    (c) a fair and accurate copy of, extract from or summary of anything published by or on the authority of Parliament.

(2) The court must stay any proceedings where the defendant shows that—

    (a) the proceedings relate to the publication of anything that falls within paragraph (a), (b) or (c) of subsection (1); or

    (b) the proceedings seek to prevent or postpone the making of any such publication.

(3) This section also has effect in relation to the Welsh Assembly and the Northern Ireland Assembly (and any reference to Parliament is to be read as a reference to the Assembly in question).

8 Other reports etc protected by qualified privilege

(1) The publication of any report or other statement mentioned in Schedule 1 to this Act is privileged unless the publication is shown to be made with malice, subject as follows.

(2) In an action for defamation in respect of the publication of a report or other statement mentioned in Part 2 of Schedule 1, there is no defence under this section if the claimant shows that the defendant—

    (a) was requested by the claimant to publish in a suitable manner a reasonable letter or statement by way of explanation or contradiction; and

(b) refused or neglected to do so without sufficient cause.

(3) For this purpose "in a suitable manner" means in the same manner as the publication complained of or in a manner that is adequate and reasonable in the circumstances.

(4) This section does not apply to the publication to the public, or a section of the public, of matter which is not of public concern and the publication of which is not for the public benefit.

(5) Nothing in this section is to be construed—

(a) as protecting the publication of matter the publication of which is prohibited by law; or

(b) as limiting or abridging any privilege subsisting apart from this section.

Publication

9   **Responsibility for publication**

(1) Any defendant in an action for defamation has a defence if the defendant shows that the defendant's only involvement in the publication of the words or matters complained of—

(a) is as a facilitator; or

(b) is as a broadcaster of a live programme in circumstances in which it was not reasonably foreseeable that those words or matters would be published.

(2) Any defendant in an action for defamation, apart from a primary publisher, has a defence unless the claimant shows that—

(a) the notice requirements specified in subsection (3) have been complied with;

(b) the notice period specified in subsection (4) has expired; and

(c) the words or matters complained of have not been removed from the publication.

(3) The notice requirements are that the substance of the claimant's complaint must be communicated in writing to the defendant, specifying—

(a) the words or matters complained of and the person (or persons) to whom they relate;

(b) the publication that contains those words or matters;

(c) why the claimant considers the words or matters to be defamatory;

(d) the details of any matters relied on in the publication which the claimant considers to be untrue; and

(e) why the claimant considers the words or matters to be harmful in the circumstances in which they were published.

(4) The notice period is—

(a) the period of 14 days starting with the date of receipt by the defendant of all the information required by subsection (3); or

(b) such other period as the court may specify (whether of its own motion or on an application by any party to the action).

(5) Employees or agents of a primary publisher, or other person who publishes the words or matters complained of, are in the same position as their principal to the extent that they are responsible for the content of what is published or the decision to publish it.

(6) In this section—

"facilitator" means a person who is concerned only with the transmission or storage of the content of the publication and has no other influence or control over it; and

"primary publisher" means an author, an editor or a person who exercises effective control of an author or editor.

(7) For the purposes of the definition of "primary publisher" in subsection (6)—

"author" means—

(a) a person who originates the words or matters complained of; but

(b) does not include a person who does not intend that they be published; and

"editor", in relation to a publication, means a person with editorial or equivalent responsibility for the content of the publication or the decision to publish it.

(8) This section does not apply to any cause of action which arose before the section came into force.

10   Multiple publications

(1) In any case to which subsection (2) applies—

   (a) the first occasion on which the publication is made available to the public generally (or to any section of the public) is to be regarded for all purposes as the date of publication of each subsequent publication; and

   (b) in an action for defamation based on any publication to which this section applies, the cause of action is to be treated as having accrued on that date.

(2) This subsection applies to any publication (such as a book, newspaper, periodical or material in an archive) which—

   (a) is published by the same person on multiple occasions; and

   (b) on each occasion, has the same, or substantially the same, content.

(3) Subsection (2) does not apply where a subsequent publication is made in a materially different manner, but this is without prejudice to that publication itself constituting a first publication for the purposes of subsection (1).

Cause of action

11   Action for defamation brought by body corporate

A body corporate which seeks to pursue an action for defamation must show that the publication of the words or matters complained of has caused, or is likely to cause, substantial financial loss to the body corporate.

12   Striking out where claimant suffers no substantial harm

(1) The court must strike out an action for defamation unless the claimant shows that—

   (a) the publication of the words or matters complained of has caused substantial harm to the claimant's reputation; or

   (b) it is likely that such harm will be caused to the claimant's reputation by the publication.

(2) Subsection (1) does not apply if, in exceptional circumstances, the court is satisfied that it would be in the interests of justice not to strike out the action.

(3) In determining whether a claimant's reputation is or may be substantially harmed, the court must have regard to all the circumstances of the case.

(4) An order under subsection (1) may be made by the court of its own motion or on an application by any party to the action.

(5) Subsection (1) does not limit any power to strike out proceedings which is exercisable apart from this section.

13   Harmful event in cases of publication outside the jurisdiction

(1) This section applies in an action for defamation where the court is satisfied that the words or matters complained of have also been published outside the jurisdiction (including publication outside the jurisdiction of any words or matters that differ only in ways not affecting their substance).

(2) No harmful event is to be regarded as having occurred in relation to the claimant unless the publication in the jurisdiction can reasonably be regarded as having caused substantial harm to the claimant's reputation having regard to the extent of publication elsewhere.

Trial by jury

14   Reversal of presumption of trial by a jury in defamation proceedings

In section 69(1)(b) of the Senior Courts Act 1981 (trial by jury) omit the words "libel, slander".

15   Determining an application for trial by a jury

(1) If the court is satisfied that it is in the interests of justice to do so, it may order trial by jury of such matter or matters arising in an action for defamation as are specified in the order.

(2) An order under subsection (1) may be made on an application by any party to the action and the court determining the application must have regard to all the circumstances of the case.

(3) Those circumstances may include (among other things)—

    (a) whether there is a public interest in the subject matter of the action or anything arising in connection with it;

    (b) the identity of any of the parties to the action;

    (c) any office or other position held by any party to the action;

    (d) whether it is in the interests of justice that the verdict of a jury or a reasoned judgment be obtained on any matter arising in the action;

    (e) the extent to which early resolution of any matter (for example, as to the meaning of the words complained of) is likely to facilitate settlement of the action, improve active case management or assist in achieving a just and equitable outcome; and

    (f) whether the trial is likely to require the prolonged examination of documents or accounts or any scientific or local investigation which cannot conveniently be made with a jury.

(4) An application must be made in accordance with such procedure as may be prescribed by rules of court.

Evidence concerning proceedings in Parliament

16 Evidence concerning proceedings in Parliament

(1) In this section "the relevant protection", in relation to the proceedings of either House of Parliament, means the protection of any enactment or rule of law which prevents proceedings in Parliament being impeached or questioned in any court or place out of Parliament.

(2) The Speaker of either House of Parliament may, in accordance with Standing Orders of that House, by notice in writing waive the application of the relevant protection to such proceedings in an action for defamation as are specified in that notice.

(3) Where the relevant protection is waived in relation to any proceedings in an action for defamation—

    (a) that protection is not to apply to prevent evidence being given, questions being asked or statements, submissions, comments or findings being made in those proceedings; and

    (b) none of those things is to be regarded as infringing the privilege of either House of Parliament.

(4) Nothing in this section affects any enactment or rule of law so far as it protects a person from legal liability for words spoken or things done in the course of, or for the purposes of or incidental to, any proceedings in Parliament.

(5) Without prejudice to the generality of subsection (4), that subsection applies to—

    (a) the giving of evidence before either House or a committee;

    (b) the presentation or submission of a document to either House or a committee;

    (c) the preparation of a document for the purposes of or incidental to the transacting of any such business;

    (d) the formulation, making or publication of a document, including a report, by or pursuant to an order of either House or a committee; and

    (e) any communication with the Parliamentary Commissioner for Standards or any person having functions in connection with the registration of members' interests.

In this subsection "a committee" means a committee of either House or a joint committee of both Houses of Parliament.

Miscellaneous and supplementary

17 Interpretation

(1) In this Act—

"the 1996 Act" means the Defamation Act 1996;

"archive" includes any collection of sound recordings, images or other information however stored (including by electronic means);

"author" has the meaning given in section 9;

"publication" and "publish", in relation to a statement, have the meaning they have for the purposes of the law of defamation generally but "primary publisher" is specially defined for the purposes of section 9;

"statement" means words, pictures, visual images, gestures or any other method of signifying meaning;

"statutory provision" means—

(a) a provision contained in an Act or in subordinate legislation within the meaning of the Interpretation Act 1978;

(b) a provision contained in an Act of the Scottish Parliament or in an instrument made under such an Act; or

(c) a statutory provision within the meaning of the Interpretation Act (Northern Ireland) 1954.

(2) In this Act any reference to—

(a) a defendant in an action for defamation includes any person against whom a counterclaim for defamation is brought; and

(b) an action for defamation is to be construed accordingly.

18 Minor and consequential provision

Schedule 2 contains minor and consequential amendments.

19 Repeals

Schedule 3 contains repeals.

20 Extent

(1) This Act extends to England, Wales and Northern Ireland.

SCHEDULES

Section 8

SCHEDULE 1

QUALIFIED PRIVILEGE

PART 1

Statements having qualified privilege without explanation or contradiction

1 A fair and accurate report of proceedings in public of a legislature anywhere in the world.

2 A fair and accurate report of—

(a) proceedings in public before a court anywhere in the world;

(b) any statements or submissions which, for the purposes of any such proceedings, are made by, or on behalf of, any of the parties.

3 A fair and accurate report of proceedings in public of a person appointed to hold a public inquiry by a government or legislature anywhere in the world.

4 A fair and accurate report of proceedings in public anywhere in the world of an international organisation or an international conference.

5 A fair and accurate copy of or extract from any register or other document required by law to be open to public inspection.

6 A notice or advertisement published by or on the authority of a court, or of a judge or officer of a court, anywhere in the world.

7 A fair and accurate copy of, extract from or summary of matter published by or on the authority of a government or legislature anywhere in the world.

8 A fair and accurate copy of, extract from or summary of matter published anywhere in the world by an international organisation or an international conference.

PART 2

Statements privileged subject to explanation or contradiction

9 (1) A fair and accurate copy of, extract from or summary of, a notice or other matter issued for the information of the public by or on behalf of—

    (a) a legislature in the United Kingdom or another member State;

    (b) a legislature in any other country or territory;

    (c) the government of the United Kingdom or another member State;

    (d) the government of any other country or territory;

    (e) the European Parliament;

    (f) the European Commission;

    (g) an authority anywhere in the world which performs governmental functions;

    (h) an international organisation or international conference.

  (2) In this paragraph "governmental functions" includes—

    (a) police functions; and

    (b) functions performed by a public authority within the meaning of section 6 of the Human Rights Act 1998.

10 A fair and accurate copy of, extract from or summary of a document made available by—

    (a) a court in the United Kingdom or another member State;

    (b) a court in any other country or territory;

    (c) any court attached to a court falling within sub-paragraph (a) or (b);

    (d) a judge or officer of any court falling within any of sub-paragraphs (a) to (c).

11 A fair and accurate copy of, extract from or summary of material in an archive where—

    (a) the material has been publicly available online for a period of at least 12 months starting with the date of first publication by or on behalf of the archive; and

    (b) in the course of that period, no challenge has been made, whether in the courts or otherwise, which indicates that the material is considered to be defamatory.

12 (1) A fair and accurate report of proceedings at any public meeting or sitting in the United Kingdom of—

    (a) a local authority or local authority committee;

    (b) in the case of a local authority which are operating executive arrangements, the executive of that authority or a committee of that executive;

    (c) a justice or justices of the peace acting otherwise than as a court exercising judicial authority;

    (d) a commission, tribunal, committee or person appointed for the purposes of any inquiry by any statutory provision, by Her Majesty or by a Minister of the Crown, a member of the Scottish Executive, the Welsh Ministers or the Counsel General to the Welsh Assembly Government, or a Northern Ireland Department;

    (e) a person appointed by a local authority to hold a local inquiry in pursuance of any statutory provision;

    (f) any other tribunal, board, committee or body constituted by or under, and exercising functions under, any statutory provision.

  (2) In the case of a local authority which are operating executive arrangements, a fair and accurate record of any decision made by any member of the executive where that record is required to be made and available for public inspection by virtue of section 22 of the Local Government Act 2000 or of any provision in regulations made under that section.

  (3) In sub-paragraphs (1)(a) and (b) and (2)—

"local authority" means— ...

  (5) A fair and accurate report of any corresponding proceedings in—

    (a) any of the Channel Islands or the Isle of Man;

    (b) another member State; or

(c) any other country or territory.

13 (1) A fair and accurate report of proceedings at any public meeting held in the United Kingdom, in another member State or in any other country or territory.

(2) In this paragraph a "public meeting" means a meeting bona fide and lawfully held for a lawful purpose and for the furtherance or discussion of a matter of public concern, whether admission to the meeting is general or restricted.

14 A fair and accurate report of proceedings at a press conference given—

    (a) by or on behalf of any body, officer or other person falling within this Schedule or designated under it; and

    (b) in respect of published material to which qualified privilege applies by virtue of section 8.

15 (1) A fair and accurate report of proceedings at a general meeting of a UK public company or an overseas company.

(2) A fair and accurate copy of, extract from or summary of any document circulated to members of a UK public company or of an overseas company—

    (a) by or with the authority of the board of directors of the company;

    (b) by the auditors of the company; or

    (c) by any member of the company in pursuance of a right conferred by any statutory provision.

(3) A fair and accurate copy of, extract from or summary of any document circulated to members of a UK public company or of an overseas company, which relates to the appointment, resignation, retirement or dismissal of directors of the company.

(5) A fair and accurate report of proceedings at any corresponding meeting of, or copy of or extract from any corresponding document circulated to members of, a public company formed under the law of—

    (a) any of the Channel Islands or the Isle of Man;

    (b) another member State; or

    (c) any other country or territory.

16 A fair and accurate report of any finding or decision of any of the following descriptions of association, formed in the United Kingdom, another member State or any other country or territory, or of any committee or governing body of such an association—

    (a) an association formed for the purpose of promoting or encouraging the exercise of or interest in any art, science, religion or learning, and empowered by its constitution to exercise control over or adjudicate on matters of interest or concern to the association, or the actions or conduct of any person subject to such control or adjudication;

    (b) an association formed for the purpose of promoting or safeguarding the interests of any trade, business, industry or profession, or of the persons carrying on or engaged in any trade, business, industry or profession, and empowered by its constitution to exercise control over or adjudicate upon matters connected with that trade, business, industry or profession, or the actions or conduct of those persons;

    (c) an association formed for the purpose of promoting or safeguarding the interests of a game, sport or pastime to the playing or exercise of which members of the public are invited or admitted, and empowered by its constitution to exercise control over or adjudicate upon persons connected with or taking part in the game, sport or pastime;

    (d) an association formed for the purpose of promoting charitable objects or other objects beneficial to the community and empowered by its constitution to exercise control over or to adjudicate on matters of interest or concern to the association, or the actions or conduct of any person subject to such control or adjudication.

17 (1) A fair and accurate report of, copy of, extract from or summary of, any adjudication, report, statement or notice issued by a body, officer or other person designated for the purposes of this paragraph—

    (a) for England and Wales or Northern Ireland, by order of the Lord Chancellor; and

    (b) for Scotland, by order of the Secretary of State.

(2) An order under this paragraph is to be made by statutory instrument which is subject to annulment in pursuance of a resolution of either House of Parliament.

<table>
<tr><td>Section 19</td><td style="text-align:center">SCHEDULE 3</td></tr>
</table>

REPEALS

Short title and chapter	*Extent of repeal*
Parliamentary Papers Act 1840	The whole Act.
	Sections 5 and 6.
	Section 9(1).
Senior Courts Act 1981	The words "libel, slander".
Broadcasting Act 1990	Paragraph 1 of Schedule 20.
Defamation Act 1996	Section 1.
	Sections 13 to 15.
	Schedule 1.

Consumer Insurance (Disclosure and Representations) Bill

A Bill to make provision about disclosure and representations in connection with consumer insurance contracts.   [16 May 2011]

Main definitions

1 Main definitions

In this Act—

"consumer insurance contract" means a contract of insurance between—
   (a) an individual who enters into the contract wholly or mainly for purposes unrelated to the individual's trade, business or profession, and
   (b) a person who carries on the business of insurance and who becomes a party to the contract by way of that business (whether or not in accordance with permission for the purposes of the Financial Services and Markets Act 2000);

"consumer" means the individual who enters into a consumer insurance contract, or proposes to do so;

"insurer" means the person who is, or would become, the other party to a consumer insurance contract.

Pre-contract and pre-variation information

2 Disclosure and representations before contract or variation

(1) This section makes provision about disclosure and representations by a consumer to an insurer before a consumer insurance contract is entered into or varied.

(2) It is the duty of the consumer to take reasonable care not to make a misrepresentation to the insurer.

(3) A failure by the consumer to comply with the insurer's request to confirm or amend particulars previously given is capable of being a misrepresentation for the purposes of this Act (whether or not it could be apart from this subsection).

(4) The duty set out in subsection (2) replaces any duty relating to disclosure or representations by a consumer to an insurer which existed in the same circumstances before this Act applied.

(5) Accordingly—

    (a) any rule of law to the effect that a consumer insurance contract is one of the utmost good faith is modified to the extent required by the provisions of this Act, and

    (b) the application of section 17 of the Marine Insurance Act 1906 (contracts of marine insurance are of utmost good faith), in relation to a contract of marine insurance which is a consumer insurance contract, is subject to the provisions of this Act.

3 Reasonable care

(1) Whether or not a consumer has taken reasonable care not to make a misrepresentation is to be determined in the light of all the relevant circumstances.

(2) The following are examples of things which may need to be taken into account in making a determination under subsection (1)—

    (a) the type of consumer insurance contract in question, and its target market,

    (b) any relevant explanatory material or publicity produced or authorised by the insurer,

    (c) how clear, and how specific, the insurer's questions were,

    (d) whether or not an agent was acting for the consumer.

(3) The standard of care required is that of a reasonable consumer: but this is subject to subsections (4) and (5).

(4) If the insurer was, or ought to have been, aware of any particular characteristics or circumstances of the actual consumer, those are to be taken into account.

(5) A misrepresentation made dishonestly is always to be taken as showing lack of reasonable care.

Qualifying misrepresentations

4 Qualifying misrepresentations: definition and remedies

(1) An insurer has a remedy against a consumer for a misrepresentation made by the consumer before a consumer insurance contract was entered into or varied only if—

    (a) the consumer made the misrepresentation in breach of the duty set out in section 2(2), and

    (b) the insurer shows that without the misrepresentation, that insurer would not have entered into the contract (or agreed to the variation) at all, or would have done so only on different terms.

(2) A misrepresentation for which the insurer has a remedy against the consumer is referred to in this Act as a "qualifying misrepresentation".

(3) The only such remedies available are set out in Schedule 1.

5 Qualifying misrepresentations: classification and presumptions

(1) For the purposes of this Act, a qualifying misrepresentation (see section 4(2)) is either—

    (a) deliberate or reckless, or

    (b) careless.

(2) A qualifying misrepresentation is deliberate or reckless if the consumer—

    (a) knew that it was untrue or misleading, or did not care whether or not it was untrue or misleading, and

    (b) knew that the matter to which the misrepresentation related was relevant to the insurer, or did not care whether or not it was relevant to the insurer.

(3) A qualifying misrepresentation is careless if it is not deliberate or reckless.

(4) It is for the insurer to show that a qualifying misrepresentation was deliberate or reckless.

(5) But it is to be presumed, unless the contrary is shown—

    (a) that the consumer had the knowledge of a reasonable consumer, and

    (b) that the consumer knew that a matter about which the insurer asked a clear and specific question was relevant to the insurer.

Specific issues

6   Warranties and representations

(1) This section applies to representations made by a consumer—

(a) in connection with a proposed consumer insurance contract, or

(b) in connection with a proposed variation to a consumer insurance contract.

(2) Such a representation is not capable of being converted into a warranty by means of any provision of the consumer insurance contract (or of the terms of the variation), or of any other contract (and whether by declaring the representation to form the basis of the contract or otherwise).

10   Contracting out

(1) A term of a consumer insurance contract, or of any other contract, which would put the consumer in a worse position as respects the matters mentioned in subsection (2) than the consumer would be in by virtue of the provisions of this Act is to that extent of no effect.

(2) The matters are—

(a) disclosure and representations by the consumer to the insurer before the contract is entered into or varied, and

(b) any remedies for qualifying misrepresentations (see section 4(2)).

(3) This section does not apply in relation to a contract for the settlement of a claim arising under a consumer insurance contract.

Final provision

12   Short title, commencement, application and extent

(5) Nothing in this Act affects the circumstances in which a person is bound by the acts or omissions of that person's agent.

SCHEDULES

Section 4(3)

SCHEDULE 1

INSURERS' REMEDIES FOR QUALIFYING MISREPRESENTATIONS

PART 1 CONTRACTS

1   General

This Part of this Schedule applies in relation to qualifying misrepresentations made in connection with consumer insurance contracts (for variations to them, see Part 2).

2   Deliberate or reckless misrepresentations

If a qualifying misrepresentation was deliberate or reckless, the insurer—

(a) may avoid the contract and refuse all claims, and

(b) need not return any of the premiums paid, except to the extent (if any) that it would be unfair to the consumer to retain them.

Careless misrepresentations—claims

3 If the qualifying misrepresentation was careless, paragraphs 4 to 8 apply in relation to any claim.

4 The insurer's remedies are based on what it would have done if the consumer had complied with the duty set out in section 2(2), and paragraphs 5 to 8 are to be read accordingly.

5 If the insurer would not have entered into the consumer insurance contract on any terms, the insurer may avoid the contract and refuse all claims, but must return the premiums paid.

6 If the insurer would have entered into the consumer insurance contract, but on different terms (excluding terms relating to the premium), the contract is to be treated as if it had been entered into on those different terms if the insurer so requires.

7 In addition, if the insurer would have entered into the consumer insurance contract (whether the terms relating to matters other than the premium would have been the same or different), but would have charged a higher premium, the insurer may reduce proportionately the amount to be paid on a claim.

8 "Reduce proportionately" means that the insurer need pay on the claim only X% of what it would otherwise have been under an obligation to pay under the terms of the contract (or, if applicable, under the different terms provided for by virtue of paragraph 6), where—

$$X = \frac{\text{Premium actually charged}}{\text{Higher premium}} \times 100$$

9 Careless misrepresentations—treatment of contract for the future

(1) This paragraph—

    (a) applies if the qualifying misrepresentation was careless, but (b) does not relate to any outstanding claim.

(2) Paragraphs 5 and 6 (as read with paragraph 4) apply as they apply where a claim has been made.

(3) Paragraph 7 (as read with paragraph 4) applies in relation to a claim yet to be made as it applies in relation to a claim which has been made.

(4) If by virtue of sub-paragraph (2) or (3), the insurer would have either (or both) of the rights conferred by paragraph 6 or 7, the insurer may—

    (a) give notice to that effect to the consumer, or

    (b) terminate the contract by giving reasonable notice to the consumer.

(5) But the insurer may not terminate a contract under sub-paragraph (4)(b) if it is wholly or mainly one of life insurance.

(6) If the insurer gives notice to the consumer under sub-paragraph (4)(a), the consumer may terminate the contract by giving reasonable notice to the insurer.

(7) If either party terminates the contract under this paragraph, the insurer must refund any premiums paid for the terminated cover in respect of the balance of the contract term.

(8) Termination of the contract under this paragraph does not affect the treatment of any claim arising under the contract in the period before termination.

(9) Nothing in this paragraph affects any contractual right to terminate the contract.

PART 2 VARIATIONS

10 This Part of this Schedule applies in relation to qualifying misrepresentations made in connection with variations to consumer insurance contracts.

11 If the subject-matter of a variation can reasonably be treated separately from the subject-matter of the rest of the contract, Part 1 of this Schedule applies (with any necessary modifications) in relation to the variation as it applies in relation to a contract.

12 Otherwise, Part 1 applies (with any necessary modifications) as if the qualifying misrepresentation had been made in relation to the whole contract (for this purpose treated as including the variation) rather than merely in relation to the variation.

PART 4 SUPPLEMENTARY

17 Section 84 of the Marine Insurance Act 1906 (return of premium for failure of consideration) is to be read subject to the provisions of this Schedule in relation to contracts of marine insurance which are consumer insurance contracts.

Part III

Statutory Instruments

Package Travel, Package Holidays and Package Tours Regulations 1992

(SI 1992, No. 3288)

2 Interpretation

(1) In these Regulations—

'brochure' means any brochure in which packages are offered for sale;

'contract' means the agreement linking the consumer to the organiser or to the retailer, or to both, as the case may be;

'the Directive' means Council Directive 90/314/EEC on package travel, package holidays and package tours;

'offer' includes an invitation to treat whether by means of advertising or otherwise, and cognate expressions shall be construed accordingly;

'organiser' means the person who, otherwise than occasionally, organises packages and sells or offers them for sale, whether directly or through a retailer;

'the other party to the contract' means the party, other than the consumer, to the contract, that is, the organiser or the retailer, or both, as the case may be;

'package' means the pre-arranged combination of at least two of the following components when sold or offered for sale at an inclusive price and when the service covers a period of more than twenty-four hours or includes overnight accommodation—

    (a) transport;

    (b) accommodation;

    (c) other tourist services not ancillary to transport or accommodation and accounting for a significant proportion of the package,

and

    (i) the submission of separate accounts for different components shall not cause the arrangements to be other than a package;

    (ii) the fact that a combination is arranged at the request of the consumer and in accordance with his specific instructions (whether modified or not) shall not of itself cause it to be treated as other than pre-arranged;

and

'retailer' means the person who sells or offers for sale the package put together by the organiser.

(2) In the definition of 'contract' in paragraph (1) above, 'consumer' means the person who takes or agrees to take the package ('the principal contractor') and elsewhere in these Regulations 'consumer' means, as the context requires, the principal contractor, any person on whose behalf the principal contractor agrees to purchase the package ('the other beneficiaries') or any person to whom the principal contractor or any of the other beneficiaries transfers the package ('the transferee').

3   Application of Regulations

(1) These Regulations apply to packages sold or offered for sale in the territory of the United Kingdom.

4   Descriptive matter relating to packages must not be misleading

(1) No organiser or retailer shall supply to a consumer any descriptive matter concerning a package, the price of a package or any other conditions applying to the contract which contains any misleading information.

(2) If an organiser or retailer is in breach of paragraph (1) he shall be liable to compensate the consumer for any loss which the consumer suffers in consequence.

5   Requirements as to brochures

(1) Subject to paragraph (4) below, no organiser shall make available a brochure to a possible consumer unless it indicates in a legible, comprehensive and accurate manner the price and adequate information about the matters specified in Schedule 1 to these Regulations in respect of the packages offered for sale in the brochure to the extent that those matters are relevant to the packages so offered.

(2) Subject to paragraph (4) below, no retailer shall make available to a possible consumer a brochure which he knows or has reasonable cause to believe does not comply with the requirements of paragraph (1).

(3) An organiser who contravenes paragraph (1) of this regulation and a retailer who contravenes paragraph (2) thereof shall be guilty of an offence and liable—

    (a) on summary conviction, to a fine not exceeding level 5 on the standard scale;

    (b) on conviction on indictment, to a fine.

(4) Where a brochure was first made available to consumers generally before 31 December 1992 no liability shall arise under this regulation in respect of an identical brochure being made available to a consumer at any time.

6   Circumstances in which particulars in brochure are to be binding

(1) Subject to paragraphs (2) and (3) of this regulation, the particulars in the brochure (whether or not they are required by regulation 5(1) above to be included in the brochure) shall constitute implied warranties (or, as regards Scotland, implied terms) for the purposes of any contract to which the particulars relate.

(2) Paragraph (1) of this regulation does not apply—

    (a) in relation to information required to be included by virtue of paragraph 9 of Schedule 1 to these Regulations; or

    (b) where the brochure contains an express statement that changes may be made in the particulars contained in it before a contract is concluded and changes in the particulars so contained are clearly communicated to the consumer before a contract is concluded.

(3) Paragraph (1) of this regulation does not apply when the consumer and the other party to the contract agree after the contract has been made that the particulars in the brochure, or some of those particulars, should not form part of the contract.

7   Information to be provided before contract is concluded

(1) Before a contract is concluded, the other party to the contract shall provide the intending consumer with the information specified in paragraph (2) below in writing or in some other appropriate form.

(2) The information referred to in paragraph (1) is—

    (a) general information about passport and visa requirements which apply to nationals of the member State or States concerned] who purchase the package in question, including information about the length of time it is likely to take to obtain the appropriate passports and visas;

    (b) information about health formalities required for the journey and the stay; and

(c) the arrangements for security for the money paid over and (where applicable) for the repatriation of the consumer in the event of insolvency.

(3) If the intending consumer is not provided with the information required by paragraph (1) in accordance with that paragraph the other party to the contract shall be guilty of an offence and liable—

(a) on summary conviction, to a fine not exceeding level 5 on the standard scale; and

(b) on conviction on indictment, to a fine.

8 Information to be provided in good time

(1) The other party to the contract shall in good time before the start of the journey provide the consumer with the information specified in paragraph (2) below in writing or in some other appropriate form.

(2) The information referred to in paragraph (1) is the following—

(a) the times and places of intermediate stops and transport connections and particulars of the place to be occupied by the traveller (for example, cabin or berth on ship, sleeper compartment on train);

(b) the name, address and telephone number—

(i) of the representative of the other party to the contract in the locality where the consumer is to stay,

or, if there is no such representative,

(ii) of an agency in that locality on whose assistance a consumer in difficulty would be able to call,

or, if there is no such representative or agency, a telephone number or other information which will enable the consumer to contact the other party to the contract during the stay; and

(c) in the case of a journey or stay abroad by a child under the age of 16 on the day when the journey or stay is due to start, information enabling direct contact to be made with the child or the person responsible at the place where he is to stay; and

(d) except where the consumer is required as a term of the contract to take out an insurance policy in order to cover the cost of cancellation by the consumer or the cost of assistance, including repatriation, in the event of accident or illness, information about an insurance policy which the consumer may, if he wishes, take out in respect of the risk of those costs being incurred.

(3) If the consumer is not provided with the information required by paragraph (1) in accordance with that paragraph the other party to the contract shall be guilty of an offence and liable—

(a) on summary conviction, to a fine not exceeding level 5 on the standard scale;

(b) on conviction on indictment, to a fine.

9 Contents and form of contract

(1) The other party to the contract shall ensure that—

(a) depending on the nature of the package being purchased, the contract contains at least the elements specified in Schedule 2 to these Regulations;

(b) subject to paragraph (2) below, all the terms of the contract are set out in writing or such other form as is comprehensible and accessible to the consumer and are communicated to the consumer before the contract is made; and

(c) a written copy of these terms is supplied to the consumer.

(2) Paragraph (1)(b) above does not apply when the interval between the time when the consumer approaches the other party to the contract with a view to entering it is impracticable to comply with the sub-paragraph.

(3) It is an implied condition (or, as regards Scotland, an implied term) of the contract that the other party to the contract complies with the provisions of paragraph (1).

10   Transfer of bookings

(1) In every contract there is an implied term that where the consumer is prevented from proceeding with the package the consumer may transfer his booking to a person who satisfies all the conditions applicable to the package, provided that the consumer gives reasonable notice to the other party to the contract of his intention to transfer before the date when departure is due to take place.

(2) Where a transfer is made in accordance with the implied term set out in paragraph (1) above, the transferor and the transferee shall be jointly and severally liable to the other party to the contract for payment of the price of the package (or, if part of the price has been paid, for payment of the balance) and for any additional costs arising from such transfer.

11   Price revision

(1) Any term in a contract to the effect that the prices laid down in the contract may be revised shall be void and of no effect unless the contract provides for the possibility of upward or downward revision and satisfies the conditions laid down in paragraph (2) below.

(2) The conditions mentioned in paragraph (1) are that—

    (a) the contract states precisely how the revised price is to be calculated;

    (b) the contract provides that price revisions are to be made solely to allow for variations in—

        (i)   transportation costs, including the cost of fuel,

        (ii) dues, taxes or fees chargeable for services such as landing taxes or embarkation or disembarkation fees at ports and airports, or

        (iii) the exchange rates applied to the particular package; and

(3) Notwithstanding any terms of a contract,

    (i)   no price increase may be made in a specified period which may not be less than 30 days before the departure date stipulated; and

    (ii) as against an individual consumer liable under the contract, no price increase may be made in respect of variations which would produce an increase of less than 2 per cent, or such greater percentage as the contract may specify ('non-eligible variations') and that the non-eligible variations shall be left out of account in the calculation.

12   Significant alterations to essential terms

In every contract there are implied terms to the effect that—

    (a) where the organiser is constrained before the departure to alter significantly an essential term of the contract, such as the price (so far as regulation 11 permits him to do so), he will notify the consumer as quickly as possible in order to enable him to take appropriate decisions and in particular to withdraw from the contract without penalty or to accept a rider to the contract specifying the alterations made and their impact on the price; and

    (b) the consumer will inform the organiser or the retailer of his decision as soon as possible.

13   Withdrawal by consumer pursuant to regulation 12 and cancellation by organiser

(1) The terms set out in paragraphs (2) and (3) below are implied in every contract and apply where the consumer withdraws from the contract pursuant to the term in it implied by virtue of regulation 12(a), or where the organiser, for any reason other than the fault of the consumer, cancels the package before the agreed date of departure.

(2) The consumer is entitled—

    (a) to take a substitute package of equivalent or superior quality if the other party to the contract is able to offer him such a substitute; or

    (b) to take a substitute package of lower quality if the other party to the contract is able to offer him one and to recover from the organiser the difference in price between the price of the package purchased and that of the substitute package; or

    (c) to have repaid to him as soon as possible all the monies paid by him under the contract.

(3) The consumer is entitled, if appropriate, to be compensated by the organiser for non-performance of the contract except where—

    (a) the package is cancelled because the number of persons who agree to take it is less than the minimum number required and the consumer is informed of the cancellation, in writing, within the period indicated in the description of the package; or

    (b) the package is cancelled by reason of unusual and unforeseeable circumstances beyond the control of the party by whom this exception is pleaded, the consequences of which could not have been avoided even if all due care had been exercised.

(4) Overbooking shall not be regarded as a circumstance falling within the provisions of sub-paragraph (b) of paragraph (3) above.

14 Significant proportion of services not provided

(1) The terms set out in paragraphs (2) and (3) below are implied in every contract and apply where, after departure, a significant proportion of the services contracted for is not provided or the organiser becomes aware that he will be unable to procure a significant proportion of the services to be provided.

(2) The organiser will make suitable alternative arrangements, at no extra cost to the consumer, for the continuation of the package and will, where appropriate, compensate the consumer for the difference between the services to be supplied under the contract and those supplied.

(3) If it is impossible to make arrangements as described in paragraph (2), or these are not accepted by the consumer for good reasons, the organiser will, where appropriate, provide the consumer with equivalent transport back to the place of departure or to another place to which the consumer has agreed and will, where appropriate, compensate the consumer.

15 Liability of other party to the contract for proper performance of obligations under contract

(1) The other party to the contract is liable to the consumer for the proper performance of the obligations under the contract, irrespective of whether such obligations are to be performed by that other party or by other suppliers of services but this shall not affect any remedy or right of action which that other party may have against those other suppliers of services.

(2) The other party to the contract is liable to the consumer for any damage caused to him by the failure to perform the contract or the improper performance of the contract unless the failure or the improper performance is due neither to any fault of that other party nor to that of another supplier of services, because—

    (a) the failures which occur in the performance of the contract are attributable to the consumer;

    (b) such failures are attributable to a third party unconnected with the provision of the services contracted for, and are unforeseeable or unavoidable; or

    (c) such failures are due to—

        (i)   unusual and unforeseeable circumstances beyond the control of the party by whom this exception is pleaded, the consequences of which could not have been avoided even if all due care had been exercised; or

        (ii) an event which the other party to the contract or the supplier of services, even with all due care, could not foresee or forestall.

(3) In the case of damage arising from the non-performance or improper performance of the services involved in the package, the contract may provide for compensation to be limited in accordance with the international conventions which govern such services.

(4) In the case of damage other than personal injury resulting from the non-performance or improper performance of the services involved in the package, the contract may include a term limiting the amount of compensation which will be paid to the consumer, provided that the limitation is not unreasonable.

(5) Without prejudice to paragraph (3) and paragraph (4) above, liability under paragraphs (1) and (2) above cannot be excluded by any contractual term.

(6) The terms set out in paragraphs (7) and (8) below are implied in every contract.

(7) In the circumstances described in paragraph (2)(b) and (c) of this regulation, the other party to the contract will give prompt assistance to a consumer in difficulty.

(8) If the consumer complains about a defect in the performance of the contract, the other party to the contract, or his local representative, if there is one, will make prompt efforts to find appropriate solutions.

(9) The contract must clearly and explicitly oblige the consumer to communicate at the earliest opportunity, in writing or any other appropriate form, to the supplier of the services concerned and to the other party to the contract any failure which he perceives at the place where the services concerned are supplied.

27 Saving for civil consequences

No contract shall be void or unenforceable, and no right of action in civil proceedings in respect of any loss shall arise, by reason only of the commission of an offence under regulations 5, 7, 8, 16 or 22 of these Regulations.

28 Terms implied in contract

Where it is provided in these Regulations that a term (whether so described or whether described as a condition or warranty) is implied in the contract it is so implied irrespective of the law which governs the contract.

Regulation 5

SCHEDULE 1

INFORMATION TO BE INCLUDED (IN ADDITION TO THE PRICE) IN BROCHURES WHERE RELEVANT TO PACKAGES OFFERED

1. The destination and the means, characteristics and categories of transport used.

2. The type of accommodation, its location, category or degree of comfort and its main features and, where the accommodation is to be provided in a member State, its approval or tourist classification under the rules of that member State.

3. The meals which are included in the package.

4. The itinerary.

5. General information about passport and visa requirements which apply for [nationals of the member State or States in which the brochure is made available] and health formalities required for the journey and the stay.

6. Either the monetary amount or the percentage of the price which is to be paid on account and the timetable for payment of the balance.

7. Whether a minimum number of persons is required for the package to take place and, if so, the deadline for informing the consumer in the event of cancellation.

8. The arrangements (if any) which apply if consumers are delayed at the outward or homeward points of departure.

9. The arrangements for security for money paid over and for the repatriation of the consumer in the event of insolvency.

Regulation 9

SCHEDULE 2

ELEMENTS TO BE INCLUDED IN THE CONTRACT IF RELEVANT TO THE PARTICULAR PACKAGE

1. The travel destination(s) and, where periods of stay are involved, the relevant periods, with dates.

2. The means, characteristics and categories of transport to be used and the dates, times and points of departure and return.

3. Where the package includes accommodation, its location, its tourist category of degree of comfort, its main features and, where the accommodation is to be provided in a member State, its compliance with the rules of that member State.

4. The meals which are included in the package.

5. Whether a minimum number of persons is required for the package to take place and, if so, the deadline for informing the consumer in the event of cancellation.

6. The itinerary.

7. Visits, excursions or other services which are included in the total price agreed for the package.

8. The name and address of the organiser, the retailer and, where appropriate, the insurer.

9. The price of the package, if the price may be revised in accordance with the term which may be included in the contract under regulation 11, an indication of the possibility of such price revisions, and an indication of any dues, taxes or fees chargeable for certain services (landing, embarkation or disembarkation fees at ports and airports and tourist taxes) where such costs are not included in the package.

10. The payment schedule and method of payment.

11. Special requirements which the consumer has communicated to the organiser or retailer when making the booking and which both have accepted.

12. The periods within which the consumer must make any complaint about the failure to perform or the inadequate performance of the contract.

| Regulation 23 | **SCHEDULE 3** |

SCHEDULE 3

ENFORCEMENT

1 Enforcement authority

(1) Every local weights and measures authority in Great Britain shall be an enforcement authority for the purposes of regulations 5, 7, 8, 16 and 22 of these Regulations ('the relevant regulations'), and it shall be the duty of each such authority to enforce those provisions within their area.

Employers' Liability (Compulsory Insurance) Regulations 1998

(SI 1998, No. 2573)

1 Citation, commencement and interpretation

(2) In these Regulations—

'the 1969 Act' means the Employers' Liability (Compulsory Insurance) Act 1969;

. . .

2 Prohibition of certain conditions in policies of insurance

(1) For the purposes of the 1969 Act, there is prohibited in any contract of insurance any condition which provides (in whatever terms) that no liability (either generally or in respect of a particular claim) shall arise under the policy, or that any such liability so arising shall cease, if—

    (a) some specified thing is done or omitted to be done after the happening of the event giving rise to a claim under the policy,

    (b) the policy holder does not take reasonable care to protect his employees against the risk of bodily injury or disease in the course of their employment;

    (c) the policy holder fails to comply with the requirements of any enactment for the protection of employees against the risk of bodily injury or disease in the course of their employment; or

(d) the policy holder does not keep specified records or fails to provide the insurer with or make available to him information from such records.

(2) For the purposes of the 1969 Act there is also prohibited in a policy of insurance any condition which requires—

(a) a relevant employee to pay; or

(b) an insured employer to pay the relevant employee, the first amount of any claim or any aggregation of claims.

(3) Paragraphs (1) and (2) above do not prohibit for the purposes of the 1969 Act a condition in a policy of insurance which requires the employer to pay or contribute any sum to the insurer in respect of the satisfaction of any claim made under the contract of insurance by a relevant employee or any costs and expenses incurred in relation to any such claim.

3   Limit of amount of compulsory insurance

(1) Subject to paragraph (2) below, the amount for which an employer is required by the 1969 Act to insure and maintain insurance in respect of relevant employees under one or more policies of insurance shall be, or shall in aggregate be not less than £5 million in respect of—

(a) a claim relating to any one or more of those employees arising out of any one occurrence; and

(b) any costs and expenses incurred in relation to any such claim.

Provision and Use of Work Equipment Regulations 1998

(SI 1998, No. 2306)

2   Interpretation

(1) In these Regulations, unless the context otherwise requires—

'the 1974 Act' means the Health and Safety at Work etc. Act 1974;

'employer' except in regulation 3(2) and (3) includes a person to whom the requirements imposed by the Regulations apply by virtue of regulation 3(3)(a) and (b);

'essential requirements' means requirements described in regulation 10(1);

'the Executive' means the Health and Safety Executive;

'inspection' in relation to an inspection under paragraph (1) or (2) of regulation 6—

(a) means such visual or more rigorous inspection by a competent person as is appropriate for the purpose described in the paragraph;

(b) where it is appropriate to carry out testing for the purpose, includes testing the nature and extent of which are appropriate for the purpose;

'power press' means a press or press brake for the working of metal by means of tools, or for die proving, which is power driven and which embodies a flywheel and clutch;

'thorough examination' in relation to a thorough examination under paragraph (1), (2), (3) or (4) of regulation 32—

(a) means a thorough examination by a competent person;

(b) includes testing the nature and extent of which are appropriate for the purpose described in the paragraph;

'use' in relation to work equipment means any activity involving work equipment and includes starting, stopping, programming, setting, transporting, repairing, modifying, maintaining, servicing and cleaning;

'work equipment' means any machinery, appliance, apparatus, tool or installation for use at work (whether exclusively or not);

and related expressions shall be construed accordingly.

4 Suitability of work equipment

(1) Every employer shall ensure that work equipment is so constructed or adapted as to be suitable for the purpose for which it is used or provided.

(2) In selecting work equipment, every employer shall have regard to the working conditions and to the risks to the health and safety of persons which exist in the premises or undertaking in which that work equipment is to be used and any additional risk posed by the use of that work equipment.

(3) Every employer shall ensure that work equipment is used only for operations for which, and under conditions for which, it is suitable.

(4) In this regulation 'suitable' [—

    (a) subject to paragraph (b), means suitable in any respect which it is reasonably foreseeable will affect the health and safety of any person; . . .]

5 Maintenance

(1) Every employer shall ensure that work equipment is maintained in an efficient state, in efficient working order and in good repair.

(2) Every employer shall ensure that where any machinery has a maintenance log, the log is kept up to date.

6 Inspection

(1) Every employer shall ensure that, where the safety of work equipment depends on the installation conditions, it is inspected—

    (a) after installation and before being put into service for the first time; or

    (b) after assembly at a new site or in a new location, to ensure that it has been installed correctly and is safe to operate.

(2) Every employer shall ensure that work equipment exposed to conditions causing deterioration which is liable to result in dangerous situations is inspected—

    (a) at suitable intervals; and

    (b) each time that exceptional circumstances which are liable to jeopardise the safety of the work equipment have occurred,

to ensure that health and safety conditions are maintained and that any deterioration can be detected and remedied in good time.

(3) Every employer shall ensure that the result of an inspection made under this regulation is recorded and kept until the next inspection under this regulation is recorded.

(4) Every employer shall ensure that no work equipment—

    (a) leaves his undertaking; or

    (b) if obtained from the undertaking of another person, is used in his undertaking, unless it is accompanied by physical evidence that the last inspection required to be carried out under this regulation has been carried out.

7 Specific risks

(1) Where the use of work equipment is likely to involve a specific risk to health or safety, every employer shall ensure that—

    (a) the use of that work equipment is restricted to those persons given the task of using it; and

    (b) repairs, modifications, maintenance or servicing of that work equipment is restricted to those persons who have been specifically designated to perform operations of that description (whether or not also authorised to perform other operations).

(2) The employer shall ensure that the persons designated for the purposes of subparagraph (b) of paragraph (1) have received adequate training related to any operations in respect of which they have been so designated.

8 Information and instructions

(1) Every employer shall ensure that all persons who use work equipment have available to them adequate health and safety information and, where appropriate, written instructions pertaining to the use of the work equipment.

(2) Every employer shall ensure that any of his employees who supervises or manages the use of work equipment has available to him adequate health and safety information and, where appropriate, written instructions pertaining to the use of the work equipment.

(3) Without prejudice to the generality of paragraphs (1) or (2), the information and instructions required by either of those paragraphs shall include information and, where appropriate, written instructions on—

    (a) the conditions in which and the methods by which the work equipment may be used;

    (b) foreseeable abnormal situations and the action to be taken if such a situation were to occur; and

    (c) any conclusions to be drawn from experience in using the work equipment.

(4) Information and instructions required by this regulation shall be readily comprehensive to those concerned.

9 Training

(1) Every employer shall ensure that all persons who use work equipment have received adequate training for purposes of health and safety, including training in the methods which may be adopted when using the work equipment, any risks which such use may entail and precautions to be taken.

(2) Every employer shall ensure that any of his employees who supervises or manages the use of work equipment has received adequate training for purposes of health and safety, including training in the methods which may be adopted when using the work equipment, any risks which such use may entail and precautions to be taken.

10 Conformity with Community requirements

[(1) Every employer shall ensure that an item of work equipment conforms at all times with any essential requirements, other than requirements which, at the time of its being first supplied or put into service in any place in which these Regulations apply, did not apply to work equipment of its type.

(2) In this regulation "essential requirements", in relation to an item of work equipment, means requirements relating to the design and construction of work equipment of its type in any of the instruments listed in Schedule 1 (being instruments which give effect to Community directives concerning the safety of products);]

(3) This regulation applies to items of work equipment provided for use in the premises or undertaking of the employer for the first time after 31 December 1992.

11 Dangerous parts of machinery

(1) Every employer shall ensure that measures are taken in accordance with paragraph (2) which are effective—

    (a) to prevent access to any dangerous part of machinery or to any rotating stock-bar; or

    (b) to stop the movement of any dangerous part of machinery or rotating stock-bar before any part of a person enters a danger zone.

[(2) The measures required by paragraph (1) shall consist of—

    (a) the provision of fixed guards enclosing every dangerous part or rotating stock-bar where and to the extent that it is practicable to do so, but where or to the extent that it is not, then

    (b) the provision of other guards or protection devices where and to the extent that it is practicable to do so, but where or to the extent that it is not, then

    (c) the provision of jigs, holders, push-sticks or similar protection appliances used in conjunction with the machinery where and to the extent that it is practicable to do so,

and the provision of such information, instruction, training and supervision as is necessary.]

(3) All guards and protection devices provided under sub-paragraphs (a) or (b) of paragraphs (2) shall—

    (a) be suitable for the purpose for which they are provided;

    (b) be of good construction, sound material and adequate strength;

    (c) be maintained in an efficient state, in efficient working order and in good repair;

    (d) not give rise to any increased risk to health or safety;

    (e) not be easily bypassed or disabled;

    (f) be situated at sufficient distance from the danger zone;

    (g) not unduly restrict the view of the operating cycle of the machinery, where such a view is necessary;

    (h) be so constructed or adapted that they allow operations necessary to fit or replace parts and for maintenance work, restricting access so that it is allowed only to the area where the work is to be carried out and, if possible, without having to dismantle the guard or protection device.

    (4) All protection appliances provided under sub-paragraph (c) of paragraph (2) shall comply with sub-paragraphs (a) to (d) and (g) of paragraph (3).

    (5) In this regulation—

'danger zone' means any zone in or around machinery in which a person is exposed to a risk to health or safety from contact with a dangerous part of machinery or a rotating stock-bar;

'stock-bar' means any part of a stock-bar which projects beyond the head-stock of a lathe.

12   Protection against specified hazards

    (1) Every employer shall take measures to ensure that the exposure of a person using work equipment to any risk to his health or safety from any hazard specified in paragraph (3) is either prevented, or, where that is not reasonably practicable, adequately controlled.

    (2) The measures required by paragraph (1) shall—

    (a) be measures other than the provision of personal protective equipment or of information, instruction, training and supervision, so far as is reasonably practicable; and

    (b) include, where appropriate, measures to minimise the effects of the hazard as well as to reduce the likelihood of the hazard occurring.

    (3) The hazards referred to in paragraph (1) are—

    (a) any article or substance falling or being ejected from work equipment;

    (b) rupture or disintegration of parts of work equipment;

    (c) work equipment catching fire or overheating;

    (d) the unintended or premature discharge of any article or of any gas, dust, liquid, vapour or other substance which, in each case, is produced, used or stored in the work equipment;

    (e) the unintended or premature explosion of the work equipment or any article or substance produced, used or stored in it.

    (4) For the purposes of this regulation 'adequately' means adequately having regard only to the nature of the hazard and the nature and degree of exposure to the risk.

    (5) This regulation shall not apply where any of the following Regulations apply in respect of any risk to a person's health or safety for which such Regulations require measures to be taken to prevent or control such risk, namely—

    (a)   the Ionising Radiations Regulations 1985;

    (b)   the [Control of Asbestos at Work Regulations 2006;

    (c)   the Control of Substances Hazardous to Health Regulations 1994];

    (d)   the [Control of Noise at Work Regulations 2005];

    (e)   the Construction (Head Protection) Regulations 1989;

    (f)   the Control of Lead at Work Regulations 1998

    [(g) the Control of Vibration at Work Regulations 2005].

13   High or very low temperature

Every employer shall ensure that work equipment, parts of work equipment and any article or substance produced, used or stored in work equipment which, in each case, is at a high or very low temperature shall have protection where appropriate so as to prevent injury to any person by burn, scald or sear.

14   Controls for starting or making a significant change in operating conditions

(1) Every employer shall ensure that, where appropriate, work equipment is provided with one or more controls for the purposes of—

(a) starting the work equipment (including re-starting after a stoppage for any reason); or

(b) controlling any change in the speed, pressure or other operating conditions of the work equipment where such conditions after the change result in risk to health and safety which is greater than or of a different nature from such risks before the change.

(2) Subject to paragraph (3), every employer shall ensure that, where a control is required by paragraph (1), it shall not be possible to perform any operation mentioned in sub-paragraph (a) or (b) of that paragraph except by a deliberate action on such control.

(3) Paragraph (1) shall not apply to re-starting or changing operating conditions as a result of the normal operating cycle of an automatic device.

15   Stop controls

(1) Every employer shall ensure that, where appropriate, work equipment is provided with one or more readily accessible controls the operation of which will bring the work equipment to a safe condition in a safe manner.

(2) Any control required by paragraph (1) shall bring the work equipment to a complete stop where necessary for reasons of health and safety.

(3) Any control required by paragraph (1) shall, if necessary for reasons of health and safety, switch off all sources of energy after stopping the functioning of the work equipment.

(4) Any control required by paragraph (1) shall operate in priority to any control which starts or changes the operating conditions of the work equipment.

16   Emergency stop controls

(1) Every employer shall ensure that, where appropriate, work equipment is provided with one or more readily accessible emergency stop controls unless it is not necessary by reason of the nature of the hazards and the time taken for the work equipment to come to a complete stop as a result of the action of any control provided by virtue of regulation 15(1).

(2) Any control required by paragraph (1) shall operate in priority to any control required by regulation 15(1).

17   Controls

(1) Every employer shall ensure that all controls for work equipment are clearly visible and identifiable, including by appropriate marking where necessary.

(2) Except where necessary, the employer shall ensure that no control for work equipment is in a position where any person operating the control is exposed to a risk to his health or safety.

(3) Every employer shall ensure where appropriate—

(a) that, so far as is reasonably practicable, the operator of any control is able to ensure from the position of that control that no person is in a place where he would be exposed to any risk to his health or safety as a result of the operation of that control, but where or to the extent that it is not reasonably practicable;

(b) that, so far as is reasonably practicable, systems of work are effective to ensure that, when work equipment is about to start, no person is in a place where he would be exposed to a risk to his health or safety as a result of the work equipment starting, but where neither of these is reasonably practicable;

(c) that an audible, visible or other suitable warning is given by virtue of regulation 24 whenever work equipment is about to start.

(4) Every employer shall take appropriate measures to ensure that any person who is in a place where he would be exposed to a risk to his health or safety as a result of the starting or stopping of work equipment has sufficient time and suitable means to avoid that risk.

18   Control systems

[(1) Every employer shall ensure, so far as is reasonably practicable, that all control systems of work equipment—

     (a) are safe; and

     (b) are chosen making due allowance for the failures, faults and constraints to be expected in the planned circumstances of use.]

  (2) Without prejudice to the generality of paragraph (1), a control system shall not be safe unless—

     (a) its operation does not create any increased risk to health or safety;

     (b) it ensures, so far as is reasonably practicable, that any fault in or damage to any part of the control system or the loss of supply of any source of energy used by the work equipment cannot result in additional or increased risk to health or safety;

     (c) it does not impede the operation of any control required by regulation 15 or 16.

19   Isolation from sources of energy

(1) Every employer shall ensure that where appropriate work equipment is provided with suitable means to isolate it from all its sources of energy.

(2) Without prejudice to the generality of paragraph (1), the means mentioned in that paragraph shall not be suitable unless they are clearly identifiable and readily accessible.

(3) Every employer shall take appropriate measures to ensure that re-connection of any energy source to work equipment does not expose any person using the work equipment to any risk to his health or safety.

20   Stability

Every employer shall ensure that work equipment or any part of work equipment is stabilised by clamping or otherwise where necessary for purposes of health or safety.

21   Lighting

Every employer shall ensure that suitable and sufficient lighting, which takes account of the operations to be carried out, is provided at any place where a person uses work equipment.

22   Maintenance operations

Every employer shall take appropriate measures to ensure that work equipment is so constructed or adapted that, so far as is reasonably practicable, maintenance operations which involve a risk to health or safety can be carried out while the work equipment is shut down, or in other cases—

     (a) maintenance operations can be carried out without exposing the person carrying them out to a risk to his health or safety; or

     (b) appropriate measures can be taken for the protection of any person carrying out maintenance operations which involve a risk to his health or safety.

23   Markings

Every employer shall ensure that work equipment is marked in a clearly visible manner with any marking appropriate for reasons of health and safety.

24   Warnings

(1) Every employer shall ensure that work equipment incorporates any warnings or warning devices which are appropriate for reasons of health and safety.

(2) Without prejudice to the generality of paragraph (1), warnings given by warning devices on work equipment shall not be appropriate unless they are unambiguous, easily perceived and easily understood.

Unfair Terms in Consumer Contracts Regulations 1999

(SI 1999, No. 2083)

3   Interpretation

  (1) In these Regulations—

'the Community' means the European Community;

'consumer' means any natural person who, in contracts covered by these Regulations, is acting for purposes which are outside his trade, business or profession;

'court' in relation to England and Wales and Northern Ireland means a county court or the High Court, and in relation to Scotland, the Sheriff or the Court of Session;

'Director' means the Director General of Fair Trading;

'EEA Agreement' means the Agreement on the European Economic Area signed at Oporto on 2nd May 1992 as adjusted by the protocol signed at Brussels on 17th March 1993;

'Member State' means a State which is a contracting party to the EEA Agreement;

'notified' means notified in writing;

'qualifying body' means a person specified in Schedule 1;

'seller or supplier' means any natural or legal person who, in contracts covered by these Regulations, is acting for purposes relating to his trade, business or profession, whether publicly owned or privately owned;

'unfair terms' means the contractual terms referred to in regulation 5.

[(1A) The references—

(a) in regulation 4(1) to a seller or a supplier, and

(b) in regulation 8(1) to a seller or supplier,

include references to a distance supplier and to an intermediary.

(1B) In paragraph (1A) and regulation 5(6)—

'distance supplier' means—

(a) a supplier under a distance contract within the meaning of the Financial Services (Distance Marketing) Regulations 2004, or

(b) a supplier of unsolicited financial services within regulation 15 of those Regulations; and 'intermediary' has the same meaning as in those Regulations.]

(2) In the application of these Regulations to Scotland for references to an 'injunction' or an 'interim injunction' there shall be substituted references to an 'interdict' or 'interim interdict' respectively.

4   Terms to which these Regulations apply

(1) These Regulations apply in relation to unfair terms in contracts concluded between a seller or a supplier and a consumer.

(2) These Regulations do not apply to contractual terms which reflect—

(a) mandatory statutory or regulatory provisions (including such provisions under the law of any Member State or in Community legislation having effect in the United Kingdom without further enactment);

(b) the provisions or principles of international conventions to which the Member States or the Community are party.

5   Unfair Terms

(1) A contractual term which has not been individually negotiated shall be regarded as unfair if, contrary to the requirement of good faith, it causes a significant imbalance in the parties' rights and obligations arising under the contract, to the detriment of the consumer.

(2) A term shall always be regarded as not having been individually negotiated where it has been drafted in advance and the consumer has therefore not been able to influence the substance of the term.

(3) Notwithstanding that a specific term or certain aspects of it in a contract has been individually negotiated, these Regulations shall apply to the rest of a contract if an overall assessment of it indicates that it is a pre-formulated standard contract.

(4) It shall be for any seller or supplier who claims that a term was individually negotiated to show that it was.

(5) Schedule 2 to these Regulations contains an indicative and non-exhaustive list of the terms which may be regarded as unfair.

[(6) Any contractual term providing that a consumer bears the burden of proof in respect of showing whether a distance supplier or an intermediary complied with any or all of the obligations placed upon him resulting from the Directive and any rule or enactment implementing it shall always be regarded as unfair.

(7) In paragraph (6)—

'the Directive' means Directive 2002/65/EC of the European Parliament and of the Council of 23 September 2002 concerning the distance marketing of consumer financial services and amending Council Directive 90/619/EEC and Directives 97/7/EC and 98/27/EC; and

'rule' means a rule made by the Financial Services Authority under the Financial Services and Markets Act 2000 or by a designated professional body within the meaning of section 326(2) of that Act.]

6   Assessment of unfair terms

(1) Without prejudice to regulation 12, the unfairness of a contractual term shall be assessed, taking into account the nature of the goods or services for which the contract was concluded and by referring, at the time of conclusion of the contract, to all the circumstances attending the conclusion of the contract and to all the other terms of the contract or of another contract on which it is dependent.

(2) In so far as it is in plain intelligible language, the assessment of fairness of a term shall not relate—

(a) to the definition of the main subject matter of the contract, or

(b) to the adequacy of the price or remuneration, as against the goods or services supplied in exchange.

7   Written contracts

(1) A seller or supplier shall ensure that any written term of a contract is expressed in plain, intelligible language.

(2) If there is doubt about the meaning of a written term, the interpretation which is most favourable to the consumer shall prevail but this rule shall not apply in proceedings brought under regulation 12.

8   Effect of unfair term

(1) An unfair term in a contract concluded with a consumer by a seller or supplier shall not be binding on the consumer.

(2) The contract shall continue to bind the parties if it is capable of continuing in existence without the unfair term.

9   Choice of law clauses

These Regulations shall apply notwithstanding any contract term which applies or purports to apply the law of a non-Member State, if the contract has a close connection with the territory of the Member States.

10   Complaints—consideration by [OFT]

(1) It shall be the duty of the [OFT] to consider any complaint made to [it] that any contract term drawn up for general use is unfair, unless—

(a) the complaint appears to the [OFT] to be frivolous or vexatious; or

(b) a qualifying body has notified the [OFT] that it agrees to consider the complaint.

(2) The [OFT] shall give reasons for [its] decision to apply or not to apply, as the case may be, for an injunction under regulation 12 in relation to any complaint which these Regulations require [it] to consider.

(3) In deciding whether or not to apply for an injunction in respect of a term which the [OFT] considers to be unfair, [it] may, if [it] considers it appropriate to do so, have regard to any undertakings given to him by or on behalf of any person as to the continued use of such a term in contracts concluded with consumers.

11   Complaints—consideration by qualifying bodies

(1) If a qualifying body specified in Part One of Schedule 1 notifies the [OFT] that it agrees to consider a complaint that any contract term drawn up for general use is unfair, it shall be under a duty to consider that complaint.

(2) Regulation 10(2) and (3) shall apply to a qualifying body which is under a duty to consider a complaint as they apply to the [OFT].

12   Injunctions to prevent continued use of unfair terms

(1) The [OFT] or, subject to paragraph (2), any qualifying body may apply for an injunction (including an interim injunction) against any person appearing to the [OFT] or that body to be using, or recommending use of, an unfair term drawn up for general use in contracts concluded with consumers.

(2) A qualifying body may apply for an injunction only where—

    (a) it has notified the [OFT] of its intention to apply at least fourteen days before the date on which the application is made, beginning with the date on which the notification was given; or

    (b) the [OFT] consents to the application being made within a shorter period.

(3) The court on an application under this regulation may grant an injunction on such terms as it thinks fit.

(4) An injunction may relate not only to use of a particular contract term drawn up for general use but to any similar term, or a term having like effect, used or recommended for use by any person.

13   Powers of the [OFT] and qualifying bodies to obtain documents and information

(1) The [OFT] may exercise the power conferred by this regulation for the purpose of—

    (a) facilitating [its] consideration of a complaint that a contract term drawn up for general use is unfair; or

    (b) ascertaining whether a person has complied with an undertaking or court order as to the continued use, or recommendation for use, of a term in contracts concluded with consumers.

(2) A qualifying body specified in Part One of Schedule 1 may exercise the power conferred by this regulation for the purpose of—

    (a) facilitating its consideration of a complaint that a contract term drawn up for general use is unfair; or

    (b) ascertaining whether a person has complied with—

        (i)   an undertaking given to it or to the court following an application by that body, or

        (ii)   a court order made on an application by that body,

as to the continued use, or recommendation for use, of a term in contracts concluded with consumers.

(3) The [OFT] may require any person to supply to [it], and a qualifying body specified in Part One of Schedule 1 may require any person to supply to it—

    (a) a copy of any document which that person has used or recommended for use, at the time the notice referred to in paragraph (4) below is given, as a pre-formulated standard contract in dealings with consumers;

    (b) information about the use, or recommendation for use, by that person of that document or any other such document in dealings with consumers.

(4) The power conferred by this regulation is to be exercised by a notice in writing which may—

    (a) specify the way in which and the time within which it is to be complied with; and

    (b) be varied or revoked by a subsequent notice.

(5) Nothing in this regulation compels a person to supply any document or information which he would be entitled to refuse to produce or give in civil proceedings before the court.

(6) If a person makes default in complying with a notice under this regulation, the court may, on the application of the [OFT] or of the qualifying body, make such order as the court thinks fit for requiring the default to be made good, and any such order may provide that all the costs or expenses of and incidental to the application shall be borne by the person in default or by any officers of a company or other association who are responsible for its default.

14 Notification of undertakings and orders to [OFT]

A qualifying body shall notify the [OFT]—
- (a) of any undertaking given to it by or on behalf of any person as to the continued use of a term which that body considers to be unfair in contracts concluded with consumers;
- (b) of the outcome of any application made by it under regulation 12, and of the terms of any undertaking given to, or order made by, the court;
- (c) of the outcome of any application made by it to enforce a previous order of the court.

15 Publication, information and advice

(1) The [OFT] shall arrange for the publication in such form and manner as [it] considers appropriate, of—
- (a) details of any undertaking or order notified to [it] under regulation 14;
- (b) details of any undertaking given to [it] by or on behalf of any person as to the continued use of a term which the [OFT] considers to be unfair in contracts concluded with consumers;
- (c) details of any application made by [it] under regulation 12, and of the terms of any undertaking given to, or order made by, the court;
- (d) details of any application made by the [OFT] to enforce a previous order of the court.

(2) The Director shall inform any person on request whether a particular term to which these Regulations apply has been—
- (a) the subject of an undertaking given to the [OFT] or notified to [it] by a qualifying body; or
- (b) the subject of an order of the court made upon application by [it] or notified to [it] by a qualifying body;

and shall give that person details of the undertaking or a copy of the order, as the case may be, together with a copy of any amendments which the person giving the undertaking has agreed to make to the term in question.

(3) The [OFT] may arrange for the dissemination in such form and manner as [it] considers appropriate of such information and advice concerning the operation of these Regulations as may appear to him to be expedient to give to the public and to all persons likely to be affected by these Regulations.

[16 The functions of the Financial Services Authority

The functions of the Financial Services Authority under these Regulations shall be treated as functions of the Financial Services Authority under the Financial Services and Markets Act 2000.]

Regulation 3

SCHEDULE 1

QUALIFYING BODIES

[PART ONE]

[1. The Information Commissioner.
2. The Gas and Electricity Markets Authority.
3. The Director General of Electricity Supply for Northern Ireland.
4. The Director General of Gas for Northern Ireland.

5. The Office of Communications.
6. The Water Services Regulation Authority.
7. The Rail Regulator.
8. Every weights and measures authority in Great Britain.
9. The Department of Enterprise, Trade and Investment in Northern Ireland.
10. The Financial Services Authority.]

PART TWO

11. Consumers' Association.

Regulation 5(5)   **SCHEDULE 2**

INDICATIVE AND NON-EXHAUSTIVE LIST OF TERMS WHICH MAY BE REGARDED AS UNFAIR

1. Terms which have the object or effect of—
   (a) excluding or limiting the legal liability of a seller or supplier in the event of the death of a consumer or personal injury to the latter resulting from an act or omission of that seller or supplier;
   (b) inappropriately excluding or limiting the legal rights of the consumer vis-à-vis the seller or supplier or another party in the event of total or partial non-performance or inadequate performance by the seller or supplier of any of the contractual obligations, including the option of offsetting a debt owed to the seller or supplier against any claim which the consumer may have against him;
   (c) making an agreement binding on the consumer whereas provision of services by the seller or supplier is subject to a condition whose realisation depends on his own will alone;
   (d) permitting the seller or supplier to retain sums paid by the consumer where the latter decides not to conclude or perform the contract, without providing for the consumer to receive compensation of an equivalent amount from the seller or supplier where the latter is the party cancelling the contract;
   (e) requiring any consumer who fails to fulfil his obligation to pay a disproportionately high sum in compensation;
   (f) authorising the seller or supplier to dissolve the contract on a discretionary basis where the same facility is not granted to the consumer, or permitting the seller or supplier to retain the sums paid for services not yet supplied by him where it is the seller or supplier himself who dissolves the contract;
   (g) enabling the seller or supplier to terminate a contract of indeterminate duration without reasonable notice except where there are serious grounds for doing so;
   (h) automatically extending a contract of fixed duration where the consumer does not indicate otherwise, when the deadline fixed for the consumer to express his desire not to extend the contract is unreasonably early;
   (i) irrevocably binding the consumer to terms with which he had no real opportunity of becoming acquainted before the conclusion of the contract;
   (j) enabling the seller or supplier to alter the terms of the contract unilaterally without a valid reason which is specified in the contract;
   (k) enabling the seller or supplier to alter unilaterally without a valid reason any characteristics of the product or service to be provided;
   (l) providing for the price of goods to be determined at the time of delivery or allowing a seller of goods or supplier of services to increase their price without in both cases giving the consumer the corresponding right to cancel the contract if the final price is too high in relation to the price agreed when the contract was concluded;

     (m) giving the seller or supplier the right to determine whether the goods or services supplied are in conformity with the contract, or giving him the exclusive right to interpret any term of the contract;

     (n) limiting the seller's or supplier's obligation to respect commitments undertaken by his agents or making his commitments subject to compliance with a particular formality;

     (o) obliging the consumer to fulfil all his obligations where the seller or supplier does not perform his;

     (p) giving the seller or supplier the possibility of transferring his rights and obligations under the contract, where this may serve to reduce the guarantees for the consumer, without the latter's agreement;

     (q) excluding or hindering the consumer's right to take legal action or exercise any other legal remedy, particularly by requiring the consumer to take disputes exclusively to arbitration not covered by legal provisions, unduly restricting the evidence available to him or imposing on him a burden of proof which, according to the applicable law, should lie with another party to the contract.

2. Scope of paragraphs 1(g), (j) and (l)

     (a) Paragraph 1(g) is without hindrance to terms by which a supplier of financial services reserves the right to terminate unilaterally a contract of indeterminate duration without notice where there is a valid reason, provided that the supplier is required to inform the other contracting party or parties thereof immediately.

     (b) Paragraph 1(j) is without hindrance to terms under which a supplier of financial services reserves the right to alter the rate of interest payable by the consumer or due to the latter, or the amount of other charges for financial services without notice where there is a valid reason, provided that the supplier is required to inform the other contracting party or parties thereof at the earliest opportunity and that the latter are free to dissolve the contract immediately.

     Paragraph 1(j) is also without hindrance to terms under which a seller or supplier reserves the right to alter unilaterally the conditions of a contract of indeterminate duration, provided that he is required to inform the consumer with reasonable notice and that the consumer is free to dissolve the contract.

     (c) Paragraphs 1(g), (j) and (l) do not apply to:
     – transactions in transferable securities, financial instruments and other products or services where the price is linked to fluctuations in a stock exchange quotation or index or a financial market rate that the seller or supplier does not control;
     – contracts for the purchase or sale of foreign currency, traveller's cheques or international money orders denominated in foreign currency;

     (d) Paragraph 1(l) is without hindrance to price indexation clauses, where lawful, provided that the method by which prices vary is explicitly described.

Consumer Protection (Distance Selling) Regulations 2000

(SI 2000, No. 2334)

3 Interpretation

    (1) In these Regulations—

['the 2000 Act' means the Financial Services and Markets Act 2000;

'appointed representative' has the same meaning as in section 39(2) of the 2000 Act;

'authorised person' has the same meaning as in section 31(2) of the 2000 Act;]

    'breach' means contravention by a supplier of a prohibition in, or failure to comply with a requirement of, these Regulations;

    'business' includes a trade or profession;

'consumer' means any natural person who, in contracts to which these Regulations apply, is acting for purposes which are outside his business;

'court' in relation to England and Wales and Northern Ireland means a county court or the High Court, and in relation to Scotland means the Sheriff Court or the Court of Session;

'credit' includes a cash loan and any other form of financial accommodation, and for this purpose 'cash' includes money in any form;

'[OFT]' means the [Office of Fair Trading];

'distance contract' means any contract concerning goods or services concluded between a supplier and a consumer under an organised distance sales or service provision scheme run by the supplier who, for the purpose of the contract, makes exclusive use of one or more means of distance communication up to and including the moment at which the contract is concluded;

'EEA Agreement' means the Agreement on the European Economic Area signed at Oporto on 2 May 1992 as adjusted by the Protocol signed at Brussels on 17 March 1993;

'enactment' includes an enactment comprised in, or in an instrument made under, an Act of the Scottish Parliament;

'enforcement authority' means the [OFT], every weights and measures authority in Great Britain, and the Department of Enterprise, Trade and Investment in Northern Ireland;

'excepted contract' means a contract such as is mentioned in regulation 5(1);

['financial service' means any service of a banking, credit, insurance, personal pension, investment or payment nature;]

'means of distance communication' means any means which, without the simultaneous physical presence of the supplier and the consumer, may be used for the conclusion of a contract between those parties; and an indicative list of such means is contained in Schedule 1;

'Member State' means a State which is a contracting party to the EEA Agreement;

'operator of a means of communication' means any public or private person whose business involves making one or more means of distance communication available to suppliers;

'period for performance' has the meaning given by regulation 19(2);

'personal credit agreement' has the meaning given by regulation 14(8);

['regulated activity' has the same meaning as in section 22 of the 2000 Act;]

'related credit agreement' has the meaning given by regulation 15(5);

'supplier' means any person who, in contracts to which these Regulations apply, is acting in his commercial or professional capacity; and

'working days' means all days other than Saturdays, Sundays and public holidays.

(2) In the application of these Regulations to Scotland, for references to an 'injunction' or an 'interim injunction' there shall be substituted references to an 'interdict' or an 'interim interdict' respectively.

4   Contracts to which these Regulations apply

These Regulations apply, subject to regulation 6, to distance contracts other than excepted contracts.

5   Excepted contracts

(1) The following are excepted contracts, namely any contract—
   (a) for sale or other disposition of an interest in land except for a rental agreement;
   (b) for the construction of a building where the contract also provides for a sale or other disposition of an interest in land on which the building is constructed, except for a rental agreement;
   (c) relating to financial services [. . .];
   (d) concluded by means of an automated vending machine or automated commercial premises;
   (e) concluded with a telecommunications operator through the use of a public pay-phone;
   (f) concluded at an auction.
(2) References in paragraph (1) to a rental agreement—

(a) if the land is situated in England and Wales, are references to any agreement which does not have to be made in writing (whether or not in fact made in writing) because of section 2(5)(a) of the Law of Property (Miscellaneous Provisions) Act 1989;

(b) if the land is situated in Scotland, are references to any agreement for the creation, transfer, variation or extinction of an interest in land, which does not have to be made in writing (whether or not in fact made in writing) as provided for in section 1(2) and (7) of the Requirements of Writing (Scotland) Act 1995; and

(c) if the land is situated in Northern Ireland, are references to any agreement which is not one to which section II of the Statute of Frauds, (Ireland) 1695 applies.

(3) Paragraph (2) shall not be taken to mean that a rental agreement in respect of land situated outside the United Kingdom is not capable of being a distance contract to which these Regulations apply.

6   Contracts to which only part of these regulations apply

[(1) Regulations 7 to 20 shall not apply to a contract which is a regulated contract within the meaning of the Timeshare, Holiday Products, Resale and Exchange Contracts Regulations 2010.]

(2) Regulations 7 to 19(1) shall not apply to—

(a) contracts for the supply of food, beverages or other goods intended for everyday consumption supplied to the consumer's residence or to his workplace by regular roundsmen; or

(b) contracts for the provision of accommodation, transport, catering or leisure services, where the supplier undertakes, when the contract is concluded, to provide these services on a specific date or within a specific period.

(3) Regulations 19(2) to (8) and 20 do not apply to a contract for a 'package' within the meaning of the Package Travel, Package Holidays and Package Tours Regulations 1992 which is sold or offered for sale in the territory of the Member States.

[(4) Regulations 7 to 14, 17 to 20 and 25 do not apply to any contract which is made, and regulation 24 does not apply to any unsolicited services which are supplied, by an authorised person where the making or performance of that contract or the supply of those services, as the case may be, constitutes or is part of a regulated activity carried on by him.

(5) Regulations 7 to 9, 17 to 20 and 25 do not apply to any contract which is made, and regulation 24 does not apply to any unsolicited services which are supplied, by an appointed representative where the making or performance of that contract or the supply of those services, as the case may be, constitutes or is part of a regulated activity carried on by him.]

7   Information required prior to the conclusion of the contract

(1) Subject to paragraph (4), in good time prior to the conclusion of the contract the supplier shall—

(a) provide to the consumer the following information—

(i) the identity of the supplier and, where the contract requires payment in advance, the supplier's address;

(ii) a description of the main characteristics of the goods or services;

(iii) the price of the goods or services including all taxes;

(iv) delivery costs where appropriate;

(v) the arrangements for payment, delivery or performance;

(vi) the existence of a right of cancellation except in the cases referred to in regulation 13;

(vii) the cost of using the means of distance communication where it is calculated other than at the basic rate;

(viii) the period for which the offer or the price remains valid; and

(ix) where appropriate, the minimum duration of the contract, in the case of contracts for the supply of goods or services to be performed permanently or recurrently;

(b) inform the consumer if he proposes, in the event of the goods or services ordered by the consumer being unavailable, to provide substitute goods or services (as the case may be) of equivalent quality and price; and

    (c) inform the consumer that the cost of returning any such substitute goods to the supplier in the event of cancellation by the consumer would be met by the supplier.

    (2) The supplier shall ensure that the information required by paragraph (1) is provided in a clear and comprehensible manner appropriate to the means of distance communication used, with due regard in particular to the principles of good faith in commercial transactions and the principles governing the protection of those who are unable to give their consent such as minors.

    (3) Subject to paragraph (4), the supplier shall ensure that his commercial purpose is made clear when providing the information required by paragraph (1).

    (4) In the case of a telephone communication, the identity of the supplier and the commercial purpose of the call shall be made clear at the beginning of the conversation with the consumer.

8 Written and additional information

    (1) Subject to regulation 9, the supplier shall provide to the consumer in writing, or in another durable medium which is available and accessible to the consumer, the information referred to in paragraph (2), either—

        (a) prior to the conclusion of the contract, or

        (b) thereafter, in good time and in any event—

            (i)   during the performance of the contract, in the case of services; and

            (ii) at the latest at the time of delivery where goods not for delivery to third parties are concerned.

    (2) The information required to be provided by paragraph (1) is—

        (a) the information set out in paragraphs (i) to (vi) of Regulation 7(1)(a);

        (b) information about the conditions and procedures for exercising the right to cancel under regulation 10, including—

            (i)   where a term of the contract requires (or the supplier intends that it will require) that the consumer shall return the goods to the supplier in the event of cancellation, notification of that requirement; [. . .]

            (ii) information as to whether the consumer or the supplier would be responsible under these Regulations for the cost of returning any goods to the supplier, or the cost of his recovering them, if the consumer cancels the contract under regulation 10;

         [(iii) in the case of a contract for the supply of services, information as to how the right to cancel may be affected by the consumer agreeing to performance of the services beginning before the end of the seven working day period referred to in regulation 12;]

        (c) the geographical address of the place of business of the supplier to which the consumer may address any complaints;

        (d) information about any after-sales services and guarantees; and

        (e) the conditions for exercising any contractual right to cancel the contract, where the contract is of an unspecified duration or a duration exceeding one year.

9 Services performed through the use of a means of distance communication

    (1) Regulation 8 shall not apply to a contract for the supply of services which are performed through the use of a means of distance communication, where those services are supplied on only one occasion and are invoiced by the operator of the means of distance communication.

    (2) But the supplier shall take all necessary steps to ensure that a consumer who is a party to a contract to which paragraph (1) applies is able to obtain the supplier's geographical address and the place of business to which the consumer may address any complaints.

10 Right to cancel

    (1) Subject to regulation 13, if within the cancellation period set out in regulations 11 and 12, the consumer gives a notice of cancellation to the supplier, or any other person previously notified by the supplier to the consumer as a person to whom notice of cancellation may be given, the notice of cancellation shall operate to cancel the contract.

(2) Except as otherwise provided by these Regulations, the effect of a notice of cancellation is that the contract shall be treated as if it had not been made.

(3) For the purposes of these Regulations, a notice of cancellation is a notice in writing or in another durable medium available and accessible to the supplier (or to the other person to whom it is given) which, however expressed, indicates the intention of the consumer to cancel the contract.

(4) A notice of cancellation given under this regulation by a consumer to a supplier or other person is to be treated as having been properly given if the consumer—

    (a) leaves it at the address last known to the consumer and addressed to the supplier or other person by name (in which case it is to be taken to have been given on the day on which it was left);

    (b) sends it by post to the address last known to the consumer and addressed to the supplier or other person by name (in which case, it is to be taken to have been given on the day on which it was posted);

    (c) sends it by facsimile to the business facsimile number last known to the consumer (in which case it is to be taken to have been given on the day on which it is sent); or

    (d) sends it by electronic mail, to the business electronic mail address last known to the consumer (in which case it is to be taken to have been given on the day on which it is sent).

(5) Where a consumer gives a notice in accordance with paragraph (4)(a) or (b) to a supplier who is a body corporate or a partnership, the notice is to be treated as having been properly given if—

    (a) in the case of a body corporate, it is left at the address of, or sent to, the secretary or clerk of that body; or

    (b) in the case of a partnership, it is left with or sent to a partner or a person having control or management of the partnership business.

11 Cancellation period in the case of contracts for the supply of goods

(1) For the purposes of regulation 10, the cancellation period in the case of contracts for the supply of goods begins with the day on which the contract is concluded and ends as provided in paragraphs (2) to (5).

(2) Where the supplier complies with regulation 8, the cancellation period ends on the expiry of the period of seven working days beginning with the day after the day on which the consumer receives the goods.

(3) Where a supplier who has not complied with regulation 8 provides to the consumer the information referred to in regulation 8(2), and does so in writing or in another durable medium available and accessible to the consumer, within the period of three months beginning with the day after the day on which the consumer receives the goods, the cancellation period ends on the expiry of the period of seven working days beginning with the day after the day on which the consumer receives the information.

(4) Where neither paragraph (2) nor (3) applies, the cancellation period ends on the expiry of the period of three months and seven working days beginning with the day after the day on which the consumer receives the goods.

(5) In the case of contracts for goods for delivery to third parties, paragraphs (2) to (4) shall apply as if the consumer had received the goods on the day on which they were received by the third party.

12 Cancellation period in the case of contracts for the supply of services

(1) For the purposes of regulation 10, the cancellation period in the case of contracts for the supply of services begins with the day on which the contract is concluded and ends as provided in paragraphs (2) to (4).

(2) Where the supplier complies with regulation 8 on or before the day on which the contract is concluded, the cancellation period ends on the expiry of the period of seven working days beginning with the day after the day on which the contract is concluded.

(3) [Subject to paragraph (3A)] Where a supplier who has not complied with regulation 8 on or before the day on which the contract is concluded provides to the consumer the information referred to in regulation 8(2) [. . .], and does so in writing or in another durable medium available and accessible

to the consumer, within the period of three months beginning with the day after the day on which the contract is concluded, the cancellation period ends on the expiry of the period of seven working days beginning with the day after the day on which the consumer receives the information.

[(3A) Where the performance of the contract has begun with the consumer's agreement before the expiry of the period of seven working days beginning with the day after the day on which the contract was concluded and the supplier has not complied with regulation 8 on or before the day on which performance began, but provides to the consumer the information referred to in regulation 8(2) in good time during the performance of the contract, the cancellation period ends—

> (a) on the expiry of the period of seven working days beginning with the day after the day on which the consumer receives the information; or
>
> (b) if the performance of the contract is completed before the expiry of the period referred to in sub-paragraph (a), on the day when the performance of the contract is completed.]

(4) Where [none of paragraphs (2) to (3A) applies], the cancellation period ends on the expiry of the period of three months and seven working days beginning with the day after the day on which the contract is concluded.

13 Exceptions to the right to cancel

(1) Unless the parties have agreed otherwise, the consumer will not have the right to cancel the contract by giving notice of cancellation pursuant to regulation 10 in respect of contracts—

> [(a) for the supply of services if the performance of the contract has begun with the consumer's agreement—
>> (i) before the end of the cancellation period applicable under regulation 12(2); and
>> (ii) after the supplier has provided the information referred to in regulation 8(2).];
>
> (b) for the supply of goods or services the price of which is dependent on fluctuations in the financial market which cannot be controlled by the supplier;
>
> (c) for the supply of goods made to the consumer's specifications or clearly personalised or which by reason of their nature cannot be returned or are liable to deteriorate or expire rapidly;
>
> (d) for the supply of audio or video recordings or computer software if they are unsealed by the consumer;
>
> (e) for the supply of newspapers, periodicals or magazines; or
>
> (f) for gaming, betting or lottery services.

14 Recovery of sums paid by or on behalf of the consumer on cancellation, and return of security

(1) On the cancellation of a contract under regulation 10, the supplier shall reimburse any sum paid by or on behalf of the consumer under or in relation to the contract to the person by whom it was made free of any charge, less any charge made in accordance with paragraph (5).

(2) The reference in paragraph (1) to any sum paid on behalf of the consumer includes any sum paid by a creditor who is not the same person as the supplier under a personal credit agreement with the consumer.

(3) The supplier shall make the reimbursement referred to in paragraph (1) as soon as possible and in any case within a period not exceeding 30 days beginning with the day on which the notice of cancellation was given.

(4) Where any security has been provided in relation to the contract, the security (so far as it is so provided) shall, on cancellation under regulation 10, be treated as never having had effect and any property lodged with the supplier solely for the purposes of the security as so provided shall be returned by him forthwith.

(5) Subject to paragraphs (6) and (7), the supplier may make a charge, not exceeding the direct costs of recovering any goods supplied under the contract, where a term of the contract provides that the consumer must return any goods supplied if he cancels the contract under regulation 10 but the consumer does not comply with this provision or returns the goods at the expense of the supplier.

(6) Paragraph (5) shall not apply where—

(a) the consumer cancels in circumstances where he has the right to reject the goods under a term of the contract, including a term implied by virtue of any enactment, or

(b) the term requiring the consumer to return any goods supplied if he cancels the contract is an 'unfair term' within the meaning of the Unfair Terms in Consumer Contracts Regulations 1999.

(7) Paragraph (5) shall not apply to the cost of recovering any goods which were supplied as substitutes for the goods ordered by the consumer.

(8) For the purposes of these Regulations, a personal credit agreement is an agreement between the consumer and any other person ('the creditor') by which the creditor provides the consumer with credit of any amount.

15   Automatic cancellation of a related credit agreement

(1) Where a notice of cancellation is given under regulation 10 which has the effect of cancelling the contract, the giving of the notice shall also have the effect of cancelling any related credit agreement.

(2) Where a related credit agreement is cancelled by virtue of paragraph (1), the supplier shall, if he is not the same person as the creditor under that agreement, forthwith on receipt of the notice of cancellation inform the creditor that the notice has been given.

(3) Where a related credit agreement is cancelled by virtue of paragraph (1)—

(a) any sum paid by or on behalf of the consumer under, or in relation to, the credit agreement which the supplier is not obliged to reimburse under regulation 14(1) shall be reimbursed, except for any sum which, if it had not already been paid, would have to be paid under subparagraph (b);

(b) the agreement shall continue in force so far as it relates to repayment of the credit and payment of interest, subject to regulation 16; and

(c) subject to subparagraph (b), the agreement shall cease to be enforceable.

(4) Where any security has been provided under a related credit agreement, the security, so far as it is so provided, shall be treated as never having had effect and any property lodged with the creditor solely for the purposes of the security as so provided shall be returned by him forthwith.

(5) For the purposes of this regulation and regulation 16, a 'related credit agreement' means an agreement under which fixed sum credit which fully or partly covers the price under a contract cancelled under regulation 10 is granted—

(a) by the supplier, or

(b) by another person, under an arrangement between that person and the supplier.

(6) For the purposes of this regulation and regulation 16—

(a) 'creditor' is a person who grants credit under a related credit agreement;

(b) 'fixed sum credit' has the same meaning as in section 10 of the Consumer Credit Act 1974;

(c) 'repayment' in relation to credit means repayment of money received by the consumer, and cognate expressions shall be construed accordingly; and

(d) 'interest' means interest on money so received.

16   Repayment of credit and interest after cancellation of a related credit agreement

(1) This regulation applies following the cancellation of a related credit agreement by virtue of regulation 15(1).

(2) If the consumer repays the whole or a portion of the credit—

(a) before the expiry of one month following the cancellation of the credit agreement, or

(b) in the case of a credit repayable by instalments, before the date on which the first instalment is due,

no interest shall be payable on the amount repaid.

(3) If the whole of a credit repayable by instalments is not repaid on or before the date referred to in paragraph (2)(b), the consumer shall not be liable to repay any of the credit except on receipt of

a request in writing, signed by the creditor, stating the amounts of the remaining instalments (recal-culated by the creditor as nearly as may be in accordance with the agreement and without extending the repayment period), but excluding any sum other than principal and interest.

(4) Where any security has been provided under a related credit agreement the duty imposed on the consumer to repay credit and to pay interest shall not be enforceable before the creditor has discharged any duty imposed on him by regulation 15(4) to return any property lodged with him as security on cancellation.

17   Restoration of goods by consumer after cancellation

(1) This regulation applies where a contract is cancelled under regulation 10 after the consumer has acquired possession of any goods under the contract other than any goods mentioned in regula-tion 13(1)(b) to (e).

(2) The consumer shall be treated as having been under a duty throughout the period prior to cancellation—

    (a) to retain possession of the goods, and

    (b) to take reasonable care of them.

(3) On cancellation, the consumer shall be under a duty to restore the goods to the supplier in accordance with this regulation, and in the meanwhile to retain possession of the goods and take rea-sonable care of them.

(4) The consumer shall not be under any duty to deliver the goods except at his own premises and in pursuance of a request in writing, or in another durable medium available and accessible to the consumer, from the supplier and given to the consumer either before, or at the time when, the goods are collected from those premises.

(5) If the consumer—

    (a) delivers the goods (whether at his own premises or elsewhere) to any person to whom, under regulation 10(1), a notice of cancellation could have been given; or

    (b) sends the goods at his own expense to such a person,

he shall be discharged from any duty to retain possession of the goods or restore them to the supplier.

(6) Where the consumer delivers the goods in accordance with paragraph (5)(a), his obligation to take care of the goods shall cease; and if he sends the goods in accordance with paragraph (5)(b), he shall be under a duty to take reasonable care to see that they are received by the supplier and not damaged in transit, but in other respects his duty to take care of the goods shall cease when he sends them.

(7) Where, at any time during the period of 21 days beginning with the day notice of cancellation was given, the consumer receives such a request as is mentioned in paragraph (4), and unreasonably refuses or unreasonably fails to comply with it, his duty to retain possession and take reasonable care of the goods shall continue until he delivers or sends the goods as mentioned in paragraph (5), but if within that period he does not receive such a request his duty to take reasonable care of the goods shall cease at the end of that period.

(8) Where—

    (a) a term of the contract provides that if the consumer cancels the contract, he must return the goods to the supplier, and

    (b) the consumer is not otherwise entitled to reject the goods under the terms of the

    (c) contract or by virtue of any enactment,

paragraph (7) shall apply as if for the period of 21 days there were substituted the period of 6 months.

(9) Where any security has been provided in relation to the cancelled contract, the duty to restore goods imposed on the consumer by this regulation shall not be enforceable before the supplier has discharged any duty imposed on him by regulation 14(4) to return any property lodged with him as security on cancellation.

(10) Breach of a duty imposed by this regulation on a consumer is actionable as a breach of statutory duty.

18   Goods given in part-exchange

(1) This regulation applies on the cancellation of a contract under regulation 10 where the supplier agreed to take goods in part-exchange (the 'part-exchange goods') and those goods have been delivered to him.

(2) Unless, before the end of the period of 10 days beginning with the date of cancellation, the part-exchange goods are returned to the consumer in a condition substantially as good as when they were delivered to the supplier, the consumer shall be entitled to recover from the supplier a sum equal to the part-exchange allowance.

(3) In this regulation the part-exchange allowance means the sum agreed as such in the cancelled contract, or if no such sum was agreed, such sum as it would have been reasonable to allow in respect of the part-exchange goods if no notice of cancellation had been served.

(4) Where the consumer recovers from the supplier a sum equal to the part-exchange allowance, the title of the consumer to the part-exchange goods shall vest in the supplier (if it has not already done so) on recovery of that sum.

19   Performance

(1) Unless the parties agree otherwise, the supplier shall perform the contract within a maximum of 30 days beginning with the day after the day the consumer sent his order to the supplier.

(2) Subject to paragraphs (7) and (8), where the supplier is unable to perform the contract because the goods or services ordered are not available, within the period for performance referred to in paragraph (1) or such other period as the parties agree ('the period for performance'), he shall—

    (a) inform the consumer; and

    (b) reimburse any sum paid by or on behalf of the consumer under or in relation to the contract to the person by whom it was made.

(3) The reference in paragraph (2)(b) to any sum paid on behalf of the consumer includes any sum paid by a creditor who is not the same person as the supplier under a personal credit agreement with the consumer.

(4) The supplier shall make the reimbursement referred to in paragraph (2)(b) as soon as possible and in any event within a period of 30 days beginning with the day after the day on which the period for performance expired.

(5) A contract which has not been performed within the period for performance shall be treated as if it had not been made, save for any rights or remedies which the consumer has under it as a result of the non-performance.

(6) Where any security has been provided in relation to the contract, the security (so far as it is so provided) shall, where the supplier is unable to perform the contract within the period for performance, be treated as never having had any effect and any property lodged with the supplier solely for the purposes of the security as so provided shall be returned by him forthwith.

(7) Where the supplier is unable to supply the goods or services ordered by the consumer, the supplier may perform the contract for the purposes of these Regulations by providing substitute goods or services (as the case may be) of equivalent quality and price provided that—

    (a) this possibility was provided for in the contract;

    (b) prior to the conclusion of the contract the supplier gave the consumer the information required by regulation 7(1)(b) and (c) in the manner required by regulation 7(2).

(8) In the case of outdoor leisure events which by their nature cannot be rescheduled, paragraph 2(b) shall not apply where the consumer and the supplier so agree.

20   Effect of non-performance on related credit agreement

Where a supplier is unable to perform the contract within the period for performance—

    (a) regulations 15 and 16 shall apply to any related credit agreement as if the consumer had given a valid notice of cancellation under regulation 10 on the expiry of the period for performance; and

(b) the reference in regulation 15(3)(a) to regulation 14(1) shall be read, for the purposes of this regulation, as a reference to regulation 19(2).

24 Inertia selling

(1) Paragraph (2) and (3) apply if—

(a) unsolicited goods are sent to a person ('the recipient') with a view to his acquiring them;

(b) the recipient has no reasonable cause to believe that they were sent with a view to their being acquired for the purposes of a business; and

(c) the recipient has neither agreed to acquire nor agreed to return them.

(2) The recipient may, as between himself and the sender, use, deal with or dispose of the goods as if they were an unconditional gift to him.

(3) The rights of the sender to the goods are extinguished.

(6) In this regulation—

'acquire' includes hire;

'send' includes deliver;

'sender', in relation to any goods, includes—

(a) any person on whose behalf or with whose consent the goods are sent;

(b) any other person claiming through or under the sender or any person mentioned in paragraph (a); and

(c) any person who delivers the goods; and

'unsolicited' means, in relation to goods sent or services supplied to any person, that they are sent or supplied without any prior request made by or on behalf of the recipient.

(10) This regulation applies only to goods sent and services supplied after the date on which it comes into force.

25 No contracting-out

(1) A term contained in any contract to which these Regulations apply is void if, and to the extent that, it is inconsistent with a provision for the protection of the consumer contained in these Regulations.

(2) Where a provision of these Regulations specifies a duty or liability of the consumer in certain circumstances, a term contained in a contract to which these Regulations apply, other than a term to which paragraph (3) applies, is inconsistent with that provision if it purports to impose, directly or indirectly, an additional duty or liability on him in those circumstances.

(3) This paragraph applies to a term which requires the consumer to return any goods supplied to him under the contract if he cancels it under regulation 10.

(4) A term to which paragraph (3) applies shall, in the event of cancellation by the consumer under regulation 10, have effect only for the purposes of regulation 14(5) and 17(8).

(5) These Regulations shall apply notwithstanding any contract term which applies or purports to apply the law of a non-Member State if the contract has a close connection with the territory of a Member State.

26 Consideration of complaints

(1) It shall be the duty of an enforcement authority to consider any complaint made to it about a breach unless—

(a) the complaint appears to the authority to be frivolous or vexatious; or

(b) another enforcement authority has notified the [OFT] that it agrees to consider the complaint.

(2) If an enforcement authority notifies the [OFT] that it agrees to consider a complaint made to another enforcement authority, the first mentioned authority shall be under a duty to consider the complaint.

(3) An enforcement authority which is under a duty to consider a complaint shall give reasons for its decision to apply or not to apply, as the case may be, for an injunction under regulation 27.

(4) In deciding whether or not to apply for an injunction in respect of a breach an enforcement authority may, if it considers it appropriate to do so, have regard to any undertaking given to it or another enforcement authority by or on behalf of any person as to compliance with these Regulations.

27 Injunctions to secure compliance with these Regulations

(1) The [OFT] or, subject to paragraph (2), any other enforcement authority may apply for an injunction (including an interim injunction) against any person who appears to the [OFT] or that authority to be responsible for a breach.

(2) An enforcement authority other than the [OFT] may apply for an injunction only where—

(a) it has notified the [OFT] of its intention to apply at least fourteen days before the date on which the application is to be made, beginning with the date on which the notification was given; or

(b) the [OFT] consents to the application being made within a shorter period.

(3) The court on an application under this regulation may grant an injunction on such terms as it thinks fit to secure compliance with these Regulations.

28 Notification of undertakings and orders to the [OFT]

An enforcement authority other than the [OFT] shall notify the [OFT]—

(a) of any undertaking given to it by or on behalf of any person who appears to it to be responsible for a breach;

(b) of the outcome of any application made by it under regulation 27 and of the terms of any undertaking given to or order made by the court;

(c) of the outcome of any application made by it to enforce a previous order of the court.

29 Publication, information and advice

(1) The [OFT] shall arrange for the publication in such form and manner as [it] considers appropriate of—

(a) details of any undertaking or order notified to [it] under regulation 28;

(b) details of any undertaking given to [it] by or on behalf of any person as to compliance with these Regulations;

(c) details of any application made by [it] under regulation 27, and of the terms of any undertaking given to, or order made by, the court;

(d) details of any application made by the [OFT] to enforce a previous order of the court.

(2) The [OFT] may arrange for the dissemination in such form and manner as [it] considers appropriate of such information and advice concerning the operation of these Regulations as it may appear to [it] to be expedient to give to the public and to all persons likely to be affected by these Regulations.

Regulation 3

SCHEDULE 1

INDICATIVE LIST OF MEANS OF DISTANCE COMMUNICATION

1. Unaddressed printed matter.
2. Addressed printed matter.
3. Letter.
4. Press advertising with order form.
5. Catalogue.
6. Telephone with human intervention.
7. Telephone without human intervention (automatic calling machine, audiotext).
8. Radio.
9. Videophone (telephone with screen).
10. Videotext (microcomputer and television screen) with keyboard or touch screen.

11. Electronic mail.
12. Facsimile machine (fax).
13. Television (teleshopping).

Electronic Commerce (EC Directive) Regulations 2002

(SI 2002, No. 2013)

2 Interpretation

(1) In these Regulations and in the Schedule . . .

'consumer' means any natural person who is acting for purposes other than those of his trade, business or profession; . . .

'the Directive' means Directive 2000/31/EC of the European Parliament and of the Council of 8 June 2000 on certain legal aspects of information society services, in particular electronic commerce, in the Internal Market (Directive on electronic commerce); . . .

'information society services' (which is summarised in recital 17 of the Directive as covering 'any service normally provided for remuneration, at a distance, by means of electronic equipment for the processing (including digital compression) and storage of data, and at the individual request of a recipient of a service') has the meaning set out in Article 2(a) of the Directive, (which refers to Article 1(2) of Directive 98/34/EC of the European Parliament and of the Council of 22 June 1998 laying down a procedure for the provision of information in the field of technical standards and regulations, as amended by Directive 98/48/EC of 20 July 1998); . . .

'recipient of the service' means any person who, for professional ends or otherwise, uses an information society service, in particular for the purposes of seeking information or making it accessible; . . .

'service provider' means any person providing an information society service;

'the Treaty' means the treaty establishing the European Community.

(3) Terms used in the Directive other than those in paragraph (1) above shall have the same meaning as in the Directive.

9 Information to be provided where contracts are concluded by electronic means

(1) Unless parties who are not consumers have agreed otherwise, where a contract is to be concluded by electronic means a service provider shall, prior to an order being placed by the recipient of a service, provide to that recipient in a clear, comprehensible and unambiguous manner the information set out in (a) to (d) below—

    (a) the different technical steps to follow to conclude the contract;

    (b) whether or not the concluded contract will be filed by the service provider and whether it will be accessible;

    (c) the technical means for identifying and correcting input errors prior to the placing of the order; and

    (d) the languages offered for the conclusion of the contract.

(2) Unless parties who are not consumers have agreed otherwise, a service provider shall indicate which relevant codes of conduct he subscribes to and give information on how those codes can be consulted electronically.

(3) Where the service provider provides terms and conditions applicable to the contract to the recipient, the service provider shall make them available to him in a way that allows him to store and reproduce them.

(4) The requirements of paragraphs (1) and (2) above shall not apply to contracts concluded exclusively by exchange of electronic mail or by equivalent individual communications.

10   Other information requirements

Regulations 6, 7, 8 and 9(1) have effect in addition to any other information requirements in legislation giving effect to Community law.

11   Placing of the order

(1)   Unless parties who are not consumers have agreed otherwise, where the recipient of the service places his order through technological means, a service provider shall—

    (a)   acknowledge receipt of the order to the recipient of the service without undue delay and by electronic means; and

    (b)   make available to the recipient of the service appropriate, effective and accessible technical means allowing him to identify and correct input errors prior to the placing of the order.

(2)   For the purposes of paragraph (1)(a) above—

    (a)   the order and the acknowledgement of receipt will be deemed to be received when the parties to whom they are addressed are able to access them; and

    (b)   the acknowledgement of receipt may take the form of the provision of the service paid for where that service is an information society service.

(3)   The requirements of paragraph (1) above shall not apply to contracts concluded exclusively by exchange of electronic mail or by equivalent individual communications.

12   Meaning of the term 'order'

Except in relation to regulation 9(1)(c) and regulation 11(1)(b) where 'order' shall be the contractual offer, 'order' may be but need not be the contractual offer for the purposes of regulations 9 and 11.

13   Liability of the service provider

The duties imposed by regulations 6, 7, 8, 9(1) and 11(1)(a) shall be enforceable, at the suit of any recipient of a service, by an action against the service provider for damages for breach of statutory duty.

14   Compliance with Regulation 9(3)

Where on request a service provider has failed to comply with the requirement in regulation 9(3), the recipient may seek an order from any court having jurisdiction in relation to the contract requiring that service provider to comply with that requirement.

15   Right to rescind contract

Where a person—

    (a)   has entered into a contract to which these Regulations apply, and

    (b)   the service provider has not made available means of allowing him to identify and correct input errors in compliance with regulation 11(1)(b),

he shall be entitled to rescind the contract unless any court having jurisdiction in relation to the contract in question orders otherwise on the application of the service provider.

Electronic Signatures Regulations 2002

(SI 2002, No. 318)

2   Interpretation

'certificate' means an electronic attestation which links signature-verification data to a person and confirms the identity of that person;

'certification-service-provider' means a person who issues certificates or provides other services related to electronic signatures;

'qualified certificate' means a certificate which meets the requirements in Schedule 1 and is provided by a certification-service-provider who fulfils the requirements in Schedule 2;

3 Supervision of certification-service-providers

(1) It shall be the duty of the Secretary of State to keep under review the carrying on of activities of certification-service-providers who are established in the United Kingdom and who issue qualified certificates to the public and the persons by whom they are carried on with a view to her becoming aware of the identity of those persons and the circumstances relating to the carrying on of those activities.

(2) It shall also be the duty of the Secretary of State to establish and maintain a register of certification-service-providers who are established in the United Kingdom and who issue qualified certificates to the public.

(3) The Secretary of State shall record in the register the names and addresses of those certification-service-providers of whom she is aware who are established in the United Kingdom and who issue qualified certificates to the public.

(4) The Secretary of State shall publish the register in such manner as she considers appropriate.

(5) The Secretary of State shall have regard to evidence becoming available to her with respect to any course of conduct of a certification-service-provider who is established in the United Kingdom and who issues qualified certificates to the public and which appears to her to be conduct detrimental to the interests of those persons who use or rely on those certificates with a view to making any of this evidence as she considers expedient available to the public in such manner as she considers appropriate.

4 Liability of certification-service-providers

(1) Where—
- (a) a certification-service-provider either—
  - (i)   issues a certificate as a qualified certificate to the public, or
  - (ii) guarantees a qualified certificate to the public,
- (b) a person reasonably relies on that certificate for any of the following matters—
  - (i)   the accuracy of any of the information contained in the qualified certificate at the time of issue,
  - (ii) the inclusion in the qualified certificate of all the details referred to in Schedule 1,
  - (iii) the holding by the signatory identified in the qualified certificate at the time of its issue of the signature-creation data corresponding to the signature-verification data given or identified in the certificate, or
  - (iv) the ability of the signature-creation data and the signature-verification data to be used in a complementary manner in cases where the certification-service-provider generates them both,
- (c) that person suffers loss as a result of such reliance, and
- (d) the certification-service-provider would be liable in damages in respect of any extent of the loss—
  - (i)   had a duty of care existed between him and the person referred to in sub-paragraph (b) above, and
  - (ii) had the certification-service-provider been negligent,

then that certification-service-provider shall be so liable to the same extent notwithstanding that there is no proof that the certification-service-provider was negligent unless the certification-service-provider proves that he was not negligent.

(2) For the purposes of the certification-service-provider's liability under paragraph (1) above there shall be a duty of care between that certification-service-provider and the person referred to in paragraph (1)(b) above.

5 Data protection

(1) A certification-service-provider who issues a certificate to the public and to whom this paragraph applies in accordance with paragraph (6) below—

(a) shall not obtain personal data for the purpose of issuing or maintaining that certificate otherwise than directly from the data subject or after the explicit consent of the data subject, and

(b) shall not process the personal data referred to in sub-paragraph (a) above—

   (i) to a greater extent than is necessary for the purpose of issuing or maintaining that certificate, or

   (ii) to a greater extent than is necessary for any other purpose to which the data subject has explicitly consented,

unless the processing is necessary for compliance with any legal obligation, to which the certification-service-provider is subject, other than an obligation imposed by contract.

(2) The obligation to comply with paragraph (1) above shall be a duty owed to any data subject who may be affected by a contravention of paragraph (1).

(3) Where a duty is owed by virtue of paragraph (2) above to any data subject, any breach of that duty which causes that data subject to sustain loss or damage shall be actionable by him.

(4) Compliance with paragraph (1) above shall also be enforceable by civil proceedings brought by the Crown for an injunction or for an interdict or for any other appropriate relief or remedy.

(5) Paragraph (4) above shall not prejudice any right that a data subject may have by virtue of paragraph (3) above to bring civil proceedings for the contravention or apprehended contravention of paragraph (1) above.

Regulation 2

SCHEDULE 2
(Annex II to the Directive)

Requirements for certification-service-providers issuing qualified certificates

Certification-service-providers must:

(a) demonstrate the reliability necessary for providing certification services;

(b) ensure the operation of a prompt and secure directory and a secure and immediate revocation service;

(c) ensure that the date and time when a certificate is issued or revoked can be determined precisely;

(d) verify, by appropriate means in accordance with national law, the identity and, if applicable, any specific attributes of the person to which a qualified certificate is issued;

(e) employ personnel who possess the expert knowledge, experience, and qualifications necessary for the services provided, in particular competence at managerial level, expertise in electronic signature technology and familiarity with proper security procedures; they must also apply administrative and management procedures which are adequate and correspond to recognised standards;

(f) use trustworthy systems and products which are protected against modification and ensure the technical and cryptographic security of the process supported by them;

(g) take measures against forgery of certificates, and, in cases where the certification- service-provider generates signature-creation data, guarantee confidentiality during the process of generating such data;

(h) maintain sufficient financial resources to operate in conformity with the requirements laid down in the Directive, in particular to bear the risk of liability for damages, for example, by obtaining appropriate insurance;

(i) record all relevant information concerning a qualified certificate for an appropriate period of time, in particular for the purpose of providing evidence of certification for the purposes of legal proceedings. Such recording may be done electronically;

(j) not store or copy signature-creation data of the person to whom the certification- service-provider provided key management services;

(k) before entering into a contractual relationship with a person seeking a certificate to support his electronic signature inform that person by a durable means of communication of the precise terms and conditions regarding the use of the certificate, including any limitations on its use, the existence of a voluntary accreditation scheme and procedures for complaints and dispute settlement. Such information, which may be transmitted electronically, must be in writing and in readily understandable language. Relevant parts of this information must also be made available on request to third parties relying on the certificate;

(l) use trustworthy systems to store certificates in a verifiable form so that:
   – only authorised persons can make entries and changes,
   – information can be checked for authenticity,
   – certificates are publicly available for retrieval in only those cases for which the certificate-holder's consent has been obtained, and
   – any technical changes compromising these security requirements are apparent to the operator.

Late Payment of Commercial Debts Regulations 2002

(SI 2002, No. 1674)

3   Proceedings restraining use of grossly unfair terms

(1) In this regulation:

(a) 'small and medium-sized enterprises' means those enterprises defined in Annex 1 to Commission Regulation (EC) No 70/2001 of 12th January 2001 on the application of Articles 87 and 88 of the EC Treaty to State aid to small and medium-sized enterprises;

(b) 'representative body' means an organisation established to represent the collective interests of small and medium-sized enterprises in general or in a particular sector or area.

(2) This regulation applies where a person acting in the course of a business has written standard terms on which he enters (or intends to enter) as purchaser into contracts to which the Late Payment of Commercial Debts (Interest) Act 1998 applies which include a term purporting to oust or vary the right to statutory interest in relation to qualifying debts created by those contracts.

(3) If it appears to the High Court that in all or any circumstances the purported use of such a term in a relevant contract would be void under the Late Payment of Commercial Debts (Interest) Act 1998, the court on the application of a representative body may grant an injunction against that person restraining him in those circumstances from using the offending term, on such terms as the court may think fit.

(4) Only a representative body may apply to the High Court under this regulation.

Financial Services (Distance Marketing) Regulations 2004

(SI 2004, No. 2095)

15   Unsolicited services

(1) A person ('the recipient') who receives unsolicited financial services for purposes other than those of his business from another person who supplies those services in the course of his business, shall not thereby become subject to any obligation (to make payment, or otherwise).

(4) In this regulation, 'unsolicited' means, in relation to financial services supplied to any person, that they are supplied without any prior request made by or on behalf of that person.

(8) This regulation is without prejudice to any right a supplier may have at any time, by contract or otherwise, to renew a distance contract with a consumer without any request made by or on behalf of that consumer prior to the renewal of that contract.

Damages (Variation of Periodical Payments) Order 2005

(SI 2005, No. 841)

1 Citation, commencement, interpretation and extent

(2) In this Order—
- (a) 'the Act' means the Damages Act 1996;
- (b) 'agreement' means an agreement by parties to a claim or action for damages which settles the claim or action and which provides for periodical payments;
- (c) 'damages' means damages for future pecuniary loss in respect of personal injury;
- (d) 'defence society' means the Medical Defence Union or the Medical Protection Society;
- (e) 'variable agreement' means an agreement which contains a provision referred to in Article 9(1);
- (f) 'variable order' means an order for periodical payments which contains a provision referred to in Article 2.

(3) In the application of this Order to Northern Ireland—
- (a) 'claimant' means plaintiff;
- (b) 'permission' means leave;
- (c) 'statements of case' means, in the High Court, the writ and pleadings and, in the county court, the civil bill and any notice of intention to defend, defence, notice for particulars, replies and counterclaim.

(4) This Order extends to England and Wales and Northern Ireland.

(5) This Order applies to proceedings begun on or after the date on which it comes into force.

2 Power to make variable orders

If there is proved or admitted to be a chance that at some definite or indefinite time in the future the claimant will—
- (a) as a result of the act or omission which gave rise to the cause of action, develop some serious disease or suffer some serious deterioration, or
- (b) enjoy some significant improvement in his physical or mental condition, where that condition had been adversely affected as a result of that act or omission,

the court may, on the application of a party, with the agreement of all the parties, or of its own initiative, provide in an order for periodical payments that it may be varied.

3 Defendant's financial resources

Unless—
- (a) the defendant is insured in respect of the claim,
- (b) the source of payment under the order for periodical payments is a government or health service body within the meaning of section 2A(2) of the Act,
- (c) the payment is guaranteed under section 6 of or the Schedule to the Act, or
- [(d) the order is made by consent and the claimant is neither a child, nor a person who lacks capacity within the meaning of the Mental Capacity Act 2005 (c.9) to administer and manage his property and affairs nor a patient within the meaning of Part VII of the Mental Health (Northern Ireland) Order 1986,]

the court will take into account the defendant's likely future financial resources in considering whether to make a variable order.

4   Award of provisional damages

The court may make a variable order in addition to an order for an award of provisional damages made by virtue of section 32A of the [Senior Courts Act 1981] or section 51 of the County Courts Act 1984 or, in relation to Northern Ireland, paragraph 10(2)(a) of Schedule 6 to the Administration of Justice Act 1982.

5   Contents of variable order

Where the court makes a variable order—

(a) the damages must be assessed or agreed on the assumption that the disease, deterioration or improvement will not occur;

(b) the order must specify the disease or type of deterioration or improvement;

(c) the order may specify a period within which an application for it to be varied may be made;

(d) the order may specify more than one disease or type of deterioration or improvement and may, in respect of each, specify a different period within which an application for it to be varied may be made;

(e) the order must provide that a party must obtain the court's permission to apply for it to be varied, unless the court otherwise orders.

6   Applications to extend period for applying for permission to vary

Where a period is specified under Article 5(c) or (d)—

(a) a party may make more than one application to extend the period, and such an application is not to be treated as an application to vary a variable order for the purposes of Article 7;

(b) a party may not make an application for the variable order to be varied after the end of the period specified or such period as extended by the court.

7   Limit on number of applications to vary

A party may make only one application to vary a variable order in respect of each specified disease or type of deterioration or improvement.

8   Case file

(1) Where the court makes a variable order, the case file documents must be preserved by the court until the end of the period or periods specified under Article 5(c) or (d) or of any extension of them or, if no such period was specified, until the death of the claimant.

(2) The case file documents are, unless the court otherwise orders—

(a) the judgment as entered;

(b) the statements of case;

(c) the schedule of expenses and losses;

(d) a transcript of the judge's oral judgment;

(e) all medical reports relied on;

(f) a transcript of any parts of the claimant's own evidence which the judge considers necessary;

(g) any subsequent orders.

(3) A court officer must ensure that the case file documents are provided by the parties where necessary and filed on the court file.

(4) Where a variable order has been made, the legal representatives of the parties and, if the parties are insured, their insurers, must also preserve their own case file until the end of the period or periods specified under Article 5(c) or (d) or of any extension of them or, if no such period was specified, until the death of the claimant.

9   Variable agreements

(1) If there is agreed to be a chance that at some definite or indefinite time in the future the claimant will—

    (a) as a result of the act or omission which gave rise to the cause of action, develop some serious disease or suffer some serious deterioration, or

    (b) enjoy some significant improvement in his physical or mental condition, where that condition had been adversely affected as a result of that act or omission,

the parties to an agreement may agree that a party to it may apply to the court subsequently for its terms to be varied.

(2) Where the parties agree to permit an application to vary the terms of an agreement, the agreement—

    (a) must expressly state that a party to it may apply to the court for its terms to be varied;

    (b) must specify the disease or type of deterioration or improvement;

    (c) may specify a period within which an application for it to be varied may be made;

    (d) may specify more than one disease or type of deterioration or improvement and may, in respect of each, specify a different period within which an application for it to be varied may be made.

(3) A party who is permitted by an agreement to apply for its terms to be varied must obtain the court's permission to apply for it to be varied.

10   Application for permission

(1) An application for permission to apply for a variable order or a variable agreement to be varied must be accompanied by evidence—

    (a) that the disease, deterioration or improvement specified in the order or agreement has occurred, and

    (b) that it has caused or is likely to cause an increase or decrease in the pecuniary loss suffered by the claimant.

(2) Where the applicant is the claimant and he knows that the defendant is insured in respect of the claim and the identity of the defendant's insurers, he must serve the application notice on the insurers as well as on the defendant.

(3) Where the applicant is the claimant and he knows that the defendant is a member of a defence society and the identity of the defence society, he must serve the application notice on the defence society as well as on the defendant.

(4) The respondent to the application may, within 28 days after service of the application, serve written representations on the applicant and, if he does, must file them with the court.

(5) The court will deal with the application without a hearing.

11   Refusal of permission

(1) Where permission is refused, the applicant may, within 14 days after service of the order, request the decision to be reconsidered at a hearing.

(2) No appeal lies from an order refusing permission after reconsideration.

12   Grant of permission

(1) Where permission is granted, the court will also give directions as to the application for the variation of the variable order or the variable agreement.

(2) Directions must include directions as to—

    (a) the date by which the application for variation must be served and filed;

    (b) the service and filing of evidence.

(3) No appeal lies from an order granting permission.

13   Order for variation

(1) On an application for the variation of a variable order or a variable agreement, if the court is satisfied—

   (a) that the disease, deterioration or improvement specified in the order or agreement has occurred, and

   (b) that it has caused or is likely to cause an increase or decrease in the pecuniary loss suffered by the claimant,

it may order—

     (i) the amount of annual payments to be varied, either from the date of the application for permission or from the date of the application to vary if the order did not require the permission of the court for an application to vary, or from such later date as it may specify in the order;

     (ii) how each payment is to be made during the year and at what intervals;

     (iii) a lump sum to be paid in addition to the existing periodical payments.

   (2) Section 2(3) to (9) of the Act applies to orders under this Order as it applies to orders for periodical payments.

14 Application of rules of court

In England and Wales, the Civil Procedure Rules 1998 and in Northern Ireland, rules of court apply to applications under this Order, except where this Order makes provision inconsistent with Civil Procedure Rules or rules of court.

General Product Safety Regulations 2005

(SI 2005, No. 1803)

PART 1 GENERAL

2. Interpretation

In these Regulations:—

'the 1987 Act' means the Consumer Protection Act 1987;

'Community law' includes a law in any part of the United Kingdom which implements a Community obligation;

'contravention' includes a failure to comply and cognate expressions shall be construed accordingly;

'dangerous product' means a product other than a safe product;

'distributor' means a professional in the supply chain whose activity does not affect the safety properties of a product;

'enforcement authority' means the Secretary of State, any other Minister of the Crown in charge of a government department, any such department and any authority or council mentioned in regulation 10;

'general safety requirement' means the requirement that only safe products should be placed on the market;

'the GPS Directive' means Directive 2001/95/EC of the European Parliament and of the Council of 3 December 2001 on general product safety;

'magistrates' court' in relation to Northern Ireland, means a court of summary jurisdiction;

'Member State' means a member State, Norway, Iceland or Liechtenstein;

'notice' means a notice in writing;

'officer', in relation to an enforcement authority, means a person authorised in writing to assist the authority in carrying out its functions under or for the purposes of the enforcement of these Regulations and safety notices, except in relation to an enforcement authority which is a government department where it means an officer of that department;

'producer' means—

    (a) the manufacturer of a product, when he is established in a Member State and any other person presenting himself as the manufacturer by affixing to the product his name, trade mark or other distinctive mark, or the person who reconditions the product;

    (b) when the manufacturer is not established in a Member State—

        (i) if he has a representative established in a Member State, the representative,

        (ii) in any other case, the importer of the product from a state that is not a Member State into a Member State;

    (c) other professionals in the supply chain, insofar as their activities may affect the safety properties of a product;

'product' means a product which is intended for consumers or likely, under reasonably foreseeable conditions, to be used by consumers even if not intended for them and which is supplied or made available, whether for consideration or not, in the course of a commercial activity and whether it is new, used or reconditioned and includes a product that is supplied or made available to consumers for their own use in the context of providing a service. 'product' does not include equipment used by service providers themselves to supply a service to consumers, in particular equipment on which consumers ride or travel which is operated by a service provider;

'recall' means any measure aimed at achieving the return of a dangerous product that has already been supplied or made available to consumers;

'recall notice' means a notice under regulation 15;

'record' includes any book or document and any record in any form;

'requirement to mark' means a notice under regulation 12;

'requirement to warn' means a notice under regulation 13;

'safe product' means a product which, under normal or reasonably foreseeable conditions of use including duration and, where applicable, putting into service, installation and maintenance requirements, does not present any risk or only the minimum risks compatible with the product's use, considered to be acceptable and consistent with a high level of protection for the safety and health of persons. In determining the foregoing, the following shall be taken into account in particular—

    (a) the characteristics of the product, including its composition, packaging, instructions for assembly and, where applicable, instructions for installation and maintenance,

    (b) the effect of the product on other products, where it is reasonably foreseeable that it will be used with other products,

    (c) the presentation of the product, the labelling, any warnings and instructions for its use and disposal and any other indication or information regarding the product, and

    (d) the categories of consumers at risk when using the product, in particular children and the elderly.

The feasibility of obtaining higher levels of safety or the availability of other products presenting a lesser degree of risk shall not constitute grounds for considering a product to be a dangerous product;

'safety notice' means a suspension notice, a requirement to mark, a requirement to warn, a withdrawal notice or a recall notice;

'serious risk' means a serious risk, including one the effects of which are not immediate, requiring rapid intervention;

'supply' in relation to a product includes making it available, in the context of providing a service, for use by consumers;

'suspension notice' means a notice under regulation 11;

'withdrawal' means any measure aimed at preventing the distribution, display or offer of a dangerous product to a consumer;

'withdrawal notice' means a notice under regulation 14.

Application

3.—(1) Each provision of these Regulations applies to a product in so far as there are no specific provisions with the same objective in rules of Community law governing the safety of the product other than the GPS Directive.

(2) Where a product is subject to specific safety requirements imposed by rules of Community law other than the GPS Directive, these Regulations shall apply only to the aspects and risks or category of risks not covered by those requirements. This means that:

(a) the definition of 'safe product' and 'dangerous product' in regulation 2 and regulations 5 and 6 shall not apply to such a product in so far as concerns the risks or category of risks covered by the specific rules, and

(b) the remainder of these Regulations shall apply except where there are specific provisions governing the aspects covered by those regulations with the same objective.

4. These Regulations do not apply to a second-hand product supplied as a product to be repaired or reconditioned prior to being used, provided the supplier clearly informs the person to whom he supplies the product to that effect.

PART 2 OBLIGATIONS OF PRODUCERS AND DISTRIBUTORS

5. General safety requirement

(1) No producer shall place a product on the market unless the product is a safe product.

(2) No producer shall offer or agree to place a product on the market or expose or possess a product for placing on the market unless the product is a safe product.

(3) No producer shall offer or agree to supply a product or expose or possess a product for supply unless the product is a safe product.

(4) No producer shall supply a product unless the product is a safe product.

6. Presumption of conformity

(1) Where, in the absence of specific provisions in rules of Community law governing the safety of a product, the product conforms to the specific rules of the law of part of the United Kingdom laying down the health and safety requirements which the product must satisfy in order to be marketed in the United Kingdom, the product shall be deemed safe so far as concerns the aspects covered by such rules.

(2) Where a product conforms to a voluntary national standard of the United Kingdom giving effect to a European standard the reference of which has been published in the Official Journal of the European Union in accordance with Article 4 of the GPS Directive, the product shall be presumed to be a safe product so far as concerns the risks and categories of risk covered by that national standard. The Secretary of State shall publish the reference number of such national standards in such manner as he considers appropriate.

(3) In circumstances other than those referred to in paragraphs (1) and (2), the conformity of a product to the general safety requirement shall be assessed taking into account—

(a) any voluntary national standard of the United Kingdom giving effect to a European standard, other than one referred to in paragraph (2),

(b) other national standards drawn up in the United Kingdom,

(c) recommendations of the European Commission setting guidelines on product safety assessment,

(d) product safety codes of good practice in the sector concerned,

(e) the state of the art and technology, and

(f) reasonable consumer expectations concerning safety.

(4) Conformity of a product with the criteria designed to ensure the general safety requirement is complied with, in particular the provisions mentioned in paragraphs (1) to (3), shall not bar an enforcement authority from exercising its powers under these Regulations in relation to that product where there is evidence that, despite such conformity, it is dangerous.

7. Other obligations of producers

(1) Within the limits of his activities, a producer shall provide consumers with the relevant information to enable them—

(a) to assess the risks inherent in a product throughout the normal or reasonably foreseeable period of its use, where such risks are not immediately obvious without adequate warnings, and

(b) to take precautions against those risks.

(2) The presence of warnings does not exempt any person from compliance with the other requirements of these Regulations.

(3) Within the limits of his activities, a producer shall adopt measures commensurate with the characteristics of the products which he supplies to enable him to—

(a) be informed of the risks which the products might pose, and

(b) take appropriate action including, where necessary to avoid such risks, withdrawal, adequately and effectively warning consumers as to the risks or, as a last resort, recall.

(4) The measures referred to in paragraph (3) include—

(a) except where it is not reasonable to do so, an indication by means of the product or its packaging of—

(i) the name and address of the producer, and

(ii) the product reference or where applicable the batch of products to which it belongs; and

(b) where and to the extent that it is reasonable to do so—

(i) sample testing of marketed products,

(ii) investigating and if necessary keeping a register of complaints concerning the safety of the product, and

(iii) keeping distributors informed of the results of such monitoring where a product presents a risk or may present a risk.

8. Obligations of distributors

(1) A distributor shall act with due care in order to help ensure compliance with the applicable safety requirements and in particular he—

(a) shall not expose or possess for supply or offer or agree to supply, or supply, a product to any person which he knows or should have presumed, on the basis of the information in his possession and as a professional, is a dangerous product; and

(b) shall, within the limits of his activities, participate in monitoring the safety of a product placed on the market, in particular by—

(i) passing on information on the risks posed by the product,

(ii) keeping the documentation necessary for tracing the origin of the product,

(iii) producing the documentation necessary for tracing the origin of the product, and cooperating in action taken by a producer or an enforcement authority to avoid the risks.

(2) Within the limits of his activities, a distributor shall take measures enabling him to cooperate efficiently in the action referred to in paragraph (1)(b)(iii).

9. Obligations of producers and distributors

(1) Subject to paragraph (2), where a producer or a distributor knows that a product he has placed on the market or supplied poses risks to the consumer that are incompatible with the general

safety requirement, he shall forthwith notify an enforcement authority in writing of that information and—

    (a) the action taken to prevent risk to the consumer; and

    (b) where the product is being or has been marketed or otherwise supplied to consumers outside the United Kingdom, of the identity of each Member State in which, to the best of his knowledge, it is being or has been so marketed or supplied.

  (2) Paragraph (1) shall not apply—

    (a) in the case of a second-hand product supplied as an antique or as a product to be repaired or reconditioned prior to being used, provided the supplier clearly informed the person to whom he supplied the product to that effect,

    (b) in conditions concerning isolated circumstances or products.

  (3) In the event of a serious risk the notification under paragraph (1) shall include the following—

    (a) information enabling a precise identification of the product or batch of products in question,

    (b) a full description of the risks that the product presents,

    (c) all available information relevant for tracing the product, and

    (d) a description of the action undertaken to prevent risks to the consumer.

  (4) Within the limits of his activities, a person who is a producer or a distributor shall co-operate with an enforcement authority (at the enforcement authority's request) in action taken to avoid the risks posed by a product which he supplies or has supplied. Every enforcement authority shall maintain procedures for such co-operation, including procedures for dialogue with the producers and distributors concerned on issues related to product safety.

PART 3 ENFORCEMENT

10. Enforcement

  (1) It shall be the duty of every authority to which paragraph (4) applies to enforce within its area these Regulations and safety notices.

  (2) An authority in England or Wales to which paragraph (4) applies shall have the power to investigate and prosecute for an alleged contravention of any provision imposed by or under these Regulations which was committed outside its area in any part of England and Wales.

  (3) A district council in Northern Ireland shall have the power to investigate and prosecute for an alleged contravention of any provision imposed by or under these Regulations which was committed outside its area in any part of Northern Ireland.

  (4) The authorities to which this paragraph applies are:

    (a) in England, a county council, district council, London Borough Council, the Common Council of the City of London in its capacity as a local authority and the Council of the Isles of Scilly,

    (b) in Wales, a county council or a county borough council,

    (c) in Scotland, a council constituted under section 2 of the Local Government etc. (Scotland) Act 1994,

    (d) in Northern Ireland any district council.

  (5) An enforcement authority shall in enforcing these Regulations act in a manner proportionate to the seriousness of the risk and shall take due account of the precautionary principle. In this context, it shall encourage and promote voluntary action by producers and distributors. Notwithstanding the foregoing, an enforcement authority may take any action under these Regulations urgently and without first encouraging and promoting voluntary action if a product poses a serious risk.

11. Suspension notices

  (1) Where an enforcement authority has reasonable grounds for suspecting that a requirement of these Regulations has been contravened in relation to a product, the authority may, for the period

needed to organise appropriate safety evaluations, checks and controls, serve a notice ('a suspension notice') prohibiting the person on whom it is served from doing any of the following things without the consent of the authority, that is to say—

    (a) placing the product on the market, offering to place it on the market, agreeing to place it on the market or exposing it for placing on the market, or

    (b) supplying the product, offering to supply it, agreeing to supply it or exposing it for supply.

(2)　A suspension notice served by an enforcement authority in relation to a product may require the person on whom it is served to keep the authority informed of the whereabouts of any such product in which he has an interest.

(3)　A consent given by the enforcement authority for the purposes of paragraph (1) may impose such conditions on the doing of anything for which the consent is required as the authority considers appropriate.

12.　Requirements to mark

(1)　Where an enforcement authority has reasonable grounds for believing that a product is a dangerous product in that it could pose risks in certain conditions, the authority may serve a notice ('a requirement to mark') requiring the person on whom the notice is served at his own expense to undertake either or both of the following, as specified in the notice—

    (a) to ensure that the product is marked in accordance with requirements specified in the notice with warnings as to the risks it may present,

    (b) to make the marketing of the product subject to prior conditions as specified in the notice so as to ensure the product is a safe product.

(2)　The requirements referred to in paragraph (1)(a) shall be such as to ensure that the product is marked with a warning which is suitable, clearly worded and easily comprehensible.

13.　Requirements to warn

Where an enforcement authority has reasonable grounds for believing that a product is a dangerous product in that it could pose risks for certain persons, the authority may serve a notice ('a requirement to warn') requiring the person on whom the notice is served at his own expense to undertake one or more of the following, as specified in the notice—

    (a) where and to the extent it is practicable to do so, to ensure that any person who could be subject to such risks and who has been supplied with the product be given warning of the risks in good time and in a form specified in the notice,

    (b) to publish a warning of the risks in such form and manner as is likely to bring those risks to the attention of any such person,

    (c) to ensure that the product carries a warning of the risks in a form specified in the notice.

14.　Withdrawal notices

(1)　Where an enforcement authority has reasonable grounds for believing that a product is a dangerous product, the authority may serve a notice ('a withdrawal notice') prohibiting the person on whom it is served from doing any of the following things without the consent of the authority, that is to say—

    (a) placing the product on the market, offering to place it on the market, agreeing to place it on the market or exposing it for placing on the market, or

    (b) supplying the product, offering to supply it, agreeing to supply it or exposing it for supply.

(2)　A withdrawal notice may require the person on whom it is served to take action to alert consumers to the risks that the product presents.

(3)　In relation to a product that is already on the market, a withdrawal notice may only be served by an enforcement authority where the action being undertaken by the producer or the distributor concerned in fulfilment of his obligations under these Regulations is unsatisfactory or insufficient to prevent the risks concerned to the health and safety of persons.

(4) Paragraph (3) shall not apply in the case of a product posing a serious risk requiring, in the view of the enforcement authority, urgent action.

(5) A withdrawal notice served by an enforcement authority in relation to a product may require the person on whom it is served to keep the authority informed of the whereabouts of any such product in which he has an interest.

(6) A consent given by the enforcement authority for the purposes of paragraph (1) may impose such conditions on the doing of anything for which the consent is required as the authority considers appropriate.

15. Recall notices

(1) Subject to paragraph (4), where an enforcement authority has reasonable grounds for believing that a product is a dangerous product and that it has already been supplied or made available to consumers, the authority may serve a notice ('a recall notice') requiring the person on whom it is served to use his reasonable endeavours to organise the return of the product from consumers to that person or to such other person as is specified in the notice.

(2) A recall notice may require—

- (a) the recall to be effected in accordance with a code of practice applicable to the product concerned, or
- (b) the recipient of the recall notice to—
  - (i)   contact consumers who have purchased the product in order to inform them of the recall, where and to the extent it is practicable to do so,
  - (ii)   publish a notice in such form and such manner as is likely to bring to the attention of purchasers of the product the risk the product poses and the fact of the recall, or
  - (iii)   make arrangements for the collection or return of the product from consumers who have purchased it or for its disposal,

and may impose such additional requirements on the recipient of the notice as are reasonable and practicable with a view to achieving the return of the product from consumers to the person specified in the notice or its disposal.

(3) In determining what requirements to include in a recall notice, the enforcement authority shall take into consideration the need to encourage distributors, users and consumers to contribute to its implementation.

(4) A recall notice may only be issued by an enforcement authority where—

- (a) other action which it may require under these Regulations would not suffice to prevent the risks concerned to the health and safety of persons,
- (b) the action being undertaken by the producer or the distributor concerned in fulfilment of his obligations under these Regulations is unsatisfactory or insufficient to prevent the risks concerned to the health and safety of persons, and
- (c) the authority has given not less than seven days notice to the person on whom the recall notice is to be served of its intention to serve such a notice and where that person has before the expiry of that period by notice required the authority to seek the advice of such person as the Institute determines on the questions of—
  - (i)   whether the product is a dangerous product,
  - (ii)   whether the issue of a recall notice is proportionate to the seriousness of the risk, and the authority has taken account of such advice.

(5) Paragraphs (4)(b) and (c) shall not apply in the case of a product posing a serious risk requiring, in the view of the enforcement authority, urgent action.

(6) Where a person requires an enforcement authority to seek advice as referred to in paragraph (4)(c), that person shall be responsible for the fees, costs and expenses of the Institute and of the person appointed by the Institute to advise the authority.

(7) In paragraphs 4(c) and (6) 'the Institute' means the charitable organisation with registered number 803725 and known as the Chartered Institute of Arbitrators.

(8) A recall notice served by an enforcement authority in relation to a product may require the person on whom it is served to keep the authority informed of the whereabouts of any such product to which the recall notice relates, so far as he is able to do so.

(9) Where the conditions in paragraph (1) for serving a recall notice are satisfied and either the enforcement authority has been unable to identify any person on whom to serve a recall notice, or the person on whom such a notice has been served has failed to comply with it, then the authority may itself take such action as could have been required by a recall notice.

(10) Where—

(a) an authority has complied with the requirements of paragraph (4); and

(b) the authority has exercised its powers under paragraph (9) to take action following the failure of the person on whom the recall notice has been served to comply with that notice,

then the authority may recover from the person on whom the notice was served summarily as a civil debt, any costs or expenses reasonably incurred by it in undertaking the action referred to in sub-paragraph (b).

(11) A civil debt recoverable under the preceding paragraph may be recovered—

(a) in England and Wales by way of complaint (as mentioned in section 58 of the Magistrates' Courts Act 1980,

(b) in Northern Ireland in proceedings under Article 62 of the Magistrate's Court (Northern Ireland) Order 1981.

16.   Supplementary provisions relating to safety notices

(1) Whenever feasible, prior to serving a safety notice the authority shall give an opportunity to the person on whom the notice is to be served to submit his views to the authority. Where, due to the urgency of the situation, this is not feasible the person shall be given an opportunity to submit his views to the authority after service of the notice.

(2) A safety notice served by an enforcement authority in respect of a product shall—

(a) describe the product in a manner sufficient to identify it;

(b) state the reasons on which the notice is based;

(c) indicate the rights available to the recipient of the notice under these Regulations and (where applicable) the time limits applying to their exercise; and

(d) in the case of a suspension notice, state the period of time for which it applies.

(3) A safety notice shall have effect throughout the United Kingdom.

(4) Where an enforcement authority serves a suspension notice in respect of a product, the authority shall be liable to pay compensation to a person having an interest in the product in respect of any loss or damage suffered by reason of the notice if—

(a) there has been no contravention of any requirement of these Regulations in relation to the product; and

(b) the exercise by the authority of the power to serve the suspension notice was not attributable to any neglect or default by that person.

(5) Where an enforcement authority serves a withdrawal notice in respect of a product, the authority shall be liable to pay compensation to a person having an interest in the product in respect of any loss or damage suffered by reason of the notice if—

(a) the product was not a dangerous product; and

(b) the exercise by the authority of the power to serve the withdrawal notice was not attributable to any neglect or default by that person.

(6) Where an enforcement authority serves a recall notice in respect of a product, the authority shall be liable to pay compensation to the person on whom the notice was served in respect of any loss or damage suffered by reason of the notice if—

(a) the product was not a dangerous product; and

(b) the exercise by the authority of the power to serve the recall notice was not attributable to any neglect or default by that person.

(7) An enforcement authority may vary or revoke a safety notice which it has served provided that the notice is not made more restrictive for the person on whom it is served or more onerous for that person to comply with.

(8) Wherever feasible prior to varying a safety notice the authority shall give an opportunity to the person on whom the original notice was served to submit his views to the authority.

17. Appeals against safety notices

(1) A person on whom a safety notice has been served and a person having an interest in a product in respect of which a safety notice (other than a recall notice) has been served may, before the end of the period of 21 days beginning with the day on which the notice was served, apply for an order to vary or set aside the terms of the notice.

(2) On an application under paragraph (1) the court or the sheriff, as the case may be, shall make an order setting aside the notice only if satisfied that—

    (a) in the case of a suspension notice, there has been no contravention in relation to the product of any requirement of these Regulations,

    (b) in the case of a requirement to mark or a requirement to warn, the product is not a dangerous product,

    (c) in the case of a withdrawal notice—

        (i) the product is not a dangerous product, or

        (ii) where applicable, regulation 14(3) has not been complied with by the enforcement authority concerned,

    (d) in the case of a recall notice—

        (i) the product is not a dangerous product, or

        (ii) regulation 15(4) has not been complied with,

    (e) in any case, the serving of the safety notice concerned was not proportionate to the seriousness of the risk.

(3) On an application concerning the period of time specified in a suspension notice as the period for which it applies, the court or the sheriff, as the case may be, may reduce the period to such period as it considers sufficient for organising appropriate safety evaluations, checks and controls.

(4) On an application to vary the terms of a notice, the court or the sheriff, as the case may be, may vary the requirements specified in the notice as it considers appropriate.

(5) A person on whom a recall notice has been served and who proposes to make an application under paragraph (1) in relation to the notice may, before the end of the period of seven days beginning with the day on which the notice was served, apply to the court or the sheriff for an order suspending the effect of the notice and the court or the sheriff may, in any case where it considers it appropriate to do so, make an order suspending the effect of the notice.

(6) If the court or the sheriff makes an order suspending the effect of a recall notice under paragraph (5) in the absence of the enforcement authority, the enforcement authority may apply for the revocation of such order.

(7) An order under paragraph (5) shall take effect from the time it is made until—

    (a) it is revoked under paragraph (6),

    (b) where no application is made under paragraph (1) in respect of the recall notice within the time specified in that paragraph, the expiration of that time,

    (c) where such an application is made but is withdrawn or dismissed for want of prosecution, the date of dismissal or withdrawal of the application, or

    (d) where such an application is made and is not withdrawn or dismissed for want of prosecution, the determination of the application.

(8) Subject to paragraph (6), in Scotland the sheriff's decision under paragraph (5) shall be final.

(9) An application under this regulation may be made—

    (a) by way of complaint to any magistrates' court in which proceedings have been brought in England and Wales or Northern Ireland—

  (i)   in respect of a contravention in relation to the product of a requirement imposed by
        or under these Regulations; or

 (ii)   for the forfeiture of the product under regulation 18;

(b) where no such proceedings have been brought, by way of complaint to any magistrates'
     court; or

(c) in Scotland, by summary application to the sheriff.

(10) A person aggrieved by an order made pursuant to an application under paragraph (1) by a
magistrates' court in England, Wales or Northern Ireland, or by a decision of such a court not to make
such an order, may appeal against that order or decision—

(a) in England and Wales, to the Crown Court;

(b) in Northern Ireland, to the county court.

18.   Forfeiture: England and Wales and Northern Ireland

(1) An enforcement authority in England and Wales or Northern Ireland may apply for an order
for the forfeiture of a product on the grounds that the product is a dangerous product.

(2) An application under paragraph (1) may be made—

(a) where proceedings have been brought in a magistrates' court for an offence in respect of
     a contravention in relation to the product of a requirement imposed by or under these
     Regulations, to that court,

(b) where an application with respect to the product has been made to a magistrates' court
     under regulation 17 (appeals against safety notices) or 25 (appeals against detention of
     products and records) to that court, and

(c) otherwise, by way of complaint to a magistrates' court.

(3) An enforcement authority making an application under paragraph (1) shall serve a copy
of the application on any person appearing to it to be the owner of, or otherwise to have an interest in, the product to which the application relates, together with a notice giving him the opportunity to appear at the hearing of the application to show cause why the product should not be
forfeited.

(4) A person on whom notice is served under paragraph (3) and any other person claiming to be
the owner of, or otherwise to have an interest in, the product to which the application relates shall
be entitled to appear at the hearing of the application and show cause why the product should not be
forfeited.

(5) The court shall not make an order for the forfeiture of a product—

(a) if any person on whom notice is served under paragraph (3) does not appear, unless ser-
     vice of the notice on that person is proved, or

(b) if no notice under paragraph (3) has been served, unless the court is satisfied that in the
     circumstances it was reasonable not to serve notice on any person.

(6) The court may make an order for the forfeiture of a product only if it is satisfied that the product is a dangerous product.

(7) Any person aggrieved by an order made by a magistrates' court for the forfeiture of a product, or by a decision of such a court not to make such an order, may appeal against that order or
decision—

(a) in England and Wales, to the Crown Court;

(b) in Northern Ireland, to the county court.

(8) An order for the forfeiture of a product shall not take effect until the later of—

  (i)   the end of the period within which an appeal under paragraph (7) may be brought or
        within which an application under section 111 of the Magistrates' Courts Act 1980
        or article 146 of the Magistrates' Courts (Northern Ireland) Order 1981 (statement
        of case) may be made, or

 (ii)   if an appeal or an application is so made, when the appeal or application is deter-
        mined or abandoned.

(9) Subject to the following paragraph, where a product is forfeited it shall be destroyed in accordance with such directions as the court may give.

(10) On making an order for forfeiture of a product a magistrates' court may, if it considers it appropriate to do so, direct that the product shall (instead of being destroyed) be delivered up to such person as the court may specify, on condition that the person—

(a) does not supply the product to any person otherwise than as mentioned in paragraph (11), and

(b) on condition, if the court considers it appropriate, that he complies with any order to pay costs or expenses (including any order under regulation 28) which has been made against him in the proceedings for the order for forfeiture.

(11) The supplies which may be permitted under the preceding paragraph are—

(a) a supply to a person who carries on a business of buying products of the same description as the product concerned and repairing or reconditioning them,

(b) a supply to a person as scrap (that is to say, for the value of materials included in the product rather than for the value of the product itself),

(c) a supply to any person, provided that being so supplied the product is repaired by or on behalf of the person to whom the product was delivered up by direction of the court and that following such repair it is not a dangerous product.

20. Offences

(1) A person who contravenes regulations 5 or 8(1)(a) shall be guilty of an offence and liable on conviction on indictment to imprisonment for a term not exceeding 12 months or to a fine not exceeding £20,000 or to both, or on summary conviction to imprisonment for a term not exceeding three months or to a fine not exceeding the statutory maximum or to both.

(2) A person who contravenes regulation 7(1), 7(3) (by failing to take any of the measures specified in regulation 7(4)), 8(1)(b)(i), (ii) or (iii) or 9(1) shall be guilty of an offence and liable on summary conviction to imprisonment for a term not exceeding three months or to a fine not exceeding level 5 on the standard scale or to both.

(3) A producer or distributor who does not give notice to an enforcement authority under regulation 9(1) in respect of a product he has placed on the market or supplied commits an offence where it is proved that he ought to have known that the product poses risks to consumers that are incompatible with the general safety requirement and he shall be liable on summary conviction to imprisonment for a term not exceeding three months or to a fine not exceeding level 5 on the standard scale or to both.

(4) A person who contravenes a safety notice shall be guilty of an offence and liable on conviction on indictment to imprisonment for a term not exceeding 12 months or to a fine not exceeding £20,000 or to both, or on summary conviction to imprisonment for a term not exceeding three months or to a fine not exceeding the statutory maximum or to both.

21. Test purchases

(1) An enforcement authority shall have power to organise appropriate checks on the safety properties of a product, on an adequate scale, up to the final stage of use or consumption and for that purpose may make a purchase of a product or authorise an officer of the authority to make a purchase of a product.

(2) Where a product purchased under paragraph (1) is submitted to a test and the test leads to—

(a) the bringing of proceedings for an offence in respect of a contravention in relation to the product of any requirement imposed by or under these Regulations or for the forfeiture of the product under regulation 18 or 19, or

(b) the serving of a safety notice in respect of the product, and

(c) the authority is requested to do so and it is practicable for the authority to comply with the request, then the authority shall allow the person from whom the product was purchased, a person who is a party to the proceedings, on whom the notice was served or who has an interest in the product to which the notice relates, to have the product tested.

22. Powers of entry and search etc.

(1) An officer of an enforcement authority may at any reasonable hour and on production, if required, of his credentials exercise any of the powers conferred by the following provisions of this regulation.

(2) The officer may, for the purposes of ascertaining whether there has been a contravention of a requirement imposed by or under these Regulations, enter any premises other than premises occupied only as a person's residence and inspect any record or product.

(3) The officer may, for the purpose of ascertaining whether there has been a contravention of a requirement imposed by or under these Regulations, examine any procedure (including any arrangements for carrying out a test) connected with the production of a product.

(4) If the officer has reasonable grounds for suspecting that the product has not been placed on the market or supplied in the United Kingdom since it was manufactured or imported he may for the purpose of ascertaining whether there has been a contravention in relation to the product of a requirement imposed by or under these Regulations—

  (a) require a person carrying on a commercial activity, or employed in connection with a commercial activity, to supply all necessary information relating to the activity, including by the production of records,

  (b) require any record which is stored in an electronic form and is accessible from the premises to be produced in a form—

  (i)   in which it can be taken away, and

  (ii)   in which it is visible and legible.

  (c) for the purpose of ascertaining (by testing or otherwise) whether there has been any such contravention, seize and detain samples of the product,

  (d) take copies of, or of an entry in, any records produced by virtue of sub-paragraph (a).

(5) If the officer has reasonable grounds for suspecting that there has been a contravention in relation to a product of a requirement imposed by or under these Regulations, he may—

  (a) for the purpose of ascertaining whether there has been any such contravention, require a person carrying on a commercial activity, or employed in connection with a commercial activity, to supply all necessary information relating to the activity, including by the production of records,

  (b) for the purpose of ascertaining whether there has been any such contravention, require any record which is stored in an electronic form and is accessible from the premises to be produced in a form—

  (i)   in which it can be taken away, and

  (ii)   in which it is visible and legible,

  (c) for the purpose of ascertaining (by testing or otherwise) whether there has been any such contravention, seize and detain samples of the product,

  (d) take copies of, or of an entry in, any records produced by virtue of sub-paragraph (a).

(6) The officer may seize and detain any products or records which he has reasonable grounds for believing may be required as evidence in proceedings for an offence in respect of a contravention of any requirement imposed by or under these Regulations.

(7) If and to the extent that it is reasonably necessary to do so to prevent a contravention of any requirement imposed by or under these Regulations, the officer may, for the purpose of exercising his power under paragraphs (4) to (6) to seize products or records—

  (a) require any person having authority to do so to open any container or to open any vending machine; and

(b) himself open or break open any such container or machine where a requirement made under sub-paragraph (a) in relation to the container or machine has not been complied with.

23. Provisions supplemental to regulation 22 and search warrants etc.

(1) An officer seizing any products or records shall, before he leaves the premises, provide to the person from whom they were seized a written notice—

(a) specifying the products (including the quantity thereof) and records seized,

(b) stating the reasons for their seizure, and

(c) explaining the right of appeal under regulation 25.

(2) References in paragraph (1) and regulation 25 to the person from whom something has been seized, in relation to a case in which the power of seizure was exercisable by reason of the product having been found on any premises, are references to the occupier of the premises at the time of the seizure.

(3) If a justice of the peace—

(a) is satisfied by written information on oath that there are reasonable grounds for believing either—

(i) that any products or records which an officer has power to inspect under regulation 22 are on any premises and that their inspection is likely to disclose evidence that there has been a contravention of any requirement imposed by or under these Regulations, or

(ii) that such a contravention has taken place, is taking place or is about to take place on any premises, and

(b) is also satisfied by such information either—

(i) that admission to the premises has been or is likely to be refused and that notice of the intention to apply for a warrant under this paragraph has been given to the occupier, or

(ii) that an application for admission, or the giving of such a notice, would defeat the object of the entry or that the premises are unoccupied or that the occupier is temporarily absent and it might defeat the object of the entry to await his return.

the justice may by warrant under his hand, which shall continue in force for a period of one month, authorise any officer of an enforcement authority to enter the premises, if need be by force.

(4) An officer entering premises by virtue of regulation 22 or a warrant under paragraph (3) may take him such other persons and equipment as may appear to him necessary.

(5) On leaving any premises which a person is authorised to enter by a warrant under paragraph (3), that person shall, if the premises are unoccupied or the occupier is temporarily absent—

(a) leave the premises as effectively secured against trespassers as he found them,

(b) attach a notice such as is mentioned in paragraph (1) in a prominent place at the premises.

(6) Where a product seized by an officer of an enforcement authority under regulation 22 or 23 is submitted to a test, the authority shall inform the person mentioned in paragraph (1) of the result of the test and, if—

(a) proceedings are brought for an offence in respect of a contravention in relation to the product of any requirement imposed by or under these Regulations or for the forfeiture of the product under regulation 18 or 19; or

(b) a safety notice is served in respect of the product; and

(c) the authority is requested to do so and it is practicable for him to comply with the request,

then the authority shall allow a person who is a party to the proceedings or, on whom the notice was served or who has an interest in the product to which the notice relates to have the product tested.

(7) If a person who is not an officer of an enforcement authority purports to act as such under regulation 22 or under this regulation he shall be guilty of an offence and liable on summary conviction to a fine not exceeding level 5 on the standard scale.

(8) In the application of this section to Scotland, the reference in paragraph (3) to a justice of the peace shall include a reference to a sheriff and the reference to written information on oath shall be construed as a reference to evidence on oath.

(9) In the application of this section to Northern Ireland, the reference in paragraph (3) to a justice of the peace shall include a reference to a lay magistrate and the references to an information on oath shall be construed as a reference to a complaint on oath.

24. Obstruction of officers

(1) A person who—

    (a) intentionally obstructs an officer of an enforcement authority who is acting in pursuance of any provision of regulations 22 or 23; or

    (b) intentionally fails to comply with a requirement made of him by an officer of an enforcement authority under any provision of those regulations; or

    (c) without reasonable cause fails to give an officer of an enforcement authority who is so acting any other assistance or information which the officer may reasonably require of him for the purposes of the exercise of the officer's functions under any provision of those regulations,

shall be guilty of an offence and liable on summary conviction to a fine not exceeding level 5 on the standard scale.

(2) A person shall be guilty of an offence if, in giving any information which is required by him by virtue of paragraph (1)(c)—

    (a) he makes a statement which he knows is false in a material particular; or

    (b) he recklessly makes a statement which is false in a material particular.

(3) A person guilty of an offence under paragraph (2) shall be liable—

    (a) on conviction on indictment, to a fine;

    (b) on summary conviction, to a fine not exceeding the statutory maximum.

25. Appeals against detention of products and records

(1) A person referred to in regulation 23(1) may apply for an order requiring any product or record which is for the time being detained under regulation 22 or 23 by an enforcement authority or by an officer of such an authority to be released to him or to another person.

(2) An application under the preceding paragraph may be made—

    (a) to any magistrates' court in which proceedings have been brought in England and Wales or Northern Ireland—

        (i)   for an offence in respect of a contravention in relation to the product of a requirement imposed by or under these Regulation, or

        (ii) for the forfeiture of the product under regulation 18,

    (b) where no such proceedings have been brought, by way of complaint to a magistrates' court;

    (c) in Scotland, by summary application to the sheriff.

(3) On an application under paragraph (1) to a magistrates' court or to the sheriff, the court or the sheriff may make an order requiring a product or record to be released only if the court or sheriff is satisfied—

    (a) that proceedings

        (i)   for an offence in respect of any contravention in relation to the product or, in the case of a record, the product to which the record relates, of any requirement imposed by or under these Regulations; or

        (ii) for the forfeiture of the product or, in the case of a record, the product to which the record relate, under regulation 18 or 19,

    have not been brought or, having been brought, have been concluded without the product being forfeited; and

(b) where no such proceedings have been brought, that more than six months have elapsed since the product or records was seized.

(4) In determining whether to make an order under this regulation requiring the release of a product or record the court or sheriff shall take all the circumstances into account including the results of any tests on the product which have been carried out by or on behalf of the enforcement authority and any statement made by the enforcement authority to the court or sheriff as to its intention to bring proceedings for an offence in respect of a contravention in relation to the product of any requirement imposed by or under these Regulations.

(5) Where—

(a) more than 12 months have elapsed since a product or records were seized and the enforcement authority has not commenced proceedings for an offence in respect of a contravention in relation to the product (or, in the case of records, the product to which the records relate) of any requirement imposed by or under these Regulations or for the forfeiture of the product under regulation 18 or 19, or

(b) an enforcement authority has brought proceedings for an offence as mentioned in subparagraph (a) and the proceedings were dismissed and all rights of appeal have been exercised or the time for appealing has expired,

the authority shall be under a duty to return the product or records detained under regulation 22 or 23 to the person from whom they were seized.

(6) Where the authority is satisfied that some other person has a better right to a product or record than the person from whom they were seized, the authority shall, instead of the duty in paragraph (5), be under a duty to return it to that other person or, as the case may be, to the person appearing to the authority to have the best right to the product or record in question.

(7) Where different persons claim to be entitled to the return of a product or record that is required to be returned under paragraph (5), then it may be retained for as long as it reasonably necessary for the determination in accordance with paragraph (6) of the person to whom it must be returned.

(8) A person aggrieved by an order made under this regulation by a magistrates' court in England and Wales or Northern Ireland, or by a decision of such a court not to make such an order, may appeal against that order or decision—

(a) in England and Wales, to the Crown Court;

(b) in Northern Ireland, to the county court;

and an order so made may contain such provision as appears to the court to be appropriate for delaying the coming into force of the order pending the making and determination of any appeal (including any application under section 111 of the Magistrates' Courts Act 1980 or article 146 of the Magistrates' Courts (Northern Ireland) Order 1981 (statement of case)).

26. Compensation for seizure and detention

Where an officer of an enforcement authority exercises any power under regulation 22 or 23 to seize and detain a product, the enforcement authority shall be liable to pay compensation to any person having an interest in the product in respect of any loss or damage caused by reason of the exercise of the power if—

(a) there has been no contravention in relation to the product of any requirement imposed by or under these Regulations, and

(b) the exercise of the power is not attributable to any neglect or default by that person.

27. Recovery of expenses of enforcement

(1) This regulation shall apply where a court—

(a) convicts a person of an offence in respect of a contravention in relation to a product of any requirement imposed by or under these Regulations, or

(b) makes an order under regulation 18 or 19 for the forfeiture of a product.

(2) The court may (in addition to any other order it may make as to costs or expenses) order the person convicted or, as the case may be, any person having an interest in the product to reimburse an enforcement authority for any expenditure which has been or may be incurred by that authority—

      (a) in connection with any seizure or detention of the product by or on behalf of the authority, or

      (b) in connection with any compliance by the authority with directions given by the court for the purposes of any order for the forfeiture of the product.

28. Power of Secretary of State to obtain information

(1) If the Secretary of State considers that, for the purposes of deciding whether to serve a safety notice, or to vary or revoke a safety notice which he has already served, he requires information or a sample of a product he may serve on a person a notice requiring him:

      (a) to furnish to the Secretary of State, within a period specified in the notice, such information as is specified;

      (b) to produce such records as are specified in the notice at a time and place so specified (and to produce any such records which are stored in any electronic form in a form in which they are visible and legible) and to permit a person appointed by the Secretary of State for that purpose to take copies of the records at that time and place;

      (c) to produce such samples of a product as are specified in the notice at a time and place so specified.

(2) A person shall be guilty of an offence if he—

      (a) fails, without reasonable cause, to comply with a notice served on him under paragraph (1); or

      (b) in purporting to comply with a requirement which by virtue of paragraph (1)(a) or (b) is contained in such a notice—

          (i) furnishes information or records which he knows are false in a material particular, or

          (ii) recklessly furnishes information or records which are false in a material particular.

(3) A person guilty of an offence under paragraph (2) shall—

      (a) in the case of an offence under sub-paragraph (a) of that paragraph, be liable on summary conviction to a fine not exceeding level 5 on the standard scale; and

      (b) in the case of an offence under sub-paragraph (b) of that paragraph, be liable—

          (i) on conviction on indictment, to a fine;

          (ii) on summary conviction, to a fine not exceeding the statutory maximum.

29. Defence of due diligence

(1) Subject to the following provisions of this regulation, in proceedings against a person for an offence under these Regulations it shall be a defence for that person to show that he took all reasonable steps and exercised all due diligence to avoid committing the offence.

(2) Where in any proceedings against any person for such an offence the defence provided by paragraph (1) involves an allegation that the commission of the offence was due—

      (a) to the act or default of another, or

      (b) to reliance on information given by another,

that person shall not, without the leave of the court, be entitled to rely on the defence unless, not less than seven clear days before, in England, Wales and Northern Ireland, the hearing of the proceedings or, in Scotland, the trial diet, he has served a notice under paragraph (3) on the person bringing the proceedings.

(3) A notice under this paragraph shall give such information identifying or assisting in the identification of the person who—

      (a) committed the act or default, or

      (b) gave the information,

as is in the possession of the person serving the notice at the time he serves it.

(4)　A person may not rely on the defence provided by paragraph (1) by reason of his reliance on information supplied by another, unless he shows that it was reasonable in all the circumstances to have relied on the information, having regard in particular—

 (a)　to the steps which he took, and those which might reasonably have been taken, for the purpose of verifying the information; and

 (b)　to whether he had any reason to disbelieve the information.

30.　Defence in relation to antiques

. . .

31.　Liability of person other than principal offender

(1)　Where the commission by a person of an offence under these Regulations is due to an act or default committed by some other person in the course of a commercial activity of his, the other person shall be guilty of the offence and may be proceeded against and punished by virtue of this paragraph whether or not proceedings are taken against the first-mentioned person.

(2)　Where a body corporate is guilty of an offence under these Regulations (including where it is so guilty by virtue of paragraph (1)) in respect of any act or default which is shown to have been committed with the consent or connivance of, or to be attributable to any neglect on the part of, any director, manager, secretary or other similar officer of the body corporate or any person who was purporting to act in any such capacity he, as well as the body corporate, shall be guilty of that offence and shall be liable to be proceeded against and punished accordingly.

(3)　Where the affairs of a body corporate are managed by its members, paragraph (2) shall apply in relation to the acts and defaults of a member in connection with his functions of management as if he were a director of the body corporate.

(4)　Where a Scottish partnership is guilty of an offence under these Regulations (including where it is so guilty by virtue of paragraph (1)) in respect of any act or default which is shown to have been committed with the consent or connivance of, or to be attributable to any neglect on the part of, a partner in the partnership, he, as well as the partnership, shall be guilty of that offence and shall be liable to be proceeded against and punished accordingly.

PART 4　MISCELLANEOUS

36.　Market surveillance

In order to ensure a high level of consumer health and safety protection, enforcement authorities shall within the limits of their responsibility and to the extent of their ability undertake market surveillance of products employing appropriate means and procedures and co-operating with other enforcement authorities and competent authorities of other Member States which may include:

 (a)　establishment, periodical updating and implementation of sectoral surveillance pro-grammes by categories of products or risks and the monitoring of surveillance activities, findings and results,

 (b)　follow-up and updating of scientific and technical knowledge concerning the safety of products,

 (c)　the periodical review and assessment of the functioning of the control activities and their effectiveness and, if necessary revision of the surveillance approach and organisation put in place.

42.　Civil proceedings

These Regulations shall not be construed as conferring any right of action in civil proceedings in respect of any loss or damage suffered in consequence of a contravention of these Regulations.

Regulatory Reform (Unsolicited Goods and Services Act 1971) (Directory Entries and Demands for Payment) Order 2005

(SI 2005, No. 55)

1   Citation, commencement, extent and interpretation
(3) Expressions used in this Order which are also used in the Unsolicited Goods and Services Act 1971 have the same meaning as in that Act.

5   The Electronic Commerce (EC Directive) Regulations 2002
The Electronic Commerce (EC Directive) Regulations 2002 apply to—
>   (a) this Order; and
>   (b) any subordinate provisions order (within the meaning of section 4(4) of the Regulatory Reform Act 2001) made in respect of the Schedule to this Order.

Article 3   SCHEDULE

PART 1 PARTICULARS OF DIRECTORY OR PROPOSED DIRECTORY WHICH MUST BE GIVEN IN A NOTE

The particulars referred to in section 3(3) of the Unsolicited Goods and Services Act 1971 are:
>   (a) the amount of the charge;
>   (b) the name of the directory or proposed directory;
>   (c) the name of the person producing the directory;
>   (d) the geographic address at which that person is established;
>   (e) if the directory is to be available in printed form, the proposed date of publication of the directory or of the issue in which the entry is to be included;
>   (f) if the directory or the issue in which the entry is to be included is to be put on sale, the price at which it is to be offered for sale and the minimum number of copies which are to be available for sale;
>   (g) if the directory or the issue of the directory in which the entry is to be included is to be distributed free of charge (whether or not it is also to be put on sale), the minimum numbers of copies which are to be so distributed; and
>   (h) if the directory is or is to be made available in a form other than printed form, adequate details of how it may be accessed.

PART 2 CONDITIONS APPLYING TO INVOICE OR SIMILAR DOCUMENT WHICH DOES NOT ASSERT RIGHT TO PAYMENT

The conditions referred to in section 6(2) of the Unsolicited Goods and Services Act 1971 are that the invoice or similar document must:
>   (a) be clear, legible and comprehensible; and
>   (b) contain the following statement, displayed in uppercase lettering and in a manner that makes that statement readily apparent to a reasonable person reading that invoice or similar document—
>> 'THIS IS NOT A DEMAND FOR PAYMENT
>> THERE IS NO OBLIGATION TO PAY
>> THIS IS NOT A BILL'

PART 3 INFORMATION REQUIRED IN WRITTEN NOTICE

The notice referred to in section 3B(1)(h)(i) of the Unsolicited Goods and Services Act 1971 must specify the following information:

    (a) the fact that the earlier contract is to be renewed or extended;

    (b) the commencement date of the new contract;

    (c) the cost to the purchaser of the new contract; and

    (d) the fact that the purchaser may, within 21 days, write to the person by whom the notice is given withdrawing his consent to the renewal or extension of the contract.

PART 4 INFORMATION TO BE GIVEN TO A PURCHASER

The following information must be given to the purchaser pursuant to section 3B(1)(i)(ii) of the Unsolicited Goods and Services Act 1971:

    (a) the name of the relevant publisher; and

    (b) the fact that, if the purchaser enters into the new contract:

        (i)   the other party to the new contract will be the relevant publisher; and

        (ii) the parties to the earlier contract and the new contract will be different.

Transfer of Undertakings (Protection of Employment) Regulations 2006

(SI 2006, No. 246)

3. A relevant transfer

    (1) These Regulations apply to—

        (a) a transfer of an undertaking, business or part of an undertaking or business situated immediately before the transfer in the United Kingdom to another person where there is a transfer of an economic entity which retains its identity;

        . . .

and in which the conditions set out in paragraph (3) are satisfied.

    (2) In this regulation 'economic entity' means an organised grouping of resources which has the objective of pursuing an economic activity, whether or not that activity is central or ancillary.

4. Effect of relevant transfer on contracts of employment

    (1) Except where objection is made under paragraph (7), a relevant transfer shall not operate so as to terminate the contract of employment of any person employed by the transferor and assigned to the organised grouping of resources or employees that is subject to the relevant transfer, which would otherwise be terminated by the transfer, but any such contract shall have effect after the transfer as if originally made between the person so employed and the transferee.

    (2) Without prejudice to paragraph (1), but subject to paragraph (6), and regulations 8 and 15(9), on the completion of a relevant transfer—

        (a) all the transferor's rights, powers, duties and liabilities under or in connection with any such contract shall be transferred by virtue of this regulation to the transferee; and

        (b) any act or omission before the transfer is completed, of or in relation to the transferor in respect of that contract or a person assigned to that organised grouping of resources or employees, shall be deemed to have been an act or omission of or in relation to the transferee.

(3) Any reference in paragraph (1) to a person employed by the transferor and assigned to the organised grouping of resources or employees that is subject to a relevant transfer, is a reference to a person so employed immediately before the transfer, or who would have been so employed if he had not been dismissed in the circumstances described in regulation 7(1), including, where the transfer is effected by a series of two or more transactions, a person so employed and assigned or who would have been so employed and assigned immediately before any of those transactions.

(4) Subject to regulation 9, in respect of a contract of employment that is, or will be, transferred by paragraph (1), any purported variation of the contract shall be void if the sole or principal reason for the variation is—

    (a) the transfer itself; or

    (b) a reason connected with the transfer that is not an economic, technical or organisational reason entailing changes in the workforce.

(5) Paragraph (4) shall not prevent the employer and his employee, whose contract of employment is, or will be, transferred by paragraph (1), from agreeing a variation of that contract if the sole or principal reason for the variation is—

    (a) a reason connected with the transfer that is an economic, technical or organisational reason entailing changes in the workforce; or

    (b) a reason unconnected with the transfer.

(7) Paragraphs (1) and (2) shall not operate to transfer the contract of employment and the rights, powers, duties and liabilities under or in connection with it of an employee who informs the transferor or the transferee that he objects to becoming employed by the transferee.

(8) Subject to paragraphs (9) and (11), where an employee so objects, the relevant transfer shall operate so as to terminate his contract of employment with the transferor but he shall not be treated, for any purpose, as having been dismissed by the transferor.

(9) Subject to regulation 9, where a relevant transfer involves or would involve a substantial change in working conditions to the material detriment of a person whose contract of employment is or would be transferred under paragraph (1), such an employee may treat the contract of employment as having been terminated, and the employee shall be treated for any purpose as having been dismissed by the employer.

(10) No damages shall be payable by an employer as a result of a dismissal falling within paragraph (9) in respect of any failure by the employer to pay wages to an employee in respect of a notice period which the employee has failed to work.

(11) Paragraphs (1), (7), (8) and (9) are without prejudice to any right of an employee arising apart from these Regulations to terminate his contract of employment without notice in acceptance of a repudiatory breach of contract by his employer.

Business Protection from Misleading Marketing Regulations 2008

(SI 2008, No. 1276)

[Implementing Directive 2006/114/EC of the European Parliament and of the Council concerning misleading and comparative advertising [2006] OJ L376/21.]

3. Prohibition of advertising which misleads traders

    (1) Advertising which is misleading is prohibited.

    (2) Advertising is misleading which—

        (a) in any way, including its presentation, deceives or is likely to deceive the traders to whom it is addressed or whom it reaches; and by reason of its deceptive nature, is likely to affect their economic behaviour; or

        (b) for those reasons, injures or is likely to injure a competitor.

(3) In determining whether advertising is misleading, account shall be taken of all its features, and in particular of any information it contains concerning—

    (a) the characteristics of the product (as defined in paragraph (4));

    (b) the price or manner in which the price is calculated;

    (c) the conditions on which the product is supplied or provided; and

    (d) the nature, attributes and rights of the advertiser (as defined in paragraph (5)).

(4) In paragraph (3)(a) the 'characteristics of the product' include—

    (a) availability of the product;

    (b) nature of the product;

    (c) execution of the product;

    (d) composition of the product;

    (e) method and date of manufacture of the product;

    (f) method and date of provision of the product;

    (g) fitness for purpose of the product;

    (h) uses of the product;

    (i) quantity of the product;

    (j) specification of the product;

    (k) geographical or commercial origin of the product;

    (l) results to be expected from use of the product; or

    (m) results and material features of tests or checks carried out on the product.

(5) In paragraph (3)(d) the 'nature, attributes and rights' of the advertiser include the advertiser's—

    (a) identity;

    (b) assets;

    (c) qualifications;

    (d) ownership of industrial, commercial or intellectual property rights; or

    (e) awards and distinctions.

6. Misleading advertising

A trader is guilty of an offence if he engages in advertising which is misleading under regulation 3.

29. Validity of agreements

An agreement shall not be void or unenforceable by reason only of a breach of these Regulations.

Consumer Protection from Unfair Trading Regulations 2008

(SI 2008, No. 1277)

PART 1 GENERAL

2. Interpretation

(1) In these Regulations—

. . .

'commercial practice' means any act, omission, course of conduct, representation or commercial communication (including advertising and marketing) by a trader, which is directly connected with the promotion, sale or supply of a product to or from consumers, whether occurring before, during or after a commercial transaction (if any) in relation to a product;

. . .

'invitation to purchase' means a commercial communication which indicates characteristics of the product and the price in a way appropriate to the means of that commercial communication and thereby enables the consumer to make a purchase;

'materially distort the economic behaviour' means in relation to an average consumer, appreciably to impair the average consumer's ability to make an informed decision thereby causing him to take a transactional decision that he would not have taken otherwise;

. . .

'professional diligence' means the standard of special skill and care which a trader may reasonably be expected to exercise towards consumers which is commensurate with either—

    (a) honest market practice in the trader's field of activity, or

    (b) the general principle of good faith in the trader's field of activity;

. . .

'transactional decision' means any decision taken by a consumer, whether it is to act or to refrain from acting, concerning—

    (a) whether, how and on what terms to purchase, make payment in whole or in part for, retain or dispose of a product; or

    (b) whether, how and on what terms to exercise a contractual right in relation to a product.

(6) Paragraph (5) is without prejudice to the common and legitimate advertising practice of making exaggerated statements which are not meant to be taken literally.

3. Prohibition of unfair commercial practices

(1) Unfair commercial practices are prohibited.

(2) Paragraphs (3) and (4) set out the circumstances when a commercial practice is unfair.

(3) A commercial practice is unfair if—

    (a) it contravenes the requirements of professional diligence; and

    (b) it materially distorts or is likely to materially distort the economic behaviour of the average consumer with regard to the product.

(4) A commercial practice is unfair if—

    (a) it is a misleading action under the provisions of regulation 5;

    (b) it is a misleading omission under the provisions of regulation 6;

    (c) it is aggressive under the provisions of regulation 7; or

    (d) it is listed in Schedule 1.

5. Misleading actions

(1) A commercial practice is a misleading action if it satisfies the conditions in either paragraph (2) or paragraph (3).

(2) A commercial practice satisfies the conditions of this paragraph—

    (a) if it contains false information and is therefore untruthful in relation to any of the matters in paragraph (4) or if it or its overall presentation in any way deceives or is likely to deceive the average consumer in relation to any of the matters in that paragraph, even if the information is factually correct; and

    (b) it causes or is likely to cause the average consumer to take a transactional decision he would not have taken otherwise.

(3) A commercial practice satisfies the conditions of this paragraph if—

    (a) it concerns any marketing of a product (including comparative advertising) which creates confusion with any products, trade marks, trade names or other distinguishing marks of a competitor; or

    (b) it concerns any failure by a trader to comply with a commitment contained in a code of conduct which the trader has undertaken to comply with, if—

        (i)   the trader indicates in a commercial practice that he is bound by that code of conduct, and

        (ii) the commitment is firm and capable of being verified and is not aspirational, and it causes or is likely to cause the average consumer to take a transactional decision he would not have taken otherwise, taking account of its factual context and of all its features and circumstances.

(4) The matters referred to in paragraph (2)(a) are—

    (a) the existence or nature of the product;

    (b) the main characteristics of the product (as defined in paragraph 5);

    (c) the extent of the trader's commitments;

    (d) the motives for the commercial practice;

    (e) the nature of the sales process;

    (f) any statement or symbol relating to direct or indirect sponsorship or approval of the trader or the product;

    (g) the price or the manner in which the price is calculated;

    (h) the existence of a specific price advantage;

    (i) the need for a service, part, replacement or repair;

    (j) the nature, attributes and rights of the trader (as defined in paragraph 6);

    (k) the consumer's rights or the risks he may face.

(5) In paragraph (4)(b), the 'main characteristics of the product' include—

    (a) availability of the product;

    (b) benefits of the product;

    (c) risks of the product;

    (d) execution of the product;

    (e) composition of the product;

    (f) accessories of the product;

    (g) after-sale customer assistance concerning the product;

    (h) the handling of complaints about the product;

    (i) the method and date of manufacture of the product;

    (j) the method and date of provision of the product;

    (k) delivery of the product;

    (l) fitness for purpose of the product;

    (m) usage of the product;

    (n) quantity of the product;

    (o) specification of the product;

    (p) geographical or commercial origin of the product;

    (q) results to be expected from use of the product; and

    (r) results and material features of tests or checks carried out on the product.

(6) In paragraph (4)(j), the 'nature, attributes and rights' as far as concern the trader include the trader's—

    (a) identity;

    (b) assets;

    (c) qualifications;

    (d) status;

    (e) approval;

    (f) affiliations or connections;

    (g) ownership of industrial, commercial or intellectual property rights; and

    (h) wards and distinctions.

(7) In paragraph (4)(k) 'consumer's rights' include rights the consumer may have under Part 5A of the Sale of Goods Act 1979 or Part 1B of the Supply of Goods and Services Act 1982.

6. Misleading omissions

(1) A commercial practice is a misleading omission if, in its factual context, taking account of the matters in paragraph (2)—

    (a) the commercial practice omits material information,

    (b) the commercial practice hides material information,

(c) the commercial practice provides material information in a manner which is unclear, unintelligible, ambiguous or untimely, or

(d) the commercial practice fails to identify its commercial intent, unless this is already apparent from the context,

and as a result it causes or is likely to cause the average consumer to take a transactional decision he would not have taken otherwise.

(2) The matters referred to in paragraph (1) are—

(a) all the features and circumstances of the commercial practice;

(b) the limitations of the medium used to communicate the commercial practice (including limitations of space or time); and

(c) where the medium used to communicate the commercial practice imposes limitations of space or time, any measures taken by the trader to make the information available to consumers by other means.

(3) In paragraph (1) 'material information' means—

(a) the information which the average consumer needs, according to the context, to take an informed transactional decision; and

(b) any information requirement which applies in relation to a commercial communication as a result of a Community obligation.

(4) Where a commercial practice is an invitation to purchase, the following information will be material if not already apparent from the context in addition to any other information which is material information under paragraph (3)—

(a) the main characteristics of the product, to the extent appropriate to the medium by which the invitation to purchase is communicated and the product;

(b) the identity of the trader, such as his trading name, and the identity of any other trader on whose behalf the trader is acting;

(c) the geographical address of the trader and the geographical address of any other trader on whose behalf the trader is acting;

(d) either—

(i) the price, including any taxes; or

(ii) where the nature of the product is such that the price cannot reasonably be calculated in advance, the manner in which the price is calculated;

(e) where appropriate, either—

(i) all additional freight, delivery or postal charges; or

(ii) where such charges cannot reasonably be calculated in advance, the fact that such charges may be payable;

(f) the following matters where they depart from the requirements of professional diligence—

(i) arrangements for payment,

(ii) arrangements for delivery,

(iii) arrangements for performance,

(iv) complaint handling policy;

(g) for products and transactions involving a right of withdrawal or cancellation, the existence of such a right.

7. Aggressive commercial practices

(1) A commercial practice is aggressive if, in its factual context, taking account of all of its features and circumstances—

(a) it significantly impairs or is likely significantly to impair the average consumer's freedom of choice or conduct in relation to the product concerned through the use of harassment, coercion or undue influence; and

(b) it thereby causes or is likely to cause him to take a transactional decision he would not have taken otherwise.

(2) In determining whether a commercial practice uses harassment, coercion or undue influence account shall be taken of—

    (a) its timing, location, nature or persistence;

    (b) the use of threatening or abusive language or behaviour;

    (c) the exploitation by the trader of any specific misfortune or circumstance of such gravity as to impair the consumer's judgment, of which the trader is aware, to influence the consumer's decision with regard to the product;

    (d) any onerous or disproportionate non-contractual barrier imposed by the trader where a consumer wishes to exercise rights under the contract, including rights to terminate a contract or to switch to another product or another trader; and

    (e) any threat to take any action which cannot legally be taken.

(3) In this regulation—

    (a) 'coercion' includes the use of physical force; and

    (b) 'undue influence' means exploiting a position of power in relation to the consumer so as to apply pressure, even without using or threatening to use physical force, in a way which significantly limits the consumer's ability to make an informed decision.

29. Validity of agreements

An agreement shall not be void or unenforceable by reason only of a breach of these Regulations.

Regulation 3(4)(d) **SCHEDULE 1**

COMMERCIAL PRACTICES WHICH ARE IN ALL CIRCUMSTANCES CONSIDERED UNFAIR

. . .

Part IV

EU Materials*

Treaty Establishing the European Economic Community

(Treaty of Rome, 25 March 1957, revised)

Article 81 (ex Art. 85)

1. The following shall be prohibited as incompatible with the common market: all agreements between undertakings, decisions by associations of undertakings and concerted practices which may affect trade between Member States and which have as their object or effect the prevention, restriction or distortion of competition within the common market, and in particular those which:

    (a) directly or indirectly fix purchase or selling prices or any other trading conditions;

    (b) limit or control production, markets, technical development, or investment;

    (c) share markets or sources of supply;

    (d) apply dissimilar conditions to equivalent transactions with other trading parties, thereby placing them at a competitive disadvantage;

    (e) make the conclusion of contracts subject to acceptance by the other parties of supplementary obligations which, by their nature or according to commercial usage, have no connection with the subject of such contracts.

2. Any agreements or decisions prohibited pursuant to this Article shall be automatically void.

3. The provisions of paragraph 1 may, however, be declared inapplicable in the case of:

    – any agreement or category of agreements between undertakings;

    – any decision or category of decisions by associations of undertakings;

    – any concerted practice or category of concerted practices;

which contributes to improving the production or distribution of goods or to promoting technical or economic progress, while allowing consumers a fair share of the resulting benefit, and which does not:

    (a) impose on the undertakings concerned restrictions which are not indispensable to the attainment of these objectives;

    (b) afford such undertakings the possibility of eliminating competition in respect of a substantial part of the products in question.

Article 82 (ex Art. 86)

Any abuse by one or more undertakings of a dominant position within the common market or in a substantial part of it shall be prohibited as incompatible with the common market in so far as it may affect trade between Member States. Such abuse may, in particular, consist in:

    (a) directly or indirectly imposing unfair purchase or selling prices or other unfair trading conditions;

    (b) limiting production, markets or technical development to the prejudice of consumers;

(c) applying dissimilar conditions to equivalent transactions with other trading parties, thereby placing them at a competitive disadvantage;

(d) making the conclusion of contracts subject to acceptance by the other parties of supplementary obligations which, by their nature or according to commercial usage, have no connection with the subject of such contracts.

Regulation (EC) No 864/2007 of the European Parliament and of the Council of 11 July 2007 on the law applicable to non-contractual obligations (Rome II)

[2007] OJ L199/40

Article 2   Non-contractual obligations

1. For the purpose of this Regulation, damage shall cover any consequence arising out of tort/delict, unjust enrichment, *negotiorum gestio* or *culpa in contrahendo*.

Regulation (EC) No 593/2008 of the European Parliament and of the Council of 17 June 2008 on the law applicable to contractual obligations (Rome I)

Article 1   Material scope

1. This Regulation shall apply, in situations involving a conflict of laws, to contractual obligations in civil and commercial matters.

Article 3   Freedom of choice

1. A contract shall be governed by the law chosen by the parties. The choice shall be made expressly or clearly demonstrated by the terms of the contract or the circumstances of the case. By their choice the parties can select the law applicable to the whole or to part only of the contract.

Article 9   Overriding mandatory provisions

3. Effect may be given to the overriding mandatory provisions of the law of the country where the obligations arising out of the contract have to be or have been performed, in so far as those overriding mandatory provisions render the performance of the contract unlawful.

Article 10   Consent and material validity

1. The existence and validity of a contract, or of any term of a contract, shall be determined by the law which would govern it under this Regulation if the contract or term were valid.

Part V

International Materials

United Nations Convention on the Use of Electronic Communications in International Contracts[*]

(2005)

Article 1. Scope of application

1. This Convention applies to the use of electronic communications in connection with the formation or performance of a contract between parties whose places of business are in different States.

Article 8. Legal recognition of electronic communications

1. A communication or a contract shall not be denied validity or enforceability on the sole ground that it is in the form of an electronic communication.

2. Nothing in this Convention requires a party to use or accept electronic communications, but a party's agreement to do so may be inferred from the party's conduct.

Article 9. Form requirements

1. Nothing in this Convention requires a communication or a contract to be made or evidenced in any particular form.

2. Where the law requires that a communication or a contract should be in writing, or provides consequences for the absence of a writing, that requirement is met by an electronic communication if the information contained therein is accessible so as to be usable for subsequent reference.

Article 10. Time and place of dispatch and receipt of electronic communications

1. The time of dispatch of an electronic communication is the time when it leaves an information system under the control of the originator or of the party who sent it on behalf of the originator or, if the electronic communication has not left an information system under the control of the originator or of the party who sent it on behalf of the originator, the time when the electronic communication is received.

2. The time of receipt of an electronic communication is the time when it becomes capable of being retrieved by the addressee at an electronic address designated by the addressee. The time of receipt of an electronic communication at another electronic address of the addressee is the time when it becomes capable of being retrieved by the addressee at that address and the addressee becomes aware that the electronic communication has been sent to that address. An electronic communication is presumed to be capable of being retrieved by the addressee when it reaches the addressee's electronic address.

---

[*] Reproduced with permission from the United Nations Commission on International Trade Law (UNCITRAL).

3. An electronic communication is deemed to be dispatched at the place where the originator has its place of business and is deemed to be received at the place where the addressee has its place of business, as determined in accordance with article 6.

4. Paragraph 2 of this article applies notwithstanding that the place where the information system supporting an electronic address is located may be different from the place where the electronic communication is deemed to be received under paragraph 3 of this article.

Article 11.   Invitations to make offers

A proposal to conclude a contract made through one or more electronic communications which is not addressed to one or more specific parties, but is generally accessible to parties making use of information systems, including proposals that make use of interactive applications for the placement of orders through such information systems, is to be considered as an invitation to make offers, unless it clearly indicates the intention of the party making the proposal to be bound in case of acceptance.

Article 12.   Use of automated message systems for contract formation

A contract formed by the interaction of an automated message system and a natural person, or by the interaction of automated message systems, shall not be denied validity or enforceability on the sole ground that no natural person reviewed or intervened in each of the individual actions carried out by the automated message systems or the resulting contract.

Article 14.   Error in electronic communications

1. Where a natural person makes an input error in an electronic communication exchanged with the automated message system of another party and the automated message system does not provide the person with an opportunity to correct the error, that person, or the party on whose behalf that person was acting, has the right to withdraw the portion of the electronic communication in which the input error was made if:

(a) The person, or the party on whose behalf that person was acting, notifies the other party of the error as soon as possible after having learned of the error and indicates that he or she made an error in the electronic communication;

and

(b) The person, or the party on whose behalf that person was acting, has not used or received any material benefit or value from the goods or services, if any, received from the other party.

2. Nothing in this article affects the application of any rule of law that may govern the consequences of any error other than as provided for in paragraph 1.

Part VI

Codes

DRAFT COMMON FRAME OF REFERENCE (DCFR)

Principles, Definitions and Model Rules of European Private Law*

BOOK I GENERAL PROVISIONS

I. – 1:101: Intended field of application

(1) These rules are intended to be used primarily in relation to contracts and other juridical acts, contractual and non-contractual rights and obligations and related property matters.

I. – 1:102: Interpretation and development

(1) These rules are to be interpreted and developed autonomously and in accordance with their objectives and the principles underlying them.

(2) They are to be read in the light of any applicable instruments guaranteeing human rights and fundamental freedoms and any applicable constitutional laws.

(3) In their interpretation and development regard should be had to the need to promote:

   (a) uniformity of application;
   (b) good faith and fair dealing; and
   (c) legal certainty.

(4) Issues within the scope of the rules but not expressly settled by them are so far as possible to be settled in accordance with the principles underlying them.

(5) Where there is a general rule and a special rule applying to a particular situation within the scope of the general rule, the special rule prevails in any case of conflict.

I. – 1:103: Good faith and fair dealing

(1) The expression "good faith and fair dealing" refers to a standard of conduct characterised by honesty, openness and consideration for the interests of the other party to the transaction or relationship in question.

(2) It is, in particular, contrary to good faith and fair dealing for a party to act inconsistently with that party's prior statements or conduct when the other party has reasonably relied on them to that other party's detriment.

I. – 1:104: Reasonableness

Reasonableness is to be objectively ascertained, having regard to the nature and purpose of what is being done, to the circumstances of the case and to any relevant usages and practices.

* Reproduced with permission of the Study Group on a European Civil Code, the Research Group on EC Private Law (Acquis Group) and Sellier European Law Publishers.

I. – 1:105:   "Consumer" and "business"

(1) A "consumer" means any natural person who is acting primarily for purposes which are not related to his or her trade, business or profession.

(2) A "business" means any natural or legal person, irrespective of whether publicly or privately owned, who is acting for purposes relating to the person's self-employed trade, work or profession, even if the person does not intend to make a profit in the course of the activity.

(3) A person who is within both of the preceding paragraphs is regarded as falling exclusively within paragraph (1) in relation to a rule which would provide protection for that person if that person were a consumer, and otherwise as falling exclusively within paragraph (2).

I. – 1:106:   "In writing" and similar expressions

(1) For the purposes of these rules, a statement is "in writing" if it is in textual form and in characters which are directly legible from paper or another tangible durable medium.

I. – 1:107:   "Signature" and similar expressions

(1) A reference to a person's signature includes a reference to that person's handwritten signature, electronic signature or advanced electronic signature, and references to anything being signed by a person are to be construed accordingly.

I. – 1:108:   Definitions in Annex

(1) The definitions in the Annex apply for all the purposes of these rules unless the context otherwise requires.

(2) Where a word is defined, other grammatical forms of the word have a corresponding meaning.

I. – 1:109:   Notice

(1) This Article applies in relation to the giving of notice for any purpose under these rules. "Notice" includes the communication of information or of a juridical act.

(2) The notice may be given by any means appropriate to the circumstances.

(3) The notice becomes effective when it reaches the addressee, unless it provides for a delayed effect.

(4) The notice reaches the addressee:
  (a) when it is delivered to the addressee;
  (b) when it is delivered to the addressee's place of business or, where there is no such place of business or the notice does not relate to a business matter, to the addressee's habitual residence;
  (c) in the case of a notice transmitted by electronic means, when it can be accessed by the addressee; or
  (d) when it is otherwise made available to the addressee at such a place and in such a way that the addressee could reasonably be expected to obtain access to it without undue delay.

(5) The notice has no effect if a revocation of it reaches the addressee before or at the same time as the notice.

(6) Any reference in these rules to a notice given by or to a person includes a notice given by or to an agent of that person who has authority to give or receive it.

(7) In relations between a business and a consumer the parties may not, to the detriment of the consumer, exclude the rule in paragraph (4)(c) or derogate from or vary its effects.

I. – 1:110:   Computation of time

. . .

BOOK II CONTRACTS AND OTHER JURIDICAL ACTS

Chapter 1: General provisions

II. – 1:101:   Meaning of "contract" and "juridical act"

(1) A contract is an agreement which is intended to give rise to a binding legal relationship or to have some other legal effect. It is a bilateral or multilateral juridical act.

(2) A juridical act is any statement or agreement, whether express or implied from conduct, which is intended to have legal effect as such. It may be unilateral, bilateral or multilateral.

II. – 1:102:   Party autonomy
(1) Parties are free to make a contract or other juridical act and to determine its contents, subject to any applicable mandatory rules.

(2) Parties may exclude the application of any of the following rules relating to contracts or other juridical acts, or the rights and obligations arising from them, or derogate from or vary their effects, except as otherwise provided.

(3) A provision to the effect that parties may not exclude the application of a rule or derogate from or vary its effects does not prevent a party from waiving a right which has already arisen and of which that party is aware.

II. – 1:103:   Binding effect
(1) A valid contract is binding on the parties.

(2) A valid unilateral undertaking is binding on the person giving it if it is intended to be legally binding without acceptance.

(3) This Article does not prevent modification or termination of any resulting right or obligation by agreement between the debtor and creditor or as provided by law.

II. – 1:104:   Usages and practices
(1) The parties to a contract are bound by any usage to which they have agreed and by any practice they have established between themselves.

(2) The parties are bound by a usage which would be considered generally applicable by persons in the same situation as the parties, except where the application of such usage would be unreasonable.

(3) This Article applies to other juridical acts with any necessary adaptations.

II. – 1:105:   Imputed knowledge etc.
If a person who with a party's assent was involved in making a contract or other juridical act or in exercising a right or performing an obligation under it:
    (a) knew or foresaw a fact, or is treated as having knowledge or foresight of a fact; or
    (b) acted intentionally or with any other relevant state of mind this knowledge, foresight or state of mind is imputed to the party.

II. – 1:106:   Form
(1) A contract or other juridical act need not be concluded, made or evidenced in writing nor is it subject to any other requirement as to form.

(2) Where a contract or other juridical act is invalid only by reason of noncompliance with a particular requirement as to form, one party (the first party) is liable for any loss suffered by the other (the second party) by acting in the mistaken, but reasonable, belief that it was valid if the first party:
    (a) knew it was invalid;
    (b) knew or could reasonably be expected to know that the second party was acting to that party's potential prejudice in the mistaken belief that it was valid; and
    (c) contrary to good faith and fair dealing, allowed the second party to continue so acting.

II. – 1:107:   Mixed contracts
(1) For the purposes of this Article a mixed contract is a contract which contains:
    (a) parts falling within two or more of the categories of contracts regulated specifically in these rules; or
    (b) a part falling within one such category and another part falling within the category of contracts governed only by the rules applicable to contracts generally.

(2) Where a contract is a mixed contract then, unless this is contrary to the nature and purpose of the contract, the rules applicable to each relevant category apply, with any appropriate adaptations, to the corresponding part of the contract and the rights and obligations arising from it.

(3) Paragraph (2) does not apply where:

   (a) a rule provides that a mixed contract is to be regarded as falling primarily within one category; or

   (b) in a case not covered by the preceding sub-paragraph, one part of a mixed contract is in fact so predominant that it would be unreasonable not to regard the contract as falling primarily within one category.

(4) In cases covered by paragraph (3) the rules applicable to the category into which the contract primarily falls (the primary category) apply to the contract and the rights and obligations arising from it. However, rules applicable to any elements of the contract falling within another category apply with any appropriate adaptations so far as is necessary to regulate those elements and provided that they do not conflict with the rules applicable to the primary category.

(5) Nothing in this Article prevents the application of any mandatory rules.

II. – 1:108: Partial invalidity or ineffectiveness

Where only part of a contract or other juridical act is invalid or ineffective, the remaining part continues in effect if it can reasonably be maintained without the invalid or ineffective part.

II. – 1:109: Standard terms

A "standard term" is a term which has been formulated in advance for several transactions involving different parties and which has not been individually negotiated by the parties.

II. – 1:110: Terms "not individually negotiated"

(1) A term supplied by one party is not individually negotiated if the other party has not been able to influence its content, in particular because it has been drafted in advance, whether or not as part of standard terms.

(2) If one party supplies a selection of terms to the other party, a term will not be regarded as individually negotiated merely because the other party chooses that term from that selection.

(3) If it is disputed whether a term supplied by one party as part of standard terms has since been individually negotiated, that party bears the burden of proving that it has been.

(4) In a contract between a business and a consumer, the business bears the burden of proving that a term supplied by the business has been individually negotiated.

(5) In contracts between a business and a consumer, terms drafted by a third person are considered to have been supplied by the business, unless the consumer introduced them to the contract.

Chapter 2: Non-discrimination

II. – 2:101: Right not to be discriminated against

A person has a right not to be discriminated against on the grounds of sex or ethnic or racial origin in relation to a contract or other juridical act the object of which is to provide access to, or supply, goods, other assets or services which are available to the public.

II. – 2:102: Meaning of discrimination

(1) "Discrimination" means any conduct whereby, or situation where, on grounds such as those mentioned in the preceding Article:

   (a) one person is treated less favourably than another person is, has been or would be treated in a comparable situation; or

   (b) an apparently neutral provision, criterion or practice would place one group of persons at a particular disadvantage when compared to a different group of persons.

(2) Discrimination also includes harassment on grounds such as those mentioned in the preceding Article. "Harassment" means unwanted conduct (including conduct of a sexual nature) which violates a person's dignity, particularly when such conduct creates an intimidating, hostile, degrading, humiliating or offensive environment, or which aims to do so.

(3) Any instruction to discriminate also amounts to discrimination.

II. – 2:103:   Exception
Unequal treatment which is justified by a legitimate aim does not amount to discrimination if the means used to achieve that aim are appropriate and necessary.

II. – 2:104:   Remedies
(1) If a person is discriminated against contrary to II. – 2:101 (Right not to be discriminated against) then, without prejudice to any remedy which may be available under Book VI (Non-contractual liability for damage caused to another), the remedies for non-performance of an obligation under Book III, Chapter 3 (including damages for economic and non-economic loss) are available.

(2) Any remedy granted should be proportionate to the injury or anticipated injury; the dissuasive effect of remedies may be taken into account.

II. – 2:105:   Burden of proof
(1) If a person who considers himself or herself discriminated against on one of the grounds mentioned in II. – 2:101 (Right not to be discriminated against) establishes, before a court or another competent authority, facts from which it may be presumed that there has been such discrimination, it falls on the other party to prove that there has been no such discrimination.

(2) Paragraph (1) does not apply to proceedings in which it is for the court or another competent authority to investigate the facts of the case.

Chapter 3: Marketing and pre-contractual duties

Section 1: Information duties

II. – 3:101:   Duty to disclose information about goods, other assets and services
(1) Before the conclusion of a contract for the supply of goods, other assets or services by a business to another person, the business has a duty to disclose to the other person such information concerning the goods, other assets or services to be supplied as the other person can reasonably expect, taking into account the standards of quality and performance which would be normal under the circumstances.

(2) In assessing what information the other person can reasonably expect to be disclosed, the test to be applied, if the other person is also a business, is whether the failure to provide the information would deviate from good commercial practice.

II. – 3:102:   Specific duties for businesses marketing to consumers
(1) Where a business is marketing goods, other assets or services to a consumer, the business has a duty not to give misleading information. Information is misleading if it misrepresents or omits material facts which the average consumer could expect to be given for an informed decision on whether to take steps towards the conclusion of a contract. In assessing what an average consumer could expect to be given, account is to be taken of all the circumstances and of the limitations of the communication medium employed.

(2) Where a business uses a commercial communication which gives the impression to consumers that it contains all the relevant information necessary to make a decision about concluding a contract, the business has a duty to ensure that the communication in fact contains all the relevant information. Where it is not already apparent from the context of the commercial communication, the information to be provided comprises:

(a) the main characteristics of the goods, other assets or services, the identity and address, if relevant, of the business, the price, and any available right of withdrawal;
(b) peculiarities related to payment, delivery, performance and complaint handling, if they depart from the requirements of professional diligence; and
(c) the language to be used for communications between the parties after the conclusion of the contract, if this differs from the language of the commercial communication.

(3) A duty to provide information under this Article is not fulfilled unless all the information to be provided is provided in the same language.

II. – 3:103:   Duty to provide information when concluding contract with a consumer who is at a particular disadvantage

(1) In the case of transactions that place the consumer at a significant informational disadvantage because of the technical medium used for contracting, the physical distance between business and consumer, or the nature of the transaction, the business has a duty, as appropriate in the circumstances, to provide clear information about the main characteristics of any goods, other assets or services to be supplied, the price, the address and identity of the business with which the consumer is transacting, the terms of the contract, the rights and obligations of both contracting parties, and any available right of withdrawal or redress procedures. This information must be provided a reasonable time before the conclusion of the contract. The information on the right of withdrawal must, as appropriate in the circumstances, also be adequate in the sense of II. – 5:104 (Adequate information on the right to withdraw).

(2) Where more specific information duties are provided for specific situations, these take precedence over the general information duty under paragraph (1).

(3) The business bears the burden of proof that it has provided the information required by this Article.

II. – 3:104:   Information duties in real time distance communication

(1) When initiating real time distance communication with a consumer, a business has a duty to provide at the outset explicit information on its name and the commercial purpose of the contact.

(2) Real time distance communication means direct and immediate distance communication of such a type that one party can interrupt the other in the course of the communication. It includes telephone and electronic means such as voice over internet protocol and internet related chat, but does not include communication by electronic mail.

(3) The business bears the burden of proof that the consumer has received the information required under paragraph (1).

(4) If a business has failed to comply with the duty under paragraph (1) and a contract has been concluded as a result of the communication, the other party has a right to withdraw from the contract by giving notice to the business within the period specified in II. – 5:103 (Withdrawal period).

(5) A business is liable to the consumer for any loss caused by a breach of the duty under paragraph (1).

II. – 3:105:   Formation by electronic means

(1) If a contract is to be concluded by electronic means and without individual communication, a business has a duty to provide information about the following matters before the other party makes or accepts an offer:

(a) the technical steps to be taken in order to conclude the contract;
(b) whether or not a contract document will be filed by the business and whether it will be accessible;
(c) the technical means for identifying and correcting input errors before the other party makes or accepts an offer;
(d) the languages offered for the conclusion of the contract;
(e) any contract terms used.

(2) The business has a duty to ensure that the contract terms referred to in paragraph (1)(e) are available in textual form.

(3) If a business has failed to comply with the duty under paragraph (1) and a contract has been concluded in the circumstances there stated, the other party has a right to withdraw from the contract by giving notice to the business within the period specified in II. – 5:103 (Withdrawal period).

(4) A business is liable to the consumer for any loss caused by a breach of the duty under paragraph (1).

II. – 3:106: Clarity and form of information

(1) A duty to provide information imposed on a business under this Chapter is not fulfilled unless the requirements of this Article are satisfied.

(2) The information must be clear and precise, and expressed in plain and intelligible language.

(3) Where rules for specific contracts require information to be provided on a durable medium or in another particular form it must be provided in that way.

(4) In the case of contracts between a business and a consumer concluded at a distance, information about the main characteristics of any goods, other assets or services to be supplied, the price, the address and identity of the business with which the consumer is transacting, the terms of the contract, the rights and obligations of both contracting parties, and any available redress procedures, as may be appropriate in the particular case, must be confirmed in textual form on a durable medium at the time of conclusion of the contract. The information on the right of withdrawal must also be adequate in the sense of II. – 5:104 (Adequate information on the right to withdraw).

II. – 3:107: Information about price and additional charges

. . .

II. – 3:108: Information about address and identity of business

. . .

II. – 3:109: Remedies for breach of information duties

(1) If a business has a duty under II. – 3:103 (Duty to provide information when concluding contract with a consumer who is at a particular disadvantage) to provide information to a consumer before the conclusion of a contract from which the consumer has the right to withdraw, the withdrawal period does not commence until all this information has been provided. Regardless of this, the right of withdrawal lapses after one year from the time of the conclusion of the contract.

(2) If a business has failed to comply with any duty imposed by the preceding Articles of this Section and a contract has been concluded, the business has such obligations under the contract as the other party has reasonably expected as a consequence of the absence or incorrectness of the information. Remedies provided under Book III, Chapter 3 apply to non-performance of these obligations.

(3) Whether or not a contract is concluded, a business which has failed to comply with any duty imposed by the preceding Articles of this Section is liable for any loss caused to the other party to the transaction by such failure. This paragraph does not apply to the extent that a remedy is available for non-performance of a contractual obligation under the preceding paragraph.

(4) The remedies provided under this Article are without prejudice to any remedy which may be available under II. – 7:201 (Mistake).

(5) In relations between a business and a consumer the parties may not, to the detriment of the consumer, exclude the application of this Article or derogate from or vary its effects.

Section 2: Duty to prevent input errors and acknowledge receipt

II. – 3:201: Correction of input errors

(1) A business which intends to conclude a contract by making available electronic means without individual communication for concluding it has a duty to make available to the other party appropriate, effective and accessible technical means for identifying and correcting input errors before the other party makes or accepts an offer.

(2) Where a person concludes a contract in error because of a failure by a business to comply with the duty under paragraph (1) the business is liable for any loss caused to that person by such failure. This is without prejudice to any remedy which may be available under II.–7:201 (Mistake).

(3) In relations between a business and a consumer the parties may not, to the detriment of the consumer, exclude the application of this Article or derogate from or vary its effects.

II. – 3:202: Acknowledgement of receipt

(1) A business which offers the facility to conclude a contract by electronic means and without individual communication has a duty to acknowledge by electronic means the receipt of an offer or an acceptance by the other party.

(2) If the other party does not receive the acknowledgement without undue delay, that other party may revoke the offer or withdraw from the contract.

(3) The business is liable for any loss caused to the other party by a breach of the duty under paragraph (1).

(4) In relations between a business and a consumer the parties may not, to the detriment of the consumer, exclude the application of this Article or derogate from or vary its effects.

Section 3: Negotiation and confidentiality duties

II. – 3:301: Negotiations contrary to good faith and fair dealing

(1) A person is free to negotiate and is not liable for failure to reach an agreement.

(2) A person who is engaged in negotiations has a duty to negotiate in accordance with good faith and fair dealing and not to break off negotiations contrary to good faith and fair dealing. This duty may not be excluded or limited by contract.

(3) A person who is in breach of the duty is liable for any loss caused to the other party by the breach.

(4) It is contrary to good faith and fair dealing, in particular, for a person to enter into or continue negotiations with no real intention of reaching an agreement with the other party.

II. – 3:302: Breach of confidentiality

(1) If confidential information is given by one party in the course of negotiations, the other party is under a duty not to disclose that information or use it for that party's own purposes whether or not a contract is subsequently concluded.

(2) In this Article, "confidential information" means information which, either from its nature or the circumstances in which it was obtained, the party receiving the information knows or could reasonably be expected to know is confidential to the other party.

(3) A party who reasonably anticipates a breach of the duty may obtain a court order prohibiting it.

(4) A party who is in breach of the duty is liable for any loss caused to the other party by the breach and may be ordered to pay over to the other party any benefit obtained by the breach.

Section 4: Unsolicited goods or services

II. – 3:401: No obligation arising from failure to respond

(1) If a business delivers unsolicited goods to, or performs unsolicited services for, a consumer:
- (a) no contract arises from the consumer's failure to respond or from any other action or inaction by the consumer in relation to the goods and services; and
- (b) no non-contractual obligation arises from the consumer's acquisition, retention, rejection or use of the goods or receipt of benefit from the services.

(2) Sub-paragraph (b) of the preceding paragraph does not apply if the goods or services were supplied:
- (a) by way of benevolent intervention in another's affairs; or
- (b) in error or in such other circumstances that there is a right to reversal of an unjustified enrichment.

(3) This Article is subject to the rules on delivery of excess quantity under a contract for the sale of goods.

(4) For the purposes of paragraph (1) delivery occurs when the consumer obtains physical control over the goods.

Section 5: Damages for breach of duty under this Chapter

II. – 3:501: Liability for damages

(1) Where any rule in this Chapter makes a person liable for loss caused to another person by a breach of a duty, the other person has a right to damages for that loss.

(2) The rules on III.–3:704 (Loss attributable to creditor) and III.–3:705 (Reduction of loss) apply with the adaptation that the reference to non-performance of the obligation is to be taken as a reference to breach of the duty.

Chapter 4: Formation

Section 1: General provisions

II. – 4:101: Requirements for the conclusion of a contract
A contract is concluded, without any further requirement, if the parties:
> (a) intend to enter into a binding legal relationship or bring about some other legal effect; and
> (b) reach a sufficient agreement.

II. – 4:102: How intention is determined
The intention of a party to enter into a binding legal relationship or bring about some other legal effect is to be determined from the party's statements or conduct as they were reasonably understood by the other party.

II. – 4:103: Sufficient agreement
> (1) Agreement is sufficient if:
>> (a) the terms of the contract have been sufficiently defined by the parties for the contract to be given effect; or
>> (b) the terms of the contract, or the rights and obligations of the parties under it, can be otherwise sufficiently determined for the contract to be given effect.

(2) If one of the parties refuses to conclude a contract unless the parties have agreed on some specific matter, there is no contract unless agreement on that matter has been reached.

II. – 4:104: Merger clause
(1) If a contract document contains an individually negotiated term stating that the document embodies all the terms of the contract (a merger clause), any prior statements, undertakings or agreements which are not embodied in the document do not form part of the contract.

(2) If the merger clause is not individually negotiated it establishes only a presumption that the parties intended that their prior statements, undertakings or agreements were not to form part of the contract. This rule may not be excluded or restricted.

(3) The parties' prior statements may be used to interpret the contract. This rule may not be excluded or restricted except by an individually negotiated term.

(4) A party may by statements or conduct be precluded from asserting a merger clause to the extent that the other party has reasonably relied on such statements or conduct.

II. – 4:105: Modification in certain form only
(1) A term in a contract requiring any agreement to modify its terms, or to terminate the relationship resulting from it, to be in a certain form establishes only a presumption that any such agreement is not intended to be legally binding unless it is in that form.

(2) A party may by statements or conduct be precluded from asserting such a term to the extent that the other party has reasonably relied on such statements or conduct.

Section 2: Offer and acceptance

II. – 4:201: Offer
> (1) A proposal amounts to an offer if:
>> (a) it is intended to result in a contract if the other party accepts it; and
>> (b) it contains sufficiently definite terms to form a contract.

(2) An offer may be made to one or more specific persons or to the public.

(3) A proposal to supply goods from stock, or a service, at a stated price made by a business in a public advertisement or a catalogue, or by a display of goods, is treated, unless the circumstances

indicate otherwise, as an offer to supply at that price until the stock of goods, or the business's capacity to supply the service, is exhausted.

II. – 4:202:   Revocation of offer

(1) An offer may be revoked if the revocation reaches the offeree before the offeree has dispatched an acceptance or, in cases of acceptance by conduct, before the contract has been concluded.

(2) An offer made to the public can be revoked by the same means as were used to make the offer.

(3) However, a revocation of an offer is ineffective if:
  (a) the offer indicates that it is irrevocable;
  (b) the offer states a fixed time for its acceptance; or
  (c) it was reasonable for the offeree to rely on the offer as being irrevocable and the offeree has acted in reliance on the offer.

(4) Paragraph (3) does not apply to an offer if the offeror would have a right under any rule in Books II to IV to withdraw from a contract resulting from its acceptance. The parties may not, to the detriment of the offeror, exclude the application of this rule or derogate from or vary its effects.

II. – 4:203:   Rejection of offer

When a rejection of an offer reaches the offeror, the offer lapses.

II. – 4:204:   Acceptance

(1) Any form of statement or conduct by the offeree is an acceptance if it indicates assent to the offer.

(2) Silence or inactivity does not in itself amount to acceptance.

II. – 4:205:   Time of conclusion of the contract

(1) If an acceptance has been dispatched by the offeree the contract is concluded when the acceptance reaches the offeror.

(2) In the case of acceptance by conduct, the contract is concluded when notice of the conduct reaches the offeror.

(3) If by virtue of the offer, of practices which the parties have established between themselves, or of a usage, the offeree may accept the offer by doing an act without notice to the offeror, the contract is concluded when the offeree begins to do the act.

II. – 4:206:   Time limit for acceptance

(1) An acceptance of an offer is effective only if it reaches the offeror within the time fixed by the offeror.

(2) If no time has been fixed by the offeror the acceptance is effective only if it reaches the offeror within a reasonable time.

(3) Where an offer may be accepted by performing an act without notice to the offeror, the acceptance is effective only if the act is performed within the time for acceptance fixed by the offeror or, if no such time is fixed, within a reasonable time.

II. – 4:207:   Late acceptance

(1) A late acceptance is nonetheless effective as an acceptance if without undue delay the offeror informs the offeree that it is treated as an effective acceptance.

(2) If a letter or other communication containing a late acceptance shows that it has been dispatched in such circumstances that if its transmission had been normal it would have reached the offeror in due time, the late acceptance is effective as an acceptance unless, without undue delay, the offeror informs the offeree that the offer is considered to have lapsed.

II. – 4:208:   Modified acceptance

(1) A reply by the offeree which states or implies additional or different terms which materially alter the terms of the offer is a rejection and a new offer.

(2) A reply which gives a definite assent to an offer operates as an acceptance even if it states or implies additional or different terms, provided these do not materially alter the terms of the offer. The additional or different terms then become part of the contract.

(3) However, such a reply is treated as a rejection of the offer if:

(a) the offer expressly limits acceptance to the terms of the offer;

(b) the offeror objects to the additional or different terms without undue delay; or

(c) the offeree makes the acceptance conditional upon the offeror's assent to the additional or different terms, and the assent does not reach the offeree within a reasonable time.

II. – 4:209:   Conflicting standard terms

(1) If the parties have reached agreement except that the offer and acceptance refer to conflicting standard terms, a contract is nonetheless formed. The standard terms form part of the contract to the extent that they are common in substance.

(2) However, no contract is formed if one party:

(a) has indicated in advance, explicitly, and not by way of standard terms, an intention not to be bound by a contract on the basis of paragraph (1); or

(b) without undue delay, informs the other party of such an intention.

II. – 4:210:   Formal confirmation of contract between businesses

If businesses have concluded a contract but have not embodied it in a final document, and one without undue delay sends the other a notice in textual form on a durable medium which purports to be a confirmation of the contract but which contains additional or different terms, such terms become part of the contract unless:

(a) the terms materially alter the terms of the contract; or

(b) the addressee objects to them without undue delay.

II. – 4:211:   Contracts not concluded through offer and acceptance

The rules in this Section apply with appropriate adaptations even though the process of conclusion of a contract cannot be analysed into offer and acceptance.

Section 3: Other juridical acts

II. – 4:301:   Requirements for a unilateral juridical act

The requirements for a unilateral juridical act are:

(a) that the party doing the act intends to be legally bound or to achieve the relevant legal effect;

(b) that the act is sufficiently certain; and

(c) that notice of the act reaches the person to whom it is addressed or, if the act is addressed to the public, the act is made public by advertisement, public notice or otherwise.

II. – 4:302:   How intention is determined

The intention of a party to be legally bound or to achieve the relevant legal effect is to be determined from the party's statements or conduct as they were reasonably understood by the person to whom the act is addressed.

II. – 4:303:   Right or benefit may be rejected

Where a unilateral juridical act confers a right or benefit on the person to whom it is addressed, that person may reject it by notice to the maker of the act, provided that is done without undue delay and before the right or benefit has been expressly or impliedly accepted. On such rejection, the right or benefit is treated as never having accrued.

Chapter 5: Right of withdrawal

Section 1: Exercise and effect

II. – 5:101:   Scope and mandatory nature

(1) The provisions in this Section apply where under any rule in Books II to IV a party has a right to withdraw from a contract within a certain period.

(2) The parties may not, to the detriment of the entitled party, exclude the application of the rules in this Chapter or derogate from or vary their effects.

II. – 5:102:   Exercise of right to withdraw

(1) A right to withdraw is exercised by notice to the other party. No reasons need to be given.

(2) Returning the subject matter of the contract is considered a notice of withdrawal unless the circumstances indicate otherwise.

II. – 5:103:   Withdrawal period

(1) A right to withdraw may be exercised at any time after the conclusion of the contract and before the end of the withdrawal period.

(2) The withdrawal period ends fourteen days after the latest of the following times;
   (a) the time of conclusion of the contract;
   (b) the time when the entitled party receives from the other party adequate information on the right to withdraw; or
   (c) if the subject matter of the contract is the delivery of goods, the time when the goods are received.

(3) The withdrawal period ends no later than one year after the time of conclusion of the contract.

(4) A notice of withdrawal is timely if dispatched before the end of the withdrawal period.

II. – 5:104:   Adequate information on the right to withdraw

Adequate information on the right to withdraw requires that the right is appropriately brought to the entitled party's attention, and that the information provides, in textual form on a durable medium and in clear and comprehensible language, information about how the right may be exercised, the withdrawal period, and the name and address of the person to whom the withdrawal is to be communicated.

II. – 5:105:   Effects of withdrawal

(1) Withdrawal terminates the contractual relationship and the obligations of both parties under the contract.

(2) The restitutionary effects of such termination are governed by the rules in Book III, Chapter 3, Section 5, Sub-section 4 (Restitution) as modified by this Article, unless the contract provides otherwise in favour of the withdrawing party.

(3) Where the withdrawing party has made a payment under the contract, the business has an obligation to return the payment without undue delay, and in any case not later than thirty days after the withdrawal becomes effective.

(4) The withdrawing party is not liable to pay:
   (a) for any diminution in the value of anything received under the contract caused by inspection and testing;
   (b) for any destruction or loss of, or damage to, anything received under the contract, provided the withdrawing party used reasonable care to prevent such destruction, loss or damage.

(5) The withdrawing party is liable for any diminution in value caused by normal use, unless that party had not received adequate notice of the right of withdrawal.

(6) Except as provided in this Article, the withdrawing party does not incur any liability through the exercise of the right of withdrawal.

(7) If a consumer exercises a right to withdraw from a contract after a business has made use of a contractual right to supply something of equivalent quality and price in case what was ordered is unavailable, the business must bear the cost of returning what the consumer has received under the contract.

II. – 5:106:   Linked contracts

(1) If a consumer exercises a right of withdrawal from a contract for the supply of goods, other assets or services by a business, the effects of withdrawal extend to any linked contract.

(2) Where a contract is partially or exclusively financed by a credit contract, they form linked contracts, in particular:

> (a) if the business supplying goods, other assets or services finances the consumer's performance;
>
> (b) if a third party which finances the consumer's performance uses the services of the business for preparing or concluding the credit contract;
>
> (c) if the credit contract refers to specific goods, assets or services to be financed with this credit, and if this link between both contracts was suggested by the supplier of the goods, other assets or services, or by the supplier of credit; or
>
> (d) if there is a similar economic link.

(3) The provisions of II.–5:105 (Effects of withdrawal) apply accordingly to the linked contract.

(4) Paragraph (1) does not apply to credit contracts financing the contracts mentioned in paragraph (2)(f) of the following Article.

Section 2: Particular rights of withdrawal

II. – 5:201:   Contracts negotiated away from business premises

(1) A consumer is entitled to withdraw from a contract under which a business supplies goods, other assets or services, including financial services, to the consumer, or is granted a personal security by the consumer, if the consumer's offer or acceptance was expressed away from the business premises.

(2) Paragraph (1) does not apply to:

> (a) a contract concluded by means of an automatic vending machine or automated commercial premises;
>
> (b) a contract concluded with telecommunications operators through the use of public payphones;
>
> (c) a contract for the construction and sale of immovable property or relating to other immovable property rights, except for rental;
>
> (d) a contract for the supply of foodstuffs, beverages or other goods intended for everyday consumption supplied to the home, residence or workplace of the consumer by regular roundsmen;
>
> (e) a contract concluded by means of distance communication, but outside of an organised distance sales or service-provision scheme run by the supplier;
>
> (f) a contract for the supply of goods, other assets or services whose price depends on fluctuations in the financial market outside the supplier's control, which may occur during the withdrawal period;
>
> (g) a contract concluded at an auction;
>
> (h) travel and baggage insurance policies or similar short-term insurance policies of less than one month's duration.

(3) If the business has exclusively used means of distance communication for concluding the contract, paragraph (1) also does not apply if the contract is for:

> (a) the supply of accommodation, transport, catering or leisure services, where the business undertakes, when the contract is concluded, to supply these services on a specific date or within a specific period;
>
> (b) the supply of services other than financial services if performance has begun, at the consumer's express and informed request, before the end of the withdrawal period referred to in II.–5:103 (Withdrawal period) paragraph (1);
>
> (c) the supply of goods made to the consumer's specifications or clearly personalised or which, by reason of their nature, cannot be returned or are liable to deteriorate or expire rapidly;
>
> (d) the supply of audio or video recordings or computer software
>> (i)   which were unsealed by the consumer, or
>> (ii) which can be downloaded or reproduced for permanent use, in case of supply by electronic means;

(e) the supply of newspapers, periodicals and magazines;

(f) gaming and lottery services.

(4) With regard to financial services, paragraph (1) also does not apply to contracts that have been fully performed by both parties, at the consumer's express request, before the consumer exercises his or her right of withdrawal.

II. – 5:202: Timeshare contracts

...

Chapter 6: Representation

...

Chapter 7: Grounds of invalidity

Section 1: General provisions

II. – 7:101: Scope

(1) This Chapter deals with the effects of:

    (a) mistake, fraud, threats, or unfair exploitation; and

    (b) infringement of fundamental principles or mandatory rules.

(2) It does not deal with lack of capacity.

(3) It applies in relation to contracts and, with any necessary adaptations, other juridical acts.

II. – 7:102: Initial impossibility or lack of right or authority to dispose

A contract is not invalid, in whole or in part, merely because at the time it is concluded performance of any obligation assumed is impossible, or because a party has no right or authority to dispose of any assets to which the contract relates.

Section 2: Vitiated consent or intention

II. – 7:201: Mistake

(1) A party may avoid a contract for mistake of fact or law existing when the contract was concluded if:

    (a) the party, but for the mistake, would not have concluded the contract or would have done so only on fundamentally different terms and the other party knew or could reasonably be expected to have known this; and

    (b) the other party;

        (i) caused the mistake;

        (ii) caused the contract to be concluded in mistake by leaving the mistaken party in error, contrary to good faith and fair dealing, when the other party knew or could reasonably be expected to have known of the mistake;

        (iii) caused the contract to be concluded in mistake by failing to comply with a pre-contractual information duty or a duty to make available a means of correcting input errors; or

        (iv) made the same mistake.

(2) However a party may not avoid the contract for mistake if:

    (a) the mistake was inexcusable in the circumstances; or

    (b) the risk of the mistake was assumed, or in the circumstances should be borne, by that party.

II. – 7:202: Inaccuracy in communication may be treated as mistake

An inaccuracy in the expression or transmission of a statement is treated as a mistake of the person who made or sent the statement.

II. – 7:203:   Adaptation of contract in case of mistake

(1) If a party is entitled to avoid the contract for mistake but the other party performs, or indicates a willingness to perform, the obligations under the contract as it was understood by the party entitled to avoid it, the contract is treated as having been concluded as that party understood it. This applies only if the other party performs, or indicates a willingness to perform, without undue delay after being informed of the manner in which the party entitled to avoid it understood the contract and before that party acts in reliance on any notice of avoidance.

(2) After such performance or indication the right to avoid is lost and any earlier notice of avoidance is ineffective.

(3) Where both parties have made the same mistake, the court may at the request of either party bring the contract into accordance with what might reasonably have been agreed had the mistake not occurred.

II. – 7:204:   Liability for loss caused by reliance on incorrect information

(1) A party who has concluded a contract in reasonable reliance on incorrect information given by the other party in the course of negotiations has a right to damages for loss suffered as a result if the provider of the information:

   (a) believed the information to be incorrect or had no reasonable grounds for believing it to be correct; and
   (b) knew or could reasonably be expected to have known that the recipient would rely on the information in deciding whether or not to conclude the contract on the agreed terms.

(2) This Article applies even if there is no right to avoid the contract.

II. – 7:205:   Fraud

(1) A party may avoid a contract when the other party has induced the conclusion of the contract by fraudulent misrepresentation, whether by words or conduct, or fraudulent non-disclosure of any information which good faith and fair dealing, or any pre-contractual information duty, required that party to disclose.

(2) A misrepresentation is fraudulent if it is made with knowledge or belief that the representation is false and is intended to induce the recipient to make a mistake. A non-disclosure is fraudulent if it is intended to induce the person from whom the information is withheld to make a mistake.

(3) In determining whether good faith and fair dealing required a party to disclose particular information, regard should be had to all the circumstances, including:

   (a) whether the party had special expertise;
   (b) the cost to the party of acquiring the relevant information;
   (c) whether the other party could reasonably acquire the information by other means; and
   (d) the apparent importance of the information to the other party.

II. – 7:206:   Coercion or threats

(1) A party may avoid a contract when the other party has induced the conclusion of the contract by coercion or by the threat of an imminent and serious harm which it is wrongful to inflict, or wrongful to use as a means to obtain the conclusion of the contract.

(2) A threat is not regarded as inducing the contract if in the circumstances the threatened party had a reasonable alternative.

II. – 7:207:   Unfair exploitation

(1) A party may avoid a contract if, at the time of the conclusion of the contract:

   (a) the party was dependent on or had a relationship of trust with the other party, was in economic distress or had urgent needs, was improvident, ignorant, inexperienced or lacking in bargaining skill; and
   (b) the other party knew or could reasonably be expected to have known this and, given the circumstances and purpose of the contract, exploited the first party's situation by taking an excessive benefit or grossly unfair advantage.

(2) Upon the request of the party entitled to avoidance, a court may if it is appropriate adapt the contract in order to bring it into accordance with what might have been agreed had the requirements of good faith and fair dealing been observed.

(3) A court may similarly adapt the contract upon the request of a party receiving notice of avoidance for unfair exploitation, provided that this party informs the party who gave the notice without undue delay after receiving it and before that party has acted in reliance on it.

II. – 7:208:   Third persons

(1) Where a third person for whose acts a party is responsible or who with a party's assent is involved in the making of a contract:

   (a) causes a mistake, or knows of or could reasonably be expected to know of a mistake; or
   (b) is guilty of fraud, coercion, threats or unfair exploitation, remedies under this Section are available as if the behaviour or knowledge had been that of the party.

(2) Where a third person for whose acts a party is not responsible and who does not have the party's assent to be involved in the making of a contract is guilty of fraud, coercion, threats or unfair exploitation, remedies under this Section are available if the party knew or could reasonably be expected to have known of the relevant facts, or at the time of avoidance has not acted in reliance on the contract.

II. – 7:209:   Notice of avoidance

Avoidance under this Section is effected by notice to the other party.

II. – 7:210:   Time

A notice of avoidance under this Section is ineffective unless given within a reasonable time, with due regard to the circumstances, after the avoiding party knew or could reasonably be expected to have known of the relevant facts or became capable of acting freely.

II. – 7:211:   Confirmation

If a party who is entitled to avoid a contract under this Section confirms it, expressly or impliedly, after the period of time for giving notice of avoidance has begun to run, avoidance is excluded.

II. – 7:212:   Effects of avoidance

(1) A contract which may be avoided under this Section is valid until avoided but, once avoided, is retrospectively invalid from the beginning.

(2) The question whether either party has a right to the return of whatever has been transferred or supplied under a contract which has been avoided under this Section, or a monetary equivalent, is regulated by the rules on unjustified enrichment.

(3) The effect of avoidance under this Section on the ownership of property which has been transferred under the avoided contract is governed by the rules on the transfer of property.

II. – 7:213:   Partial avoidance

If a ground of avoidance under this Section affects only particular terms of a contract, the effect of an avoidance is limited to those terms unless, giving due consideration to all the circumstances of the case, it is unreasonable to uphold the remaining contract.

II. – 7:214:   Damages for loss

(1) A party who has the right to avoid a contract under this Section (or who had such a right before it was lost by the effect of time limits or confirmation) is entitled, whether or not the contract is avoided, to damages from the other party for any loss suffered as a result of the mistake, fraud, coercion, threats or unfair exploitation, provided that the other party knew or could reasonably be expected to have known of the ground for avoidance.

(2) The damages recoverable are such as to place the aggrieved party as nearly as possible in the position in which that party would have been if the contract had not been concluded, with the further limitation that, if the party does not avoid the contract, the damages are not to exceed the loss caused by the mistake, fraud, coercion, threats or unfair exploitation.

(3) In other respects the rules on damages for non-performance of a contractual obligation apply with any appropriate adaptation.

II. – 7:215:   Exclusion or restriction of remedies

(1) Remedies for fraud, coercion, threats and unfair exploitation cannot be excluded or restricted.

(2) Remedies for mistake may be excluded or restricted unless the exclusion or restriction is contrary to good faith and fair dealing.

II. – 7:216:   Overlapping remedies

A party who is entitled to a remedy under this Section in circumstances which afford that party a remedy for non-performance may pursue either remedy.

Section 3: Infringement of fundamental principles or mandatory rules

II. – 7:301:   Contracts infringing fundamental principles

A contract is void to the extent that:
- (a) it infringes a principle recognised as fundamental in the laws of the Member States of the European Union; and
- (b) nullity is required to give effect to that principle.

II. – 7:302:   Contracts infringing mandatory rules

(1) Where a contract is not void under the preceding Article but infringes a mandatory rule of law, the effects of that infringement on the validity of the contract are the effects, if any, expressly prescribed by that mandatory rule.

(2) Where the mandatory rule does not expressly prescribe the effects of an infringement on the validity of a contract, a court may:
- (a) declare the contract to be valid;
- (b) avoid the contract, with retrospective effect, in whole or in part; or
- (c) modify the contract or its effects.

(3) A decision reached under paragraph (2) should be an appropriate and proportional response to the infringement, having regard to all relevant circumstances, including:
- (a) the purpose of the rule which has been infringed;
- (b) the category of persons for whose protection the rule exists;
- (c) any sanction that may be imposed under the rule infringed;
- (d) the seriousness of the infringement;
- (e) whether the infringement was intentional; and
- (f) the closeness of the relationship between the infringement and the contract.

II. – 7:303:   Effects of nullity or avoidance

(1) The question whether either party has a right to the return of whatever has been transferred or supplied under a contract, or part of a contract, which is void or has been avoided under this Section, or a monetary equivalent, is regulated by the rules on unjustified enrichment.

(2) The effect of nullity or avoidance under this Section on the ownership of property which has been transferred under the void or avoided contract, or part of a contract, is governed by the rules on the transfer of property.

(3) This Article is subject to the powers of the court to modify the contract or its effects.

II. – 7:304:   Damages for loss

(1) A party to a contract which is void or avoided, in whole or in part, under this Section is entitled to damages from the other party for any loss suffered as a result of the invalidity, provided that the first party did not know and could not reasonably be expected to have known, and the other party knew or could reasonably be expected to have known, of the infringement.

(2) The damages recoverable are such as to place the aggrieved party as nearly as possible in the position in which that party would have been if the contract had not been concluded or the infringing term had not been included.

Chapter 8: Interpretation

Section 1: Interpretation of contracts

II. – 8:101:   General rules

(1) A contract is to be interpreted according to the common intention of the parties even if this differs from the literal meaning of the words.

(2) If one party intended the contract, or a term or expression used in it, to have a particular meaning, and at the time of the conclusion of the contract the other party was aware, or could reasonably be expected to have been aware, of the first party's intention, the contract is to be interpreted in the way intended by the first party.

(3) The contract is, however, to be interpreted according to the meaning which a reasonable person would give to it:

    (a) if an intention cannot be established under the preceding paragraphs; or

    (b) if the question arises with a person, not being a party to the contract or a person who by law has no better rights than such a party, who has reasonably and in good faith relied on the contract's apparent meaning.

II. – 8:102:   Relevant matters

(1) In interpreting the contract, regard may be had, in particular, to:

    (a) the circumstances in which it was concluded, including the preliminary negotiations;

    (b) the conduct of the parties, even subsequent to the conclusion of the contract;

    (c) the interpretation which has already been given by the parties to terms or expressions which are the same as, or similar to, those used in the contract and the practices they have established between themselves;

    (d) the meaning commonly given to such terms or expressions in the branch of activity concerned and the interpretation such terms or expressions may already have received;

    (e) the nature and purpose of the contract;

    (f) usages; and

    (g) good faith and fair dealing.

(2) In a question with a person, not being a party to the contract or a person such as an assignee who by law has no better rights than such a party, who has reasonably and in good faith relied on the contract's apparent meaning, regard may be had to the circumstances mentioned in sub-paragraphs (a) to (c) above only to the extent that those circumstances were known to, or could reasonably be expected to have been known to, that person.

II. – 8:103:   Interpretation against supplier of term or dominant party

(1) Where there is doubt about the meaning of a term not individually negotiated, an interpretation of the term against the party who supplied it is to be preferred.

(2) Where there is doubt about the meaning of any other term, and that term has been established under the dominant influence of one party, an interpretation of the term against that party is to be preferred.

II. – 8:104:   Preference for negotiated terms

Terms which have been individually negotiated take preference over those which have not.

II. – 8:105:   Reference to contract as a whole

Terms and expressions are to be interpreted in the light of the whole contract in which they appear.

II. – 8:106:   Preference for interpretation which gives terms effect

An interpretation which renders the terms of the contract lawful, or effective, is to be preferred to one which would not.

II. – 8:107: Linguistic discrepancies

Where a contract document is in two or more language versions none of which is stated to be authoritative, there is, in case of discrepancy between the versions, a preference for the interpretation according to the version in which the contract was originally drawn up.

Section 2: Interpretation of other juridical acts

II. – 8:201: General rules

(1) A unilateral juridical act is to be interpreted in the way in which it could reasonably be expected to be understood by the person to whom it is addressed.

(2) If the person making the juridical act intended the act, or a term or expression used in it, to have a particular meaning, and at the time of the act the person to whom it was addressed was aware, or could reasonably be expected to have been aware, of the first person's intention, the act is to be interpreted in the way intended by the first person.

(3) The act is, however, to be interpreted according to the meaning which a reasonable person would give to it:

(a) if neither paragraph (1) nor paragraph (2) applies; or

(b) if the question arises with a person, not being the addressee or a person who by law has no better rights than the addressee, who has reasonably and in good faith relied on the contract's apparent meaning.

II. – 8:202: Application of other rules by analogy

The provisions of Section 1, apart from its first Article, apply with appropriate adaptations to the interpretation of a juridical act other than a contract.

Chapter 9: Contents and effects of contracts

Section 1: Contents

II. – 9:101: Terms of a contract

(1) The terms of a contract may be derived from the express or tacit agreement of the parties, from rules of law or from practices established between the parties or usages.

(2) Where it is necessary to provide for a matter which the parties have not foreseen or provided for, a court may imply an additional term, having regard in particular to:

(a) the nature and purpose of the contract;

(b) the circumstances in which the contract was concluded; and

(c) the requirements of good faith and fair dealing.

(3) Any term implied under paragraph (2) should, where possible, be such as to give effect to what the parties, had they provided for the matter, would probably have agreed.

(4) Paragraph (2) does not apply if the parties have deliberately left a matter unprovided for, accepting the consequences of so doing.

II. – 9:102: Certain pre-contractual statements regarded as contract terms

(1) A statement made by one party before a contract is concluded is regarded as a term of the contract if the other party reasonably understood it as being made on the basis that it would form part of the contract terms if a contract were concluded. In assessing whether the other party was reasonable in understanding the statement in that way account may be taken of:

(a) the apparent importance of the statement to the other party;

(b) whether the party was making the statement in the course of business; and

(c) the relative expertise of the parties.

(2) If one of the parties to a contract is a business and before the contract is concluded makes a statement, either to the other party or publicly, about the specific characteristics of what is to be

supplied by that business under the contract, the statement is regarded as a term of the contract unless:

    (a) the other party was aware when the contract was concluded, or could reasonably be expected to have been so aware, that the statement was incorrect or could not otherwise be relied on as such a term; or

    (b) the other party's decision to conclude the contract was not influenced by the statement.

(3) For the purposes of paragraph (2), a statement made by a person engaged in advertising or marketing on behalf of the business is treated as being made by the business.

(4) Where the other party is a consumer then, for the purposes of paragraph (2), a public statement made by or on behalf of a producer or other person in earlier links of the business chain between the producer and the consumer is treated as being made by the business unless the business, at the time of conclusion of the contract, did not know and could not reasonably be expected to have known of it.

(5) In the circumstances covered by paragraph (4) a business which at the time of conclusion of the contract did not know and could not reasonably be expected to have known that the statement was incorrect has a right to be indemnified by the person making the statement for any liability incurred as a result of that paragraph.

(6) In relations between a business and a consumer the parties may not, to the detriment of the consumer, exclude the application of this Article or derogate from or vary its effects.

II. – 9:103:   Terms not individually negotiated

(1) Terms supplied by one party and not individually negotiated may be invoked against the other party only if the other party was aware of them, or if the party supplying the terms took reasonable steps to draw the other party's attention to them, before or when the contract was concluded.

(2) If a contract is to be concluded by electronic means, the party supplying any terms which have not been individually negotiated may invoke them against the other party only if they are made available to the other party in textual form.

(3) For the purposes of this Article

    (a) "not individually negotiated" has the meaning given by II.–1:110 (Terms "not individually negotiated"); and

    (b) terms are not sufficiently brought to the other party's attention by a mere reference to them in a contract document, even if that party signs the document.

II. – 9:104:   Determination of price

Where the amount of the price payable under a contract cannot be determined from the terms agreed by the parties, from any other applicable rule of law or from usages or practices, the price payable is the price normally charged in comparable circumstances at the time of the conclusion of the contract or, if no such price is available, a reasonable price.

II. – 9:105:   Unilateral determination by a party

Where the price or any other contractual term is to be determined by one party and that party's determination is grossly unreasonable then, notwithstanding any provision in the contract to the contrary, a reasonable price or other term is substituted.

II. – 9:106:   Determination by a third person

(1) Where a third person is to determine the price or any other contractual term and cannot or will not do so, a court may, unless this is inconsistent with the terms of the contract, appoint another person to determine it.

(2) If a price or other term determined by a third person is grossly unreasonable, a reasonable price or term is substituted.

II. – 9:107:   Reference to a non-existent factor

Where the price or any other contractual term is to be determined by reference to a factor which does not exist or has ceased to exist or to be accessible, the nearest equivalent factor is substituted unless this would be unreasonable in the circumstances, in which case a reasonable price or other term is substituted.

II. – 9:108:   Quality
Where the quality of anything to be supplied or provided under the contract cannot be determined from the terms agreed by the parties, from any other applicable rule of law or from usages or practices, the quality required is the quality which the recipient could reasonably expect in the circumstances.

II. – 9:109:   Language
Where the language to be used for communications relating to the contract or the rights or obligations arising from it cannot be determined from the terms agreed by the parties, from any other applicable rule of law or from usages or practices, the language to be used is that used for the conclusion of the contract.

Section 2: Simulation

II. – 9:201:   Effect of simulation
(1) When the parties have concluded a contract or an apparent contract and have deliberately done so in such a way that it has an apparent effect different from the effect which the parties intend it to have, the parties' true intention prevails.

(2) However, the apparent effect prevails in relation to a person, not being a party to the contract or apparent contract or a person who by law has no better rights than such a party, who has reasonably and in good faith relied on the apparent effect.

Section 3: Effect of stipulation in favour of a third party

II. – 9:301:   Basic rules
(1) The parties to a contract may, by the contract, confer a right or other benefit on a third party. The third party need not be in existence or identified at the time the contract is concluded.

(2) The nature and content of the third party's right or benefit are determined by the contract and are subject to any conditions or other limitations under the contract.

(3) The benefit conferred may take the form of an exclusion or limitation of the third party's liability to one of the contracting parties.

II. – 9:302:   Rights, remedies and defences
Where one of the contracting parties is bound to render a performance to the third party under the contract, then, in the absence of provision to the contrary in the contract:
  (a) the third party has the same rights to performance and remedies for non-performance as if the contracting party was bound to render the performance under a binding unilateral undertaking in favour of the third party; and
  (b) the contracting party may assert against the third party all defences which the contracting party could assert against the other party to the contract.

II. – 9:303:   Rejection or revocation of benefit
(1) The third party may reject the right or benefit by notice to either of the contracting parties, if that is done without undue delay after being notified of the right or benefit and before it has been expressly or impliedly accepted. On such rejection, the right or benefit is treated as never having accrued to the third party.

(2) The contracting parties may remove or modify the contractual term conferring the right or benefit if this is done before either of them has given the third party notice that the right or benefit has been conferred. The contract determines whether and by whom and in what circumstances the right or benefit can be revoked or modified after that time.

(3) Even if the right or benefit conferred is by virtue of the contract revocable or subject to modification, the right to revoke or modify is lost if the parties have, or the party having the right to revoke

or modify has, led the third party to believe that it is not revocable or subject to modification and if the third party has reasonably acted in reliance on it.

Section 4: Unfair terms

II. – 9:401: **Mandatory nature of following provisions**

The parties may not exclude the application of the provisions in this Section or derogate from or vary their effects.

II. – 9:402: **Duty of transparency in terms not individually negotiated**

(1) A person who supplies terms which have not been individually negotiated has a duty to ensure that they are drafted and communicated in plain, intelligible language.

(2) In a contract between a business and a consumer a term which has been supplied by the business in breach of the duty of transparency imposed by paragraph (1) may on that ground alone be considered unfair.

II. – 9:403: **Meaning of "unfair" in contracts between a business and a consumer**

In a contract between a business and a consumer, a term [which has not been individually negotiated] is unfair for the purposes of this Section if it is supplied by the business and if it significantly disadvantages the consumer, contrary to good faith and fair dealing.

II. – 9:404: **Meaning of "unfair" in contracts between non-business parties**

In a contract between parties neither of whom is a business, a term is unfair for the purposes of this Section only if it is a term forming part of standard terms supplied by one party and significantly disadvantages the other party, contrary to good faith and fair dealing.

II. – 9:405: **Meaning of "unfair" in contracts between businesses**

A term in a contract between businesses is unfair for the purposes of this Section only if it is a term forming part of standard terms supplied by one party and of such a nature that its use grossly deviates from good commercial practice, contrary to good faith and fair dealing.

II. – 9:406: **Exclusions from unfairness test**

(1) Contract terms are not subjected to an unfairness test under this Section if they are based on:

    (a) provisions of the applicable law;

    (b) international conventions to which the Member States are parties, or to which the European Union is a party; or

    (c) these rules.

(2) For contract terms which are drafted in plain and intelligible language, the unfairness test extends neither to the definition of the main subject matter of the contract, nor to the adequacy of the price to be paid.

II. – 9:407: **Factors to be taken into account in assessing unfairness**

(1) When assessing the unfairness of a contractual term for the purposes of this Section, regard is to be had to the duty of transparency under II.–9:402 (Duty of transparency in terms not individually negotiated), to the nature of what is to be provided under the contract, to the circumstances prevailing during the conclusion of the contract, to the other terms of the contract and to the terms of any other contract on which the contract depends.

(2) For the purposes of II.–9:403 (Meaning of "unfair" in contracts between a business and a consumer) the circumstances prevailing during the conclusion of the contract include the extent to which the consumer was given a real opportunity to become acquainted with the term before the conclusion of the contract.

II. – 9:408: **Effects of unfair terms**

(1) A term which is unfair under this Section is not binding on the party who did not supply it.

(2) If the contract can reasonably be maintained without the unfair term, the other terms remain binding on the parties.

II. – 9:409: Exclusive jurisdiction clauses

(1) A term in a contract between a business and a consumer is unfair for the purposes of this Section if it is supplied by the business and if it confers exclusive jurisdiction for all disputes arising under the contract on the court for the place where the business is domiciled.

(2) Paragraph (1) does not apply if the chosen court is also the court for the place where the consumer is domiciled.

II. – 9:410: Terms which are presumed to be unfair in contracts between a business and a consumer

(1) A term in a contract between a business and a consumer is presumed to be unfair for the purposes of this Section if it is supplied by the business and if it:

(a) excludes or limits the liability of a business for death or personal injury caused to a consumer through an act or omission of that business;

(b) inappropriately excludes or limits the remedies, including any right to set-off, available to the consumer against the business or a third party for non-performance by the business of obligations under the contract;

(c) makes binding on a consumer an obligation which is subject to a condition the fulfilment of which depends solely on the intention of the business;

(d) permits a business to keep money paid by a consumer if the latter decides not to conclude the contract, or perform obligations under it, without providing for the consumer to receive compensation of an equivalent amount from the business in the reverse situation;

(e) requires a consumer who fails to perform his or her obligations to pay a disproportionately high amount of damages;

(f) entitles a business to withdraw from or terminate the contractual relationship on a discretionary basis without giving the same right to the consumer, or entitles a business to keep money paid for services not yet supplied in the case where the business withdraws from or terminates the contractual relationship;

(g) enables a business to terminate a contractual relationship of indeterminate duration without reasonable notice, except where there are serious grounds for doing so; this does not affect terms in financial services contracts where there is a valid reason, provided that the supplier is required to inform the other contracting party thereof immediately;

(h) automatically extends a contract of fixed duration unless the consumer indicates otherwise, in cases where such terms provide for an unreasonably early deadline;

(i) enables a business to alter the terms of the contract unilaterally without a valid reason which is specified in the contract; this does not affect terms under which a supplier of financial services reserves the right to change the rate of interest to be paid by, or to, the consumer, or the amount of other charges for financial services without notice where there is a valid reason, provided that the supplier is required to inform the consumer at the earliest opportunity and that the consumer is free to terminate the contractual relationship with immediate effect; neither does it affect terms under which a business reserves the right to alter unilaterally the conditions of a contract of indeterminate duration, provided that the business is required to inform the consumer with reasonable notice, and that the consumer is free to terminate the contractual relationship;

(j) enables a business to alter unilaterally without a valid reason any characteristics of the goods, other assets or services to be provided;

(k) provides that the price of goods or other assets is to be determined at the time of delivery or supply, or allows a business to increase the price without giving the consumer the right to withdraw if the increased price is too high in relation to the price agreed at the conclusion of the contract; this does not affect price-indexation clauses, where lawful, provided that the method by which prices vary is explicitly described;

(l) gives a business the right to determine whether the goods, other assets or services supplied are in conformity with the contract, or gives the business the exclusive right to interpret any term of the contract;

(m) limits the obligation of a business to respect commitments undertaken by its agents, or makes its commitments subject to compliance with a particular formality;

(n) obliges a consumer to fulfil all his or her obligations where the business fails to fulfil its own;

(o) allows a business to transfer its rights and obligations under the contract without the consumer's consent, if this could reduce the guarantees available to the consumer;

(p) excludes or restricts a consumer's right to take legal action or to exercise any other remedy, in particular by referring the consumer to arbitration proceedings which are not covered by legal provisions, by unduly restricting the evidence available to the consumer, or by shifting a burden of proof on to the consumer;

(q) allows a business, where what has been ordered is unavailable, to supply an equivalent without having expressly informed the consumer of this possibility and of the fact that the business must bear the cost of returning what the consumer has received under the contract if the consumer exercises a right to withdraw.

(2) Subparagraphs (g), (i) and (k) do not apply to:

(a) transactions in transferable securities, financial instruments and other products or services where the price is linked to fluctuations in a stock exchange quotation or index or a financial market rate beyond the control of the business;

(b) contracts for the purchase or sale of foreign currency, traveller's cheques or international money orders denominated in foreign currency.

BOOK III: OBLIGATIONS AND CORRESPONDING RIGHTS

Chapter 1: General

III. – 1:101: Scope of Book
This Book applies, except as otherwise provided, to all obligations within the scope of these rules, whether they are contractual or not, and to corresponding rights to performance.

III. – 1:102: Definitions
(1) An obligation is a duty to perform which one party to a legal relationship, the debtor, owes to another party, the creditor.

(2) Performance of an obligation is the doing by the debtor of what is to be done under the obligation or the not doing by the debtor of what is not to be done.

(3) Non-performance of an obligation is any failure to perform the obligation, whether or not excused, and includes delayed performance and any other performance which is not in accordance with the terms regulating the obligation.

(4) An obligation is reciprocal in relation to another obligation if:

(a) performance of the obligation is due in exchange for performance of the other obligation;

(b) it is an obligation to facilitate or accept performance of the other obligation; or

(c) it is so clearly connected to the other obligation or its subject matter that performance of the one can reasonably be regarded as dependent on performance of the other.

(5) The terms regulating an obligation may be derived from a contract or other juridical act, the law or a legally binding usage or practice, or a court order; and similarly for the terms regulating a right.

III. – 1:103: Good faith and fair dealing
(1) A person has a duty to act in accordance with good faith and fair dealing in performing an obligation, in exercising a right to performance, in pursuing or defending a remedy for non-performance, or in exercising a right to terminate an obligation or contractual relationship.

(2) The duty may not be excluded or limited by contract or other juridical act.

(3) Breach of the duty does not give rise directly to the remedies for non-performance of an obligation but may preclude the person in breach from exercising or relying on a right, remedy or defence which that person would otherwise have.

III. – 1:104:   Co-operation

The debtor and creditor are obliged to co-operate with each other when and to the extent that this can reasonably be expected for the performance of the debtor's obligation.

III. – 1:105:   Non-discrimination

Chapter 2 (Non-discrimination) of Book II applies with appropriate adaptations to:

(a) the performance of any obligation to provide access to, or supply, goods, other assets or services which are available to members of the public;

(b) the exercise of a right to performance of any such obligation or the pursuing or defending of any remedy for non-performance of any such obligation; and

(c) the exercise of a right to terminate any such obligation.

III. – 1:106:   Conditional rights and obligations

(1) The terms regulating a right, obligation or contractual relationship may provide that it is conditional upon the occurrence of an uncertain future event, so that it takes effect only if the event occurs (suspensive condition) or comes to an end if the event occurs (resolutive condition).

(2) Upon fulfilment of a suspensive condition, the relevant right, obligation or relationship takes effect.

(3) Upon fulfilment of a resolutive condition, the relevant right, obligation or relationship comes to an end.

(4) When a party, contrary to the duty of good faith and fair dealing or the obligation to co-operate, interferes with events so as to bring about the fulfilment or non-fulfilment of a condition to that party's advantage, the other party may treat the condition as not having been fulfilled or as having been fulfilled as the case may be.

(5) When a contractual obligation or relationship comes to an end on the fulfilment of a resolutive condition any restitutionary effects are regulated by the rules in Chapter 3, Section 5, Sub-section 4 (Restitution) with appropriate adaptations.

III. – 1:107:   Time-limited rights and obligations

(1) The terms regulating a right, obligation or contractual relationship may provide that it is to take effect from or end at a specified time, after a specified period of time or on the occurrence of an event which is certain to occur.

(2) It will take effect or come to an end at the time or on the event without further steps having to be taken.

(3) When a contractual obligation or relationship comes to an end under this Article any restitutionary effects are regulated by the rules in Chapter 3, Section 5, Sub-section 4 (Restitution) with appropriate adaptations.

III. – 1:108:   Variation or termination by agreement

(1) A right, obligation or contractual relationship may be varied or terminated by agreement at any time.

(2) Where the parties do not regulate the effects of termination, then:

(a) it has prospective effect only and does not affect any right to damages, or a stipulated payment, for non-performance of any obligation performance of which was due before termination;

(b) it does not affect any provision for the settlement of disputes or any other provision which is to operate even after termination; and

(c) in the case of a contractual obligation or relationship any restitutionary effects are regulated by the rules in Chapter 3, Section 5, Sub-section 4 (Restitution) with appropriate adaptations.

III. – 1:109: Variation or termination by notice

(1) A right, obligation or contractual relationship may be varied or terminated by notice by either party where this is provided for by the terms regulating it.

(2) Where, in a case involving continuous or periodic performance of a contractual obligation, the terms of the contract do not say when the contractual relationship is to end or say that it will never end, it may be terminated by either party by giving a reasonable period of notice. In assessing whether a period of notice is reasonable, regard may be had to the interval between performances or counter-performances.

(3) Where the parties do not regulate the effects of termination, then:

    (a) it has prospective effect only and does not affect any right to damages, or a stipulated payment, for non-performance of any obligation performance of which was due before termination;

    (b) it does not affect any provision for the settlement of disputes or any other provision which is to operate even after termination; and

    (c) in the case of a contractual obligation or relationship any restitutionary effects are regulated by the rules in Chapter 3, Section 5, Sub-section 4 (Restitution) with appropriate adaptations.

III. – 1:110: Variation or termination by court on a change of circumstances

(1) An obligation must be performed even if performance has become more onerous, whether because the cost of performance has increased or because the value of what is to be received in return has diminished.

(2) If, however, performance of a contractual obligation or of an obligation arising from a unilateral juridical act becomes so onerous because of an exceptional change of circumstances that it would be manifestly unjust to hold the debtor to the obligation a court may:

    (a) vary the obligation in order to make it reasonable and equitable in the new circumstances; or

    (b) terminate the obligation at a date and on terms to be determined by the court.

(3) Paragraph (2) applies only if:

    (a) the change of circumstances occurred after the time when the obligation was incurred;

    (b) the debtor did not at that time take into account, and could not reasonably be expected to have taken into account, the possibility or scale of that change of circumstances;

    (c) the debtor did not assume, and cannot reasonably be regarded as having assumed, the risk of that change of circumstances; and

    (d) the debtor has attempted, reasonably and in good faith, to achieve by negotiation a reasonable and equitable adjustment of the terms regulating the obligation.

III. – 1:111: Tacit prolongation

Where a contract provides for continuous or repeated performance of obligations for a definite period and the obligations continue to be performed by both parties after that period has expired, the contract becomes a contract for an indefinite period, unless the circumstances are inconsistent with the tacit consent of the parties to such prolongation.

Chapter 2: Performance

III. – 2:101: Place of performance

(1) If the place of performance of an obligation cannot be otherwise determined from the terms regulating the obligation it is:

    (a) in the case of a monetary obligation, the creditor's place of business;

    (b) in the case of any other obligation, the debtor's place of business.

(2) For the purposes of the preceding paragraph:

    (a) if a party has more than one place of business, the place of business is that which has the closest relationship to the obligation; and

(b) if a party does not have a place of business, or the obligation does not relate to a business matter, the habitual residence is substituted.

(3) If, in a case to which paragraph (1) applies, a party causes any increase in the expenses incidental to performance by a change in place of business or habitual residence subsequent to the time when the obligation was incurred, that party is obliged to bear the increase.

III. – 2:102:   Time of performance

(1) If the time at which, or a period of time within which, an obligation is to be performed cannot otherwise be determined from the terms regulating the obligation it must be performed within a reasonable time after it arises.

(2) If a period of time within which the obligation is to be performed can be determined from the terms regulating the obligation, the obligation may be performed at any time within that period chosen by the debtor unless the circumstances of the case indicate that the creditor is to choose the time.

(3) Unless the parties have agreed otherwise, a business must perform the obligations incurred under a contract concluded at a distance for the supply of goods, other assets or services to a consumer no later than 30 days after the contract was concluded.

(4) If a business has an obligation to reimburse money received from a consumer for goods, other assets or services supplied, the reimbursement must be made as soon as possible and in any case no later than 30 days after the obligation arose.

III. – 2:103:   Early performance

(1) A creditor may reject an offer to perform before performance is due unless the early performance would not cause the creditor unreasonable prejudice.

(2) A creditor's acceptance of early performance does not affect the time fixed for the performance by the creditor of any reciprocal obligation.

III. – 2:104:   Order of performance

If the order of performance of reciprocal obligations cannot be otherwise determined from the terms regulating the obligations then, to the extent that the obligations can be performed simultaneously, the parties are bound to perform simultaneously unless the circumstances indicate otherwise.

III. – 2:105:   Alternative obligations or methods of performance

(1) Where a debtor is bound to perform one of two or more obligations, or to perform an obligation in one of two or more ways, the choice belongs to the debtor, unless the terms regulating the obligations or obligation provide otherwise.

(2) If the party who is to make the choice fails to choose by the time when performance is due, then:
   (a) if the delay amounts to a fundamental non-performance, the right to choose passes to the other party;
   (b) if the delay does not amount to a fundamental non-performance, the other party may give a notice fixing an additional period of reasonable length within which the party to choose is required to do so. If the latter still fails to do so, the right to choose passes to the other party.

III. – 2:106:   Performance entrusted to another

A debtor who entrusts performance of an obligation to another person remains responsible for performance.

III. – 2:107:   Performance by a third person

(1) Where personal performance by the debtor is not required by the terms regulating the obligation, the creditor cannot refuse performance by a third person if:
   (a) the third person acts with the assent of the debtor; or
   (b) the third person has a legitimate interest in performing and the debtor has failed to perform or it is clear that the debtor will not perform at the time performance is due.

(2) Performance by a third person in accordance with paragraph (1) discharges the debtor except to the extent that the third person takes over the creditor's right by assignment or subrogation.

(3) Where personal performance by the debtor is not required and the creditor accepts performance of the debtor's obligation by a third party in circumstances not covered by paragraph (1) the debtor is discharged but the creditor is liable to the debtor for any loss caused by that acceptance.

III. – 2:108: Method of payment

(1) Payment of money due may be made by any method used in the ordinary course of business.

(2) A creditor who accepts a cheque or other order to pay or a promise to pay is presumed to do so only on condition that it will be honoured. The creditor may not enforce the original obligation to pay unless the order or promise is not honoured.

III. – 2:109: Currency of payment

(1) The debtor and the creditor may agree that payment is to be made only in a specified currency.

(2) In the absence of such agreement, a sum of money expressed in a currency other than that of the place where payment is due may be paid in the currency of that place according to the rate of exchange prevailing there at the time when payment is due.

(3) If, in a case falling within the preceding paragraph, the debtor has not paid at the time when payment is due, the creditor may require payment in the currency of the place where payment is due according to the rate of exchange prevailing there either at the time when payment is due or at the time of actual payment.

(4) Where a monetary obligation is not expressed in a particular currency, payment must be made in the currency of the place where payment is to be made.

III. – 2:110: Imputation of performance

(1) Where a debtor has to perform several obligations of the same nature and makes a performance which does not suffice to extinguish all of the obligations, then subject to paragraph (5), the debtor may at the time of performance notify the creditor of the obligation to which the performance is to be imputed.

(2) If the debtor does not make such a notification the creditor may, within a reasonable time and by notifying the debtor, impute the performance to one of the obligations.

(3) An imputation under paragraph (2) is not effective if it is to an obligation which is not yet due, or is illegal, or is disputed.

(4) In the absence of an effective imputation by either party, and subject to the following paragraph, the performance is imputed to that obligation which satisfies one of the following criteria in the sequence indicated:

(a) the obligation which is due or is the first to fall due;
(b) the obligation for which the creditor has the least security;
(c) the obligation which is the most burdensome for the debtor;
(d) the obligation which has arisen first.

If none of the preceding criteria applies, the performance is imputed proportionately to all the obligations.

(5) In the case of a monetary obligation, a payment by the debtor is to be imputed, first, to expenses, secondly, to interest, and thirdly, to principal, unless the creditor makes a different imputation.

III. – 2:111: Property not accepted

(1) A person who has an obligation to deliver or return corporeal property other than money and who is left in possession of the property because of the creditor's failure to accept or retake the property, has an ancillary obligation to take reasonable steps to protect and preserve it.

(2) The debtor may obtain discharge from the obligation to deliver or return and from the ancillary obligation mentioned in the preceding paragraph:

(a) by depositing the property on reasonable terms with a third person to be held to the order of the creditor, and notifying the creditor of this; or

(b) by selling the property on reasonable terms after notice to the creditor, and paying the net proceeds to the creditor.

(3) Where, however, the property is liable to rapid deterioration or its preservation is unreasonably expensive, the debtor has an obligation to take reasonable steps to dispose of it. The debtor may obtain discharge from the obligation to deliver or return by paying the net proceeds to the creditor.

(4) The debtor left in possession is entitled to be reimbursed or to retain out of the proceeds of sale any costs reasonably incurred.

III. – 2:112:   Money not accepted

(1) Where a creditor fails to accept money properly tendered by the debtor, the debtor may after notice to the creditor obtain discharge from the obligation to pay by depositing the money to the order of the creditor in accordance with the law of the place where payment is due.

(2) Paragraph (1) applies, with appropriate adaptations, to money properly tendered by a third party in circumstances where the creditor is not entitled to refuse such performance.

III. – 2:113:   Costs and formalities of performance

(1) The costs of performing an obligation are borne by the debtor.

(2) In the case of a monetary obligation the debtor's obligation to pay includes taking such steps and complying with such formalities as may be necessary to enable payment to be made.

III. – 2:114:   Extinctive effect of performance

Full performance extinguishes the obligation if it is:

(a) in accordance with the terms regulating the obligation; or
(b) of such a type as by law to afford the debtor a good discharge.

Chapter 3: Remedies for non-performance

Section 1: General

III. – 3:101:   Remedies available

(1) If an obligation is not performed by the debtor and the non-performance is not excused, the creditor may resort to any of the remedies set out in this Chapter.

(2) If the debtor's non-performance is excused, the creditor may resort to any of those remedies except enforcing specific performance and damages.

(3) The creditor may not resort to any of those remedies to the extent that the creditor caused the debtor's non-performance

III. – 3:102:   Cumulation of remedies

Remedies which are not incompatible may be cumulated. In particular, a creditor is not deprived of the right to damages by resorting to any other remedy.

III. – 3:103:   Notice fixing additional period for performance

(1) In any case of non-performance of an obligation the creditor may by notice to the debtor allow an additional period of time for performance.

(2) During the additional period the creditor may withhold performance of the creditor's reciprocal obligations and may claim damages, but may not resort to any other remedy.

(3) If the creditor receives notice from the debtor that the debtor will not perform within that period, or if upon expiry of that period due performance has not been made, the creditor may resort to any available remedy.

III. – 3:104:   Excuse due to an impediment

(1) A debtor's non-performance of an obligation is excused if it is due to an impediment beyond the debtor's control and if the debtor could not reasonably be expected to have avoided or overcome the impediment or its consequences.

(2) Where the obligation arose out of a contract or other juridical act, non-performance is not excused if the debtor could reasonably be expected to have taken the impediment into account at the time when the obligation was incurred.

(3) Where the excusing impediment is only temporary the excuse has effect for the period during which the impediment exists. However, if the delay amounts to a fundamental non-performance, the creditor may treat it as such.

(4) Where the excusing impediment is permanent the obligation is extinguished. Any reciprocal obligation is also extinguished. In the case of contractual obligations any restitutionary effects of extinction are regulated by the rules in Chapter 3, Section 5, Sub-section 4 (Restitution) with appropriate adaptations.

(5) The debtor has a duty to ensure that notice of the impediment and of its effect on the ability to perform reaches the creditor within a reasonable time after the debtor knew or could reasonably be expected to have known of these circumstances. The creditor is entitled to damages for any loss resulting from the non-receipt of such notice.

III. – 3:105: Term excluding or restricting remedies

(1) A term of a contract or other juridical act which purports to exclude or restrict liability to pay damages for personal injury (including fatal injury) caused intentionally or by gross negligence is void.

(2) A term excluding or restricting a remedy for non-performance of an obligation, even if valid and otherwise effective, having regard in particular to the rules on unfair contract terms in Book II, Chapter 9, Section 4, may nevertheless not be invoked if it would be contrary to good faith and fair dealing to do so.

III. – 3:106: Notices relating to non-performance

(1) If the creditor gives notice to the debtor because of the debtor's non-performance of an obligation or because such non-performance is anticipated, and the notice is properly dispatched or given, a delay or inaccuracy in the transmission of the notice or its failure to arrive does not prevent it from having effect.

(2) The notice has effect from the time at which it would have arrived in normal circumstances.

III. – 3:107: Failure to notify non-conformity

(1) If, in the case of an obligation to supply goods, other assets or services, the debtor supplies goods, other assets or services which are not in conformity with the terms regulating the obligation, the creditor may not rely on the lack of conformity unless the creditor gives notice to the debtor within a reasonable time specifying the nature of the lack of conformity.

(2) The reasonable time runs from the time when the goods or other assets are supplied or the service is completed or from the time, if it is later, when the creditor discovered or could reasonably be expected to have discovered the non-conformity.

(3) The debtor is not entitled to rely on paragraph (1) if the failure relates to facts which the debtor knew or could reasonably be expected to have known and which the debtor did not disclose to the creditor.

(4) This Article does not apply where the creditor is a consumer.

III. – 3:108: Business unable to fulfil consumer's order by distance communication

(1) Where a business is unable to perform its obligations under a contract concluded with a consumer by means of distance communication, it is obliged to inform the consumer immediately and refund any sums paid by the consumer without undue delay and in any case within 30 days. The consumer's remedies for non-performance remain unaffected.

(2) The parties may not, to the detriment of the consumer, exclude the application of this Article or derogate from or vary its effects.

Section 2: Cure by debtor of non-conforming performance

III. – 3:201:   Scope
This Section applies where a debtor's performance does not conform to the terms regulating the obligation.

III. – 3:202:   Cure by debtor: general rules
(1) The debtor may make a new and conforming tender if that can be done within the time allowed for performance.

(2) If the debtor cannot make a new and conforming tender within the time allowed for performance but, promptly after being notified of the lack of conformity, offers to cure it within a reasonable time and at the debtor's own expense, the creditor may not pursue any remedy for non-performance, other than withholding performance, before allowing the debtor a reasonable period in which to attempt to cure the non-conformity.

(3) Paragraph (2) is subject to the provisions of the following Article.

III. – 3:203:   When creditor need not allow debtor an opportunity to cure
The creditor need not, under paragraph (2) of the preceding Article, allow the debtor a period in which to attempt cure if:
> (a) failure to perform a contractual obligation within the time allowed for performance amounts to a fundamental non-performance;
> (b) the creditor has reason to believe that the debtor's performance was made with knowledge of the non-conformity and was not in accordance with good faith and fair dealing;
> (c) the creditor has reason to believe that the debtor will be unable to effect the cure within a reasonable time and without significant inconvenience to the creditor or other prejudice to the creditor's legitimate interests; or
> (d) cure would be inappropriate in the circumstances.

III. – 3:204:   Consequences of allowing debtor opportunity to cure
(1) During the period allowed for cure the creditor may withhold performance of the creditor's reciprocal obligations, but may not resort to any other remedy.

(2) If the debtor fails to effect cure within the time allowed, the creditor may resort to any available remedy.

(3) Notwithstanding cure, the creditor retains the right to damages for any loss caused by the debtor's initial or subsequent non-performance or by the process of effecting cure.

III. – 3:205:   Return of replaced item
(1) Where the debtor has, whether voluntarily or in compliance with an order under III. – 3:302 (Enforcement of non-monetary obligations), remedied a non-conforming performance by replacement, the debtor has a right and an obligation to take back the replaced item at the debtor's expense.

(2) The creditor is not liable to pay for any use made of the replaced item in the period prior to the replacement.

Section 3: Right to enforce performance

III. – 3:301:   Enforcement of monetary obligations
(1) The creditor is entitled to recover money payment of which is due.

(2) Where the creditor has not yet performed the reciprocal obligation for which payment will be due and it is clear that the debtor in the monetary obligation will be unwilling to receive performance, the creditor may nonetheless proceed with performance and may recover payment unless:
> (a) the creditor could have made a reasonable substitute transaction without significant effort or expense; or
> (b) performance would be unreasonable in the circumstances.

III. – 3:302:   Enforcement of non-monetary obligations

(1) The creditor is entitled to enforce specific performance of an obligation other than one to pay money.

(2) Specific performance includes the remedying free of charge of a performance which is not in conformity with the terms regulating the obligation.

(3) Specific performance cannot, however, be enforced where:
- (a) performance would be unlawful or impossible;
- (b) performance would be unreasonably burdensome or expensive; or
- (c) performance would be of such a personal character that it would be unreasonable to enforce it.

(4) The creditor loses the right to enforce specific performance if performance is not requested within a reasonable time after the creditor has become, or could reasonably be expected to have become, aware of the non-performance.

(5) The creditor cannot recover damages for loss or a stipulated payment for non-performance to the extent that the creditor has increased the loss or the amount of the payment by insisting unreasonably on specific performance in circumstances where the creditor could have made a reasonable substitute transaction without significant effort or expense.

III. – 3:303:   Damages not precluded

The fact that a right to enforce specific performance is excluded under the preceding Article does not preclude a claim for damages.

Section 4: Withholding performance

III. – 3:401:   Right to withhold performance of reciprocal obligation

(1) A creditor who is to perform a reciprocal obligation at the same time as, or after, the debtor performs has a right to withhold performance of the reciprocal obligation until the debtor has tendered performance or has performed.

(2) A creditor who is to perform a reciprocal obligation before the debtor performs and who reasonably believes that there will be non-performance by the debtor when the debtor's performance becomes due may withhold performance of the reciprocal obligation for as long as the reasonable belief continues. However, the right to withhold performance is lost if the debtor gives an adequate assurance of due performance.

(3) A creditor who withholds performance in the situation mentioned in paragraph (2) has a duty to give notice of that fact to the debtor as soon as is reasonably practicable and is liable for any loss caused to the debtor by a breach of that duty.

(4) The performance which may be withheld under this Article is the whole or part of the performance as may be reasonable in the circumstances.

Section 5: Termination

III. – 3:501:   Scope and definition

(1) This Section applies only to contractual obligations and contractual relationships.

(2) In this Section "termination" means the termination of the contractual relationship in whole or in part and "terminate" has a corresponding meaning.

Sub-section 1: Grounds for termination

III. – 3:502:   Termination for fundamental non-performance

(1) A creditor may terminate if the debtor's non-performance of a contractual obligation is fundamental.

(2) A non-performance of a contractual obligation is fundamental if:
- (a) it substantially deprives the creditor of what the creditor was entitled to expect under the contract, as applied to the whole or relevant part of the performance, unless at the

time of conclusion of the contract the debtor did not foresee and could not reasonably be expected to have foreseen that result; or

(b) it is intentional or reckless and gives the creditor reason to believe that the debtor's future performance cannot be relied on.

III. – 3:503:   Termination after notice fixing additional time for performance

(1) A creditor may terminate in a case of delay in performance of a contractual obligation which is not in itself fundamental if the creditor gives a notice fixing an additional period of time of reasonable length for performance and the debtor does not perform within that period.

(2) If the period fixed is unreasonably short, the creditor may terminate only after a reasonable period from the time of the notice.

III. – 3:504:   Termination for anticipated non-performance

A creditor may terminate before performance of a contractual obligation is due if the debtor has declared that there will be a non-performance of the obligation, or it is otherwise clear that there will be such a non-performance, and if the non-performance would have been fundamental.

III. – 3:505:   Termination for inadequate assurance of performance

A creditor who reasonably believes that there will be a fundamental non-performance of a contractual obligation by the debtor may terminate if the creditor demands an adequate assurance of due performance and no such assurance is provided within a reasonable time.

Sub-section 2: Scope, exercise and loss of right to terminate

III. – 3:506:   Scope of right to terminate

(1) Where the debtor's obligations under the contract are not divisible the creditor may only terminate the contractual relationship as a whole.

(2) Where the debtor's obligations under the contract are to be performed in separate parts or are otherwise divisible, then:

(a) if there is a ground for termination under this Section of a part to which a counter-performance can be apportioned, the creditor may terminate the contractual relationship so far as it relates to that part;

(b) the creditor may terminate the contractual relationship as a whole only if the creditor cannot reasonably be expected to accept performance of the other parts or there is a ground for termination in relation to the contractual relationship as a whole.

III. – 3:507:   Notice of termination

(1) A right to terminate under this Section is exercised by notice to the debtor.

(2) Where a notice under III.–3:503 (Termination after notice fixing additional time for performance) provides for automatic termination if the debtor does not perform within the period fixed by the notice, termination takes effect after that period or a reasonable length of time from the giving of notice (whichever is longer) without further notice.

III. – 3:508:   Loss of right to terminate

(1) If performance has been tendered late or a tendered performance otherwise does not conform to the contract the creditor loses the right to terminate under this Section unless notice of termination is given within a reasonable time.

(2) Where the creditor has given the debtor a period of time to cure the non-performance under III.–3:202 (Cure by debtor: general rules) the time mentioned in paragraph (1) begins to run from the expiry of that period. In other cases that time begins to run from the time when the creditor has become, or could reasonably be expected to have become, aware of the tender or the non-conformity.

(3) A creditor loses a right to terminate by notice under III.–3:503 (Termination after notice fixing additional time for performance), III.–3:504 (Termination for anticipated non-performance) or

III. – 3:505 (Termination for inadequate assurance of performance) unless the creditor gives notice of termination within a reasonable time after the right has arisen.

Sub-section 3: Effects of termination

III. – 3:509:   Effect on obligations under the contract

(1) On termination under this Section, the outstanding obligations or relevant part of the outstanding obligations of the parties under the contract come to an end.

(2) Termination does not, however, affect any provision of the contract for the settlement of disputes or other provision which is to operate even after termination.

(3) A creditor who terminates under this Section retains existing rights to damages or a stipulated payment for non-performance and in addition has the same right to damages or a stipulated payment for non-performance as the creditor would have had if there had been non-performance of the now extinguished obligations of the debtor. In relation to such extinguished obligations the creditor is not regarded as having caused or contributed to the loss merely by exercising the right to terminate.

Sub-section 4: Restitution

III. – 3:510:   Restitution of benefits received by performance

(1) On termination under this Section a party (the recipient) who has received any benefit by the other's performance of obligations under the terminated contractual relationship or terminated part of the contractual relationship is obliged to return it. Where both parties have obligations to return, the obligations are reciprocal.

(2) If the performance was a payment of money, the amount received is to be repaid.

(3) To the extent that the benefit (not being money) is transferable, it is to be returned by transferring it. However, if a transfer would cause unreasonable effort or expense, the benefit may be returned by paying its value.

(4) To the extent that the benefit is not transferable it is to be returned by paying its value in accordance with III.–3:512 (Payment of value of benefit).

(5) The obligation to return a benefit extends to any natural or legal fruits received from the benefit.

III. – 3:511:   When restitution not required

(1) There is no obligation to make restitution under this Sub-section to the extent that conforming performance by one party has been met by conforming performance by the other.

(2) The terminating party may elect to treat performance as non-conforming if what was received by that party is of no, or fundamentally reduced, value to that party because of the other party's non-performance.

(3) Restitution under this Sub-section is not required where the contract was gratuitous.

III. – 3:512:   Payment of value of benefit

(1) The recipient is obliged to:
   (a) pay the value (at the time of performance) of a benefit which is not transferable or which ceases to be transferable before the time when it is to be returned; and
   (b) pay recompense for any reduction in the value of a returnable benefit as a result of a change in the condition of the benefit between the time of receipt and the time when it is to be returned.

(2) Where there was an agreed price the value of the benefit is that proportion of the price which the value of the actual performance bears to the value of the promised performance. Where no price was agreed the value of the benefit is the sum of money which a willing and capable provider and a willing and capable recipient, knowing of any non-conformity, would lawfully have agreed.

(3) The recipient's liability to pay the value of a benefit is reduced to the extent that as a result of a non-performance of an obligation owed by the other party to the recipient:
   (a) the benefit cannot be returned in essentially the same condition as when it was received; or

(b) the recipient is compelled without compensation either to dispose of it or to sustain a disadvantage in order to preserve it.

(4) The recipient's liability to pay the value of a benefit is likewise reduced to the extent that it cannot be returned in the same condition as when it was received as a result of conduct of the recipient in the reasonable, but mistaken, belief that there was no non-conformity.

III. – 3:513:   Use and improvements

(1) The recipient is obliged to pay a reasonable amount for any use which the recipient makes of the benefit except in so far as the recipient is liable under III.–3:512 (Payment of value of benefit) paragraph (1) in respect of that use.

(2) A recipient who has improved a benefit which the recipient is obliged under this Section to return has a right to payment of the value of improvements if the other party can readily obtain that value by dealing with the benefit unless:

    (a) the improvement was a non-performance of an obligation owed by the recipient to the other party; or

    (b) the recipient made the improvement when the recipient knew or could reasonably be expected to know that the benefit would have to be returned.

III. – 3:514:   Liabilities arising after time when return due

(1) The recipient is obliged to:

    (a) pay the value (at the time of performance) of a benefit which ceases to be transferable after the time when its return was due; and

    (b) pay recompense for any reduction in the value of a returnable benefit as a result of a change in the condition of the benefit after the time when its return was due.

(2) If the benefit is disposed of after the time when return was due, the value to be paid is the value of any proceeds, if this is greater.

(3) Other liabilities arising from non-performance of an obligation to return a benefit are unaffected.

Section 6: Price reduction

III. – 3:601:   Right to reduce price

(1) A creditor who accepts a performance not conforming to the terms regulating the obligation may reduce the price. The reduction is to be proportionate to the decrease in the value of what was received by virtue of the performance at the time it was made compared to the value of what would have been received by virtue of a conforming performance.

(2) A creditor who is entitled to reduce the price under the preceding paragraph and who has already paid a sum exceeding the reduced price may recover the excess from the debtor.

(3) A creditor who reduces the price cannot also recover damages for the loss thereby compensated but remains entitled to damages for any further loss suffered.

(4) This Article applies with appropriate adaptations to a reciprocal obligation of the creditor other than an obligation to pay a price.

Section 7: Damages and interest

III. – 3:701:   Right to damages

(1) The creditor is entitled to damages for loss caused by the debtor's non-performance of an obligation, unless the non-performance is excused.

(2) The loss for which damages are recoverable includes future loss which is reasonably likely to occur.

(3) "Loss" includes economic and non-economic loss. "Economic loss" includes loss of income or profit, burdens incurred and a reduction in the value of property. "Non-economic loss" includes pain and suffering and impairment of the quality of life.

III. – 3:702:   General measure of damages

The general measure of damages for loss caused by non-performance of an obligation is such sum as will put the creditor as nearly as possible into the position in which the creditor would have been if the obligation had been duly performed. Such damages cover loss which the creditor has suffered and gain of which the creditor has been deprived.

III. – 3:703: Foreseeability

The debtor in an obligation which arises from a contract or other juridical act is liable only for loss which the debtor foresaw or could reasonably be expected to have foreseen at the time when the obligation was incurred as a likely result of the non-performance, unless the non-performance was intentional, reckless or grossly negligent.

III. – 3:704: Loss attributable to creditor

The debtor is not liable for loss suffered by the creditor to the extent that the creditor contributed to the non-performance or its effects.

III. – 3:705: Reduction of loss

(1) The debtor is not liable for loss suffered by the creditor to the extent that the creditor could have reduced the loss by taking reasonable steps.

(2) The creditor is entitled to recover any expenses reasonably incurred in attempting to reduce the loss.

III. – 3:706: Substitute transaction

A creditor who has terminated a contractual relationship in whole or in part under Section 5 and has made a substitute transaction within a reasonable time and in a reasonable manner may, in so far as entitled to damages, recover the difference between the value of what would have been payable under the terminated relationship and the value of what is payable under the substitute transaction, as well as damages for any further loss.

III. – 3:707: Current price

Where the creditor has terminated a contractual relationship in whole or in part under Section 5 and has not made a substitute transaction but there is a current price for the performance, the creditor may, in so far as entitled to damages, recover the difference between the contract price and the price current at the time of termination as well as damages for any further loss.

III. – 3:708: Interest on late payments

(1) If payment of a sum of money is delayed, whether or not the non-performance is excused, the creditor is entitled to interest on that sum from the time when payment is due to the time of payment at the average commercial bank short-term lending rate to prime borrowers prevailing for the currency of payment at the place where payment is due.

(2) The creditor may in addition recover damages for any further loss.

III. – 3:709: When interest to be added to capital

(1) Interest payable according to the preceding Article is added to the outstanding capital every 12 months.

(2) Paragraph (1) of this Article does not apply if the parties have provided for interest upon delay in payment.

III. – 3:710: Interest in commercial contracts

(1) If a business delays the payment of a price due under a contract for the supply of goods, other assets or services without being excused under III.–3:104 (Excuse due to an impediment), interest is due at the rate specified in paragraph (4), unless a higher interest rate is applicable.

(2) Interest at the rate specified in paragraph (4) starts to run on the day which follows the date or the end of the period for payment provided in the contract. If there is no such date or period, interest at that rate starts to run:

    (a) 30 days after the date when the debtor receives the invoice or an equivalent request for payment; or

    (b) 30 days after the date of receipt of the goods or services, if the date under (a) is earlier or uncertain, or if it is uncertain whether the debtor has received an invoice or equivalent request for payment.

(3) If conformity of goods or services to the contract is to be ascertained by way of acceptance or verification, the 30 day period under paragraph (2)(b) starts to run on the date of acceptance or verification.

(4) The interest rate for delayed payment is the interest rate applied by the European Central Bank to its most recent main refinancing operation carried out before the first calendar day of the half-year in question ("the reference rate"), plus seven percentage points. For the currency of a Member State which is not participating in the third stage of economic and monetary union, the reference rate is the equivalent rate set by its national central bank.

(5) The creditor may in addition recover damages for any further loss.

III. – 3:711: Unfair terms relating to interest

(1) A term whereby a business pays interest from a date later than that specified in the preceding Article paragraph (2) (a) and (b) and paragraph (3), or at a rate lower than that specified in paragraph (4), is not binding to the extent that this would be unfair.

(2) A term whereby a debtor is allowed to pay the price for goods, other assets or services later than the time when interest starts to run under the preceding Article paragraph (2)(a) and (b) and paragraph (3) does not deprive the creditor of interest to the extent that this would be unfair.

(3) Something is unfair for the purposes of this Article if it grossly deviates from good commercial practice, contrary to good faith and fair dealing.

III. – 3:712: Stipulated payment for non-performance

(1) Where the terms regulating an obligation provide that a debtor who fails to perform the obligation is to pay a specified sum to the creditor for such non-performance, the creditor is entitled to that sum irrespective of the actual loss.

(2) However, despite any provision to the contrary, the sum so specified in a contract or other juridical act may be reduced to a reasonable amount where it is grossly excessive in relation to the loss resulting from the non-performance and the other circumstances.

III. – 3:713: Currency by which damages to be measured

Damages are to be measured by the currency which most appropriately reflects the creditor's loss.

[*Chapters 4 (Plurality of debtors and creditors), 5 (Change of parties), 6 (Set-off and merger) and 7 (Prescription) are omitted.*]

BOOK V BENEVOLENT INTERVENTION IN ANOTHER'S AFFAIRS

Chapter 1: Scope

V. – 1:101: Intervention to benefit another

(1) This Book applies where a person, the intervener, acts with the predominant intention of benefiting another, the principal, and:
  (a) the intervener has a reasonable ground for acting; or
  (b) the principal approves the act without such undue delay as would adversely affect the intervener.
(2) The intervener does not have a reasonable ground for acting if the intervener:
  (a) has a reasonable opportunity to discover the principal's wishes but does not do so; or
  (b) knows or can reasonably be expected to know that the intervention is against the principal's wishes.

V. – 1:102: Intervention to perform another's duty

Where an intervener acts to perform another person's duty, the performance of which is due and urgently required as a matter of overriding public interest, and the intervener acts with the predominant intention of benefiting the recipient of the performance, the person whose duty the intervener acts to perform is a principal to whom this Book applies.

V. – 1:103:   Exclusions

This Book does not apply where the intervener:

    (a) is authorised to act under a contractual or other obligation to the principal;

    (b) is authorised, other than under this Book, to act independently of the principal's consent; or

    (c) is under an obligation to a third party to act.

Chapter 2: Duties of intervener

V. – 2:101:   Duties during intervention

(1) During the intervention, the intervener must:

    (a) act with reasonable care;

    (b) except in relation to a principal within V.–1 :102 (Intervention to perform another's duty), act in a manner which the intervener knows or can reasonably be expected to assume accords with the principal's wishes; and

    (c) so far as possible and reasonable, inform the principal about the intervention and seek the principal's consent to further acts.

(2) The intervention may not be discontinued without good reason.

V. – 2:102:   Reparation for damage caused by breach of duty

(1) The intervener is liable to make reparation to the principal for damage caused by breach of a duty set out in this Chapter if the damage resulted from a risk which the intervener created, increased or intentionally perpetuated.

(2) The intervener's liability is reduced or excluded in so far as this is fair and reasonable, having regard to, among other things, the intervener's reasons for acting.

(3) An intervener who at the time of intervening lacks full legal capacity is liable to make reparation only in so far as that intervener is also liable to make reparation under Book VI (Non-contractual liability arising out of damage caused to another).

V. – 2:103:   Obligations after intervention

(1) After intervening the intervener must without undue delay report and account to the principal and hand over anything obtained as a result of the intervention.

(2) If at the time of intervening the intervener lacks full legal capacity, the obligation to hand over is subject to the defence which would be available under VII.–6:101 (Disenrichment).

(3) The remedies for non-performance in Book III, Chapter 3 apply but with the modification that any liability to pay damages or interest is subject to the qualifications in paragraphs (2) and (3) of the preceding Article.

Chapter 3: Rights and authority of intervener

V. – 3:101:   Right to indemnification or reimbursement

The intervener has a right against the principal for indemnification or, as the case may be, reimbursement in respect of an obligation or expenditure (whether of money or other assets) in so far as reasonably incurred for the purposes of the intervention.

V. – 3:102:   Right to remuneration

(1) The intervener has a right to remuneration in so far as the intervention is reasonable and undertaken in the course of the intervener's profession or trade.

(2) The remuneration due is the amount, so far as reasonable, which is ordinarily paid at the time and place of intervention in order to obtain a performance of the kind undertaken. If there is no such amount a reasonable remuneration is due.

V. – 3:103: Right to reparation

An intervener who acts to protect the principal, or the principal's property or interests, against danger has a right against the principal for reparation for loss caused as a result of personal injury or property damage suffered in acting, if:

(a) the intervention created or significantly increased the risk of such injury or damage; and

(b) that risk, so far as foreseeable, was in reasonable proportion to the risk to the principal.

V. – 3:104: Reduction or exclusion of intervener's rights

(1) The intervener's rights are reduced or excluded in so far as the intervener at the time of acting did not want to demand indemnification, reimbursement, remuneration or reparation, as the case may be.

(2) These rights are also reduced or excluded in so far as this is fair and reasonable, having regard among other things to whether the intervener acted to protect the principal in a situation of joint danger, whether the liability of the principal would be excessive and whether the intervener could reasonably be expected to obtain appropriate redress from another.

V. – 3:105: Obligation of third person to indemnify or reimburse the principal

If the intervener acts to protect the principal from damage, a person who would be accountable under Book VI (Non-contractual liability arising out of damage caused to another) for the causation of such damage to the principal is obliged to indemnify or, as the case may be, reimburse the principal's liability to the intervener.

V. – 3:106: Authority of intervener to act as representative of the principal

(1) The intervener may conclude legal transactions or perform other juridical acts as a representative of the principal in so far as this may reasonably be expected to benefit the principal.

(2) However, a unilateral juridical act by the intervener as a representative of the principal has no effect if the person to whom it is addressed rejects the act without undue delay.

BOOK VI NON-CONTRACTUAL LIABILITY ARISING OUT OF DAMAGE CAUSED TO ANOTHER

Chapter 1: Fundamental provisions

VI. – 1:101: Basic rule

(1) A person who suffers legally relevant damage has a right to reparation from a person who caused the damage intentionally or negligently or is otherwise accountable for the causation of the damage.

(2) Where a person has not caused legally relevant damage intentionally or negligently that person is accountable for the causation of legally relevant damage only if Chapter 3 so provides.

VI. – 1:102: Prevention

Where legally relevant damage is impending, this Book confers on a person who would suffer the damage a right to prevent it. This right is against a person who would be accountable for the causation of the damage if it occurred.

VI. – 1:103: Scope of application

VI.–1:101 (Basic rule) and VI.–1:102 (Prevention):

(a) apply only in accordance with the following provisions of this Book;

(b) apply to both legal and natural persons, unless otherwise stated;

(c) do not apply in so far as their application would contradict the purpose of other private law rules; and

(d) do not affect remedies available on other legal grounds.

Chapter 2: Legally relevant damage

Section 1: General

VI. – 2:101:   Meaning of legally relevant damage

(1) Loss, whether economic or non-economic, or injury is legally relevant damage if:

(a) one of the following rules of this Chapter so provides;

(b) the loss or injury results from a violation of a right otherwise conferred by the law; or

(c) the loss or injury results from a violation of an interest worthy of legal protection.

(2) In any case covered only by sub-paragraphs (b) or (c) of paragraph (1) loss or injury constitutes legally relevant damage only if it would be fair and reasonable for there to be a right to reparation or prevention, as the case may be, under VI.–1:101 (Basic rule) or VI.–1:102 (Prevention).

(3) In considering whether it would be fair and reasonable for there to be a right to reparation or prevention regard is to be had to the ground of accountability, to the nature and proximity of the damage or impending damage, to the reasonable expectations of the person who suffers or would suffer the damage, and to considerations of public policy.

(4) In this Book:

(a) economic loss includes loss of income or profit, burdens incurred and a reduction in the value of property;

(b) non-economic loss includes pain and suffering and impairment of the quality of life.

Section 2: Particular instances of legally relevant damage

VI. – 2:201:   Personal injury and consequential loss

(1) Loss caused to a natural person as a result of injury to his or her body or health and the injury as such are legally relevant damage.

(2) In this Book:

(a) such loss includes the costs of health care including expenses reasonably incurred for the care of the injured person by those close to him or her; and

(b) personal injury includes injury to mental health only if it amounts to a medical condition.

VI. – 2:202:   Loss suffered by third persons as a result of another's personal injury or death

(1) Non-economic loss caused to a natural person as a result of another's personal injury or death is legally relevant damage if at the time of injury that person is in a particularly close personal relationship to the injured person.

(2) Where a person has been fatally injured:

(a) legally relevant damage caused to the deceased on account of the injury to the time of death becomes legally relevant damage to the deceased's successors;

(b) reasonable funeral expenses are legally relevant damage to the person incurring them; and

(c) loss of maintenance is legally relevant damage to a natural person whom the deceased maintained or, had death not occurred, would have maintained under statutory provisions or to whom the deceased provided care and financial support.

VI. – 2:203:   Infringement of dignity, liberty and privacy

(1) Loss caused to a natural person as a result of infringement of his or her right to respect for his or her dignity, such as the rights to liberty and privacy, and the injury as such are legally relevant damage.

(2) Loss caused to a person as a result of injury to that person's reputation and the injury as such are also legally relevant damage if national law so provides.

VI. – 2:204:   Loss upon communication of incorrect information about another

Loss caused to a person as a result of the communication of information about that person which the person communicating the information knows or could reasonably be expected to know is incorrect is legally relevant damage.

VI. – 2:205:   Loss upon breach of confidence

Loss caused to a person as a result of the communication of information which, either from its nature or the circumstances in which it was obtained, the person communicating the information knows or could reasonably be expected to know is confidential to the person suffering the loss is legally relevant damage.

VI. – 2:206:   Loss upon infringement of property or lawful possession

(1) Loss caused to a person as a result of an infringement of that person's property right or lawful possession of a movable or immovable thing is legally relevant damage.

(2) In this Article:

(a) loss includes being deprived of the use of property;

(b) infringement of a property right includes destruction of or physical damage to the subject-matter of the right (property damage), disposition of the right, interference with its use and other disturbance of the exercise of the right.

VI. – 2:207:   Loss upon reliance on incorrect advice or information

Loss caused to a person as a result of making a decision in reasonable reliance on incorrect advice or information is legally relevant damage if:

(a) the advice or information is provided by a person in pursuit of a profession or in the course of trade; and

(b) the provider knew or could reasonably be expected to have known that the recipient would rely on the advice or information in making a decision of the kind made.

VI. – 2:208:   Loss upon unlawful impairment of business

(1) Loss caused to a person as a result of an unlawful impairment of that person's exercise of a profession or conduct of a trade is legally relevant damage.

(2) Loss caused to a consumer as a result of unfair competition is also legally relevant damage if Community or national law so provides.

VI. – 2:209:   Burdens incurred by the state upon environmental impairment

Burdens incurred by the State or designated competent authorities in restoring substantially impaired natural elements constituting the environment, such as air, water, soil, flora and fauna, are legally relevant damage to the State or the authorities concerned.

VI. – 2:210:   Loss upon fraudulent misrepresentation

(1) Without prejudice to the other provisions of this Section loss caused to a person as a result of another's fraudulent misrepresentation, whether by words or conduct, is legally relevant damage.

(2) A misrepresentation is fraudulent if it is made with knowledge or belief that the representation is false and it is intended to induce the recipient to make a mistake.

VI. – 2:211:   Loss upon inducement of non-performance of obligation

Without prejudice to the other provisions of this Section, loss caused to a person as a result of another's inducement of the non-performance of an obligation by a third person is legally relevant damage only if:

(a) the obligation was owed to the person sustaining the loss; and

(b) the person inducing the non-performance:

(i)   intended the third person to fail to perform the obligation, and

(ii) did not act in legitimate protection of the inducing person's own interest.

Chapter 3: Accountability

Section 1: Intention and negligence

VI. – 3:101: Intention

A person causes legally relevant damage intentionally when that person causes such damage either:

    (a) meaning to cause damage of the type caused; or

    (b) by conduct which that person means to do, knowing that such damage, or damage of that type, will or will almost certainly be caused.

VI. – 3:102: Negligence

A person causes legally relevant damage negligently when that person causes the damage by conduct which either:

    (a) does not meet the particular standard of care provided by a statutory provision whose purpose is the protection of the person suffering the damage from that damage; or

    (b) does not otherwise amount to such care as could be expected from a reasonably careful person in the circumstances of the case.

VI. – 3:103: Persons under eighteen

(1) A person under eighteen years of age is accountable for causing legally relevant damage according to VI.–3:102 (Negligence) sub-paragraph (b) only in so far as that person does not exercise such care as could be expected from a reasonably careful person of the same age in the circumstances of the case.

(2) A person under seven years of age is not accountable for causing damage intentionally or negligently.

(3) However, paragraphs (1) and (2) do not apply to the extent that:

    (a) the person suffering the damage cannot obtain reparation under this Book from another; and

    (b) liability to make reparation would be equitable having regard to the financial means of the parties and all other circumstances of the case.

VI. – 3:104: Accountability for damage caused by children or supervised persons

(1) Parents or other persons obliged by law to provide parental care for a person under fourteen years of age are accountable for the causation of legally relevant damage where that person under age caused the damage by conduct that would constitute intentional or negligent conduct if it were the conduct of an adult.

(2) An institution or other body obliged to supervise a person is accountable for the causation of legally relevant damage suffered by a third party when:

    (a) the damage is personal injury, loss within VI.–2:202 (Loss suffered by third persons as a result of another's personal injury or death) or property damage;

    (b) the person whom the institution or other body is obliged to supervise caused that damage intentionally or negligently or, in the case of a person under eighteen, by conduct that would constitute intention or negligence if it were the conduct of an adult; and

    (c) the person whom the institution or other body is obliged to supervise is a person likely to cause damage of that type.

(3) However, a person is not accountable under this Article for the causation of damage if that person shows that there was no defective supervision of the person causing the damage.

Section 2: Accountability without intention or negligence

VI. – 3:201: Accountability for damage caused by employees and representatives

(1) A person who employs or similarly engages another is accountable for the causation of legally relevant damage suffered by a third person when the person employed or engaged:

(a) caused the damage in the course of the employment or engagement; and

(b) caused the damage intentionally or negligently, or is otherwise accountable for the causation of the damage.

(2) Paragraph (1) applies correspondingly to a legal person in relation to a representative causing damage in the course of their engagement. A representative is a person who is authorised to effect juridical acts on behalf of the legal person by its constitution.

VI. – 3:202: Accountability for damage caused by the unsafe state of an immovable

(1) A person who independently exercises control over an immovable is accountable for the causation of personal injury and consequential loss, loss within VI.–2:202 (Loss suffered by third persons as a result of another's personal injury or death), and loss resulting from property damage (other than to the immovable itself) by a state of the immovable which does not ensure such safety as a person in or near the immovable is entitled to expect having regard to the circumstances including:

(a) the nature of the immovable;

(b) the access to the immovable; and

(c) the cost of avoiding the immovable being in that state.

(2) A person exercises independent control over an immovable if that person exercises such control that it is reasonable to impose a duty on that person to prevent legally relevant damage within the scope of this Article.

(3) The owner of the immovable is to be regarded as independently exercising control, unless the owner shows that another independently exercises control.

VI. – 3:203: Accountability for damage caused by animals

A keeper of an animal is accountable for the causation by the animal of personal injury and consequential loss, loss within VI.–2:202 (Loss suffered by third persons as a result of another's personal injury or death), and loss resulting from property damage.

VI. – 3:204: Accountability for damage caused by defective products

(1) The producer of a product is accountable for the causation of personal injury and consequential loss, loss within VI.–2:202 (Loss suffered by third persons as a result of another's personal injury or death), and, in relation to consumers, loss resulting from property damage (other than to the product itself) by a defect in the product.

(2) A person who imported the product into the European Economic Area for sale, hire, leasing or distribution in the course of that person's business is accountable correspondingly.

(3) A supplier of the product is accountable correspondingly if:

(a) the producer cannot be identified; or

(b) in the case of an imported product, the product does not indicate the identity of the importer (whether or not the producer's name is indicated), unless the supplier informs the person suffering the damage, within a reasonable time, of the identity of the producer or the person who supplied that supplier with the product.

(4) A person is not accountable under this Article for the causation of damage if that person shows that:

(a) that person did not put the product into circulation;

(b) it is probable that the defect which caused the damage did not exist at the time when that person put the product into circulation;

(c) that person neither manufactured the product for sale or distribution for economic purpose nor manufactured or distributed it in the course of business;

(d) the defect is due to the product's compliance with mandatory regulations issued by public authorities;

(e) the state of scientific and technical knowledge at the time that person put the product into circulation did not enable the existence of the defect to be discovered; or

(f) in the case of a manufacturer of a component, the defect is attributable to:

       (i)   the design of the product into which the component has been fitted; or

       (ii) instructions given by the manufacturer of the product.

(5) "Producer" means:

    (a) in the case of a finished product or a component, the manufacturer;

    (b) in the case of raw material, the person who abstracts or wins it; and

    (c) any person who, by putting a name, trade mark or other distinguishing feature on the product, gives the impression of being its producer.

(6) "Product" means a movable, even if incorporated into another movable or an immovable, or electricity.

(7) A product is defective if it does not provide the safety which a person is entitled to expect, having regard to the circumstances including:

    (a) the presentation of the product;

    (b) the use to which it could reasonably be expected that the product would be put; and

    (c) the time when the product was put into circulation,

but a product is not defective merely because a better product is subsequently put into circulation.

VI. – 3:205: Accountability for damage caused by motor vehicles

(1) A keeper of a motor vehicle is accountable for the causation of personal injury and consequential loss, loss within VI.–2:202 (Loss suffered by third persons as a result of another's personal injury or death), and loss resulting from property damage (other than to the vehicle and its freight) in a traffic accident which results from the use of the vehicle.

(2) "Motor vehicle" means any vehicle intended for travel on land and propelled by mechanical power, but not running on rails, and any trailer, whether or not coupled.

VI. – 3:206: Accountability for damage caused by dangerous substances or emissions

(1) A keeper of a substance or an operator of an installation is accountable for the causation by that substance or by emissions from that installation of personal injury and consequential loss, loss within VI.–2:202 (Loss suffered by third persons as a result of another's personal injury or death), loss resulting from property damage, and burdens within VI.–2:209 (Burdens incurred by the State upon environmental impairment), if:

    (a) having regard to their quantity and attributes, at the time of the emission, or, failing an emission, at the time of contact with the substance it is very likely that the substance or emission will cause such damage unless adequately controlled; and

    (b) the damage results from the realisation of that danger.

(2) "Substance" includes chemicals (whether solid, liquid or gaseous). Microorganisms are to be treated like substances.

(3) "Emission" includes:

    (a) the release or escape of substances;

    (b) the conduction of electricity;

    (c) heat, light and other radiation;

    (d) noise and other vibrations; and

    (e) other incorporeal impact on the environment.

(4) "Installation" includes a mobile installation and an installation under construction or not in use.

(5) However, a person is not accountable for the causation of damage under this Article if that person:

    (a) does not keep the substance or operate the installation for purposes related to that person's trade, business or profession; or

    (b) shows that there was no failure to comply with statutory standards of control of the substance or management of the installation.

VI. – 3:207:   Other accountability for the causation of legally relevant damage

A person is also accountable for the causation of legally relevant damage if national law so provides where it:

> (a) relates to a source of danger which is not within VI.–3:104 (Accountability for damage caused by children or supervised persons) to VI.–3:205 (Accountability for damage caused by motor vehicles);
>
> (b) relates to substances or emissions; or
>
> (c) disapplies VI.–3:204 (Accountability for damage caused by defective products) paragraph (4)(e).

VI. – 3:208:   Abandonment

For the purposes of this section, a person remains accountable for an immovable, vehicle, substance or installation which that person abandons until another exercises independent control over it or becomes its keeper or operator. This applies correspondingly, so far as reasonable, in respect of a keeper of an animal.

Chapter 4: Causation

VI. – 4:101:   General rule

> (1) A person causes legally relevant damage to another if the damage is to be regarded as a consequence of that person's conduct or the source of danger for which that person is responsible.
>
> (2) In cases of personal injury or death the injured person's predisposition with respect to the type or extent of the injury sustained is to be disregarded.

VI. – 4:102:   Collaboration

A person who participates with, instigates or materially assists another in causing legally relevant damage is to be regarded as causing that damage.

VI. – 4:103:   Alternative causes

Where legally relevant damage may have been caused by any one or more of a number of occurrences for which different persons are accountable and it is established that the damage was caused by one of these occurrences but not which one, each person who is accountable for any of the occurrences is rebuttably presumed to have caused that damage.

Chapter 5: Defences

Section 1: Consent or conduct of the person suffering the damage

VI. – 5:101:   Consent and acting at own risk

> (1) A person has a defence if the person suffering the damage validly consents to the legally relevant damage and is aware or could reasonably be expected to be aware of the consequences of that consent.
>
> (2) The same applies if the person suffering the damage, knowing the risk of damage of the type caused, voluntarily takes that risk and is to be regarded as accepting it.

VI. – 5:102:   Contributory fault and accountability

> (1) Where the fault of the person suffering the damage contributes to the occurrence or extent of legally relevant damage, reparation is to be reduced according to the degree of such fault.
>
> (2) However, no regard is to be had to:
>
> > (a) an insubstantial fault of the person suffering the damage;
> >
> > (b) fault or accountability whose contribution to the causation of the damage is insubstantial;
> >
> > (c) the injured person's want of care contributing to that person's personal injury caused by a motor vehicle in a traffic accident, unless that want of care constitutes profound failure to take such care as is manifestly required in the circumstances.

(3) Paragraphs (1) and (2) apply correspondingly where the fault of a person for whom the person suffering the damage is responsible within the scope of VI.–3:201 (Accountability for damage caused by employees and representatives) contributes to the occurrence or extent of the damage.

(4) Compensation is to be reduced likewise if and in so far as any other source of danger for which the person suffering the damage is responsible under Chapter 3 (Accountability) contributes to the occurrence or extent of the damage.

VI. – 5:103: Damage caused by a criminal to a collaborator

Legally relevant damage caused unintentionally in the course of committing a criminal offence to another person participating or otherwise collaborating in the offence does not give rise to a right to reparation if this would be contrary to public policy.

Section 2: Interests of accountable persons or third parties

VI. – 5:201: Authority conferred by law

A person has a defence if legally relevant damage is caused with authority conferred by law.

VI. – 5:202: Self-defence, benevolent intervention and necessity

(1) A person has a defence if that person causes legally relevant damage in reasonable protection of a right or of an interest worthy of legal protection of that person or a third person if the person suffering the legally relevant damage is accountable for endangering the right or interest protected. For the purposes of this paragraph VI.–3:103 (Persons under eighteen) is to be disregarded.

(2) The same applies to legally relevant damage caused by a benevolent intervener to a principal without breach of the intervener's duties.

(3) Where a person causes legally relevant damage to the patrimony of another in a situation of imminent danger to life, body, health or liberty in order to save the person causing the damage or a third person from that danger and the danger could not be eliminated without causing the damage, the person causing the damage is not liable to make reparation beyond providing reasonable recompense.

VI. – 5:203: Protection of public interest

A person has a defence if legally relevant damage is caused in necessary protection of values fundamental to a democratic society, in particular where damage is caused by dissemination of information in the media.

Section 3: Inability to control

VI. – 5:301: Mental incompetence

(1) A person who is mentally incompetent at the time of conduct causing legally relevant damage is liable only if this is equitable, having regard to the mentally incompetent person's financial means and all the other circumstances of the case. Liability is limited to reasonable recompense.

(2) A person is to be regarded as mentally incompetent if that person lacks sufficient insight into the nature of his or her conduct, unless the lack of sufficient insight is the temporary result of his or her own misconduct.

VI. – 5:302: Event beyond control

A person has a defence if legally relevant damage is caused by an abnormal event which cannot be averted by any reasonable measure and which is not to be regarded as that person's risk.

Section 4: Contractual exclusion and restriction of liability

VI. – 5:401: Contractual exclusion and restriction of liability

(1) Liability for causing legally relevant damage intentionally cannot be excluded or restricted.

(2) Liability for causing legally relevant damage as a result of a profound failure to take such care as is manifestly required in the circumstances cannot be excluded or restricted:

(a) in respect of personal injury (including fatal injury); or

(b) if the exclusion or restriction is otherwise illegal or contrary to good faith and fair dealing.

(3) Liability for damage for the causation of which a person is accountable under VI.–3:204 (Accountability for damage caused by defective products) cannot be restricted or excluded.

(4) Other liability under this Book can be excluded or restricted unless statute provides otherwise.

Section 5: Loss within VI.–2:202
(Loss suffered by third persons as a result of another's personal injury or death)

VI. – 5:501:   Extension of defences against the injured person to third persons

A defence which may be asserted against a person's right of reparation in respect of that person's personal injury or, if death had not occurred, could have been asserted, may also be asserted against a person suffering loss within VI.–2:202 (Loss suffered by third persons as a result of another's personal injury or death).

Chapter 6: Remedies

Section 1: Reparation in general

VI. – 6:101:   Aim and forms of reparation

(1) Reparation is to reinstate the person suffering the legally relevant damage in the position that person would have been in had the legally relevant damage not occurred.

(2) Reparation may be in money (compensation) or otherwise, as is most appropriate, having regard to the kind and extent of damage suffered and all the other circumstances of the case.

(3) Where a tangible object is damaged, compensation equal to its depreciation of value is to be awarded instead of the cost of its repair if the cost of repair unreasonably exceeds the depreciation of value. This rule applies to animals only if appropriate, having regard to the purpose for which the animal was kept.

(4) As an alternative to reinstatement under paragraph (1), but only where this is reasonable, reparation may take the form of recovery from the person accountable for the causation of the legally relevant damage of any advantage obtained by the latter in connection with causing the damage.

VI. – 6:102:   De minimis rule

Trivial damage is to be disregarded.

VI. – 6:103:   Equalisation of benefits

(1) Benefits arising to the person suffering legally relevant damage as a result of the damaging event are to be disregarded unless it would be fair and reasonable to take them into account.

(2) In deciding whether it would be fair and reasonable to take the benefits into account, regard shall be had to the kind of damage sustained, the nature of the accountability of the person causing the damage and, where the benefits are conferred by a third person, the purpose of conferring those benefits.

VI. – 6:104:   Multiple persons suffering damage

Where multiple persons suffer legally relevant damage and reparation to one person will also make reparation to another, Book III, Chapter 4, Section 2 (Plurality of creditors) applies with appropriate adaptation to their rights to reparation.

VI. – 6:105:   Solidary liability

Where several persons are liable for the same legally relevant damage, they are liable solidarily.

VI. – 6:106:   Assignment of right to reparation

The person suffering the damage may assign a right to reparation, including a right to reparation for non-economic loss.

Section 2: Compensation

VI. – 6:201: Right of election

The person suffering the damage may choose whether or not to spend compensation on the reinstatement of the damaged interest.

VI. – 6:202: Reduction of liability

Where it is fair and reasonable to do so, a person may be relieved of liability to compensate, either wholly or in part, if, where the damage is not caused intentionally, liability in full would be disproportionate to the accountability of the person causing the damage or the extent of the damage or the means to prevent it.

VI. – 6:203: Capitalisation and quantification

(1) Compensation is to be awarded as a lump sum unless a good reason requires periodical payment.

(2) National law determines how compensation for personal injury and non-economic loss is to be quantified.

VI. – 6:204: Compensation for injury as such

Injury as such is to be compensated independent of compensation for economic or non-economic loss.

Section 3: Prevention

VI. – 6:301: Right to prevention

(1) The right to prevention exists only in so far as:
    (a) reparation would not be an adequate alternative remedy; and
    (b) it is reasonable for the person who would be accountable for the causation of the damage to prevent it from occurring.

(2) Where the source of danger is an object or an animal and it is not reasonably possible for the endangered person to avoid the danger the right to prevention includes a right to have the source of danger removed.

VI. – 6:302: Liability for loss in preventing damage

A person who has reasonably incurred expenditure or sustained other loss in order to prevent that person from suffering an impending damage, or in order to limit the extent or severity of damage suffered, has a right to compensation from the person who would have been accountable for the causation of the damage.

Chapter 7: Ancillary rules

VI. – 7:101: National constitutional laws

The provisions of this Book are to be interpreted and applied in a manner compatible with the constitutional law of the court.

VI. – 7:102: Statutory provisions

National law determines what legal provisions are statutory provisions.

VI. – 7:103: Public law functions and court proceedings

This Book does not govern the liability of a person or body arising from the exercise or omission to exercise public law functions or from performing duties during court proceedings.

VI. – 7:104: Liability of employees, employers, trade unions and employers' associations

This Book does not govern the liability of:
    (a) employees (whether to co-employees, employers or third parties) arising in the course of employment;
    (b) employers to employees arising in the course of employment; and

(c) trade unions and employers' associations arising in the course of an industrial dispute.

VI. – 7:105:   Reduction or exclusion of liability to indemnified persons
If a person is entitled from another source to reparation, whether in full or in part, for that person's damage, in particular from an insurer, fund or other body, national law determines whether or not by virtue of that entitlement liability under this Book is limited or excluded.

BOOK VII   UNJUSTIFIED ENRICHMENT

Chapter 1:   General

VII. – 1:101:   Basic rule
(1) A person who obtains an unjustified enrichment which is attributable to another's disadvantage is obliged to that other to reverse the enrichment.
(2) This rule applies only in accordance with the following provisions of this Book.

Chapter 2:   When enrichment unjustified

VII. – 2:101:   Circumstances in which an enrichment is unjustified
(1) An enrichment is unjustified unless:
  (a) the enriched person is entitled as against the disadvantaged person to the enrichment by virtue of a contract or other juridical act, a court order or a rule of law; or
  (b) the disadvantaged person consented freely and without error to the disadvantage.
(2) If the contract or other juridical act, court order or rule of law referred to in paragraph (1)(a) is void or avoided or otherwise rendered ineffective retrospectively, the enriched person is not entitled to the enrichment on that basis.
(3) However, the enriched person is to be regarded as entitled to an enrichment by virtue of a rule of law only if the policy of that rule is that the enriched person is to retain the value of the enrichment.
(4) An enrichment is also unjustified if:
  (a) the disadvantaged person conferred it:
    (i)   for a purpose which is not achieved; or
    (ii) with an expectation which is not realised;
  (b) the enriched person knew of, or could reasonably be expected to know of, the purpose or expectation; and
  (c) the enriched person accepted or could reasonably be assumed to have accepted that the enrichment must be reversed in such circumstances.

VII. – 2:102:   Performance of obligation to third person
Where the enriched person obtains the enrichment as a result of the disadvantaged person performing an obligation or a supposed obligation owed by the disadvantaged person to a third person, the enrichment is justified if:
  (a) the disadvantaged person performed freely; or
  (b) the enrichment was merely the incidental result of performance of the obligation.

VII. – 2:103:   Consenting or performing freely
(1) If the disadvantaged person's consent is affected by incapacity, fraud, coercion, threats or unfair exploitation, the disadvantaged person does not consent freely.
(2) If the obligation which is performed is ineffective because of incapacity, fraud, coercion threats or unfair exploitation, the disadvantaged person does not perform freely.

Chapter 3: Enrichment and disadvantage

VII. – 3:101:   Enrichment

(1) A person is enriched by:

(a) an increase in assets or a decrease in liabilities;

(b) receiving a service or having work done; or

(c) use of another's assets.

(2) In determining whether and to what extent a person obtains an enrichment, no regard is to be had to any disadvantage which that person sustains in exchange for or after the enrichment.

VII. – 3:102:   Disadvantage

(1) A person is disadvantaged by:

(a) a decrease in assets or an increase in liabilities;

(b) rendering a service or doing work; or

(c) another's use of that person's assets.

(2) In determining whether and to what extent a person sustains a disadvantage, no regard is to be had to any enrichment which that person obtains in exchange for or after the disadvantage.

Chapter 4: Attribution

VII. – 4:101:   Instances of attribution

An enrichment is attributable to another's disadvantage in particular where:

(a) an asset of that other is transferred to the enriched person by that other;

(b) a service is rendered to or work is done for the enriched person by that other;

(c) the enriched person uses that other's asset, especially where the enriched person infringes the disadvantaged person's rights or legally protected interests;

(d) an asset of the enriched person is improved by that other; or

(e) the enriched person is discharged from a liability by that other.

VII. – 4:102:   Intermediaries

Where one party to a juridical act is an authorised intermediary indirectly representing a principal, any enrichment or disadvantage of the principal which results from the juridical act, or from a performance of obligations under it, is to be regarded as an enrichment or disadvantage of the intermediary.

VII. – 4:103:   Debtor's performance to a non-creditor; onward transfer in good faith

(1) An enrichment is also attributable to another's disadvantage where a debtor confers the enrichment on the enriched person and as a result the disadvantaged person loses a right against the debtor to the same or a like enrichment.

(2) Paragraph (1) applies in particular where a person who is obliged to the disadvantaged person to reverse an unjustified enrichment transfers it to a third person in circumstances in which the debtor has a defence under VII.–6:101 (Disenrichment).

VII. – 4:104:   Ratification of debtor's performance to a non-creditor

(1) Where a debtor purports to discharge a debt by paying a third person, the creditor may ratify that act.

(2) Ratification extinguishes the creditor's right against the debtor to the extent of the payment with the effect that the third person's enrichment is attributable to the creditor's loss of the claim against the debtor.

(3) As between the creditor and the third person, ratification does not amount to consent to the loss of the creditor's right against the debtor.

(4) This Article applies correspondingly to performances of non-monetary obligations.

(5) Other rules may exclude the application of this Article if an insolvency or equivalent proceeding has been opened against the debtor before the creditor ratifies.

VII. – 4:105: Attribution resulting from an act of an intervener

(1) An enrichment is also attributable to another's disadvantage where a third person uses an asset of the disadvantaged person without authority so that the disadvantaged person is deprived of the asset and it accrues to the enriched person.

(2) Paragraph (1) applies in particular where, as a result of an intervener's interference with or disposition of goods, the disadvantaged person ceases to be owner of the goods and the enriched person becomes owner, whether by juridical act or rule of law.

VII. – 4:106: Ratification of intervener's acts

(1) A person entitled to an asset may ratify the act of an intervener who purports to dispose of or otherwise uses that asset in a juridical act with a third person.

(2) The ratified act has the same effect as a juridical act by an authorised intermediary. As between the person ratifying and the intervener, ratification does not amount to consent to the intervener's use of the asset.

VII. – 4:107: Where type or value not identical

An enrichment may be attributable to another's disadvantage even though the enrichment and disadvantage are not of the same type or value.

Chapter 5: Reversal of enrichment

VII. – 5:101: Transferable enrichment

(1) Where the enrichment consists of a transferable asset, the enriched person reverses the enrichment by transferring the asset to the disadvantaged person.

(2) Instead of transferring the asset, the enriched person may choose to reverse the enrichment by paying its monetary value to the disadvantaged person if a transfer would cause the enriched person unreasonable effort or expense.

(3) If the enriched person is no longer able to transfer the asset, the enriched person reverses the enrichment by paying its monetary value to the disadvantaged person.

(4) However, to the extent that the enriched person has obtained a substitute in exchange, the substitute is the enrichment to be reversed if:

    (a) the enriched person is in good faith at the time of disposal or loss and the enriched person so chooses; or

    (b) the enriched person is not in good faith at the time of disposal or loss, the disadvantaged person so chooses and the choice is not inequitable.

(5) The enriched person is in good faith if that person neither knew nor could reasonably be expected to know that the enrichment was or was likely to become unjustified.

VII. – 5:102: Non-transferable enrichment

(1) Where the enrichment does not consist of a transferable asset, the enriched person reverses the enrichment by paying its monetary value to the disadvantaged person.

(2) The enriched person is not liable to pay more than any saving if the enriched person:

    (a) did not consent to the enrichment; or

    (b) was in good faith.

(3) However, where the enrichment was obtained under an agreement which fixed a price or value for the enrichment, the enriched person is at least liable to pay that sum if the agreement was void or voidable for reasons which were not material to the fixing of the price.

(4) Paragraph (3) does not apply so as to increase liability beyond the monetary value of the enrichment.

VII. – 5:103:   Monetary value of an enrichment; saving

(1) The monetary value of an enrichment is the sum of money which a provider and a recipient with a real intention of reaching an agreement would lawfully have agreed as its price. Expenditure of a service provider which the agreement would require the recipient to reimburse is to be regarded as part of the price.

(2) A saving is the decrease in assets or increase in liabilities which the enriched person would have sustained if the enrichment had not been obtained.

VII. – 5:104:   Fruits and use of an enrichment

(1) Reversal of the enrichment extends to the fruits and use of the enrichment or, if less, any saving resulting from the fruits or use.

(2) However, if the enriched person obtains the fruits or use in bad faith, reversal of the enrichment extends to the fruits and use even if the saving is less than the value of the fruits or use.

Chapter 6: Defences

VII. – 6:101:   Disenrichment

(1) The enriched person is not liable to reverse the enrichment to the extent that the enriched person has sustained a disadvantage by disposing of the enrichment or otherwise (disenrichment), unless the enriched person would have been disenriched even if the enrichment had not been obtained.

(2) However, a disenrichment is to be disregarded to the extent that:
   (a) the enriched person has obtained a substitute;
   (b) the enriched person was not in good faith at the time of disenrichment, unless:
      (i)   the disadvantaged person would also have been disenriched even if the enrichment had been reversed; or
      (ii) the enriched person was in good faith at the time of enrichment, the disenrichment was sustained before performance of the obligation to reverse the enrichment was due and the disenrichment resulted from the realisation of a risk for which the enriched person is not to be regarded as responsible; or
   (c) paragraph (3) of VII.–5:102 (Non-transferable enrichment) applies.

(3) Where the enriched person has a defence under this Article as against the disadvantaged person as a result of a disposal to a third person, any right of the disadvantaged person against that third person is unaffected.

VII. – 6:102:   Juridical acts in good faith with third parties

The enriched person is also not liable to reverse the enrichment if:
   (a) in exchange for that enrichment the enriched person confers another enrichment on a third person; and
   (b) the enriched person is still in good faith at that time.

VII. – 6:103:   Illegality

Where a contract or other juridical act under which an enrichment is obtained is void or avoided because of an infringement of a fundamental principle (II. – 7:301 (Contracts infringing fundamental principles)) or mandatory rule of law, the enriched person is not liable to reverse the enrichment to the extent that the reversal would contravene the policy underlying the principle or rule.

Chapter 7: Relation to other legal rules

VII. – 7:101:   Other private law rights to recover

(1) The legal consequences of an enrichment which is obtained by virtue of a contract or other juridical act are governed by other rules if those rules grant or exclude a right to reversal of an enrichment, whether on withdrawal, termination, price reduction or otherwise.

(2) This Book does not address the proprietary effect of a right to reversal of an enrichment.

(3) This Book does not affect any other right to recover arising under contractual or other rules of private law.

VII. – 7:102:   Concurrent obligations

(1) Where the disadvantaged person has both:

    (a) a claim under this Book for reversal of an unjustified enrichment; and

    (b) (i) a claim for reparation for the disadvantage (whether against the enriched person or a third party); or

        (ii) a right to recover under other rules of private law as a result of the unjustified enrichment,

the satisfaction of one of the claims reduces the other claim by the same amount.

(2) The same applies where a person uses an asset of the disadvantaged person so that it accrues to another and under this Book:

    (a) the user is liable to the disadvantaged person in respect of the use of the asset; and

    (b) the recipient is liable to the disadvantaged person in respect of the increase in assets.

VII. – 7:103:   Public law claims

This Book does not determine whether it applies to enrichments which a person or body obtains or confers in the exercise of public law functions.

ANNEX DEFINITIONS

Advanced electronic signature   An "advanced electronic signature" is an electronic signature which is (a) uniquely linked to the signatory (b) capable of identifying the signatory (c) created using means which can be maintained under the signatory's sole control; and (d) linked to the data to which it relates in such a manner that any subsequent change of the data is detectable. (I.–1:108(4))

Agent   An "agent" is a person who is authorised to act for another.

Assets   "Assets" means anything of economic value, including property; rights having a monetary value; and goodwill.

Assignment   "Assignment", in relation to a right, means the transfer of the right by one person, the "assignor", to another, "the assignee". (III.–5:102(1))

Avoidance   "Avoidance" of a juridical act or legal relationship is the process whereby a party or, as the case may be, a court invokes a ground of invalidity so as to make the act or relationship, which has been valid until that point, retrospectively ineffective from the beginning.

Barter, contract for   A contract for the "barter" of goods is a contract under which each party undertakes to transfer the ownership of goods, either immediately on conclusion of the contract or at some future time, in return for the transfer of ownership of other goods. (IV. A.–1:203)

Benevolent intervention in another's affairs   "Benevolent intervention in another's affairs" is the process whereby a person, the intervener, acts with the predominant intention of benefiting another, the principal, but without being authorised or bound to do so. (V.–1:101)

Business   "Business" means any natural or legal person, irrespective of whether publicly or privately owned, who is acting for purposes relating to the person's self-employed trade, work or profession, even if the person does not intend to make a profit in the course of the activity. (I.–1:106(2))

Claim   A "claim" is a demand for something based on the assertion of a right.

Claimant   A "claimant" is a person who makes, or who has grounds for making, a claim.

Commercial agency   A "commercial agency" is the legal relationship arising from a contract under which one party, the commercial agent, agrees to act on a continuing basis as a self-employed intermediary to negotiate or to conclude contracts on behalf of another party, the principal, and the principal agrees to remunerate the agent for those activities. (IV. E.–3:101)

Compensation   "Compensation" means reparation in money. (VI.–6:101(2))

Complete substitution of debtor   There is complete substitution of a debtor when a third person is substituted as debtor with the effect that the original debtor is discharged. (III.–5:203)

Condition   A "condition" is a provision which makes a legal relationship or effect depend on the occurrence or non-occurrence of an uncertain future event. A condition may be suspensive or resolutive. (III.–1:106)

Conduct   "Conduct" means voluntary behaviour of any kind, verbal or nonverbal: it includes a single act or a number of acts, behaviour of a negative or passive nature (such as accepting something without protest or not doing something) and behaviour of a continuing or intermittent nature (such as exercising control over something).

Confidential information   "Confidential information" means information which, either from its nature or the circumstances in which it was obtained, the party receiving the information knows or could reasonably be expected to know is confidential to the other party. (II.–2:302(2))

Consumer   A "consumer" means any natural person who is acting primarily for purposes which are not related to his or her trade, business or profession. (I.–1:106(1))

Consumer contract for sale   A "consumer contract for sale" is a contract for sale in which the seller is a business and the buyer is a consumer. (IV. A.–1:204)

Contract   A "contract" is an agreement which is intended to give rise to a binding legal relationship or to have some other legal effect. It is a bilateral or multilateral juridical act. (II.–1:101(1))

Contractual obligation   A "contractual obligation" is an obligation which arises from a contract, whether from an express term or an implied term or by operation of a rule of law imposing an obligation on a contracting party as such.

Contractual relationship   A "contractual relationship" is a legal relationship resulting from a contract.

Co-ownership   "Co-ownership", when created under Book VIII, means that two or more co-owners own undivided shares in the whole and each co-owner can dispose of that co-owner's share by acting alone, unless otherwise provided by the parties. (Cf. VIII.–1:203)

Corporeal   "Corporeal", in relation to property, means having a physical existence in solid, liquid or gaseous form.

Costs   "Costs" includes expenses.

Counter-performance   A "counter-performance" is a performance which is due in exchange for another performance.

Court   "Court" includes an arbitral tribunal.

Creditor   A "creditor" is a person who has a right to performance of an obligation, whether monetary or non-monetary, by another person, the debtor.

Damage   "Damage" means any type of detrimental effect.

Damages   "Damages" means a sum of money to which a person may be entitled, or which a person may be awarded by a court, as compensation for some specified type of damage.

Debtor   A "debtor" is a person who has an obligation, whether monetary or non-monetary, to another person, the creditor.

Default   "Default", in relation to proprietary security, means any non-performance by the debtor of the obligation covered by the security; and any other event or set of circumstances agreed by the secured creditor and the security provider as entitling the secured creditor to have recourse to the security. (IX.–1:201(5))

Defence   A "defence" to a claim is a legal objection or a factual argument, other than a mere denial of an element which the claimant has to prove which, if well-founded, defeats the claim in whole or in part.

Delivery   "Delivery" to a person, for the purposes of any obligation to deliver goods, means transferring possession of the goods to that person or taking such steps to transfer possession as are required by the terms regulating the obligation. ...

Direct physical control   Direct physical control is physical control which is exercised by the possessor personally or through a possession-agent exercising such control on behalf of the possessor (direct possession). (VIII.–1:205)

Discrimination   "Discrimination" means any conduct whereby, or situation where, on grounds such as sex or ethnic or racial origin, (a) one person is treated less favourably than another person is, has been or would be treated in a comparable situation; or (b) an apparently neutral provision, criterion or practice would place one group of persons at a particular disadvantage when compared to a different group of persons. (II.–2:102(1))

Divided obligation   An obligation owed by two or more debtors is a "divided obligation" when each debtor is bound to render only part of the performance and the creditor may require from each debtor only that debtor's part. (III.–4:102(2))

Divided right   A right to performance held by two or more creditors is a "divided right" when the debtor owes each creditor only that creditor's share and each creditor may require performance only of that creditor's share. (III.–4:202(2))

Durable medium   A "durable medium" means any material on which information is stored so that it is accessible for future reference for a period of time adequate to the purposes of the information, and which allows the unchanged reproduction of this information. (I.–1:107(3))

Duty   A person has a "duty" to do something if the person is bound to do it or expected to do it according to an applicable normative standard of conduct. A duty may or may not be owed to a specific creditor. A duty is not necessarily an aspect of a legal relationship. There is not necessarily a sanction for breach of a duty. All obligations are duties, but not all duties are obligations.

Economic loss   See "Loss".

Electronic   "Electronic" means relating to technology with electrical, digital, magnetic, wireless, optical, electromagnetic, or similar capabilities.

Electronic signature   An "electronic signature" means data in electronic form which are attached to, or logically associated with, other data and which serve as a method of authentication. (I.–1:108(3))

Fraudulent   A misrepresentation is fraudulent if it is made with knowledge or belief that it is false and is intended to induce the recipient to make a mistake to the recipient's prejudice. A non-disclosure is fraudulent if it is intended to induce the person from whom the information is withheld to make a mistake to that person's prejudice. (II.–7:205(2))

Fundamental non-performance   A non-performance of a contractual obligation is fundamental if (a) it substantially deprives the creditor of what the creditor was entitled to expect under the contract, as applied to the whole or relevant part of the performance, unless at the time of conclusion of the contract the debtor did not foresee and could not reasonably be expected to have foreseen that result or (b) it is intentional or reckless and gives the creditor reason to believe that the debtor's future performance cannot be relied on. (III.–3:502(2))

Good faith   "Good faith" is a mental attitude characterised by honesty and an absence of knowledge that an apparent situation is not the true situation.

Good faith and fair dealing   "Good faith and fair dealing" is a standard of conduct characterised by honesty, openness and consideration for the interests of the other party to the transaction or relationship in question. (I.–1:103)

Goods   "Goods" means corporeal movables. It includes ships, vessels, hovercraft or aircraft, space objects, animals, liquids and gases. See also "movables".

Gross negligence   There is "gross negligence" if a person is guilty of a profound failure to take such care as is self-evidently required in the circumstances.

Harassment   "Harassment" means unwanted conduct (including conduct of a sexual nature) which violates a person's dignity, particularly when such conduct creates an intimidating, hostile, degrading, humiliating or offensive environment, or which aims to do so. (II.–2:102(2))

Immovable property   "Immovable property" means land and anything so attached to land as not to be subject to change of place by usual human action.

Incomplete substitution of debtor   There is incomplete substitution of a debtor when a third person is substituted as debtor with the effect that the original debtor is retained as a debtor in case the original debtor does not perform properly.

Incorporeal   "Incorporeal", in relation to property, means not having a physical existence in solid, liquid or gaseous form.

Indemnify   To "indemnify" means to make such payment to a person as will ensure that that person suffers no loss.

Individually negotiated   See "not individually negotiated" and II.–1:110.

Ineffective   "Ineffective" in relation to a contract or other juridical act means having no effect, whether that state of affairs is temporary or permanent, general or restricted.

Insolvency proceeding   An "insolvency proceeding" means a collective judicial or administrative proceeding, including an interim proceeding, in which the assets and affairs of a person who is, or who is believed to be, insolvent are subject to control or supervision by a court or other competent authority for the purpose of reorganisation or liquidation.

Interest   "Interest" means simple interest without any assumption that it will be capitalised from time to time.

Invalid   "Invalid" in relation to a juridical act or legal relationship means that the act or relationship is void or has been avoided.

Joint obligation   An obligation owed by two or more debtors is a "joint obligation" when all the debtors are bound to render the performance together and the creditor may require it only from all of them. (III.–4:102(3))

Joint right   A right to performance held by two or more creditors is a "joint right" when the debtor must perform to all the creditors and any creditor may require performance only for the benefit of all. (III.–4:202(3))

Juridical act   A "juridical act" is any statement or agreement, whether express or implied from conduct, which is intended to have legal effect as such. It may be unilateral, bilateral or multilateral. (II.–1:101(2))

Keeper   A keeper, in relation to an animal, vehicle or substance, is the person who has the beneficial use or physical control of it for that person's own benefit and who exercises the right to control it or its use.

Lease   A "lease" is the legal relationship arising from a contract under which one party, the lessor, undertakes to provide the other party, the lessee, with a temporary right of use in exchange for rent. (IV. B.–1:101)

Loan contract   A loan contract is a contract by which one party, the lender, is obliged to provide the other party, the borrower, with credit of any amount for a definite or indefinite period (the loan period), in the form of a monetary loan or of an overdraft facility and by which the borrower is obliged to repay the money obtained under the credit, whether or not the borrower is obliged to pay interest or any other kind of remuneration the parties have agreed upon. (IV. F.–1:101(2))

Loss   "Loss" includes economic and non-economic loss. "Economic loss" includes loss of income or profit, burdens incurred and a reduction in the value of property. "Non-economic loss" includes pain and suffering and impairment of the quality of life. (III.–3:701(3) and VI.–2:101(4))

Merger of debts   A "merger of debts" means that the attributes of debtor and creditor are united in the same person in the same capacity. (III.–6:201)

Merger clause   A "merger clause" is a term in a contract document stating that the document embodies all the terms of the contract. (II.–4:104)

Monetary loan   A monetary loan is a fixed sum of money which is lent to the borrower and which the borrower agrees to repay either by fixed instalments or by paying the whole sum at the end of the loan period. (IV. F.–1:101(3))

Movables   "Movables" means corporeal and incorporeal property other than immovable property.

Negligence   There is "negligence" if a person does not meet the standard of care which could reasonably be expected in the circumstances.

Non-economic loss   See "Loss".

Non-performance   "Non-performance", in relation to an obligation, means any failure to perform the obligation, whether or not excused. It includes delayed performance and defective performance. (III.–1:101(3))

Notice   "Notice" includes the communication of information or of a juridical act. (I.–1:105)

Not individually negotiated   A term supplied by one party is not individually negotiated if the other party has not been able to influence its content, in particular because it has been drafted in advance, whether or not as part of standard terms. (II.–1:110)

Obligation   An obligation is a duty to perform which one party to a legal relationship, the debtor, owes to another party, the creditor. (III.–1:101(1))

Ownership   "Ownership" is the most comprehensive right a person, the owner, can have over property, including the exclusive right, so far as consistent with applicable laws or rights granted by the owner, to use, enjoy, modify, destroy, dispose of and recover the property. (VIII.–1:202)

Performance   "Performance", in relation to an obligation, is the doing by the debtor of what is to be done under the obligation or the not doing by the debtor of what is not to be done. (III.–1:101(2))

Person   "Person" means a natural or legal person.

Physical control   "Physical control", in relation to goods, means direct physical control or indirect physical control. (Cf. VIII.–1:205)

Possession   Possession, in relation to goods, means having physical control over the goods. (VIII.–1:205)

Prescription   "Prescription", in relation to the right to performance of an obligation, is the legal effect whereby the lapse of a prescribed period of time entitles the debtor to refuse performance.

Presumption   A "presumption" means that the existence of a known fact or state of affairs allows the deduction that something else should be held true, until the contrary is demonstrated.

Price   The "price" is what is due by the debtor under a monetary obligation, in exchange for something supplied or provided, expressed in a currency which the law recognises as such.

Proceeds   "Proceeds", in relation to proprietary security, is every value derived from an encumbered asset, such as value realised by sale, collection or other disposition; damages or insurance payments in respect of defects, damage or loss; civil and natural fruits, including distributions; and proceeds of proceeds. (IX.–1:201(11))

Producer   "Producer" includes, in the case of something made, the maker or manufacturer; in the case of raw material, the person who abstracts or wins it; and in the case of something grown, bred or raised, the grower, breeder or raiser. A special definition applies for the purposes of VI.–3:204.

Property   "Property" means anything which can be owned: it may be movable or immovable, corporeal or incorporeal.

Ratify   "Ratify" means confirm with legal effect.

Reasonable   What is "reasonable" is to be objectively ascertained, having regard to the nature and purpose of what is being done, to the circumstances of the case and to any relevant usages and practices. (I.–1:104)

Reciprocal   An obligation is reciprocal in relation to another obligation if (a) performance of the obligation is due in exchange for performance of the other obligation; (b) it is an obligation to facilitate or accept performance of the other obligation; or (c) it is so clearly connected to the other obligation or its subject matter that performance of the one can reasonably be regarded as dependent on performance of the other. (III.–1:101(4))

Recklessness   A person is "reckless" if the person knows of an obvious and serious risk of proceeding in a certain way but nonetheless voluntarily proceeds without caring whether or not the risk materialises.

Rent   "Rent" is the money or other value which is due in exchange for a temporary right of use. (IV. B.–1:101)

Reparation   "Reparation" means compensation or another appropriate measure to reinstate the person suffering damage in the position that person would have been in had the damage not occurred. (VI.–6:101)

Representative   A "representative" is a person who has authority to affect the legal position of another person, the principal, in relation to a third party by acting in the name of the principal or otherwise in such a way as to indicate an intention to affect the principal's legal position directly. (II.–6:102(1))

Requirement   A "requirement" is something which is needed before a particular result follows or a particular right can be exercised.

Resolutive   A condition is "resolutive" if it causes a legal relationship or effect to come to an end when the condition is satisfied. (III.–1:106)

Retention of ownership device   There is a retention of ownership device when ownership is retained by the owner of supplied assets in order to secure a right to performance of an obligation. (IX.–1:103)

Revocation   "Revocation", means (a) in relation to a juridical act, its recall by a person or persons having the power to recall it, so that it no longer has effect and (b) in relation to something conferred or transferred, its recall, by a person or persons having power to recall it, so that it comes back or must be returned to the person who conferred it or transferred it.

Right   "Right", depending on the context, may mean (a) the correlative of an obligation or liability (as in "a significant imbalance in the parties' rights and obligations arising under the contract"); (b) a proprietary right (such as the right of ownership); (c) a personality right (as in a right to respect for dignity, or a right to liberty and privacy); (d) a legally conferred power to bring about a particular result (as in "the right to avoid" a contract); (e) an entitlement to a particular remedy (as in a right to have performance of a contractual obligation judicially ordered) or (f) an entitlement to do or not to do something affecting another person's legal position without exposure to adverse consequences (as in a "right to withhold performance of the reciprocal obligation").

Sale, contract for   A contract for the "sale" of goods or other assets is a contract under which one party, the seller, undertakes to another party, the buyer, to transfer the ownership of the goods or other assets to the buyer, or to a third person, either immediately on conclusion of the contract or at some future time, and the buyer undertakes to pay the price. (IV.A.–1:202)

Set-off   "Set-off" is the process by which a person may use a right to performance held against another person to extinguish in whole or in part an obligation owed to that person. (III.–6:101)

Signature   "Signature" includes a handwritten signature, an electronic signature or an advanced electronic signature. (I.–1:108(2))

Solidary obligation   An obligation owed by two or more debtors is a "solidary obligation" when all the debtors are bound to render one and the same performance and the creditor may require it from any one of them until there has been full performance. (III.–4:102(1))

Solidary right   A right to performance held by two or more creditors is a "solidary right" when any of the creditors may require full performance from the debtor and the debtor may render performance to any of the creditors. (III.–4:202(1))

Standard terms   "Standard terms" are terms which have been formulated in advance for several transactions involving different parties, and which have not been individually negotiated by the parties. (II.–1:109)

Subrogation   "Subrogation", in relation to rights, is the process by which a person who has made a payment or other performance to another person acquires by operation of law that person's rights against a third person.

Substitution of debtor   "Substitution" of a debtor is the process whereby, with the agreement of the creditor, a third party is substituted completely or incompletely for the debtor, the contract remaining in force. (III.–5:202) See also "complete substitution of debtor" and "incomplete substitution of debtor".

Supply   To "supply" goods or other assets means to make them available to another person, whether by sale, gift, barter, lease or other means: to "supply" services means to provide them to another person, whether or not for a price. Unless otherwise stated, "supply" covers the supply of goods, other assets and services.

Suspensive   A condition is "suspensive" if it prevents a legal relationship or effect from coming into existence until the condition is satisfied. (III.–1:106)

Tacit prolongation   "Tacit prolongation" is the process whereby, when a contract provides for continuous or repeated performance of obligations for a definite period and the obligations continue to be performed by both parties after that period has expired, the contract becomes a contract for an indefinite period, unless the circumstances are inconsistent with the tacit consent of the parties to such prolongation. (III.–1:111)

Term   "Term" means any provision, express or implied, of a contract or other juridical act, of a law, of a court order or of a legally binding usage or practice: it includes a condition.

Termination   "Termination", in relation to an existing right, obligation or legal relationship, means bringing it to an end with prospective effect except in so far as otherwise provided.

Textual form   In "textual form", in relation to a statement, means expressed in alphabetical or other intelligible characters by means of any support which permits reading, recording of the information contained in the statement and its reproduction in tangible form. (I.–1:107(2))

Transfer of contractual position   "Transfer of contractual position" is the process whereby, with the agreement of all three parties, a new party replaces an existing party to a contract, taking over the rights, obligations and entire contractual position of that party. (III.–5:302)

Treatment, contract for   A contract for treatment is a contract under which one party, the treatment provider, undertakes to provide medical treatment for another party, the patient, or to provide any other service in order to change the physical or mental condition of a person. (IV. C.–8:101)

Trust   A "trust" is a legal relationship in which a trustee is obliged to administer or dispose of one or more assets (the trust fund) in accordance with the terms governing the relationship (trust terms) to benefit a beneficiary or advance public benefit purposes. (X.–1:201)

Trustee   A "trustee" is a person in whom a trust fund becomes or remains vested when the trust is created or subsequently on or after appointment and who has the obligation set out in the definition of "trust" above. (X.–1:203(2))

Unjustified enrichment   An "unjustified enrichment" is an enrichment which is not legally justified.

Valid   "Valid", in relation to a juridical act or legal relationship, means that the act or relationship is not void and has not been avoided.

Void   "Void", in relation to a juridical act or legal relationship, means that the act or relationship is automatically of no effect from the beginning.

Voidable   "Voidable", in relation to a juridical act or legal relationship, means that the act or relationship is subject to a defect which renders it liable to be avoided and hence rendered retrospectively of no effect.

Withdraw   A right to "withdraw" from a contract or other juridical act is a right, exercisable only within a limited period, to terminate the legal relationship arising from the contract or other juridical act, without having to give any reason for so doing and without incurring any liability for non-performance of the obligations arising from that contract or juridical act. (II.–5:101 to II.–5:105)

Withholding performance   "Withholding performance", as a remedy for non-performance of a contractual obligation, means that one party to a contract may decline to render due counter-performance until the other party has tendered performance or has performed. (III.–3:401)

Writing   In "writing" means in textual form, on paper or another durable medium and in directly legible characters. (I.–1:107(1))

Index

A

Access to Neighbouring Land Act 1992
ss. 1–4, 6 **172–7**
Administration of Justice Act 1970
s. 40 **23**
Administration of Justice Act 1982
ss. 1, 2, 5 **121**
Animals Act 1971
ss. 1–12 **28–32**
Anti-social Behaviour Act 2003
ss. 9, 10, 11A, 30, 36, 40, 65, 66, 68, 69,
75–7 **268–73**
Apportionment Act 1870
ss. 2, 3, 5–7 **4–5**
Arbitration Act 1996
ss. 8, 29, 40, 87, 89–91 **204–5**

B

Banking Act 2009
ss. 191, 244 **307**
Broadcasting Act 1990
s. 166, Sched. 20 **160–1**
Building Act 1984
s. 38 **133**
Business Protection from Misleading Marketing
Regulations 2008
regs 3, 6, 29 **408–9**

C

Carriage of Goods by Sea Act 1971
ss. 1–3, Sched. **32–8**
Carriage of Goods by Sea Act 1992
ss. 1–5 **177–80**
Civil Aviation Act 1982
ss. 38A, 38C, 76, 77 **121–2**
Civil Evidence Act 1968
ss. 11, 13 **21**
Civil Liability (Contribution) Act 1978
ss. 1–7 **77–9**
Civil Partnership Act 2004
ss. 1, 69, 73 **277**
Companies Act 2006
ss. 17, 33, 39–41, 43, 51, 83, 170, 174, 176, 178,
189, 195, 196, 222, 232, 463, 532, 534, 537,
655, 847, 942, 954, 956, 1218 **288–94**
Compensation Act 2006
ss. 1–4. **294–6**
Congenital Disabilities (Civil Liability) Act 1976
ss. 1–5 **59–61**
Consumer Credit Act 1974
ss. 55–7, 60, 65, 67–71, 75, 76, 87, 88, 94, 96, 99,
100, 113, 127, 129, 132, 140A–B, 162, 163, 165,
170, 173, 175, 181, 189 **48–56**

Consumer Insurance (Disclosure and
Representations) Bill
ss. 1–6, 10, 12, Sched. 1 **348–51**
Consumer Protection Act 1987
ss. 1–9, 11, 12, 29, 30, 32–4, 39, 41, 45 **139–47**
Consumer Protection (Distance Selling)
Regulations 2000
regs 3–20, 24–9, Sched. 1 **370–81**
Consumer Protection from Unfair
Trading Regulations 2008
regs 2, 3, 5–7, 29, Sched. 1 **409–13**
Contracts (Rights of Third Parties) Act 1999
ss. 1–10 **250–4**
Copyright, Designs and Patents Act 1988
ss. 96, 97, 229, 253 **148**
Corporate Manslaughter and Corporate
Homicide Act 2007
ss. 1–9, 11 **301–4**
Countryside and Rights of Way Act 2000
ss. 1, 2, 12 **254–5**
Courts and Legal Services Act 1990
ss. 8, 61 **161**
Criminal Injuries Compensation Act 1995
ss. 1–3, 7, 9 **197–201**
Criminal Justice Act 2003
s. 329 **273**
Criminal Justice and Public Order Act 1994
ss. 60–6, 68, 69 **192–4**
Criminal Law Act 1967
ss. 3, 14 **19–20**
Crown Proceedings Act 1947
s. 2 **14–15**
Customs and Excise Management Act 1979
s. 137A **79–80**

D

Damages Act 1996
ss. 1–4, 6, 7 **205–9**
Damages (Scotland) Act 2011
ss. 1–14 **314–19**
Damages (Variation of Periodical Payments)
Order 2005
arts 1–14 **386–9**
Dangerous Wild Animals Act 1976
ss. 1, 4 **61–2**
Data Protection Act 1998
ss. 10, 13, 57 **233**
Defamation Act 1952
ss. 2, 3, 5, 6, 9–13, 16 **16–17**
Defamation Act 1996
ss. 1–4, 7–10, 13–15, 17, Sched. 1 **209–18**
Defamation Bill
ss. 1–20, Scheds 1, 3 **339–48**

Defective Premises Act 1972
    ss. 1–6 **41–4**
Dormant Bank and Building Society Accounts Act 2008
    ss. 1, 4, 5, 10 **306–7**
Draft Common Frame of Reference (DCFR)
    Principles, Definitions and Model Rules of
        European Private Law
    Books I–III, V–VII and Annex Definitions **418–76**

E

Electronic Commerce (EC Directive) Regulations 2002
    regs 2, 9–15 **381–2**
Electronic Signatures Regulations 2002
    regs 2–5, Sched. 2 **382–5**
Employers' Liability (Compulsory Insurance) Act 1969
    ss. 1, 2 **22**
Employers' Liability (Compulsory Insurance)
        Regulations 1998
    regs 1–3 **358–9**
Employer's Liability (Defective Equipment) Act 1969
    s. 1 **22–3**
Employment Act 1989
    s. 11 **158**
Enterprise Act 2002
    ss. 1, 108, 173 **267**
Environmental Protection Act 1990
    ss. 33, 34, 58B, 73, 78A–80A, 82 **161–8**
Equality Act 2010
    ss. 4, 13, 26–9, 31–3, 39, 66, 114, 119,
        142–6, 212 **307–11**

F

Factors Act 1889
    ss. 1, 2 **6**
Fatal Accidents Act 1976
    ss. 1–5 **62–4**
Finance Act 2000
    Sched. 6 **256**
Financial Services and Markets Act 2000
    ss. 19, 26, 27, 71, 80, 90, 102, 131, 139, 150,
        213, 222, 291, 380–6 **256–62**
Financial Services (Distance Marketing)
        Regulations 2004
    reg. 15 **385–6**
Fires Prevention (Metropolis) Act 1774
    s. 86 **1**
Food Safety Act 1990
    s. 44 **168**
Forfeiture Act 1982
    ss. 1, 2, 5 **122–3**
Freedom of Information Act 2000
    ss. 56, 79 **263**

G

Gambling Act 2005
    ss. 335–8 **278–9**
General Product Safety Regulations 2005
    regs 2–18, 20–31, 36, 42 **389–405**

Government of Wales Act 2006
    ss. 1, 42, 130 **296**

H

Health and Safety at Work Act 1974
    ss. 2–4, 17, 47 **56–8**
Health and Social Care (Community Health and
        Standards) Act 2003
    ss. 150–1, 153, 155, 162–6 **274–7**
Highways Act 1980
    ss. 41, 58, 102, 129A, 129B, 129G, 165 **101–2**
Housing Act 1985
    s. 118 **137**
Housing Act 1988
    ss. 16, 27, 28 **149–50**
Human Rights Act 1998
    ss. 1–13, 19, 21, 22, Sched. 1 **234–44**

I

Income Tax Act 2007
    s. 762 **304**
Insolvency Act 1986
    s. 238 **137–8**

L

Landlord and Tenant Act 1985
    s. 8 **137**
Landlord and Tenant (Covenants) Act 1995
    ss. 3, 5, 13, 23–5 **201–3**
Late Payment of Commercial Debts
        (Interest) Act 1998
    ss. 1–11, 13–17 **244–9**
Late Payment of Commercial Debts
        Regulations 2002
    reg. 3 **385**
Latent Damage Act 1986
    ss. 1, 3 **138–9**
Law of Libel Amendment Act 1888
    s. 5 **5**
Law of Property Act 1925
    ss. 41, 49, 56, 136, 146, 205 **9–10**
Law of Property (Miscellaneous Provisions) Act 1989
    ss. 1–3 **158–60**
Law Reform (Contributory Negligence) Act 1945
    ss. 1, 4 **13–14**
Law Reform (Frustrated Contracts) Act 1943
    ss. 1–3 **12–13**
Law Reform (Husband and Wife) Act 1962
    s. 1 **19**
Law Reform (Married Women and Tortfeasors)
        Act 1935
    ss. 3, 4 **11–12**
Law Reform (Miscellaneous Provisions) Act 1934
    s. 1 **10–11**
Law Reform (Personal Injuries) Act 1948
    ss. 1–3 **15**
Legal Services Act 2007
    ss. 131, 154, 176 **304–5**

Libel Act 1843
  ss. 1, 2 **3**
Libel Act 1845
  s. 2 **3**
Limitation Act 1980
  ss. 1–6, 8–24, 26–33, 35–9 **102–19**
Local Government (Contracts) Act 1997
  ss. 1, 2 **219**

M

Marine Insurance Act 1906
  ss. 17, 18, 20, 22, 33–5, 49, 82–4, 87 **7–9**
Mental Capacity Act 2005
  ss. 1–8, 24–8, 30–7, 42 **279–88**
Mercantile Law Amendment Act 1856
  ss. 3, 5 **3–4**
Merchant Shipping Act 1995
  ss. 92, 93, 234 **203–4**
Minors' Contracts Act 1987
  ss. 2, 3 **147**
Misrepresentation Act 1967
  ss. 1–3 **20**

N

National Health Service Act 2006
  s. 9 **296–7**
National Minimum Wage Act 1998
  s. 1 **249**
National Parks and Access to the Countryside Act 1949
  s. 60 **15**
Negligence (Psychiatric Illness) Bill
  (Law Com. No. 249) (Draft)
  ss. 1–5 **320–2**
NHS Redress Act 2006
  ss. 1–3, 6–14 **297–300**

O

Occupiers' Liability Act 1957
  ss. 1–3, 5, 6 **17–19**
Occupiers' Liability Act 1984
  ss. 1, 1A, 3 **133–4**
Offences Against the Person Act 1861
  ss. 44, 45 **4**

P

Package Travel, Package Holidays and Package
  Tours Regulations 1992
  regs 2–15, 27, 28, Scheds 1–3 **352–8**
Parliamentary Papers Act 1840
  ss. 1–4 **2**
Pneumoconiosis etc. (Workers' Compensation)
  Act 1979
  ss. 1, 2, 5, 9 **80–1**
Police Act 1996
  s. 88 **218–19**
Police and Criminal Evidence Act 1984
  ss. 17, 19, 22, 24, 32, 34, 55, 62, 65 **134–7**

Postal Services Act 2000
  ss. 89–91 **263–4**
Powers of Criminal Courts (Sentencing) Act 2000
  ss. 73, 130, 134, 137, 143, 145, 148, 149 **264–7**
Proceeds of Crime Act 2002
  ss. 7, 304–7 **267–8**
Protection from Eviction Act 1977
  ss. 1–3 **64–5**
Protection from Harassment Act 1997
  ss. 1–5A, 7, 12 **219–21**
Provision and Use of Work Equipment
  Regulations 1998
  regs 2, 4–24 **359–64**

R

Railways Act 1993
  s. 122 **191–2**
Regulation (EC) No 864/2007 (Non-contractual
  obligations) (Rome II)
  Art. 2 **415**
Regulation (EC) No 593/2008 (Law applicable to
  contractual obligations) (Rome I)
  Arts 1, 3, 9, 10 **415**
Regulatory Reform (Unsolicited Goods and
  Services Act 1971) (Directory Entries and
  Demands for Payment) Order 2005
  arts 1, 5, Sched. **406–7**
Rehabilitation of Offenders Act 1974
  ss. 4, 8 **58**
Reserve and Auxiliary Forces
  (Protection of Civil Interests) Act 1951
  s. 13 **16**
Reservoirs Act 1975
  s. 28 **59**
Road Traffic Act 1988
  ss. 38, 143–5, 148, 149, 151, 153, 157–9 **150–7**
Road Traffic (Consequential Provisions) Act 1988
  s. 7 **157**

S

Sale of Goods Act 1979
  ss. 1–21, 23–39, 41–57, 59–62 **81–99**
Senior Courts Act 1981
  ss. 32, 32A, 35, 35A, 8, 49, 50, 69 **119–21**
Slander of Women Act 1891
  s. 1 **6–7**
Social Security Contributions and Benefits Act 1992
  ss. 94, 97, 98, 100, 101, 174 **180–1**
Social Security (Recovery of Benefits) Act 1997
  ss. 1–23, 28–32, Scheds 1, 2 **221–32**
State Immunity Act 1978
  ss. 1, 3, 5 **79**
Statute of Frauds 1677
  s. 4 **1**
Statute of Frauds Amendment Act 1828
  s. 6 **1**
Supply of Goods and Services Act 1982
  ss. 1–16, 18–19 **123–33**

Supply of Goods (Implied Terms) Act 1973
   ss. 8–12, 14, 15 44–7

T

Taxes Management Act 1970
   ss. 30, 33, Sched. 1AB 24–8
Theatres Act 1968
   s. 4 22
Third Parties (Rights against Insurers) Act 2010
   ss. 1, 2, 4, 6, 8, 10, 14, 16, 17 311–14
Torts (Interference with Goods) Act 1977
   ss. 1–14, 16, Sched. 1 65–71
Trade Descriptions Act 1968
   s. 35 22
Trade Union and Labour Relations (Consolidation)
      Act 1992
   ss. 1, 10, 11, 20, 22, 127, 128, 137, 138, 140,
      142–5, 166, 178–80, 186, 187, 219–22,
      224–6, 236, 237, 240, 241, 244, 245, 273,
      288 181–91
Transfer of Undertakings (Protection of Employment)
      Regulations 2006
   regs 3, 4 407–8
Treaty Establishing the European Economic
      Community (Treaty of Rome, 1957)
   Arts 81, 82 414–15
Tribunals, Courts and Enforcement Act 2007
   ss. 62, 63, 65, 85, 89 305–6

U

Unfair Contract Terms Act 1977
   ss. 1–7, 9–14, 26, 27, 29, Scheds 1, 2 71–7
Unfair Contract Terms Bill (Law Com. No. 292; Scot.
      Law Com. No. 199) (Draft)
   ss. 1–17, 21–35, Scheds 1–4 322–39
Unfair Terms in Consumer Contracts
      Regulations 1999
   regs 3–16, Scheds 1, 2 364–70
United Nations Convention on the Use of Electronic
      Communications in International
      Contracts (2005)
   Arts 1, 8–12, 14 416–17
Unsolicited Goods and Services Act 1971
   ss. 2–6 38–41

V

Vaccine Damage Payments Act 1979
   ss. 1–3, 6, 12 99–101
Value Added Tax Act 1994
   ss. 80, 80A 195–7

W

Water Industry Act 1991
   s. 209 168–9
Water Resources Act 1991
   ss. 161, 208, 221 169–72